AMERICAN ART ANALOG

VOLUME II
1842–1874

Compiled by
Michael David Zellman

CHELSEA HOUSE PUBLISHERS
in association with
AMERICAN ART ANALOG

1986

Director : Michael David Zellman
Editor : Rebecca Stefoff
Production Management and Coordination : Richard Alan Zakroff
Editorial and Project Consultant : Don Sugarman
Photo Research and Registration : Elizabeth Preston
Computer Operations : Sheila Mulligan
Administrative Assistant : Evelyn Kobler
Production Support : Phil DiPiero

Photographers : James D. Dee
Ali Elai
Theodore Flagg
Robert Grove
Richard Haynes, Jr.
John Kasparian
M.S. Rezny
Clive Russ
Neil Scholl
Paul Wilson

Researchers : Edmond Bassetti
Cheryl Cibulka
Roberta Geier
Joan Irving
Rebecca Rackin
David Sellin
Cynthia Seibels
Michelle Stricker
J. Gray Sweeney
Linda Sykes
Diane Tepfer
Jennifer Way

Designer : Richard Goettel
Typesetting : The Kingswood Group, Inc.
Printed in Japan

Library of Congress Cataloging-in-Publication Data

American art analog.

Includes bibliographies and indexes.
Contents: v. 1. 1688–1842—v. 2. 1842–1874—v.3. 1874–1930.
1. Art, American.   2. Art, American—Prices.
3. Art as an investment.   4. Art—Collectors and collecting.
I. Zellman, Michael David.
N6505.A56   1986   759.13   85-29085
ISBN 1-555-46000-3 (set)
ISBN 1-555-46002-X (Volume II)

CONTENTS

─────────────────────── **VOLUME III** ───────────────────────

ARTWORK CONTRIBUTORS

MUSEUMS AND UNIVERSITIES

Abby Aldrich Rockefeller Folk Art Center
Alabama Department of Archives and History
Amon Carter Museum
Anchorage Historical and Fine Arts Museum
Art Institute of Chicago
Bayly Museum
University of Virginia
Baltimore Museum of Art
Board of Selectmen, Abbot Hall
Boston Athenaeum
Bowdoin College Museum of Art
Brandywine River Museum, Brandywine Conservancy
Brooklyn Museum
Butler Institute of American Art
Cahoon Museum
Carnegie Institute
Colby College Museum of Art
Connecticut Historical Society
Corcoran Gallery of Art
Crocker Art Museum
Delaware Art Museum
Detroit Institute of Art
Florence Griswold Museum, Lyme Historical Society
Fogg Museum, Harvard University
Gilcrease Institute of American History and Art
Grand Rapids Art Museum
Hirshhorn Museum and Sculpture Garden
Historical Society of Pennsylvania
Independence National Historical Park Services
Indianapolis Museum of Art
La Salle University Art Museum
Los Angeles County Museum of Art
Metropolitan Museum of Art
Montclair Art Museum
Monterey Peninsula Museum of Art
Montgomery Museum of Fine Arts
Morse Gallery
Mount Vernon Ladies Association
Munson-Williams-Proctor Art Institute
Museum of American Folk Art
Museum of Fine Arts, Boston
Museum of the Confederacy
Muskegon Museum of Art
Nassau County Museum of Fine Art
National Academy of Design

National Center of Afro-American Artists
National Cowboy Hall of Fame
National Gallery of Art
National Museum of American Art
National Portrait Gallery
Neuberger Museum State University of New York
New Jersey State Museum
New York Historical Society
New York State Historical Association
Newark Museum
North Carolina Museum of Art
Oakland Museum
Palm Springs Desert Museum
Passaic County Historical Society
Peale Museum
Pennsylvania Academy of the Fine Arts
Perry Public Library
Philadelphia Museum of Art
Phillips Collection
Princeton University Art Museum
Reading Public Museum and Art Gallery
Sagamore Hill National Historical Site
Schomberg Center for Research in Black Culture, New York Public Library
Shelburne Museum
Sheldon Memorial Art Gallery, University of Nebraska
Smithsonian Institution
Stark Museum of Art
Strong Museum
Studio Museum in Harlem
Vassar College Art Gallery
Walters Art Gallery
Whitney Museum of American Art
William A. Farnsworth Library and Art Museum
Winterthur Museum
Worcester Art Museum
Yale University Art Gallery

GALLERIES

A.B. Closson Gallery
ACA Galleries
Adams Davidson Galleries
Andre Emmerich Gallery
Arvest Galleries, Inc.
Balogh Gallery
Borghi Galleries
Braarud Fine Art
Chapellier Gallery
Connecticut Gallery, Inc.

County Store Gallery, Inc.
Daniel B. Grossman, Inc.
Deru's Fine Art
Driscoll & Walsh Fine Art
GWS Galleries
Gallery Schlesinger-Boisante, Incorporated
Gerald Peters Gallery (The Peters Corporation)
Gimpel & Weitzenhoffer Gallery
Graham Gallery
Grand Central Gallery
Henry B. Holt, Inc.
Hirschl & Adler Galleries, Inc.
James Maroney Gallery
Jeffery Hoffeld & Co., Inc.
Jeffrey Allen Gallery
John H. Garzoli
Kennedy Galleries
Kraushaar Galleries
M. Knoedler & Co., Inc.
Marbella Gallery, Inc.
Martin Diamond Gallery
Maxwell Galleries
Newman Galleries
O.K. Harris Works of Art
Oliphant and Company, LTD.
Oscarsson Hood Gallery
Peter Tillou Gallery
Petersen Galleries
Raydon Galleries
Richard Love Galleries
Robert Elkon Gallery
Robert M. Hicklin, Jr., Inc.
SIMIC Gallery
Schwarz & Son, Philadelphia
Smith Gallery
Sperone Westwater Gallery
Taggart, Jorgensen & Putman, Dealers in Fine Paintings
Thaler, Frederic Gallery
Vose Galleries of Boston, Inc.
Whistler Gallery, Inc.
Whitehall Gallery
Wunderlich & Company, Inc.

CORPORATE COLLECTIONS

Chase Manhattan Bank, N.A.
Coca-Cola Company
Early California and Western Art Research
George Demont Otis Foundation
Sotheby's
Sterling Regal, Inc.

ESSAY CONTRIBUTORS

Matthew Baigell, Rutgers University

Robert Bishop, Museum of American Folk Art

Thomas W. Bower, National Museum of American Art, Smithsonian Institution

Richard Boyle, Philadelphia College of Art

Patricia Janis Broder

George M. Cohen, Hofstra University

Edmund Barry Gaither, Museum of the National Center of Afro-American Artists

Piri Halasz

Mary F. Holahan, Delaware Art Museum

Robert F. Looney, Free Library of Philadelphia

Henry Niemann

A.J. Peluso

Oswaldo Rodriguez Roque, Metropolitan Museum of Art

David Sellin

J. Gray Sweeney, Arizona State University

Diane Tepfer

Mary Jo Viola, Baruch College, City University of New York

ART HISTORY CONSULTANTS

Roland Elzea, Delaware Art Museum

Jonathan Harding, Boston Athenaeum

Elizabeth H. Hawkes, Delaware Art Museum

Richard Love, Richard Love Galleries

David Sellin

Diane Tepfer

BIOGRAPHY WRITERS

Craig Ruffin Bailey
John Bolles
Jessica Chapin
Sandra Chatfield
Barbara Craig
Robert Cullers
Sondra Donner
Jeanne Doseff Dority
Anne C. Dougherty
Thomas M. Duthie
Randee Dutton
Andrea Fine
Donalyn Frank
Jeanne Gampe

Patricia Gibbon
Jonathan Gross
George M. Harding, Jr.
Joan G. Hauser
Joan Irving
Nina Jaroslav
Evelyn Kobler
Patricia McBroom
Márguerite Morris
Marc M. Narducci
Doris Patterson
Rebecca Rackin
Susan Shiber
Lisa Silverman
Peter Simoneaux

Vic Skrowronski
Yvonne Sobel
William Sokolic
Rebecca Stefoff
Michele Stricker
Donald Sugarman
J. Gray Sweeney
Ruth Tallmadge
Delia Turner
Dan Vitale
Kate Walbert
Deidre Watters
Anne Werner
Steve Witte

The three-volume *American Art Analog* contains information about 820 artists. Unlike most other reference works, it does not present its subjects in alphabetical order. Instead they are listed chronologically, so that the *Analog* reflects the overall history of American art and at the same time gives you a close look at each artist. To find the entry for a particular artist, check the Index, which is repeated in full at the back of each volume.

Artists are presented in order by the year of their birth—or, in cases where the birth year is unknown, by the year in which their artistic activity began. Volume I includes artists born from 1688 to the second quarter of the nineteenth century; Volume II, artists born during the second and third quarters of the nineteenth century; and Volume III, those born from the fourth quarter of the nineteenth century through 1930.

In addition to the biographical entries on individual artists, each volume of the *Analog* also contains four or more special essays—concise articles about various periods or types of American painting, written for the *Analog* by expert scholars in the field of art history. They are designed both to introduce the era of American art covered in each volume and to amplify your understanding of the individual artists.

Each of the three volumes includes a glossary of art terms and a bibliographical list of further reading on American art. The Glossary and the Bibliography, like the Index, are repeated in full at the end of every volume.

The biographical entries are the backbone of the *American Art Analog*. Each biography consists of three elements, which together give a succinct picture of the artist's life, work and performance at recent auctions. The three elements are: one or more full-color reproductions of representative paintings; an article giving information about the painter's education and training, important influences, significant works, critical reputation, and the like; and a chart or graph of financial data based on recent sales of the artist's work.

This financial data is unique to the *Analog*. It gives you a quick, clear general idea of the auction performance of the artist's work. From this you can arrive at an approximation of the current auction worth of a painting by the artist, for purposes of investment or valuation.

Because it is impossible to analyze private sales, the values analyzed in the *Analog* are international auction figures, generally regarded by the art-purchasing community as the most reliable guide to value. Although the relationship of these auction-house or wholesale values to the retail value of a painting can vary, certain factors influence the difference between the two figures. Some of the factors which may contribute to a dealer's asking price for a painting are: the value of the dealer's counsel in helping you build a specialized collection, as of the Ashcan School, the Hudson River School, or Western art; conservation or restoration services, which can amount to 25 percent or more of the ultimate asking price; framing costs; scheduled insurance costs; photographic costs, promotional fees and exhibition costs; the cost of researching and creating a properly executed monograph; general overhead expenses; and examination and research by outside experts to determine authenticity.

Perhaps the most important of these factors is authentication: a $50,000 work of art which is obtained for $20,000 is no bargain, if at a later date it is determined to be a forgery.

As a general rule, the markup between the auction and retail values of art is directly related to the asking price. Generally, the lower a piece's value, the higher the percentage of markup—the markup percentage of a $100,000 item is less than that of a $2,000 item.

Of course, many factors affect the value of individual paintings. Such factors include the painting's condition, size and restoration history, the rarity of the artist's work and the period during which he executed the painting, the subject matter and provenance of the painting, and its exhibition history.

The *Analog* financial data represents the percentages of change in auction price based on averages only. With the exception of record sales, they do not identify specific paintings. However, bidding between two aggressive buyers can sometimes drive a particular painting's price well beyond the anticipated estimate, resulting in a mathematical skew. Such skews are greatly reduced in a ten-year analysis, but the possibility exists that some of the values given here reflect these unusual situations.

The *American Art Analog* financial analysis is based on the aggregate surface area of the paintings sold in a given year and the dollars paid for those paintings, as compared with the base year, 1975.

The ten-year financial analysis will appear in the form of either a four-line chart or a chart plus a bar graph (in a very few cases, information on recent sales activity was insufficient or unavailable, so no analysis is given).

The chart consists of four elements (see Example A on the following page). The top line identifies the auction season. (Each auction season actually includes parts of two calendar years, because most auction house sales seasons follow the academic year from September through August.) The second line, "Paintings," gives the number of paintings analyzed for each auction season. The third line, "Dollars," gives the aggregate dollars paid for those paintings.

The bottom line of each chart describes the artist's record sale—the highest price paid for a painting during the decade. It tells you: the price paid for the painting, the auction house which sold it (identified by initials which are explained in the Auction House List at the back of each volume), the date of the sale, and the title and dimensions of the painting.

In cases where sufficient data exists, the chart is supplemented by a bar graph, which appears immediately above it (see Example B). The graph represents the percentage of change in the sales of the artist's work in each season of the decade, taking the 1975-1976 season as the base of comparison for each succeeding season. At the top of the graph, the average change over ten years is given as a percentage. Note that the ranges covered by the graphs differ, depending on the different levels of performance of various artists' work. In cases where the bar rises above or falls below the borders of the graph, the increment shown is a standard one, not necessarily representative of the actual percentage.

In summary, the *American Art Analog* graphs and charts reflect average changes only, and if properly employed can be of inestimable value for the art professional, appraiser, investor, collector, estate specialist, and all others interested in the field of American art. They provide an excellent overview of the gross auction activity of a particular artist.

The financial data in these three volumes is expanded and updated in other elements of the *American Art Analog* reference system. The Blue Book is published annually and adds each new season's auction figures to the ten-year data base. In addition, Special Reports are available for amplified financial analysis of a specific artist, including painting-by-painting sales information.

Ignoti nulla cupido.

Example A

SEASON	75-76	76-77	77-78	78-79	79-80	80-81	81-82	82-83	83-84	84-85
Paintings	1	1		3	5	6	8	2	5	6
Dollars	$2,500	$4,250		$4,950	$6,700	$12,000	$18,950	$2,900	$7,175	$19,675

Record Sale: $11,000, CH, 3/15/85, "Tropical Landscape at Dusk," 24 × 49 in.

Example B

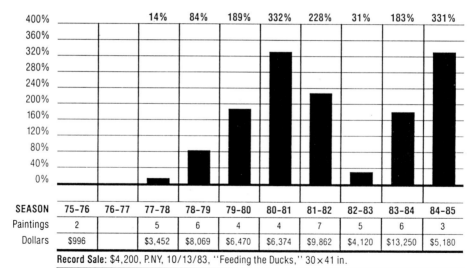

10-Year Average Change From Base Years '75-'76: 155%

		14%	84%	189%	332%	228%	31%	183%	331%

SEASON	75-76	76-77	77-78	78-79	79-80	80-81	81-82	82-83	83-84	84-85
Paintings	2		5	6	4	4	7	5	6	3
Dollars	$996		$3,452	$8,069	$6,470	$6,374	$9,862	$4,120	$13,250	$5,180

Record Sale: $4,200, P.NY, 10/13/83, "Feeding the Ducks," 30 × 41 in.

ESSAYS

AMERICAN MARINE ART AND SHIP PORTRAITURE

A.J. PELUSO, JR.

Anton Otto Fischer, *Home Again,* 24 x 30 in. Courtesy of Oliphant & Company, LTD., New York, New York.

An often-reproduced anonymous painting in the Museum of Fine Arts in Boston is called *Meditation by the Sea.* It is thought to have been done in the 1860s, perhaps copied from a magazine illustration. The center of its focus is a small man in uniform, dwarfed by the sea and the rocks of the shore. He gives the impression of a contemplative man taken up by his private thoughts. What does this American think of the sea? About what does he wonder?

Our contemporary perception of the sea is that it is something on which we cruise, or over which we fly. It wasn't always thus.

The sea was a source of mystery, even of terror. In the earliest times, it was the great unknown, the beginning of the end, the terra incognita. It was a place for heroes and for the voyages of Jonah or Odysseus. Later, man invented tools to conquer the sea, with better sails and

James Bard, *Brother Jonathan,* 1871, 32 x 52 in., signed l.r. Courtesy of Smith Gallery, New York, New York.

then with steam. As artists reflected on each advance, they never ceased to express man's underlying fear and respect for the power of the sea.

There is in all marine art a mix of two elements, never in the same proportion. One concerns the sea as a subject of metaphor and of mystery: God's work, to which Emerson referred when he said, "A nobler want of man is served by nature." The other concerns the sea as a subject of fact: man's work.

This dual theme permeates all American marine art and flows from our experience as seafarers. We had come here as immigrants to shed and shun a European past. Without a useful past we sought one of our own making, discovering the limits of our existence in the dimensions and potentialities of our new nation. The history of that endeavour was shaped by the oceans and rivers that defined our earliest America. Having discovered the limits of our new domain, we exploited it with an explosion of inventive American genius. Robert Fulton invented the steamboat; Donald McKay invented the clipper, the *Grand Republic;* George Steers invented the first of the many winners of the 100 Guineas Cup, the *America.* We knew that we had come from the sea and that the sea was the source of life, of commerce and of our national greatness.

As could be expected, the first manifestations of "American" marine art were painted by immigrants.

Michele Felice Corne was born on the island of Elba, and came to America from the Kingdom of Naples. He finished his career at Newport, Rhode Island. Thomas Birch was born in London but died in Philadelphia. Robert Salmon was born in England, emigrated from Liverpool and died in Boston. Thomas Chambers was also born in England and died in the Hudson Valley.

Fortunately, America was a snug harbor for native marine artists. Massachusetts gave us William Bradford; New Hampshire, Alfred Thompson Bricher; New Jersey, Asher Durand; New York, Ralph Blakelock, Jasper Cropsey, Sanford Robinson Gifford, George Inness, Homer Dodge Martin and William Sidney Mount; Ohio, Thomas Worthington Wittredge; Pennsylvania, Thomas Eakins, Martin John Heade and William Trost Richards; South Carolina, Washington Allston; Virginia, George Caleb Bingham.

Most of these artists worked close to home. The East coast was clearly the center of early activity, but there is much yet to be discovered and appreciated from the rest of the nation. Until now, both scholars and the marketplace have concentrated on the artists of the East, but it is clear that the Great Lakes, the Ohio and Mississippi Rivers, the Gulf of Mexico and the Pacific were as inspiring as the Atlantic and the Hudson River. There are many regional champions of marine art, and their time will soon come.

James Gayle Tyler, *Volunteer,* 14 x 18½ in., signed l.l. Courtesy of Henry B. Holt, Inc., Essex Fells, New Jersey.

There is also a body of marine work which comes to us from travelers such as Gilbert Davis Munger and Herman Herzog, who spent their working lives covering the length and breadth of the country and visiting the full range of American marine venues. Typical of their work in this vein are Munger's *View of Golden Gate* (1871, Phelan Collection) and Herzog's *The Pacific Coast Near Monterey* (1875, Phelan Collection).

There are many types of American marine art—ship portraits, seascapes, views of historic battles or disasters, genre scenes of maritime commerce or harbor activity, and more. In most cases, marine painters worked in more than one of these categories; some of them produced works in all categories.

But the major and most often seen type of marine art is the ship portrait—a painting which is, in effect, a portrait of a particular ship, usually commissioned for the ship's owner, captain, or crew. Ship portraiture is an art which

has been aptly described as a "celebration of commerce." It reflects pride, but its philosophy also squares with the pious sentiments of Emerson: "When its errands are noble and adequate, a steamboat bridging the Atlantic between Old and New England and arriving at its ports with the punctuality of a planet, is a step of man into harmony with nature."

For a time, in the early nineteenth century, "captain's pictures," as ship portraits are sometimes called, were obtained from European or Far Eastern sources. In Hong Kong, scores of "port painters" appeased the pride of shipowners and sailors. In Marseilles, the Roux family had painted ship portraits for generations. Cammillieri and Pelligrin were active there as well. There were also artists in Genoa, in Livorno, in Naples, Malta, Le Havre, Copenhagen and Liverpool. It was a most difficult market for Americans to break into. They eventually did so, however, and from the mid-nineteenth century until

James E. Buttersworth, *Yacht "Dauntless"*, 12¼ x 18 in. Courtesy of Vose Galleries of Boston, Inc., Massachusetts.

well into the twentieth, Americans dominated the field, which continued to occupy both native-born and immigrant artists.

Corne made the first lucrative market, in New England. According to Salem diarist Reverend William Bentley, "Mr. Corne continues to enjoy his reputation as a painter of Ships. In every house we see the ships of our harbour delineated for those who have navigated them." In Corne's case, the buyer got his "European" portrait at home. Later, every house was filled with American-made portraits.

American-born brothers James and John Bard carved out a market painting portraits of Hudson River steamboats, such as *Daniel Drew* (1861, Smith Gallery). English-born James Edward Buttersworth painted yachts, as in *Sandbaggers* (Henry Holt). (The Mystic Seaport Museum in Mystic, Connecticut has the most extensive collection of Buttersworths.) Their subjects were, at least initially, not ocean-going vessels, so they had little competition.

Ship portraiture spans a wide range of talents and techniques, from naive folk art to the most meticulous precisionist, from the derivative to the innovative. In the folk mode are the paintings of James and John Bard and James Guy Evans, the early work of James Gale Tyler, the

works of German-born Julius Stockfleth of Galveston, Texas, and the work of Otto Muhlenfeld in Baltimore, Maryland. Among the precisionists you will find the work of the mature James Bard, Hoboken's Danish-born Antonio Jacobsen, New Bedford's English-born Charles Sidney Raleigh, Irishman William Coulter of San Francisco and Samuel Finley Morse Badger of Boston. A large middle ground of competence was occupied by William P. Stubbs of Boston, by Percy Sanborn of Belfast, Maine, by Englishman Joseph Lee of San Francisco and by Great Lakes specialist Seth Arca Whipple. Among the innovative ship portraits are the works of German Fred Pansing, the rare but exceptional works of Samuel Ward Stanton and the equally rare and luminous works of Elisha Taylor Baker, as well as the oil-on-canvas and embroidered works of Brooklyn-based Dane Thomas Willis.

The most prolific of these painters, those whose works are most often encountered, were Antonio Jacobsen, who painted the *John E. Moore* (1884, Smith Gallery), and William P. Stubbs, who painted the *Annie Pendleton* (1891, Penobscot Marine Museum).

All had draftsmanship in common. It was unacceptable for a ship-portrait painter to paint inaccurately. Whether he was painting waves or sails, every detail had to be correct and meticulous; the client was an expert in such

Antonio Jacobsen, *I.F. Chapman,* 40 x 50 in. Courtesy of Oliphant and Company, LTD., New York, New York.

Antonio Jacobsen, *G.W. Jones,* 1888, 22 x 36 in., signed l.r. Courtesy of Smith Gallery, New York, New York.

Charles Sidney Raleigh, *Mary Bates,* 1878, 25½ x 35½ in., signed l.l. Courtesy of Smith Gallery, New York, New York.

William Bradford, *Seining off Labrador,* 16 x 24 in. Courtesy of Oliphant and Company, LTD., New York, New York.

things and would not tolerate a departure from the reality he knew.

The largest collections of ship portraits in the United States may be seen at the Mariners Museum in Newport News, Virginia and the Peabody Museum in Salem, Massachusetts.

Many other types of marine paintings either were produced by artists who also painted ship portraits or have elements in common with ship portraiture.

One such is the marine landscape, or seascape, discussed in detail in another essay in this book. It most often takes the form of a view of the meeting of sea and land, the marriage of the coastal rocks and the relentless sea. Seascapes often included representations of ships, as in Thomas Doughty's *Desert Rock Lighthouse* (1847, Newark Museum). Ice is another subject found in this category, one commanded by William Bradford, who virtually built his career upon ice paintings, such as *Ice Dwellers Watching the Invaders* (ca. 1870, Whaling Museum of New Bedford). This painting and scores like it speak eloquently of the loneliness of the sea, the daring of those who explored its limits, and the challenge of nature's elemental cold.

Also at the Whaling Museum in New Bedford is a large collection of the works of Charles Sidney Raleigh, who developed his own niche with many larger-than-life portraits of ice-dwelling polar bears (at the same time that animal painter William Beard was devoting himself to the allegorical depiction of land animals).

Paintings which depict man's interaction with the sea— genre views of maritime commerce or harbor scenes— often include detailed pictures of ships and boats. Many of them portrayed whaling or fishing activities, as in Raleigh's work or Bradford's *Seining off Labrador.* In a more sporting vein, Bradford and Buttersworth painted yacht races. Harbor scenes were also important. James Hamilton painted a *View of Chesapeake Bay with Baltimore in the Background* (1859, Trinity College). Fitz Hugh Lane, whose gentle but ardent work is in a class by itself, painted *Gloucester Harbor* (1848, Virginia Museum) and *New York Harbor* (1850, Museum of Fine Arts, Boston).

Another form of marine art which has affinities with the ship portrait is the sea-battle painting, the epitome of what has been called "naval nationalism." The Revolutionary War and the War of 1812 were favored subjects, and the Civil War and the Spanish-American War added subjects to this category. Thomas Birch painted *The Battle of Lake Erie.* Thomas Chambers painted several scenes from the War of 1812, including *Constitution Capturing*

Thomas Chambers, *Constitution Capturing Java,* 21¼ x 30 in. Courtesy of Wunderlich and Company, Inc., New York, New York.

Antonio Jacobsen, *County of Edinburgh,* 1903, 22 x 36 in., signed l.r. Courtesy of Smith Gallery, New York, New York.

Java and *The Constitution and the Guerriere* (ca. 1845, Metropolitan Museum of Art). Even Fitz Hugh Lane found inspiration in *The United States Frigate President Engaging the British Squadron, 1815* (1850, Corcoran Gallery of Art). The United States Naval Academy in Annapolis, Maryland has a splendid collection of sea-battle subjects.

Paintings of disasters at sea or on the water also featured ships, as in William Wheeler's *Great Lakes Marine Disaster* (ca. 1860, Phelan Collection). It features a pitiable group adrift in a lifeboat in the moonlight, watching as their ship burns. The circumstance and the fine detail suggest that it may commemorate an actual event.

All these artists painted in oils. There were, however, two exceptional marine artists who established their reputations as watercolorists.

Frederic Schiller Cozzens was a journeyman artist who created an impressively large body of work which is often seen and readily available. (Many of his paintings were lithographically reproduced.) He concentrated on America's domestic and international yachting experiences and bore historical witness to those exciting events.

His compatriot, and the pre-eminent marine artist regardless of medium, was Winslow Homer. His work is the most sought-after in the marketplace—understandably so, as it was unique, far ahead of its time, possessed of fresh themes and a forward-looking style. Whereas much marine art was derivative and looked to the past or to European sources, the work of Winslow Homer found personal, and particularly American, inspiration.

Be encouraged to participate in and enjoy the marine art of America. It is as rich, as broad in scope, as varied in subject matter, as extensive in the range of talent and style, and as bountiful as America itself.

A.J. Peluso, Jr. is the author of *J. & J. Bard Picture Painters* and many articles on marine and ship portrait art.

SEASCAPE: MARINE LANDSCAPE PAINTING

J. GRAY SWEENEY

John Singleton Copley, *Watson and the Shark,* 1778, 72 x 90¼ in., signed l.c. Gift of Mrs. George von Lengerke Meyer; Courtesy of the Museum of Fine Arts, Boston, Massachusetts.

For purposes of discussion, marine painting can be divided into two broad categories. One is ship portraiture, or the depiction of specific ships. Although ship portraiture, which is discussed in another essay in these volumes, is a long-established and well-recognized aspect of marine painting, we are concerned here with the other type of marine painting: the marine landscape. Some of the most illuminating masterpieces in American art were created in this genre.

The felicitous term "seascape" has been used by Professor Roger B. Stein to describe this type of marine art; *Seascape* was the title of his 1975 exhibition at the Whitney Museum of American Art. Earlier, John Wilmerding had pioneered the study of American marine painting with his 1968 publication of *A History of American Marine Painting*. The work of these scholars demonstrated that paintings of the seascape reflect the historical and artistic development of the nineteenth century.

Thomas Birch, *Perry Leaving the Lawrence,* Courtesy of Private Collection.

The seascapes discussed in this essay, excluding portraits of ships, include: views of harbors and ports where the landscape is given at least equal importance with the ships represented; coastal scenes or views of the sea from the land; views of sea battles and ships on the sea; and symbolic seascapes. Marine landscape paintings of masterpiece stature, when carefully considered, possess the same aesthetic and symbolic importance as terrestrial landscapes, and the pattern of development in this art form closely parallels the mainstream of American art. An important relationship exists between the irreplaceable masterpieces which are discussed here and the typical marine landscape painting available to collectors, for the masterpiece provides a standard, a benchmark, against which the value and art-historical importance of other works may be measured.

The mythological and symbolic aspects of seascapes had appeared by the late eighteenth century, in works by Benjamin West and John Singleton Copley. West's *Telemachus and Calypso* (ca. 1809, Corcoran Gallery of Art) subordinates the human drama to the powers of nature. It contrasts the world of men on the left, characterized by dark storm and shipwreck, with the world of women on the right, a sensuous, beautiful landscape. Copley's *Watson and the Shark* (1778, Museum of Fine Arts, Boston) has long been a benchmark of American marine art. Recent studies have emphasized its complex symbolic meaning in the context of nationalism and revolution.

The emergence of romanticism in the early nineteenth century profoundly affected paintings of the seascape. Washington Allston's *Rising of a Thunderstorm at Sea* (1804, Museum of Fine Arts, Boston) places the helpless figures in a pilot boat at the mercy of a sublime sea which is rising in fury. The sunlit sky and the mysterious form in the clouds seem to offer the only prospect for release from this psychologically resonant view of a wilderness of waves.

Seascapes of this period also frequently incorporated images of nationalism and national identity. In addition, images of the divinity of nature are dominant in the mid-nineteenth century. Ship portraits, images of man's commercial use and control of the seas, continued as the most

Fitz Hugh Lane, *Stage Fort Across Gloucester Harbor,* 1862, 38 x 60 in., signed l.r. Courtesy of the Metropolitan Museum of Art, Photograph courtesy of Vose Galleries, Inc., Boston, Massachusetts.

Martin Johnson Heade, *Thunderstorm Over Narragansett Bay,* 1868, 32⅛ x 54½ in., signed l.l. Courtesy of Amon Carter Museum, Fort Worth, Texas.

Martin Johnson Heade, *Spouting Rock, Newport,* 1862, 25 x 50 in., signed l.c. Courtesy of Vose Galleries of Boston, Inc., Massachusetts.

prevalent type of marine painting. In the latter part of the nineteenth century, images of man's loneliness and vulnerability to nature would appear in Winslow Homer's work.

Art received a creative impetus from the melding of romanticism and nationalism after the War of 1812. Artists and patrons placed new emphasis on depicting native heroes and using native materials. On the inland seas of America's Great Lakes, the Battle of Lake Erie in the War of 1812 was an American victory that led to Thomas Birch's *Perry Leaving the Lawrence* (1838, private collection). It depicts a crucial moment in the naval battle, when Perry abandoned his sinking flagship, carrying his battle flag—which bore the famous words "Don't Give Up the Ship"—to the sister ship *Niagara.* He resumed, and won, the battle. With its idealized action and its emphasis on heroism for the sake of one's country, Birch's painting is a characteristically nationalistic depiction of a sea battle. The Civil War would later inspire numerous sea-battle paintings, such as those by Xanthus R. Smith.

Some of the prime early-nineteenth-century expressions of America's emerging pride in its maritime power were created by Robert Salmon. His *View of Boston Harbor from Constitution Wharf (View of Charlestown)* (1833, United States Naval Academy) is an expansive, sun-drenched view of American naval ships entering Boston Harbor. Its sharp, crisp detail and precisely ordered geometry of space emphasize the new nation's pride in its naval power.

In the work of the first generation of romantic landscape painters, the seascape is further refined as an artistic vision of nature. Thomas Birch, Thomas Cole, Thomas Doughty and Joshua Shaw created remarkable seascapes,

full of romantic sentiment. A significant number of the landscape painters of the Hudson River School painted seascapes as well. Foremost among them was Frederic Edwin Church. His *Sunrise Off the Maine Coast* (1863, Wadsworth Atheneum) is a powerful romantic meditation painted with the scrupulous attention to "truth to nature" prescribed by leading English art critic John Ruskin. Yet Church's work is more than merely a view of a place where land and sea meet in foaming rage. For Church, a glorious sunrise over the shores of New England would have been symbolically associated with the young nation's belief in its errand in the wilderness and the fulfillment of its manifest destiny on the North American continent. Church's contemporary Albert Bierstadt also painted a number of important marine landscapes, while William Bradford followed Church's lead in painting the Arctic.

The artists of the Hudson River School powerfully expressed their romantic vision of nature's divinity and nationalistic importance, especially in their marine landscapes. For these painters, the seascape was yet another aspect of nature's beauty and sublimity. Many of the artists who have been called luminists often painted seascapes. For example, Fitz Hugh Lane's *Ships and an Approaching Storm Off Owl's Head, Maine* (1860, John D. Rockefeller IV) captures the hushed stillness of nature before the storm. It expresses in an optimistic way the presence of American maritime enterprise in the face of nature's power.

Strongly contrasting with Lane's optimistic, pre-Civil War treatment of the approaching storm is Martin J. Heade's *Thunderstorm Over Narragansett Bay* (1868, Amon Carter Museum). The painting puzzled its audience

John Frederick Kensett, *Along the Hudson,* 1852, 18⅛ x 24 in. Courtesy of National Museum of American Art, Smithsonian Institution, Washington, D.C., Bequest of Helen Huntington Hull.

when it was first exhibited in 1868; its power over specta-tors has been renewed in the mid-twentieth century, as it has been enshrined as a benchmark of the so-called lumi-nist movement. Heade's thunderstorm is far more than a picture of some becalmed sailboats. Its somber mood and dark color recall the final scene of *Old Age* from Thomas Cole's allegorical series "The Voyage of Life," with its dark, brooding atmosphere and flat, calm sea. Perhaps, like the discreet symbolism found in the contemporary art of the English pre-raphaelites or even that of Frederic Edwin Church, Heade's work may be interpreted as a pro-found meditation on the stages of life's journey and its fragile transience. Whatever the exact meaning of Heade's elusive painting, it demonstrates that seascape can express the deepest and most complex feelings and ideas about nature, and that such works of art are—like Herman Melville's *Moby-Dick*—barometers of American civilization.

At yet another extreme from Heade's masterpiece are the seascapes of Sanford R. Gifford, John F. Kensett, T. Worthington Whittredge and Alfred T. Bricher. Gif-ford's marine landscapes are charged with a warm golden light that speaks of the beneficence of nature. Kensett emphasizes the impassive yet vital presence of rocks, sand, sea and sun. His marine paintings are seldom stormy or dark, yet they uniquely reflect the awesome, immutable presence of the created order. One of the prolific Kensett's last works captures the essence of his vision: *Sunrise over the Sea* (1872, Metropolitan Museum of Art) distills light and water to their purest and most transcendent forms.

American seascape painting changed with the advent of new, more painterly styles in art. James A.M. Whistler, George Inness, Ralph A. Blakelock and Albert P. Ryder moved marine landscape painting toward a personal rather than a nationalistic or romantic involvement with nature. Ryder's brooding seascapes and images of lonely ships sailing under a baleful moon gave a new dimension to marine painting. Poorly crafted as they are, his paint-ings speak poetically of loneliness and of life's fearful journey over a forbidding deep. Ryder's special place in American art links him with those few artists who empha-sized seascape as a psychological exploration. In his *The Flying Dutchman* (ca. 1887, National Museum of Ameri-can Art), the mad Hollander sails phantom-like from the

Alfred Thompson Bricher, *A Quiet Day Near Manchester, Cape Ann,* 1873, 20 x 38¼ in., signed l.l. Courtesy of Wunderlich and Company, Inc., New York, New York.

Winslow Homer, *The Gulf Stream,* 1899, 29⅛ x 49⅛ in., signed l.l. Courtesy of The Metropolitan Museum of Art, Wolfe Fund, 1906. Catharine Lorillard Wolfe Collection.

external world to an internal one of feeling and ultimate search.

At the end of the nineteenth century, Winslow Homer made the seascape one of his primary subjects and elevated the genre to a new level of importance. His life on Maine's coast, in England and in the Bahamas enabled him to add new images to marine painting: heroic fishermen toiling in adversity and stalwart women waiting by the seashore.

Homer's masterpiece, *The Gulf Stream* (Metropolitan Museum of Art), painted in the last year of the nineteenth century, is the culminating image of American marine art. A forlorn sailor on a derelict ship, surrounded by sharks, looks defiantly away from the symbols of his salvation: a passing ship on the distant horizon and a cross-shaped stanchion on the bow of his boat. Homer's revelation of the grim indifference of nature creates a terrifyingly modern feeling, as if the beneficent deity of the earlier part of the century had been withdrawn. Emerging in Homer's late marine paintings is an existential vision of nature appropriate to the twentieth century.

The appreciation and collection of seascape is a long-established American tradition. Today, renewed attention is being given to works in this genre, because scholars, curators, collectors and art dealers now recognize that through their seascapes American artists have taught us to better understand the range and variety of our encounters with nature. While emphasis has been placed here on the recognized masterpieces—or benchmarks—of American marine art, it is important to stress that there are numerous other artists and works which also share the importance and vitality of this major American artistic genre. Through the marine landscape we can come to understand how Americans have seen and interpreted themselves in the New World.

J. Gray Sweeney's primary area of research is mid-nineteenth-century American landscape painting. He has organized many exhibitions and in 1984-1985 was Senior Fellow at the National Museum of American Art in Washington, D.C., where he researched a major study of Thomas Cole's influence. He is currently an associate professor of art history at Arizona State University.

Albert Pinkham Ryder, *Flying Dutchman,* ca. 1887, 14¼ X 17¼ in. Courtesy of National Museum of American Art, Smithsonian Institution, Gift of John Gellatly.

GENRE PAINTING IN AMERICA

GEORGE M. COHEN

Charles Willson Peale, *George Washington at Princeton,* 1779, 93 x 58½ in. Courtesy of the Pennsylvania Academy of the Fine Arts, Philadelphia, Gift of the Executors of Elizabeth Wharton McKean estate.

America possesses a peculiarly fresh and distinct nationalistic spirit which emphasizes individualism and the doctrine of equality. It is from this ideology that our painters of genre life arose in the middle decades of the nineteenth century.

By definition genre means genus, kind or type. It is a category of painting in which the subject matter represents typical scenes from ordinary life, as distinguished from the specific scenes recorded in landscape, portrait or history painting.

Genre art records commonplace, everyday activities which show the pleasures, vices and follies, the work, play and amusements of ordinary people in a realistic and straightforward manner. It represents common people engaged in mundane, recognizable pursuits.

Although its themes are universal, genre painting deals with the actual, not the ideal. Its aspirations and achievements belong to the common world and no other. It records the struggles, the character, the happiness and the folly of mankind. It is everyman's history, and its painters are observers. They have little prejudice because they have no prepossessions.

But genre art also has certain subjective qualities. It may be satiric, didactic, sentimental, romantic, even religious. Such qualities as the absurd, the pathetic, the exaggerated, the ironical, or the kindly play of humor may be part of its pictorial philosophy. Genre themes usually possess an optimistic outlook—a so-called "affirmative positivism." Familiarity and sympathy between the seer and the seen are the wellsprings of the genre painter.

Genre recorders feel and convey the immediacy and importance of the themes they deal with. Their goal is to depict our moods and manners and to record the incidents of the passing minute. Genre art is best when there is least public preoccupation with questions of politics or religion, and when the human figures are anonymously depicted.

Anonymity is genre art's idiosyncrasy. In this type of painting, one is not really concerned with actual human names; only the common human condition is important and revealed. Genre painters do not interpret history, religion or myth. They are preoccupied with what real people are accustomed to—whether it is from instinct or inclination. Whereas the historical picture says, "That happened once," the genre picture says, "This happens often."

Genre painters are true realists, interpreting what they have seen with the physical eye. Their subject is always, though, a typical situation—characteristic of a time, a place, a social class, an age or a profession—that will

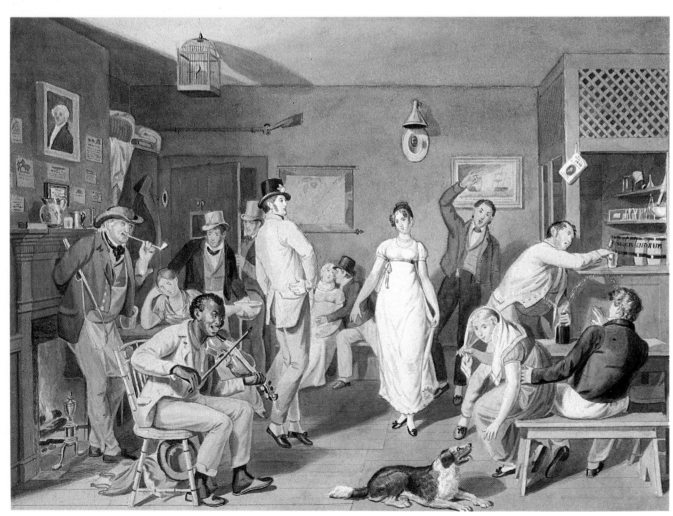

John Lewis Krimmel, *Barroom Dancing.* Courtesy of Frank S. Schwarz & Son, Philadelphia, Pennsylvania.

Francis Guy, *Carter's Tavern at the Head of Lake George*, 39 x 66 in. Courtesy of the Detroit Institute of Arts, Founders Society Purchase, Robert H. Tannahill Fund.

touch or even entertain the viewer. The real theme of a genre painting is condition, not event.

The highest form of genre painting was first reached in seventeenth-century Holland, Flanders and France. Such noted Dutch painters as Jan Vermeer, Gerard Terborch, Jan Steen, Gabriel Metsu, Pieter de Hooch and Adrian van Ostade, as well as the Flemings David Teniers, Frans Snyders, Jacob Jordaens and Adrian van Brouwer, were but a few who excelled in all levels of genre portrayals of subjects ranging from well-to-do burghers to lowly peasants.

In France, the Brothers Le Nain were credited with creating similar oils. Like the Dutch and Flemish works, their paintings were poignant and immediate vignettes from the lives of the middle classes and peasants. They isolated mundane incidents from everyday life in a down-to-earth, factual way.

In a similar manner, Spanish painter Diego Velazquez poignantly recorded episodes of street life during his early Seville period. Many art historians assert that if he had remained in Seville (he was later called to the court of Philip IV in Madrid) he would have been the greatest genre painter of his time.

By the late eighteenth century, sentimental, rustic genre painting prevailed in England and on the Continent. It included the work of Jean Baptiste Greuze, Francis Wheatley, George Morland and David Wilkie, as well as the heritage of political and social satire represented by William Hogarth, James Gillray, Thomas Rowlandson and George Cruikshank.

Meanwhile, in eighteenth-century America, scenes of everyday life were portrayed in a wide variety of media: commercial signs, banknotes, embroidery, fire screens and literary illustrations. It was not, however, until the second decade of the following century that true genre painting emerged in America. It was to resemble the European prototypes, with emphasis on gestures, anecdotal elements, and moralizing or humorous stories.

American painting had always included a latent genre tradition. For a long time, however, the would-be art patron was for the most part limited to portraiture or historical narration. But as life in the United States became less difficult, as new wealth and a new leisure society arose within the middle classes, and as artistic competence developed, American art assumed a more varied naturalism based on the observation of character. Scenes which depicted rigidly posed sitters or formally grouped soldiers gave way to more natural scenes of recognizable, everyday events.

This change did not occur overnight. A desire still existed for historical battle pictures, views of cities and topographical landscapes; the ever-growing national and historical consciousness of Americans created a demand for such subjects.

It was not until after the introduction of lithography in the late 1840s that true genre art really came into its own. This new graphic medium, with its journalistic ability to be reproduced for a mass culture, encouraged less-well-

George Caleb Bingham, *Wood-Boatman on a River,* 1854, 29 x 36¼ in. Courtesy of Amon Carter Museum, Fort Worth, Texas.

known artists—among whom were many genre painters.

At the same time, powerful political and socioeconomic forces were at work in the United States. The "Age of Jackson," with its emphasis on democratization and the common man's quest for equality, coupled with the increased nationalism brought about by the geographic expansion of the nation's frontier posts, helped shatter the old aristocratic oligarchy of the original colonial states. Unfamiliar names such as St. Louis, Pittsburgh, Kansas City, Fort Benton and Fort Laramie became economic and political focal points, just as Boston, New York, Philadelphia and New Orleans had been a few years earlier.

Although high culture and wealth were still confined to the Eastern seaboard, the spirit of the American people was now directed toward the frontier—and toward the homely, natural aspects of life. A strengthening democracy encouraged a national mood of realistic, good-natured self-examination. Thus, by the middle decades of the nineteenth century, America was a land which looked proudly at itself. American painters, too, became in-

trospective and began to record a national, homespun culture.

In addition, American and Western European artists at this time shared a sense of the passing or fading of the agrarian way of life. With the Industrial Revolution spreading to America, many artists turned away from city life and painted either virgin terrain (such as that favored by the Hudson River School painters) or the life of the farmer.

Rural, rustic America was studied, observed and documented—although some artists did interpret genre scenes of city life. In short, self-examination with a dominant note of nostalgia was to become a significant feature of America's genre-painting tradition.

Before the rise of America's true genre artists, there were a few who foreshadowed genre painting. For example, Philadelphian Charles Willson Peale painted *The Exhumation of the First American Mastodon* (1806-1808, Peale Museum, Baltimore). The rural picture showed some 25 workmen drawing buckets of water from a marl

Winslow Homer, *The Morning Bell,* ca. 1866, 24 x 38¼ in., signed l.r. Courtesy of Yale University Art Gallery, New Haven, Connecticut, Bequest of Stephen Carlton Clark, BA 1903.

pit containing mastodon bones. Peale's direct observation and the scientific accuracy of his pictorial information made the work a harbinger of later genre painting.

Between 1815 and 1820, Henry Sargent painted *The Tea Party* and *The Dinner Party* (Museum of Fine Arts, Boston). These oils were essentially transcripts of social life, depicting the manners, modes and mores of fashionable Beacon Hill society in Boston.

Another early genre painter of polite society was John Lewis Krimmel. He learned genre art by copying imported engravings by Europeans Wilkie, Hogarth and Greuze, and went on to produce such works as *A Fourth of July Celebration in Centre Square, Philadelphia* (1819, Pennsylvania Academy of the Fine Arts). The setting of this picture is Benjamin Latrobe's "water-works" plant, where socializing crowds mill around before William Rush's wooden statue *Water Nymph and Bittern.* The contrived, theatrical setting is pervaded with an English decorativeness and superficiality. Yet through his keen observation of society and its recreational pleasures, Krimmel imbues the work with an urban colloquialism.

This spirit continued in the oils of Francis Guy, who painted topographical scenes of New York City and especially of early village life in Brooklyn. *Winter Scene in Brooklyn* (1817-1820, Brooklyn Museum), an overall view of the locale, is like a Pieter Brueghel painting from the Flemish Renaissance, abounding in the activities of people going about their everyday affairs.

Finally, Henry Inman's *Rip Van Winkle Awakening from His Sleep* (1823) relates to the sub-category of literary genre art, depicting scenes from popular literature. Through such scenes as this, Inman introduced to America a new category of genre painting. Literary genre was to remain a separate category within American art. Its best-known exponent was John Quidor, who evoked nostalgia for bygone rural life, using scenes from literature to portray the common man in a bucolic setting. He often consulted the works of authors Washington Irving and James Fenimore Cooper, borrowing from their tales to suit his own artistic purposes.

But the most popular inspiration for genre art was found in America's rural areas. It seemed that wherever pastoral folk gathered or performed a task, their activities were recorded in the most direct and immediate manner. Scenes of farm labor—ranging from corn husking, wood hauling and bargaining for livestock to colloquial vignettes of hoe-downing, swapping yarns or tasting maple sugar—formed the repertoire of many genre artists.

Among the more noted of these artists was William Sidney Mount, who was considered the first American-born painter to devote himself entirely to genre subjects. Mount was a "character," full of Yankee idiosyncracies, who preferred the little rural community of Stony Brook, Long Island to the urban clamor of nearby New York City. A close and happy relationship developed between his envi-

Eastman Johnson, *Cranberry Pickers, Nantucket*, 1880, signed l.r. Courtesy of Vose Galleries of Boston, Inc., Massachusetts.

ronment and his art. Mount's works became the purest pictorial expressions of the agrarian, Jacksonian democracy which existed before the full impact of the Industrial Revolution was felt in America.

A Western counterpart of Mount was frontier painter George Caleb Bingham. His work presented a lively pageant of talkative politicians, loutish backwoodsmen, solid citizens, staggering drunks and roistering boatmen. His paintings possess an air of sincerity, suggesting that his characters lived lives of their own and were real personalities, truthfully interpreted.

Like Mount, Bingham caught the feelings and impulses which act upon his casual, sometimes careless crowds and individuals. His genre work showed people at ease with the world, well-rooted and impersonal as they performed their daily tasks in a way that echoed the paintings of sixteenth-century Fleming Pieter Brueghel. Bingham gave the final humanizing touch to the generation which tamed the Western lands, waters and wildlife. He understood the compelling motive which brought most of the immigrants to the West—an insatiable land hunger.

Perhaps America's finest rural genre painter was Winslow Homer. Although he is usually thought of as a marine painter, his early scenes of rustic New England life were poignant, bucolic pictures, both illustrative and anecdotal.

Some say Homer's genre work grew out of his early background in lithographs and woodcuts for magazine illustrations in *Harper's Weekly*. Whatever the case, his genre art, like Mount's and Bingham's, contained an undertone of humor and quiet optimism. With a detached and realistic eye, he studied and monumentalized common folk. Plain, prosaic scenes from the farm and countryside were represented in a non-idealistic manner. His people were genuine rustics. Tanned and freckled, dressed in straw hats, cotton sunbonnets and cowhide boots, they were recorded with the utmost detail and concern for realism.

Homer evoked a nostalgic yearning for the peaceful country—free from the pressures, chaos and squalor of urban industrialism. Without deviating from truth and authenticity, he attempted to capture the positive pleasures of America's old, rural environs.

Another well-known rural genre artist was Eastman Johnson, who portrayed scenes of New England and the East coast. Like that of Mount, Bingham and Homer, his genre art was filled with humor, good nature and optimism. As a result, his bucolic scenes emanate a happy, objective healthiness, a vitality and gentle human appeal.

Some artists chose to depict the common man in urban surroundings. Although fewer in number than their rural peers, they recorded street panoramas with the same sincerity and truthfulness. Among the more esteemed in this category were Richard Caton Woodville of Baltimore and David Gilmore Blythe of Pittsburgh. Both imbued city vignettes with vitality, good-nature and nostalgia.

Woodville was one of the first American artists to achieve financial success with genre art. His themes were acceptable to the rising man of affairs and means of the day, and the American Art-Union found a customer for each of his oils. His humorous, impersonal subject matter portrayed common city people favorably, while its universality permitted the viewer to enter vicariously into the intimate urban scenes. His canvases even included an element of nostalgia, recalling familiar and pleasurable past experiences that an urbanite might have seen or participated in.

On the other hand, Blythe looked upon his city's "gen-

Richard C. Woodville, *Two Figures at a Stove,* 1845, 8½ x 6¾ in., signed l.r. Courtesy of Kennedy Galleries, New York, New York.

John Quidor, *Ichabod Crane Flying from the Headless Horseman,* ca. 1828, 22⅝ x 30¹/₁₆ in. Courtesy of Yale University Art Gallery, New Haven, Connecticut, The Mabel Brady Garvan Collection.

try" with a humorous but satirical eye. His wit emphasized the essentials of a scene and sometimes developed a strain of almost caricatural madness. Blythe's satire was sometimes bitter and coarse. Like the eighteenth-century English painter William Hogarth or the nineteenth-century French caricaturist Honore Daumier, he painted only the ridiculous side of humanity, commenting on his subjects' self-importance—a trait often found in city dwellers. His travels took him into taverns, marketplaces, even prisons.

Of course, there were others whose creativity and talent contributed to and perpetuated genre painting in America. Albertus Del Orient Browere, John George Brown, James Goodwyn Clooney, George Henry Durrie, Francis William Edmonds, Edward Lamson Henry, David Claypool Johnston and Arthur Fitzwilliam Tait produced genre accounts of everyday rural and urban activity. Their aim, whether they depicted the rugged, agrarian farmer or the sophisticated, prosperous city-dweller, was not only to record scenes of everyday life but to serve other functions: literary narration, psychological portraiture and sociopolitical documentation. They were attuned to the spirit of nationalism embodied in the nineteenth-century concept of America's "manifest destiny" as an extraordinary nation of democratically ordinary people.

American genre painting, by the last decade of the nineteenth century, had come a long way from its rudimentary beginnings. It became so popular a mode of artistic expression that it began to rival portrait and landscape art.

We owe a debt of gratitude to the genre artists who carried forth the American spirit of equality. They possessed both skill and passion for life. They presented America with a necessary heritage, saying to the world, "We have something to offer. Look at us!"

George M. Cohen is an associate professor of art history and humanities at Hofstra University. He has written numerous articles on American art for *College Art Journal, Art Voices, American Artist, Art and Antiques, Art and Artists* and *Valuation.* He has also published *A History of American Art.* In addition, Cohen is a senior member and past president of the Long Island (NY) chapter of the American Society of Appraisers and a member of the Appraisers Association of America.

George Henry Durrie, *Hunter in Winter Landscape,* 12 x 9⅞ in., signed l.r. Courtesy of Wunderlich and Company, Inc., New York, New York.

AMERICAN LANDSCAPE PAINTING IN THE NINETEENTH CENTURY

ROBERT F. LOONEY

Thomas Doughty, *Fishing,* 1830, 13½ x 17 in., signed l.r. Courtesy of Vose Galleries of Boston, Inc., Massachusetts.

It has been said that the reason the ancient Greeks were sculptors and architects rather than painters is because of the extraordinary quality of the light in Greece: it is so very clear that it sharpened the ability of the artists to see dimension and depth. Light is also one of the salient char-

acteristics of landscape painting in nineteenth-century America: the particular quality of American light is the way it seemed to enhance the color of the natural world. Successive generations of painters responded to light in a variety of ways, but their response is a common thread

Thomas Cole, *View of Boston,* 34 x 47⅛ in. Photograph courtesy of Hirshl & Adler Galleries, Inc., New York, New York.

that is traceable through the entire century, almost like a principal theme in a great musical composition. It has its introduction, development, climax and finally its coda, or denouement.

Another characteristic of equal importance was spatial magnitude, or panoramic grandeur, which went hand in hand with the rise of a nationalistic spirit. America was then a new nation, and nineteenth-century Americans grew more and more interested in the land itself: its vastness, the wonders of its scenery, the character of its wilderness. These Americans were a proud people, and they wanted to see the distant reaches of their country's boundaries. Underlying this interest was a sense of "manifest destiny," the belief that the United States was destined to become a great nation, as was manifest in its great size and in the principles upon which it was founded. Thus a kind of rediscovery of America was to take place at the hands of its landscape painters.

A new reverence for nature found its way into painting, partly through its expression in literature in the great romantic movement. Poets in England and Europe looked at nature in all its glorious detail and found in it a Divine Presence, and life itself took on a new meaning as this pantheist philosophy touched all people. There was a new exulation in the wilderness, a feeling of awe for its power and might and of inspiration drawn from its mystical beauty.

During the first decades of the nineteenth century, a number of printed views, chiefly of American cities and all derived from paintings and drawings, were published. Important among these were the views of Philadelphia by William Russell Birch. They were the first such prints to depict the vitality of life as it was being lived in an American city. These views became popular in Europe and thus instigated a succession of similar publications, including *Picturesque Views of American Scenery* in 1820 and the *Hudson River Portfolio* in 1826, both engraved by John Hill after paintings by Joshua Shaw and William G. Wall. The significance of these so-called travel books was that they stimulated a direct interest in the American landscape, helping to set in motion a landscape tradition that would be distinctly American in character.

In the vanguard of this tradition was Thomas Doughty, who had begun to paint American landscapes by 1820. He traveled about in the Eastern states as far North as Maine, and presumably South into the Carolinas, finding subject

Asher B. Durand, *Showery Day Among the Mountains,* 20 x 30 in. Courtesy of Vose Galleries of Boston, Inc., Massachusetts.

matter for his paintings along the way. He was particularly inspired by his visits to the Hudson River Valley; his pictures of this region are among his best. His dramatic use of light heightened the quality of his paintings, especially as it was reflected from the silvery surfaces of rivers and lakes and glowed from skies and mountainsides bathed by the sun. Although his paintings were not literal renderings of what he actually saw, they were American in character and detail, and they gained him much popularity.

Doughty initiated the discovery of the American landscape as a worthy subject for painting, but he was very much overshadowed by his contemporary Thomas Cole. Doughty's works, realistic although not literal, were pleasing enough in their poetic rendering of scenes his audience could relate to. But Thomas Cole was not content to reproduce what he saw in the natural setting before him. Caught up in the ideals of romanticism he sought to portray the sublime, the passionate, the dramatic elements present in nature for the visionary.

Cole's early pictures were fresh and innovative, and like Doughty's they suggested the reality of the settings. In his works of the 1830s, however, he turned to moral and religious allegory, and painted great epics in series, with nature as the stage upon which he worked out his themes. Among these epics was *The Course of Empire* (1836,

New-York Historical Society), an allegory of the rise and fall of an empire in five panels. Perhaps his most famous work is *The Voyage of Life* (1840, Munson-Williams-Proctor Institute), four panels illustrating man's journey through life. In these vast epics he used light to intensify the dramatic treatment of space, which he had learned from studying the landscape drawings of Claude Lorraine and the etchings of Rembrandt. In his pure landscapes Cole depicted America as another Eden, a demi-paradise.

Cole was considered the founder of what became known as the Hudson River School of painters, chiefly because he more than any other painter of the 1820s and 1830s defined through his work the characteristics and focus common to the various members of the group. They were by no means confined to a geographic location, although they drew heavily upon the Hudson River Valley for their subject matter. The Northeastern United States was their territory; the beauty of the American wilderness, overlaid with the ideals of nationalistic spirit and romantic transcendentalism, was their subject.

Cole, however, did not transcribe nature literally in his work, but adjusted it to his themes and ideas and embroidered upon it. It remained for Asher B. Durand to focus on the faithful and detailed rendering of natural settings. Durand became the central figure of the Hudson River School, and after Cole's death in 1848 was the major land-

John F. Kensett, *Coast of Narragansett,* 1861, 14 x 24 in., signed l.c. Courtesy of Vose Galleries of Boston, Inc., Massachusetts.

Jasper F. Cropsey, *Figures on Hudson,* 1874, 12 x 20 in., signed l.r. Courtesy of Taggart, Jorgensen & Putman Gallery, Washington, D.C.

Frederic Edwin Church, *Aurora Borealis,* 1865, 56⅛ x 83½ in. Courtesy of the National Museum of American Art, Smithsonian Institution, Washington, D.C., Gift of Eleanor Blodgett.

scape painter in America. He became famous early in life as a master engraver. In this medium he produced genre scenes, portraits and landscapes; he scored a great triumph with his reproduction of John Trumbull's painting of the signing of the Declaration of Independence. In the late 1830s, Durand turned his attention to painting. His early work in this medium included portraits as well as landscapes very much in the manner of Cole.

Durand traveled to Europe in 1840, in the company of three of his pupils who were to become famous as landscape painters: John F. Kensett, John W. Casilear and Thomas P. Rossiter. In 1855 he published "Letters On Landscape Painting," an important document that defined the principles and style of the Hudson River painters. The style described, which was essentially his own, involved a close attention to the details of nature. He asserted that in order to learn how to paint nature, the artist must study nature directly. The most effective pictures were those painted on the scene and not in the studio. And in observing nature in all its energetic splendor, one also observed the very presence of God.

Durand's pictures were at first very formally arranged; planes of depth or distance were achieved by careful use of atmospheric tones, which lightened with distance. Their

configuration allowed the framing of a view into the distance with trees and foliage painted in exact design and proportion. He was intensely interested in trees, and made many individual studies which later showed up in his pictures. Durand frequently placed a figure in the center of his paintings as a point of reference before the distant view. This compositional formula was derived from Durand's studies of the landscape engravings of Claude Lorraine. Among Durand's most famous works using the formula is *Kindred Spirits* (1849, New York Public Library), which shows Thomas Cole and his friend, poet William Cullen Bryant, contemplating the sublimity of nature. The two figures stand on a rock framed by trees and overhanging limbs, through which glows a luminous distant sky, its light reflected in a cascading stream below.

John Frederick Kensett, who traveled to Europe with Durand, was also a student of the works of Claude Lorraine. Kensett was chiefly a painter of the mountains and seacoasts of New England. His canvases show a distinct preference for quiet scenes in which a luminous atmosphere veils roughness, light shines with clarity, and stillness is achieved by means of even brushstrokes.

Architect-painter Jasper Cropsey was another artist influenced by Thomas Cole. He traveled much in Europe

Albert Bierstadt, *Bridal Veil Fall, Yosemite,* 1873, 22 x 16 in., signed l.l. Courtesy of John H. Garzoli, San Francisco, California.

in the 1840s and 1850s, finally settling in New York in the 1860s. He painted in the luminist tradition, and is often called America's "painter of autumn" because of the golden light that suffused his autumnal landscapes of the White Mountains and the Hudson River Valley, as in *Autumn on the Hudson* (1860, National Gallery of Art). He moved with the times, however, and included details in his pictures that indicated in a positive and optimistic manner the encroachment of industry upon the landscape, as in *Starucca Viaduct* (1865, Toledo Museum), which focuses on a railroad bridge in the Susquehanna River Valley.

Landscape painter Frederick Edwin Church had been a student of Thomas Cole, whose influence is recognizable in his paintings. The brilliant play of light, the drama, and

the reverence for nature are there, but the drama of Church's work is of different quality. If in Cole's pictures the drama was of theme and subject, derived from consideration of the past, in Church's it existed in the scene in nature at the moment of observation. Church was interested in the contemporary America, the present experience, the wild energy of the new continent at its most passionate. He rejected the religious and moral intensity of Cole.

Church traveled in the New World, rather than in Europe as his contemporaries had done. He went from South America to the Arctic in search of subject matter. His first great success was *Niagara* (1857, Corcoran Gallery of Art), which startles the viewer because of its unusual point of view: it shows the fierce energy of the falls

Thomas Moran, *Grand Canyon,* 1912, 30 x 25 in., signed l.r. Courtesy of Frank S. Schwarz & Son, Philadelphia.

from a point above the river's bank and includes the whole vast arc of the falls in a great panoramic sweep. His interest in natural science, particularly the writings of Alexander von Humboldt, drew him to such remote places as Labrador and inspired his painting of icebergs. Other natural phenomena also appear in his pictures; his painting of *Cotapaxi* (1862, Detroit Institute of Arts) shows the volcano in eruption—its dark smoke not dense enough, however, to obscure the brilliant light of the sunrise. The culmination of his epic landscapes was *Twilight in the Wilderness* (1860, Cleveland Museum of Art), one of a series of impassioned sunset views of North America. It exhibits Church's mature style, a combination of luminism, realism, and the historical and "operatic" tendencies of his teacher.

An important artistic development in the 1850s was the invention of chemical pigments, which replaced the earlier mineral-based paints. These new and brilliant colors gave the artist more flexibility and range, especially in depicting the effects of light, as in *Twilight in the Wilderness.*

Church's contemporary Albert Bierstadt was trained in Dusseldorf and painted many scenes while traveling in Europe. In 1858, he traveled to the American West and began painting the landscapes upon which his fame rests: grandiose, topographically accurate panoramas in which he attempted to show America as another Eden. Among his successful canvases were *The Rocky Mountains* (1863, Metropolitan Museum of Art) and *Storm in the Rocky Mountains* (1868, Brooklyn Museum). The disillusionment of the post-Civil War period, however, affected American taste, and by the 1880s Bierstadt was considered out of step with his time.

George Inness, *Approaching Storm,* 1844, 27 x 40 in., signed l.l. Photograph courtesy of Borghi & Co. Fine Art Dealers, New York, New York.

More than any other painter, Thomas Moran was instrumental in familiarizing Eastern Americans with the scenery of the West. He painted, among other subjects, many views of the canyons and mountains that are now part of the great national parks, such as the Grand Canyon, the Yellowstone and the Rocky Mountains. His work was influenced by that of British painter J.M.W. Turner, in whose paintings details were minimized and overall impressions heightened. In a similar manner, Moran painted great panoramic scenes but omitted small details; he softened the rugged appearance of the landscape by the play of light and atmosphere across his surface. To him the literal landscape was of less importance than the idealized one.

In post-Civil War America, landscape painting was reduced from the epic proportions of grand vistas and panoramas to more individual responses. Artists began to interpret nature less from prescribed or popular notions than from their own emotions and intellects. The idealized view of nature and the prevailing pantheism gave way to the more realistic vision of the painter himself. The same techniques continued to be used, replication of the details of scenery continued to be emphasized, but allegorical content was for the most part abandoned.

To George Inness, the interpretation of landscape through painting was an emotional response. He filled his canvases with poetic atmosphere in the manner of Turner, whose work had impressed him on his visit abroad in the 1850s, and combined this with a pastoral quality derived from the barbizon painters of France. The result was a luminous vision of gentle scope to which the viewer could respond on a private level. He depicted quiet personal moments as opposed to the earlier landscapists' visions of universal drama.

Among more deliberately poetic interpreters of the American landscape was Alexander H. Wyant. He was a great admirer of George Inness, whose tonalist style he adopted and turned to his own uses. After study abroad, where he was deeply impressed by the work of J.M.W. Turner and Camille Corot, among others, Wyant settled in the Northeast United States. True to tonalist characteristics—such as a gentle and personal, rather than an exact, rendering of natural detail, and an atmosphere charged with mood—Wyant painted many scenes of the Adirondack Mountains. Outstanding among his works are *An Old Clearing* (1881, Metropolitan Museum of Art) and *The Mohawk Valley* (1866, Metropolitan Museum of Art).

Although he was primarily a portraitist, Thomas Eakins painted occasional landscapes very much in the

Alexander H. Wyant, *White Mountains (Mt. Washington).* Courtesy of Vose Galleries of Boston, Inc., Massachusetts.

luminist tradition. His pictures, illuminated with a clear penetrating light, are executed with a mathematical and photographic attention to detail.

Winslow Homer's exposure to Manet and other impressionists sharpened his sense of design and his attention to the details of nature. He painted New England seascapes and landscapes, mostly in watercolor, which are spontaneous in feeling and vital in their portrayal of the intense energy of nature. The work of Eakins and Homer indicates a new realism in American painting.

Hand in hand with the realistic optical experience afforded by photography was the interpretative experience of the French impressionists. Their influence upon American painting is observable in the work of James McNeill Whistler and Julian Alden Weir, among others. Once again their concern was for light—specifically, light as it was reflected from surfaces. To the impressionists, the purpose of painting was essentially to give pleasure to the viewer, as opposed to the appeal on more introspective levels that had been made by earlier painters.

Not until the end of the century did these concerns become formulated into what could be seen as abstract landscapes, as in the work of Albert Pinkham Ryder. In his work, the landscape themes were expressed in large areas of color rather than in the carefully wrought objects of the scene. The effect of the whole was a vision of inner essence, rather than of surface reality.

American painters in the final decades of the nineteenth century moved steadily into the transition heralded by George Inness, from the great groundswell of heroic, nationalistic landscape into a phase more personally visionary. Their painting focused less on the exact replication of nature than on scenery as a spiritual manifestation; it tended toward impressions and depictions of personal experience. In the face of social expansion and industrial advance, landscape painting in one way was escapist, but it also paradoxically embraced the symbols of technology. It recorded changes, and thus laid the foundation for a new realism. By the end of the century, landscape painting had come full circle and was emerging into a generation burgeoning with new perspectives.

Robert F. Looney is head of the Print and Picture Department of the Free Library of Philadelphia. He is the author of *Old Philadelphia In Early Photographs* and of several articles on early American printmaking for the American Historical Print Collectors Society. He also edited *Philadelphia Printmaking: American Prints Before 1860.*

PAINTINGS OF THE AMERICAN WEST

PATRICIA JANIS BRODER

George Catlin, *Comanche War Party on the March, Fully Equipped,* 1846-1848, 20 x 27⅜ in. Courtesy of National Museum of American Art (formerly National Collection of Fine Arts), Smithsonian Institution. Gift of Mrs. Joseph Harrison, Jr.

Western art is truly one of America's most valuable cultural treasures. Since the 1830s, paintings of the West have served to document America's unique history and to celebrate the natural wonders of a world of majestic snow-capped peaks, spectacular vistas and fantastic land forms.

The world of Western art is the world of the explorer and the pioneer, the trapper and the trader, the frontier farmer and the soldier, the cowboy and the Indian. Western paintings celebrate the discovery, settlement and challenges of each successive frontier and depict the joys and sorrows of life in pioneer settlements, farming communities, mining camps and military posts. Paintings of the West also document the evolution of transportation across the country—the wagon train, the freighter, the stage-coach, the Pony Express and the first transcontinental railroad. They extol the glories of the great cattle empires and the search for fortunes in gold, silver and oil.

Generation after generation of painters worked with a sense of mission to record the changing face of the Indian world: the great buffalo hunts and the subsequent destruction of the buffalo herds, the establishment of military forts and trading posts, decades of armed conflict between Indians and whites, historic battles, treaties signed and broken, forced marches, the relocation of

Alfred Jacob Miller, *Buffalo Hunt,* 30¼ x 50⅛ in. Courtesy of Amon Carter Museum, Fort Worth, Texas.

entire tribes, the confinement of many tribes to reservations, and the ultimate destruction of all or part of many Indian cultures.

The art of the West has many dimensions and the importance of Western paintings is not limited to their historical or ethnological value. The men and women—even the land—of the West are symbols of America, not only for Americans but for people around the world. Western art stands as visual testimony to the changing ideals, values and beliefs of the developing United States.

Western art offers a truly American blend of realism and romanticism. Since the earliest expeditions, painters of the West have used precisely determined, historically accurate images, the results of their firsthand observation and painstaking research, to express the hopes and fears, ideals and aspirations of each age. These artists shared the beliefs and prejudices of their contemporaries, and their work mirrors their ideologies as well as the physical world they painted.

The first images of the American West were created by the expeditionary artists—independent adventurers as well as those who accompanied government and privately funded expeditions to the West. These painters preserved for posterity glimpses of the Indian world before the arrival of the white man changed it forever. George Catlin, Karl Bodmer, Alfred J. Miller, John Mix Stanley, Carl Wimar, Charles Deas, Seth Eastman, Jules Tavernier and William Cary are among the outstanding artists who journeyed across the country to record the natural wonders of the West and document the lives and likenesses of its original inhabitants.

George Catlin traveled from the Great Plains to the Rocky Mountains and from the upper Missouri River to the Mexican border, painting the daily and ceremonial activities of each tribe he visited and portraits of the leaders. Catlin's drawings, watercolors, oil studies and sketches, dating from 1832, are the first comprehensive record of the Indian tribes of the trans-Mississippi West.

In 1833, Karl Bodmer traveled along the historic route of Lewis and Clark as the official artist of German Prince Maximillian of Wied Neuwied. In 1843, Maximillian published *Travels in the Interior of North America,* a folio of polychrome engravings which today is considered the best and most comprehensive pictorial record of the Missouri frontier.

In 1837, artist Alfred Jacob Miller accompanied Captain William Drummond Stewart, a nobleman from Scotland, on an expedition to the Rocky Mountains. As the Stewart party traveled from the Great Plains to the Green River Rendezvous, Miller sketched the daily events, the tribesmen and women and the scenery of each area.

From 1839 to 1853, John Mix Stanley traveled the major overland routes to the West. In 1846, he joined the Magoffin Expedition, which traveled over the Santa Fe Trail to New Mexico Territory. In Santa Fe, Stanley joined Major Stephen Kearny's expedition to San Diego.

Seth Eastman, *Indian Mode of Travel*, 1869, 31 x 44 in., signed l.l. Photograph courtesy of The Gerald Peters Gallery, Santa Fe, New Mexico.

The prevailing attitudes toward the land of the West and its native inhabitants illustrate the facility with which people accept contradictory beliefs: untamed nature was viewed both as a wilderness to be conquered and given the gift of civilization and, at the same time, as a paradisiacal Eden, contact with which offered a chance for redemption and spiritual purification.

The settlement of the West represented the achievement of the goal of "manifest destiny," America's destiny as a great nation. Nineteenth-century Americans were idealists who believed in the perfectability of man and viewed the conquest and settlement of the West as a confirmation of mankind's inevitable progress. The man of the future was the pioneer, who would tame the wilderness and bring civilization to its savage inhabitants.

The heroic landscape painters of nineteenth-century America saw the wonders of nature as evidence of divine grace. They worked to capture both the physical reality and the spiritual essence of the American West. Some insisted on absolute fidelity to nature; others, like Albert Bierstadt, rearranged the land forms in order to maximize the effect of the majestic mountain scenes. In 1858, Bierstadt joined a military expedition led by General Frederick W. Lander to lay a wagon train route across the Rocky Mountains from Fort Laramie to the Pacific coast. His giant canvases of the wonders of the Rockies epitomize the romantic dream of the glories of a sublime wilderness.

In 1871, Thomas Moran served as guest painter on the government-funded expedition led by F.W. Haden to survey the area of the Yellowstone River. In 1873, he joined the expedition of John Wesley Powell, who had been the first to explore the Colorado River and its tributaries, on a survey of the Colorado-Plateau province; in the course of this trip, Moran made a boat trip down the Grand Canyon. Moran's paintings and the photographs of William Henry Jackson influenced Congress to establish the Yellowstone country as America's first national park in 1872. Today most of the areas Moran painted have been preserved in their natural state as national parks.

The nineteenth-century vision of the Indian was also a composite of contradictory stereotypes. Artists idealized the Indian both as nature's nobleman, a child of nature who instinctively lived in harmony with the physical world, and as a savage, an obstacle to progress and to the inevitable course of civilization. After the defeat of Sitting Bull at the battle of Wounded Knee, however, the Indians were romanticized as a dying race driven to the edge of the continent—the end of the trail.

Each generation of painters knew that its work would

Albert Bierstadt, *The Wind River,* 1870, 54 x 84 in., signed l.r. Courtesy of Wunderlich and Company, Inc., New York.

Thomas Moran, *Cliffs of the Upper Colorado River, Wyoming Territory,* 1882, 16 x 24 in., signed l.r. Courtesy of National Museum of American Art, Smithsonian Institution, Bequest of Henry Ward Ranger through the National Academy of Design.

Henry F. Farny, *Buffalo Trail Over the Divide,* 1914, 26 x 30 in., signed l.r. Photograph courtesy of Hirschl & Adler Galleries, Inc., New York, New York.

chronicle a world lost forever and herald the emergence of a new world. While some artists in the late nineteenth and early twentieth centuries were inspired by the heroic lives of those who settled the West, many of the most important Western artists of the period strove to document a world which would soon belong to history. For the expeditionary artists, the West had represented a dream of the future; the late-nineteenth-century artists saw the West as a symbol of the glory and beauty of the past. Some worked to complete accurate ethnological records of historic figures and specific customs and rituals, while others idealized Indian life as the symbol of a harmonious world destroyed by the march of industrial progress. Henry Farny, Charles M. Russell, Joseph Sharp, Ernest Blumenschein, Olaf Seltzer and W.R. Leigh are among the many master painters whose major inspiration was the Indian world.

As a young man, Charles M. Russell spent the happiest years of his life working as a wrangler in the Judith Basin of Montana. He sang to the cattle as a night herder and lived among the Blackfeet Indians. The America he loved belonged to the past. He became the poet laureate of an idyllic Indian world—a world which belonged only to memory.

Frederic Remington first traveled to the West in 1880. During his youth he worked as a hired cowhand, sheep rancher and gold prospector. He served in the military during the final campaign against the Sioux. These experiences—and Remington's travels through the Dako-

tas, Wyoming, Montana, Kansas and the Indian Territory—were the primary inspiration for his career as chronicler of the heroic West of the 1880s, a world of cowboys, Indians and cavalrymen.

Throughout the twentieth century, the artists who followed in Russell's footstep; would focus on the Indian world as a symbol of a noble and harmonious past. Those who followed the Remington tradition would celebrate the West of the cavalrymen and cowboy as a symbol of a glorious, brave and heroic America.

Charles Schreyvogel dramatized the dangers and glories of the Western military; Edward Borein, William Gollings and Frank Tenney Johnson romanticized the life of the new American hero, the cowboy. They celebrated life on the range, the long trail drives and the virtuoso feats of horsemanship which live on in today's rodeo events. Like the Indian, the American cowboy embodied contradictory images. On one hand, he was a hard-drinking, happy-go-lucky man, full of high spirits; a jovial companion, he was brave and fearless, in love with excitement and danger. But he was also portrayed as a sober, serious and hard-working loner, frequently introspective, given at times to an almost romantic melancholy. Like the Indian, he was a man of nature, doomed to extinction by industrial progress.

Traditional Western paintings include very few images of white women. While Indian women were sufficiently poetic and exotic to be part of the romantic West, white women were limited to the roles of Indian Captive and

Charles Marion Russell, *When the Plains Were His,* 15⅛ x 15⅛ in., signed l.l. Courtesy of Wunderlich and Company, Inc., New York, New York.

Pioneer Mother. The West of fantasy was a masculine world—the world of the conquering hero, the enterprising individual. Even such opposites as the lawman and the outlaw confirm or violate the same ethical and spiritual codes. Heroes and villains symbolize the success or failure of the same dreams and ideals.

During the first decades of the twentieth century, the American West became known as a mecca for painters, a special source of artistic inspiration. The brilliant light of the high desert country and the spectacular land forms and vistas attracted artists from all parts of the world.

The Taos Society of Artists, founded in 1915, annually mounted exhibitions which traveled across the nation and to Europe and South America. In 1917, Mabel Dodge moved to Taos, New Mexico and transformed the desert community into a cultural oasis. Among the visitors she

brought to Taos were Leo Stein, Robert Edmund Jones, D.H. Lawrence, Paul Strand, Max Weber, Carl Jung, Leopold Stokowski, Marsden Hartley, John Marin, Andrew Dasburg and Georgia O'Keeffe. By 1920, Santa Fe was recognized as the first cultural capital of the Southwest. Both Santa Fe and Taos gained fame as tri-cultural communities, where artists could view firsthand the life and land of the Pueblo Indians, the Spanish-Americans and the Anglos (everyone neither Indian nor Spanish-American).

Although traditional Western art is dominated by images of an idealized romantic world, many mainstream twentieth-century American artists accepted the challenge to paint the reality of the modern West. The West has been portrayed in styles that can be described as impression-ism, post-impressionism, fauvism, cubism, futurism, syn-

Frederic Remington, *El Vaquero,* 15 x 7½ in., signed l.r. Photograph courtesy of The Gerald Peters Gallery, Santa Fe, New Mexico.

Edward Borein, *Roping A Steer,* 8½ x 13¼ in., signed l.r. Courtesy of Henry B. Holt, Inc., Essex Fells, New Jersey.

chromism, expressionism, structuralism, precisionism, surrealism and—during the past three decades—abstract-expressionism, pop and photo-realism. The West not only inspired artists who wished to document the narrative of the historical West or celebrate the beauty of its spectacular scenery, but provided the perfect catalyst for modern realist and abstract painters. Inspiration came from the fundamental realities of the West—the lives of contemporary rural and urban people and the forms, colors and light of both landscape and cityscape.

During the nineteenth century, outstanding American mainstream painters such as Titian Ramsay Peale, Worthington Whittredge, Sanford Gifford, John Kensett and Thomas Eakins had made major contributions to America's heritage of Western art. In the twentieth century, such giants of American art as Robert Henri, John Sloan, Marsden Hartley, Edward Hopper, John Marin and Georgia O'Keeffe gave new vitality to the art of the American West.

Modern paintings of the West had two basic sets of roots: the realist vision heralded by Robert Henri and the modernist vision inspired by European abstraction. Henri believed that art must be a record of life, focusing on the present rather than the past, the human rather than the heroic. Among Henri's friends, students and disciples who made outstanding contributions to the realist vision of the West were John Sloan, George Bellows, Randall Davey, Leon Kroll, Yasuo Kuniyoshi, Homer Boss and Edward Hopper.

European abstraction was introduced to America at the Armory Show of 1913 and at the New York City gallery of Alfred Steiglitz. Inspired by European avant-garde art, Marsden Hartley, Jan Matulka, Walt Kuhn, Stuart Davis, John Marin and Georgia O'Keeffe were pioneers of a tradition of Western modernism that has been continued by Max Ernst, Milton Avery, Arshile Gorky, Adolph Gottlieb, Helen Frankenthaler and Richard Diebenkorn. During the 1960s and 1970s, pop and photo-realist images of the West became a new and important part of America's cultural heritage. In addition, the evolution of non-ritual painting among American Indian artists during the twentieth century is one of the most dynamic and interesting developments in Western art.

Today, myth and history, reality and fantasy, tradition and innovation, all contribute to the energy and power of the multi-dimensional world that is the American West. And today as in the past, paintings of the American West offer a special challenge, the challenge to explore the mind, the heart and the soul of America.

Patricia Janis Broder is an art historian, lecturer and writer and an authority on the art of the American West. Her books include *Bronzes of the American West, Hopi Painting: The World of the Hopis, Great Paintings of the Old American West, American Indian Painting & Sculpture, Taos: A Painter's Dream* and *The American West: The Modern Vision.* She is the recipient of the Herbert Adams Medal awarded by the National Sculpture Society for Outstanding Service to American Sculpture and the Trustee Gold Medal for Outstanding Contribution to the West awarded by the National Academy of Western Art.

THE SPIRAL OF AFRO-AMERICAN ART

EDMUND BARRY GAITHER

Robert Duncanson, *Valley of Lake Pepin, Minnesota,* 1869, 12 x 21⅝ in. Courtesy of National Center of Afro-American Artists, Roxbury, Massachusetts.

No image better represents the development of Afro-American art than the spiral, for Afro-American art history begins with a narrow thematic and stylistic conservatism in the late eighteenth century and moves forward in rising, ever more encompassing upward-curving lines. Its growth is inescapably and profoundly affected by the general condition of the larger black community. Socioeconomic, political and cultural issues addressed by blacks in their struggle toward fuller inclusion in American life provided the context for the black artist. His contribution was part of the progressive striving of black people toward participation in American—and European—cultural life.

Some of the questions confronting Afro-American artists have been identical to those facing other American artists: What is American art? Where shall I study? And who will evaluate and appreciate my work? But the Afro-American artist had to go to a deeper level: Am I truly American? Where is my place in American art? Have I a distinct and even unique heritage? Who will be my sponsors? And what institutions will accept and exhibit my work? He found himself at a perpetual crossroads, where personal artistic priorities intersected confusingly with political and cultural imperatives. This dichotomy remains a central problem in Afro-American art.

Afro-American fine arts have had several periods of accelerated activity and flowering: the early portraits; international recognition of nineteenth-century landscapists and painters of historical, literary and religious subjects; the new self-image and enhanced sense of African heritage explored during the "New Negro" era or

Henry O. Tanner, *The Annunciation*, 1898, 57 x 71¼ in., signed l.l. Courtesy of National Center of Afro-American Artists, Roxbury, Massachusetts.

"Harlem Renaissance" of the 1920s; and the application of art to political and cultural purposes in the 1960s. Each of these periods built on the accumulated work that preceded it. The result was a tradition that by the 1980s was—in its most liberal manifestations—indistinguishable from the American art mainstream.

Late in the eighteenth century, black urban communities formed in the mid-Atlantic and New England cities and provided the matrix from which the Afro-American artist emerged. Scipio Moorhead, perhaps the best exemplar of the early Afro-American artist, illustrated these artists' basic embracing of European and American cultural standards. Moorhead, who was the house servant to the Reverend John Moorhead, pastor of the Church of the Presbyterian Stranger in Boston, and his friend Phyllis Wheatley, the earliest Afro-American formalist poet, wrestled with the dilemma of how to internalize Euro-American cultural and social values and yet remain black in America. Their evident solution was to adopt prevailing aesthetic and technical traditions governing art. For them,

the "classics," such as Milton and Virgil, provided both appropriate subject matter and correct models. They honored European values even though their own circumstances contradicted these values.

Thus black American artists began in alliance with the values of the colonial governing class, and worked within the Euro-American fine arts tradition. From this narrow, conservative—perhaps even defensive—base, Afro-American fine arts took form.

Before the nineteenth century, portraiture comprised almost the whole of American art. Limners, provincial portrait painters, documented and promulgated family status through portraiture in the republican era, as they had in the earlier colonial period. Baltimore, a lively port city, figured prominently in the economic and political life of the young nation and was home to many wealthy and powerful families. It was also a slave-holding city. Yet within a few decades after the Revolutionary War, black artist Joshua Johnson (also given as Johnston) was active there as a portrait painter.

Edward Mitchell Bannister, *Under the Oak Tree,* 1895, 16 x 24 in., signed l.r. Courtesy of Raydon Gallery, New York, New York.

Although details of Johnson's life are unclear, he probably was slave-born and self-taught. Occasional references associate him with the Charles Willson Peale family, sometimes suggesting that James Peale was his teacher, but such a direct relationship is improbable. It is likely, however, that he visited the Peale Museum, and that he studied the works of outstanding portraitists in Baltimore. By 1798, he was sufficiently successful and confident to advertise in the *Baltimore Intelligence,* a local newspaper. Several of his major commissions were executed at the turn of the nineteenth century.

Johnson mastered the generally accepted conventions for the placement of sitters, the use of props and the devices of composition, but infused his best works, such as *Sea Captain John Murphy* (ca. 1810) and *The McCormick Family* (ca. 1805) with a fascinating visual directness. His sitters possess a personal integrity not always captured by naive painters, and his economical use of linear elements for both descriptive and decorative purposes merits appreciation, particularly in the context of the American preference for simplicity and honesty in art.

Negro Cleric (ca. 1805-1810), one of the few portraits of black sitters attributed to Johnson, is one of his most psychologically successful paintings. It is difficult to understand why there were not more black sitters among his clients, for while the Baltimore black community was

not rich, it boasted many prominent blacks and included important black religious and fraternal organizations.

Johnson was the first black American artist to leave behind a large body of work and the first to gain regional recognition in his lifetime and to earn his living from his art; he competed for a place by internalizing American social values, which gave him acceptance among the planter and maritime families who were his patrons.

In addition to Johnson, a number of other Afro-American portraitists were active in the nineteenth century, including Robert M. Douglass, Jr., Patrick Henry Reason, David Bustill Bowser, William Simpson, Julian Hudson, Jules Lion and Eugene Warburg. Of these, several deserve particular attention. Reason, a New York City printmaker who created lithographic portraits of many noted abolitionists, was one of the earliest Afro-American artists to reflect sociopolitical themes. Hudson, a free black who painted *The Battle of New Orleans* (1815), was the first Afro-American artist to leave a *Self-Portrait* (1839). And in Louisiana, far from the English-speaking Atlantic seaboard, the wealthy Franco-African families of the turn of the nineteenth century produced artists and patrons. Three portraits of members of the Metoyer family in Natchitoches are believed to be the work of an unidentified black artist.

Several Afro-American painters won acclaim in Europe

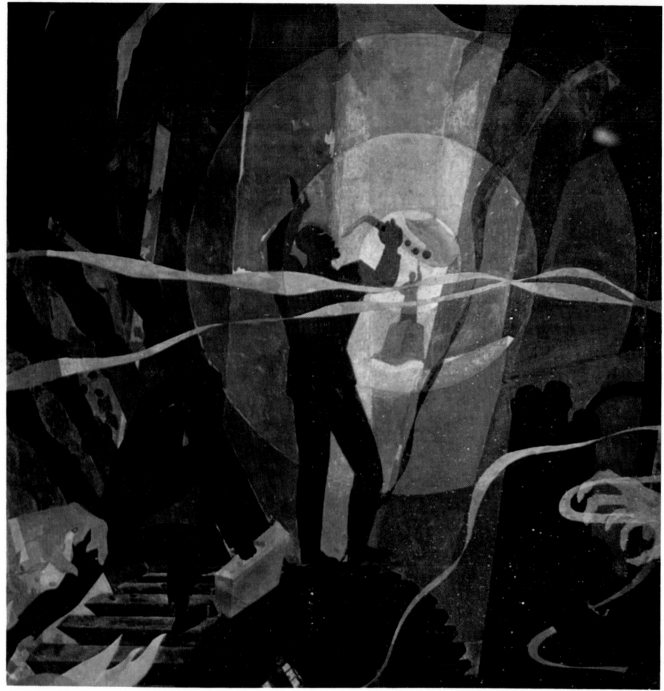

Aaron Douglas, *Aspects of Negro Life: Song of the Towers,* 1934, 72 x 72 in. Courtesy of Schomburg Center for Research in Black Culture, New York Public Library, New York.

during the nineteenth century. Especially notable were Robert Scott Duncanson and Henry Ossawa Tanner.

Although Duncanson painted portraits and still lifes, he was chiefly a landscapist who alternated between the realism of the Hudson River School and the romantic European style. He enjoyed wide acceptance in Ohio and Michigan in the mid-nineteenth century, and his *Blue Hole, Flood Waters, Little Miami River* (1851) is an important American painting of remarkable beauty. Yet Duncanson, who had been born near Cincinnati and had grown up there during the fugitive slave and Dred Scott controversies, felt unrecognized in the United States and

longed for Europe, with its "more expansive idea of art" and more supportive atmosphere.

His landscapes, with their non-racial themes, are his most dramatic and artistically resolved paintings. His work derived from classical themes, as in *Landscape with Classical Ruins: Temple of Sibilla* (1850), from American luminism, as in *Valley of Lake Pepin, Minnesota* (ca. 1862), or from both, as in *Dog's Head, Scotland* (1871). Other works, such as *Uncle Tom and Little Eva* (1853) and several portraits of abolitionists, are uninspired. Race-related themes exerted little influence on his work. But, although Duncanson was favorably received by crit-

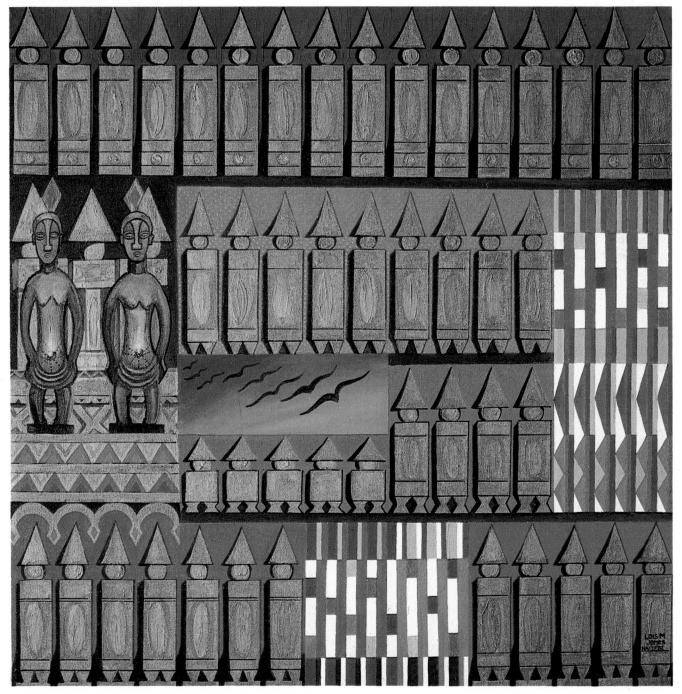

Lois Mailou Jones, *Les Ancesters,* 1982, 36 x 36 in., signed l.r. Courtesy of National Center of Afro-American Artists, Roxbury, Massachusetts.

ics in Britain, he remained unsure of himself and his place among his American peers, and seems never to have shaken off the corrosive personal effects of racism.

Without question, the foremost nineteenth-century Afro-American artist was Henry Ossawa Tanner. Not only was he honored and respected in France, then the center of the art world, but he also became the principal inspiration for early-twentieth-century black artists.

Tanner studied with Thomas Eakins at the Pennsylvania Academy of Fine Arts, after which he became a realist painter and photographer. Late in the 1880s, he moved to Atlanta, where he taught art and practiced photography.

In the South, Tanner sketched black people in the mountains of North Carolina, who later appeared in works such as *The Thankful Poor* (1894). In 1891, Tanner departed for Europe. His intended destination was Rome, but he stopped in France and remained there until his death in 1937.

Tanner's mature style evolved from genre works, such as the famous *Banjo Lesson* (1893) or *The Sabot Maker* (1895), toward more mystical, introspective religious works, such as *Abraham's Oaks* (1897) and *Burning of Sodom and Gomorrah* (1907). The hallmarks of his style were his preference for blue-green blazes, his sketchy, almost dematerialized, figures and his fascination with suffused light. Like Ralph Blakelock and Albert Ryder, Tanner cultivated an inner vision, a nocturnal, spiritual vision.

Tanner had a successful career and received many honors; he had made a place for himself in the conservative wing of the international art world. He gave Afro-American artists a heritage of unquestioned brilliance and success, and also gave them a model for escaping American racism through expatriation.

Perhaps the most reclusive of the major nineteenth-century Afro-American artists was Edward Mitchell Bannister. Born in Canada, he moved to Boston in the early 1850s and studied art with William Rimmer while practicing photography. He traveled little and never visited Europe. Between 1865 and 1900, he was active primarily as a painter of landscapes in the barbizon mood, although he did sometimes paint genre scenes, religious themes and portraits.

Bannister's *Under the Oak Tree* received the bronze medal and a certificate of merit at the Philadelphia Centennial Exposition in 1876. Like other Bannister landscapes of the 1870s and 1880s, *Under the Oak Tree* is a rural pastoral scene, probably in Rhode Island, with cows or sheep and peasant-like figures. A few of Bannister's late paintings show the effect of impressionism, particularly *Street Scene* (1895).

Nineteenth-century Afro-American artists shared several characteristics: They were dynamic, willful personalities. They were professionals, masters of their concepts and materials. Although racism was omnipresent, they overwhelmingly preferred neutral or non-racial themes. Most were born in the West or North. For the most part, they lacked both a strong communal sense and the supportive institutions which could have exhibited and sold their works. They lacked patrons who could help artists make a living. And, finally, they fully accepted Euro-American canons as correct guides in their creative work.

If the nineteenth century was the period when Afro-American artists first secured an honorable place within American art in the United States and abroad, the twentieth century was the era when these artists asserted their identity as heirs of both a unique black American experience and an ancient African legacy.

Three factors brought about dramatic changes in pre-World War II Afro-America: the great migration to the North, which brought about the urban attitudes subsumed under the characterization "the New Negro"; the discovery of Afro-American artists by the black colleges of the South and the mid-Atlantic region; and the opportunities made available to black artists by the Works Progress Administration. The most important was the emergence of the "New Negro" concept.

In the wake of the reconstruction era, there appeared in the South a very strong self-help movement led by Booker T. Washington. Simultaneously, W.E.B. Dubois was advancing the concept of the "talented tenth" in the black intellectual communities of the North. In the North and Midwest, the onset of World War I stimulated economic

growth. The result was a tremendous migration of blacks from the South to the North, which had come to be regarded as the "land of promise." Concentrated black urban communities developed in Philadelphia, Chicago, Detroit and New York City. Sharing these new communities were large pockets of black immigrants from the Caribbean. By 1920, the nucleus of the Northern black ghetto was in place.

An immediate consequence of the appearance of these densely populated urban communities was a new and expanded black identity. Assertive, exuberant, progressive, artistic, intellectual—these were the attributes of "the New Negro." He claimed both his African heritage and his subsequent experiences outside of Africa, and made them the basis of a bold new manhood, buttressed by participation in World War I, heightened nationalism, a fledgling vanguard of creative intellectuals and the political muscle born of sheer numbers. Shedding their rural, parochial identity and discovering a more aggressive self-image, blacks found allies within the American political left.

For black creative intellectuals and artists, this ferment led to two mighty actions: the reclamation of the African legacy in the arts, and the sympathetic depiction of black life—whether rural or urban, Afro-American or Caribbean. The black subject was now legitimate; the black physiognomy was now projected without apology or shame.

Alain Leroy Locke, an advocate of racial art, asserted that black artists had lost contact with their true heritage and needed to study African art in order to rediscover their original genius. He made his own collection of African art available to artists, several of whom thereupon embraced African stylistic idioms. One was Aaron Douglas, whose *Aspects of Negro Life* (1934) and other murals and illustrations were inspired by the study of African decorative patterns and motifs.

Painting (and sculpture) celebrating black physiognomy flourished. One contributing factor was the rapid growth of portraiture of prominent blacks, such as May Howard Jackson's *Dean Kelley Miller* and the inspired rendering of intimate, often family, portraits, such as *Gussie* by Edwin A. Harleston. Another was the popularity of pictures of types, such as Archibald Motley's *Mending Socks* (1924), Richmond Barthe's *West Indian Girl* (1930), or Lois Mailou Jones's *Negro Student* (1930). A third was the interest in West Indian and Afro-American genre art evidenced by William E. Scott's *Haitian Fisherman* (1931) and Malvin Gray Johnson's *The Orphan Bank, Harlem* (1934).

Several Afro-American artists showed the influence of African art through cubist techniques. Conspicuous among them were Hale Woodruff (*The Card Players,* 1930) and Malvin Gray Johnson (*African Masks*). Other artists allied themselves with broad directions in American art. For example, Palmer Hayden's *Battery March* is closely akin in spirit to William Larson's cityscapes of lower Manhattan.

In 1927, William Harmon established the Harmon

Allan Crite, *The Choir Singer,* 1941, signed l.l. Collection of St. Augustine's and St. Martin's Episcopal Church, Boston, Massachusetts. Photograph courtesy of National Center of Afro-American Artists, Roxbury.

Jacob Lawrence, *Hiroshima Series,* 1983, 23½ x 18 in., signed l.r. Private collection. Photograph courtesy of The Studio Museum, Harlem, New York.

Foundation in New York City to promote the education and cultural development of minorities. For nearly a decade, it was perhaps disproportionately significant because it provided the only regularly scheduled annual exhibition for Afro-American artists. Moreover, the catalogue of each show documented the early careers of many artists. During its early years, the Harmon Foundation presented virtually every recognized black artist in the nation. Another benefit of its work was to give a sense of association to the artists. This sense of "groupness" was also linked to the self-awareness that was part of the "New Negro" concept.

For the most part, the directions set in Afro-American art during the 1920s continued into the 1930s. But the black colleges and the WPA laid the groundwork for increased interaction between the different generations of Afro-American artists and between these artists and the professional art world.

Black colleges and universities made three significant contributions to black fine arts. First, the art departments at schools such as Howard University offered the first systematic visual-arts training within a black context in the South. Also prominent in this development were Atlanta University, Hampton Institute and Fisk University. Second, the black colleges also offered economic support to older black visual artists after the waning of the "New Negro" movement in the North; artists like Aaron Douglas of Fisk became the teachers of the next generation. Third, black colleges and universities established their own museum and galleries. Atlanta University established an annual exhibition in 1941 which eventually superseded that of the Harmon Foundation.

By 1933, the Works Projects Administration was set up. It proved to be vitally important to black artists. Its mural, graphics, easel and sculpture projects employed artists to create works for public buildings and also paid other artists to conduct community workshops.

Under the WPA, more Afro-American artists were at work in their profession than at any other time in American history. Charles H. Alston and Henry Bannarn were in charge of workshops in Harlem. Many young artists, such as Jacob Lawrence, Charles White, and Ernest Crichlow began their careers under the WPA, often receiving their initial training from other Afro-American artists paid with WPA funds. In addition to being able both to paint and to eat, the Afro-American artists associated with the WPA found their horizons widened through their increasing contact with white artists. Common professional problems and social philosophies became the basis for friendships between men who might otherwise never have met. Although equal access was not yet the rule of the day, the black artists sometimes made useful contacts with the official art world.

Many Afro-American artists who began working in the 1930s found themselves influenced by social realism. Even those whose styles were relatively abstract, such as Jacob Lawrence, were still associated with social, narrative art. Hale Woodruff, who worked in a Midwestern regional style, and Charles White, whose work had the flavor of Mexican social art, were exponents of social commentary focusing on rural and labor abuses, tragic events and hard times. Their works depict lynchings, sharecropping and natural disasters. Sometimes they chose to illustrate history with an eye toward ennobling the black past. Lawrence's "Toussaint L'Ouverture Series" (1938), Woodruff's "Amistead Murals" (1939) and White's "Five Famous Negroes" (1940) demonstrate this tendency.

Not all Afro-American artists were preoccupied with large sociopolitical movements and issues, although most did share a sense of community that had not existed before World War I. Some painters and sculptors pursued more academic directions or more lyrical themes. William H. Johnson, Lois Mailou Jones, Allan R. Crite, Augusta Savage, Ernest Crichlow and others often preferred nonpolitical subject matter—still lifes, genre, city views or personal visions. They were not in creative conflict with their more politically and socially oriented peers; rather they demonstrated the diversity of Afro-American art.

The earliest sustained relationships between black artists and the professional world of galleries and museums developed late in the 1930s. Those artists who were perceived as naives or primitives were recognized first. Folk painter Horace Pippin's works were accepted for exhibition at the Museum of Modern Art well before more sophisticated painters drew notice. Jacob Lawrence, whose early works were regarded as intuitive, was featured in a 1940 article in *Fortune* magazine and became the subject of great interest in the New York art world. Pippin and Lawrence spearheaded the breakthrough that eventually allowed Afro-American artists to penetrate beyond the outer reaches of American art.

"The Negro Artist Comes of Age" (1945) was a milestone in the recognition of black artists by museums. Organized by John David Hatch in association with Alain Locke and presented at the Albany Institute of History and Art, this exhibition featured more than a score of artists and set a precedent which would not be revived until the late 1960s.

The decades immediately after World War II were uneventful for Afro-American artists. Those able to survive without WPA support continued to create. Many adopted styles like those of their white peers in the hope of integrating themselves into the art scene. Others followed individual directions and achieved individual successes. A small but growing number were now handled by galleries—but often through arrangements which compromised their integrity. Many black artists felt themselves eclipsed by white peers whose work was not superior to their own. Outstanding among the Afro-American artists of this era were Norman Lewis, Lois Mailou Jones, John Rhoden, Hughie Lee-Smith and Eldzier Cortor.

The 1960s and 1970s brought unprecedented growth, development and consolidation to the Afro-American artists. As in the 1920s, social and political forces led to the new burst of activity. As the old civil rights movement with its pro-integration principles lost energy, a vigorous nationalism appeared in black America.

The generation of artists born during or just after World War II felt called upon—indeed commissioned—to become "artists for the people," to translate the new ethic of black power into visual forms. A number of nationalist and pro-nationalist arts groups sprang up, and other less emphatically political artists adjusted their styles to harmonize more closely with the historical moment.

Rooted in nationalist political ideology and pro-African sentiments, new black artists led in the fight to take art to the community, to make it affordable, to find a basis for mass appreciation of art and to make art the servant of a larger world view. Africobra (the African Commune of Black Relevant Artists) was a school of such artists. Its direct predecessor, OBAC (Organization of Black American Culture) had in 1967 created the "Wall of Respect" in Chicago. That mural, which depicted popular black heroes such as Muhammed Ali and Malcolm X, proved potent. Within a year of its completion, scores of similar walls dotted black and other inner-city neighborhoods across the nation. They were an expression of art for the "African" community in America.

The "Wall of Respect" launched "Black Art," a didactic art form characterized by its commitment to: the use of the past and its heroes to inspire heroic and revolutionary ideals; the use of recent political and social events to teach recognition, control and extermination of the "enemy"; and the visualization of the future which the nation can anticipate after its struggle is won. Dana Chandler's *Fred Hampton's Door* (1969) and Jeff Donaldson's *Amos and Andy* (1971) are Black Art paintings. Other painters associated with the movement include Faith Ringgold, Benny Andrews, Cliff Joseph, Emory Douglass and Bill Walker.

Closely related to Black Art, yet distinctly different, is

Romare Bearden, *Serenade,* 1941, 38¾ x 53¾ in. Courtesy of National Center of Afro-American Artists, Roxbury, Massachusetts.

the work of the Neo-African School, which studies traditional and contemporary African art, examining its formal organization, palette and psychology. The Neo-Africanists produce their own art as an extension of their rediscovered Africanity. They intimately share with the didactic black artist a sense of common nationalist roots. Proponents of the Neo-African approach include James Phillips, Alfred Smith, Ademola Olugebefola and Arthur Carraway.

Although they were highly visible, the Afro-American artists concerned with social or political issues were not the only ones active in the 1960s and 1970s. Major careers were shaped by others who emphasized the resolution of formal artistic problems over narrative or thematic content. Still others—including Sam Gilliam, Joe Overstreet, Barbara Chase-Riboud, Martin Puryear and Manuel Hughes—chose to become part of conceptual, hard-edge, color-field or other critically acknowledged artistic movements.

Afro-American artists have always displayed a very strong bias toward figuration. Barkley Hendricks and Pheoris West have extended this interest toward new horizons. Similarly, Marie Johnson and Betty Saar have expanded the parameters of personal iconography interpreted by means of assemblage techniques.

Romare Bearden is a figure of gigantic proportions in post-1950s Afro-American art, not only because of the wide critical acclaim for his work but also because of his role as a mentor to younger artists and an advocate of

Afro-American exhibitions and art history.

The institutional framework in which the black artist exists is a factor in his struggle for recognition. On that count, two recent developments must be cited. First, the role of "black shows" as they reappeared in the late 1960s cannot be overstated. Exhibitions such as "The Evolution of Afro-American Art: 1800-1950" (City College of New York, 1967) and "Afro-American Artists: New York and Boston" (Museum of Fine Arts, Boston, 1970) made the work of black artists accessible to a large and diverse audience for the first time. Second, the effect of black museums—such as the Studio Museum in Harlem and the Museum of the National Center of Afro-American Artists—must not be underestimated. They provide sustained and sympathetic support for Afro-American art and artists.

The spiral of Afro-American art is the movement toward full participation in the American art world. Still, even a spiral must have a base, a sense of relationship to a central core: in this case, the self-image of the black artist. In the aftermath of the 1970s, the spiral continues to rise and widen, but its pull toward a center may be waning.

Edmund Barry Gaither is a co-founder of the African-American Museums Association and director of the National Center of Afro-American Artists in Boston. He has organized numerous exhibitions of the work of black artists, including "Afro-American Artists: New York and Boston" at the Museum of Fine Arts in Boston in 1970.

BIOGRAPHIES

WILLIAM PIERCE STUBBS
(1842-1909)

Ship Lydia M. Deering, 26¼ x 42 in., signed l.l. Courtesy of Taggart, Jorgensen, & Putman Gallery, Washington, D.C.

William Pierce Stubbs, or Billy Stubbs, as he was called, painted genre scenes and portraits of ships in the folk art manner. He worked in Maine and Boston. All his known works are oils and pastels.

Stubbs was born in Bucksport, Maine in 1842, the son of Captain Reuben Stubbs. He was self-taught as an artist. Although he worked in and around Bucksport during his career, he also worked in Boston. A Boston directory of 1876 lists him as a painter; a directory of 1877 lists him as a marine artist. In 1882, he was living in Charlestown, but he maintained a studio in Boston.

Typical of Stubbs's early work are genre paintings, showing scenes from everyday life in Bucksport, executed in primitive style. One such is variously titled *Packing Fish for the Boston Market* or *Packing the Catch* (ca. 1850, privately owned). It shows workers among old-fashioned smelt tents, barrels and boats, with a farm, woods and hills in the background.

Stubbs also worked in the popular tradition of the ship portraitists, painting highly detailed pictures of specific ships, including the Nantucket and New Bedford whaling ships which were an integral part of the American economy

during the period. Examples of Stubbs's work in this school are *Ship in Storm* (1901, Marine Arts, Salem), *The Ship Carrie E. Phillips* (date unknown, privately owned), and *American Square-Rigged Ship Under Full Sail* (1881, Flayderman Galleries, New Milford).

Stubbs exhibited at the International Maritime Exhibition in Boston in 1890, where his paintings were priced from $25 to $500. Suffering from melancholia, he was committed to Worcester State Hospital in 1894. He died in Medfield State Hospital in 1909.

SEASON	75-76	76-77	77-78	78-79	79-80	80-81	81-82	82-83	83-84	84-85
Paintings									7	1
Dollars									$27,500	$1,300

Record Sale: $5,700, RB.HM, 3/20/84, "The Schooner Andrew H. Edwards," 24 × 36 in.

CONRAD WISE CHAPMAN
(1842-1910)

Among Southern artists of the Civil War years, Conrad Wise Chapman was considered the principal painter of the Confederacy. Chapman's paintings, particularly those executed in the vicinity of Charleston, South Carolina, depict the everyday events, duties and settings of military life.

Born in Washington, D.C. in 1842, Conrad Chapman was the son of Virginia-born expatriate artist John Gadsby Chapman. He spent much of his youth in Rome, where he was trained in large part by his father. Despite his European upbringing, Chapman acquired a love of the South, and returned to Virginia in 1861 at the outbreak of the Civil War. He enlisted in the Confederate army, and his fellow soldiers soon nicknamed him "Old Rome."

At Shiloh, Chapman received head wounds when his weapon exploded during reloading, and was transferred to Charleston, due in part to family connections. He was attached to the staff of General P.G.T. Beauregard, who ordered him to illustrate the city's forts and batteries.

Chapman's sketches, executed between September, 1863 and March, 1864, form the basis for 31 small oil-on-board paintings. These panels record various military installations, including *Battery Marshall, Sullivan's Island* (1863, Valentine Museum), *Submarine Torpedo Boat* (1863-1864, Museum of the Confederacy) and *Fort Sumter Interior* (1864, Valentine Museum). These painterly renderings, important as historical documents, are noted for their clarity of color, strong contrasts and deep perspective.

After General Lee's surrender in 1865, Chapman decided to join the Confederate General Magruder in supporting the Mexican Emperor Maximilian; however, Chapman remained in Mexico for several years. Enamored of the Mexi-

Fort Moultrie Interior, September 16, 1863, 9½ x 13 in., signed l.r. Courtesy of Museum of the Confederacy, Richmond, Virginia.

can landscape, the artist painted an impressive, 14-foot panoramic view entitled *Valley of Mexico* (1866, Valentine Museum). This work is considered one of the finest paintings of Mexican terrain, and has been compared to works by Mexico's great nineteenth-century landscapist Jose Maria Velasco.

Much of Chapman's later life was spent in Mexico, where he worked as an itinerant artist who painted directly on photographs. He died in 1910.

PUBLIC COLLECTIONS
Museum of the Confederacy, Richmond, Virginia
Valentine Museum, Richmond, Virginia

SEASON	75-76	76-77	77-78	78-79	79-80	80-81	81-82	82-83	83-84	84-85
Paintings	1			2		1			1	
Dollars	$725			$8,360		$900			$12,000	

Record Sale: $12,000, SPB, 1/27/84, "On the Beach," 9 × 16 in.

ARTHUR PARTON
(1842-1914)

Born in New York City in 1842, Arthur Parton was a landscape painter who studied in Philadelphia under William T. Richards and at the Pennsylvania Academy of the Fine Arts. Parton gained from Richards a sound grounding in the technical aspects of his art.

Parton settled in New York City in 1865 and became a regular exhibitor at the National Academy of Design. In 1886, he received the gold medal of the American Art Association and the Temple Medal from the Pennsylvania Academy of the Fine Arts in Philadelphia. He also won the competitive prize in the Paris Exposition in 1900. His works are represented at the Metropolitan Museum of Art.

In 1869, Parton spent a year in Europe, where he was influenced by the barbizon painters. His first pictures were shown in Philadelphia in 1862, but the works that brought him public prominence were *On the Road to Mt. Marcy* (1873, location unknown), *A Mountain Brook* (1874, location unknown) and *Evening, Harlem River* (1887, location unknown).

His *November, Loch Lomond,* and *Solitude* (dates and locations unknown) attracted a great deal of attention at the Centennial Exposition of 1876 and gave him a national reputation. "In any foreign collection of paintings," the *New York Evening Post* said, "Mr. Parton's work would be distinctly American." He died in 1914 at age 71.

Coming to the Deer Lick, 28 x 44½ in., signed l.c. Collection of Janice Mooney Knight. Photograph courtesy of Kennedy Galleries, New York, New York.

MEMBERSHIPS
American National Academy
American Water Color Society
Artist's Fund Society
National Academy of Design

PUBLIC COLLECTIONS
Metropolitan Museum of Art, New York City

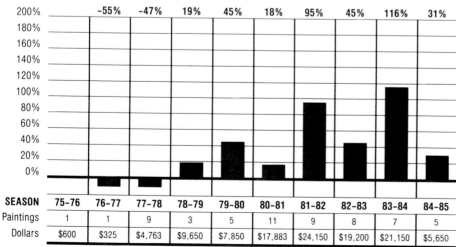

10-Year Average Change From Base Years '75-'76: 27%

	-55%	-47%	19%	45%	18%	95%	45%	116%	31%

SEASON	75-76	76-77	77-78	78-79	79-80	80-81	81-82	82-83	83-84	84-85
Paintings	1	1	9	3	5	11	9	8	7	5
Dollars	$600	$325	$4,763	$9,650	$7,850	$17,883	$24,150	$19,200	$21,150	$5,650

Record Sale: $11,500, SPB, 4/23/82, "On the Hudson," 12 x 25 in.

FREDERICK STUART CHURCH
(1842-1924)

Girl with Rabbits, 1886, 14¾ x 31⅜ in., signed l.l. Courtesy of National Museum of American Art, Smithsonian Institution, Gift of John Gellatly.

Born in Grand Rapids, Michigan in 1842, Frederick Stuart Church became known for his whimsical and decorative works.

Church first studied drawing at age 10, under Marinus Harting. School and his hometown were left behind when he was 13; he moved to Chicago to work for the American Express Company. He continued to draw in his spare time. During the Civil War he joined the Union Army, serving as a private for more than three years. He returned to his job in Chicago after the war and then studied at the Chicago Academy of Design under Walter Shirlaw.

In 1870, Church moved to New York City, where he lived until his death in 1924. He continued his training at the National Academy of Design, under Lemuel Wilmarth, and at the Art Students League.

Church initially made his living in New York City as a magazine illustrator, gaining popularity from his captivating black-and-white drawings of anthropomorphic animals. His more serious works, in watercolors and oils, developed after sales of the illustrations declined. He is also known for his original etchings. He studied nature thoroughly, and although his style of treating animals was often fanciful or inventive, knowledge of his subjects is evident.

One of Church's imaginative paintings, *Lily of the Jungle* (date and location unknown), is typical of the fairy-tale quality of his work. A wood sprite, posed for by Evelyn Nesbit, a famous actress of the day, ties a flower garland to a tiger beside a lily pond. Wood sprites, flamingos, polar bears, rabbits, peacocks, swans, and lions were typically found in his work. Believing that beauty was the soul of art, Church often painted lightly-clad young women in a "shepherdess" role with wild animals; he used delicate hues and a wide range of greens.

Church exhibited widely and was elected to the National Academy of Design.

MEMBERSHIPS
American Water Color Society
National Academy of Design
New York Etching Club
Society of American Artists
Society of Illustrators

PUBLIC COLLECTIONS
Detroit Institute of Arts
Grand Rapids Art Museum
Metropolitan Museum of Art, New York City
National Gallery of Art, Washington, D.C.

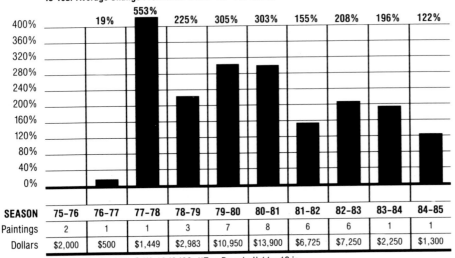

10-Year Average Change From Base Years '75-'76: 209%

SEASON	75-76	76-77	77-78	78-79	79-80	80-81	81-82	82-83	83-84	84-85
		19%	553%	225%	305%	303%	155%	208%	196%	122%
Paintings	2	1	1	3	7	8	6	6	1	1
Dollars	$2,000	$500	$1,449	$2,983	$10,950	$13,900	$6,725	$7,250	$2,250	$1,300

Record Sale: $3,250, S.W, 10/3/82, "Two Dryads," 11 × 19 in.

ALBERT INSLEY
(1842-1937)

Landscape artist Albert Insley, associated with the American barbizon painters, enjoyed an active career depicting inland and marine subjects around the New England and Middle Atlantic states, from the early 1850s to 1935.

Insley was raised in Jersey City, New Jersey, the son of a photographer. He received his first painting commission at age 12, and worked for his father as an apprentice photographer during his teens.

During the early 1860s, Insley continued his artistic development, first as an art instructor with Henry Hillyer at New York University, then, from 1864 to 1865, as a student of Jasper Francis Cropsey. The artist painted some historically interesting views of New York Harbor, Bayonne, New Jersey and Staten Island, and began to exhibit his work regularly at the National Academy of Design beginning in 1862.

Insley exhibited annually at the Academy from 1862 to 1898, and at the Brooklyn Art Association from 1869 to 1891. From 1873 to 1918, he maintained a residence and studio at the prestigious Tenth Street Studio Building in New York City, making regular painting trips to Rockland County, New Jersey, the Hudson River Valley, New Hampshire, Massachusetts, Maine, Connecticut and Long Island.

After 1881, Insley's paintings became more expressive under the tutelage of

A Terraced Garden (the old Marshall House, Nanuet, New York), 1889, 12 x 18 in., signed l.l. Collection of Roy Blankenship.

George Inness, and more poetic under the influence of the French barbizon painters. From 1905 to 1915, the artist painted many memorable impressionistic works. Insley used a bright palette of colors from the early 1920s to his death in 1937.

Insley died after 83 years of painting, at age 95, in Nyack, New York.

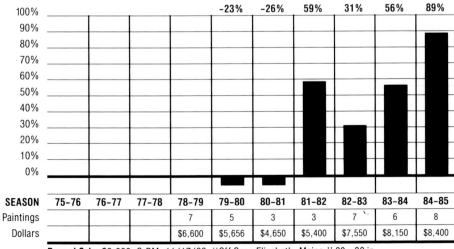

10-Year Average Change From Base Years '78-'79: 27%

SEASON	75-76	76-77	77-78	78-79	79-80	80-81	81-82	82-83	83-84	84-85
					-23%	-26%	59%	31%	56%	89%
Paintings				7	5	3	3	7	6	8
Dollars				$6,600	$5,656	$4,650	$5,400	$7,550	$8,150	$8,400

Record Sale: $3,000, S.BM, 11/17/83, "Off Cape Elizabeth, Maine," 20 x 32 in.

MEMBERSHIPS
Boston Arts Club
Brooklyn Art Association
Nanuet Painters and Sculptors Guild
National Academy of Design
Pennsylvania Academy of Fine Arts
Salmagundi Club

PUBLIC COLLECTIONS
Archives of American Art, Washington, D.C.
Cragsmoor Free Library, New York
Delaware Art Museum, Wilmington
Harding Museum, Chicago
Jersey City Museum, New Jersey
Preservation Society, Newport,
   Rhode Island
Rockland County Historical Society,
   New York

JOHN M. TRACY
(1843-1893)

Field Trial-On a Point, ca. 1890, 30 x 50 in., signed l.r. Courtesy of Wunderlich and Company, Inc., New York, New York.

Some have called John M. Tracy the American Landseer because of his skill at painting gun dogs, but to others the comparison is not valid. As one knowledgeable dog-lover put it, Landseer humanized his animal subjects "in a manner suggesting Aesop's fables," whereas Tracy painted them as true representatives of their breeds. Tracy knew dogs, was an early field-trial judge and today is considered one of the finest gun dog painters of his generation. He also was known for his paintings of thoroughbred horses.

He was born near Rochester, Ohio in 1843, soon after his father, an abolitionist preacher, was killed during an antislavery riot. To support her family, his mother, an intelligent, self-reliant woman, became a female journalist. Tracy was a high-strung and precocious youngster, who spent much of his childhood with his maternal grandmother. He attended Oberlin College in Ohio and Northwestern University in Chicago.

Before age 17, he had helped to rescue survivors of a shipwreck in Lake Michigan. At the outbreak of the Civil War, although he was under age, he enlisted in the 19th Illinois Infantry. He served for four years, was wounded twice and was discharged as a lieutenant.

After the war, Tracy taught school and picked fruit in southern Illinois until he had saved enough money to go to Paris to study at the Ecole des Beaux Arts. Later he recalled that, of all his studies in Paris, the most valuable had been training in drawing from memory at a small school just behind the Beaux Arts.

Returning to the United States in 1869, he spent three years in California painting landscapes. While they painted much of the same scenery, Tracy avoided what some consider the sensationalism of Bierstadt. Instead, he concentrated on an Inness-influenced fidelity to nature that became his hallmark.

After another stay in Paris for more study and to complete his only battle scene—commissioned by the United States government—Tracy settled in St. Louis and started to paint portraits. His sitters at first were predominantly women and children, but gradually the focus shifted to men in fields with their guns and dogs, the milieu in which he was to do his best work.

In 1881, Tracy moved to Greenwich, Connecticut, where he painted most of his sporting scenes. Because of his health he later moved his family to the milder climate of Ocean Springs, Mississippi. He died there in 1893, as he was finishing one of his largest and best paintings of horses.

SEASON	75-76	76-77	77-78	78-79	79-80	80-81	81-82	82-83	83-84	84-85
Paintings		1					3		1	1
Dollars		$2,250					$7,350		$46,000	$1,900

Record Sale: $46,000, D.NY, 9/28/83, "Field Trials in North Carolina," 30 × 50 in.

JAMES WELLS CHAMPNEY
(1843-1903)

James Wells "Champ" Champney was a prolific artist whose work was of high quality and broad scope. He was very successful as an oil painter of genre scenes, and later was perhaps the foremost pastelist of his day. A lecturer, illustrator, watercolorist and photographer, he was also one of the first Americans to grasp and utilize the spirit of impressionism.

Champney was born in Boston in 1843. At Lowell Institute he studied drawing and took courses in anatomy under Oliver Wendell Holmes. He was apprenticed to a Boston wood-engraver at 16, but left in 1862 to serve in the Civil War. Discharged because of malaria, he taught drawing from 1864 to 1866 at Dr. Dio Lewis's Young Ladies' Seminary.

In 1866, Champney decided to become a professional artist and went to Europe to study. He left for London in October, then journeyed on to Ecouen, France a month later to be tutored by Edouard Frere. Champney spent 1868 in Antwerp studying under Van Lerius, and 1869 in Italy. That year he exhibited his first genre painting at the Paris Salon.

In 1870 he returned to Boston, where he opened a studio and continued to produce genre paintings, popular with the American public. These paintings quaintly depicted the young, as in *Teetering at the Saw Mill* (date and location unknown); the old, as in *Second Childhood* (date and location unknown); or the two together, as in *Helping Grandma* (date and location unknown).

In 1873, Champney was commissioned by *Scribner's* to illustrate "The Great South," a series of articles by Edward King. The two traveled more than 25,000 miles, and Champney contributed at least 500 illustrations. Afterwards, Champney visited Europe, where

Spring in the Connecticut Valley of Western Massachusetts, 20 x 30 in., signed l.r. Courtesy of Arvest Galleries, Inc., Boston, Massachusetts.

he again exhibited at the Salon, and was commissioned by *L'Illustration,* the French magazine, to do figure drawings of American life. In 1876, Champney settled in Deerfield, Massachusetts and showed his paintings at the Centennial Exhibition in Philadelphia.

While teaching art at Smith College between 1877 and 1884, Champney began experimenting with pastels. His pastel "translations," or copies, of European masterpieces, as well as portraits of New York society and theater personalities, boosted his artistic growth

and popularity. In fact, to have one's portrait rendered in Champney's pastels was an affirmation of status.

The high point of his career, however, was his exhibition at Knoedler's Gallery in 1897. He displayed 40 pastels, 12 comprising a series called "Types of American Girlhood." These large paintings bore such titles as *The Bicyclist, The College Graduate* and *At the Golf Links.*

Champney died in an elevator mishap while leaving the Camera Club in New York City in 1903.

SEASON	75-76	76-77	77-78	78-79	79-80	80-81	81-82	82-83	83-84	84-85
Paintings									7	1
Dollars									$56,100	$3,250

Record Sale: $42,000, CH, 6/1/84, "Deerfield Valley," 26 × 18 in.

MEMBERSHIPS
American Watercolor Society
Black and White Club
Camera Club
Century Club
Metropolitan Museum of Art
National Academy of Design
Salmagundi Club
Society of American Artists

WILLIAM EDWARD NORTON
(1843-1916)

Sailing Ships, 1871, 24 x 36 in., signed l.r. Courtesy of Henry B. Holt, Inc., Essex Fells, New Jersey.

His New England ancestry inspired a love of the sea in William Edward Norton, but it was his artistic vision which brought him to prominence as a maritime painter. Norton was acclaimed by both his peers and the public, earning many honors—including the coveted Osborn Prize, awarded him twice for his marine paintings.

Born in 1843 to a Boston family of shipbuilders, Norton went to sea in his teens. When his duties permitted, he sketched the ship, the sea and his mates, subjects he continued to paint throughout his life.

Norton attended art and science classes at the Lowell Institute, and used the dissecting rooms of Harvard Medical College to perfect his anatomy sketches.

George Inness, Norton's teacher, encouraged him to open a small studio. Married at 25 and supporting himself by sign painting, he settled down to serious work and produced 107 paintings, which sold at auction for $10,000.

The sale allowed Norton to travel and study abroad. In Paris, he studied with Antoine Vollon and Chevreuse, and painted a number of oils of the Normandy coast and its fishermen.

The Nortons settled in London, where he was well received and regularly exhibited at the Royal Academy. He represented the United States at the International Exposition, and also had

South Sea Whaling, 20 x 30 in. Courtesy of Oliphant & Company, LTD., New York, New York.

two paintings accepted by the Paris Salon.

Although exposed to exciting new ideas in European art, he remained aloof from impressionism, preferring the barbizon style of Millet and Corot. Norton's fine composition, perspective, form and color can be seen in such paintings as *Fight of the Alabama and Kearsarge* (date unknown, Historical Society, Portland, Maine), *Fish Market, Dieppe, France* (date unknown, Public Library, Malden, Massachusetts) and *Tranquility* (1895, location unknown).

Twenty-five years later, Norton returned to his native land as a renowned painter. He lived and worked in New York City until his death there in 1916.

MEMBERSHIPS
Black Heath Art Club
Boston Art Club
Salmagundi Club

PUBLIC COLLECTIONS
Essex Hall, Salem, Massachusetts
Historical Society, Portland, Maine
Museum of Fine Arts, Boston
National Collection of Fine Arts,
 Washington, D.C.
Public Library, Malden, Massachusetts

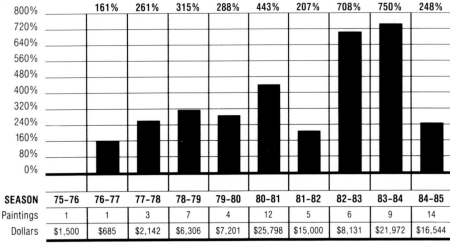

10-Year Average Change From Base Years '75-'76: 338%

	75-76	76-77	77-78	78-79	79-80	80-81	81-82	82-83	83-84	84-85
(% change)		161%	261%	315%	288%	443%	207%	708%	750%	248%
Paintings	1	1	3	7	4	12	5	6	9	14
Dollars	$1,500	$685	$2,142	$6,306	$7,201	$25,798	$15,000	$8,131	$21,972	$16,544

Record Sale: $8,000, SPB, 6/4/82, "Hauling the Nets," 34 x 47 in.

WILLIAM SARTAIN
(1843-1924)

A Summer Afternoon, 22 x 26 in., signed l.r. Courtesy of Raydon Gallery, New York, New York.

William Sartain is known for serene landscapes of verdant marshes and coastal wetlands, with broad expanses of clouded sky over long, low horizons. Compositions tend to be frontal, elements parallel to the picture plane, as abstract as possible within the requirements of factual on-site representation. Detail is subordinate to general effect; surfaces are painterly and without "finish"; broad masses are reinforced at the edges without outline. Generally Sartain can be called a tonalist.

Sartain was born in Philadelphia in 1843, the son of John Sartain, mezzotint artist, publisher, art administrator and entrepreneur. Thomas Eakins was his school chum and lifelong friend. Like his brother Samuel and sister Emily, William was trained in art by his father, starting his professional career as a mezzotint engraver. Aspiring to higher art, he attended the old Pennsylvania Academy, studying with Christian Schussele.

Early in 1869, Sartain sailed for France with Eakins, and shared his Paris studio. Through his friend he quickly was assimilated into French student life, and was particularly close to the family of Rosa Bonheur. After brief study with Adolphe Yvon, he enrolled in the atelier of Leon Bonnat, realist painter and advocate of Spanish seventeenth-century art; he also regularly attended courses at the Ecole des Beaux-Arts.

With Eakins and H. Humphrey Moore, Sartain traveled in Spain in 1870; during the Commune he was in Rome. With Charles Sprague Pearce he went to Algiers, but lived mostly in Paris until he returned to Philadelphia in 1875.

His father was then secretary of the new Pennsylvania Academy (under construction) and director of the art department of the coming 1876 International Centennial Exposition. Sartain's application for space in the exhibition was denied. His father thought little of the achievements of his son, who destroyed much of his own early work in a fit of depression.

He then moved to New York City, where he became a founding member of the Society of American Artists in 1877, in rebellion against the reactionary National Academy of Design. He did show a painting in 1876 in Philadelphia in the inaugural exhibition of the new Pennsylvania Academy; a strongly modeled head of a Negro, done in France, titled *Bedouin Chieftain* (French National Collection).

Sartain was a solid painter and teacher. On occasion he filled in for "the Boss" (as Eakins was called by his Academy students). On the invitation of parents unwilling to submit their daughters to the Academy life classes, Sartain came regularly from New York to Philadelphia to criticize the work of a group of girls; one was Cecilia Beaux, who credited him with her first real instruction. Around 1880 most of the serious art students in Philadelphia were either in "The Boss's Gang" or the "Billy Girls."

Sartain traveled frequently to France, and occasionally to North Africa. His paintings were of modest dimensions, sent back to his dealer William Macbeth for framing and exposition. They were seldom dated. He numbered his paintings, but as yet no key to his system has been found.

Sartain's early works include darkly modeled heads reminiscent of Bonnat (Brooklyn Museum, Philadelphia Museum of Art) and street and canal views in Venice and Algiers (National Museum of American Art). But he found his "motif" in the simplest of landscapes. With others who enjoyed the uncomplicated union of sky and horizon, he was part of the weekend and summer colony at Nutley, New Jersey.

Sartain never married. While he was a prolific painter, his sales were modest. He died in 1924 at age 81, leaving many unsold works, a good portion of which are known to have been destroyed.

PUBLIC COLLECTIONS
Brooklyn Museum
Corcoran Gallery of Art, Washington, D.C.
National Museum of American Art, Washington, D.C.
National Collection, Musees de France
Pennsylvania Academy of the Fine Arts, Philadelphia
Philadelphia Museum of Art

SEASON	75-76	76-77	77-78	78-79	79-80	80-81	81-82	82-83	83-84	84-85
Paintings				1	1	1				
Dollars				$1,300	$600	$1,200				

Record Sale: $1,300, SPB, 5/1/79, "Meadow Brook," 10 × 20 in.

JOHN APPLETON BROWN
(1844-1902)

Often identified with his popular depictions of blossoming apple orchards, John Appleton Brown painted a variety of subjects, including nocturnal scenes, the sea and grazing cattle. Brown was considered one of America's most prominent exponents of the French barbizon tradition of landscape painting, popular during the late nineteenth century.

Brown was born in West Newbury, Massachusetts in 1844. After only one year in Boston's Studio Building, where William Morris Hunt and George Inness were working, Brown traveled to Paris in 1866. As with generations of Boston artists before him, Brown rendered copies of old-master paintings in the Louvre and undertook private tutelage.

Brown's earliest work reflects the subtle palette and feathery textures of the barbizon painters, such as Corot and Daubigny. After a second trip to France in 1875, Brown returned to Boston and was embraced by local art patrons, who were eagerly buying works by barbizon painters and by American artists who emulated their style.

The artist was nicknamed "Appleblossom Brown" because of his predilection for spring scenes and blossoming apple orchards. His paintings won favor because of the optimism and sense of well-being they conveyed. The zenith of his popularity coincided with Boston's first exposure to impressionist landscapes in the late 1880s. Following the

A Showery May Morning, 31 x 42 in., signed l.r. Courtesy of the Museum of Fine Arts, Boston, Massachusetts. Bequest of Charles T. and Susan P. Baker.

example of other American impressionists, Brown adopted a bright palette, loose brushwork, informal compositions and a commitment to painting out-of-doors.

Paintings such as *Early Summer* (ca. 1880, Museum of Fine Arts, Boston), rendered with grainy brushstrokes and high-keyed colors, parallel in a conservative way the landscapes of Monet at Giverny. Like many American artists of the era, Brown retained the draftsman's traditional concern for volume, solidity and form. In terms of color, he favored cool greens, deep blues and purples. Typically, he enlivened the foreground of his compositions with daubs of white, lavender and yellow.

Before his death in 1902, Brown was widely praised and exhibited frequently in the United States and at the Salon in Paris.

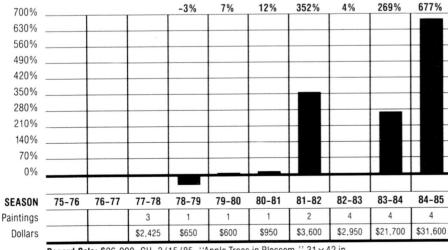

10-Year Average Change From Base Years '77-'78: 165%

				-3%	7%	12%	352%	4%	269%	677%

SEASON	75-76	76-77	77-78	78-79	79-80	80-81	81-82	82-83	83-84	84-85
Paintings			3	1	1	1	2	4	4	4
Dollars			$2,425	$650	$600	$950	$3,600	$2,950	$21,700	$31,600

Record Sale: $26,000, CH, 3/15/85, "Apple Trees in Blossom," 31 x 42 in.

MEMBERSHIPS
National Academy of Design

PUBLIC COLLECTIONS
Museum of Fine Arts, Boston

FRANKLIN D. BRISCOE
(1844-1903)

Evening Passage, 20 x 30 in., signed l.r. Courtesy of Newman Galleries, Philadelphia, Pennsylvania.

Best known for his masterful renderings of marine views, Franklin Dulin Briscoe established a successful painting career and was highly regarded in his day. He was a versatile artist whose work included history painting and portraiture as well as seascapes.

Briscoe was born in Baltimore in 1844. At age four, he moved with his parents to Philadelphia, where he received his art training.

Interested in painting, the young Briscoe became a pupil of Edward Moran at age 16, and subsequently supplemented his studies by travel abroad. Like many artists of the time, Briscoe drew inspiration from the galleries of London, Paris and other continental cities.

The subjects of Briscoe's earliest works were marine views based on his numerous, extended voyages. One of the most successful paintings of this group is entitled *A Breezy Day off Dieppe* (date and location unknown), which attracted favorable critical attention when it was exhibited in the Philadelphia Centennial Exposition in 1876. Another noted work inspired by nautical imagery is *The North Atlantic* (date and location unknown), a powerful depiction of the open sea and the forces of wind and water.

In 1885, the artist completed a major work entitled *The Battle of Gettysburg* (location unknown), which was later exhibited throughout the country. This painting is composed of a series of 10 panels, each 13 by 23 feet. When presented together, they depict that famous and decisive combat, from the firing of the first shot to the closing rout of Hill's corps and Pickett's division.

In addition to his accomplishment in painting historic events and marine views, Briscoe was a skilled portraitist. His work was exhibited at the Pennsylvania Academy of the Fine Arts in 1863, and at the Brooklyn Art Association in 1873. Briscoe remained in Philadelphia, where he died in 1903.

10-Year Average Change From Base Years '77-'78: 104%

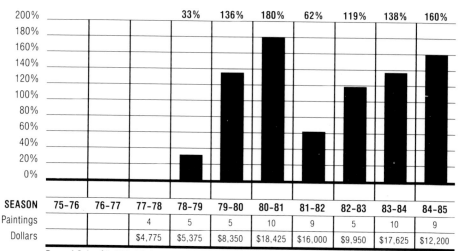

SEASON	75-76	76-77	77-78	78-79	79-80	80-81	81-82	82-83	83-84	84-85
				33%	136%	180%	62%	119%	138%	160%
Paintings			4	5	5	10	9	5	10	9
Dollars			$4,775	$5,375	$8,350	$18,425	$16,000	$9,950	$17,625	$12,200

Record Sale: $5,750, YG.P, 1/28/84, "Fisherman and Boats on Beach," 30 x 50 in.

FRED PANSING
(1844-1912)

In the days when travel between continents was by ship or not at all, there was a great demand for ship paintings. Even when the great, picturesque sailing ships became outdated, the public appetite for pictures of ships remained undiminished. Steamships, tugboats and paddle wheelers were all, from time to time, favorites of marine painters.

Not surprisingly, America's busiest seaport, New York City, was home to many painters who specialized in ships. One such artist was German-born Fred Pansing, who emigrated to New York in 1865 after five years at sea. Pansing at first found it necessary to earn his living in his brother's grocery store, but his years on shipboard, when every spare minute was spent sketching, made him eminently suited for a career as a painter of ships.

Eventually, Pansing went to work for the American Lithographic Company. His lithographs feature luminous color and finely detailed lines. Occasionally, he presented his steamers in a three-quarter, foreshortened view that added drama and interest. He also worked in oils, but Pansing oil paintings are relatively rare.

From 1910 to 1911, he served as manager of the Arts Club of Jersey City. He died in 1912 at age 68.

MEMBERSHIPS
Arts Club of Jersey City

Priscilla, 23 x 37 in., signed l.l. Courtesy of Henry B. Holt, Inc., Essex Fells, New Jersey.

10-Year Average Change From Base Years '75-'76: 95%

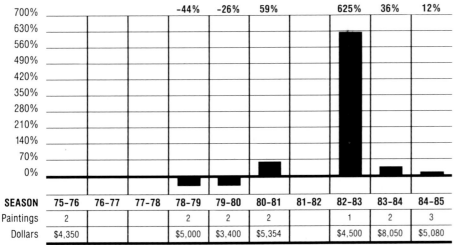

SEASON	75-76	76-77	77-78	78-79	79-80	80-81	81-82	82-83	83-84	84-85
				−44%	−26%	59%		625%	36%	12%
Paintings	2			2	2	2		1	2	3
Dollars	$4,350			$5,000	$3,400	$5,354		$4,500	$8,050	$5,080

Record Sale: $4,500, RB.HM, 8/10/82, "Outward Bound," 11 × 14 in.

424

CHARLES EDWIN LEWIS GREEN
(1844-1915)

Charles Edwin Lewis Green was a New England marine painter of the nineteenth century. At age 35, he gave up his career as a businessman and devoted the remaining 35 years of his life to painting.

Born in 1844 in Lynn, Massachusetts, Green was the son of a shoemaker. He worked in various trades, including straw, paper, twine, ink and leatherboard businesses. Little is known about Green's early life, but he probably began painting professionally in 1879. After his father died in 1881, Green's career as an artist accelerated. He had his first professional exhibition at the Boston Art Club in 1882.

Green was probably primarily self-taught, although he may have studied with Joshua Sheldon in Lynn. He probably also studied with Boston artist Otis Weber. Green became friendly with such Lynn artists as Edward Burrill, T. Clark Oliver and Charles H. Woodbury.

Green's work may be divided into two major categories. First, he painted countless coastal scenes, which often included boats and small figures. Second, he painted country scenes, with quaint buildings and grazing cows. In both, Green emphasized dramatic skies, weather and atmospheric conditions.

Most of Green's paintings were of the Massachusetts Bay area. In the summer of 1887, he made a trip to Nova Scotia and Cape Breton to find new motifs. He painted many scenes of fishermen, boathouses, fishing boats and nets. Over the next couple of decades, Green continued to use Northern settings for inspiration.

Around 1889, Green made a trip to Europe; it had a significant effect on his subsequent work. He traveled to England, Holland and Germany, and became very interested in the open-air painting made popular by Jules Bastien-Lepage in Concarneau, France. Green painted a great number of landscapes in the English version of Concarneau—Newlyn. His paintings of Newlyn and the nearby towns captured the wet atmosphere and natural light of the fishing villages.

Green's picturesque shore and landscape paintings were widely exhibited and collected. His work found prominent buyers, including the wife of President Rutherford B. Hayes and the first president of the Museum of Fine Arts in Boston, Martin Brimmer.

Green died in Lynn in 1915.

Steps, 10 x 14 in. Courtesy of Mr. and Mrs. Abbot W. Vose, Boston.

MEMBERSHIPS
Paint and Clay Club

SEASON	75-76	76-77	77-78	78-79	79-80	80-81	81-82	82-83	83-84	84-85
Paintings							1	3	3	
Dollars							$1,000	$5,100	$3,350	

Record Sale: $2,000, S.BM, 11/18/82, "Swampscott Dories," 10 × 14 in.

THOMAS COWPERTHWAIT EAKINS
(1844-1916)

Walt Whitman, 1887, 30 x 24 in., signed u.r. Courtesy of The Pennsylvania Academy of the Fine Arts, Philadelphia.

Thomas Cowperthwait Eakins was the foremost realist and the strongest figure painter of his time in America. His expertise in anatomy and perspective gave a powerful, unequalled solidity to his work. He did not flatter his subjects; instead, his portraits often became compelling psychological studies. The men and women who were his models are usually shown in action—rowing, lecturing, singing, wrestling or playing an instrument.

Eakins was born in Philadelphia in 1844. Aside from a few years abroad, he lived all his life in his native city, teaching there and in New York City. His father wanted the best for his son and allowed him free rein to pursue his studies, both at the Pennsylvania Academy of the Fine Arts and at Jefferson Medical College. Between 1866 and 1870 Eakins studied at the Ecole des Beaux-Arts in Paris with Jean-Leon Gerome and Augustin-Alexandre Dumont, and with Leon Bonnat. He spent six months in Spain, where he was influenced by the work of Diego Velasquez. He admired the naturalistic style of the famous Spanish painter, and he also acquired Velasquez's technique of using multilayered glazes rather than thick opaque paint. In Seville, Eakins painted families enjoying their Sunday outings.

In 1870, Eakins returned to the United States and began working on his rowing scenes. The long lines of the sculls and the angles made by the oars allowed him to dwell lovingly on the problems of perspective and to use his "trigonometric tables." *Max Schmitt in a Single Scull* (1871, Metropolitan Museum of Art), one of his earliest and best-known paintings, is an example.

Eakins studied surgery at Jefferson Medical College in 1873. One of his most famous paintings, *The Gross Clinic* (1875, Jefferson Medical College), dates from this period. Famous surgeon Samuel D. Gross is pictured with bloody scalpel in hand, lecturing before a group of serious medical students. The graphic realism of this work shocked the art world but established Eakins as a leader of naturalism.

In 1877, Eakins was invited to instruct at the Pennsylvania Academy of the Fine Arts. He was a skillful teacher and quickly became professor of drawing and painting. He later became director of the Academy schools. Dissection was an important part of the curriculum.

Photography was another of Eakins's interests. In 1884, with Eadweard Muybridge, he did a special study of animal and human locomotion. He improved on the pioneer photographer's methods by inventing a single camera to replace several.

Eakins never made much money from his paintings; his total earnings from his work came to less than $15,000. Collector Albert C. Barnes bought one oil in 1914 for about $5,000, but Eakins remained almost unknown in his home town.

In 1886, Eakins was forced to resign from the Academy because of a disagreement about his teaching practices. Many of the male students left the Academy with him, and together they established the Philadelphia Art Students' League, where Eakins taught without pay for about seven years.

Eakins's only one-man show was held in 1896, at the Earles' Galleries. He died in 1916. Memorial exhibitions of his work were held at the Metropolitan Museum of Art and the Pennsylvania Academy of the Fine Arts from 1917 to 1918.

SEASON	75-76	76-77	77-78	78-79	79-80	80-81	81-82	82-83	83-84	84-85
Paintings			2	2		2	1	5	1	
Dollars			$281,000	$50,400		$16,500	$25,000	$969,000	$8,000	

Record Sale: $500,000, CH, 6/3/83, "Spinning," 15 × 11 in.

THAD WELCH
(1844-1919)

Landscape, 1902, 20 x 36⅛ in., signed l.l. Courtesy of National Museum of American Art, Smithsonian Institution, Gift of Mrs. Clarence Baumert Kell.

Thad Welch was a California landscape painter known for his treatments of Spanish and Indian subjects in Santa Fe and his scenes of Colorado and the Southwest.

Welch was born in Indiana in 1844. His pioneer family traveled by prairie schooner and raft to an Oregon farm when he was three years old.

At age 20, Welch began working for an Oregon printer. He moved to San Francisco in 1866 and worked as a printer and laborer while studying art and sketching. A patron of the arts sponsored his education at the Royal Academy in Munich, where his fellow students included American artists Henry Raschen and Frank Duveneck, as well as John Twachtman, who befriended Welch, and traveled with him through Europe.

While he was studying in Munich, Welch used a very dark palette. In 1878, he went to Paris, and his painting became lighter and brighter, with some influence from the barbizon painters.

He returned to the United States in 1881 and worked in New York and Boston. He married artist Ludmilla Pilat, and they settled in Boston, where Welch worked for lithographer Louis Prang. At this time, he painted with American landscape painters Thomas Hill, George Inness and Thomas Moran.

Welch and his wife settled in California. Plagued by ill health and poverty, Welch was awarded landscape commis-sions by Leland Stanford, but was too poor to rent a studio.

In 1905, the Welches moved from the Marin County hills to Santa Barbara. His reputation as a landscape painter was growing and his paintings were beginning to command high prices.

A versatile and inventive man, Welch created a rapid shutter for a camera and an electric dynamo. He also carved violins. He died in 1919 in Santa Barbara.

MEMBERSHIPS
San Francisco Art Club

PUBLIC COLLECTIONS
California Palace of the Legion of Honor,
  San Francisco
Fine Arts Gallery of San Diego
Oakland Art Museum, California

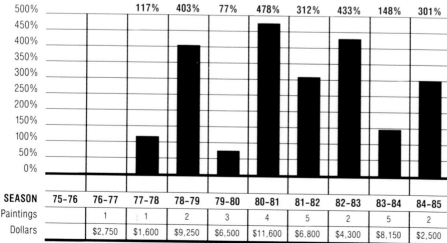

10-Year Average Change From Base Years '76-'77: 252%

SEASON	75-76	76-77	77-78	78-79	79-80	80-81	81-82	82-83	83-84	84-85
			117%	403%	77%	478%	312%	433%	148%	301%
Paintings		1	1	2	3	4	5	2	5	2
Dollars		$2,750	$1,600	$9,250	$6,500	$11,600	$6,800	$4,300	$8,150	$2,500

Record Sale: $7,000, BB.SF, 10/16/78, "Cattle Grazing Marin County," 29 × 49 in.

MARY CASSATT
(1844-1926)

A major impressionistic painter and one of the most significant American artists, Mary Cassatt was widely acclaimed in France during her lifetime, but fame in her homeland came only toward the end of her career.

She stood in the vanguard of impressionism, exhibiting side-by-side with Renoir, Monet and her friend, Degas, who influenced her early style, although not her subjects. While Degas painted prostitutes and dancers, Cassatt typically portrayed middle-class women, often with their children. Her technique shows an extraordinary grasp of intimacy.

Born in Allegheny City, now a part of Pittsburgh, to a wealthy family, Cassatt was expected to take her place among the social elite; instead, she chose to be a painter, to the dismay of her family. Her father is said to have exclaimed, "I would almost rather see you dead!"

Cassatt persevered, enrolling in the Pennsylvania Academy of the Fine Arts in 1861, where the education—copying antique casts and third-rate paintings—bored her. Insisting on an European education, Cassatt went to Paris in 1866, never to remain as a resident in her native country for very long. For years, she toured European museums, copying old masters, and studying privately with such artists as Jean Leon Gerome, Edouard Frere and Charles Bellay. By 1873 she was an established artist, exhibiting at the Paris Salon.

The Caress, 1902, 32⅞ x 27⅜ in., signed l.r. Courtesy of National Museum of American Art, Smithsonian Institution, Gift of William T. Evans. © ADAGP, Paris/VAGA, New York 1985

Cassatt, a strong and independent thinker, was devoted to the philosophy that art should portray life as honestly as possible—and in brilliant color. Increasingly impressionistic, her work was rejected for display by the Paris Salon in 1876. That same year, a new group of painters, including Degas, invited her to join the independents and she exhibited with them beginning in 1877 and for the next decade.

From creamy yellow and orange shimmering paints in her early impressionistic period, Cassatt evolved a more solid style in the 1880s, using strong patterns and clear outlines. The figures are firm, well-rounded forms done in parallel brushstrokes. In 1890, a Japanese exhibition of prints inspired her to do a series of 10 prints in drypoint and aqua-

tint that are among her most beautiful productions. She held her first individual show in 1891 and a second in 1893, leaving no doubt about her prominence as an artist.

Still, the American critics ignored her, as they had done 15 years earlier when she sent impressionistic works to the United States. Not until after the turn of the century when Cassatt was named a chevalier in the French Legion of Honor did American art institutions recognize her greatness.

Cassatt never married. Beginning in 1877, her parents and her sister, Lydia, lived with her in Paris and she nursed them during varying stages of illness for 18 years. Throughout her life, she was, in growing measure, a feminist and a humanist who hated war and disliked the dissonance of the twentieth century, including cubism. On her estate in Oise, she would expound—a tall, straight figure in designer clothes—on the social and political issues of the day, a rebel in white gloves.

In addition to her own body of work, including paintings, prints and pastels, Cassatt was also responsible for encouraging American collectors to buy European impressionistic works, many of which are now held by American museums.

MEMBERSHIPS
Legion of Honor
National Academy of Design

PUBLIC COLLECTIONS
Metropolitan Museum of Art, New York City
Museum of Fine Arts, Boston
National Gallery of Art, Washington, D.C.

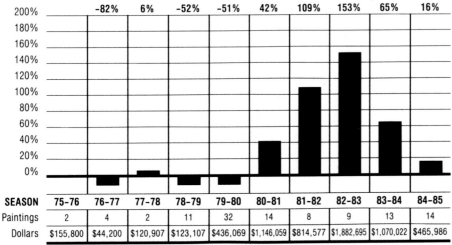

10-Year Average Change From Base Years '75-'76: 21%

	-82%	6%	-52%	-51%	42%	109%	153%	65%	16%

SEASON	75-76	76-77	77-78	78-79	79-80	80-81	81-82	82-83	83-84	84-85
Paintings	2	4	2	11	32	14	8	9	13	14
Dollars	$155,800	$44,200	$120,907	$123,107	$436,069	$1,146,059	$814,577	$1,882,695	$1,070,022	$465,986

Record Sale: $1,000,000, CH, 5/17/83, "Reading 'le Figaro'," 40 × 32 in.

HENRY A. FERGUSON
(1845-1911)

Island of San Francisco in Deserto, Venice. ca. 1900, 6 x 14 ½ in., signed l.r. Courtesy of Bowdoin College Museum of Art, Brunswick, Maine.

Landscape painter Henry Augustus Ferguson's art covered more than four decades and spanned several continents.

Born in 1845 in Glens Falls, New York, he received no art training until he moved to Albany in the 1860s to join an older brother, who was a successful wood engraver. There he became a friend and pupil of painters Homer D. Martin and George Boughton and sculptors Launt Thompson and Charles Calverly. After developing a market for his landscapes and architectural paintings, he followed Martin to New York City, where he set up a studio.

Ferguson later traveled extensively in Mexico, South America, Europe (where he spent three years in Venice) and Egypt. Wherever he went, he successfully captured the mood and ambience of his surroundings. He crossed the Andes Mountains six times, and depicted their grandeur in his vividly romantic style. He first achieved artistic prominence with his striking paintings of tropical vegetation. *City of Santiago* (date and location unknown) sold for $10,000, a fortune at that time.

When Ferguson returned to New York City after his years of travel, artists and men of letters seemed to gravitate to his studio. He often spent the summer painting the Berkshire Mountains; his scenes of the Hudson River area reflect the beauty of that environment. Ferguson's style is characterized by meticulous attention to detail, possibly attributable to his training in graphic techniques.

As Ferguson grew older, he exhibited great skill at restoring old canvases, and was employed by galleries and many private collectors.

Ferguson died in 1911 in New York City.

MEMBERSHIPS
Century Association
National Academy of Design

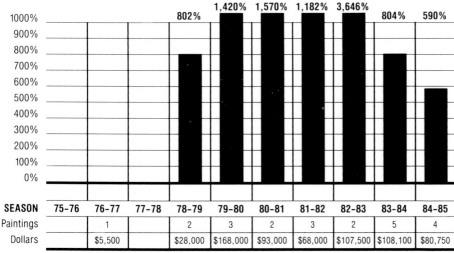

10-Year Average Change From Base Years '76-'77: 1,252%

SEASON	75-76	76-77	77-78	78-79	79-80	80-81	81-82	82-83	83-84	84-85
Paintings		1		2	3	2	3	2	5	4
Dollars		$5,500		$28,000	$168,000	$93,000	$68,000	$107,500	$108,100	$80,750

Bar chart percentages: 78-79: 802%, 79-80: 1,420%, 80-81: 1,570%, 81-82: 1,182%, 82-83: 3,646%, 83-84: 804%, 84-85: 590%

Record Sale: $140,000, SPB, 4/25/80, "Indian Woman with Children," 36 × 30 in.

429

MARIA OAKEY DEWING
(1845-1927)

Garden in May, 1895, 25⅝ x 32½ in., signed l.r. Courtesy of National Museum of American Art, Smithsonian Institution, Washington, D.C. Gift of John Gellatly.

In 1927, art critic Royal Cortissoz wrote at the death of Maria Oakey Dewing: "There was no mistaking her quality, her accent. She had her own vision. . . . Save for La Farge, we have had no one who could work with flowers the magic that was hers."

Much of Maria Oakey's early professional career centered in New York City, where she was born in 1845. By age 17, she started painting. From 1866 to 1871, she studied at the Cooper Union School of Design for Women, then at the National Academy of Design, from 1871 to 1875. William Morris Hunt in Boston taught her briefly, and in 1876, in Paris, she studied with Thomas Couture.

The years leading up to her 1881 marriage to figure-painter Thomas Wilmer Dewing were stimulating. In the late 1860s, sharing a Broadway studio with Helena de Kay, she associated with the inner circle of New York writers and artists, including John La Farge, with whom she had studied earlier in the decade, and who decidedly influenced her work.

Spending their summers in the lively art colony of Cornish, New Hampshire from 1885 to 1903, the Dewings cultivated a lovely garden at their home, "Doveridge"; many of her outdoor garden studies painted there, using an innovative brushy technique, express her knowledge of botany.

Possibly not wanting to compete with her husband in figure work, on which she concentrated in earlier years, Dewing made flowers her specialty. However, she is thought to have collaborated on some of his paintings. She resumed figure studies in 1900.

Her outdoor paintings, such as *Garden in May* (1895, National Collection of Fine Arts), were often asymmetrically arranged, close-up views. An affinity with oriental art is felt in her still lifes, influenced by Japanese artist Sotatsu.

A cultivated, witty woman, Maria Oakey Dewing was a poet and author of three books; her magazine articles appeared in *Art and Progress.* She stopped writing after her daughter's birth.

The paintings of this talented artist were brought to light in the 1970s, after a period of little attention, by art historian Jennifer A. Martin, who uncovered about 15 of Dewing's works.

PUBLIC COLLECTIONS
Addison Gallery of American Art, Andover,
  Massachusetts
National Collection of Fine Arts,
  Washington, D. C.

SEASON	75-76	76-77	77-78	78-79	79-80	80-81	81-82	82-83	83-84	84-85
Paintings										1
Dollars										$850

Record Sale: $850, P.NY, 10/3/84, "Philosopher's Corner," 21 × 14 in.

JULIAN SCOTT
(1846-1901)

The career of Julian Scott, whose illustrations and paintings dominated the landmark 1890 census book *Report on Indians Taxed and Indians Untaxed,* was launched by a Civil War injury.

In 1861, at age 15, Scott enlisted as a musician in the Third Vermont Regiment. He singlehandedly captured a rebel nearing the Union camp. Injured in the incident, Scott received the first Congressional Medal of Honor for bravery, and was given a staff post with General William F. "Baldy" Smith.

As he recuperated, Scott sketched pictures of Army camp life and soldiers' portraits on the hospital walls. A visiting New York merchant was taken with Scott's untutored skill and became his benefactor, later underwriting Scott's art education.

After the war, Scott enrolled at the National Academy of Design, New York City. He was a pupil of Emmanuel Gottlieb until 1868. Scott opened a New York studio in 1864, successfully selling his Civil War military scenes and genre paintings.

His work continued in popularity. In 1890, Scott was among the group of artists chosen by the federal government to conduct the 11th census of American Indians. The other artists included Henry Poore, Gilbert Gaul, Peter Moran and Walter Shirlaw.

Scott worked for more than three years on the project among the Moqui Pueblos of Arizona and New Mexico, as well as Comanche, Wichita and other Oklahoma tribes.

In the resulting 683-page report, over 30 drawings and paintings by Scott comprise more than three-quarters of the illustrations, both in color and black-and-white. Scott also created 11 aquatint illustrations for the 1892 book, *The Song of the Ancient People,* by Edna Dean Proctor.

A Break: Playing Cards, 1881, 27 x 22 in., signed l.r. Courtesy of Indianapolis Museum of Art; James E. Roberts Fund and Martha Delzell Memorial Fund.

Scott was born in 1846 in Johnson, Vermont. He died in 1901 in Plainfield, New Jersey.

MEMBERSHIPS
National Academy of Design

PUBLIC COLLECTIONS
Smithsonian Institution, Division of
  Ethnology, Washington, D.C.
Vermont State House
University of Pennsylvania Museum of Art,
  Philadelphia

SEASON	75-76	76-77	77-78	78-79	79-80	80-81	81-82	82-83	83-84	84-85
Paintings		1			1		2	1	2	1
Dollars		$1,000			$7,000		$6,250	$30,000	$1,250	$2,250

Record Sale: $30,000, SPB, 6/2/83, "Vermont Divis. @ Battle of Chancellorsvi," 48 × 72 in.

FRANCIS DAVIS MILLET
(1846-1912)

Francis Davis Millet was an active and conscientious artist, skilled in writing as well as painting, and highly respected as a decorator and muralist. His varied career and travels, which he recorded in word and paint, helped him become a noted painter of the historical genre.

Born in Massachusetts in 1846, Millet served as a drummer boy for the Union Army in the Civil War. In 1869, he graduated from Harvard University and began working as a lithographer. He studied painting from 1871 to 1873 at the Royal Academy in Antwerp, Belgium. This was followed by studies in Venice and Rome.

In 1876, Millet gained important exposure; he exhibited his work at the Philadelphia Centennial and helped John La Farge decorate Boston's Trinity Church. Through his association with La Farge, he became a permanent committee member of Boston's Museum School.

Millet's paintings and murals often depict American Indian themes or scenes such as mail delivery in the American West and in Alaska. His production of decoration and murals was prolific. In 1873, he was in charge of decoration at the World's Columbian Exposition.

He led a diverse life, serving as an artist-correspondent during the Russo-Turkish War in 1877, and later during the Spanish-American War. With John

Girl with Silver Platter of Oranges, 1890, 20½ x 14½ in., signed l.l. Photograph courtesy of Borghi & Co. Fine Art Dealers, New York, New York.

Singer Sargent and Edwin A. Abbey, he founded a "Bohemian" colony in England in 1884.

Millet was a noted leader of art societies who served as a trustee for the Metropolitan Museum of Art in New York City. He was lost at sea in the *Titanic* disaster of 1912, while he was director of the American Academy in Rome.

MEMBERSHIPS
National Academy of Design

PUBLIC COLLECTIONS
Minnesota Capitol Building, St. Paul
Museum of Modern Art, New York City
Tate Gallery, London
Wisconsin Capitol Building, Madison

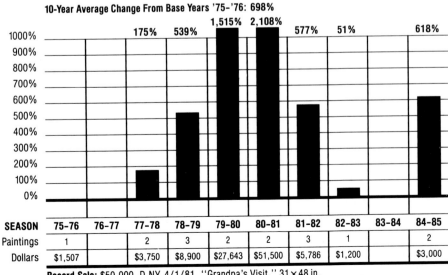

10-Year Average Change From Base Years '75-'76: 698%

SEASON	75-76	76-77	77-78	78-79	79-80	80-81	81-82	82-83	83-84	84-85
Paintings	1		2	3	2	2	3	1		2
Dollars	$1,507		$3,750	$8,900	$27,643	$51,500	$5,786	$1,200		$3,000

(Percentages above bars: 175%, 539%, 1,515%, 2,108%, 577%, 51%, 618%)

Record Sale: $50,000, D.NY, 4/1/81, "Grandpa's Visit," 31 × 48 in.

432

MARSHALL JOHNSON
(1846?-1921)

Very little is known about the life of Marshall Johnson, Jr. When he died, only two signed sketchbooks survived him. However, at the height of his career he was a popular maritime artist.

A native of Boston, Johnson was born either in 1846 or 1850 (sources differ). As a boy he attended Lowell Institute. In 1870, Johnson shipped out as a sailor on an ill-fated voyage of the *Sunbeam*. The ship caught fire off the coast of South America, and all but 12 men lost their lives. Johnson was one of the survivors.

Returning to Boston, Johnson studied art for three years under marine painter William E. Norton, before setting up his own studio. In the late 1880s, he traveled to Europe and studied marine art in Holland, England and France.

It was this European trip which critics believe reinforced Johnson's romantic rendering of the ships he painted. Despite high detailing, the overall effect of his work is more dramatic than realistic. Upon his return to the United States, he maintained a studio on India Wharf in Boston.

During the 1880s and 1890s, Johnson's work was widely collected, and he exhibited at the Boston Art Club, the Copley Society and the Jordan Art Gallery. His ship painting of *The Constitution* (1883, Marine Arts Gallery, Salem, Massachusetts) became the advertising symbol of a major New England life insurance company.

When Johnson died in 1921, no obituary was written and no memorial was offered. Twenty-nine of his oil paintings were featured in a successful exhibition at the Vose Galleries in Boston two years later. Most of his surviving work is held in private collections.

Homeward Bound, 25 x 30 in., signed l.l. Courtesy of Arvest Galleries, Inc., Boston, Massachusetts.

SEASON	75-76	76-77	77-78	78-79	79-80	80-81	81-82	82-83	83-84	84-85
Paintings				1		1	4	4	1	7
Dollars				$450		$900	$5,150	$3,900	$750	$12,904

Record Sale: $3,250, RB.HM, 8/7/84, ''The Bark Sunbeam,'' 24 × 36 in.

FREDERIC SCHILLER COZZENS

(1846-1928)

Every year for 50 years Frederic Schiller Cozzens painted the America's Cup Race held off New York Harbor. His work is an invaluable documentation of the marine and yachting scene of his era, illustrating every type of English and American watercraft.

Cozzens was born in New York City in 1846. When he was six years old the family moved to Yonkers, New York, to a house overlooking the Hudson River and the Palisades. His father, Frederic S. Cozzens, Sr., was a wine merchant and a published author who numbered among his friends William Cullen Bryant, James Fenimore Cooper, William Makepeace Thackeray and Washington Irving.

From 1864 to 1867, Cozzens attended Renselaer Polytechnic Institute in Troy, New York.

His illustrations appeared in New York's *Daily Graphic* and *Harper's Weekly* from the mid-1870s to 1898. Besides the yachting pictures, he also painted warships and fishing vessels, and in 1920 and 1921, paintings of North American Indians.

His best known work is a series of watercolors for *Kelley's American Yachts: Their Clubs and Races,* published in 1884 by Scribner's.

From a *New York Times* interview with Cozzens published on June 13, 1926, it is clear that the artist was famil-

Plate XX, *The America Cup 1881 The Start-Atlanta-Mischief*, 1883, 14 x 20½ in., signed l.l. Private Collection, Photograph courtesy of Kennedy Galleries, New York, New York.

Houqua, 14 x 20 in. Courtesy of Oliphant and Company, LTD., New York, New York.

iar with every aspect of yacht racing. According to Brockmeyer, the *Times* writer, "Mr. Cozzens is, or has been, a thoroughly practiced yachtsman. His pictures show it. Not a detail in his drawings of a boat's construction but (what) is plain to the naval architect; not a fine line in the graceful sweep of a hull or in the towering 'stick' of the big sloops carrying a smother of canvas but (what) is faithfully set down in pigments true to hue and seemingly alive with the pert flippancy of a gay flapper of the seas."

Cozzens died in New York City in 1928. The first large exhibition of his work was held at the Mystic Seaport Museum, Connecticut, in 1983.

PUBLIC COLLECTIONS
Mariner's Museum, Newport News, Virginia
Massachusetts Institute of Technology
New York Yacht Club, New York
Peabody Museum of Salem, Massachusetts
United States Coast Guard Academy,
   New London, Connecticut

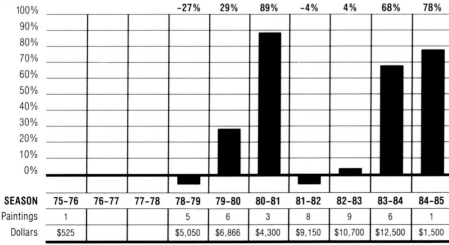

10-Year Average Change From Base Years '75-'76: 30%

				-27%	29%	89%	-4%	4%	68%	78%
SEASON	75-76	76-77	77-78	78-79	79-80	80-81	81-82	82-83	83-84	84-85
Paintings	1			5	6	3	8	9	6	1
Dollars	$525			$5,050	$6,866	$4,300	$9,150	$10,700	$12,500	$1,500

Record Sale: $4,000, CH, 9/28/83, "Race Between Bedoinn, Katrina & Emerald," 13 × 22 in.

LUCIEN WHITING POWELL
(1846-1930)

Landscape artist Lucien Whiting Powell enjoyed a long and prolific career, and was exceedingly popular in his day. Powell was equally renowned for his fresh, colorful renderings of the city of Venice and of the Grand Canyon.

Powell, whose family was descended from Jamestown settlers, was born in Levinworth Manor, Virginia in 1846. His early education included several years in Virginia District schools, as well as private tutelage. Before leaving for Philadelphia to undertake a fine arts education, he entered the 11th Virginia Cavalry at age 17 in order to serve in the Civil War. After the war, he studied in Philadelphia with Thomas Moran and at the Pennsylvania Academy of the Fine Arts.

Continuing his education abroad, Powell traveled to London in 1875. There, he studied at the West London School of Art and was impressed by the paintings of J.M.W. Turner. While in Europe, he went on several sketching tours and visited the great galleries of London, Paris and Rome.

It was 15 years before Powell visited Europe again. By that time, his reputation as a professional artist was firmly established. When he returned to Europe, he became known as a painter of Venetian scenes. These dream-like landscapes, executed in watercolor and oil, convey a sense of light and color reminiscent of the work of Turner.

In Virginia, 1910, 20 x 30 in., signed l.l. Courtesy of Raydon Gallery, New York, New York.

In 1901, the 55-year-old artist took a trip to the American West which resulted in a number of landscape paintings. His powerful depictions of canyons and mountains are considered among his finest works. Most notable are *The Afterglow—Grand Canyon* (date unknown, Corcoran Gallery of Art) and *Grand Canyon of the Yellowstone River* (date unknown, National Gallery of Art).

In 1910, Powell and his wife traveled to the Middle East and Palestine, stopping over in Egypt and Italy. From this voyage, the artist brought back a series of picturesque, spontaneous watercolors depicting the Holy Land.

Powell was a fortunate artist, as he received liberal financial patronage. But despite his good fortune and great popularity, biographical sources note that he was a pessimistic man who did not enjoy his successes. Represented in private and public collections throughout the world, Powell died in Washington, D.C. in 1930.

MEMBERSHIPS
Landscape Club of Washington, D.C.
Society of Washington Artists
Washington Water Color Club

PUBLIC COLLECTIONS
American University of Washington, D.C.
Atlanta Museum of Art
Carnegie Library, Pittsburgh
Corcoran Gallery of Art, Washington, D.C.
Georgetown University, Washington, D.C.
National Gallery of Art, Washington, D.C.

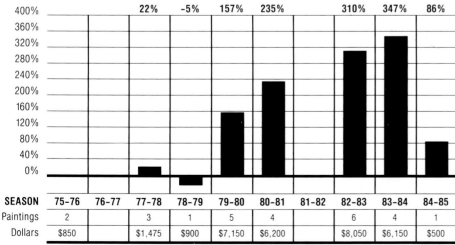

10-Year Average Change From Base Years '75-'76: 144%

		22%	-5%	157%	235%		310%	347%	86%

SEASON	75-76	76-77	77-78	78-79	79-80	80-81	81-82	82-83	83-84	84-85
Paintings	2		3	1	5	4		6	4	1
Dollars	$850		$1,475	$900	$7,150	$6,200		$8,050	$6,150	$500

Record Sale: $3,400, W.W, 6/12/83, "Grand Canyon," 17 x 23 in.

435

CHARLES CRAIG
(1846-1931)

Throughout his life, Charles Craig was imaginatively inspired by Western and Indian life. His important genre paintings are characterized by detailed accuracy, gained from several years spent living with various Western tribes.

Born in 1846 on a farm in Morgan County, Ohio, Craig began painting as a boy—creating his palette from natural materials and using an oil-and-flour-treated bedsheet as his canvas.

When he was 19, Craig traveled West, living for four years with Indian tribes. Eager to record what he had seen, but knowing he lacked technical expertise, Craig returned to Ohio. He set up a studio and painted portraits to earn enough money to finance his art education.

Craig studied at the Pennsylvania Academy of the Fine Arts from 1872 to 1873. He then worked briefly under the tutelage of Peter Moran, who himself was a painter of Indian life.

In 1881, Craig moved to Colorado Springs, where he set up a studio; he was one of the first resident artists in that resort community. Craig's paintings during this period were literal and reflected his frequent trips to the Ute reservation in Southwestern Colorado.

During Craig's 50 years in Colorado Springs, he supplemented his income by giving art lessons. He exhibited regularly in the town's Antlers Hotel; a fire there in 1895 destroyed many of his works. Others are exhibited in private collections throughout the United States and Europe.

Indian Chief on a White Horse, 1898, 30 x 25 in., signed l.r. Courtesy of Vose Galleries of Boston, Inc.

Craig died in Colorado Springs in 1931.

PUBLIC COLLECTIONS
Denver Art Museum, Colorado

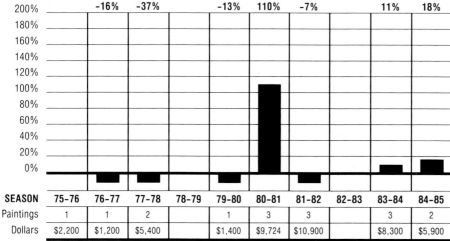

10-Year Average Change From Base Years '75-'76: 8%

		−16%	−37%		−13%	110%	−7%		11%	18%

SEASON	75-76	76-77	77-78	78-79	79-80	80-81	81-82	82-83	83-84	84-85
Paintings	1	1	2		1	3	3		3	2
Dollars	$2,200	$1,200	$5,400		$1,400	$9,724	$10,900		$8,300	$5,900

Record Sale: $7,500, SPB, 10/22/81, ''Indian Hunting From a Canoe,'' 36 × 50 in.

436

DE SCOTT EVANS
(1847-1898)

Known in his day principally for portraits of elegant women in stylish interiors or sunny fields, De Scott Evans today receives more attention for his trompe l'oeil still lifes. They were unusual in that most were vertical. Their subjects were luscious fruits—usually apples or pears—hanging by strings against boards of which every detail of grain, knothole and nail hole was scrupulously portrayed.

Ironically, Evans seemed to paint these still lifes almost as a private joke for himself. Most of the painted paper labels bear pseudonyms or variations of his given name. Nearly all are undated.

Evans was born David Scott Evans in Wayne County, Indiana in 1847. He Gallicized his name on his return from a trip to France in the 1870s. Little is known of his early art training, but after attending Miami University in Oxford, Ohio, he went to Cincinnati and entered the studio of Alfred Beaugureau, where he studied drawing. By 1874, he settled in Cleveland and began painting portraits. Three years later he went to Paris and studied under Adolphe William Bouguereau.

When he came back to Cleveland, his career as a portraitist flourished. He was much admired for his skill in handling background draperies. At the same time he became an instructor and later co-director of the Cleveland Academy of Fine Arts, a post he held until he moved to New York.

Lady by the Fire, 36 x 24 in., signed l.r. Courtesy of Vose Galleries of Boston, Inc., Massachusetts.

Several tabletop still lifes which Evans painted in Cleveland are extant, but his most interesting works are the compositions done after he settled in New York.

In an amusing variation from the fruit still life, he also painted a series on peanuts in a rustic wall compartment, covered by a cracked piece of glass, with several of the peanuts seemingly about to spill out through a hole in the glass.

Evans occasionally painted interior decorations as well. In 1898, he boarded the *S.S. Burgoyne,* on his way to Paris to paint decorations for the music room of a Cleveland patron. The ship sank and Evans was drowned.

PUBLIC COLLECTIONS
Carnegie Institute, Pittsburgh
Portland Art Museum, Oregon
Yale University Art Gallery

10-Year Average Change From Base Years '75–'76: 2,656%

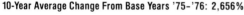
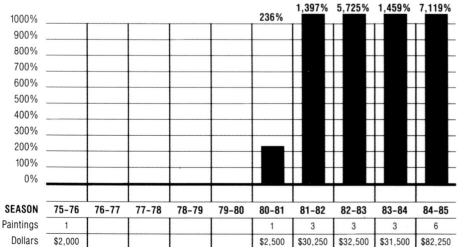

SEASON	75–76	76–77	77–78	78–79	79–80	80–81	81–82	82–83	83–84	84–85
						236%	1,397%	5,725%	1,459%	7,119%
Paintings	1					1	3	3	3	6
Dollars	$2,000					$2,500	$30,250	$32,500	$31,500	$82,250

Record Sale: $24,000, CH, 9/21/84, "Leave Message," 12 × 10 in.

SARAH PAXTON BALL DODSON

(1847-1906)

Sarah Paxton Ball Dodson was a leader among the expatriate Americans who worked in the academic tradition of smooth-surfaced, large-scale allegorical and historical paintings, often with classical or biblical subjects.

Dodson was born in Philadelphia in 1847. She studied under history painter Christian Schussele at the Pennsylvania Academy of the Fine Arts in 1872. Moving to Paris, she became the pupil of Jules Lefebvre and Evariste Luminais. She began exhibiting large academic canvases at the Paris Salon.

The best-known of her works from this period is *The Bacidae* (1883, Indianapolis Museum of Art), a dramatic study of two priestesses of the ancient world. The painting is noted for its vigorous brushwork, rich color scheme and masterful modeling of the human figures. In a more contemporary vein, Dodson also painted a *Signing of the Declaration of Independence* (1883, location unknown).

In her later paintings, Dodson moved toward more personal and poetic subjects, often with religious overtones. This phase of her work has been compared with that of Henry Tanner, the black religious painter, and also with the work of the symbolists.

Dodson settled in Brighton, England, where she painted landscapes as well as figure paintings. Despite serious illness, she continued to paint until her death in 1906.

PUBLIC COLLECTIONS
Indianapolis Museum of Art

Une Martyre (Saint Thechla), 1891, 29½ x 21½ in., signed l.l. Courtesy of National Museum of American Art, Smithsonian Institution, Gift of Richard Ball Dodson.

SEASON	75-76	76-77	77-78	78-79	79-80	80-81	81-82	82-83	83-84	84-85
Paintings								2		
Dollars								$3,300		

Record Sale: $2,000, S.W, 10/2/82, "The Morning Stars," 23 × 30 in.

MILNE RAMSEY
(1847-1915)

Milne Ramsey was a landscape, figure and still-life painter. When he was in his prime, his work was sufficiently well-known to warrant visits to his studio in Paris by such notables as Mary Cassatt and Ulysses S. Grant. Yet soon after his death in 1915 he was almost totally forgotten. Only in recent years has interest in him been revived.

Born in Philadelphia in 1847, Ramsey studied at the Pennsylvania Academy of the Fine Arts. He had his own studio for a time, then went to Paris to study for close to five years in the atelier of Leon Bonnat. Altogether he spent more than 10 years in Europe, studying and painting. He did many landscapes, especially in rural Normandy and Brittany. Some of his work also was based on narrative themes.

After his return to the United States, he lived in Philadelphia for several years. He then took a studio in New York City and divided his time between it and a seaside home in Atlantic City, New Jersey. He returned to Philadelphia for good in 1900.

In his European landscapes, Ramsey used a thick impasto. There was no evidence of it, however, in his still lifes, for which he now is gaining recognition. They were crisp, well-organized compositions that revealed his mastery of both color and technique, particularly in his handling of fabrics.

Like James McNeill Whistler and others of his generation in Paris, Ramsey was fascinated by, and collected, oriental artifacts. He used them in some of his most appealing still lifes.

PUBLIC COLLECTIONS
Mint Museum of Art, Charlotte, North Carolina

Still Life with Apples, 18 x 22 in., signed l.r. Photograph courtesy of M. Knoedler & Co., Inc., New York, New York.

SEASON	75-76	76-77	77-78	78-79	79-80	80-81	81-82	82-83	83-84	84-85
Paintings									3	
Dollars									$7,350	

Record Sale: $5,500, CH, 12/9/83, ''Metal,'' 20 × 30 in.

HENRY F. FARNY
(1847-1916)

Henry F. Farny, the candid chronicler of the American Indian, was born in Ribeauville, Alsace, France in 1847. His family fled to the United States when the Napoleonic party came to power in 1853.

They settled first in Western Pennsylvania, where young Farny got to know the Seneca Indians, beginning his lifelong fascination. The Farny family moved to Cincinnati, Ohio in 1859.

By age 18, Farny, an accomplished lithographer and engraver, was published in *Harper's* magazine. In Cincinnati he met influential artist and teacher Frank Duveneck, who became a lifelong friend.

Farny moved to New York City in 1867, working as an illustrator for *Harper's*. He traveled back and forth to Europe, where he studied in Dusseldorf, Munich, Rome and Vienna, but he remained based in Cincinnati.

Farny became a successful illustrator. He exhibited a 90-foot-long cartoon at the Vienna Exposition of 1873; the work had been commissioned by the Cincinnati Chamber of Commerce.

His work as an illustrator led Farny to the American West, which fascinated the readers of the magazine articles and books he illustrated. In 1878, he began the first of his many American expeditions, traveling 1,000 miles down the Missouri River in a canoe. Later, he was present when the final spike was driven to complete the transcontinental railroad.

These journeys awakened his childhood fascination with the Indians, and in 1881 he began to paint the vignettes of Indian life which gave him lasting fame. They were an immediate success and sold almost as soon as he finished them. By 1890, he had largely abandoned his illustration jobs for full-time painting.

Though at one point he was adopted by a tribe of Sioux, who gave him the name "Long Boots," Farny retained a

Indians in Winter-Moving Camp, 1904, 10½ x 7½ in., signed l.r. Courtesy of Wunderlich and Company, Inc., New York, New York.

perspective on Indian ways which imbued his quiet, matter-of-fact paintings with a particular poignancy. He knew he was preserving a dying way of life, but neither glorified nor denigrated it. His many oils and gouaches are beautifully observed, neither too hasty nor over-detailed.

Farny married his ward, 18-year-old Ann Ray, when he was 59. He continued to visit the dwindling native American tribes until his death in Cincinnati in 1916. Because of his patient observation of the Indian way of life, much has been preserved which might otherwise have been lost.

SEASON	75-76	76-77	77-78	78-79	79-80	80-81	81-82	82-83	83-84	84-85
Paintings			1	7	4	9	5	5	6	
Dollars			$195,000	$230,000	$21,750	$892,750	$153,400	$323,000	$27,800	

Record Sale: $460,000, SPB, 4/23/81, "Nomads," 22 × 40 in.

PUBLIC COLLECTIONS
Taft Museum, Cincinnati, Ohio
Cincinnati Art Museum

ALBERT PINKHAM RYDER
(1847-1917)

The Watering Place, 8¾ x 11⅜ in., signed l.l. Courtesy of Vose Galleries of Boston, Inc., Massachusetts.

A romantic visionary painter, Albert Pinkham Ryder now is considered one of the most important American artists of the nineteenth and early twentieth centuries. His haunting, moonlit seascapes and evocations of passages from the Bible, great poetry and even Wagnerian operas—all were steeped in his deep reverence for nature.

Going beyond his individual paintings, however, what is significant about Ryder is the way in which his simplified, rhythmic forms foreshadowed much of what was to come in modern art. To him painting was not simply a representation of what was seen, but rather a manifestation of an inner vision. It was a creative language which spoke to the senses through color, form and tone.

New Bedford, Massachusetts, where Ryder was born in 1847, was the center of the whaling industry; his forebears had been mariners for generations. An infection damaged his eyes when he was a boy, cutting short his education. Some speculate that Ryder's predilection for eerie moonlight and vague forms, rather than detail, may have stemmed from his sight problems.

His father bought him paints and canvas to occupy his time and, coached by a local amateur painter, the boy went into the fields to try his hand at painting. He was delighted to discover one day that he saw the scene he was trying to paint in terms of only three masses—sky, foliage and earth. Putting aside his brushes, he applied his paint vigorously in large areas with a palette knife. "It was better than nature," he said, "for it was vibrating with the thrill of a new creation."

Around 1867, Ryder and his family moved to New York City. The first time he applied for admission to the National Academy of Design school he was turned down, and instead studied with portrait painter William Edgar Marshall, whose naive approach to religious and romantic subjects influenced him deeply. In 1871, the Academy relented and accepted Ryder.

Most of his works of the 1870s were small landscapes, recalled from his days in the countryside around New Bedford. While naturalistic, they had an artless simplicity and, even then, highly individualized forms were beginning to appear.

In 1877 and again in 1882, Ryder went to Europe, but was impressed neither by the contemporary paintings he saw nor by the old masters in the museums. He went to Europe on two other occasions, but each time it was more for rest and to study the effect of moonlight on water than from any desire to study European art. In the 1880s, he began his work based on biblical and poetic episodes, manifesting his deeply religious inner vision.

Seldom satisfied with his paintings, Ryder sometimes worked on them for years. He had little technical knowledge and applied layer upon layer of paint, glazes and varnish, frequently not letting one dry before painting on top of it. The result was that many of his works darkened and deteriorated deplorably, until today some are hardly recognizable.

Ryder often did not sign his works and rarely dated them. This negligence, added to his small output, made him an easy target for forgers. When he died, one expert estimates, forgeries outnumbered his own work by 10 to one.

In his last years, Ryder became more and more reclusive and eccentric. After a serious illness in 1915, kindly friends took him into their Long Island home and cared for him until his death in 1917.

MEMBERSHIPS
National Academy of Design
Society of American Artists

PUBLIC COLLECTIONS
Art Institute of Chicago
Brooklyn Museum
Cleveland Museum of Art
Detroit Institute of Arts
Metropolitan Museum of Art, New York City
Museum of Fine Arts, Boston
National Collection of Fine Arts,
    Washington, D.C.
National Gallery, Washington, D.C.
Phillips Collection, Washington, D.C.
Worcester Art Museum, Massachusetts

(No sales information available.)

RALPH ALBERT BLAKELOCK
(1847-1919)

Woodland Brook, 16 x 24 in., signed l.r. Courtesy of Vose Galleries of Boston, Inc., Massachusetts.

Acclaim for his haunting, innovative painting came too late to rescue Ralph Albert Blakelock from the tragedy of insanity spurred by poverty. Blakelock's mysterious landscapes—jewel-like, brooding, glowing—have caused him to be linked with Albert Ryder as one of the chief painters in the subjective, romantic mode of the late nineteenth century.

The beginning of Blakelock's career was auspicious. Born in 1847, the son of a New York City physician, Blakelock became adept early at both music and painting (he sometimes discussed his art in musical terms).

Self-taught, he had already begun painting landscapes of the White and Adirondack Mountains by 1864, when he enrolled at the Free Academy of the City of New York (now City College). Three semesters later, in 1866, he left. He may have learned the late Hudson River School techniques at Cooper Union. But here his formal art training ended.

In 1867, at age 20, he began to show his work, then in the admired realistic style, at the National Academy of Design, where he was represented for several consecutive years.

Blakelock's life and art were changed irrevocably by his long journeys to the far West from 1869 to 1871—through Indian country to California and the Pacific Coast, and down to the Isthmus of Panama. On his return East, Blakelock painted landscapes reflecting his new preoccupations with mood over representation, and with his own imagination over realism.

His technique also changed. He began to layer his paint thickly, scraping some away and adding more to build a complex tonality.

Blakelock's extreme departures from the accepted academic fashion were too great; his work did not sell well enough for him to support his growing family. He was often forced to sell paintings for a pittance.

Blakelock was declared insane and placed in an asylum in 1899. He spent most of the remaining years of his life in a mental hospital.

Reportedly, his descent into madness came on the day his ninth child was born. Asking $1,000 of a collector for a painting, Blakelock was offered $500, which he refused. Unable to sell the picture, he returned and the collector then offered only $300. Blakelock took the money and tore it up; he was seized and institutionalized.

Shortly thereafter, his work began to gain recognition. Within a few years, paintings he had sold for very little were commanding high prices—as high as $20,000 by 1916, when Blakelock, still destitute and incarcerated, was named an academician by the National Academy of Design.

Soon forgeries of the now-acclaimed artist abounded—so many that collectors find Blakelock's work hard to authenticate. Blakelock's family remained poverty-stricken. A daughter of the artist is said to have lost her mind after being duped by a forger.

A visitor to the artist in 1916 reports that Blakelock appeared lucid until, at parting, he pulled out a roll of bills and gave three to the visitor, telling him to invest them. The "bills" were three small landscapes painted to resemble money.

Blakelock was frequently hospitalized after 1916. He died in 1919.

SEASON	75-76	76-77	77-78	78-79	79-80	80-81	81-82	82-83	83-84	84-85
Paintings	1	2	11	13	20	12	12	13	12	10
Dollars	$560	$6,850	$21,267	$44,250	$51,874	$42,850	$76,000	$29,700	$22,850	$20,400

Record Sale: $30,000, SPB, 4/23/82, "Coastal Scene, Jamaica," 36 × 56 in.

AUGUST LAUX
(1847-1921)

German-born August Laux achieved a considerable reputation in the 1870s for his frescoes and decorative painting, but switched to genre scenes and still lifes a decade later. His work, always traditional in style, was highly regarded in his day but forgotten soon after his death.

He was born in the Pfalz area of the Rhineland in 1847 to French parents. Members of his mother's family held important positions in the government of Strasburg; one of his uncles and a cousin were sculptors in Paris.

One story has it that, during a visit to his uncle's studio while he was a child, the young Laux took mallet and chisel to try his hand at sculpting, unbeknown to his elders, and managed to ruin a work in progress. True or not, the boy did show an aptitude for sculpting and was encouraged to work in clay. Soon after his parents emigrated to New York City in 1863, he began studying sculpture.

In 1867, however, he switched to painting and enrolled in classes at the National Academy of Design. His first painting was exhibited there in 1870.

Three years later Laux was commissioned to paint the scenery for the private theater of a club in Manhattan. The results were so successful that he was soon much in demand for frescoes and decorations in hotels and other buildings, as well as in such magnificent private homes as those of financier Jay Gould and Andrew Garvey.

Still Life with Flowers, 19½ 23½ in., signed l.r. Courtesy of Private Collection.

Laux turned to genre painting, still lifes and landscape sketches after 1880. He continued to work in this vein until his death in Brooklyn in 1921.

10-Year Average Change From Base Years '80-'81: 93%

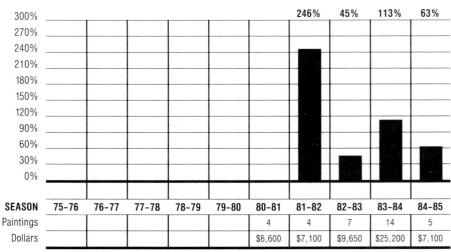

SEASON	75-76	76-77	77-78	78-79	79-80	80-81	81-82	82-83	83-84	84-85
Paintings						4	4	7	14	5
Dollars						$6,600	$7,100	$9,650	$25,200	$7,100

Record Sale: $4,500, SPB, 1/27/84, "Strawberries and Blossoms," 10×12 in.

FREDERIC ARTHUR BRIDGMAN
(1847-1927)

Afternoon in Dreams, 1878, 11½ x 17 in., signed l.r. Photograph courtesy of The Gerald Peters Gallery, Santa Fe, New Mexico.

The orientalist and archaeological works of Frederic Arthur Bridgman made his fortune and reputation as the outstanding American expatriate artist in the 1870s and 1880s.

By the 1890s, public taste for these themes had faded. But Bridgman has been so identified with his North African portraits and scenes of antique mythology that his versatility is sometimes slighted.

Bridgman was born in Tuskegee, Alabama. By 1863, he was an apprentice steel engraver at the American Bank Note Company in New York City, studying at the Brooklyn Art Studio and the National Academy of Design.

In 1866, Bridgman sailed for Europe, becoming one of the earliest members of the Pont-Aven artists' colony in Brittany. From 1867 to 1871, he was among the first American students of Jean-Leon Gerome, renowned for his academic, detailed paintings of North African scenes.

Contemporaries described Bridgman as personable, observant and absolutely addicted to art. He worked constantly. His first entry at the 1868 Paris Salon, *Breton Games* (date and location unknown), was praised, and was reproduced in *Le Monde Illustre.*

Having completed his academic work in 1872, Bridgman painted in the Pyrenees and spent five months in Tangiers and Algeria, the first of many visits to North Africa.

While his Pyrenees work attracted attention at the 1873 Salon for its vivacity and artistic assurance, Bridgman was in Egypt, traveling up the Nile.

He began concentrating on portrayals, both realistic and romanticized, of North African scenes and mythology. His orientalist pictures soon surpassed Gerome's in expressiveness and in the handling of atmospheric effect and light.

Bridgman's fame skyrocketed in the mid-1870s. In 1877, his first archaeolog-

ical painting, *The Funeral of a Mummy* (date and location unknown), earned him a Paris Salon award, rare for a non-Frenchman. He married that year and settled permanently in France. In 1878, he received the award of the French Legion of Honor for *The Past-Times of the Assyrian King* (date and location unknown).

In 1881, the critical and financial success of Bridgman's first one-man show in New York City led to his election to the American Academy of Design. The show, at the American Art Gallery, included 300 oil sketches and finished paintings.

The decline in popular taste for exotic scenes did not affect Bridgman's artistic dedication and growth. Some critics find the freer line, vitality and lighter touch of his later work, particularly his oil sketches, more appealing than some of his earlier, acclaimed works.

Bridgman taught, chaired art projects, wrote commentary, poetry and music, and painted. His final show was in 1926. He died in 1927 in Rouen, France.

MEMBERSHIPS
National Academy of Design

PUBLIC COLLECTIONS
Art Institute of Chicago
Corcoran Gallery of Art, Washington, D.C.

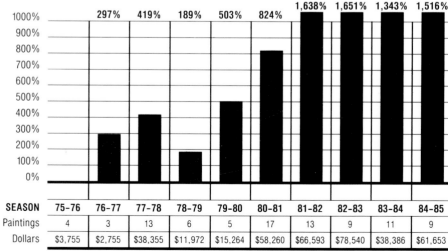

10-Year Average Change From Base Years '75-'76: 838%

SEASON	75-76	76-77	77-78	78-79	79-80	80-81	81-82	82-83	83-84	84-85
		297%	419%	189%	503%	824%	1,638%	1,651%	1,343%	1,516%
Paintings	4	3	13	6	5	17	13	9	11	9
Dollars	$3,755	$2,755	$38,355	$11,972	$15,264	$58,260	$66,593	$78,540	$38,386	$61,653

Record Sale: $33,400, S, 6/21/83, "Towing on the Nile," 35 x 59 in.

444

HAMILTON HAMILTON
(1847-1928)

Hamilton Hamilton was known mostly for his landscapes, although he took up genre painting in the 1890s. He was one of the founders of the Silvermine Guild of Artists in Norwalk, Connecticut.

The young Hamilton studied painting, but was not particularly encouraged by his parents. After some years, however, they became reconciled to his interest in art. In 1870, they sent him abroad to study. Eventually, he joined the American colony in Pont-Aven, Brittany. These artists identified themselves with the English artist John Constable and the barbizon landscape painters in France.

Just when he had gotten settled, however, Hamilton was called back home in 1872 to help support his family. Works such as *Lil' Southern Belles* (ca. 1894, location unknown), in which he used his twin daughters as models, are softly realistic and show a fine sense of composition. In the early 1900s, when he went to California for his health, he lightened his palette and began to experiment with color more. *The House of the Astronomers* (date and location unknown) illustrates his newly-found use of color imagery. The general tone of the painting is an otherworldly blue. He worked as a portrait painter in Buffalo, New York.

When Hamilton went to England for a year or two in 1895, he painted on the Cornish coast and became a protege of

Blowing Bubbles, 30 x 36 in., signed l.l. Courtesy of Henry B. Holt, Inc., Essex Fells, New Jersey.

John Ruskin, the critic, artist and writer.

In 1896, he came back and settled in Peekskill, New York. Landscape paintings of this period include *Hayfield, Chestnut Blossoms* and *Verplanck's Point* (dates and locations unknown).

Hamilton died in 1928.

MEMBERSHIPS
American Watercolor Society
Etchers Club
National Academy of Design

PUBLIC COLLECTIONS
Albright-Knox Museum, Buffalo, New York

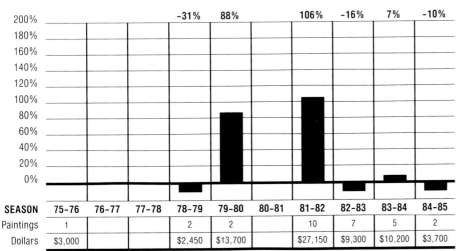

10-Year Average Change From Base Years '75-'76: 21%

SEASON	75-76	76-77	77-78	78-79	79-80	80-81	81-82	82-83	83-84	84-85
				-31%	88%		106%	-16%	7%	-10%
Paintings	1			2	2		10	7	5	2
Dollars	$3,000			$2,450	$13,700		$27,150	$9,300	$10,200	$3,700

Record Sale: $12,000, SPB, 2/13/82, ''Cabin in the Mountains,'' 18 x 28 in.

CHARLES DORMAN ROBINSON
(1847-1933)

High in the Mountains, 30 x 38 in., signed l.r. Courtesy of Marbella Gallery, Inc., New York, New York. Photograph by Richard Haynes.

Charles Dorman Robinson came to be known as "the dean of Pacific Coast artists" and is best remembered for his marine paintings, but his major fascination was with that large-scale amalgam of theater and painting known as the panorama. His favorite subject was the awe-inspiring Yosemite Valley in California. He never tired of attempting to portray its grandeur, despite the destruction of most of his work by human perfidy, fire and earthquake.

Robinson was born in East Monmouth, Maine in 1847. The family soon moved to Vermont, and Robinson's father, a man of grand schemes, went to California in 1848. The family joined him in San Francisco in 1850 and young Charles grew up sketching the ships in the harbor.

In 1860, scene painter and panoramist George Tirrell gave Robinson some leftover paint and canvas after finishing a series of immense views of the Northern California landscape. Robinson quickly created his own smaller and less polished panorama and exhibited it in a neighbor's barn.

After Robinson's father disappeared in 1857, his mother moved the family back to Vermont in 1861. Robinson remained on the East coast until 1874, and there received most of his instruction. He came into contact with Albert Bierstadt, the major American landscape artist, and James Hamilton, the "American Turner." The influence of Turner through Hamilton was especially strong in Robinson's later work.

He migrated across the country to San Francisco in 1874, and by 1875 was painting full-time, establishing himself as a major painter within three years.

In 1880, Robinson discovered the Yosemite Valley in California. He summered there for 24 years, and made it the subject of what he considered his most important work.

In 1892 he began construction of an immense canvas (50 feet high by 380 feet long, weighing five tons), portraying the valley. After exhibition in the United States he shipped it to Paris for the 1900 Exposition, but found when he arrived that his agent had failed him and exhibition was impossible. He had to cut it up and sell it for canvas in order to get home.

Later in Robinson's life, many of his other paintings of the valley were demolished by a series of fires and an earthquake. In spite of this, his enthusiasm for his life and work never diminished. He continued to paint pictures of the Yosemite until his death in 1933 in San Rafael, California.

MEMBERSHIPS
Bohemian Club
Palette Club
San Francisco Art Association

PUBLIC COLLECTIONS
California Historical Society, San Francisco
Crocker Art Museum, Sacramento, California
Oakland Art Museum, California
Society of California Pioneers, San Francisco

SEASON	75-76	76-77	77-78	78-79	79-80	80-81	81-82	82-83	83-84	84-85
Paintings				2	7	7	5	3	5	3
Dollars				$1,850	$6,400	$7,650	$5,900	$3,000	$5,250	$2,300

Record Sale: $2,250, BB.SF, 6/24/81, "Ruins in a Sublime Setting," 41 × 67 in.

446

SEVERIN ROESEN

(Active 1848-1871)

Severin Roesen was one of the most important still-life painters of the mid-nineteenth century. His canvases overflowing with fruits and flowers seem vulgar by modern standards, but they faithfully reflect Victorian opulence and the optimistic perspective of a New World filled with abundance.

Little is known of Roesen's life. It is thought he was born in 1815 in the German Rhineland and immigrated to the United States in the wake of the European revolutions of 1848. Roesen settled first in New York City, then moved to Philadelphia, Harrisburg and finally to Williamsport, Pennsylvania, where he stayed for a decade, becoming the resident master of still-life painting in that North-central Pennsylvania city. He disappeared from the Williamsport scene about 1872 and nothing more is known of his life.

Roesen's work seems to have had a substantial impact on the mid-Victorian art world. Several artists, including Paul Lacroix, imitated his work; his productivity, which included porcelain and enamel painting, appears to have given the art of still-life painting in America a major boost. Roesen derived his artistic principles from late-seventeenth- and early-eighteenth-century Dutch still life. His style reflects that of the Dusseldorf Academy, Europe's then-favorite art school, where Roesen may have studied.

Roesen painted 300 to 400 canvases, all very similar. Fruits from all seasons mix with flowers, bird's nests, half-filled wine glasses and ceramic objects. The whole is set upon a marble slab—sometimes a double-tiered table—to convey an image of incredible richness. The paintings, most of them large, would have dominated the interior of a Victorian dining room, and there is reason to believe that many were commissioned for that purpose.

His method of painting was synthetic. Roesen probably did not work solely

Still Life in Landscape, 29 x 36 in., signed l.r. Courtesy of Vose Galleries of Boston, Inc., Massachusetts.

from living objects (his botanical cornucopia ignores natural seasons). He may have painted from prints or used templates which he rearranged for each new painting. The same groups repeat themselves in several canvases, and there is little development over time in his art.

PUBLIC COLLECTIONS
Delaware Art Museum, Wilmington

SEASON	75-76	76-77	77-78	78-79	79-80	80-81	81-82	82-83	83-84	84-85
Paintings						4	3	5	12	2
Dollars						$141,500	$100,500	$136,000	$288,500	$25,500

Record Sale: $52,500, SPB, 10/17/80, "Still Life with Fruit," 36 × 51 in.

447

WILLIAM MICHAEL HARNETT
(1848-1892)

William Michael Harnett, born in Clonakilty, county Cork, Ireland in 1848, was considered the most influential American still-life painter of the late nineteenth century. As a leading exponent of American trompe d'oeil, he influenced an entire generation of still-life painters, such as Jefferson D. Chalfant, John F. Peto and John Haberle.

Harnett grew up in Philadelphia. From a family of artisans, he first trained as an engraver of silver—a technique reflected in his later precise, linear style. He also attended classes at the Pennsylvania Academy of the Fine Arts. In 1871, he moved to New York City and attended classes at the National Academy and Cooper Union. He continued to work at his trade as an engraver. By 1874, he was able to devote himself fully to his painting. In 1876, he returned to Philadelphia and resumed his studies at the Academy.

Harnett's early period, from 1874 to 1880, featured intricately detailed, small still lifes of tabletops cluttered with casually arranged, simple objects. These early works demonstrate his lifelong concern with texture, exemplified by his meticulous brushwork.

The Artist's Letter Rack (1879, location unknown) is a precursor of his next period. This tour de force of illusionism shows a bulletin board covered with memorabilia. The painter's choice of flat

The Banker's Table II, 1877, 8 x 12 in., signed l.r. Courtesy of Kennedy Galleries, New York, New York.

objects displayed in a shallow space creates a trompe d'oeil effect.

During his second period, from 1880 to 1886, Harnett studied in Europe. Beginning in London, he moved to Frankfurt and then in 1881 to Munich, where he studied the old masters for four years. During this period his subjects changed from the ordinary to the exotic, and he began to use older objects from which he could reproduce mellower tones and richer, yet transparent hues. The fourth version of his large still life of game, *After the Hunt* (1885, location unknown), was shown to great acclaim at the Paris Salon of 1885.

Upon his return to the United States, *After the Hunt* was purchased by Theo-

dore Stewart, who hung it in his popular New York saloon. The painting was so much admired that imitations abounded. In later years, works by other artists, especially those of John F. Peto, were falsely signed with Harnett's name, and confused collectors and scholars for many years.

From 1886 until his death in 1892, Harnett continued to produce work that was still realistic but was more subtle; his choice of subjects became almost symbolic. An example is *Still Life— Violin and Music* (1888, location unknown). Harnett also painted a number of single subjects, such as a pistol, a bird, or a horseshoe silhouetted against a monochrome wall to create an effect of almost classic simplicity.

Harnett was crippled with arthritis, which severely limited his artistic production in his later years. He is estimated to have produced about 500 paintings, of which nearly two-thirds are lost. Although he was considered old-fashioned by influential critics of his time, his exacting realism was later esteemed by twentieth-century artists.

PUBLIC COLLECTIONS
Addison Gallery of American Art, Andover, Massachusetts
Art Museum, Wichita, Kansas
Butler Institute of Art, Youngstown, Ohio
Fine Arts Museums of San Francisco
Gallery of Fine Arts, Columbus, Ohio
Graves Art Gallery, Sheffield, England
Metropolitan Museum of Art, New York City
Museum of Fine Arts, Boston

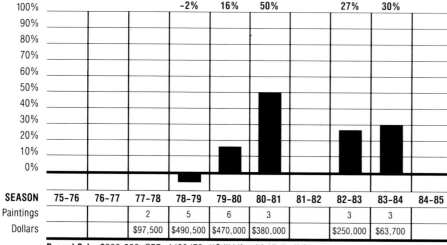

10-Year Average Change From Base Years '77-'78: 20%

			-2%	16%	50%		27%	30%	
SEASON	75-76	76-77	77-78	78-79	79-80	80-81	81-82	82-83	83-84	84-85
Paintings			2	5	6	3		3	3	
Dollars			$97,500	$490,500	$470,000	$380,000		$250,000	$63,700	

Record Sale: $300,000, SPB, 4/20/79, "Still Life with Violin," 21 x 18 in.

448

GEORGE HERBERT McCORD
(1848-1909)

George Herbert McCord, a painter known for his watercolors, oils and pastels, as well as his black-and-white drawings, was born in New York City in 1848.

McCord was a pupil of Samuel F.B. Morse and James Fairman in 1866, and had exhibited at the National Academy of Design by 1870. He gained public attention in 1875 for two paintings, *Sleepy Hollow* and *Sunny Side—Home of Washington Irving* (dates and locations unknown), which were exhibited in New York City as part of a fundraising drive for a Washington Irving monument.

McCord made frequent trips to sketch in New England, Canada, Florida and the Upper Mississippi. He was one of an elite group of artists invited by the Santa Fe Railroad to paint scenes of the Grand Canyon. He was also invited on the Arkell Erie Canal trip.

McCord's marine scenes and landscapes were popular in their time for their atmospheric quality and highly-developed sense of color. He was sought after for commissions and was invited by Andrew Carnegie to paint the scenery around his castle in Cluny, Scotland.

McCord was named an associate of the National Academy of Design in 1880. He was active in other artists' organizations in New York City, and was frequently honored at exhibitions nationwide.

Though he maintained a permanent studio at his Morristown, New Jersey home, McCord spent much time abroad. He lived and painted for three years in Venice, and later in Paris. During these trips, he was joined by his wife and daughters, two of whom became accomplished artists. McCord's only sister, who was also a painter, joined the family in Venice and Italy.

McCord died in New York City in 1909.

Adirondack Lake, Twilight, 1875, 20 x 36 in., signed l.l. Courtesy of Driscoll & Walsh Fine Art, Boston, Massachusetts.

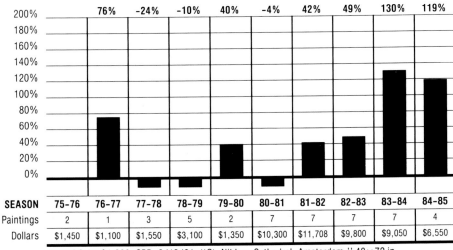

10-Year Average Change From Base Years '75-'76: 42%

	76%	-24%	-10%	40%	-4%	42%	49%	130%	119%
SEASON	75-76	76-77	77-78	78-79	79-80	80-81	81-82	82-83	83-84	84-85
Paintings	2	1	3	5	2	7	7	7	7	4
Dollars	$1,450	$1,100	$1,550	$3,100	$1,350	$10,300	$11,708	$9,800	$9,050	$6,550

Record Sale: $4,000, SPB, 6/19/81, "St. Niklaas Cathedral, Amsterdam," 48 × 72 in.

MEMBERSHIPS
American Water Color Society
Artists Fund Society
Brooklyn Art Club
Lotos Club
National Academy of Design
Newspaper Artists' Society
New York Water Color Club
Salmagundi Club

PUBLIC COLLECTIONS
Albany Institute of History and Art, New York

FRANK KNOX MORTON REHN
(1848-1914)

Frank Knox Morton Rehn was one of the most successful American marine painters of the nineteenth century. Although he chose not to travel abroad, in an effort to ensure that his work remained thoroughly American in character, he achieved international recognition.

Born in Philadelphia in 1848, Rehn enrolled at the Pennsylvania Academy of the Fine Arts at age 18, studying under Christian Schussell. His studies included mechanical art, portraiture, landscapes, marines, still lifes and figures.

He earned a living by painting commissioned portraits for friends, and by selling painted terra-cotta plaques.

Early in his career, Rehn painted many different subjects—landscapes, portraits and still lifes—with equal skill; he won awards for these varied subjects.

After a trip to the New Jersey shore, Rehn began to concentrate on painting seascapes. His decision to specialize in marine paintings was probably influenced by Russell Smith's suggestion to him that he concentrate his talents on one subject.

In 1881, Rehn moved to New York City and set up a studio with some other artists in the Hotel Chelsea. He kept this studio until his death. Rehn spent his summers in Magnolia, Massachusetts, where he painted with John Henry

Sunrise, Coast of New England, 20 x 35 in., signed l.l. Courtesy of Newman Galleries, Philadelphia, Pennsylvania.

Twachtman, Childe Hassam and William Merritt Chase.

Although he retained the American character of his painting, Rehn was deeply influenced by the French impressionists, and was one of the first Americans to introduce the impressionist style of painting to his fellow countrymen. It is thus ironic that he was one of the few nineteenth-century American painters who did not travel abroad.

Rehn won an impressively long list of prestigious awards, for his skillfully painted watercolors as well as his oils. He was elected an associate member of the National Academy of Design in 1899, and a member in 1908.

Rehn died in Magnolia in 1914.

MEMBERSHIPS
American Watercolor Society
Fine Arts Federation of New York
Lotos Club
National Academy of Design
New York Watercolor Club
Salmagundi Club

PUBLIC COLLECTIONS
Corcoran Gallery of Art, Washington, D.C.
Detroit Institute of Arts

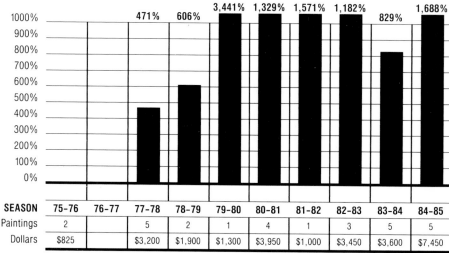

10-Year Average Change From Base Years '75-'76: 1,235%

SEASON	75-76	76-77	77-78	78-79	79-80	80-81	81-82	82-83	83-84	84-85
(% change)			471%	606%	3,441%	1,329%	1,571%	1,182%	829%	1,688%
Paintings	2		5	2	1	4	1	3	5	5
Dollars	$825		$3,200	$1,900	$1,300	$3,950	$1,000	$3,450	$3,600	$7,450

Record Sale: $4,500, S.BM, 11/20/84, ''Gloucester Harbour,'' 16 × 28 in.

450

WALTER CLARK
(1848-1917)

Walter Clark is best remembered as a landscape painter, although he also worked as a sculptor and studied architecture.

Clark was born in New York City in 1848. Educated at a military academy in Brattleboro, Vermont, as well as at the Massachusetts Institute of Technology, he studied mechanical engineering, which may have stimulated his interest in drawing.

After leaving the Institute in 1869, Clark toured Europe with his uncle and guardian, visiting the principal cities and observing their art and architecture. He went on to travel alone through Egypt, India, China, Japan and the Pacific. Upon his return to the United States, he first joined a classmate, Wheelock Willard, in establishing a ranch on the plains of Wyoming, at that time still "wild West" country. He then went to New York City in the mid-1870s to resume the serious study of art.

He studied drawing under Lemuel Wilmarth of the National Academy of Design, and sculpture under J. Scott Hartley, at whose studio the recently formed Salmagundi Club met. There Clark met landscape painter George Inness, Hartley's brother-in-law, who influenced Clark in the direction of landscape painting. Clark and Inness had adjoining studios in the Holbein Studio building.

Clark began exhibiting widely. His paintings, like those of the barbizon landscapists, emphasized subjective mood. His later work shows the influence of impressionism. *Matanzas, Cuba* (ca. 1878, location unknown) and *Farmland, Chadd's Ford, Pennsylvania* (ca. 1890, location unknown) are typical landscapes.

Clark died in 1917. His son, Eliot, was also a painter.

Cows on the Brandywine, 19¾ x 30 in. Photograph courtesy of Balogh Gallery, Inc., Charlottesville, Virginia.

MEMBERSHIPS
Century Association
National Academy of Design
New York Water Color Club
Salmagundi Club
Society of American Artists

SEASON	75-76	76-77	77-78	78-79	79-80	80-81	81-82	82-83	83-84	84-85
Paintings				1				2	2	
Dollars				$600				$1,700	$1,300	

Record Sale: $1,100, CH, 6/3/83, "Grey Day," 20 × 24 in.

WILLIAM PRESTON PHELPS
(1848-1917)

By the Stream, 36 x 48 in., signed l.l. Courtesy of John H. Garzoli Gallery, San Francisco, California.

William Preston Phelps was born in 1848 in Chesham, New Hampshire. As a child growing up on the Phelps family homestead, he developed an abiding love for the mountains and the people of New England. This deep affection later became the dominating force behind his art.

Phelps displayed an aptitude for drawing at an early age. His first professional art work was sign painting. He studied in Germany for three years under Velten, Meissner and Barth, and showed his work in the International Exhibition at Munich's Glass Palace.

He returned to the United States in 1878, and exhibited *Morning, Evening* and *Forest Scene near Munich* (dates and locations unknown) at the National Academy of Design. He then went to Paris, where he studied the principles of landscape art established by Pelouse and Guillemette. Phelps spent a total of seven years in Europe before setting up a studio in Lowell, Massachusetts.

During his years in Lowell, Phelps painted numerous landscapes of the Merrimack Valley, and at least several pictures of farm animals. He would leave the studio to paint along the New England coast and in Western states. In the summer of 1886, Phelps undertook his most monumental work, a seven-by-12-foot canvas called *The Grand Canyon of the Colorado River in Arizona* (location unknown), a faithful depiction of this natural marvel.

In 1889, Phelps returned to the homestead, in the region of Monadnock Mountain. The remainder of his career was spent capturing on canvas the many moods of the region and the unique ways of New England life. Unlike many of his contemporaries who studied in Europe, Phelps retained a deep attachment to his roots, and his paintings reflect a boyish innocence and idealism.

Technically, however, Phelps was a perfectionist, who always worked at on site. In fact, the Grand Canyon painting was done entirely on location, with the huge canvas held on a specially-constructed frame at the Canyon's brink, 6,000 feet above the Colorado River.

In his later career, Phelps concentrated on painting scenes of New England life, earning the title "the Painter of Monadnock." Illness forced his retirement to a hospital at age 69, and the Phelps homestead and many of his works were put up for public sale in August of 1917, the year of his death.

SEASON	75-76	76-77	77-78	78-79	79-80	80-81	81-82	82-83	83-84	84-85
Paintings			1	5	4	6	2	3	6	2
Dollars			$900	$5,675	$5,050	$12,400	$1,950	$2,150	$8,342	$1,200

Record Sale: $4,500, B.P, 4/7/84, "Autumn in New Hampshire," 30 × 50 in.

EDWARD TOBY ROSENTHAL
(1848-1917)

Edward Toby Rosenthal was a significant turn-of-the-century portrait and genre artist. However, it was Rosenthal's rendering of a fictional character which brought him public acclaim and critical acknowledgement.

Born in 1848 in New Haven, Connecticut, Rosenthal first studied art under Henri Bacon and Fortunato Arriola in San Francisco, where his family had moved. When he was 16 years old, Rosenthal's parents, though poor, sent their son to study in Munich—then an art center rivaling Paris. Rosenthal enrolled in Munich's Royal Academy, and subsequently studied under Carl Raupp and Carl von Piloty.

Except for extended periodic trips to the United States, Rosenthal spent most of his life abroad, where he received portrait commissions from notable and royal personages.

In 1871, Rosenthal was commissioned by American millionaire art patron Tibercio Parrott to do a painting depicting "Elaine," the central figure in a poem by Alfred Lord Tennyson. Elaine, Tennyson wrote, died of unrequited love for the legendary Sir Lancelot.

Completed four years later, *Elaine* (University of Illinois, Urbana) shows a beautiful woman lying under a canopy on a funeral barge. To achieve artistic verisimilitude, Rosenthal used the corpse of a young woman as his model, until neighbors began to complain.

When the painting was exhibited in San Francisco, thousands stood in line to view it. This was one of the few times Rosenthal's work was shown in the United States.

Primarily figure and genre paintings, Rosenthal's works show well-balanced color and composition, often rendered with humor.

Rosenthal died in Munich in 1917.

Portrait of William Seligsberg, 1878, 29¼ x 23¾ in., signed l.l. Courtesy of the Collection of David and Jeanne Carlson, San Francisco, California.

PUBLIC COLLECTIONS
Art Institute of Chicago
Leipzig Museum
M.H. de Young Memorial Museum, San Francisco
San Francisco Museum of Art

SEASON	75-76	76-77	77-78	78-79	79-80	80-81	81-82	82-83	83-84	84-85
Paintings					2		2		2	1
Dollars					$11,000		$20,600		$3,300	$588

Record Sale: $18,000, SPB, 6/29/82, "Trial of Constance de Beverley," 57 × 91 in.

FRANK DUVENECK
(1848-1919)

Frank Duveneck was one of the first American realist painters to work in the robust Munich style, using low-life genre subjects. He was also an able teacher and exerted considerable influence on many younger artists. Some attribute the origins of the Ashcan School to the vigor and candor of Duveneck's work.

Born Francis Decker in Covington, Kentucky in 1848, he later adopted his stepfather's name. As a young man he spent several years working for Wilhelm Lamprecht, a German-born church decorator.

Encouraged by a Franciscan brother, Duveneck went to Munich in 1870 to continue his studies in church decoration. Once there, however, his interests changed and he enrolled at the Royal Academy to study under Wilhelm von Diez. Through Diez he became a follower of Wilhelm Liebl, the noted realist painter.

Upon his return to the United States, Duveneck began painting portraits, decorating churches again and teaching in Cincinnati. His paintings attracted little attention at first, but a successful show in Boston in 1875 established his reputation.

Duveneck returned to Munich that same year with painters John H. Twachtman and Henry Farny, two friends from Cincinnati. His reputation soon spread among his American contemporaries and his enthusiastic coterie became known as "Duveneck's Boys."

Walter Shirlaw, ca. 1873, 24 x 18 in. Courtesy of National Museum of American Art, Smithsonian Institution, Gift of Mrs. Walter Shirlaw.

Duveneck opened his own painting classes, first in Munich, then in Polling, a village in Bavaria. His gregarious bohemianism attracted many American students. Later he moved the school to Italy, with winters in Florence and summers in Venice. In reaction to the light and color of Italy, Duveneck's own work became brighter, with smoother brushwork.

In 1880, he was introduced to etching and learned much from James McNeill Whistler, who was in Venice at the time. In fact, when Duveneck exhibited three etchings in London the following year, several critics mistook them for Whistler's.

Duveneck married one of his pupils in 1886; she died in Paris two years later. Deeply saddened, he returned to Cincinnati to sculpt a memorial for her.

He settled permanently in Cincinnati and joined the faculty of the Cincinnati Art Academy, but frequently traveled to France and Italy in the summer. Later he spent his summers in Gloucester, Massachusetts, painting landscapes and seascapes in a more impressionistic style than his earlier work. He died in Cincinnati in 1919.

MEMBERSHIPS
Cincinnati Art Club
National Academy of Design
National Institute of Arts and Letters
Society of American Artists
Society of Western Artists

PUBLIC COLLECTIONS
Cincinnati Art Museum
Indianapolis Museum of Art
Metropolitan Museum of Art, New York City
Montclair Art Museum, New Jersey
Museum of Fine Arts, Boston
National Gallery of Art, Washington, D.C.
Pennsylvania Academy of the Fine Arts, Philadelphia

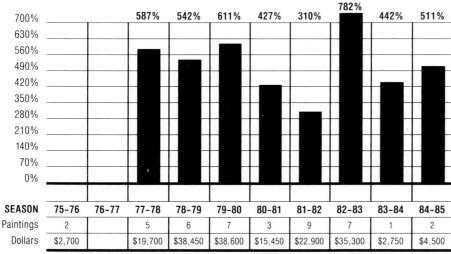

10-Year Average Change From Base Years '75-'76: 468%

SEASON	75-76	76-77	77-78	78-79	79-80	80-81	81-82	82-83	83-84	84-85
			587%	542%	611%	427%	310%	782%	442%	511%
Paintings	2		5	6	7	3	9	7	1	2
Dollars	$2,700		$19,700	$38,450	$38,600	$15,450	$22,900	$35,300	$2,750	$4,500

Record Sale: $18,000, D.NY, 4/20/83, "Seated Nude," 34 x 26 in.

HUGH BOLTON JONES
(1848-1927)

The Old Pasture, 39 x 60 in., signed l.r. Courtesy of John H. Garzoli Gallery, San Francisco, California.

H. Bolton Jones was an award-winning landscape artist of the late nineteenth century, whose paintings of pastoral scenes were widely exhibited in the United States around the turn of the century.

Born in 1848 in Baltimore, Jones began his formal studies at the Maryland Institute. In 1865, he studied under Horace W. Robbins in New York City, and two years later exhibited at the National Academy of Design.

From 1865 to 1876, Jones painted many landscapes of well-known scenes of the Eastern United States, from Maryland and West Virginia north to the Berkshire Mountains of Western Massachusetts. In style and subject matter, his paintings of this period tend to reflect the dominant influence of the Hudson River School.

In 1876, Jones traveled to Europe with his younger brother, eventually joining former Baltimore acquaintance Thomas Hovenden in the artists' colony at Pont-Aven, Brittany. Here he painted his first mature plein-air works, depicting scenes of winter light, as in *Edge of the Moor, Brittany* (1877, location unknown).

In 1880, Jones returned to the United States, where he continued to paint American landscapes in a manner emphasizing the effects of seasonal light or time of day on his rural subjects. He was elected an associate of the National Academy of Design in 1893; he received awards at the Paris expositions of 1889 and 1900 and the St. Louis exposition of 1904. He continued to paint until his death in 1927, in New York City.

MEMBERSHIPS
National Academy of Design
National Institute of Arts and Letters

PUBLIC COLLECTIONS
Brooklyn Museum
Corcoran Gallery of Art, Washington, D.C.
Metropolitan Museum of Art, New York City

10-Year Average Change From Base Years '76-'77: 86%

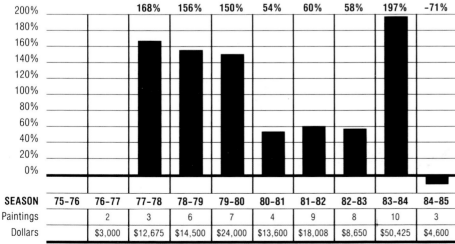

SEASON	75-76	76-77	77-78	78-79	79-80	80-81	81-82	82-83	83-84	84-85
			168%	156%	150%	54%	60%	58%	197%	-71%
Paintings		2	3	6	7	4	9	8	10	3
Dollars		$3,000	$12,675	$14,500	$24,000	$13,600	$18,008	$8,650	$50,425	$4,600

Record Sale: $15,000, CH, 6/1/84, "Old Road to the River," 38 × 60 in.

JOHN CARLETON WIGGINS
(1848-1932)

Carleton Wiggins (who did not use his first name) was a landscape painter in the group of Old Lyme, Connecticut artists in the early 1900s. He is especially noted for his use of sheep or cattle as focal points of pastoral scenes. For many years the inspiration for his work came from the countryside of Old Lyme, a natural setting for the art colony whose work reflected the influence of the French barbizon painters.

Born in Turners (now Harriman), New York in 1848, Wiggins studied under eminent American landscape painter George Inness at the National Academy of Design, after being educated in the public schools of Brooklyn. When he studied in France from 1880 to 1881, he became dedicated to plein-air painting. He exhibited in the Paris Salon in 1881.

The Royal Academy in London reproduced his work in *Royal Academy Pictures* in 1896 and 1897, in addition to hanging his pictures "on the line" (at eye level at the Academy exhibitions).

Wiggins had technical skill, never losing his structural composition, and Inness's influence is noted in his use of soft edges, warm colors and subtle lights and shadows. A critic once said, "His pictures have atmosphere and repose."

Wiggins was the father and grandfather of painters Guy C. Wiggins (1883-1962) and Guy A. Wiggins (1921-   ). A major exhibition of their work was held in 1979 in Connecticut at the

Boathouse - Lake George, 1871, 12 x 30 in., signed l.l. Courtesy of John H. Garzoli Gallery, San Francisco, California.

Loomis Chaffee School and New Britain Museum of American Art, representing "Three Generations of Wigginses."

The work of Carleton Wiggins is represented in numerous major museums and collections. He was president of the Salmagundi Club in 1911 and 1912, and dean of the Lyme Art Association. He made his permanent home in Old Lyme, Connecticut in 1915, after being a summer resident for many years, and died there in 1932.

MEMBERSHIPS
American Federation of Arts
American Watercolor Society
Artists' Fund Society
Brooklyn Art Club
Connecticut Academy of Fine Arts
Lotus Club
National Academy of Design
Salmagundi Club
Society of American Artists
Society of Landscape Painters

PUBLIC COLLECTIONS
Art Institute of Chicago
Brooklyn Museum
Corcoran Gallery of Art, Washington, D.C.
Metropolitan Museum of Art, New York City
National Gallery of Art, Washington, D.C.
Newark Museum, New Jersey

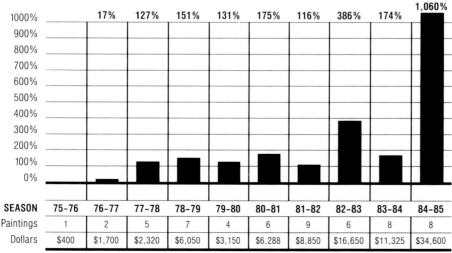

10-Year Average Change From Base Years '75-'76: 234%

	75-76	76-77	77-78	78-79	79-80	80-81	81-82	82-83	83-84	84-85
(% change)		17%	127%	151%	131%	175%	116%	386%	174%	1,060%
SEASON	75-76	76-77	77-78	78-79	79-80	80-81	81-82	82-83	83-84	84-85
Paintings	1	2	5	7	4	6	9	6	8	8
Dollars	$400	$1,700	$2,320	$6,050	$3,150	$6,288	$8,850	$16,650	$11,325	$34,600

Record Sale: $17,000, CH, 12/7/84, "January in New York," 28 x 42 in.

LILLA CABOT PERRY
(1848-1933)

Wealthy, cultured Bostonian Lilla Cabot Perry came late to painting and poetry, but she earned awards for her direct, airy portraits and landscapes. She was instrumental, with Mary Cassatt, in introducing impressionism to the United States.

Descended from the elite Lowells and Cabots, the artist was married in 1874 to fellow aristocrat Thomas Sargent Perry, a professor of eighteenth-century literature. The Perry home became a gathering-place for such cultural lights as William Dean Howells, Henry James and painter John La Farge, Lilla's brother-in-law.

During the 1880s, Perry studied at Boston's Cowles School, with Robert Vonnoh and Dennis Bunker; later she worked in Paris at the Academies Julien and Colarossi, and with Alfred Stevens.

She also began to write poetry, publishing four volumes between 1886 and 1923.

In 1889, the Perrys went to Normandy, France, for the first of 10 seasons they spent there at intervals until 1909.

Perry's visit to French impressionist Claude Monet, a near neighbor at Giverny, began a lasting friendship. In order to promote Monet's work in America, she brought his *Entretat* to Boston, but was surprised that few liked it, except La Farge.

Perry became an advocate for Monet and impressionism. For many years, she

Lady at the Tea Table, 45 x 34½ in., signed u.r. Private Collection, Photograph courtesy of Hirschl & Adler, Inc., New York, New York.

lectured, wrote and encouraged American patronage of the style. Monet's influence on Perry's work is seen in her landscapes. Her figure painting retained its early clear definition and structure, with diffused effects of light. The freshness of her work was enhanced by her preference for painting directly on the canvas without preliminary sketches.

From 1893 to 1901, when her husband taught at Keiojiku College in Tokyo, Perry painted more than 80 pictures of Japanese life and landscapes. In her later years, fashionably spent in Boston with summers in Hancock, New Hampshire, she produced portraits and landscapes in oil and pastels.

Perry died in 1933, at age 85.

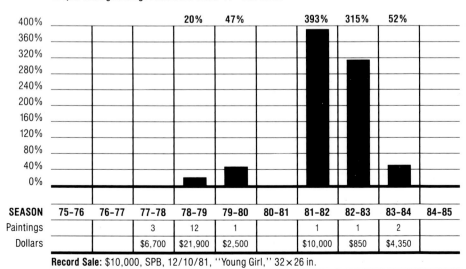

10-Year Average Change From Base Years '77-'78: 138%

			20%	47%		393%	315%	52%	

SEASON	75-76	76-77	77-78	78-79	79-80	80-81	81-82	82-83	83-84	84-85
Paintings			3	12	1		1	1	2	
Dollars			$6,700	$21,900	$2,500		$10,000	$850	$4,350	

Record Sale: $10,000, SPB, 12/10/81, ''Young Girl,'' 32 × 26 in.

457

LOUIS COMFORT TIFFANY
(1848-1933)

My Family at Somesville, ca. 1888, 24 x 36 in. Courtesy of The Morse Gallery of Art, Winter Park, Florida, through the courtesy of the Charles Hosmer Morse Foundation.

While most people today associate his name with the design and manufacture of highly original art nouveau glass, Louis Comfort Tiffany began his career as a painter of landscapes, genre scenes and still lifes in both oil and watercolor. His lifelong fascination with exotic art and culture was apparent in much of this early work.

He was born in 1848 in New York City, where his father was the founder of the prestigious jewelry store that still bears the family name. Young Tiffany had no interest in business, however, and chose instead to study art. George Inness, the landscape painter, saw his early sketches and encouraged him.

Tiffany's interest in Islamic and Far Eastern art was sparked by Edward C. Moore, chief designer for the Tiffany store, who was a collector himself. Later, when he went to Paris, Tiffany studied with Leon Bally, who specialized in landscapes and Middle Eastern genre paintings.

In the spring of 1869 Tiffany accompanied painter Samuel Colman on a trip to Spain and North Africa. At Colman's urging, he started making watercolor sketches, which he developed into paintings after his return to New York. In 1874, he made another trip to France, this time spending the summer painting in Brittany.

He painted and exhibited regularly through the 1870s. His rich colors and dramatic lighting clearly showed the influence of Colman. In 1879, however, he gave up painting altogether in favor of interior design, joining with Colman and others to form Louis C. Tiffany and Associated Artists. This collaboration was the origin of his famous glass designs, as well as work in various other media.

Tiffany established a foundation at his Long Island estate to encourage young artists and craftsmen. By the time of his death in 1933, however, his innovative work in glass had already been overshadowed by the stark functionalism of the German Bauhaus.

MEMBERSHIPS
American Federation of Arts
American Institute of Graphic Arts
American Watercolor Society
Century Association
Imperial Society of Fine Arts, Japan
National Academy of Design
National Arts Club
National Sculpture Society
New York Architectural League
New York Municipal Art Society
Societe Nationale des Beaux Arts
Society of American Artists

PUBLIC COLLECTIONS
Louis Comfort Tiffany Foundation, Oyster Bay, Long Island
Metropolitan Museum of Art, New York City

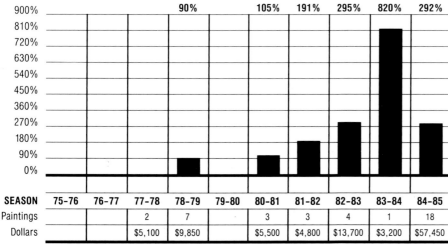

10-Year Average Change From Base Years '77-'78: 256%

| | 90% | 105% | 191% | 295% | 820% | 292% |

SEASON	75-76	76-77	77-78	78-79	79-80	80-81	81-82	82-83	83-84	84-85
Paintings			2	7		3	3	4	1	18
Dollars			$5,100	$9,850		$5,500	$4,800	$13,700	$3,200	$57,450

Record Sale: $7,000, P.NY, 2/1/85, "Sarah Painting, Florida Shore," 23 × 15 in.

458

EDWIN H. BLASHFIELD
(1848-1936)

Edwin Howland Blashfield was a prolific and renowned late-nineteenth-century mural painter, whose decorative works have enhanced numerous American landmarks.

Along with contemporaries William Morris Hunt and John La Farge, Blashfield became a vital force in spurring the revival of the mural-painting movement.

Born in 1848 in Brooklyn, Blashfield was educated in Boston at the Massachusetts Institute of Technology. His initial intention to become an architect or engineer was eclipsed by an interest in painting. This led him to Hunt, who urged him to seek further instruction in Paris.

Blashfield heeded Hunt's advice. In 1867, he came under the tutelage of the French academic master, Jean-Leon Gerome. After three years' work in New York, from 1871 to 1874, he went back to Paris and studied under portraitist Leon Bonnat for six years.

Blashfield began exhibiting at the Paris Salon in the 1870s. His works, which included genre paintings, portraits and decorations, were also exhibited at the Royal Academy in London.

Blashfield's reputation as an easel painter grew, and in 1881 he returned to New York City to set up a studio.

In 1893, Blashfield was catapulted into prominence when he was judged the most significant muralist exhibiting at the World's Columbian Exposition in

Mary Age Five, 1882,
60 x 36 in., signed l.r.
Courtesy of Henry B. Holt, Inc.,
Essex Fells, New Jersey.

Chicago. This success, followed by work on the dome of the Library of Congress, on the Appellate Courthouse in New York and on a decorative panel for the Bank of Pittsburgh, won him national acclaim.

Blashfield's grand style was characterized by strong drawing, vibrant color, shallow spacing and symmetrical arrangements. His well-defined composition, emphasizing the female form, made him one of the most popular mural painters of his time. He was besieged with commissions to work on state capitols, libraries, universities and commercial buildings throughout the East and Midwest.

A highly literate man who was a notable contributor to the arts until his death in 1936, Blashfield co-authored a book, *Italian Cities,* with his first wife, writer Evangeline Wilbour. He also wrote *Mural Painting in America* (1914) and edited, with his wife and T.A. Hopkins, Vasari's *Lives of the Painters.* Active in many art organizations, he was an important member of the art community.

MEMBERSHIPS
American Federation of Art
American Institute of Arts and Letters
Architectural League of New York
National Academy of Design
National Arts Club
National Commission of Fine Arts
National Institute of Arts and Letters
National Society of Mural Painters
New York Federation of Fine Arts
Pennsylvania Academy of the Fine Arts
Salmagundi Club
Society of American Artists
Society of Illustrators
Washington Art Club

PUBLIC COLLECTIONS
Baltimore Courthouse
Cleveland Federal Building
Detroit Public Library
Essex County Court House, Newark, New Jersey
Hudson County Court House, Jersey City, New Jersey
State Capitol, Madison, Wisconsin
Massachusetts Institute of Technology
Metropolitan Museum of Art, New York City
New-York Historical Society, New York City
Williams College, Williamstown, Massachusetts

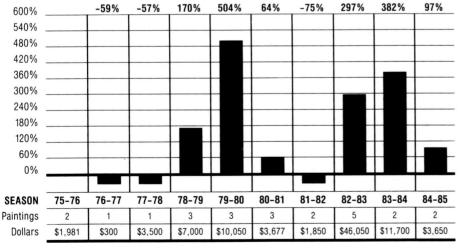

10-Year Average Change From Base Years '75-'76: 132%

	-59%	-57%	170%	504%	64%	-75%	297%	382%	97%

SEASON	75-76	76-77	77-78	78-79	79-80	80-81	81-82	82-83	83-84	84-85
Paintings	2	1	1	3	3	3	2	5	2	2
Dollars	$1,981	$300	$3,500	$7,000	$10,050	$3,677	$1,850	$46,050	$11,700	$3,650

Record Sale: $36,000, SPB, 12/2/82, "The Orientalist," 32 x 40 in.

SCOTT LEIGHTON
(1849-1898)

Called "one of the most famous animal painters of the day" by the *Boston Evening Transcript* and dubbed "the Landseer of the United States" by the *New York Times,* Scott Leighton specialized in painting horses. The technical excellence of his drawing, and his depiction of animal comfort and content, create a priceless record of horses and the part they played in late-nineteenth-century America.

Born in Auburn, Maine, the artist had saved nearly $2,000 by age 17 from horse-trading. He moved to Portland, Maine, where he studied painting with Harrison Bird Brown, and sold his work for an average of $2.50 per portrait. From 1869 to 1879, he taught Delbert D. Coombs, who later became known for his landscapes and paintings of cows.

By 1880, Leighton had set up his studio in Boston. His home in Revere House "was ever a delightful lounging place, and one was ever sure to meet prominent owners, breeders, and roadites," a veritable mecca for sportsmen, according to one newspaper account. It was there that entries closed for the famous Mystic Park Trotter Race won by Smuggler in 1874. The artist's portrait of Smuggler was later lithographed by Haskell and Allen in 1878 and by S.E. Cassino in 1881.

Public demand for color lithographs of famous harness-racing winners was widespread. Leighton was most well-known for 33 pictures he executed for

Familiar Friends, 9 x 14 in., signed l.r. Courtesy of Arvest Galleries, Inc., Boston, Massachusetts.

Currier and Ives between 1880 and 1889. All but two had horses as their main subject.

In 1883, Leighton began to paint landscapes, cattle and fowl. His sense of humor is apparent in these oils, mostly painted on canvas.

In 1897, the artist was placed in the McLean Insane Asylum in Waverly, Massachusetts, where he died a pauper. His paintings were sold at auction to pay his debts.

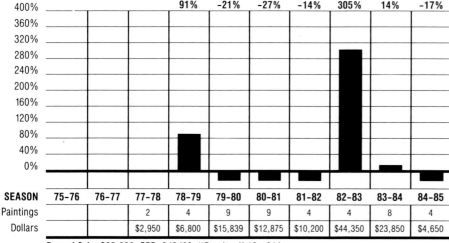

10-Year Average Change From Base Years '77-'78: 41%

			91%	-21%	-27%	-14%	305%	14%	-17%

SEASON	75-76	76-77	77-78	78-79	79-80	80-81	81-82	82-83	83-84	84-85
Paintings			2	4	9	9	4	4	8	4
Dollars			$2,950	$6,800	$15,839	$12,875	$10,200	$44,350	$23,850	$4,650

Record Sale: $25,000, SPB, 6/2/83, "Passing," 16 x 24 in.

MEMBERSHIPS
Art Club of Boston
Paint and Clay Club

PUBLIC COLLECTIONS
Addison Gallery of American Art, Andover, Massachusetts
Clark Art Institute, Williamstown, Massachusetts
Phoenix Art Museum, Arizona
Portland Museum of Art, Maine
West Point Museum, New York

EDWIN LORD WEEKS
(1849-1903)

Arab with Camel, 1870,
18¼ x 13 in., signed l.l.
Photograph courtesy of
Borghi & Co. Fine Art Dealers,
New York, New York.

Although Edwin Lord Weeks was born and raised in the United States, less than one year of his career was spent in his native country. Influenced by his Paris teacher, Jean-Leon Gerome, Weeks concentrated on the architecture and life of the Orient.

Edwin Weeks was born near Boston in 1849, and was educated in the public schools of Boston and Newton. Financed by his father's import business, Weeks began his career in 1869 with a sketching trip to Florida, and on to Surinam and other South American points. Following this, Weeks returned to Boston for a short time and painted historical pictures and landscapes.

The same year, Weeks went to Paris to study with Bonnat, and at the Ecole des Beaux-Arts under Gerome. Weeks shared Gerome's interest in oriental subject matter, and traveled to North Africa, Spain and the Middle East while still a student.

In 1872, Weeks returned to Massachusetts, where he set up a studio and married his cousin, Frances Rollins Hale. Less than a year later, Weeks and his wife joined Robert Gavin, a Scottish painter, on a trip to the Mediterranean and Morocco. Weeks spent the remainder of the decade there, occasionally returning to Boston to exhibit and do illustration work.

Weeks emulated Gerome in the 1870s, and *Departure from the Stronghold* (date and location unknown) shows the

painterly style he favored during this period. Weeks's paintings in the 1880s, however, became more technical and detailed, as in *The Gate at the Fortress of Agra* (date and location unknown). One theory is that the rigors of travel required that Weeks, also a photographer, capture a scene on film, and then paint from the photograph when conditions permitted.

Weeks made Paris his base of operations in 1880. He exhibited his first paintings of India at the Salon in 1884;

after he was recognized in Paris, international acclaim soon followed. He continued his painting expeditions to India, Turkey and Persia.

In addition to being an illustrator, painter and photographer, Weeks was also a writer. His illustrated accounts of his travels were published in *Harper's* and *Scribner's* magazines between 1893 and 1895, and then in book form as *From the Black Sea through Persia and India* in 1896. He also continued to illustrate books.

Little is known of Weeks's paintings after the 1890s. Only one from that period, *Three Beggars of Cordova* (date unknown, Pennsylvania Academy of the Fine Arts), is known, and it seems to indicate a return to the painterly style of the 1870s. Weeks received many honors and awards in his international career, and he belonged to several art organizations. He died in Paris in 1903.

MEMBERSHIPS
Boston Art Club
Legion of Honor
Paris Society of American Painters

PUBLIC COLLECTIONS
Art Institute of Chicago
Brooklyn Museum
Metropolitan Museum of Art, New York City
Pennsylvania Academy of the Fine Arts,
   Philadelphia

10-Year Average Change From Base Years '75-'76: 1,042%

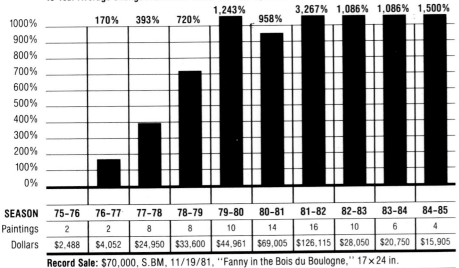

SEASON	75-76	76-77	77-78	78-79	79-80	80-81	81-82	82-83	83-84	84-85
Paintings	2	2	8	8	10	14	16	10	6	4
Dollars	$2,488	$4,052	$24,950	$33,600	$44,961	$69,005	$126,115	$28,050	$20,750	$15,905

(chart percentages: 170%, 393%, 720%, 1,243%, 958%, 3,267%, 1,086%, 1,086%, 1,500%)

Record Sale: $70,000, S.BM, 11/19/81, "Fanny in the Bois du Boulogne," 17 x 24 in.

461

WILLIAM MERRITT CHASE
(1849-1916)

Feeding Baby, 20 x 16 in. Photograph courtesy of Borghi & Co. Fine Art Dealers, New York, New York.

William Merritt Chase, master of a full spectrum of techniques and painting styles, was also one of the most influential art teachers of the late nineteenth and early twentieth centuries.

Although he has been identified with the late realist school, the range of his work exceeds categorization. A vigorous teacher, Chase remained an avid student. He incorporated into his store of abilities every style and technical approach, new or old, that he found admirable.

His paintings reflect his enthusiasms. A landscape might draw on the boldest impressionism; a still life, on the vigorous brushwork of the Munich school; a portrait, on lush classicism or on interior, subdued tonalism.

No matter how eclectic, Chase's canvases maintain unerring harmony through his surety in composition, form, light and modeling. His work is characteristically fresh and energetic, with lustrous surfaces.

Chase, born in 1849 in Ninevah, Indiana, first studied art in Indianapolis. In 1870, he studied for a year at the National Academy of Design in New York City. Afterward, he supported himself painting still lifes. On a trip to visit his family in St. Louis he obtained patronage that enabled him to study in Europe.

From 1872 to 1876, Chase attended the Royal Academy in Munich. The curriculum emphasized the dramatic high-lighting, dark backgrounds and full pigments of the seventeenth-century masters.

In 1877, Chase visited Venice for nine months with other Munich students, Franch Duveneck and John H. Twachtman. He returned in 1878 to New York City, where his work had gained notice at the previous year's National Academy show. He had also won a medal at the Centennial Exhibition in Philadelphia.

Chase began to teach at the Art Students League and opened his own studio, soon a mecca for artists breaking with academic conventions. Gregarious, forceful and unconventional, Chase encouraged his students' individual artistry. To train others in his rapid facility, he had students do a portrait in one hour, wipe it away, and do another in less time.

Chase also taught at his summer home in Shinnecock, Long Island, for 11 years; for more than 10 years at the Chase School, later the New York School of Art; and at the Pennsylvania Academy of the Fine Arts. He also pioneered summer classes abroad.

His students, many of whom became famous, included Kenneth Hayes Miller, Marsden Hartley, Rockwell Kent, Charles Demuth, Charles Sheeler, and Georgia O'Keeffe.

Chase died in 1916, in New York City.

MEMBERSHIPS
National Academy of Design
National Institute of Arts and Letters
Society of American Artists
Ten American Painters

PUBLIC COLLECTIONS
Art Institute of Chicago
Brooklyn Museum
Cincinnati Art Museum
Cleveland Museum of Art
Detroit Institute of Arts
Museum of Fine Arts, Boston
Metropolitan Museum of Art, New York City
National Gallery of Art, Washington, D.C.
Parrish Art Museum, Southampton, New York
St. Louis Museum

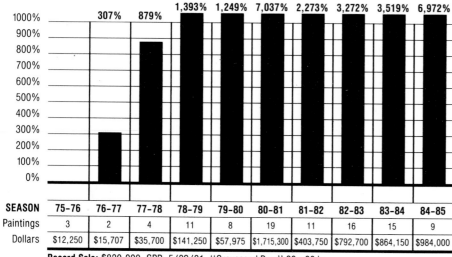

10-Year Average Change From Base Years '75-'76: 2,690%

	307%	879%	1,393%	1,249%	7,037%	2,273%	3,272%	3,519%	6,972%

SEASON	75-76	76-77	77-78	78-79	79-80	80-81	81-82	82-83	83-84	84-85
Paintings	3	2	4	11	8	19	11	16	15	9
Dollars	$12,250	$15,707	$35,700	$141,250	$57,975	$1,715,300	$403,750	$792,700	$864,150	$984,000

Record Sale: $820,000, SPB, 5/29/81, "Gravesend Bay," 20 x 30 in.

462

HENRY S. BISBING
(1849-1933)

Henry Bisbing made his mark as a painter of rural scenes. After an early career as a wood engraver, he found his major influences and greatest triumphs in late-nineteenth-century Europe. Outside of his native Philadelphia, he was not well known in the United States.

Henry Singlewood Bisbing was born in 1849 to a Philadelphia family descended from early Prussian colonists. He studied at the Pennsylvania Academy of the Fine Arts under noted engraver John Sartain.

At Sartain's urging, Bisbing took up drawing on wood to be engraved for illustrations. In 1872, he moved to New York City, where he worked as an illustrator for *Appleton's Art Journal* and *The Aldine Press*, among other publications.

Four years later Bisbing left for Europe, embarking in a new direction as a painter. He studied initially with Barth and Loefftz in Munich. By 1879, he had become a pupil and protege of J.H.L. de Haas, the famed animal painter from Brussels. De Haas, more than any other artist, exerted the dominant influence on Bisbing's career, although Bisbing did further work with Parisian figure-painter Felix du Vuillefroy.

Although Bisbing continued to dabble in engraving (he served on the international jury of engraving awards at the 1889 Paris exposition), he spent the remainder of the century developing his abilities as a chronicler of rural life. Most of his subject matter was found in and around Etaples, France and Zwolle, Holland, where Bisbing spent many of his summers.

His work during this period is characterized by a pastoral, serene realism, as evidenced in *Afternoon In The Meadow* (date and location unknown), his entry at the World Columbian Exposition in 1893. The painting won the silver medal, one of many awards Bisbing received in the 1890s.

In The Meadow, 1888, 79 x 138 in., signed l.l. Courtesy of the Pennsylvania Academy of the Fine Arts, Philadelphia, Pennsylvania. Gift of Colonel Thomas Fitzgerald.

Eventually, Bisbing returned to the United States, settling in Ledyard, Connecticut. He died in 1933, without ever achieving in this country the esteem he enjoyed in Europe.

MEMBERSHIPS
Paris Salon
Paris Society of American Painters

PUBLIC COLLECTIONS
Pennsylvania Academy of the Fine Arts,
  Philadelphia
Stadtsgalerie, Berlin

SEASON	75-76	76-77	77-78	78-79	79-80	80-81	81-82	82-83	83-84	84-85
Paintings					1	2	2	4		2
Dollars					$1,400	$2,900	$1,700	$3,720		$1,850

Record Sale: $1,900, SPB, 6/5/81, "Dappled Herds a' Grazing," 15 x 27 in.

WILLIAM HENRY LIPPINCOTT

(1849-1920)

Infantry in Arms, 1887, 32 x 53¼ in., signed l.r. Courtesy of The Pennsylvania Academy of the Fine Arts, Philadelphia.

Born in Philadelphia in 1849, William Henry Lippincott began his art studies at the Pennsylvania Academy of the Fine Arts. He excelled first as an illustrator, then as a scenic artist.

Later, during his eight years in Paris, the young American turned to genre painting. One of his most important works, *Love's Ambush* (1890, location unknown), is a refined version of his Breton peasant interiors.

While in Paris, Lippincott studied under Leon Bonnat and shared a studio with American artists Edwin Blashfield, Charles Pearce and Milne Ramsey. He exhibited regularly in the Paris salons. In 1882 he returned to the United States and established a studio in New York City.

Lippincott served for years as professor of painting at the National Academy of Design, during which time he was

instrumental in establishing regular still-life studies as part of the students' basic training. He felt, as did many other well-respected artists of his day, that the study of color and form was as important as long years of drawing instruction—maybe more so.

Lippincott was elected an associate member of the National Academy in 1884 and became a full member in 1896. He died in New York City in 1920.

SEASON	75-76	76-77	77-78	78-79	79-80	80-81	81-82	82-83	83-84	84-85
Paintings			2	2		1		2	2	
Dollars			$2,350	$8,900		$1,500		$17,300	$1,650	

Record Sale: $14,000, SPB, 6/2/83, "Love's Ambush," 29 × 43 in.

ABBOTT HANDERSON THAYER
(1849-1921)

Abbott Thayer was a leading figure painter of the late nineteenth century, best known for his idealized portrayals of female models as madonnas flanked by young children, and as virgins dressed in flowing robes. Thayer is also remembered for his semi-impressionistic landscapes of Mount Monadnock in New Hampshire, and his study of protective coloration in nature.

Thayer was born in 1849 in Boston, the son of a physician. He began his artistic training around 1865 under amateur animal painter Henry D. Morse. Between 1868 and 1874, he studied at the Brooklyn Art School and the National Academy of Design, where he began exhibiting his work around 1868.

In 1875, Thayer went to Paris, where he studied at the Ecole des Beaux Arts under Henri Lehmann and Jean-Leon Gerome. In 1879, he returned to New York City, where he set up his studio, and began to develop the style of painting for which he achieved great popularity in the 1890s.

Thayer's paintings of virgins and madonnas were in keeping with the sentiment and fashion of the time, and have much in common with the work of his friends and contemporaries George de Forest Brush and sculptor Augustus Saint Gaudens.

Throughout the 1880s, Thayer exhibited regularly with the Society of American Artists. By the 1890s, he enjoyed the

Young Lady, 1881, 20 x 16 in., signed l.r. Courtesy of Raydon Gallery, New York, New York.

patronage of such major collectors as Charles Lang Freer and J. Montgomery Sears. His painting *Virgin Enthroned* (1891, National Collection of American Art) won high praise at the Columbian Exposition of 1893, and Thayer went on to win awards from the Pennsylvania Academy of the Fine Arts in 1896, and the Paris Exposition in 1900.

After 1901, Thayer settled in Dublin, New Hampshire, where he turned increasingly to the painting of landscapes and to the study of nature. His depictions of Mount Monadnock, visible from his studio, are notable for their impressionistic tonal qualities, much in contrast to the artist's earlier paintings.

Thayer's study of protective coloring in nature, *Concealing Coloration in the Animal Kingdom* (1909), is both original and authoritative, and provided the basis of camouflage techniques employed in both World Wars.

MEMBERSHIPS
National Academy of Design
Society of American Artists

PUBLIC COLLECTIONS
Bowdoin College, Brunswick, Maine
Corcoran Gallery of Art, Washington, D.C.
Freer Gallery of Art, Washington, D.C.
Metropolitan Museum of Art, New York City
Museum of Fine Art, Boston
National Collection of Fine Art,
  Washington, D.C.
Princeton University Art Museum, New Jersey
Rhode Island School of Design, Providence
Smith College, Northampton, Massachusetts
Wadsworth Atheneum, Hartford, Connecticut

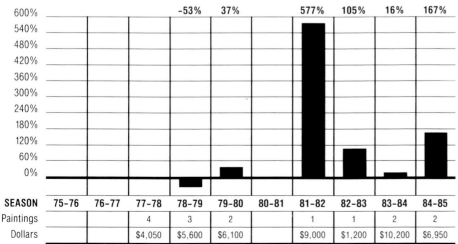

10-Year Average Change From Base Years '77-'78: 121%

				−53%	37%		577%	105%	16%	167%
SEASON	75-76	76-77	77-78	78-79	79-80	80-81	81-82	82-83	83-84	84-85
Paintings			4	3	2		1	1	2	2
Dollars			$4,050	$5,600	$6,100		$9,000	$1,200	$10,200	$6,950

Record Sale: $9,000, CH, 12/11/81, ''Pensive Model,'' 19 x 14 in.

465

THOMAS BIGELOW CRAIG
(1849-1924)

A landscape painter of primarily regional interest, Thomas Bigelow Craig made a fairly good living from his work. He specialized in landscapes with cattle, which were popular at the time. However, he received no recognition from the critics.

Craig was born in Philadelphia in 1849, and lived there for the first 40 years of his life. Most records indicate that he was self-taught, but some suggest that he may also have studied for a short time at the Pennsylvania Academy of the Fine Arts. He began to exhibit at the academy in 1869, when he was 20. Later he frequently exhibited at the Art Club in Philadelphia and at the National Academy of Design in New York.

Craig moved to New York City in 1889, and then 10 years later to Rutherford, New Jersey, which overlooks the Passaic River valley. Until his death in 1924, he divided his time between Rutherford and Woodland, New York, where he had a summer house.

Grazing cows, quiet streams and dramatically highlighted pastures were hallmarks of Craig's work. Generally speaking, it can be divided into three periods. His early works were landscapes, in which small cows figured simply as accessories. In mid-career he painted pleasantly-composed scenes, in which cows and landscape were given roughly equal weight. And his late

Indian War Party-Denver, 1893, 12 x 20 in., signed l.r. Photograph courtesy of M. Knoedler & Co., Inc., New York, New York.

works, done at the height of what some art observers called "the cow craze," were in effect bovine portraits, with little air or landscape to be seen around the bulk of the animal.

MEMBERSHIPS
Artists' Fund Society
Chicago Water Color Club
National Academy of Design
Salmagundi Club

PUBLIC COLLECTIONS
Newark Museum, New Jersey
Pennsylvania Academy of the Fine Arts,
  Philadelphia

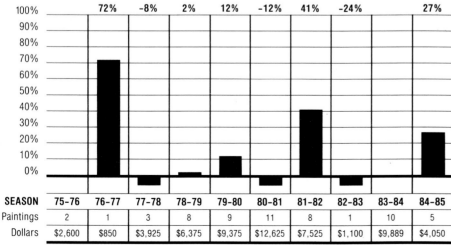

10-Year Average Change From Base Years '75-'76: 11%

	72%	-8%	2%	12%	-12%	41%	-24%		27%

SEASON	75-76	76-77	77-78	78-79	79-80	80-81	81-82	82-83	83-84	84-85
Paintings	2	1	3	8	9	11	8	1	10	5
Dollars	$2,600	$850	$3,925	$6,375	$9,375	$12,625	$7,525	$1,100	$9,889	$4,050

Record Sale: $3,200, CH, 1/30/81, "In the Evening Light," 39 x 53 in.

466

ALEXANDER POPE
(1849-1924)

Alexander Pope was an animal sculptor and painter, whose best known work, in the trompe l'oeil manner, was his least favorite. He preferred animal portraiture to the often illusionary still-life technique inspired by William Michael Harnett.

Pope was born in Boston in 1849. Working in his family's lumber business probably sparked his interest in woodworking, and he began carving animals and hunting trophies.

His art career started in earnest in the late 1870s. Pope apparently studied perspective and drawing with sculptor William Rimmer, and took up painting birds and other animals in addition to his woodwork. Two portfolios of lithographs, *Upland Game Birds and Water Fowl of the United States* and *Celebrated Dogs of America,* earned him the title "Landseer of America."

Pope began using oils in 1883, concentrating at first on sentimental animal portraits. By 1887, however, he had become Boston's representative of the trompe l'oeil school, ultimately producing about a dozen canvases in this style, the most heralded being *The Trumpeter Swan* (1900, location unknown).

Of all the artists representative of this school, Pope was the closest to Harnett in his use of rich, dark colors. He arranged his paintings in a geometric fashion. *The Oak Door* (1887, location unknown) featured an actual oak panel, on which were painted an assortment of

Hanging Brace of Bobwhite Quail with Holly, 1908. Private Collection, Photograph courtesy of Kennedy Galleries, New York, New York.

metal attachments, a shotgun and a gamebag. Like all of Pope's trompe l'oeil works, it featured hunting and military paraphernalia.

Despite their success, Pope was not very fond of his trompe l'oeil paintings. By 1912, in fact, he had all but given up the style, returning again to animal portraits until his death in 1924.

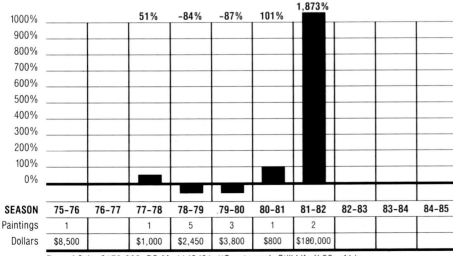

10-Year Average Change From Base Years '75-'76: 309%

SEASON	75–76	76–77	77–78	78–79	79–80	80–81	81–82	82–83	83–84	84–85
			51%	–84%	–87%	101%	1,873%			
Paintings	1		1	5	3	1	2			
Dollars	$8,500		$1,000	$2,450	$3,800	$800	$180,000			

Record Sale: $170,000, RG.M, 11/6/81, "Sportsman's Still Life," 53 × 41 in.

DWIGHT WILLIAM TRYON
(1849-1925)

Autumn Morning, 1919, 17½ x 27 in., signed l.l. Courtesy of Vose Galleries of Boston, Inc., Massachusetts.

One of America's first impressionists, Dwight William Tryon produced muted, serene landscapes and seascapes that remained popular from the 1880s until his death in 1925.

Strongly influenced by the barbizon mode, Tryon brought to it his own exceptionally refined vision of diffused light and atmospheric effect.

His compositions emphasize placid horizontals. His early palette, lightened in his later work, was singularly low-key, often monochromatic. A tonalist, he has also been called a "quietist."

Although few modern critics find Tryon's approach more inert than contemplative, his colors more muddy than subtle, in his time he was called "the complete painter's painter." He received numerous awards and became wealthy enough to endow the Tryon Gallery at Smith College.

Born in Hartford, Connecticut in 1849, Tryon painted New England scenes while working as a bookstore clerk.

In 1876, he auctioned all of his work for $2,000 and, with his wife, went to France to study art. His teachers included Jacquesson de la Chevreuse (once a pupil of Ingres), Charles Daubigny, Antoine Guillemet and Henri Harpignies. He spent some summers with figure painter Abbott Thayer, and traveled in Normandy, Holland and Venice; his Norman and Dutch scenes were accepted by the 1881 Paris Salon.

Tryon returned that year to open a New York City studio and was greeted almost immediately by recognition and honors. He acquired a lifelong patron, Charles Lang Freer. In 1892 and 1893, he painted a series on the seasons for Freer's Detroit home. A large portion of Tryon's work is in the Freer Gallery in Washington, D.C.

In 1883, Tryon opened a summer studio in Dartmouth, Massachusetts. From 1885 to 1923, he was professor of art at Smith College in Northampton, Massachusetts.

In the 1890s, Tryon moved from massy, somber tonalities into a lighter, poetic coloration, with increasingly delicate brushwork. He painted fewer oils, working more in pastels.

Tryon appears never to have been driven by urgent impulses of the impressionists. His later work shows diminished intensity.

He died in 1925 at South Dartmouth, Massachusetts.

MEMBERSHIPS
American Water Color Society
National Academy of Design
Society of American Artists

PUBLIC COLLECTIONS
Brooklyn Museum
Freer Gallery of Art, Washington, D.C.
National Collection of Fine Arts, Washington, D.C.
Tryon Gallery, Smith College, Northampton, Massachusetts
University of Connecticut Museum of Art
Washington University, St. Louis, Missouri

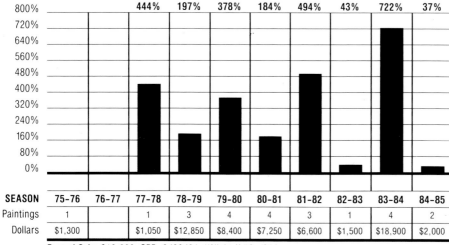

10-Year Average Change From Base Years '75-'76: 278%

		444%	197%	378%	184%	494%	43%	722%	37%
SEASON	75-76	76-77	77-78	78-79	79-80	80-81	81-82	82-83	83-84	84-85
Paintings	1		1	3	4	4	3	1	4	2
Dollars	$1,300		$1,050	$12,850	$8,400	$7,250	$6,600	$1,500	$18,900	$2,000

Record Sale: $12,000, SPB, 6/22/84, "Night," 16 x 24 in.

JULIAN WALBRIDGE RIX
(1850-1903)

Indian Lake - Vermont, ca. 1875-1876, 30 x 60 in., signed l.l. Courtesy of John H. Garzoli Gallery, San Francisco, California.

Julian Walbridge Rix is a classic example of the self-taught, self-made artist who is willing to turn his hand to any art-related occupation that will further his career.

Rix was born in Vermont in 1850 to a family that traced its descent to the first settlers of Massachusetts. Although his father, Judge Alfred Rix, moved the family to San Francisco when young Julian was four, the boy was soon returned to Vermont to live with an uncle. He returned to California when he was 15 to finish his schooling. He showed both talent and interest in art, but his father discouraged him and he received no art education. While apprenticed to a trading firm, he found the time to paint, and became a sign and decorative painter by age 22.

By the late 1880s, Rix was highly respected in California as a landscape artist and was a member of the Bohemian Club in San Francisco. He mingled with an unconventional group of artists including Strong, Jollin and the "bohemian of bohemians," Jules Tavernier, his close friend and studio-mate.

It was only when he moved to the East Coast that Rix began to receive national recognition for his work. After first living in Paterson, New Jersey, he moved to New York City, where he maintained a studio and residence until his death in 1903. He continued to work outdoors—on both coasts, in Colorado and abroad—for much of every year. He also made etchings and provided illustrations for *Harper's Magazine* and *Harper's Weekly.*

Rix, who never married, led an unconventional and free-spirited life. He experimented with unusual applications of his media, such as using watercolors as if they were oils, and learned all he knew about art by working directly from nature. Yet he was accepted as one of the best landscape artists of the day, and his paintings are neither awkward nor uncontrolled, but vivid and vigorous.

MEMBERSHIPS
American Water Color Society
Bohemian Club of San Francisco
New York Etching Club

PUBLIC COLLECTIONS
Corcoran Gallery of Art, Washington, D.C.
Minneapolis Art Museum, Minnesota
Toledo Art Museum, Ohio

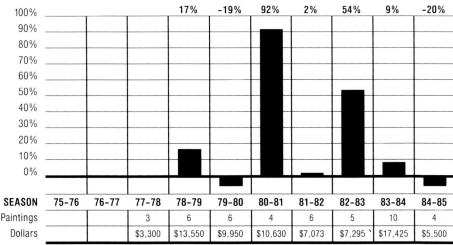

10-Year Average Change From Base Years '77–'78: 17%

			17%	–19%	92%	2%	54%	9%	–20%

SEASON	75-76	76-77	77-78	78-79	79-80	80-81	81-82	82-83	83-84	84-85
Paintings			3	6	6	4	6	5	10	4
Dollars			$3,300	$13,550	$9,950	$10,630	$7,073	$7,295	$17,425	$5,500

Record Sale: $4,780, S, 10/22/80, "Lake in the Rockies," 30 × 50 in.

GEORGE HITCHCOCK
(1850-1913)

George Hitchcock was a leading American expatriate artist of the late nineteenth century. He was critically acclaimed on both sides of the Atlantic for his renditions of Dutch landscapes and people, painted in an impressionistic mood, emphasizing the effects of outdoor light.

Born in 1850 in Providence, Rhode Island, George Hitchcock received his law degree from Harvard University before deciding to pursue his career as an artist. He left the United States for Europe in 1879, and proceeded to study painting in London, Paris, Dusseldorf and the Hague.

In Paris, Hitchcock studied for a year at the Academie Julien under Gustave Boulanger and Jules Lefebvre. He also spent several summers in succession at the Hague, working under Dutch marine painter Hendrik Willem Mesdag.

By the early 1880s, Hitchcock had settled in Holland, where he was to maintain a studio throughout his life. He is best known for his paintings of Dutch landscapes, portraying peasant women in colorful dress and fields of tulips in shimmering rows. His work was especially noted for its use of bright sunlight and shadows to create auras and halos around many of his subjects, a practice that earned him the title "painter of sunlight."

Both in Europe and the United States, George Hitchcock was regarded by critics as one of the best American painters of his period. He was given major exhibitions in New York, Providence, and Detroit in 1905, and was elected an associate member of the National Academy of Design in 1909. He died in 1913 on the Island of Maarken, Holland.

The Annunciation, 66 x 39½ in. Courtesy of Raydon Gallery, New York, New York.

10-Year Average Change From Base Years '75-'76: 193%

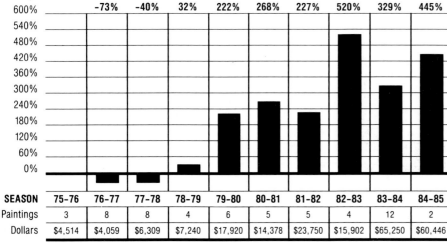

SEASON	75-76	76-77	77-78	78-79	79-80	80-81	81-82	82-83	83-84	84-85
		-73%	-40%	32%	222%	268%	227%	520%	329%	445%
Paintings	3	8	8	4	6	5	5	4	12	2
Dollars	$4,514	$4,059	$6,309	$7,240	$17,920	$14,378	$23,750	$15,902	$65,250	$60,446

Record Sale: $60,000, CH, 12/7/84, "Poppy Field," 51 × 65 in.

MEMBERSHIPS
Franz Joseph Order
National Academy of Design

PUBLIC COLLECTIONS
Brooklyn Museum
Rhode Island School of Design, Providence
University of Rochester, New York

470

CHARLES YARDLEY TURNER
(1850-1918)

Charles Yardley Turner was a painter known for his large mural decorations in government buildings, theaters and hotels.

Born in Baltimore in 1850, he graduated from the Maryland Institute College of Art in 1870. He then went to New York City and entered the school of the National Academy of Design. He also studied in Paris under Jean Paul Laurens, Baron Munkacsy and Leon Bonnat.

He became an associate of the National Academy of Design in 1893 and was named an academician three years later.

Turner adapted American historical themes to his murals, often depicting Puritans, Indians and scenes from the Revolutionary War. He maintained studios in Baltimore and New York.

His mural, *The Burning of the Peggy Stuart,* was painted for the Baltimore Court House and illustrates the entrance of the brig *Peggy Stuart* into Annapolis Harbor in 1774.

Turner painted panels for the Congressional Library, the Wisconsin state capitol and numerous public buildings in New York, New Jersey, Ohio and Maryland. He also painted drop curtains for theaters and decorated hotels in New York.

He was named assistant director of decorations at the Columbian Exposi-

The Interesting Chapter, 27 x 18 in., signed l.r. Courtesy of Grand Central Art Galleries, Inc., New York, New York.

tion in Chicago in 1893 and director of color at the Pan-American Exposition in Buffalo. He also was a founder and

president of the Art Students League in New York.

In 1912, Turner became director of the Maryland Institute.

At the time of his death in New York City in 1918, he was considered one of the three greatest mural artists in the United States.

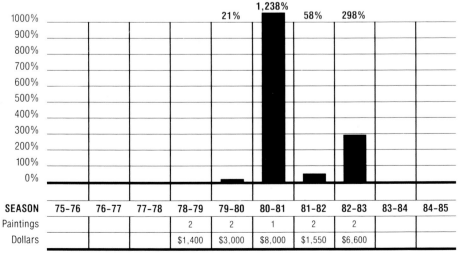

10-Year Average Change From Base Years '78-'79: 323%

SEASON	75-76	76-77	77-78	78-79	79-80	80-81	81-82	82-83	83-84	84-85
Paintings				2	2	1	2	2		
Dollars				$1,400	$3,000	$8,000	$1,550	$6,600		

Percentages shown on chart: 21% (78-79), 1,238% (80-81), 58% (81-82), 298% (82-83)

Record Sale: $8,000, D.NY, 4/1/81, "Interesting Chapter," 27 x 18 in.

MEMBERSHIPS
American Water Color Society
Century Association
National Academy of Design
National Society of Mural Painters

PUBLIC COLLECTIONS
Brooklyn Museum
Metropolitan Museum of Art,
  New York City
Union League Club of New York
Wisconsin State Capitol, Madison

ANTONIO JACOBSEN
(1850-1921)

New York Harbor, 1886, 36 x 72 in., signed l.r. Courtesy of Smith Gallery, New York, New York.

Probably the most prolific marine painter ever, Antonio Jacobsen was not, in his own words, an artist, "but a painter of floating property; of ship portraits." He painted every sort of vessel in meticulous detail.

Most of Jacobsen's customers were ship masters or owners, and they were not interested in fine art; they wanted an accurate record of what the vessel looked like. Since the period in which Jacobsen was active spanned the transition from sail to steam propulsion, he left an invaluable historical record of transatlantic and coastal shipping.

Jacobsen was born in Copenhagen, Denmark in 1850. Because his father was a violin-maker, he was trained as a musician, but his real love was for ships and the sea. He spent much time sketching on the waterfront.

When the Franco-Prussian War broke out in 1871, Jacobsen had no desire to be conscripted into the Danish army and came to the United States instead. His sketching ability soon got him a job painting decorative scenes on the doors of iron safes. This, in turn, attracted the attention of an executive of the Old Dominion Steamship Company, who asked him to paint pictures of some of the firm's ships. With this, Jacobsen was launched on his lifetime career.

He was a prodigious worker. If a customer was in a hurry, he could turn out a finished ship portrait in a single day. Some 3,000 of his paintings are extant;

one knowledgeable collector estimates that the total of his output might have been as high as 6,000.

Before starting a painting, Jacobsen would make detailed pencil sketches of the vessel, often covering four or five pages in a notebook. Each notebook was numbered and filed for reference.

He spent his entire career either in New York City or in a large home in West Hoboken, New Jersey, which commanded a magnificent view of the har-

bor. Over the years he painted every imaginable type of vessel, small and large, from tugboats to racing sloops. In the mid-1880s, he did some forward-quarter views of yachts with sails billowing that, in the opinion of one expert, came closer to fine art than any of his work.

Thinking that they would ruin the value of his paintings, Jacobsen refused to allow lithographs to be made from his work (although a few were made anyway). Diminishing demand after the turn of the century, however, affected the quality of his work. He began selling paintings to a gallery in lots of 10 at very reduced prices. Even so, he continued to paint until shortly before his death in 1921.

PUBLIC COLLECTIONS
Mariners Museum, Norfolk, Virginia
Museum of the City of New York
National Museum of American Art, Washington, D.C.
Newark Museum, New Jersey
New-York Historical Society, New York City
Old Dartmouth Historical Society and Whaling Museum, New Bedford, Massachusetts
Peabody Museum, Salem, Massachusetts
Philadelphia Maritime Museum
Smithsonian Institution, Washington, D.C.
South Street Seaport Museum, New York City

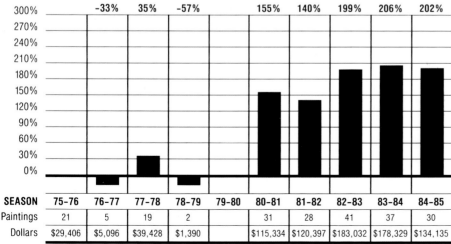

10-Year Average Change From Base Years '75-'76: 94%

	75-76	76-77	77-78	78-79	79-80	80-81	81-82	82-83	83-84	84-85
(% change)	-33%	35%	-57%			155%	140%	199%	206%	202%
SEASON	75-76	76-77	77-78	78-79	79-80	80-81	81-82	82-83	83-84	84-85
Paintings	21	5	19	2		31	28	41	37	30
Dollars	$29,406	$5,096	$39,428	$1,390		$115,334	$120,397	$183,032	$178,329	$134,135

Record Sale: $16,500, SPB, 9/23/81, "Shelter Island," 22 x 36 in.

472

THOMAS P. ANSHUTZ
(1851-1912)

Thomas Anshutz was a Kentucky-born painter and teacher who influenced the art world more through his students than through his own work. Anshutz was the director of the Pennsylvania Academy of the Fine Arts, succeeding his mentor, Thomas Eakins, in that post. He trained many leaders of the next generation of artists: John Sloan, Robert Henri and William Glackens.

In his own work, Anshutz, influenced by Eakins, shows a strong interest in anatomy. The majority of his oils depict a female figure in a contemplative or coquettish posture. He also painted landscapes and was an excellent watercolorist. Recognition came late in Anshutz's life; his importance as a painter has been acknowledged only in the twentieth century.

Anshutz was born in 1851 in Newport, Kentucky. He studied at the National Academy of Design in New York City before coming to Philadelphia. In 1892, Anshutz traveled to Paris, studying for a year at the Academie Julien with Henri-Lucien Doucet and Adolphe William Bouguereau.

Often compared unfavorably to Eakins, Anshutz is thought to lack his mentor's vigor and innovative spirit, while sharing his inclination to depict the human body in a variety of positions within a naturalistic setting.

Anshutz's most famous work, *Ironworkers Noontime* (ca. 1882, private collection), anticipated the realism of later artists in its working-men, partially stripped, taking a break from work.

His watercolors, frequently beach scenes with children, are lighter and brighter than his oils, but it is his large oil portraits of women, subtle in tone and color, that have most attracted contemporary interest. Solidly constructed, the interpretive figures demonstrate an intimate knowledge of anatomy.

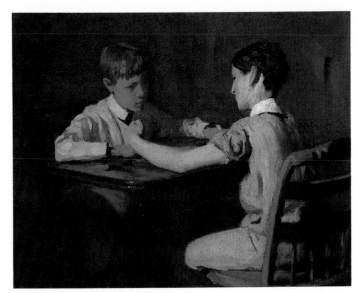

Checker Players, ca. 1895, 16⅛ x 20⅛ in. Courtesy of National Museum of American Art, Smithsonian Institution, Gift of Orrin Wickersham June.

Woman Reading at a Desk, 26 x 24 in., signed l.r. Photograph courtesy of Hirschl & Adler Galleries, New York, New York.

SEASON	75-76	76-77	77-78	78-79	79-80	80-81	81-82	82-83	83-84	84-85
Paintings	1			3	4	2	2	1		3
Dollars	$3,000			$114,050	$20,450	$2,000	$19,200	$1,100		$3,346

Record Sale: $110,000, SPB, 4/20/79, ''Farmer and Son at Harvesting,'' 24 × 17 in.

HENRY STULL
(1851-1913)

Along with Edward Troye, Henry Stull is considered by many to have been the outstanding painter of thoroughbred race horses in the United States in the late nineteenth century.

He painted many of the winners of some of the most prestigious stakes races of the day, and was commissioned to paint many notable horses in English and continental stables. In his typical horse portraits, Stull would paint the animal as realistically as possible, centered in his composition, and then paint the background in a freer, almost impressionistic style.

Stull was born in Hamilton, Ontario, Canada, reportedly above a stable. His earliest ambition was to be an actor. While serving an apprenticeship as a clerk for a Toronto firm, he joined an amateur theatrical company. When he moved to Brooklyn in 1870, he joined another company; he painted scenery and acted.

In 1873, he moved to Manhattan and went to work with *Leslie's Weekly* as an illustrator. Three years later, he went over to *The Spirit of the Times,* a magazine devoted to horses and sports events, as a cartoonist and caricaturist. Within a few years, he began to paint portraits of race horses. To help him in his work, he studied anatomy at a local veterinary college.

Stull's usual practice was to make many preliminary sketches of a horse in the field and then paint the portrait in

Ornament, 1898, signed l.r. Courtesy of Keeneland Association, Lexington, Kentucky.

his New York City studio. Over the years, he made so many trips to the horse farms of Kentucky that he considered one of them, McGrathiana, his home-away-from-home. His last trip to the bluegrass country was in 1912, a year before his death.

MEMBERSHIPS
Coney Island Jockey Club

PUBLIC COLLECTIONS
Jockey Club, New York City

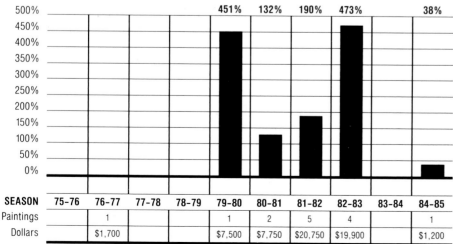

10-Year Average Change From Base Years '76-'77: 214%

SEASON	75-76	76-77	77-78	78-79	79-80	80-81	81-82	82-83	83-84	84-85
					451%	132%	190%	473%		38%
Paintings		1			1	2	5	4		1
Dollars		$1,700			$7,500	$7,750	$20,750	$19,900		$1,200

Record Sale: $8,800, CH, 6/4/82, ''Racehorse in Landscape,'' 28 × 39 in.

474

ARTHUR BURDETT FROST, SR.
(1851-1928)

Arthur Burdett Frost was one of America's foremost illustrators, and an important painter of sporting scenes. He is best known for illustrating the seven Uncle Remus books, written by Joel Chandler Harris; Frost helped to immortalize Br'er Rabbit in American literature. During his long career Frost illustrated more than 90 books, including those of Lewis Carroll, Charles Dickens, Mark Twain, William Thackeray and Owen Wister.

He is less well known for his still-life and landscape paintings, which show the influence of his teachers, Thomas Eakins and William Merritt Chase.

There is nothing glamorous about Frost's work: it is absolutely true to life. His characters are genuine. Very often he added excitement by showing something about to happen.

Frost was born in Philadelphia in 1851; Robert Frost was a distant cousin.

After attending the Pennsylvania Academy of the Fine Arts, Frost was working as a novice lithographer in 1874 when he was given an opportunity to illustrate a book. It turned out to be a sensation and sold more than a million copies. The book was *Out of the Hurly Burly* by Charles Heber Clarke, who used the pseudonym Max Adeler. Raved the *Philadelphia Item:* "... more amusement and entertainment can be found in this one volume than any other half-dozen comical books we have read

His Antlers Were Not Record Ones, 24 x 21 in., signed l.l. Courtesy of Grand Central Art Galleries, Inc., New York, New York.

this season. It contains 400 of the best American illustrations we have ever seen."

For Frost, this was the beginning of 50 prolific years of work for the top

magazines of the country, including *Harper's, Scribner's, Life* and *Collier's.*

Frost died in Pasadena, California in 1928.

PUBLIC COLLECTIONS
Brandywine River Museum, Chadds Ford, Pennsylvania
Delaware Art Museum, Wilmington
Library of Congress, Washington, D.C.

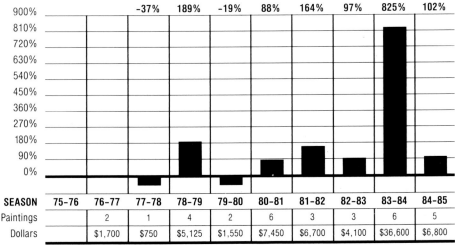

10-Year Average Change From Base Years '76-'77: 157%

		-37%	189%	-19%	88%	164%	97%	825%	102%

SEASON	75-76	76-77	77-78	78-79	79-80	80-81	81-82	82-83	83-84	84-85
Paintings		2	1	4	2	6	3	3	6	5
Dollars		$1,700	$750	$5,125	$1,550	$7,450	$6,700	$4,100	$36,600	$6,800

Record Sale: $17,000, CH, 6/8/84, "Cautious Approach," 11 × 14 in.

475

LEVI WELLS PRENTICE
(1851-1935)

Levi Wells Prentice is remembered principally for his Adirondack Mountain and lake landscapes, painted in the 1870s and early 1880s.

He had a second artistic specialty that has received recent attention—his late-nineteenth-century still lifes of fruit, executed with almost photographic exactitude. Prentice's best work is a table-top still life, *Apples in a Pail* (1892, location unknown).

Prentice was born in 1851 at Harrisburgh, New York, in the Adirondacks. Little is known of his training, but his aptitude had developed into skill by his late teens. In the early 1870s, the Prentice family moved to Syracuse, New York, where the artist opened a studio in 1875. He married in 1882 and moved to Buffalo, New York in 1883.

Prentice's mountain landscapes gained favor. He also painted portraits, decorated parlor ceilings, and designed and built furniture and houses. He made some of his own brushes, palettes and frames.

In the late 1880s, Prentice moved to Brooklyn, a center for artists of trompe l'oeil still lifes, then very much in vogue. Prentice's earliest still life is dated 1892. From then on, still lifes with fruits—apples and plums were his favorites—were his principal subjects. These still lifes are very sharp in definition, gaining further emphasis from the artist's habit of dark outlining.

Green and Red Plums, 16 x 20 in., signed l.r. Courtesy of Henry B. Holt, Inc., Essex Fells, New Jersey.

Prentice's work has been compared to that of William Mason Brown and William Michael Harnett, the preeminent painters in the ultra-realist "illusionist" mode. However, Prentice was more concerned with textural precision than Harnett, who strove for a complete illusion of three-dimensionality. And while Brown's fruits and vegetables have a voluptuous, almost preternatural glow, Prentice's are plainer, more of this world, and in that sense, more realistic than Brown's.

The artist, who lived in Manhattan, Connecticut and New Jersey, settled finally in Philadelphia, where he died in 1935.

MEMBERSHIPS
Brooklyn Art Association

PUBLIC COLLECTIONS
Adirondack Museum, Blue Mountain Lake, New York

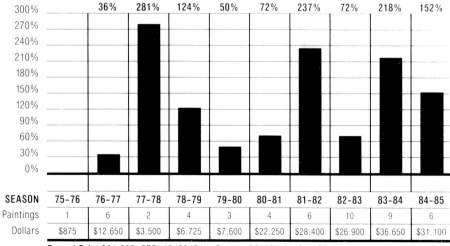

10-Year Average Change From Base Years '75-'76: 124%

SEASON	75-76	76-77	77-78	78-79	79-80	80-81	81-82	82-83	83-84	84-85
		36%	281%	124%	50%	72%	237%	72%	218%	152%
Paintings	1	6	2	4	3	4	6	10	9	6
Dollars	$875	$12,650	$3,500	$6,725	$7,600	$22,250	$28,400	$26,900	$36,650	$31,100

Record Sale: $21,000, SPB, 10/26/84, "Basket of Apples," 12 x 18 in.

476

THOMAS WILMER DEWING
(1851-1938)

Figure-painter Thomas Dewing specialized in painting introspective, refined women, either singly or in groups. His ethereal, idealized women are often seated in quiet rooms, posing with musical instruments, or wandering through hazy green fields.

Dewing is often considered a tonalist because of his limited subject range, soft brushwork, restrained but harmonious colors and elegiac mood. Tonalists usually painted landscapes; only Dewing adapted the tonalist style to figure painting.

Born in 1851 in Boston, Dewing possessed an early talent for drawing. He attended the School of the Museum of Fine Arts, and drew chalk portraits in Albany to finance a three-year trip to Paris and Munich in 1876. He studied at the Academie Julien in Paris, and with Frank Duveneck in Munich.

Upon his return, Dewing settled in New York City where he gained recognition for his portraits of women and his delicate figure studies. He married noted flower-painter Maria Oakey, who occasionally painted a floral background for her husband's contemplative figures.

Dewing taught at the Art Students League for seven years, and in 1879 exhibited at the National Academy of Design. Elected to the Society of American Artists in 1880, he resigned in 1897 to join the Ten American Painters, a group composed mostly of American impressionists such as John Twachtman, J. Alden Weir, Childe Hassam and Edmund Tarbell.

Influences on Dewing's work are derived from American painter James McNeill Whistler, from seventeenth-century Dutch master Jan Vermeer, and from Japanese arrangements. *Lady with a Lute* (1886, St. Louis Art Museum) is reminiscent of Whistler's style; it is a formal study of color in its varied hues of dark greens, and of shapes and forms in the repeated curves of the lady's body

June, 19¾ x 8¾ in., signed l.r. Courtesy of Kennedy Galleries, New York, New York.

and the lute. Vermeer's influence is evident in the sparse, austere interiors in which Dewing places his figures.

Dewing was considered an excellent draftsman and arranger of forms. His figures are integral to the picture's structure, in a style comparable to that of impressionist Mary Cassatt's paintings.

Dewing also painted elegant screens, a popular decorative form derived from the early-nineteenth-century interest in Japanese objects.

A prolific painter, Dewing worked in oil, pastel and silverpoint. He died in New York City at age 87, having painted until a decade before his death.

MEMBERSHIPS
National Academy of Design
National Institute of Arts and Letters
Ten American Painters

PUBLIC COLLECTIONS
Addison Gallery of American Art, Andover, Massachusetts
Albright-Knox Gallery, Buffalo
Art Institute of Chicago
Brooklyn Museum
Canajoharie Library and Art Gallery, New York
Carnegie Institute, Pittsburgh
Corcoran Gallery, Washington, D.C.
Freer Gallery, Washington, D.C.
Metropolitan Museum of Art, New York City
Musee d'Orsay, Paris
National Gallery of Art, Washington, D.C.
National Museum of American Art, Washington, D.C.
Rhode Island School of Design
St. Louis Art Museum, St. Louis
Toledo Museum of Art, Ohio

SEASON	75-76	76-77	77-78	78-79	79-80	80-81	81-82	82-83	83-84	84-85
Paintings		1					1	1	2	1
Dollars		$2,600					$8,200	$6,000	$32,000	$15,000

Record Sale: $20,000, SPB, 5/31/84, "Seated Woman," 10 × 8 in.

SUSAN H. MACDOWELL EAKINS
(1851-1938)

Portrait of Clarence Crammer, ca. 1930, 36 x 25 in. Courtesy of Wunderlich and Company, Inc., New York, New York.

Susan H. Macdowell Eakins, though not as well-known as her famous husband Thomas Eakins, was an accomplished painter, pianist and amateur photographer. Primarily a portraitist, she emphasized in her paintings the qualities of solid construction, subtle coloration, and a probing sense of characterization.

The daughter of liberal, intellectual parents, Susan Hannah Macdowell was born in Philadelphia in 1851. Fostered by a creative environment, the young artist painted and drew for years at home before attending art school. In 1876, she saw her future husband in the Haseltine Gallery in Philadelphia, where his controversial masterpiece *The Gross Clinic* was on display. Although reportedly too shy to approach Eakins, she resolved to study with him that year at the Pennsylvania Academy of the Fine Arts.

For six years, from 1876 to 1882, she attended the Pennsylvania Academy and studied under noted history painter Christian Schussele and, later, under Eakins. During this period she won respect for her work and remained in the forefront as a leader in student activities. Her paintings from this period, both watercolors and oils, demonstrate the essentially private and domestic nature of her subject matter. One of her best works from these years, *Two Sisters* (1879, private collection), is a nearly photographic rendering of two figures set against a background of deep, rich color.

During the 1870s and early 1880s, she also maintained an avid interest in photography. Like her husband, she often used photographs as reference material for her paintings.

In 1884, she married Thomas Eakins and the couple set up a residence and studio in Philadelphia. Although Susan

Eakins was considerably less productive after her marriage, she never stopped painting. During her married years, which art historians have called her "middle period," she again concentrated on portraiture. She adopted many of the pictorial elements of her husband's painting, such as solid draftsmanship, a restrained palette, and a structured harmony of all forms.

Typical of her work are *Kate Lewis* (1884, Allentown Art Museum) and *Portrait of Thomas Eakins* (1889, Philadelphia Museum of Art), paintings which display Susan Eakins's characteristic loose brushwork, dark background, and sensitively rendered facial features and hands.

Although Thomas Eakins's death in 1916 was a grievous shock to his wife, she did not abandon painting. The deep, mellow palette she inherited from her husband, however, underwent a change. She began to use vivid primary colors, often somewhat acrid in context, that would emerge from a dark background to create dramatic contrasts of light and dark. Yet this fresh exuberant pictorial sensibility was not compromised by sentimentality, as seen in the psychologically revealing portrait entitled *The Bibliophile* (1932, private collection). During the 1920s, Eakins produced a number of still lifes in addition to works in oil. She drew inspiration from such examples as William Merritt Chase, Maria Oakley and J. Alden Weir.

Eakins continued to paint until her death in 1938. Although her work undeniably reflects the influence of her husband, in recent years it has gained recognition for its skillful draftsmanship and solid composition. In 1973, 35 years after her death, Eakins was given her first solo exhibition at the Pennsylvania Academy of the Fine Arts.

SEASON	75-76	76-77	77-78	78-79	79-80	80-81	81-82	82-83	83-84	84-85
Paintings	1						1			
Dollars	$900						$650			

Record Sale: $900, W.W, 9/25/75, "The Three Fates," 27 x 43 in.

PUBLIC COLLECTIONS
Allentown Art Museum, Pennsylvania
Dallas Museum of Fine Arts
Joslyn Art Museum, Omaha, Nebraska
Philadelphia Museum of Art

THEODORE ROBINSON
(1852-1896)

Evening at the Lock (Nappanock, New York), 1893, 22 x 32 in., signed l.r. Courtesy of Vose Galleries of Boston, Inc., Massachusetts.

One of the first and most important of the American impressionist painters, Theodore Robinson was responsible for introducing French impressionism to many Americans.

He was born in Irasburg, Vermont in 1852, and moved with his family to Wisconsin when he was three. He was a sickly child, with asthma that plagued him throughout his life and was responsible for his premature death at age 44.

Robinson's studies began in Chicago, but in 1874 he moved to New York City to study at the National Academy of Design. In 1876, he went to Paris to study under Emile Auguste Carolus-Duran, but left to study at the Ecole de Beaux Arts under Jean-Leon Gerome. His paintings were of landscapes and figures, and at that time he still preferred tight realism. He spent summers in the village of Grez-sur-Loing with a colony of American artists, painting under the barbizon influence.

Struggling and poor, he returned to America in 1879. He taught in New York City and Boston, and did decorative work with John La Farge. By 1884, he had accumulated enough money to return to his beloved France to paint.

The turning point in Robinson's artistic life came when he went to live at Giverny, near Rouen, and met Claude Monet. Although never Monet's student, Robinson became part of his inner circle. He was greatly influenced by Monet, but did not imitate him. His colors were softer, his brushstrokes lighter, and his paintings more sensitive. Robinson's forms still had decisive contours, where Monet's seemed almost to dissolve.

Like Monet, he often painted the same scene outdoors in different lights. His well-known subject *Valley of the Seine from Giverny Heights* (1892, Addison Gallery of American Art; Corcoran Gallery; Randolph-Macon Women's College) was painted three times: in sunlight, on a gray day and on a slightly overcast day.

Robinson returned to America in 1892, to paint American subjects. By 1895, a year before his death, he began to achieve satisfaction with his own work. He told a friend, "I am just now beginning to paint subjects that touch me."

His style at this time had grown close to Monet's. The outlines of the forms were hazy and the colors were applied with loosened strokes. Before this style (which might have become post-impressionist) had fully developed, Robinson died in New York City in 1896.

PUBLIC COLLECTIONS
Addison Gallery of American Art,
   Andover, Massachusetts
Baltimore Museum of Art
Corcoran Gallery of Art, Washington, D.C.
Metropolitan Museum of Art, New York City
Randolph-Macon Women's College,
   Lynchburg, Virginia

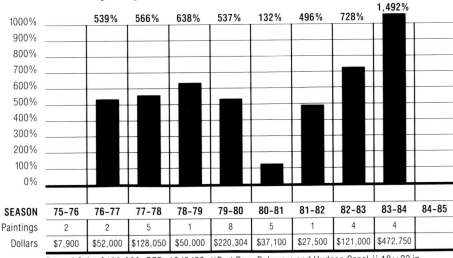

10-Year Average Change From Base Years '75-'76: 570%

	75-76	76-77	77-78	78-79	79-80	80-81	81-82	82-83	83-84	84-85
(% change)	539%	566%	638%	537%	132%	496%	728%	1,492%		
SEASON	75-76	76-77	77-78	78-79	79-80	80-81	81-82	82-83	83-84	84-85
Paintings	2	2	5	1	8	5	1	4	4	
Dollars	$7,900	$52,000	$128,050	$50,000	$220,304	$37,100	$27,500	$121,000	$472,750	

Record Sale: $190,000, SPB, 12/8/83, "Port Ben, Delaware and Hudson Canal," 18 x 22 in.

EDWIN AUSTIN ABBEY
(1852-1911)

Edwin Austin Abbey was perhaps the best-known American illustrator of the late nineteenth century. Historic England was his favorite subject, and from a base in the publishing world with Harper and Brothers, Abbey illustrated many English classics, including a multi-volume edition of Shakespeare's plays. He was also a painter and a muralist, again with a preference for English history as his subject matter.

Born in Philadelphia, Abbey studied at the Pennsylvania Academy of the Fine Arts before beginning a long association with *Harper's Weekly* in 1870. Eight years later, the publisher sent Abbey to England to illustrate a book of poems by Robert Herrick. *Selections from the Poetry of Robert Herrick* (1882) was an artistic triumph for Abbey; critics hailed it as the best-illustrated book by an American publisher.

This was followed by illustrations for a series of classics by Goldsmith, Marvell and Pope, for which Abbey provided scenes of seventeenth- and eighteenth-century England. The drawings were always archaeologically and historically accurate; Abbey was highly precise with detail. In 1886, he began the Shakespeare illustrations, some of which appeared in *Harper's*.

Abbey never returned as a resident to the United States, although he made many visits, on one occasion to paint a mural for the Boston Public Library (a major monument of the American Renaissance). In 15 panels, it depicts the quest for the Holy Grail and was completed in 1902. That same year Abbey was chosen to paint the official coronation picture of Edward VII in Westminster Abbey.

From an early naturalism, Abbey's work became more and more stylized. In the late 1890s, he turned increasingly to flattened forms crowded to the edges of the canvas. His figures are often arranged in a frieze-like procession across the pictorial field; in some ways,

A Measure, signed l.l. Photograph courtesy of Hirschl & Adler Galleries, Inc., New York, New York.

his style can be related to art nouveau and the symbolist movement.

Abbey died in 1911.

MEMBERSHIPS
National Academy of Design

PUBLIC COLLECTIONS
Boston Public Library
Capetown Museum, South Africa
Liverpool Museum, England
Metropolitan Museum of Art, New York City

SEASON	75-76	76-77	77-78	78-79	79-80	80-81	81-82	82-83	83-84	84-85
Paintings				1	2	3	2			3
Dollars				$640	$1,500	$3,500	$7,320			$6,950

Record Sale: $6,020, S, 11/10/81, "Richard, Duke of Gloucester & Lady Anne," 48 × 98 in.

JAMES CARROLL BECKWITH
(1852-1917)

Carroll Beckwith was a landscape, genre and portrait painter whose work was basically academic, but showed a strong impressionist influence in later years.

Beckwith did some mural work, first while a student in Paris and later at the Columbian Exposition in Chicago in 1893. In all probability, said one of his colleagues, mural painting would have brought out Beckwith's best powers, but portraiture paid the most during his lifetime, so he painted portraits.

He also taught for many years at the Art Students League in New York City; his influence on a younger generation of painters has been compared to that of Thomas Eakins at the Pennsylvania Academy of the Fine Arts.

Beckwith was born in Hannibal, Missouri in 1852, with the given name of James Carroll Beckwith. He disliked "James" and he tried assiduously all his life to lose both the name and the initial. His family moved to Chicago while he was young, and in 1868 he began to study art there with Walter Shirlaw.

Three years later, he moved to New York City to study at the National Academy of Design under Lemuel Wilmarth. In 1873, he went to Paris and studied for several years in the atelier of Emile Auguste Carolus-Duran. He also studied for brief periods at the Ecole des Beaux Arts and with Leon Bonnat.

A fellow student and close friend in Paris was John Singer Sargent. They

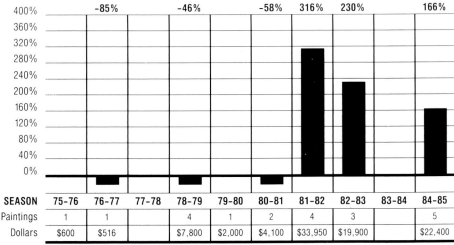

Marguerite, 1882, 30 x 25 in., signed l.l. Photograph courtesy of Borghi & Co. Fine Art Dealers, New York, New York.

shared a studio for a time, and in 1877 they helped Carolus-Duran paint a large ceiling decoration in the Louvre.

Beckwith returned to Chicago in 1878, but, after Paris, he could not bear

it and moved to New York City. The same year he began teaching an antique class at the Art Students League. He taught until 1882 and then again from 1886 until 1897. During this time he became a great success as a portrait painter.

Beckwith made many trips to Europe. He lived in Italy from 1910 to 1914 and painted many plein-air studies of monuments, buildings and landscapes. They were full of sun and bright color in the impressionist manner.

Although he was in poor health for two years before his death in New York City in 1917, Beckwith continued to paint almost until the end.

MEMBERSHIPS
American Watercolor Society
National Academy of Design
National Institute of Arts and Letters

PUBLIC COLLECTIONS
Metropolitan Museum of Art, New York City
National Gallery of Art, Washington, D.C.

10-Year Average Change From Base Years '75-'76: 65%

	-85%		-46%		-58%	316%	230%		166%
SEASON	75-76	76-77	77-78	78-79	79-80	80-81	81-82	82-83	83-84	84-85
Paintings	1	1		4	1	2	4	3		5
Dollars	$600	$516		$7,800	$2,000	$4,100	$33,950	$19,900		$22,400

Record Sale: $17,500, S, 6/8/83, "Interior of Country Study," 28 x 20 in.

481

EDGAR SAMUEL PAXSON
(1852-1919)

Edgar Samuel Paxson is still identified with the one large painting that brought him fame in the late 1800s and initiated his continuing success: *Custer's Last Battle on the Little Big Horn.* Many pictures were made of Custer's "last stand," but Paxson's six-by-10-foot canvas is the largest, and may be the most accurate.

Not one of Custer's troops survived to tell of the massacre. However, some of the Indian chiefs who participated in the actual battle posed for Paxson. The massive, detailed oil took him six or eight (some say 20) years to complete. It went on a tour that focused national attention on the artist, who remained in Montana as a successful painter, illustrator and muralist of Western Indian and frontier scenes.

Born near Buffalo, New York in 1852, Paxson was educated in a log schoolhouse, with one year at the Friend's Institute in East Hamburg, New York. His only art training was as partner to his father, a sign painter and carriage decorator.

James Fenimore Cooper's Indian tales, and the 1876 Big Horn battle, apparently fired Paxson's resolve to go West. In 1877, he left his wife and child in Buffalo and headed for Montana. There he held jobs as a ranch hand, meat hunter, dispatch rider and finally, scout in the Nez Perce War (1877-1878).

In 1879, he settled in Deer Lodge, Montana, sent for his family and began

Old Sioux, 1917, 10⅞ x 7⅛ in., signed l.r. Photograph courtesy of M. Knoedler & Co., Inc., New York, New York.

to paint in oil. He made a slim living as a commercial artist, painting signs, carriages, saloons and theater sets.

Seeking more work, Paxson moved in 1881 to Butte, Montana, his home for 24 years. Paxson served in the Montana National Guard for 10 years, and spent eight months in the Philippines during the Spanish-American War.

Paxson's Custer success gained him important commissions—eight murals of the Lewis and Clark expedition for the Missoula County (Montana) Courthouse, and six murals for the state capitol building at Helena, Montana. Though his reputation was made by his oils and murals, Paxson's small watercolors are considered his best work.

In 1905, he moved to Missoula, Montana, where he died in 1919.

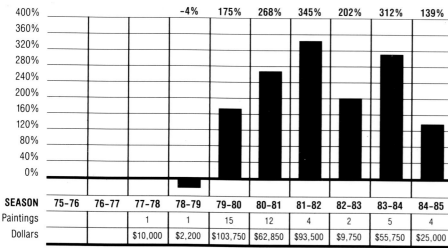

10-Year Average Change From Base Years '77-'78: 180%

					-4%	175%	268%	345%	202%	312%	139%

SEASON	75-76	76-77	77-78	78-79	79-80	80-81	81-82	82-83	83-84	84-85
Paintings			1	1	15	12	4	2	5	4
Dollars			$10,000	$2,200	$103,750	$62,850	$93,500	$9,750	$55,750	$25,000

Record Sale: $60,000, SPB, 4/23/82, "The Pipe of Peace," 30 x 49 in.

PUBLIC COLLECTIONS
Missoula, Montana, County Courthouse
State Capitol, Helena, Montana
University of Montana

482

JULIAN ALDEN WEIR
(1852-1919)

One of the chief exponents of American impressionism, Julian Alden Weir came from a family of painters.

His father, Robert Walker Weir, taught drawing at the United States Military Academy at West Point, and his brother, John Ferguson Weir, was the first director of Yale University's School of Fine Arts.

Painter and etcher Julian Alden Weir was born in West Point in 1852. He studied under his father, then at the National Academy of Design, and in Paris with Jean-Leon Gerome in 1873.

Weir felt that French impressionism lacked drawing and form. However, he exhibited at the Paris Salon in 1875. During his European studies, he met and was influenced by James A. M. Whistler.

He returned to New York City in 1883, supporting himself by painting portraits and teaching. He became a founding member of the Society of American Artists.

During the 1890s, Weir married Anna Baker, made many trips to Europe, and became one of the first Americans to introduce Edouard Manet's paintings to the United States. As a recognized authority in the modern art world, Weir was a major advisor to American collectors, encouraging them to buy works by Manet and Gustave Courbet.

Although his figure and portrait paintings were dark and dramatic, impressionism was beginning to influ-

Cattle in the Woods, 1903, 34 x 27 in., signed l.l. Courtesy of Vose Galleries of Boston, Inc., Massachusetts.

ence his work. He turned to landscape painting, where he adopted the broken brushwork and heightened color of the impressionist style. His etchings at this time ranged from portraits of family members to landscapes with fishermen's cottages.

With his friends John Twachtman, Childe Hassam and Theodore Robinson, Weir helped pioneer the impressionist movement in America. He was a major figure in the Ten American Painters, an American impressionist group formed in 1898.

One of Weir's best-known impressionist paintings is *The Red Bridge* (1895, Metropolitan Museum of Art), which shows a freshly painted vermilion iron bridge set against a green landscape.

Weir contributed a mural decoration to the World's Columbian Exposition in 1893 in Chicago.

As president of the Association of American Painters and Sculptors, organized in 1911, he was involved in planning the controversial New York City Armory Show of 1913. Always receptive to new movements in art, Weir is recognized as a strong progressive force in American art.

He died in 1919. Five years later, the Metropolitan Museum of Art honored him with a memorial exhibition.

MEMBERSHIPS
American Water Color Society
National Academy of Design
National Institute of Arts and Letters
Ten American Painters

PUBLIC COLLECTIONS
Albright-Knox Art Gallery, Buffalo
Art Institute of Chicago
Corcoran Gallery of Art, Washington, D.C.
Detroit Institute of Arts
Metropolitan Museum of Art, New York City
Museum of Fine Arts, Boston
National Museum of American Art, Washington, D.C.
Phillips Collection, Washington, D.C.
Wadsworth Atheneum, Hartford, Connecticut

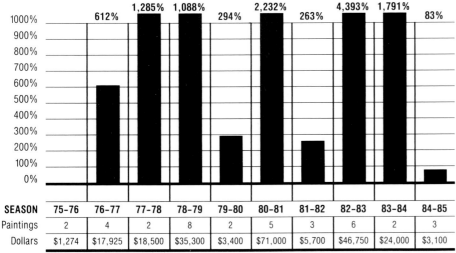

10-Year Average Change From Base Years '75-'76: 1,204%

SEASON	75-76	76-77	77-78	78-79	79-80	80-81	81-82	82-83	83-84	84-85
		612%	1,285%	1,088%	294%	2,232%	263%	4,393%	1,791%	83%
Paintings	2	4	2	8	2	5	3	6	2	3
Dollars	$1,274	$17,925	$18,500	$35,300	$3,400	$71,000	$5,700	$46,750	$24,000	$3,100

Record Sale: $18,000, DM.D, 11/23/80, "The Truants," 29 x 38 in.

483

BEN
FOSTER
(1852-1926)

Ben Foster, born in Maine in 1852, had an inauspicious beginning as an artist. The younger brother of painter Charles Foster (1850-1931),. he was forced by straitened financial circumstances to pursue a commercial career.

When he was almost 30, however, he began his long-deferred studies at the Art Students League in New York City. He studied under Abbott H. Thayer, and from 1886 to 1887 he made the traditional American artist's pilgrimage to Europe and studied with Aime Morot and Luc Oliver Merson in Paris.

After his return, Foster settled in his country home in Cornwall Hollow, Connecticut, and began his lifelong devotion to the beauty of the New England countryside.

Like his contemporaries, J. Alden Weir and Emil Carlsen, Foster had adopted many of the painting techniques of the impressionists without being rigidly bound to their ideas of the direct apprehension of light as pure color. His colors were almost exclusively those of autumn, muted and sensitive browns, grays, and rusts. The outlines of his forms were as crisp as the Connecticut autumn air. Most of his painting was done in the studio; perhaps because of this, his work is distinguished by the distillation of mood and the poetry of his landscapes.

Despite his late start, Foster received awards from the National Academy of

Birch-Clad Hills, N.D., 30 x 30 in. Courtesy of National Museum of American Art, Smithsonian Institution, Gift of William T. Evans.

Design and substantial recognition. He was also a successful art critic. He died in New York City in 1926.

MEMBERSHIPS
American Water Color Society
Century Association
National Academy of Design
National Institute of Arts and Letters
New York Water Color Club
Society of American Artists

10-Year Average Change From Base Years '77-'78: 26%

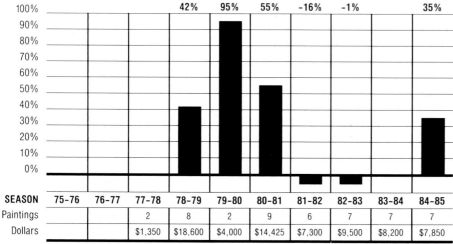

	75-76	76-77	77-78	78-79	79-80	80-81	81-82	82-83	83-84	84-85
				42%	95%	55%	-16%	-1%		35%
SEASON	75-76	76-77	77-78	78-79	79-80	80-81	81-82	82-83	83-84	84-85
Paintings			2	8	2	9	6	7	7	7
Dollars			$1,350	$18,600	$4,000	$14,425	$7,300	$9,500	$8,200	$7,850

Record Sale: $9,500, D.NY, 9/20/78, "At Longpre," 41 × 48 in.

484

EDWARD E. SIMMONS
(1852-1931)

Although he was a charter member of The Ten, the group of impressionist painters formed in 1898 to counter prevailing academic tastes, Edward Simmons was never an impressionist himself. Moreover, he was an easel painter only at the start of his career. His reputation rests principally on the many murals he painted in prominent public buildings. When he exhibited with The Ten, often the works he showed were sketches for murals on which he was working.

Born in Concord, Massachusetts in 1852, he grew up in the "Old Manse" which Hawthorne immortalized. Such luminaries as Ralph Waldo Emerson and Thoreau were regular visitors. As might be expected, he went to Harvard.

After graduation he went to Cincinnati, Ohio to work for an oil company, but soon was fired because of an error he made. When a cousin offered him a job as a clerk in San Francisco, he accepted and immediately was enthralled by the spectacular scenery and vibrant color of California.

He met Henry Casey, a young architect who had come West on doctor's orders. The two camped and hunted together in the wilds for several years. When Casey returned East to die, Simmons followed, determined now to become a painter.

He studied painting at the Boston Museum School, and anatomy with Dr. Rimmer. In 1879, he went to Paris and enrolled at the Academie Julien. Two years later, his first painting was accepted by the Paris Salon.

For several years Simmons was the focus of a small colony of American landscape painters established at Concarneau on the coast of Brittany. In 1887, he moved across the Channel to St. Ives in Cornwall. The marine paintings he did at St. Ives are considered the best of all his easel canvases.

He returned to America in 1891, and

Le Printemps, 58 x 38 in., signed l.l. Photograph courtesy of Sterling Regal, Incorporated, New York. Collection of Mr. and Mrs. Haig Tashjian.

The Lake Shore, 1910, 24 x 24 in., signed l.c. Courtesy of Frederic L. Thaler, Cornwall Bridge, Connecticut.

took a studio in New York City which he maintained until his death in 1931. At first he painted portraits. The commission to paint murals for the 1893 Columbian Exposition in Chicago set him on the path he was to follow for the rest of his career.

His murals were distinguished by meticulous drawing, freedom of execution and rich colors. He was excellent with the human figure, nude or draped.

His figures, wrote one critic, were "grandly forceful." Among his most notable murals were those in the State House in Boston and those in the State Capitol in St. Paul, Minnesota.

SEASON	75-76	76-77	77-78	78-79	79-80	80-81	81-82	82-83	83-84	84-85
Paintings				2	2	1			2	1
Dollars				$11,750	$16,100	$6,500			$10,800	$3,000

Record Sale: $13,500, S, 2/6/80, "Young Boy on Toy Horse," 29 × 20 in.

JAMES EVERETT STUART

(1852-1941)

Goat Island, Niagara Falls, 1906, 12 x 18 in., signed l.l. Courtesy of Frederic I. Thaler Gallery, Cornwall Bridge, Connecticut.

James Everett Stuart was a prolific painter of landscapes, especially of the American West and Northwest. He is also noted for having originated a method of painting on aluminum.

Born in Maine in 1852, Stuart was brought to San Francisco at age eight. He studied art in Sacramento under Virgil Williams and Raymond Yelland; later he was a pupil of Thomas Hill and William Keith at the San Francisco Studio of Design.

Stuart made early sketches and paintings of California scenes, such as the Sierra Mountains and the Sacramento and San Joaquin rivers. He made his first trip to the Pacific Northwest in 1876, and opened his studio in San Francisco in 1881. From that time on, he traveled extensively, sketching landscapes from Alaska to Panama. He lived in New York City for a time, and painted in New England. He also set up studios in Chicago, where he lived for 15 years, and in Oregon. He returned to San Francisco in 1912.

It was Stuart's practice to make large oil "sketches" in the field; later he produced large, elaborate studio paintings from them. He wrote on the backs of his paintings, and is known to have made more than 5,000 of them. His style, with suggestions of mystery, shows some barbizon influence.

Stuart developed a method of painting on aluminum which increased the permanence of his pigments, although it did not render them indestructible, as he claimed. Some of these paintings sold for $15,000. He also painted on wood.

Stuart died in San Francisco in 1941.

MEMBERSHIPS
National Art Club
San Francisco Art Association
Society of Independent Artists

PUBLIC COLLECTIONS
Los Angeles Museum of Science,
  History, and Art
Otis Art Institute, Los Angeles
White House, Washington, D.C.

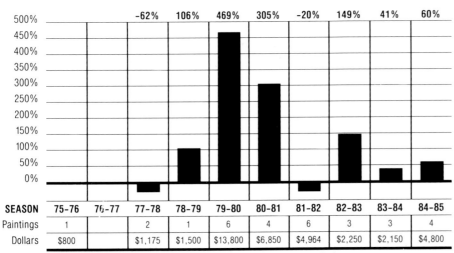

10-Year Average Change From Base Years '75-'76: 116%

	75-76	76-77	77-78	78-79	79-80	80-81	81-82	82-83	83-84	84-85
			-62%	106%	469%	305%	-20%	149%	41%	60%
SEASON	75-76	76-77	77-78	78-79	79-80	80-81	81-82	82-83	83-84	84-85
Paintings	1		2	1	6	4	6	3	3	4
Dollars	$800		$1,175	$1,500	$13,800	$6,850	$4,964	$2,250	$2,150	$4,800

Record Sale: $3,750, BB.SF, 1/21/81, "Yellowstone Canyon," 14 x 21 in.

486

WILLIAM LAMB PICKNELL
(1853-1897)

William Lamb Picknell's landscapes were never conventional studio creations, nor were they idealized, romanticized or embellished. He painted directly from nature in the open light, often in the raw glare of broad sunlight. Even winter snows were directly painted, sometimes from temporary glass enclosures. With loaded brush and palette-knife he thickly buttered his canvases with a rapidity that was legendary. A master figure painter, he depicted the activities of the Portuguese and Yankee fishermen of the New England coast with direct objectivity. He was a realist.

Born in Vermont in 1853, Picknell was orphaned at age 14, when he went to live with relatives in Boston, then a center for American landscape painting. George Inness was particularly conspicuous, and his example may have inclined the boy to study art, a career not acceptable to his family. At some point, however, Picknell convinced an uncle to support his study abroad with the sum of $1,000, which was given with the understanding that there would be no more.

Inness was at the time in Italy. Available biographical information conflicts in detail, but not in substance. Picknell received criticism from Inness in Italy, where the student might have spent several years before going to Paris. He did enroll in the atelier of Jean-Leon Gerome at the Ecole des Beaux-Arts in December of 1874, and remained there until his money ran out. By 1876 he was established in the artists' colony at Pont-Aven, in Brittany, where he remained until 1880. There he could live and work for next to nothing—in fact, for less.

Under the tutelege of the Manx-American expatriate Robert Wylie, Picknell painted alongside Thomas Hovenden and H. Bolton Jones, and his French friend Louis Pelouse. Wylie, himself largely self-taught, insisted on

Pont Aven, 1879, 22 x 18 in., signed l.l. Courtesy of Raydon Gallery, New York, New York.

accurate and truthful representation of nature, and on the importance of painting before the subject, inside or outside. Wylie taught Picknell to use the palette-knife, partially mixing colors and wiping them in broad passages on the foreground, loading the brush with some pure hue observed in nature and dragging it across crusty surfaces representing masonry or foliage. At the Hotel Julia, Picknell's bill ran for years, and Mlle. Julia contributed art supplies and transportation for his larger canvases to distant sites.

In 1880, her faith was justified when *The Road to Concarneau* (Corcoran Gallery of Art) won acclaim and honorable mention in the Salon, and a contract with the dealer Goupil. His triumph at hand and his future assured, Picknell left for two years of painting in England's New Forest, exhibiting with equal success in England. He returned home empty-handed, his pictures were so much in demand abroad.

Opening a studio in Boston in 1882, Picknell painted along the Massachusetts coast. Many of his old Brittany companions joined him to paint at Anisquam. He was accorded critical recognition at home, and traveled the United States from California to Florida, and to Pennsylvania, where he painted again with his friend Hovenden.

Picknell married in 1889, returning to France with his wife. There he painted in Grez and Moret, wintering in the Midi at Antibes, as seen in his painting *The Road to Nice* (Pennsylvania Academy of the Fine Arts). In 1895, he won a medal at the Salon for a Moret landscape, and the French nation acquired a painting from the Salon of 1898. But this honor was posthumous.

In ill-health, and grief-stricken by the death of his only child, Picknell returned to Boston in 1897 and died at age 43. Augustus St. Gaudens commemorated his friend in a portrait medal.

SEASON	75-76	76-77	77-78	78-79	79-80	80-81	81-82	82-83	83-84	84-85
Paintings			2				1	2		
Dollars			$5,100				$6,500	$6,574		

Record Sale: $6,500, CH, 12/11/81, "Near a Village," 30 × 36 in.

PUBLIC COLLECTIONS
Metropolitan Museum of Art, New York City
Museum of Fine Arts, Boston
National Collection, Musees de France
Pennsylvania Academy of the Fine Arts, Philadelphia
Walker Art Gallery, Liverpool, England

JOHN HENRY TWACHTMAN
(1853-1902)

John Henry Twachtman, a founding member of The Ten American Painters, is regarded as one of the most original and significant American impressionist landscape painters.

Born in Cincinnati, Ohio in 1853, Twachtman began his artistic career by painting floral window-shade decorations for his father's business and attending night school at the Ohio Mechanics Institute. At the Cincinnati School of Design, Twachtman studied with Frank Duveneck, who in 1875 asked the young artist to accompany him to Germany for two years of further study at the Munich Academy.

Twachtman's early style reflects the solid modeling, direct brushwork and dark tonality of Duveneck and the Munich School. It was a style Twachtman would sustain for the next eight years, during which he returned to the United States to live in Cincinnati and in New York City. He then taught for a year at Duveneck's school in Florence.

An 1883 trip to Paris proved artistically significant for Twachtman, who stayed three years. He attended the Academie Julien, where he studied under Jules Lefebvre and Louis Boulanger, and was strongly influenced by the works of James A.M. Whistler and the French impressionists.

The rich brushwork, delicate composition and low-key harmonies of Twachtman's *Arques-la-Bataille* (1885, Metro-

Beach Scene, 14 x 20 in., signed l.l. Photograph courtesy of Borghi & Co. Fine Art Dealers, New York, New York.

politan Museum of Art) exemplify the artist's early impressionist style and show the influence not only of Whistler but also of Japanese painting, reflected in the precise and elegant treatment of the reeds in the picture's foreground.

Twachtman returned to the United States in 1885. Four years later he purchased a farm near Greenwich, Connecticut. The farm would serve as inspiration for many of Twachtman's landscapes.

Twachtman's paintings of the 1890s are light and impressionist in tone, with more stress on poetic atmosphere than on objective rendering. His paintings are rarely dated. Twachtman had a particular fondness for snow scenes, which permitted him to exploit hazy atmosphere,

as exemplified by *Winter Harmony* (ca. 1900, National Gallery, Washington, D.C.). The artist often painted the same subject, as did Claude Monet; unlike Monet, however, his intent was not to capture the same scene in varying light but to elicit different emotional responses.

In addition to painting, Twachtman was a notable etcher. He also taught at the Cooper Union Institution and the Art Students League in New York.

In 1893, Twachtman and J. Alden Weir exhibited their works in New York City, along with paintings by Monet. While the French artist's paintings sold well, not a single canvas by Weir or Twachtman was purchased. Twachtman's increasing anger about American attitudes toward art prompted him, in 1897, to join with friends to form the Ten American Painters—a group of notable artists who exhibited their works together from 1898 in an attempt to promote modern American art.

Toward the end of his life, Twachtman conducted summer art classes in Gloucester, Massachusetts, where he died in 1902, just after his fiftieth birthday.

MEMBERSHIPS
American Art Club, Munich

PUBLIC COLLECTIONS
Art Institute of Chicago
Brooklyn Museum
Corcoran Gallery, Washington, D.C.
Metropolitan Museum of Art, New York City
Museum of Modern Art, New York City
National Gallery of Art, Washington, D.C.

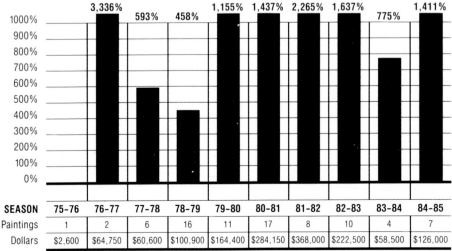

10-Year Average Change From Base Years '75-'76: 1,307%

SEASON	75-76	76-77	77-78	78-79	79-80	80-81	81-82	82-83	83-84	84-85
(% change)		3,336%	593%	458%	1,155%	1,437%	2,265%	1,637%	775%	1,411%
Paintings	1	2	6	16	11	17	8	10	4	7
Dollars	$2,600	$64,750	$60,600	$100,900	$164,400	$284,150	$368,000	$222,500	$58,500	$126,000

Record Sale: $130,000, SPB, 6/4/82, "Winter Landscape," 30 x 30 in.

488

HOWARD PYLE
(1853-1911)

Unquestionably the renaissance man of American illustration, Howard Pyle carried it to new heights as an art form. Working in virile, decorative pen-and-ink, as well as in color, he produced a prodigious number of illustrations for popular magazines and young people's books, some of which he wrote himself. He also did murals on historical subjects.

Perhaps his greatest influence, however, was as a teacher. Through his enthusiasm and willingness to share his knowledge, he inspired a generation of outstanding American illustrators. He was the founder of the Brandywine School of painters and illustrators.

Born in Wilmington, Delaware in 1853, he began to draw and write stories at an early age. As a teenager he commuted to Philadelphia to study with F.A. van der Wielen, a Belgian painter, while still working in his father's leather business. When his first illustrated poem was published in *Scribner's Magazine* in 1876, he moved to New York City to study at the Art Students League and to be closer to the magazine publishers there.

Pyle met not only editors but other successful illustrators as well, many of whom gave him advice. By 1880, when he returned to Wilmington, he was securely established as an illustrator.

In 1894, the Drexel Institute of Art, Science and Technology, a new college in Philadelphia, invited him to teach

The Pirate was a Picturesque Fellow, signed l.l.
Courtesy of Delaware Art Museum,
Howard Pyle Collection, Wilmington.

classes in illustration, giving him a free hand in his curriculum. He taught his students to think in terms of works to be reproduced on the printed page, not hung on an exhibition wall. He encouraged them also to imagine the scenes they were working on so intently that they projected themselves into the pictures.

In the summer of 1897, Drexel provided scholarships for a few top students to study with Pyle at his summer home in Chadds Ford, near Wilmington. The experiment worked so well and the students advanced so rapidly that, in 1900, Pyle resigned from Drexel and opened his own school for carefully selected students.

Pyle encouraged his students to submit their work to magazines, wrote letters of introduction for them to art editors and, when he himself was overloaded with work, sometimes passed on some of his own assignments to his most talented pupils.

Pyle was at the height of his creative powers when he died unexpectedly on a trip to Italy in 1911.

MEMBERSHIPS
National Academy of Design

PUBLIC COLLECTIONS
Brandywine River Museum,
    Chadds Ford, Pennsylvania
Delaware Art Museum, Wilmington
St. Louis Art Museum

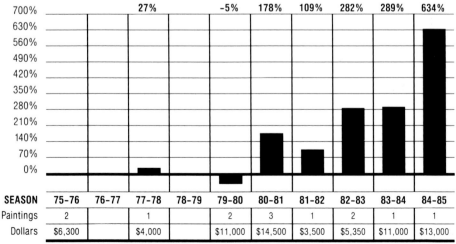

10-Year Average Change From Base Years '75-'76: 189%

		27%		-5%	178%	109%	282%	289%	634%

SEASON	75-76	76-77	77-78	78-79	79-80	80-81	81-82	82-83	83-84	84-85
Paintings	2		1		2	3	1	2	1	1
Dollars	$6,300		$4,000		$11,000	$14,500	$3,500	$5,350	$11,000	$13,000

Record Sale: $13,000, B.P, 9/22/84, ''The Death of Braddock,'' 18×12 in.

489

LEMUEL EVERETT WILMARTH
(1853-1918)

Born in Attleboro, Massachusetts in 1985, and raised in Boston, Massachusetts, Lemuel Everett Wilmarth was trained as a watchmaker. Though he pursued this craft for a time, he doggedly studied art at night, first in the Pennsylvania Academy of the Fine Arts in Philadelphia and later at the National Academy of Design in New York City.

Wilmarth turned permanently to art in 1859 and went to Germany to study in the Munich Royal Academy of the Fine Arts. After three and a half years in Munich, he went to the Ecole des Beaux-Arts in Paris, and was the first American to study under the famous painter Gerome. He remained two and a half years. Wilmarth's genre scenes, perhaps influenced by his earlier profession, were meticulously detailed and exactingly finished.

On his return to the United States, he became active in teaching and organizing classes at the Brooklyn Academy of Fine Arts. Because of this work, he was made the first full-time instructor in the National Academy of Design School.

The history of art institutions in America has been marked by the conflict between the desire for respectability and the admiration of independence. The National Academy of Design, for instance, was founded as a reaction against the American Academy of the Fine Arts, but it has been the source of further offshoots over the years. Wilmarth himself, despite his position, accompanied a group of dissident National Academy students away from the Academy between 1875 and 1877. After that brief rebellion, he returned to stay with the Academy until 1889. He died in 1918 in Brooklyn, New York.

MEMBERSHIPS
National Academy of Design

Raisins, Oranges and Nuts, 1889, 9 x 13 in., signed l.c. Courtesy of the Munson-Williams-Proctor Institute, Utica, New York.

Country Artist, 1885, 20 x 24 in., signed l.l. Courtesy of Private Collection.

SEASON	75-76	76-77	77-78	78-79	79-80	80-81	81-82	82-83	83-84	84-85
Paintings	1			2			1		1	
Dollars	$550			$5,250			$7,280		$6,500	

Record Sale: $7,280, CSK, 5/12/82, "Fresh Gathered," 21 × 17 in.

490

J. FRANCIS MURPHY
(1853-1921)

J. Francis Murphy, landscape painter, watercolorist and illustrator, was called "the American Corot" by his contemporaries for his poetic landscapes with bare trees and marshy terrain. His work generally reflects influences of tonalism due to Murphy's use of simplified, nearly-symbolic subject matter, unified with a single atmospheric tone.

Murphy was born in 1853 in Oswego, New York. His family moved to Chicago in 1868, where he worked as a stage and scene painter. Though primarily self-taught, he likely attended some classes at the Chicago Academy of Design, later called the Art Institute of Chicago. His first paintings appeared in 1870.

After viewing paintings of the Keene Valley, located in New York's Adirondacks Mountains, Murphy decided to make a sketching trip to this area that had inspired Wyant, Inness and Homer. To pay for the trip, he sold much of his finished work in 1874.

The trip was a personal success for Murphy, who was even photographed with Winslow Homer. However, the work he completed from sketches of his trip was not nearly as good as that which he sold to get there.

Though he did return to Chicago soon after, he stayed only briefly. In 1875, he moved to New York City, where he made a living as a magazine illustrator and artist for a greeting-card company.

Over the next 10 years, Murphy refined his instinctive gift for painting

Arkville, N.Y., 6½ x 10 in., signed l.r. Courtesy of Henry B. Holt, Inc., Essex Fells, New Jersey.

rural scenes. He worked from direct observation and made precise pencil sketches on site. But after an 1886 trip to France with his wife, also a painter, Murphy's work became more poetic and formularized.

Starting with an overall tone on canvas that he allowed to dry for as long as a year, Murphy added paint in thin layers. He used transparent glazes and scrumbling to produce delicate, translu-

cent effects, while allowing some accidental brushstrokes to hint at natural forms.

He preferred to work in a palette of pink and green, grayish green and golden browns. During the 1890s, he produced watercolors and numerous twilight scenes in oil, all roughly 5 by 7 inches or 6 by 8 inches, often mounted in heavy gilt frames and shadowboxes. *Landscape* (date unknown, Metropolitan Museum of Art) is an example of his small expressive oil paintings.

Although his most successful oils date from 1910 to 1916, Murphy continued to paint until six months before his death in 1921. He received many medals and awards during his life and saw one of his paintings, *Landscape* (1898, Corcoran Gallery of Art), sold at auction for $15,600 in 1918.

MEMBERSHIPS
National Academy of Design
Salmagundi Club

PUBLIC COLLECTIONS
Corcoran Gallery of Art, Washington, D.C.
Metropolitan Museum of Art, New York City
Freer Gallery of the Smithsonian Institution, Washington, D.C.

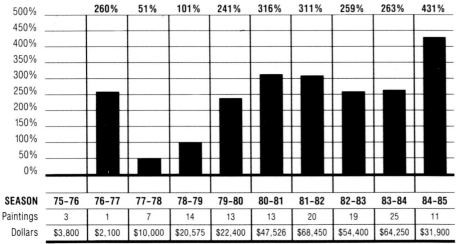

10-Year Average Change From Base Years '75-'76: 223%

	75-76	76-77	77-78	78-79	79-80	80-81	81-82	82-83	83-84	84-85
		260%	51%	101%	241%	316%	311%	259%	263%	431%
SEASON	75-76	76-77	77-78	78-79	79-80	80-81	81-82	82-83	83-84	84-85
Paintings	3	1	7	14	13	13	20	19	25	11
Dollars	$3,800	$2,100	$10,000	$20,575	$22,400	$47,526	$68,450	$54,400	$64,250	$31,900

Record Sale: $18,000, SPB, 9/23/81, "Meadow Farm," 24 × 33 in.

JOSEPH DECKER
(1853-1924)

Joseph Decker was a brilliant individualist who received cold treatment from contemporary critics. In the latter half of the nineteenth century, coherence, conventionality and refinement were valued; Decker's early paintings were unsettling, surreal and harsh. Though in his later period he adopted a tasteful, mellow style—so different that for a time he was believed to be two different artists—it brought him little positive notice. Only comparatively recently has he begun to be appreciated.

Born the son of a carpenter in Wurttemberg, Germany in 1853, he came to the United States in 1867. Though he first lived in Reading, Pennsylvania, he soon settled permanently in Brooklyn. He continued to return to Germany for long periods throughout his life, but Brooklyn was his permanent home.

Decker was apprenticed to a house painter and also worked as a sign painter. He studied art at night at the National Academy of Design, and in 1877 he began showing paintings at the annual Brooklyn Art Association show. In 1879, he enrolled at the Munich Academy. There, studying under history painter Wilhelm Lingenschmidt, he was exposed to the fluid, dark-toned, bravura style that characterized the school. But when he returned to the United States a year later, he proceeded to paint still lifes which are harsh, full of vibrating color, and strikingly original.

He entered juried shows in the National Academy of Design, the Brooklyn Art Association and others, with paintings such as *Pears* (1883, private collection), a realistic still life of pears on tree boughs. Due to the hostile reception his work received, he ceased exhibiting in juried shows almost entirely after 1889. A valuable relationship with collector Thomas B. Clark ended with the sale of Clark's collection in 1899, and Decker seems to have found

Melon and Grape Still Life, 1884, 13¾ x 20 in., signed l.l. Photograph courtesy of Kennedy Galleries, New York, New York. Private Collection.

no other patrons. By 1924, Decker was a patient in the charity ward of a Brooklyn hospital; his death certificate of that year listed his occupation as "laborer."

Decker's work falls into two distinct styles. His earlier work, mostly still life and some genre, has an unsettling detachment of viewpoint, a close focus, and a dramatically cropped composition that was similar to the twentieth-century photography of Alfred Stieglitz and others. The flatness of the picture plane and the boldness of Decker's colors repelled the art critics of his time but appeal to a modern eye.

Decker's later work is mistier, softer and more conventional. His brushstroke was much influenced by impressionism; his landscapes followed the style of George Inness, and his still lifes adopted a balanced, classical composition.

PUBLIC COLLECTIONS
Yale University Art Gallery,
New Haven, Connecticut

SEASON	75-76	76-77	77-78	78-79	79-80	80-81	81-82	82-83	83-84	84-85
Paintings					1				1	
Dollars					$1,500				$20,000	

Record Sale: $20,000, CH, 12/9/83, "Greenings," 9 × 11 in.

(THOMAS) ALEXANDER HARRISON
(1853-1930)

Thomas Alexander Harrison, an expatriate painter who spent much of his life in Paris, was born in Philadelphia in 1853.

He studied briefly at the Pennsylvania Academy of the Fine Arts before joining the United States Coastal and Geodetic Survey in 1872. He spent six years charting the East and West coasts. In 1877, he left Seattle, Washington to begin his artistic studies in San Francisco. Two years later, he arrived in Paris, where he studied with Jean Leon Gerome at the Ecole des Beaux-Arts. He also studied with Bastien-Lepage.

Harrison exhibited in the 1881 Paris Salon. His experience with the coastal survey seems to have left him with a strong feeling for seascapes. Over the next two decades, he achieved critical and popular success with these seascapes, as well as with paintings of pastoral scenes with women, sometimes nude, bathing or relaxing. He also painted landscapes and scenes of children at play on the beach.

Castles in Spain (1882, Metropolitan Museum of Art) is typical of Harrison's plein-air realism. Of his style he said, "I have always loved big nature and the sky and the feeling of space."

When Meissonier founded a new Salon in 1890, Harrison became a charter member. He served on juries and exhibited annually with the new group. He also exhibited in the United States at the Society of American Artists and at the National Academy of Design, as well as at annual exhibitions at Carnegie Institute and the Pennsylvania Academy of the Fine Arts.

At the time of his death in 1930, Harrison was called "dean of American Painters in Paris" by the *New York Times*.

Pleine Mer (High Tide with Rainbow), 27½ x 40 in., signed l.l. Courtesy of Kennedy Galleries, New York, New York.

10-Year Average Change From Base Years '79-'80: 158%

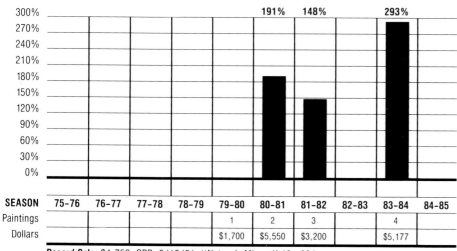

SEASON	75-76	76-77	77-78	78-79	79-80	80-81	81-82	82-83	83-84	84-85
Paintings					1	2	3		4	
Dollars					$1,700	$5,550	$3,200		$5,177	

Record Sale: $4,750, SPB, 3/16/81, "Nature's Mirror," 48×63 in.

MEMBERSHIPS
Art Club of Philadelphia
Century Association of New York City
National Academy of Design
Paris Society of Arts and Crafts
Philadelphia Water Color Club
Society of American Artists

PUBLIC COLLECTIONS
Art Institute of Chicago
Corcoran Gallery of Art, Washington, D.C.
Metropolitan Museum of Art, New York City
Musee d'Orsay
Pennsylvania Academy of the Fine Arts, Philadelphia
Royal Gallery, Dresden

EMIL CARLSEN
(1853-1932)

Chrysanthemums, 1885, 25¾ x 46¼ in., signed l.l. Photograph courtesy of Hirschl & Adler, Inc., New York, New York.

Emil Carlsen was a still-life and landscape painter noted for his serious, classical studies in the eighteenth-century tradition of Jean Baptiste Chardin. As part of a Chardinesque revival in the nineteenth century, Carlsen depicted gleaming bottles, copper kettles and dead game animals with a rich, sensuous beauty.

His still-life subjects, shining with light, merge into a dark background, creating an emphasis on subtle light and form. By contrast, his large, square landscapes and studies of flowers employ light, bright impressionistic colors.

Carlsen, born in Denmark, studied architecture for four years before coming to the United States in 1872. After a brief, unsatisfying apprenticeship in architecture, Carlsen turned to painting, studying briefly under Danish painter Laurits Holst. He was, however, primarily a self-taught painter; he eventually became one of New England's most successful still-life artists.

In 1875, Carlsen undertook European travel and study of the old masters. He was captivated by the work of Chardin; his subsequent subjects and their treatment—the wet scales of a fish, the glint of a glass bottle or the sheen of a copper urn—reflect the influence of the French painter. So believable are Carlsen's visual effects that it almost seems the objects can be touched.

Carlsen struggled with poverty until he was nearly 30. By 1884, however, with an established reputation, he was retained by a dealer to produce an annual quota of still lifes. But his style was changing. After a second visit to Paris, he returned in 1886 with a lighter palette and an interest in landscapes. His backgrounds can be found in some of the fox-hunting scenes of Alexander Pope.

Formally established as a landscape painter, Carlsen spent the next four years in San Francisco, sharing a studio with Arthur Mathews and teaching at the California School of Design, where he also served as director. Eventually, better money and opportunity drew Carlsen back to the East Coast, where he spent the rest of his career in New York and Connecticut, associating with prominent American impressionists.

He is recognized particularly for combining traditional representational art with impressionistic approaches to color and light. Carlsen was faithful to the visual truth of his subjects and is credited with endowing the still-life painting with a dignity that would soon be lost in changing artistic fashion.

MEMBERSHIPS
American Federation of Arts
Century Association
National Academy of Design
National Arts Club
National Institute of Arts and Letters
Pennsylvania Academy of the Fine Arts
Society of American Artists

PUBLIC COLLECTIONS
Albright-Knox Art Gallery, Buffalo
Brooklyn Museum
Corcoran Art Gallery, Washington, D.C.
Metropolitan Museum of Art, New York City
National Gallery of Art, Washington, D.C.
Pennsylvania Academy of the Fine Arts, Philadelphia
Rhode Island School of Design, Providence

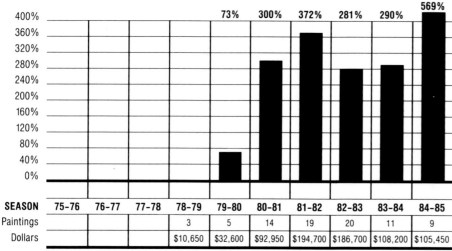

10-Year Average Change From Base Years '78-'79: 269%

SEASON	75-76	76-77	77-78	78-79	79-80	80-81	81-82	82-83	83-84	84-85
					73%	300%	372%	281%	290%	569%
Paintings				3	5	14	19	20	11	9
Dollars				$10,650	$32,600	$92,950	$194,700	$186,700	$108,200	$105,450

Record Sale: $85,000, CH, 12/11/81, "Still Life with Jars," 25 × 30 in.

WILL H. LOW
(1853-1932)

A leading American muralist, innovative illustrator and decorative painter in the 1880s and 1890s, Will H. Low participated in the American arts and crafts movement.

He painted many murals, such as the ceiling decorations for the Waldorf-Astoria Hotel in New York City and an ambitious series of murals for the New York State Education Building in Albany. His beaux-arts classicism inspired other artists of the time—notably Louis Comfort Tiffany, who adapted Low's *Aurora* (1894, Metropolitan Museum of Art) for a stained-glass window entitled *Young Woman at a Fountain*.

Born in Albany, New York, Low was first exposed to art in the studio of sculptor Erastus Dow Palmer. At 17, Low came to New York City and worked as an illustrator. He exhibited at the National Academy of Design beginning in 1872.

In 1873, Low studied first with Jean Leon Gerome at the Ecole des Beaux-Arts in Paris and later with Emile Augustus Carolus-Duran. He also began to spend his summers in Barbizon, where he was influenced by Francois Millet. He exhibited at the Paris Salon in 1874.

Low returned to New York City in 1877. He taught at the Women's Art School at Cooper Union, while doing illustrations and decorative work. In 1886, his illustrations for Keats's *Lamia,*

A Basket of Oranges, 37¼ x 19¼ in., signed l.r.
Photograph courtesy of Hirschl & Adler Galleries, Inc., New York, New York.

published the previous year, brought him great financial and critical success.

The artist continued to travel, paint and write art criticism for such publications as *McClure's, Scribner's* and *The Century.* As styles changed, there was less demand for his work after 1900.

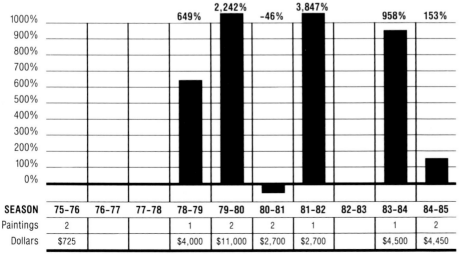

10-Year Average Change From Base Years '75-'76: 1,115%

	75-76	76-77	77-78	78-79	79-80	80-81	81-82	82-83	83-84	84-85
				649%	2,242%	-46%	3,847%		958%	153%

SEASON	75-76	76-77	77-78	78-79	79-80	80-81	81-82	82-83	83-84	84-85
Paintings	2			1	2	2	1		1	2
Dollars	$725			$4,000	$11,000	$2,700	$2,700		$4,500	$4,450

Record Sale: $10,000, CH, 5/22/80, ''Idyll,'' 19 × 30 in.

JOHN HABERLE
(1853-1933)

John Haberle, along with contemporaries William Michael Harnett and John F. Peto, was a trompe l'oeil painter of the late nineteenth century. Because of his gift for satire and humor, he was recently rediscovered as a forerunner of the pop art of the l960s.

Most of Haberle's trompe l'oeil paintings date from about 1887 to the early 1900s, when failing eyesight forced him to abandon this genre and concentrate on a broader style. Although he did make a few more attempts with the method as late as 1909, most of his later still lifes of flowers and fruit are very different in style.

Pictures of money were a Haberle specialty. The most complex of these is *The Changes of Time* (1888, private collection), in which objects such as currency, cancelled stamps, coins and a magnifying glass are framed by medallion heads of the presidents of the United States, with room left on the lower right for future presidents. Haberle's money paintings were so convincing that he actually received a warning from federal agents to stop painting them, as he was in effect making counterfeit bills.

He painted a series called *Torn in Transit* (Brandywine River Museum), in which most of the space is taken up by landscapes that are less than meticulously painted, sometimes even amateurish, while the rest of the work, showing torn paper, label and string, is pure trompe l'oeil.

Grandma's Hearthstone (1890-1894, Detroit Institute of Arts), a three-dimensional work and one of the largest trompe l'oeil paintings known, inspired an article in the *New Haven Evening Leader* of June 10, 1893. Entitled "It Fooled the Cat," it describes an incident about a cat that curled up in front of the painting when it was first shown.

A Mistaken Tidbit, 1892, 12 x 18 in., signed l.r. Courtesy of Wunderlich and Company, Inc., New York, New York.

Little is known about Haberle's life, except that he was born in New Haven, Connecticut, where he lived all his life. He began drawing as a young man, sometimes using himself as a model. In the late 1870s or early 1880s, he was a preparator at Yale University for paleontologist Othneil Charles Marsh.

Around 1887, he took classes at the National Academy of Design in New York City. In the autumn of the same year he exhibited one of his money paintings called *Imitation* (date and location unknown).

Haberle died in 1933.

PUBLIC COLLECTIONS
Brandywine River Museum, Chadds Ford,
    Pennsylvania
Detroit Institute of Arts
Metropolitan Museum of Art, New York City
New Britain Museum of American Art,
    Connecticut

SEASON	75-76	76-77	77-78	78-79	79-80	80-81	81-82	82-83	83-84	84-85
Paintings							1			1
Dollars							$800			$50,000

Record Sale: $50,000, CH, 12/7/84, "A Misunderstanding," 16 × 11 in.

JOHN FREDERICK PETO
(1854-1907)

Obscurity was the lot of John Frederick Peto, whose trompe l'oeil still lifes rivaled those of his better-known contemporary William Harnett.

Not until 1949, 42 years after his death, did Peto's work receive recognition for his fine work, in which arranged objects are painted so precisely that they "fool the eye" with an illusion of three-dimensional reality.

Peto's career held no surprises except intermittent disappointment at the failure of his work to gain attention, despite its quality and current popular tastes.

Born in Philadelphia in 1854, Peto was largely self-taught. He did study briefly in 1878 at the Pennsylvania Academy of the Fine Arts; he exhibited there in 1879 and 1887.

He evidently knew Harnett, an established painter who lived in Philadelphia from 1876 to 1880. Harnett's trompe l'oeil style and subject matter were often copied, but Peto's work was less imitative than that of other artists. His approach was soft and tonal, showing an interest in the effects of light. His brushwork was less meticulous and more evident than Harnett's, and Peto worked more with opaques, often achieving a Vermeer-like silvery cast.

Both artists turned out so-called "rack" paintings, in which fairly shallow objects, mounted bulletin-board fashion, appear to stand forward from

The First Fire Chief: the Artist's Father, 1878, signed l.r. Courtesy of The Pennsylvania Academy of the Fine Arts, Philadelphia.

the picture plane. Peto painted unaffectedly personal, commonplace things, worn by ordinary use. He did not glamorize his light-suffused subjects.

Harnett's work sold and was critically admired; Peto worked in vain. In 1889, Peto moved to Island Heights, New Jersey, to make a marginal living playing cornet at camp meetings and taking in summer boarders. He continued to paint, selling his work locally.

In 1905, two years before Peto's death, a Philadelphia dealer purchased a number of his trompe l'oeil works and forged Harnett's name to them. Ironically, they brought high prices and found their way into private collections and leading museums.

For years, the forgeries were accepted. In 1949, Alfred Frankenstein identified 20 paintings which had been attributed to Harnett as Peto's, by studying obvious differences in style, technique and pigment. Tracking clues from the painted objects (photos, newspapers and written notes), he also deduced that Peto, not Harnett, was probably the initiator of the "rack" paintings.

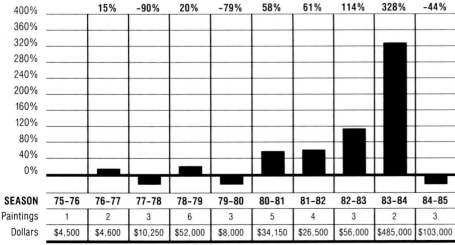

10-Year Average Change From Base Years '75-'76: 38%

	15%	-90%	20%	-79%	58%	61%	114%	328%	-44%

SEASON	75-76	76-77	77-78	78-79	79-80	80-81	81-82	82-83	83-84	84-85
Paintings	1	2	3	6	3	5	4	3	2	3
Dollars	$4,500	$4,600	$10,250	$52,000	$8,000	$34,150	$26,500	$56,000	$485,000	$103,000

Record Sale: $460,000, CH, 6/1/84, "For the Track," 43 × 30 in.

PUBLIC COLLECTIONS
Metropolitan Museum of Art, New York City
Museum of Fine Arts, Boston
Smith College Museum of Art,
 Northampton, Massachusetts

HENRY PEMBER SMITH
(1854-1907)

Landscape painter Henry Pember Smith was born in Waterford, Connecticut in 1854.

Little is known about his early training or his career before 1877, when he set up a studio in New York City. It is generally assumed that he was self-taught.

From 1877 on, Smith exhibited regularly at the National Academy of Design, although he never became a member.

His landscapes are his best-known works, particularly those of New England, England, Italy, New York State and France. Working primarily in oils and watercolors, and using a tighter technique than the emerging impressionists of his time, Smith was a realist. He portrayed his scenery in natural colors and allowed the daylight of each view to bring subtle richness or dramatic brilliance to his paintings.

Around 1901, he moved to Asbury Park, New Jersey to seek relief from ill health and rheumatism. When he died in 1907, suicide was rumored, but doctors confirmed that his death was due to a heart condition resulting from his rheumatism.

MEMBERSHIPS
American Watercolor Society
Artists' Fund Society

Homestead, 30 x 40 in., signed l.r. Courtesy of Connecticut Gallery, Marlborough, Connecticut.

Thatcher Island, Gloucester, Massachusetts, 17 x 28 in., signed l.l. Courtesy of Newman Galleries, Philadelphia, Pennsylvania.

SEASON	75-76	76-77	77-78	78-79	79-80	80-81	81-82	82-83	83-84	84-85
Paintings	3	1	7	15	13	11	12	3	20	11
Dollars	$4,900	$900	$14,850	$28,702	$26,132	$32,550	$21,750	$6,200	$41,020	$22,800

Record Sale: $5,500, CH, 4/24/81, "Old Homestead in Summer," 20 × 28 in.

ARTHUR HOEBER
(1854-1915)

Landscape painter, illustrator and art critic, Arthur Hoeber produced work very much in the barbizon vein. Following the fashion of his day, he painted large genre canvases of peasants while he was living and working in France.

After he returned to the United States, however, he became largely a painter of marshlands, contrasting the long, parallel sweeps of land and sky. He has been called a "semi-impressionist" because, while he did not actually embrace the impressionist aesthetic insofar as line and composition were concerned, his work was full of vibrancy and color.

He was born in New York City in 1854, and studied at Cooper Union and at the Art Students League under J. Carroll Beckwith. In 1881, he set off for Europe with letters of introduction from Lew Wallack, a noted actor, to his brother-in-law, painter Sir John Everett Millais. Millais recommended that the young Hoeber study at the Ecole des Beaux Arts under Jean-Leon Gerome and then with Gustave Courtois.

During his six years in France, Hoeber was an active member of the colony of American artists living there. Like them, he spent his summers painting the peasants in Normandy and at Concarneau in Brittany.

After returning to the United States, he spent considerable time on Cape Cod and Long Island, and it was then that he began painting his marshland scenes. Later he became one of the first painters

Salt Marshes in Northern New Jersey, 20 x 24 in., signed l.l. Courtesy of the Reading Public Museum, Pennsylvania.

to settle in the embryonic art colony developing in Nutley, New Jersey, not far from New York. He lived there until his death in 1915.

Along with his painting, Hoeber was a prominent art critic, writing for the *New York Globe, Harper's Weekly* and various leading monthly magazines. He was a staunch supporter of traditionalism in art, and continually attacked the "new art" that was appearing on both

sides of the Atlantic. Max Weber, he wrote, was the "high-water mark of eccentricity." And the first work by Matisse that he saw was, in his opinion, "insolent . . . foolish . . . graceless."

MEMBERSHIPS
National Academy of Design
Salmagundi Club

10-Year Average Change From Base Years '77-'78: 238%

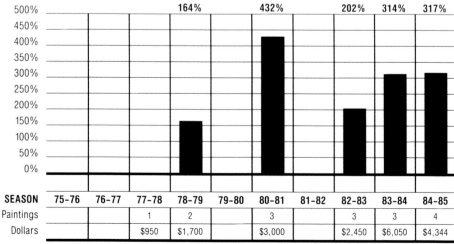

SEASON	75-76	76-77	77-78	78-79	79-80	80-81	81-82	82-83	83-84	84-85
				164%		432%		202%	314%	317%
Paintings			1	2		3		3	3	4
Dollars			$950	$1,700		$3,000		$2,450	$6,050	$4,344

Record Sale: $3,250, YG.P, 11/26/83, "Marshes at Hyannis Port," 12 x 30 in.

499

HERMAN WENDELBORG HANSEN

(1854-1924)

At an all-out scrambling gallop, wild-eyed horses with grim, vigilant riders charge out of Herman Wendelborg Hansen's watercolors as if to bowl over the unwary viewer. Hansen's watercolors of the American West capture vividly the danger, desperation and romance of a land which became myth even before it had completely passed away. Hansen, fed on that myth as a young boy in Germany, was among those responsible for the growth of the legend in the Eastern United States and in Europe, even as the West itself struggled to attain a much less exciting respectability.

Born in Dithmarschen, Germany in 1854, Hansen showed enough artistic talent that his father sent him to study at age 16 in Hamburg, Germany, under the painters Heimerdinger and Simmonsen. He studied in England in 1876 and arrived the next year in New York City.

He found work as a commercial artist there and in Chicago, but, while painting a locomotive in the Dakotas for a railroad advertisement, fell in love with the West again. For a time he spent only his summers sketching in the frontier states, but he moved to San Francisco at age 28 and made California his home until his death in Oakland in 1924.

By the time Hansen was in his fifties, he was a popular painter in the East and in Europe. He sold every watercolor and etching he produced. His *Pony Express* (1900, location unknown), his most famous painting, is still a familiar reproduction. Foreign-born Hansen had this advantage over a native Westerner: he could see romance and vigor where the inhabitants could see only inconvenience and poverty.

Buffalo Trouble, 24 x 36 in., signed l.r. Courtesy of John H. Garzoli Gallery, San Francisco, California.

PUBLIC COLLECTIONS
Denver Art Museum, Colorado
Eastman Memorial Foundation, Laurel, Mississippi

SEASON	75-76	76-77	77-78	78-79	79-80	80-81	81-82	82-83	83-84	84-85
Paintings				2		1	1	1	1	
Dollars				$8,000		$25,000	$18,000	$12,000	$13,200	

Record Sale: $25,000, BB.SF, 10/8/80, ''Renegade Apaches,'' 16 × 23 in.

500

GEORGE INNESS, JR.

(1854-1926)

George Inness, Jr. won several awards during his lifetime for his paintings of animals, but none compared to the personal reward of liberating himself from the power of the example set by his famous father, one of the greatest painters of the nineteenth century.

Inness, Jr. (as he signed his works) chose to paint figures and animals, the better to distinguish himself from his father's landscape work. In the latter years of his career, he turned to religious subjects.

Born in Paris, Inness, Jr. grew up in the Boston area. Before he was 20, he had been taught by his father for two years in Rome and had studied for a year with Leon Bonnat in Paris. In 1875, the family returned to the United States. They lived in New York City, where father and son shared a studio, and then in Montclair, New Jersey. By 1887, Inness, Jr. was exhibiting at the National Academy of Design.

His father's death in 1894 changed Inness, Jr.'s life dramatically. He went to Paris, opened a studio there and exhibited annually at the Paris Salon, where he won a gold medal.

He claimed that his father appeared to him in a vision to discuss the younger man's future. Subsequently, Inness, Jr. turned to religious subjects, the culmination of which came in a series of religious allegories he painted between 1918 and 1922. The series—on such themes as promise, realization and fulfillment—is held by the Church of the Good Shepherd in Tarpon Springs, Florida.

Inness, Jr. returned to the United States in 1900, residing in Cragsmoor, New York and Tarpon Springs, Florida.

The Newborn, 32 x 25¾ in., signed l.r. Courtesy of John H. Garzoli Gallery, San Francisco, California.

MEMBERSHIPS
Academie des Beaux Arts
National Academy of Design

PUBLIC COLLECTIONS
Metropolitan Museum of Art, New York City

SEASON	75-76	76-77	77-78	78-79	79-80	80-81	81-82	82-83	83-84	84-85
Paintings		2	2	2	2	7	8		2	2
Dollars		$9,350	$1,125	$2,400	$2,900	$15,500	$17,850		$5,850	$10,600

Record Sale: $10,000, D.NY, 4/24/85, "The Coming Storm," 30 × 45 in.

BIRGE HARRISON

(1854-1929)

Birge Harrison was one of a group of gifted young American painters, among them John Singer Sargent and Abbott Thayer, who studied in Paris in the 1870s and later helped to win serious recogniton for American art in the eyes of the art world. He was known principally for poetic winter landscapes and street scenes.

He was also the pivotal figure in the growth of the art colony at Woodstock, New York, where the Art Students League established a school of landscape painting in 1905. Harrison headed this school.

Harrison was born in Philadelphia in 1854. After school he worked first as a farmer, then went into business with his father for two years. In 1876 he met Sargent, who persuaded him to come to Paris to study art. That set the course for the rest of his life. He stayed in Paris for six years, studying for four of them at the Ecole des Beaux Arts.

In 1883, illness forced him to abandon painting for several years. To regain his health, he traveled widely. On his trips he often wrote and illustrated articles for popular magazines.

Harrison admired the work of the French impressionists, but disliked their use of intense color and the aggressiveness of their brushwork. He was far more attuned to the evocative style of the barbizon painters.

Harrison had a romantic concept of nature: its moods, he believed, should be

The Artist's Farm, Woodstock, N.Y., 18½ x 23 in., signed l.l. Courtesy of Taggart, Jorgensen, & Putman Gallery, Washington, D.C.

the source of inspiration for artistic expression. He avoided strong contrasts; his edges were soft.

In 1909, Harrison published a book, *Landscape Painting,* which became a standard text for many years. In it he

quotes Millet as saying, "Technique should always hide itself modestly behind the thing expressed." He adhered to this theory all through the years he lived and painted in Woodstock.

By the time of his death in 1929, however, most of the other artists in the colony had abandoned his techniques and ideals, sometimes even deriding them as "the moonlight and mist formula."

MEMBERSHIPS
Century Association
National Arts Club
National Institute of Arts and Letters
New York Water Color Club
Philadelphia Sketch Club
Salmagundi Club
Union Internationale des Arts et des Lettres

PUBLIC COLLECTIONS
Art Institute of Chicago
Brooks Memorial Art Gallery, Memphis, Tennessee
Detroit Institute of Arts
Philadelphia Museum of Art
St. Louis Art Museum, Missouri
Toledo Museum of Art, Ohio

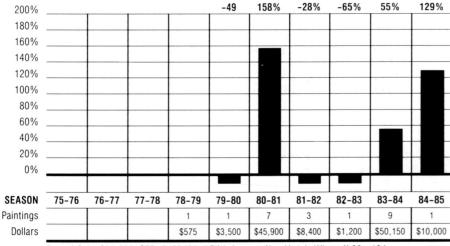

10-Year Average Change From Base Years '78-'79: 29%

				-49	158%	-28%	-65%	55%	129%

SEASON	75-76	76-77	77-78	78-79	79-80	80-81	81-82	82-83	83-84	84-85
Paintings				1	1	7	3	1	9	1
Dollars				$575	$3,500	$45,900	$8,400	$1,200	$50,150	$10,000

Record Sale: $25,000, SPB, 6/23/81, "Fifth Avenue, New York in Winter," 30 × 18 in.

WALTER LAUNT PALMER
(1854-1932)

The landscapes of Walter Launt Palmer, particularly his snow scenes, were popular prizewinners throughout a long professional career that began before the artist was 20.

Born in 1854, in Albany, New York, the son of sculptor Erastus Dow Palmer, Walter Palmer grew up with art and artists. His first lessons, in his teens, were with portraitist Charles Elliott and Hudson River School landscapist Frederic Church. Palmer's work was first accepted for the National Academy of Design show in 1872, when he was only 18.

After a European tour in 1873, Palmer continued art studies in Paris until 1876. One of his masters was Emile Auguste Carolus-Duran, whose influence is seen in the controlled tonality that modified the academic tightness of Palmer's early work. Subtlety of color, texture and light became characterisitic of all of Palmer's work.

Palmer opened a New York studio in 1876. A trip to Italy in 1881 provided material for numerous Venetian scenes in the early 1880s. Another significant trip was to the Orient. Palmer was one of the first American artists to draw inspiration from Japanese and Chinese cultures.

In 1882, Palmer returned to Albany. He began to exhibit widely, accumulating awards and critical success for his oils and watercolors, particularly for his snowscapes.

De Forest Interior, 1878, 24⅛ x 18 in. Courtesy of National Museum of American Art, Smithsonian Institution, Museum Purchase.

Reflecting several influences—academic precision, oriental delicacy, impressionist effect—these snowscapes demonstrate Palmer's belief in the vivid colorist potential of snow. He said, "Snow, being colorless, lends itself to every effect of complement and reflec-tion." Palmer painted his outdoor scenes in the studio, prefacing each with painstaking preliminary notes, sketches and photographs, which he put aside when he began to paint.

Palmer's best-known work and his own favorite is *Silent Dawn* (1920, Metropolitan Museum of Art), a picture of snow-laden trees above a still brook.

He died in 1932 in Albany.

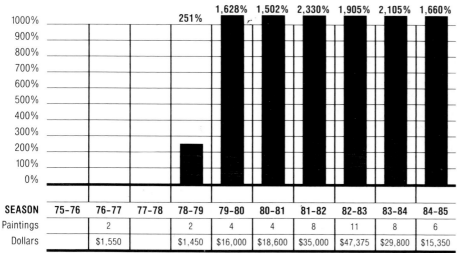

10-Year Average Change From Base Years '76-'77: 1,423%

					1,628%	1,502%	2,330%	1,905%	2,105%	1,660%
			251%							

SEASON	75-76	76-77	77-78	78-79	79-80	80-81	81-82	82-83	83-84	84-85
Paintings		2		2	4	4	8	11	8	6
Dollars		$1,550		$1,450	$16,000	$18,600	$35,000	$47,375	$29,800	$15,350

Record Sale: $12,000, SPB, 1/28/82, "Woman in Interior," 24 × 18 in.

LEONARD OCHTMAN
(1854-1934)

Leonard Ochtman's subtle, delicate, tonal landscapes brought him national prominence as a leading American impressionist at the turn of the century.

He was born in Zonnemaire, Holland in 1854. The Ochtmans came to Albany, New York in 1866.

From 1870 until 1880, Ochtman was a draftsman in an Albany engraving plant. Self-taught, he endeavored to launch his career as a painter. His work was accepted for the 1880 spring National Academy of Design show; in the 1882 fall show, his *Early Summer in Schoharie Valley* (date and location unknown) received critical notice.

In late 1883, Ochtman's work was accepted again by the Academy and, for the first time, by the American Water Color Society. Within two years, his clear, light landscapes were being shown and sold in these and other prestigious exhibitions.

He used the proceeds of his sales to travel in England, France and Holland, returning in 1887 to open a New York City studio with fellow Albany artist Charles Warren Eaton. Within a year, Ochtman was well established, exhibiting and teaching.

After his 1891 marriage to a student, Nina Fonda, he settled in Greenwich, Connecticut. The fields, rivers and harbors surrounding his home, "Grayledge," on the Mianus River, were his favorite subjects in the next several decades.

Ochtman was active in the Cos Cob, Connecticut art colony, at the heart of the new native impressionist movement. Others there included Theodore Robinson, Childe Hassam, J. Alden Weir and Elmer MacRae.

Ochtman's prestige was highest in the early twentieth century, when his award-winning oils and watercolors were demanded by public and private collectors.

After his death in 1934, Ochtman's

Frosty Fields, 1895, 24 x 36 in., signed l.l. Courtesy of Helen Fusscas, Connecticut Gallery, Marlborough.

work, like that of other American impressionists well known in their time, was neglected as critical taste turned away from "traditionalism." He and others are being restored to rightful importance in the recent renewal of interest in American impressionism.

MEMBERSHIPS
American Federation of Arts
American Water Color Society
Artists Fund Society
Brooklyn Art Club
Greenwich Society of Artists
National Academy of Design
National Arts Club
National Institute of Arts and Letters
New York Water Color Club

PUBLIC COLLECTIONS
Albany Institute of History and Art,
  New York
Brooklyn Museum
Bruce Museum, Greenwich, Connecticut
Butler Institute of American Art,
  Youngstown, Ohio
Corcoran Gallery of Art, Washington, D.C.
Dallas Museum of Fine Arts
Fort Worth Art Museum, Texas
Metropolitan Museum of Art, New York City
National Gallery of Art, Washington, D.C.
St. Louis Art Museum

SEASON	75-76	76-77	77-78	78-79	79-80	80-81	81-82	82-83	83-84	84-85
Paintings		1	4	5	2	3	4	7	6	6
Dollars		$1,100	$4,500	$6,350	$2,950	$5,750	$4,900	$11,300	$12,500	$8,800

Record Sale: $4,750, SPB, 1/27/84, "Twilight," 24 × 36 in.

HENRY RASCHEN
(1854-1937)

Whether painting portraits, Indians, landscapes or still lifes, Henry Raschen had a talent for realism and a sureness of technique that distinguished his work. During the last two decades of the nineteenth century, he was considered one of the most important painters of Indians in the country. It was in his landscapes of California, however, with their contrasts of sunlight and purple shadows, that he seemed to find his truest mode of expression.

He was born in Oldenburg, Germany in 1854, and his family emigrated to Fort Ross, California when he was 14. He began his art studies at the San Francisco Art Academy but, like many others of his day, felt the need for broader training in Europe.

At 21, he went to Munich for several years of study, where he met William Merritt Chase. After traveling for a time in Italy and France, he returned to San Francisco in 1883. For the next eight years, accompanied by a landscape painter friend, he made many visits to the Indian tribes of California. His paintings of them were recognized for their lifelike quality.

On one trip he accompanied the army's General Nelson A. Miles when he captured famous Indian chief Geronimo. Years later, after his return from another trip to Germany, Raschen visited Geronimo in prison at Fort Sill, Oklahoma.

Around the turn of the century, Raschen's career was aided greatly by the patronage of Phoebe Hearst, mother of publisher William Randolph Hearst. It was she who helped to establish him as a major artist in San Francisco.

After the earthquake and fire destroyed much of San Francisco in 1906, Raschen moved across the bay to Oakland and continued to paint there until his death in 1937.

Campfire Stories, 24 x 36 in., signed l.l. Courtesy of Vose Galleries of Boston, Inc., Massachusetts.

Still Life—Fort Ross, 20 x 30 in., signed l.r. Courtesy of John H. Garzoli Gallery, San Francisco, California.

MEMBERSHIPS
Bohemian Club
San Francisco Art Association

SEASON	75-76	76-77	77-78	78-79	79-80	80-81	81-82	82-83	83-84	84-85
Paintings						3	1	3	3	1
Dollars						$29,300	$20,000	$84,000	$56,000	$2,500

Record Sale: $50,000, SPB, 6/2/83, ''Indian Stories,'' 26 × 46 in.

ALBERT F. KING

(1854-1945)

Nineteenth-century Pittsburgh was a thriving center of industry. The bankers and industrialists who had acquired money and power by their efforts were now eager to acquire culture and social standing, and the city nourished an enthusiastic group of artists. One of these was Albert F. King, whose conservative style and skill at capturing likenesses ensured his portraits a place in many an important hall of commerce. Yet King is now more valued for his controlled, eye-deceiving still lifes, genre scenes and landscapes.

A native of Pittsburgh, he was born in that city in 1854, and lived most of his life there. Though he studied with his friend and fellow Pittsburgh painter Martin B. Leisser for a time, King was essentially self-taught. Stubborn and independent, he seemingly rejected all the movements in the art world which postdated his birth, choosing instead a severe, hard-edged realism.

King's rejection did not extend to his fellow artists, particularly the Pittsburgh painters known as the "Scalp Level Group." Led by successful artist George Hetzel, they frequently set out in the summers to paint in the countryside near the village of Scalp Level. King was among the second generation of this fellowship, and a charter member of the Artists' Association of Pittsburgh.

Although King enjoyed a comfortable living as a portraitist, painting the likenesses of Steven Foster and his friend

Still Life with Apples and Chip Basket, 12 x 18¼ in., signed l.r. Courtesy of La Salle University Art Museum, Philadelphia, Pennsylvania.

Leisser as well as those of the solid citizens of Pittsburgh, his regular submissions to the Artists' Association shows never included any portraits.

As King grew older and Pittsburgh grew more cosmopolitan, the cohesiveness of the art community weakened and new ideas filtered in. Embittered, King endeavored for a few years to live with his son in Omaha, Nebraska, but a tornado reinforced his homesickness and he returned to take up his brush again until his death at the age of 91 in 1945.

MEMBERSHIPS
Artists' Association of Pittsburgh
Pittsburgh Artists Society
Duquesne Club

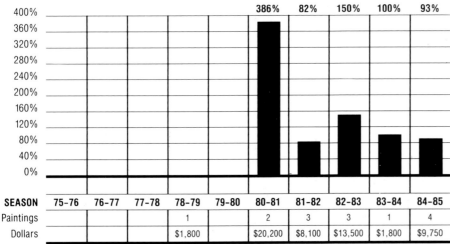

10-Year Average Change From Base Years '78-'79: 135%

						386%	82%	150%	100%	93%

SEASON	75-76	76-77	77-78	78-79	79-80	80-81	81-82	82-83	83-84	84-85
Paintings				1		2	3	3	1	4
Dollars				$1,800		$20,200	$8,100	$13,500	$1,800	$9,750

Record Sale: $19,000, SPB, 6/19/81, "Still Life," 22 × 27 in.

506

PAUL DE LONGPRE
(1855-1911)

Known in his lifetime as "the king of flower painters," Paul de Longpre devoted his career to floral still lifes. Whether painting a sunflower or an exquisite orchid, he was able to capture its very essence in his work. He was a top-flight floriculturalist as well as a painter, and he grew the blossoms he used to perfection.

Although he was born in 1855 into an aristocratic family, de Longpre was not born to wealth. As a boy he loved nature and roamed the countryside around Paris, sketching and painting, then selling his work for pocket money.

Later he joined his father and other relatives in painting silk and ivory fans, which were sold in fashionable Parisian shops. From the start, his work was notable for his originality and delicacy in the treatment of flowers.

He married at age 18, and at 21 had a floral still life exhibited in the Paris Salon. His good fortune was interrupted a few years later, however, when the bank where his money was deposited failed. In 1890, de Longpre and his wife came to America with what little money was left.

The first years in New York City were a constant struggle against poverty, but he kept painting flowers. In 1896, disregarding warnings of failure, de Longpre had an exhibition of nothing but floral paintings. It was a resounding success and his international reputation was made.

In 1899, de Longpre and his family moved to Hollywood where he built a Moorish house that was described as more beautiful than anything in Morocco. Its three acres of gardens attracted 25,000 visitors in a single year. He died there in 1911, after a long illness.

Hollyhocks, 1901, 29⅜ x 14¾ in., signed l.r. Photograph courtesy of Hirschl & Adler Galleries, Inc., New York, New York.

SEASON	75-76	76-77	77-78	78-79	79-80	80-81	81-82	82-83	83-84	84-85
Paintings				2				1	6	2
Dollars				$3,200				$1,600	$8,450	$3,500

Record Sale: $2,600, CH, 1/23/85, "Holly Hocks," 30 × 14 in.

507

WILLIAM GILBERT GAUL
(1855-1919)

William Gilbert Gaul was known for his portrayals of Civil War army life and his later paintings and illustrations of Western Indian themes.

Born in 1855 in Jersey City, New Jersey, Gaul attended Newark schools and Claverack Military Academy. Poor health prevented a Navy career, but Gaul took up art, studying in the 1870s at the National Academy of Design and the Art Students League in New York City.

Gaul spent four years on a farm he inherited in Van Buren, Tennessee, painting the remnants of the Union and Confederate armies, as well as some rural scenes.

His career as an artist and illustrator for magazines, notably *Harper's Monthly,* was successful. He traveled West many times, living on Army posts and among Indians, photographing and sketching frontier scenes to complete later at his New York City studio or Tennessee home.

His most popular works show soldierly action, notably *Charging the Battery* (date and location unknown), an 1889 Paris Exposition gold medal winner, and *Wounded to the Rear* (date and location unknown).

His most impressive single work is *Issuing Government Beef* (date unknown, Gilcrease Institute), depicting the final lot of once-proud Plains Indians. The Indians, in the clothing of their conquerors, sit and stand stolidly on a

The Indian Prisoner, 1899, 36½ x 44 in., signed l.r. Photograph courtesy of Kennedy Galleries, New York, New York. Private Collection.

hillside in their former hunting lands, while soldiers distribute beef.

Painted with Gaul's characteristic accurate, spare, painterly style and compositional insight, it avoids demeaning melodrama. The contrast of the broad open landscape and sky with the scattering of passive Indians conveys the stark message.

In 1890, he was among artists commissioned by the federal government to conduct a census of American Indians.

Gaul not only drew and painted the Indians, he added his observations to a *Report on Indians Taxed and Indians Not Taxed,* a now-rare 683-page work.

Gaul traveled widely to record subjects in Mexico, the West Indies, Panama and Nicaragua. An illustrated account of his travels was exhibited at the 1893 World Columbian Exposition in Chicago.

Gaul died in 1919 in New York City.

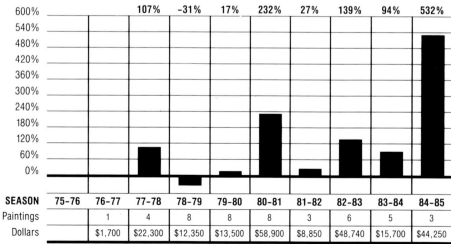

10-Year Average Change From Base Years '76-'77: 124%

		107%	-31%	17%	232%	27%	139%	94%	532%
SEASON	75–76	76–77	77–78	78–79	79–80	80–81	81–82	82–83	83–84	84–85
Paintings		1	4	8	8	8	3	6	5	3
Dollars		$1,700	$22,300	$12,350	$13,500	$58,900	$8,850	$48,740	$15,700	$44,250

Record Sale: $28,000, CH, 12/7/84, "Union Soldier," 20 × 16 in.

MEMBERSHIPS
National Academy of Design

PUBLIC COLLECTIONS
Birmingham Museum of Art, Alabama
Thomas Gilcrease Institute of American History and Art, Tulsa

JULIUS L. STEWART
(1855-1919)

Julius Stewart was a figure and genre painter from Philadelphia who spent almost his entire life in Paris. He painted the life he thoroughly enjoyed—Parisian high society.

Stewart's canvases are spirited and realistic, full of fashionable women, sumptuous fabrics and elegant drawing-rooms. He was following a genre begun by his friend, Jean Beraud, but Stewart's more vivacious work was considered especially American. In *Ready for the Ball* (1877, Jordan-Volpe Gallery, New York), a young woman rests on a sofa in an elaborate evening gown, a look of dreamy anticipation on her face.

The artist was born in 1855. His father, an expatriate art collector named William Stewart, specialized in works of the contemporary Spanish-Roman school, particularly Zamacois, Fortuny and de Madrazo. These artists had a great influence on the young Stewart; in the 1880s, he studied with Zamacois and de Madrazo, as well as with Gerome.

Stewart's first success was in being exhibited in 1883 at the Salon. His reputation was firmly established with *The Hunt Ball* (1885, Essex Club, Newark). A sequel, *The Hunt Supper* (1889, Buffalo Club, New York) was shown at the Paris Exposition.

At the same time that Stewart was painting society scenes, he painted nudes out-of-doors, a subject more acceptable in France than in America in the 1890s.

Stewart remained a bachelor, and died in 1919.

MEMBERSHIPS
Paris Society of American Painters
Societe Nationale
Societe Nationale des Beaux Arts

PUBLIC COLLECTIONS
Art Institute of Chicago
Buffalo Museum, New York
Detroit Institute of Arts
Pennsylvania Academy of the Fine Arts,
    Philadelphia

Portrait of Mrs. Francis Stanton Black, 1908, 78¾ x 44½ in., signed l.l. Walters Art Gallery, Baltimore, Maryland.

SEASON	75-76	76-77	77-78	78-79	79-80	80-81	81-82	82-83	83-84	84-85
Paintings							2	1	1	4
Dollars							$2,609	$1,600	$32,000	$177,659

Record Sale: $155,000, SPB, 12/6/84, "Summer's Promenade," 33 × 59 in.

WILLIAM ANDERSON COFFIN
(1855-1925)

Stoyestown Valley, Pa. 1909, 24 x 30 in., signed l.r. Courtesy of Driscoll & Walsh, Fine Art, Boston, Massachusetts.

William Anderson Coffin was a landscape and figure painter who was also recognized for his art criticism and for his services to art organizations and expositions.

Coffin was born in 1855 in Allegheny, Pennsylvania. He attended Yale University, where he became interested in drawing from the casts of classical sculpture in the art school. He went to Paris to study art in 1877; he continued his classical drawing and, in 1878, he enrolled in Leon Bonnat's art class, where he studied for between three and five years.

In 1879, Coffin exhibited a painting of Bonnat's life class in the Paris Salon, where he also showed work in 1880 and 1882. He settled in New York City, where he opened a studio, in 1883.

Coffin continued to paint and to exhibit widely. *The Rain* (1889, Metropolitan Museum of Art) was shown at the National Academy of Design in 1889. In 1891, it was awarded the Webb Prize by the Society of American Artists. Its simple composition—gentle hills and a cloudy sky—and its thin finish are similar to the work of tonalists such as John H. Twachtman. Its moodiness, however, suggests a link with the barbizon painters.

As a writer for the *New York Evening Post* from 1886 to 1891, and art editor for the *New York Sun* from 1896 to 1901, Coffin gained a reputation as a critic. He also wrote articles on French and American art for periodicals, including *Scribner's* and *Harper's Weekly.*

Coffin helped found the Municipal Art Society and the American Fine Arts Society; he held office in these and several other artists' organizations. In 1901, he served as director of fine arts for the Pan-American Exposition, and in 1915, he helped organize the Panama-Pacific Exposition.

He died in New York City in 1925.

10-Year Average Change From Base Years '77-'78: 190%

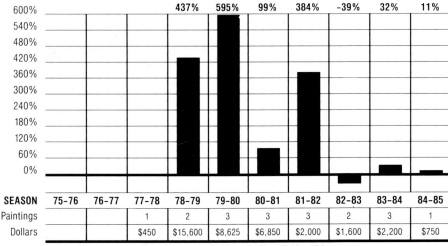

SEASON	75-76	76-77	77-78	78-79	79-80	80-81	81-82	82-83	83-84	84-85
				437%	595%	99%	384%	-39%	32%	11%
Paintings			1	2	3	3	3	2	3	1
Dollars			$450	$15,600	$8,625	$6,850	$2,000	$1,600	$2,200	$750

Record Sale: $13,500, SPB, 4/20/79, "Stroll by the River," 16 × 13 in.

MEMBERSHIPS
American Fine Arts Society
Architectural League of New York
Lotos Club
Municipal Art Society
National Academy of Design

PUBLIC COLLECTIONS
Metropolitan Museum of Art, New York City
National Museum of American Art,
    Washington, D.C.

510

GEORGE COPE
(1855-1929)

George Cope was a skilled practitioner of trompe l'oeil painting, in which familiar objects are depicted with such precise detail as to create the illusion of reality. In addition to his trompe l'oeil paintings, Cope is also known to have painted tabletop still lifes, as well as landscapes.

Cope was born to a respectable Quaker family near West Chester, Pennsylvania, where he was to spend most of his life. As a youth, he was an enthusiastic hunter and fisherman, who inherited his mother's talent for painting.

In 1876, Cope met German-born landscape painter Herman Herzog at the Philadelphia Centennial, and subsequently studied under Herzog for a number of years. His work of this period consisted mostly of landscapes in the barbizon style, and still-life paintings of dead game, without the trompe l'oeil effect.

Cope is said to have adopted the trompe l'oeil manner around 1887, in response to the great popularity of the new style, recently introduced by the painter William Harnett. Although looked down upon as a gimmick in academic circles, the style's technical virtuosity and subject matter (e.g., wild game, hunting and fishing gear, Civil War memorabilia) appealed strongly to businessmen and politicians, and Cope was only one of a number of artists to adopt it.

After his marriage in 1883, Cope lived for the remainder of his life in West Chester. Although his work was featured by a number of prominent Philadelphia art galleries during the 1890s, the majority of his paintings were sold to West Chester area residents.

After 1900, Cope turned increasingly to the painting of domestic still lifes and miniature landscapes inspired by a trip to Florida. In the final years of his life, he was reduced to selling fruit baskets

Fisherman's Accoutrements, 1887, 42 x 30 in., signed l.r. Courtesy of The Butler Institute of American Art, Youngstown, Ohio.

and sketches to his neighbors, yet he remained an active and well-liked member of the West Chester community until his death in 1929.

PUBLIC COLLECTIONS
Brandywine River Museum, Pennsylvania
Butler Institute of American Art,
   Youngstown, Ohio

SEASON	75–76	76–77	77–78	78–79	79–80	80–81	81–82	82–83	83–84	84–85
Paintings				2			1			1
Dollars				$23,600			$30,000			$7,500

Record Sale: $30,000, SPB, 4/23/82, "Union Mementoes on a Door," 52 × 32 in.

LOUIS CHARLES MOELLER
(1855-1930)

A popular genre painter of the late nineteenth century, Louis Charles Moeller became known as a specialist in cabinet-size paintings. He won the National Academy of Design's Hallgarten Prize in 1884, at age 29, for his small work entitled *Puzzled* (date and location unknown).

A native of New York, born in 1855, Moeller received his earliest training from his father, a portrait and decorative painter. He went on to study at Cooper Union and the National Academy of Design, under Lemuel Wilmarth. During six years, he worked with Frank Duveneck and Wilhelm von Diez, then returned to New York City in 1882. He began to concentrate on cabinet-size paintings instead of the large scale of his earlier work.

Moeller's compositions were characterized by attention to facial expressions and gestures by figures posed in stage-like interiors. Accessory elements, such as framed pictures and arranged objects, precisely rendered, were typical. His works of the 1880s, with pale and neutral colors on smooth surfaces, are a contrast to his rich, dark, heavily applied colors of the 1890s.

Two of Moeller's most stirring works, *The Sculptor's Studio* (ca. 1880, Metropolitan Museum of Art) and *The Old Armchair* (date unknown, Oberlin College) are without people; they use objects as clues to their owners' identities. Often his accurately detailed small works were done on wood panels.

Reading the News, 1901, 18 x 24 in., signed l.r. Courtesy of Henry B. Holt, Inc., Essex Fells, New Jersey.

Called "one of the most dramatic painters of the day" by *Quarterly Illustrator* in 1894, Moeller gave up painting in later years because of illness. He died in Weehawken, New Jersey in 1930.

MEMBERSHIPS
National Academy of Design

PUBLIC COLLECTIONS
Allen Memorial Art Museum,
  Oberlin, Ohio
Corcoran Gallery of Art,
  Washington, D.C.
Metropolitan Museum of Art,
  New York City
Newark Museum, New Jersey

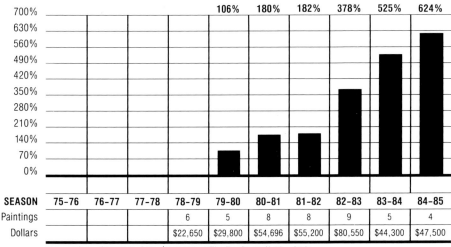

10-Year Average Change From Base Years '78-'79: 285%

	75-76	76-77	77-78	78-79	79-80	80-81	81-82	82-83	83-84	84-85
					106%	180%	182%	378%	525%	624%
SEASON	75-76	76-77	77-78	78-79	79-80	80-81	81-82	82-83	83-84	84-85
Paintings				6	5	8	8	9	5	4
Dollars				$22,650	$29,800	$54,696	$55,200	$80,550	$44,300	$47,500

Record Sale: $29,000, SPB, 12/6/84, "The Tea Party," 18 × 24 in.

JAMES GALE TYLER
(1855-1931)

James G. Tyler was one of the most notable maritime painters and illustrators of his day. His popularity can be gauged by the fact that his works were often forged. It is estimated that in New York City in 1918, more than 100 works falsely carried the artist's name.

Tyler was born in 1855 in Oswego, New York. At age 15, Tyler, already fascinated by the sea and its vessels, moved to New York, where he studied under marine artist A. Cary Smith. This brief tutelage was the only formal art training Tyler ever received.

No aspect of maritime life escaped Tyler's attention. In addition to painting all types of boats—from old sloops to clipper ships—he painted a variety of seamen, coastal scenes and seascapes.

From 1900 to 1930, Tyler traveled each year to Newport, Rhode Island, where he painted the annual America's Cup Race. Some of these paintings were commissioned; the remainder were widely exhibited and critically acclaimed.

In fact, Tyler received a number of important commissions in his lifetime. He also capitalized on the money to be made through magazines, and was a regular contributing writer and illustrator for some of the major publications of the time, including *Harper's, Century* and *Literary Digest*.

Tyler's artistic style is vivid and poetic, infused with his unique and specific enthusiasm. As seen in his *Freshen-*

Yachting, 1892, 36 x 55¾ in. Courtesy of Smith Gallery, New York, New York.

The Fortunes of War, 1887, 50 x 40 in. Courtesy of Oliphant and Company, LTD, New York, New York.

ing Breeze (date unknown, Kennedy Galleries), his emphasis is more on mood and impression than on the exact-ing details conveyed by more realistic painters. His works have been critically compared with those of Albert Ryder.

When, at the height of his career, Tyler became aware of the number of paintings falsely circulated under his name in New York, he complained to the district attorney and was able to successfully pursue several civil action suits.

Having lived for most of his life in Greenwich, Connecticut, Tyler moved to Pelham, New York in 1931, before he died.

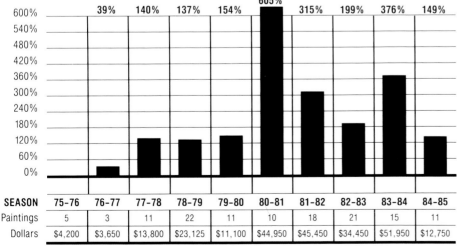

10-Year Average Change From Base Years '75-'76: 211%

		39%	140%	137%	154%	605%	315%	199%	376%	149%

SEASON	75-76	76-77	77-78	78-79	79-80	80-81	81-82	82-83	83-84	84-85
Paintings	5	3	11	22	11	10	18	21	15	11
Dollars	$4,200	$3,650	$13,800	$23,125	$11,100	$44,950	$45,450	$34,450	$51,950	$12,750

Record Sale: $32,500, D.NY, 9/24/80, "Tug A.C. Cheney Towing Barges," 36 x 54 in.

513

GEORGE de FOREST BRUSH
(1855-1941)

Portrait of Lydia Treby, 1881, 36⅜ x 44¼ in., signed l.r. Photograph courtesy of Hirschl & Adler Galleries, Inc., New York, New York.

George de Forest Brush painted in an academic manner which reflects the influences of his European training and his interest in Italian renaissance art. He drew upon two distinct bodies of subject matter—American Indian scenes and mother-and-child poses—for the bulk of his work.

Brush was born in Shelbyville, Tennessee, but he moved to Connecticut as a child. His mother, an amateur artist, was the earliest influence on his career. At age 16, he went to New York City to study at the National Academy of Design, and three years later he was off to Paris to study under Jean Leon Gerome at the Ecole des Beaux-Arts. Gerome, who taught and influenced many American artists, was noted for his precise academic style. Brush remained in Paris for almost six years.

Back home, far from the Paris salon, Brush focused on American Indian themes in the 1880s. He was praised for his accuracy and ability to present the philosophical side of his subjects, a change from other painters' attention to Indian pomp and warfare. He visited the Western Indians over a four-year period and came to know the Crow especially well.

Although his Indian paintings drew approval, they were not financially rewarding. In the 1890s, Brush turned to the theme of mother and child, which was the title of several of his paintings. (An 1895 version is in the Museum of Fine Arts, Boston; another is in the Corcoran Gallery of Art, Washington, D.C.) His family served as models for these works, which continued in a traditional, academic style much like portraits. They show Brush's interest in works of the Italian Renaissance. From 1898 until 1917, he spent part of most years in Florence.

Brush's secular madonnas are frequently sentimental, and less compelling

Polly, 1916, 36⅛ x 27⅛, signed l.r. Courtesy of National Museum of American Art, Smithsonian Institution, Gift of John Gellatly.

to the modern reviewer than his Indians.

Brush maintained a studio in Dublin, New Hampshire, for almost 50 years. He continued to travel in Europe in the 1920s. He also taught off and on for many years at the Art Students League in New York City as well as in Dublin. At age 85, he died in Hanover, New Hampshire.

MEMBERSHIPS
American Academy of Arts and Letters
Artists Fund Society
National Academy of Design
Society of American Artists

PUBLIC COLLECTIONS
Brooklyn Museum
Butler Art Institute, Youngstown, Ohio
Carnegie Institute, Pittsburgh
Corcoran Gallery of Art, Washington, D.C.
Metropolitan Museum of Art, New York City
Museum of Fine Arts, Boston
National Gallery of Art, Washington, D.C.
Pennsylvania Academy of the Fine Arts,
    Philadelphia
Worcester Art Museum, Massachusetts

SEASON	75-76	76-77	77-78	78-79	79-80	80-81	81-82	82-83	83-84	84-85
Paintings				1	3		2	3	1	1
Dollars				$70,000	$28,950		$27,750	$10,800	$1,100	$3,800

Record Sale: $70,000, CH, 5/23/79, "The Artist Sketching His Family," 20 × 24 in.

514

CECILIA BEAUX
(1855-1942)

Cecilia Beaux was a leading turn-of-the-century portraitist, ranked today with Mary Cassatt as an outstanding painter.

Beaux's greatest works were of women and children, painted with fluent, sensuous brushstrokes, but she also did portraits of leading political figures. Her subjects were often drawn from the social elite, like those of John Singer Sargent, with whom she is frequently compared.

Although her talent was evident early, she did not aspire to be a painter until she enrolled in a women's class and discovered the joy of brushwork. Once she had decided to beome a serious painter, she rejected marriage and dedicated her life to her work.

Born in Philadelphia and trained under the tutelage of William Sartain, Beaux began her career with a traditional approach to portraiture. Beautifully-modeled heads shine with mellow light against the darkness of rich, brown backgrounds. Character is evident in the faces; Beaux possessed great talent for conveying psychological insight through her figures.

When she was 32, she went abroad for the first of seven visits to France, and her style changed dramatically. At the Academie Julien, and later at the Concarneau in Brittany, Beaux discarded the "brown sauce" approach to portraits and adopted a vibrant, fluent style with whites, yellows and lavenders playing off against bright black.

Beaux's first major work was *Les Dernier Jours d'Enfance* (1883, location unknown), a profile of her sister; its composition resembles the painting Whistler did of his mother. It won awards on both sides of the Atlantic, establishing Beaux as a major portraitist.

Her magnificent double portrait *The Dancing Lesson* (1898, location unknown) looks as if it were done

Man with the Cat (Henry Sturgis Drinker), 1898, 48 x 34⅝ in., signed l.r. Courtesy of National Museum of American Art, Smithsonian Institution, Bequest of Henry Ward Ranger through the National Academy of Design.

quickly; actually, Beaux took a year to complete the work. She took similar care with the underlying composition of her portraits. Her most daring work, a calligraphic study entitled *After the Meeting* (1914, Toledo Museum of Art) was described by Frank Goodyear as "a masterpiece of animation, spatial ambience, brilliant color and bold fabric design."

She was later appointed to the faculty of the Pennsylvania Academy of the Fine Arts, the first full-time woman instructor there. She taught for 20 years, journeying frequently to France, which she considered the source of her artistic inspiration.

MEMBERSHIPS
American Federation of Arts
National Academy of Design
National Arts Club
National Association of Women Painters and Sculptors
Societaire des Beaux-Arts
Society of American Artists

PUBLIC COLLECTIONS
Art Institute of Chicago
Brooks Memorial Gallery, Memphis
Corcoran Gallery of Art, Washington, D.C.
Luxembourg Gallery, Paris
Metropolitan Museum of Art, New York City
Museum of Fine Arts, Boston
Pennsylvania Academy of the Fine Arts, Philadelphia
Toledo Museum of Art, Ohio
Ufizzi Gallery, Florence

SEASON	75-76	76-77	77-78	78-79	79-80	80-81	81-82	82-83	83-84	84-85
Paintings					1	1	2	2	1	1
Dollars					$800	$1,200	$7,100	$2,150	$650	$700

Record Sale: $3,600, CH, 12/11/81, "Rocky Landscape," 27 × 33 in.

CLAUDE RAGUET HIRST
(1855-1942)

Claude Raguet Hirst was the only important woman artist in the trompe l'oeil school of still-life painting that flourished toward the end of the nineteenth century. Hirst's unique emphasis on certain objects and her use of watercolors rather than oils set her apart as one of the most innovative trompe l'oeil painters.

Born in Cincinnati in 1855, Hirst studied at the Cincinnati Art Academy under Noble. She also studied with Agnes D. Abbatt, George Smillie and Charles C. Curran in New York City.

Hirst's early subjects were traditional still lifes of flowers and fruit. She began exhibiting these paintings at the National Academy of Design in 1884 and 1885, and continued to paint the same subjects until 1890.

Around 1890, the famous trompe l'oeil painter William Michael Harnett became her neighbor in New York City. Under Harnett's influence, Hirst began to paint table-top still lifes, including objects that were primarily associated with men, such as pipes, tobacco, spectacles and books.

Hirst's paintings differed from Harnett's in some very important ways. While Harnett and the other members of the trompe l'oeil school used oils, Hirst painted with watercolors. Of even greater significance, Hirst was more concerned with emphasizing certain objects—such as bowls, vases, candlesticks, and cannisters—rather than with simply creating an illusion of reality. In some of her paintings, Hirst replaced the traditional masculine objects with objects associated with women, such as yarn, thimbles, needles and pottery.

Hirst did not achieve much recognition as an artist during her lifetime and died in poverty in 1942.

Still Life: Ink Stand, Pipe, Tobacco Pouch and Newspaper, 9 x 13 in., signed l.l. Private Collection, Photograph courtesy of Hirschl & Adler Galleries, Inc., New York, New York.

MEMBERSHIPS
National Association of Women Painters
  and Sculptors
New York Watercolor Club

SEASON	75-76	76-77	77-78	78-79	79-80	80-81	81-82	82-83	83-84	84-85
Paintings				1	2	1	2		1	1
Dollars				$8,000	$10,500	$8,750	$7,100		$2,600	$8,000

Record Sale: $8,750, SPB, 1/29/81, "An Old Volume," 7 × 9 in.

JOHN WHITE ALEXANDER
(1856-1915)

Widely traveled and sophisticated, John White Alexander was an internationally recognized portrait painter and an accomplished muralist. His portraits were in great demand during the late nineteenth century, and among his many sitters were eminent artists, actors and authors of the day. Influenced early in his career by the decorative qualities of James McNeill Whistler's paintings, Alexander became one of the leading American exponents of the aesthetic principles of art nouveau.

Born in 1856 in Allegheny City, Pennsylvania, Alexander was orphaned at an early age. After several years of employment at the Atlantic Pacific Telegraph Company, where he worked from age 12, Alexander left for New York City in 1875. In Manhattan, he found work as a cartoonist at *Harper's Weekly*. With the money he earned as an illustrator, the young artist sailed for Europe in 1877. He enrolled in the Royal Academy in Munich.

From 1878 until his return to the United States in 1881, Alexander worked with American expatriate artist Frank Duveneck and the group of American students known as the "Duveneck Boys," first in Germany and later in Northern Italy.

Alexander's earliest works were landscapes and portraits of local people, painted with thick layers of pigment, or impasto, as used by Duveneck. Later, he developed the delicate brushwork and thinly painted surfaces characteristic of the work of Whistler, after meeting that famed artist in Venice.

Upon his return to New York City, Alexander resumed his work at *Harper's,* executing not only magazine illustrations, but a number of portraits in oil as well. In 1886, he began a series of portraits of distinguished authors for *Century Magazine*. It eventually included such writers as Thomas Hardy,

Changeable Taffeta (Portrait of Mrs. John W. Alexander), 1894, 79 x 47½ in., signed l.r. Courtesy of Graham Gallery, New York, New York.

George Bancroft and Robert Louis Stevenson.

In February of 1886, Alexander undertook to paint a portrait of the irascible, spirited poet Walt Whitman. His *Walt Whitman* (1899, Metropolitan Museum of Art), portrayed the poet in a dignified pose that belied his exuberant personality, with sophisticated design combined with thin application of paint, that suggests the influence of his friend Whistler.

In 1891, the artist married and moved with his bride to Paris. The couple remained in Paris for a decade; their friends included such notables as Oscar Wilde, Henry James and Auguste Rodin.

In his portraiture and figure paintings, Alexander developed a decorative, eclectic style associated with the growing art nouveau movement. His masterpiece *Isabella and the Pot of Basil* (1897, Boston Museum of Fine Arts), after a poem of that name by Keats, displays the

sweeping lines, broad patterns and decorative tendencies of this style.

Back in New York City in 1901, Alexander was elected to the National Academy of Design, and became an academician the following year. In 1905, he accepted a large commission to execute murals depicting the *Apotheosis of Pittsburgh* for the staircase hall of the Carnegie Institute. Although the project remained incomplete at the time of his death, he is said to have completed 47 of the total 67 panels without assistants.

Throughout the early 1900s, Alexander's portraits continued to show the influence of his Parisian experience. They became increasingly sentimental, however, more gestural in texture and less subtle coloristically. Between 1909 and his death in 1915, Alexander was president of the National Academy of Design and trustee of the Metropolitan Museum of Art.

MEMBERSHIPS
Legion of Honor
Societe Nationale des Beaux Arts
Society of British Artists

PUBLIC COLLECTIONS
Carnegie Institute, Pittsburgh
Metropolitan Museum of Art, New York City
Museum of Fine Arts, Boston
Philadelphia Museum of Art
Rhode Island School of Design, Providence

SEASON	75-76	76-77	77-78	78-79	79-80	80-81	81-82	82-83	83-84	84-85
Paintings					1		1	3	1	1
Dollars					$900		$3,000	$6,900	$22,000	$23,800

Record Sale: $23,800, PE, 12/7/84, "Kathleen Cowan Playing a Violin," 60 × 40 in.

KENYON COX

(1856-1918)

An eloquent defender of traditional values in art, Kenyon Cox was one of the finest draftsmen of his day. He did easel paintings, portraits and illustrations for books and magazines, but it was for mural paintings that he became best known. The murals, classically inspired, simple in composition and muted in color, were commissioned for public and collegiate buildings in many parts of the country.

Born in Warren, Ohio in 1856, Cox came from distinguished parentage. His maternal grandfather was the first president of Oberlin College in Ohio. His father, a brigadier general during the Civil War, became governor of Ohio, then Secretary of the Interior under President Grant and finally president of the University of Cincinnati.

At the McMicken Institute of Arts and Design in Cincinnati, the young Cox became enamored with the vitality of the work of Mariano Fortuny, and wanted to go to Paris to study with Fortuny's followers. His parents demurred, and sent him to the Pennsylvania Academy of the Fine Arts in Philadelphia. Cox considered the instruction stodgy, and in 1877 he went to Paris.

The Fortuny circle had waned by that time, and he decided to study with Carolus-Duran, whose vigorous style had attracted Sargent, among others. But in that atelier there was no emphasis on drawing, which had become almost an obsession with Cox.

He took courses with Alexandre Cabanel. At the Ecole des Beaux-Arts he chose to study with Gerome, whose work, ironically, he had dismissed as "artless" only two years before.

He stayed with Gerome until 1882, concentrating on developing an economical delineation of form. Back in New York City later that same year, however, Cox joined other young artists in challenging the National Academy of Design

An Eclogue, 1890, 48 x 60½ in., signed l.l. Courtesy of National Museum of American Art, Smithsonian Institution, Gift of Allyn Cox.

as old-hat. But the public was not ready for Cox's sensuous, beautifully rendered nudes, painted in the French academic style. This, combined with the old-guard reluctance to admit such works to National Academy shows, made Cox turn to illustration and portrait painting to earn his living during the 1880s.

The World's Columbian Exposition in Chicago in 1893 finally provided Cox with an opportunity to paint murals on a grand scale. It also gave impetus to a much broader interest in murals for public spaces. From then until 1913, Cox created a series of monumental allegorical murals for the Library of Congress, the Appellate Court House in New York City and many other buildings.

In his final years Cox argued vehemently for his views of art. "The Classic Spirit is the disinterested search for perfection," he declared. He railed against the New York City Armory Show in 1913, but few listened. When he died in 1918, the tide of opinion was running against him.

MEMBERSHIPS
American Academy of Arts and Letters
National Academy of Design
National Institute of Arts and Letters
National Society of Mural Painters
New York Architectural League
Society of American Artists

PUBLIC COLLECTIONS
Appellate Court House, New York City
Bowdoin College, Maine
Cooper-Hewitt Museum, New York City
Library of Congress, Washington, D.C.
Luzerne County Court House, Wilkes-Barre, Pennsylvania
National Academy of Design, New York City
National Collection of Fine Arts, Washington, D.C.
National Museum of American Art, Washington, D.C.

SEASON	75-76	76-77	77-78	78-79	79-80	80-81	81-82	82-83	83-84	84-85
Paintings					2			1		1
Dollars					$6,800			$2,600		$4,000

Record Sale: $4,000, SPB, 4/25/80, "The End of Summer," 23 × 9 in.

518

ASTLEY D.M. COOPER
(1856-1924)

Astley David Montague Cooper was a prolific painter, aware of what the public wanted to see and well equipped to deliver it. His highly sensitive work, depicting the stark reality of the American Western frontier, made him known as a popular and respected visual historian of that period.

The St. Louis, Missouri, in which Cooper was born in 1856 was known as the gateway to the West, but his primary influence and inspiration as a child came from relatives who had already made their mark in the West. The distinguished explorer William Clark and the renowned frontier soldier George Rogers Clark were his great-uncles. His maternal grandfather, an Indian agent for the Missouri River tribes, was Major Benjamin O'Fallon, a close friend of painter George Catlin; he had commissioned Catlin to do portraits of notable Indian chiefs. It was young Cooper's fascination with those works that drove him to become an artist.

Cooper had already gained the respect of the art community for his portraits of Indian chiefs by the time he was 21. After his schooling at Washington University in St. Louis, followed by a couple of years of field work in Colorado, Cooper was well on his way to national acclaim.

Keeping in close contact with art dealers in New York City, Philadelphia and Chicago, he made a significant move by setting up his studio in San Jose, Cali-

Indian on Horseback, Morning Rocky Mountains, 48¼ x 30 in., signed l.l. Photograph courtesy of M. Knoedler & Co., Inc., New York, New York.

fornia, in 1883. From there he gained international acclaim for his Western wildlife paintings, which often appeared in periodicals.

The San Jose studio, which was designed in the Egyptian motif, was Cooper's home base until his death in 1924. It was visited by many of the world's art lovers, as well as by public characters like General Ulysses S. Grant, who was a subject of many portraits by Cooper.

In the 1890s, Cooper's barroom murals of realistically-portrayed nudes gained him some notoriety. His real genius, however, was his ability to poignantly represent the changes that progress was bringing to the West. He vividly recorded victims in the throes of Western expansion. An example is *An Inquest on the Plains* (1890, R.W. Norton Art Gallery, Shreveport, Louisiana). Clearly, Cooper took into account the inevitable doom of life as it was on the prairies. The seven buffalo standing around a dead Indian seem to be judging their own futures. Cooper was well aware that the dominant figures of the West were soon to be gone.

MEMBERSHIPS
Salmagundi Club of St. Louis
San Francisco Art Association

PUBLIC COLLECTIONS
Stanford University Museum, California

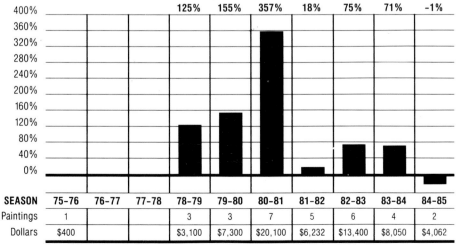

10-Year Average Change From Base Years '75-'76: 100%

	75–76	76–77	77–78	78–79	79–80	80–81	81–82	82–83	83–84	84–85
				125%	155%	357%	18%	75%	71%	-1%
SEASON	75–76	76–77	77–78	78–79	79–80	80–81	81–82	82–83	83–84	84–85
Paintings	1			3	3	7	5	6	4	2
Dollars	$400			$3,100	$7,300	$20,100	$6,232	$13,400	$8,050	$4,062

Record Sale: $7,500, CH, 4/24/81, "Indian Encampment on the Plains," 20 × 35 in.

JOHN SINGER
SARGENT
(1856-1925)

Mr. and Mrs. John W. Field. Courtesy of the Pennsylvania Academy of the Fine Arts, Philadelphia.

John Singer Sargent was America's premier portraitist of international society, one of the most brilliant lights of the Gilded Age. He also became, with Winslow Homer, its leading exponent of watercolor.

Sargent was born in Florence, Italy in 1856. The pace of his cosmopolitan life was set early. He traveled constantly, often recording observations in a sketchbook. His mother, an amateur painter, nurtured his precocious talent. At age 12, he studied with landscapist Carl Welsch in Rome. He entered the Accademia delle Belle Arti in Florence in 1870, and attended the Ecole des Beaux Arts in Paris in 1874.

He quickly switched to the less academic tutelage of Carolus-Duran, a fashionable yet adventurous portraitist. Carolus-Duran's cool sophistication, and his blend of brio and tightly handled realism, affected Sargent deeply. He soon began painting quickly from life to capture essentials.

Meanwhile, he was also absorbing Whistler's tonalism, Degas's composition, and impressionist color. *Oyster Gatherers of Cancale* (1878, Corcoran Gallery of Art), which won honorable mention at the 1878 Salon, treated the coast of Brittany with a directness and luminosity worthy of Sargent's friend Monet.

He traveled in 1879 and 1880 to see works by Velasquez and Hals. *El Jaleo* (1882, Gardner Museum) and *The Daughters of Edward Darley Boit* (1882, Museum of Fine Arts, Boston), reflect their composition, values and bravura brushwork.

In 1883, Sargent began to expand his portrait trade. However, the uproar around *Portrait of Mme. X* (1884, Metropolitan Museum of Art), an unsettlingly accurate portrayal of a notorious and exotic American beauty, ended Sargent's hopes in Paris.

London became his home from 1885 until his death in 1925. He flourished there but demand took him increasingly to America which, by the late 1880s, provided much of his clientele.

Sargent's career peaked in the early 1900s. He had painted hundreds of portraits, earned a fortune, and waded in prizes and honors (even an offer of knighthood). But by 1908, he tired of both his demanding practice and international society, and largely limited portraiture to charcoal sketches.

He began to concentrate on murals and watercolors. With Abbey and Puvis de Chavannes, Sargent decorated the new Boston public library. From 1890, he spent three decades on this project, depicting the rise of Western religion. In the 1910s and 1920s, he painted murals for the Boston Museum and the Widener Library at Harvard, and a major war picture, *Gassed* (1918, Imperial War Museum, London). Sargent traveled extensively, sketching ethnic types, ancient architecture, and battlefields; but the works lacked his usual vitality. They were generally more restrained and classic, in the manner of Puvis de Chavannes.

Sargent's curiosity, energy and vast facility found an outlet in watercolor. Always a compulsive sketcher, he turned to this medium purely for pleasure. The results were marvels of finely tuned observation, fond glimpses into the dynamism of color and light.

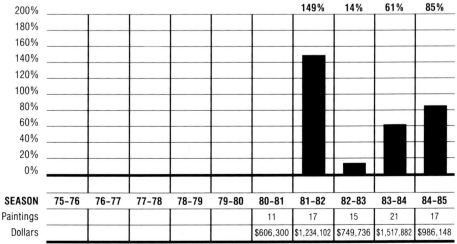

10-Year Average Change From Base Years '80-'81: 62%

| | | 149% | 14% | 61% | 85% |

SEASON	75-76	76-77	77-78	78-79	79-80	80-81	81-82	82-83	83-84	84-85
Paintings						11	17	15	21	17
Dollars						$606,300	$1,234,102	$749,736	$1,517,882	$986,148

Record Sale: $550,000, CH, 12/11/81, ''Women at Work,'' 22 × 28 in.

JEFFERSON DAVID CHALFANT
(1856-1931)

The Chess Players, signed u.l. Photograph courtesy of the Brandywine River Museum, Chadds Ford, Pennsylvania, Collection of Mrs. J. David Chalfant.

Jefferson David Chalfant, one of the foremost still-life painters in the trompe l'oeil style, was born in Lancaster, Pennsylvania in 1856. His artistic career can be divided into three thematic periods: still lifes of the late 1880s; genre paintings, which followed his formal art training; and portraits, which occupied the end of his career.

Trained by his father as a cabinet-maker, Chalfant worked in Pennsylvania and Delaware in the 1870s, finishing railroad cars and painting parlor-car interiors. In 1883, after moving to Wilmington, Delaware, he took a studio and began to paint trompe l'oeil still lifes, which were influenced by the work of William Michael Harnett.

Chalfant's still-life period was concentrated upon a series of violin paintings: *Violin* (1887, location unknown); *Violin and Music* (1887, Newark Museum); *The Old Violin* (1888, Delaware Art Museum); *Violin and Bow* (1889, Metropolitan Museum of Art). The series reveals Chalfant's progression from foreshortened forms to forms which project\into the viewer's space, and from complexity to simplicity of composition. Although they are obvious emulations of Harnett's work, they are simpler, more delicate compositions, expressing a lyric rather than a dramatic mood.

Chalfant's work is further distinguished by the golden and silver tones achieved through his preference for a monochromatic palette. The violin series also displays Chalfant's interest in pattern and decoration, through his attention to wallpapers, tablecloths and wood surfaces.

Chalfant began to exhibit his works in 1887. In 1890, Alfred Corning Clark, a leading patron of art, sent Chalfant to study in Paris at the Academie Julien under Adolphe William Bouguereau and Jules Joseph Lefebvre. The train-

ing strengthened Chalfant's realistic style without significantly altering it, and encouraged him to experiment thematically.

Upon his return to Wilmington in 1892, he embarked upon a series of genre paintings, many of which depicted interior scenes of craftsmen at their trades. The genre series reflected an artisan tradition threatened by industrialization.

Between 1894 and 1898, Chalfant received patents for a bicycle saddle, a pedal crank attachment and a machine for justifying type. In the early 1900s, he turned to portraiture under the patronage of a Senator Saulsbury. After suffering a stroke in 1927, he was unable to continue his work. He died four years later.

PUBLIC COLLECTIONS
Brandywine River Museum, Pennsylvania
Delaware Art Museum, Wilmington
Fine Arts Museums of San Francisco
Metropolitan Museum of Art, New York City
Newark Museum, New Jersey

SEASON	75–76	76–77	77–78	78–79	79–80	80–81	81–82	82–83	83–84	84–85
Paintings					2				1	
Dollars					$8,550				$20,000	

Record Sale: $20,000, SPB, 12/8/83, "Playing Soldier," 6 × 4 in.

CHARLES H. DAVIS
(1856-1933)

Born in Amesbury, Massachusetts in 1856, Charles Davis was an American impressionist whose paintings were overlaid with sentiment and a decided emotionalism. Not for him the calm, cool, reflective art of other impressionists—men like Twachtman and Hassam who were active at the same time. Instead Davis strove for dramatic effect; his best works are vivid and highly energetic.

Davis did not set out to be an artist—he began work in a carriage factory. Only after attending an exhibition highlighted by the landscapes of French painter Jean Francois Millet did he decide to enroll in drawing classes. His instructor encouraged him to enter the Boston Museum School, where the young painter-to-be studied under Otto Grundmann. In 1880 he went to France, where he remained for almost a decade.

While in France, Davis studied for a brief time at the Academie Julien under Jules Lefebvre and Gustave Boulanger. He first exhibited at the Paris Salon in 1881, and two years later his first American exhibition was mounted in Boston. Even though he remained in France, his reputation at home grew. In 1886, he was elected to the Society of American Artists. On returning to the United States, Davis settled in Mystic, Connecticut.

Davis's early works were marked by the subdued palette and dreamy quality of the barbizon painters, but after his return to America he adopted a more vigorous style. By 1895, he was displaying a penchant for depicting clouds in

Wind Driven, 50 x 40 in., signed l.l. Courtesy of John H. Garzoli Gallery, San Francisco, California.

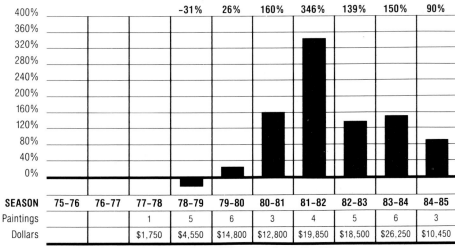

Clouds and Pond, 1889, 18 x 26 in., signed l.r. Courtesy of Connecticut Gallery, Marlborough, Connecticut.

varying weather conditions. These cloud studies eventually became his specialty. A successful and popular painter, he was elected to the National Academy of Design in 1903. He remained an active member, working until his death in 1933 at age 77.

10-Year Average Change From Base Years '77-'78: 110%

		-31%	26%	160%	346%	139%	150%	90%

SEASON	75-76	76-77	77-78	78-79	79-80	80-81	81-82	82-83	83-84	84-85
Paintings			1	5	6	3	4	5	6	3
Dollars			$1,750	$4,550	$14,800	$12,800	$19,850	$18,500	$26,250	$10,450

Record Sale: $11,500, S.BM, 11/19/81, "Winter Morning," 15 x 18 in.

MEMBERSHIPS
American Federation of Arts
Copley Society of Boston
Lotus Club
National Academy of Design
National Arts Club
Society of American Artists
Society of Mystic Artists

PUBLIC COLLECTIONS
Art Institute of Chicago
Carnegie Institute, Pittsburgh
Corcoran Institute, Washington, D.C.
Metropolitan Museum of Art,
    New York City
Museum of Fine Arts, Boston
National Gallery, Washington, D.C.
Pennsylvania Academy of the Fine Arts,
    Philadelphia

HOWARD RUSSELL BUTLER
(1856-1934)

Accomplished in several fields, including law, business and physics, Howard Russell Butler combined his artistic talent with an abiding interest in science. Although he painted portraits and figure studies, Butler preferred marine subjects, and also developed a special interest in depicting solar and lunar phenomena.

Born in 1856, Butler began drawing as a boy in Yonkers, New York. He graduated with a degree in science from Princeton University in 1876, and later received a law degree from Columbia University in 1882. In 1884, despite many business commitments and a law practice, he decided to pursue a career in the fine arts.

Butler began his formal art training at the Art Students League in New York City, and later spent two years abroad, studying for a time at the Atelier Colarossi under Raphael Collin and Gustave Courtois. While abroad, he painted his noted work *The Seaweed Gatherers* (1886, Smithsonian Institution), an oil painting derived from studies completed during a summer at Concarneau in Brittany, France. The highly skilled rendering of the transparent sea, solid earth and grainy sand demonstrates Butler's remarkable textural sensitivity.

Butler returned to the United States in 1887 and settled in New York City, where he became active in a number of art organizations. At the turn of the century, many of his business activities stemmed from his friendship with industrialist Andrew Carnegie, whose portrait he painted at least 17 times. Butler lived in California from 1905 to 1907, and again from 1921 to 1926.

In 1918, Butler accompanied a group from the United States Naval Observatory to Baker, Oregon, where he began to paint a series of solar eclipses. These works are preserved in *The Eclipse*

Portrait of Thomas Moran (1837-1926), 40 x 36 in. Courtesy of Kennedy Galleries, New York, New York.

Triptych, 1918, 1923, 1925 (American Museum, Hayden Planetarium, New York).

Between 1921 and 1926, Butler painted what he termed his "last California marine," entitled *Yankee Point, Monterey* (1921-1926, Metropolitan Museum of Art). Rendered in a bold, impressionist style, this painting shows a flattened perspective reminiscent of Winslow Homer. Fascinated by the coloristic qualities of water, Butler mastered

the illusion of transparency by depicting the reflected sky above and the varied tones of rock and sand below.

The recipient of a number of prestigious awards and honors, Butler continued to paint until his death in Princeton, New Jersey at age 78.

MEMBERSHIPS
American Astronomical Society
American Federation of the Arts
American Fine Arts Society
Architectural League of New York
Century Association
Lotus Club
National Academy of Design
National Institute of Arts and Letters
New York Water Color Club

PUBLIC COLLECTIONS
American Museum, Hayden Planetarium,
 New York City
Metropolitan Museum of Art, New York City
National Museum of American Art,
 Washington, D.C.

SEASON	75-76	76-77	77-78	78-79	79-80	80-81	81-82	82-83	83-84	84-85
Paintings			2		1		4	4	2	1
Dollars			$1,430		$700		$5,800	$4,450	$1,100	$1,000

Record Sale: $2,200, CH, 3/18/83, "Pink Phlox," 18 × 21 in.

FRANKLIN DE HAVEN
(1856-1934)

Franklin De Haven, a contemporary of Arthur Hoeber and Birge Harrison, was known as a landscape artist in the classic tradition. His paintings are characterized by variety, excellent draftsmanship and a thorough understanding of nature. Dramatic skies are almost always a major element. Said Edgar Mayhew Bacon in *Essays on American Art and Artists,* published in New York in 1896, "He filches . . . whole acres of sand-dunes and miles of breaking surf and brings them bodily to New York."

De Haven was born in Bluffton, Indiana in 1856. He came to New York City in 1886, where he became a student of George Smillie.

Evening at Manomet (date and location unknown) is De Haven's most famous and probably his best painting. Exhibited at the Prize Fund Exhibition held in the American Art Galleries of New York City in 1889, it is a beautiful evocation of a sunset on the Maine coast. Dunes are bathed in a golden light, with dark shadows counterpointed dramatically.

At an exhibition organized by the Grand Central Art Galleries Art Education Association, De Haven was called a landscape painter-musician. The violin was his favorite instrument; he numbered a Cremona among his prize possessions. His elegant *At Twilight* (date and location unknown) is full of synesthesia: the tall intertwining branches of the trees suggest the symmetry of music.

Another dramatic piece is *Woodland Scene* (date unknown, Colby College Art Museum), full of somber reflections and stark contrasts. A 1975 Colby catalog suggests, "It is like a setting for a tale by Edgar Allan Poe."

In 1926 and 1927, De Haven was president of the Salmagundi Club in New York City. He died in 1934.

The Harvest, 1897, 9½ x 13½ in., signed l.r. Courtesy of Private Collection, Radnor, Pennsylvania.

MEMBERSHIPS
Allied Artists of America
National Academy of Design
National Arts Club
Salmagundi Club

PUBLIC COLLECTIONS
Brooklyn Institute Museum
Butler Art Institute, Youngstown, Ohio
Colby College, Waterville, Maine
National Gallery, Washington, D.C.

SEASON	75-76	76-77	77-78	78-79	79-80	80-81	81-82	82-83	83-84	84-85
Paintings						1		1		1
Dollars						$650		$1,300		$500

Record Sale: $1,300, W.W, 9/26/82, "Woodland Pool at Dusk," 24 × 36 in.

MANUEL VALENCIA
(1856-1935)

17 Mile Ridge, Monterey, California, ca. 1910, 20 x 30 in., signed l.l. Courtesy of DeRu's Fine Art, Bellflower, California.

Although his art is represented in the California state capitol and a United States president purchased one of his paintings, Manuel Valencia produced Western landscapes and California historical scenes for almost 30 years before he gained attention.

The artist lived all of his life in the San Francisco area. He was born in 1856 at the Valencia hacienda, the "Rancho San Jose," in Marin County, California. A direct descendant of General Gabriel Valencia, first governor of the state of Sonora, Mexico under Spanish rule, he attended what is now Santa Clara University and took lessons from several leading artists of the area. He became art editor of the *San Francisco Chronicle* under art patron M.H. de Young.

Valencia also was the first illustrator of the Salvation Army newspaper, *War Cry,* published in San Francisco.

Despite his connections and his productivity, Valencia gleaned neither acclaim nor material reward for his art.

In 1912, when he was 56, Valencia sold 80 of his paintings in San Francisco; he had nine children and needed to pay his mortgage.

The show and sale surprised Valencia by bringing his work into popular demand, and he enjoyed a successful career until his death in 1935.

President William McKinley bought Valencia's painting of the Yosemite Valley, and a painting on another California theme was acquired by the state government for the capitol building at Sacramento.

MEMBERSHIPS
Esquela de Bellas Artes de Mexico

PUBLIC COLLECTIONS
California State Capitol, Sacramento
Huntington Art Gallery, San Marino, California

SEASON	75-76	76-77	77-78	78-79	79-80	80-81	81-82	82-83	83-84	84-85
Paintings				4	2	3	2	2	1	
Dollars				$3,900	$2,400	$1,900	$1,150	$2,600	$850	

Record Sale: $2,000, BB.SF, 2/24/83, "View of Yosemite Valley," 50 × 30 in.

COLIN CAMPBELL COOPER
(1856-1937)

Colin Campbell Cooper was an internationally successful painter, famous for his impressionistic street scenes, landscapes and architectural subjects. The recipient of numerous prestigious awards, Cooper painted oils and watercolors capturing the changing light and atmosphere of urban life at the turn of the century.

Born in Philadelphia in 1856, Cooper was the son of a surgeon. Encouraged by his well-educated parents, Cooper studied with Thomas Eakins at the Pennsylvania Academy of the Fine Arts.

Cooper made the first of many trips to Europe in 1885. He studied at the Academie Julien and the Ecole Delecluse in Paris. Traveling to Belgium, Holland and France, Cooper painted numerous picturesque scenes of European architectural treasures. These paintings gained him wide recognition, and he continued to travel in search of unusual landscape and architectural subjects throughout his career. Unfortunately, most of his early works were destroyed in a fire in 1896.

In 1897, Cooper married painter Emma Lampert (1855-1920). In 1902, he began a series of important oil paintings of New York City skyscrapers. He became particularly well known for his depictions of skyscrapers in New York City and Philadelphia.

Cooper's use of impressionist palette and brushstrokes in his oil paintings of American urban life was inspired by

Beauvais Cathedral, 36 x 26 in., signed l.r. Courtesy of Newman Galleries, Philadelphia, Pennsylvania.

Childe Hassam, who painted impressionist views of New York as early as 1890. Equally competent at watercolor painting, Cooper developed a technique of applying watercolors on canvas in a

way that makes the finished work look like an oil painting.

After spending some time in Philadelphia and abroad, Cooper settled in California in 1921, and became dean of the School of Painting at the Santa Barbara School for the Arts. He died in 1937.

MEMBERSHIPS
American Federation of Arts
American Water Color Society
Associate of the National Academy of Design
New York National Arts Club
New York Society of Painters
New York Water Color Club
Pennsylvania Academy of the Fine Arts
Philadelphia Art Center
Philadelphia Water Color Club

PUBLIC COLLECTIONS
Art Club of Philadelphia
Boston Art Club
Cincinnati Art Museum
Dallas Art Association
Lotos Club, New York City
Pennsylvania Academy of the Fine Arts, Philadelphia
Reading Museum, New York
St. Louis Museum of Fine Arts

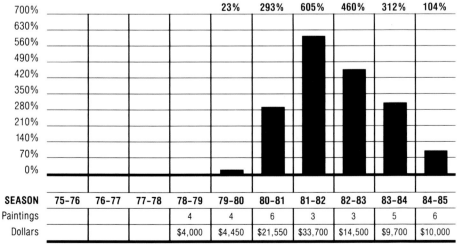

10-Year Average Change From Base Years '78-'79: 257%

	23%	293%	605%	460%	312%	104%

SEASON	75-76	76-77	77-78	78-79	79-80	80-81	81-82	82-83	83-84	84-85
Paintings				4	4	6	3	3	5	6
Dollars				$4,000	$4,450	$21,550	$33,700	$14,500	$9,700	$10,000

Record Sale: $30,000, SPB, 6/4/82, "Chatham Square Station, New York," 40 x 50 in.

WALTER GAY
(1856-1937)

Novembre, Etaples, ca. 1885, 43¼ x 64¼ in., signed l.l. Courtesy of National Museum of American Art, Smithsonian Institution, Museum Purchase.

Walter Gay achieved success in four different subjects and painting styles. He is best known for the fourth—elegant interiors.

Born in 1856 in Hingham, Massachusetts, Gay grew up in Dorchester, now part of Boston. His early art studies were with an uncle, W. Allan Gay, a landscapist in the barbizon manner.

In 1873, Gay shared a studio with landscapist John Bernard Johnston and took night classes at Boston's Lowell Institute. In three years, he had gained a reputation as a specialist in floral still lifes.

In 1876, Gay became a favorite pupil of Leon Bonnat, in Paris, France. He undertook a second subject—precise, delicate figures in eighteenth-century costume—in the brilliant, mannered style of Jean Louis and Mariano Fortuny. In 1882, Gay became one of the early members of the Concarneau group of artists living and working in Brittany, on the coast of France.

By 1884, he had turned to realistic, spare, darkly monochromatic paintings of Breton peasants and their austere way of life. In 1889, the Luxembourg Museum acquired Gay's first large figure painting in this genre. He married that year.

In 1895, Gay moved to a country home near Paris and entered upon the fourth phase of his career. He painted interiors, often with eighteenth-century appointments. These accurate pictures of exquisitely furnished rooms in public buildings and distinguished private homes are done in a light, accurate manner with animated surfaces. Though the rooms are empty, they convey a sense of the people who inhabited them.

Gay enjoyed international recognition throughout his career. He lived and worked in his Chateau du Breau until his death in 1937, at age 81.

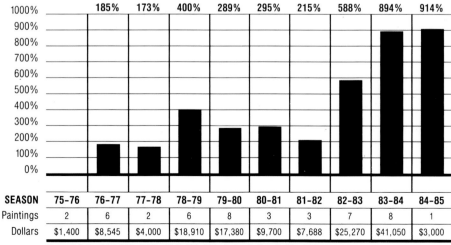

10-Year Average Change From Base Years '75-'76: 395%

SEASON	75-76	76-77	77-78	78-79	79-80	80-81	81-82	82-83	83-84	84-85
		185%	173%	400%	289%	295%	215%	588%	894%	914%
Paintings	2	6	2	6	8	3	3	7	8	1
Dollars	$1,400	$8,545	$4,000	$18,910	$17,380	$9,700	$7,688	$25,270	$41,050	$3,000

Record Sale: $14,000, SPB, 12/8/83, "Bachelor Duties," 16 × 12 in.

MEMBERSHIPS
American Federation of the Arts
National Academy of Design
National Institute of Arts and Letters
Royal Society of Water Colors
Societe des Amis du Louvre
Societe de la Peinture a l'Eau
Society of American Artists
Societe Nationale des Beaux Arts
Committee des Amis du Musee de Luxemborg

PUBLIC COLLECTIONS
Art Institute of Chicago
Carnegie Institute, Pittsburgh
Detroit Institute of Arts
Metropolitan Museum of Art, New York City
Musee d' Orsay, Paris
Museum of Fine Arts, Boston
Pennsylvania Academy of the Fine Arts, Philadelphia
Rhode Island School of Design, Providence
Yale University

WARREN J. SHEPPARD
(1856-1937)

A yachtsman and marine painter, Warren Sheppard was a fortunate individual who was able to build two successful careers around his one true love—the sea. Most of his work, including illustrations for magazines, was related to ships and ports. He was an expert on the design and rigging of ships of earlier times, and when he depicted them in some of his paintings the ships were accurate in every detail.

The scenes he painted of the canals and landmarks of Venice are particularly celebrated. And when he painted pictures of the yachts of rich men, he depicted the largest and costliest vessels of the time.

Sheppard was born in 1856 in Greenwich, New Jersey, a town on the Delaware River below Philadelphia which has been associated with ships and shipping since the earliest colonial times. He came by his love of the sea naturally; his father was captain of a ship that carried lumber. He made many trips with his father, sometimes simply to study the many moods of the sea for his own work.

His only formal art training was at Cooper Union in New York, where he took classes in perspective drawing. In 1879, he spent four months sketching such ports along the Mediterranean coast as Gibraltar, Genoa, Naples and Messina in Sicily.

Sheppard was in Paris and Venice between 1888 and 1893, and studied

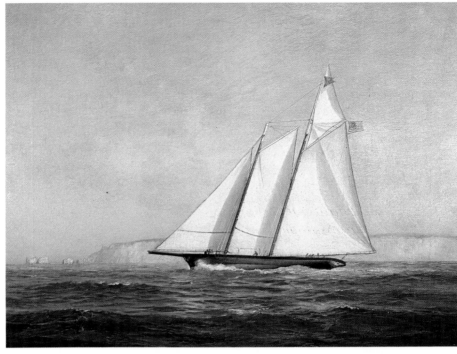

America Heading for the Needles, 16 x 22 in. Courtesy of Oliphant and Company, LTD., New York, New York.

painting in both cities, but there is no record of where or with whom he might have studied. He was in his mid-thirties by then, and already a successful illustrator and painter.

Sheppard did not spend all of his time sketching and painting, however; he designed a large sailing yacht for himself. He was an expert navigator, and took over as captain of other owners' boats in sailing races. Twice, for instance, he was in command of Frank Maier's *Tamerlane* when it won the New York-to-Bermuda race. He also wrote the book *Practical Navigation,* which was considered sufficiently authoritative to be used as a standard textbook for many years by the United States Naval Academy.

Although he had retired from the sea some years before, Sheppard continued to paint until his death in Brooklyn, New York in 1937.

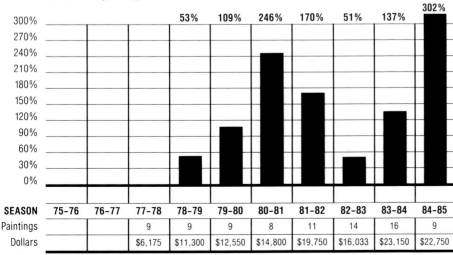

10-Year Average Change From Base Years '77-'78: 134%

SEASON	75-76	76-77	77-78	78-79	79-80	80-81	81-82	82-83	83-84	84-85
				53%	109%	246%	170%	51%	137%	302%
Paintings			9	9	9	8	11	14	16	9
Dollars			$6,175	$11,300	$12,550	$14,800	$19,750	$16,033	$23,150	$22,750

Record Sale: $11,000, CH, 3/15/85, "Lower New York Bay," 15 x 23 in.

PUBLIC COLLECTIONS
Albright-Knox Art Gallery, Buffalo
Phillips Academy, Andover, Massachusetts
Toledo Museum of Art, Ohio

ROBERT F. BLUM
(1857-1903)

Robert Frederick Blum was an active and successful artist, versatile in a number of media and highly regarded as a pastelist. His vibrant and atmospheric work, which incorporated many of impressionism's techniques, helped pave the way in America for acceptance of impressionism.

The Cincinnati in which Blum was born in 1857 was an artistic center, but he received his major inspiration when, like many other American artists of the time, he visited the Centennial Exhibition in 1876 in Philadelphia. There he was very impressed with works by artists of the Romano-Spanish School. He became such an important disciple of the well-respected Giovanni Boldini and Mariano Fortuny that he became known as "Blumtuny."

In 1880, he encountered another profound influence when he joined fellow Cincinnatian Frank Duveneck in Venice. Duveneck's group was then associated with James McNeill Whistler. Whistler's pictorial technique, if not his rejection of narrative interest in painting, can be seen reflected in much of Blum's work, and Whistler was also a strong influence on Blum's interest in etching and pastel.

Indeed, in New York City in the 1880s, Blum became president of the Society of Painters in Pastel. Through this society, and with his colleague and friend William Merritt Chase, Blum exerted a perceptible sway over the development of American taste.

Repose, 7½ x 11 in., signed u.l. Photograph courtesy of Hirschl & Adler Galleries, Inc., New York, New York.

Blum's paintings combine energetic and fluid brushwork with great attention to atmosphere and light. His subject matter was often drawn from his travels, first in Europe and later in Japan, where he was one of the first American artists to paint and travel. His important *Venetian Lace Makers* (1887, Cincinnati Museum) and *Italian Bead Stringers* (1887-1888, Otesaga Hotel, Cooperstown, New York) exemplify his concentration on contemporary but exotic material, a combination which was highly popular with the American art public.

Blum was successful not only as a painter but also as an illustrator and muralist. A series of his illustrations, created during his trip to Japan, was published in *Scribner's Magazine,* and he demonstrated his skill as a muralist in the wall panels he created for the old Mendelssohn Glee Club Hall in New York City, which are preserved in the Brooklyn Museum. Another mural work he began shortly before his death in 1903 was in the New Amsterdam Theater (since destroyed).

MEMBERSHIPS
National Academy of Design
Society of Painters in Pastel

PUBLIC COLLECTIONS
Brooklyn Museum
Cincinnati Art Museum
Metropolitan Museum of Art, New York City

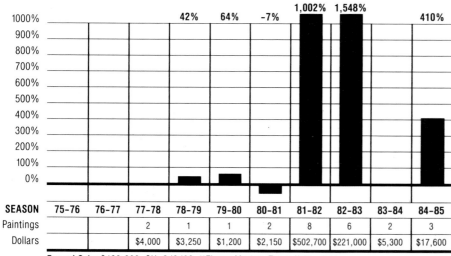

10-Year Average Change From Base Years '77-'78: 382%

SEASON	75-76	76-77	77-78	78-79	79-80	80-81	81-82	82-83	83-84	84-85
				42%	64%	-7%	1,002%	1,548%		410%
Paintings			2	1	1	2	8	6	2	3
Dollars			$4,000	$3,250	$1,200	$2,150	$502,700	$221,000	$5,300	$17,600

Record Sale: $430,000, CH, 6/3/82, "Flower Market, Tokyo," 31 x 25 in.

530

CHARLES S. PEARCE
(1857-1914)

A grandson of poet Charles Sprague, Charles S. Pearce was born and educated in Boston. He embarked upon a career as a painter in 1872, after working in his father's mercantile office.

On the advice of William Morris Hunt, Pearce entered the atelier of Leon Bonnat in Paris in 1873. One of his fellow students was John Singer Sargent. Pearce soon became a member of an artists' circle consisting of other expatriates—Loomis, Blashfield, Ramsey and Bridgeman. When poor health led Pearce to travel on the Nile for several months in 1873 and 1874, he was accompanied by Bridgeman.

In 1876, Pearce began sending works to the Paris Salon, exhibiting mainly portraits, religious subjects and oriental genre scenes. He also exhibited at the 1876 Centennial in Philadelphia.

The artist executed sentimental interpretations of rural life in Northern France, allied in style and subject matter to the French academic peasant painters, Jules Bastien-Lepage and Jules Breton. His work was solidly modeled, details were meticulously recorded and textures were sensuous. His subjects were often exotic versions of the craftsman themes popularized in the United States during the 1880s and 1890s by such artists as Edgar Melville Ward and Jefferson David Chalfant.

Pearce remained an expatriate, settling 20 miles outside of Paris in Auvers-sur-Oise in 1885. There he worked all year long in a glass-enclosed outdoor

Going to Work, 29 x 24 in., signed l.r. Courtesy of Vose Galleries of Boston, Inc., Massachusetts.

studio. He held positions on many international art juries and, as the climax of his career, contributed a series of six lunette murals to the decoration of the Library of Congress at the turn of the century.

10-Year Average Change From Base Years '76-'77: 161%

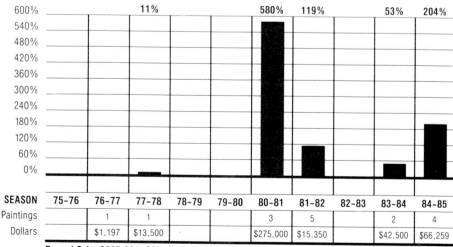

SEASON	75-76	76-77	77-78	78-79	79-80	80-81	81-82	82-83	83-84	84-85
Paintings		1	1			3	5		2	4
Dollars		$1,197	$13,500			$275,000	$15,350		$42,500	$66,259

Record Sale: $225,000, SPB, 6/19/81, "Reading by the Shore," 11 x 18 in.

JOSEPH H. GREENWOOD
(1857-1927)

Joseph H. Greenwood was an art instructor for many years, but it is for his New England landscapes that he is best known.

Greenwood was born in 1857 in Spencer, Massachusetts. Even as a boy, he strongly desired to paint, but he received little encouragement from his family. In his teens, Greenwood left home to work at a wire mill and devoted all his spare time to painting.

The mill owners, impressed with Greenwood's commitment, financed a trip to Boston, where the young man was able to study the rudiments of painting with a private instructor. Soon, however, his funds ran out, and he was forced to return to work at the mill.

Greenwood finally moved to Worcester, Massachusetts. After holding several factory jobs, he began to support himself by teaching art. At first he had only one pupil, but over time his classes grew in size. During those years, Greenwood painted constantly, and friends provided what financial support they could. Artistically, he was inspired and critically guided by painter R. Swain Gifford.

Greenwood taught for 20 years, until his own work gained recognition and painting became more remunerative than teaching.

For subjects, Greenwood almost exclusively painted the hills and lakes around Worcester. He avoided artists' colonies and steadfastly eschewed any particular school of art. "Men who follow a school are always behind," Greenwood said. "If you have anything to say, say it in your own way. The strong painters could not be budged one way or another."

Although many of the artist's landscapes were individually purchased, he is best represented in the Worcester Art Museum.

New England Farm Scene, ca. 1894, 13⅛ x 21 in., signed l.r. Courtesy of Colby College of Art, Waterville, Maine.

Greenwood died in 1927 in Worcester at the age of 70. Of his own life and early financial struggles, he said, "It gives you backbone to have to fight for what you get."

MEMBERSHIPS
Bohemian Club
Connecticut Academy of Fine Arts

PUBLIC COLLECTIONS
Worcester Art Museum, Massachusetts

SEASON	75-76	76-77	77-78	78-79	79-80	80-81	81-82	82-83	83-84	84-85
Paintings					1	3	3	1	2	2
Dollars					$800	$3,700	$2,475	$1,200	$2,050	$2,150

Record Sale: $1,600, S.BM, 5/15/85, "Autumn Landscape," 28 × 32 in.

EDWARD HENRY POTTHAST
(1857-1927)

Edward Henry Potthast was one of a number of significant American artists to emerge from Cincinnati during the nineteenth century. At the time of Potthast's birth in 1857, the Ohio city was a burgeoning art center, as well as a refuge for a number of recent German-immigrant families such as the Potthasts.

Potthast received his early art training at the McMicken School of Design, and at the Art Academy of Cincinnati. Many years before he would take up full-time painting, he established a career as a lithographer and illustrator in his native city.

Although Potthast first visited Munich at age 25 in 1882, he was 30 before he returned abroad to study for three years in Germany and Paris.

Moving to New York City in 1892, Potthast worked in his studio, dividing his time between painting and drawing illustrations for *Harper's* and *Scribner's* magazines. He would later give up lithography entirely to devote himself to painting.

Frequent trips West gave Potthast an opportunity to paint landscapes and to experiment with tonalist-inspired night scenes. But he is best known for his sun-drenched beach scenes. These enabled him to combine vigorous brushwork with an impressionist luminiscence inspired by Robert Vonnoh, an American artist Potthast had met during his Paris studies.

The Village Carpenter, ca. 1895, 30 x 20 in., signed l.l. Courtesy of Wunderlich and Company, Inc., New York, New York.

Splashing, 12½ x 16 in. Courtesy of Vose Galleries of Boston, Inc., Massachusetts.

As exemplified by *Swimming in the Surf* (date unknown, Kennedy Galleries), Potthast conveyed life and movement through a direct and almost sensual approach to landscape.

10-Year Average Change From Base Years '75-'76: 1,060%

SEASON	75-76	76-77	77-78	78-79	79-80	80-81	81-82	82-83	83-84	84-85
(% change)		205%	669%	128%	79%	2,864%	2,134%	2,182%	758%	1,579%
Paintings	5	7	15	17	7	5	37	22	17	11
Dollars	$6,600	$22,400	$126,950	$52,448	$15,250	$200,350	$1,110,400	$544,800	$238,150	$236,200

Record Sale: $160,000, SPB, 12/10/81, "Bathers by the Sea," 24×30 in.

MEMBERSHIPS
National Academy of Design

PUBLIC COLLECTIONS
Albright-Knox Art Gallery, Buffalo
Art Institute of Chicago
Brooklyn Museum
Cincinnati Art Museum

FRANCIS COATES JONES
(1857-1932)

The Serenade, 1890, 21½ x 32 in., signed l.l. Photograph courtesy of Borghi & Co. Fine Art Dealers, New York, New York.

Born in Baltimore in 1857, Francis Jones was a figure painter who specialized in genre scenes set in interiors, opulently decorated with elaborate furniture and accessories. His work was at once richly painted and academically precise, reflecting a style that was eventually influenced by impressionism, as in *Won't Play* (1880, Museum of Fine Arts, Springfield).

Jones first demonstrated an interest in art when visiting Edwin Austine Abbey in 1876. Traveling with his brother, landscape painter H. Bolton Jones, Francis Jones spent a year at the artists' colony in Pont-Aven, Brittany with such artists as Thomas Hovenden and Robert Wylie.

In the autumn of 1877, Jones left Pont-Aven for Paris, where he enrolled at the Ecole des Beaux-Arts and worked in the antique class under Henri Lehmann. He remained abroad for five years, making sketching tours of Italy, Switzerland and France.

During the winter of 1879 to 1880, Jones was in London, working on a military panorama. Returning to France, he continued his studies under the direction of William Adolphe Bouguereau and Jules Joseph Lefebvre, and attended a special class at the Ecole des Beaux-Arts.

As an illustrator, Jones did views of historic houses in Washington for *Scribner's* (October, 1893). Beginning in 1895, he worked as a mural painter. He also taught at the National Academy of

Design and spent summers painting in the Berkshire Mountains of South Egremont, Massachusetts.

Although his paintings reflected contemporary scenes, Jones's interest in costumes and decorative objects was always apparent. He died in 1932.

MEMBERSHIPS
American Federation of Artists
American Watercolor Society
Century Association
Lotus Club
National Academy of Design
National Arts Club
National Institute of Arts and Letters
National Society of Mural Painters
Salmagundi Club
Society of American Artists

PUBLIC COLLECTIONS
Art Institute of Chicago
Museum of Fine Arts, Springfield, Massachusetts

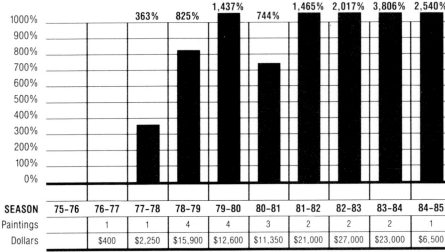

10-Year Average Change From Base Years '76-'77: 1,466%

SEASON	75-76	76-77	77-78	78-79	79-80	80-81	81-82	82-83	83-84	84-85
		363%	825%	1,437%		744%	1,465%	2,017%	3,806%	2,540%
Paintings		1	1	4	4	3	2	2	2	1
Dollars		$400	$2,250	$15,900	$12,600	$11,350	$21,000	$27,000	$23,000	$6,500

Record Sale: $17,000, BB.SF, 2/16/84, "Mother and Child," 20 × 27 in.

CHARLES WARREN EATON
(1857-1937)

Charles Warren Eaton was a watercolorist and landscape painter noted chiefly for his subtle brushwork and the sensitivity and intimacy of his work. In his early years he used subdued colors, employing delicate effects of light to create vague, suggestive moods. Some say that the strength of his paintings is in his depiction of the sky.

Today Eaton is best remembered for paintings of pine trees, done in his middle years. He did so many, in fact, that he was sometimes referred to as "The Pine Tree Painter."

During his childhood in Buffalo, New York, where he was born in 1857, he showed no interest in art. In his early twenties, however, he was so attracted to it that he quit his job as a dry goods clerk, moved to New York City and studied at the Arts Students League and at the National Academy of Design. By 1882, his work was good enough to be exhibited at the National Academy and one of his paintings was purchased by Oscar Wilde, who was visiting the city.

In the mid-1880s Eaton toured Europe, visiting great museums and the countrysides that had inspired Rembrandt, Constable and Corot. On his return to America, he met George Inness, the distinguished landscape painter. Despite a disparity of ages, the two became close friends. Inness also became the most important artistic influence in Eaton's life.

Evening Landscape, 20 x 24 in., signed l.r. Courtesy of Henry B. Holt, Inc., Essex Fells, New Jersey.

The paintings of Eaton's mature years generally fall into three groups: scenes in and around Bruges, Belgium; his paintings of pine forests; and views of hillside villages on Lake Como in Italy. Some of his paintings of canals near Bruges feature stark tree trunks as a repetitive motif.

In his Lake Como paintings, Eaton's usual understated technique gave way to impasto and choppier brush strokes, combined with a richer and much livelier palette.

After World War I Eaton went to Europe less frequently, preferring instead to paint at his summer studio in Connecticut. In 1921, he was one of several artists commissioned to paint scenes of Glacier National Park in Montana.

Realizing that both his technique and his inspiration were declining, Eaton gave up painting altogether in the decade before his death in 1937.

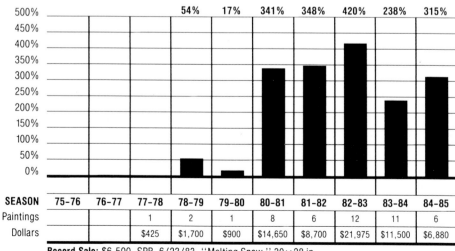

10-Year Average Change From Base Years '77-'78: 217%

			54%	17%	341%	348%	420%	238%	315%

SEASON	75-76	76-77	77-78	78-79	79-80	80-81	81-82	82-83	83-84	84-85
Paintings			1	2	1	8	6	12	11	6
Dollars			$425	$1,700	$900	$14,650	$8,700	$21,975	$11,500	$6,880

Record Sale: $6,500, SPB, 6/23/83, "Melting Snow," 30 × 28 in.

MEMBERSHIPS
American Federation of Arts
American Watercolor Society
Artists' Fund Society
Lotos Club
National Academy
New York Watercolor Club
Salmagundi Club

PUBLIC COLLECTIONS
Bloomfield Public Library, New Jersey
Brooklyn Museum
Butler Institute of American Art,
   Youngstown, Ohio
Cincinnati Art Museum
Historical Society of Bloomfield, New Jersey
Montclair Art Museum, New Jersey
Nashville Museum, Tennessee
National Gallery, Washington, D.C.
National Museum of American Art, Washington, D.C.
New Jersey Historical Society, Newark

HARRY WILLSON WATROUS
(1857-1940)

Harry Willson Watrous was a highly successful academic portrait painter. During his distinguished career he specialized in a wide variety of subjects, including genre paintings, idealized portraits of women, landscapes, night scenes and still lifes.

Born in San Francisco in 1857, Watrous spent his childhood in New York. He attended private schools in New York City.

After a trip to California in 1881, Watrous went abroad for approximately five years. He first studied with Humphrey Moore in Malaga and traveled through Southern Spain and Morocco. He studied at the Academie Julien in Paris under Leon Bonnat, Gustave Boulanger and Jules Joseph Lefebvre. The most important influence on Watrous's early work was genre painter Jean Louis Meissonier.

Watrous established himself as an academic genre painter early in his career. He painted finely detailed genre scenes, which included men in historical costumes and decorative interiors.

Around 1905, Watrous began to lose his eyesight and he began more innovative paintings. From 1905 to 1918, Watrous specialized in painting highly stylized women in seductive costumes. These pictures often included unusual birds or insects; their symbolic content contributed to their uniqueness.

From 1918 to 1923, Watrous changed his focus from the female figure to landscapes and night scenes. These paintings were influenced by the works of Watrous's friend, Ralph Blakelock. Both painters used contrasts of light and shadow in broad compositions.

After 1923, Watrous concentrated on detailed still lifes of decorative objects. He used antiques from his collection in these carefully observed paintings.

Regardless of subject matter, Watrous's work was rather academic in style. The surface of the oil paintings was smooth and highly polished. He drew the outlines of the objects with precision, and the compositions were classic in their simplicity.

Watrous was married to painter and author Elizabeth Snowden Nichols. He served as secretary of the National Academy of Design from 1898 to 1920, and as president of the Academy in 1933. Watrous died in New York City in 1940.

Oriental Still Life, 14 x 10 in., signed l.r. Photograph courtesy of M. Knoedler & Co., Inc., New York, New York.

MEMBERSHIPS
American Federation of Arts
Century Association
Lotus Club
National Academy of Design
National Arts Club
Salmagundi Club
Society of American Artists
Society of Painters

PUBLIC COLLECTIONS
Brooklyn Museum
City Art Museum, St. Louis
Corcoran Gallery, Washington, D.C.
Fort Worth Museum, Texas
Metropolitan Museum of Art, New York City
Montpelier Museum, Vermont
Portland Museum, Maine

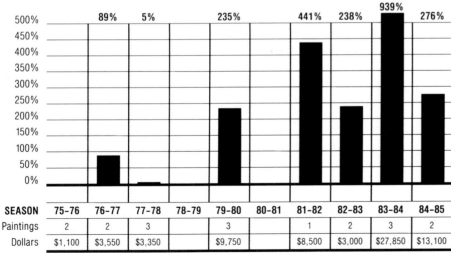

10-Year Average Change From Base Years '75-'76: 278%

SEASON	75-76	76-77	77-78	78-79	79-80	80-81	81-82	82-83	83-84	84-85
		89%	5%		235%		441%	238%	939%	276%
Paintings	2	2	3		3		1	2	3	2
Dollars	$1,100	$3,550	$3,350		$9,750		$8,500	$3,000	$27,850	$13,100

Record Sale: $16,000, SPB, 12/8/83, "The Magician," 32 × 25 in.

BRUCE CRANE
(1857-1937)

An acclaimed landscape painter of autumnal and twilight scenes, Robert Bruce Crane used a literal and detailed style before adopting the tonalism that characterized his later work. His popularity in the early 1900s attests to the continuing success of the barbizon and impressionist modes in America.

Born in New York City in 1857, Crane gained practical experience as a draftsman for an architect and builder. He began to paint in his spare time, later opening a studio in New York City. He received formal training from landscape painter Alexander H. Wyant, who influenced him to follow the barbizon style. Crane continued to study in Paris for a year and a half, painting outdoors near Grez-sur-Loing.

When he returned to New York in 1881, Crane achieved recognition for his plein-air landscapes of Eastern American scenes—the Adirondacks, Long Island, New Jersey and Connecticut. His greatest popularity, however, came in the late 1890s, when he won the Webb prize given by the Society of American Artists.

Crane spent a great number of his summers after 1904 in the popular artists' colony of Old Lyme, Connecticut. The artist sketched outdoors, as he once said, "to fill the memory with facts." He used light-tone pigments, applied to the canvas with a scrubby brush to achieve a rough, dry effect. This is well illustrated

Across the Marshes, 20 x 30 in., signed l.r. Courtesy of Henry B. Holt, Inc., Essex Fells, New Jersey.

in paintings such as *Autumn Uplands* (1908, Metropolitan Museum of Art) and *March* (date unknown, Brooklyn Museum), which rely less on detail and more upon beige, russet and brown tones to achieve their effect.

In 1915, Crane joined with Emil Carlsen, Charles H. Davis, and J. Alden Weir to establish Twelve Landscape Painters, an exhibiting organization of artists working in popular representational styles. He died in Bronxville, New York in 1937.

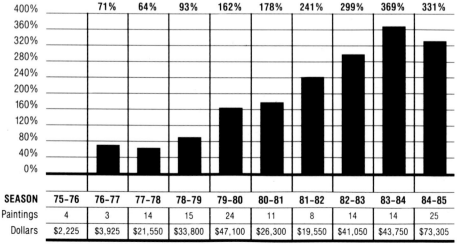

10-Year Average Change From Base Years '75-'76: 181%

	71%	64%	93%	162%	178%	241%	299%	369%	331%
SEASON	75-76	76-77	77-78	78-79	79-80	80-81	81-82	82-83	83-84	84-85
Paintings	4	3	14	15	24	11	8	14	14	25
Dollars	$2,225	$3,925	$21,550	$33,800	$47,100	$26,300	$19,550	$41,050	$43,750	$73,305

Record Sale: $12,000, W.W, 3/2/85, ''Autumn Interlude,'' 38 × 47 in.

MEMBERSHIPS
American Water Color Society
Artists' Fund Society
Associate National Academy of Design
Lotus Club
National Academy of Design
Salmagundi Club
Society of American Artists
Union Internationale des Beaux-Arts et des Lettres

PUBLIC COLLECTIONS
Brooklyn Museum
Corcoran Gallery of Art, Washington, D.C.
Fort Worth Museum, Texas
Hackley Art Gallery, Muskegon, Minnesota
Metropolitan Museum of Art, New York City
Montclair Art Museum, New Jersey
National Gallery of Art, Washington, D.C.
Peabody Institute, Baltimore
Pennsylvania Academy of the Fine Arts, Philadelphia
National Museum of American Art, Washington, D.C.
Syracuse Museum of Art, New York

PHILIP LITTLE
(1857-1942)

Philip Little was a painter and etcher who achieved some measure of success in the first three decades of the twentieth century with his paintings of coastal New England.

Little was born in Swampscott, Massachusetts, the son of one of the principal owners of the Pacific Mills factory in Lawrence, Massachusetts. He resisted his father's desire for him to enter the business, choosing instead to study design at the Massachusetts Institute of Technology from 1875 to 1877.

Following an unhappy year working in the Pacific Mills office, Little obtained a job with the Forbes Lithograph Company in Boston. Soon after, he entered the school of the Museum of Fine Arts in Boston, where he studied painting and etching from 1881 to 1882.

Little said that he did not begin to find his inspiration until around 1903, when he set up his studio on Derby Wharf in the old whaling port of Salem, Massachusetts. Here, he began to paint his mature work, scenes of the New England coast, reflecting the poetic influences of the barbizon style and some impressionistic lighting techniques.

By 1911, Little had begun to receive recognition in Europe and the Americas for his paintings, exhibiting his work in Buenos Aires and Rome, and at the Paris Salon of 1912. In the United States, Little won an honorable mention from the Art Institute of Chicago in 1912, and a silver medal at the Panama-Pacific International Exhibition of 1915 in San Francisco.

Philip Little was active in Salem civic affairs, serving as a councilman and a member of the board of health. He remained socially and professionally active until his death in Salem in 1942.

Watching the Tide, 36 x 36 in., signed l.r. Courtesy of Arvest Galleries, Inc., Boston, Massachusetts.

MEMBERSHIPS
American Society of Etchers
Minneapolis Institute of Art
National Arts Club
Portland (Maine) Society of the Arts

PUBLIC COLLECTIONS
Bowdoin College Museum of Art,
   Brunswick, Maine
Essex Institute, Salem, Massachusetts
Library of Congress, Washington, D.C.
Minneapolis Institute of Art
Museum of Fine Arts, Boston
New York Public Library, New York City
Rhode Island School of Design, Providence
St. Louis Art Museum

SEASON	75-76	76-77	77-78	78-79	79-80	80-81	81-82	82-83	83-84	84-85
Paintings				2	3	5	3	3	1	2
Dollars				$4,900	$3,475	$12,500	$4,950	$1,850	$475	$8,600

Record Sale: $8,000, BB.SF, 11/8/84, ''Train Crossing a Harbor,'' 36 × 50 in.

ERNEST ALBERT
(1857-1946)

A distinguished theatrical and scenic designer, Ernest Albert worked in New York, St. Louis and Chicago. Born in Brooklyn in 1857, he showed early talent and received the Graham Art Medal at age 15, while he was studying at the Brooklyn Art Institute. Though Albert had some early success as a newspaper artist, his introduction to the theater world in 1877 began a career in stage design; he worked on productions starring most of the best-known performers of the day. During this time, in 1879, he employed and befriended young Jules Guerin, who went on to become the Lincoln Memorial muralist.

From New York City, Albert went to St. Louis in 1880 and five years later to Chicago. In 1892, he became involved with the World's Columbian Exposition in Chicago. He was responsible for the color schemes and ornamental design of many of the interiors of buildings in that renowned and successful fair. While in Chicago, he helped found the American Society of Scenic Painters.

In 1894, Albert returned to New York City, where his work in scenic design was centered from then on. His Albert Studios did the sets for many successful productions.

All along, he had painted whenever he could snatch the time. At the pinnacle of his career in 1905, he began to withdraw gradually from his theater work. His family was settled in the striking new

Yellow Mill, 26 x 28 in., signed l.r. Courtesy of Connecticut Gallery, Marlborough, Connecticut.

house he had built in New Rochelle, New York and his financial independence was established. From then on, he devoted most of his considerable talent and energy to his landscapes.

Albert's landscapes, painted mostly in Old Lyme, Connecticut and later on Monhegan Island, Maine (as well as a few on the West Coast), are simple in composition but subtle in effect. His impressionistic rendering of color and light imbue his quiet country scenes with all the magic of the moment. The gentle strength of these pictures and of his still lifes ensured their popularity and earned him a place as one of America's respected artists.

Albert was active in several organizations and was a founder and first president of the Allied Artists of America. Ernest Albert, Jr. (1891-1955), his son, was also a painter.

Albert died at age 88 in New Canaan, Connecticut in 1946.

MEMBERSHIPS
Allied Artists of America
American Society of Scenic Painters
American Water Color Society
Chicago Society of Artists
Connecticut Academy of Fine Arts
Lyme Art Association
National Academy of Design
National Arts Club
New Haven Paint and Clay Club
New Rochelle Art Association
St. Louis Sketch Club
Salmagundi Club
Silvermine Guild of Artists

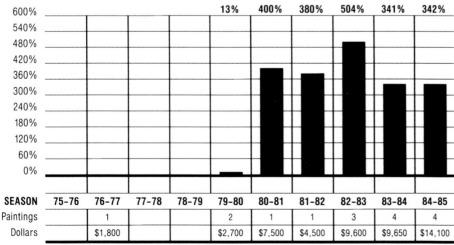

10-Year Average Change From Base Years '76-'77: 283%

					13%	400%	380%	504%	341%	342%

SEASON	75-76	76-77	77-78	78-79	79-80	80-81	81-82	82-83	83-84	84-85
Paintings		1			2	1	1	3	4	4
Dollars		$1,800			$2,700	$7,500	$4,500	$9,600	$9,650	$14,100

Record Sale: $7,500, SPB, 5/29/81, "Summer Pastoral," 30 × 40 in.

CHARLES FREDERIC ULRICH
(1858-1908)

Charles Frederic Ulrich was encouraged by his father, a painter and photographer, to study art. He was at the National Academy of Design in New York City in 1875. Shortly thereafter, he enrolled in the Royal Academy at Munich, learning the techniques and realistic styles of its popular artists.

Ulrich was influenced by his appreciation of the Dutch old masters. His work was characterized by detailed costumes and still lifes, and by the use of dark, rich colors. The German genre painters' scenes of peasant life also permanently influenced Ulrich's style.

Returning to the United States sometime before 1882, he exhibited at the National Academy of Design and was elected an associate a year later.

The Pennsylvania Dutch and their costumes caught Ulrich's interest, which later turned to immigrants. In 1884 his painting *In the Land of Promise—Castle Garden* (date and location unknown) won the National Academy of Design's first Thomas B. Clarke prize.

In 1885, Ulrich went to Holland, where he was influenced by the work of Vermeer and de Hooch. Venice became home in 1886, and he painted *Glass Blowers of Murano* (location unknown), which won a large cash prize and was superior to his earlier *Glass Blowers* (1883).

Critics praised Ulrich's purity of color and exquisite technique. While executing almost photographic precision and control, Ulrich tailored tonal changes and composition to his subjects. A series on workers at their crafts, sometimes painted on wood, attracted further praise and prominent collectors.

Except for a visit to New York City in 1891, Ulrich lived abroad for the rest of his life. He retained contact with Robert Blum and William Merritt Chase in the 1880s, and the 1890s and helped organize American exhibits in Munich. From 1900 until his death in Berlin in 1908, he worked and exhibited in Paris, London and Munich.

At the Embroidery Hoop, 15¾ x 14⅝ in., signed u.l. Photograph courtesy of Hirschl & Adler Galleries, Inc., New York, New York.

MEMBERSHIPS
National Academy of Design
Society of American Artists
Society of Painters in Pastel

PUBLIC COLLECTIONS
Corcoran Art Gallery, Washington, D.C.
Metropolitan Museum of Art, New York City

SEASON	75-76	76-77	77-78	78-79	79-80	80-81	81-82	82-83	83-84	84-85
Paintings								1		
Dollars								$27,000		

Record Sale: $27,000, SPB, 6/2/83, "Vanitas," 9 × 17 in.

540

WILLIAM VERPLANCK BIRNEY
(1858-1909)

Two Men Conversing, 12 x 15¼ in. Courtesy of Vose Galleries of Boston, Inc., Massachusetts.

William Verplanck Birney's first success seems to have charted his course for the rest of his life. He was one of two Americans who sold pictures in 1883 at the International Exhibition in Munich. His painting *A Quiet Corner* (date and location unknown) was a simple scene portraying a daydreaming young German peasant girl, but the important thing was that it told a story.

Moments in time—sentimental, poignant, sometimes merely thoughtful—are what Birney wanted to catch. The moments are occasionally painful in the extreme. In *Deserted* (date and location unknown), a village girl watches from a window with a sympathetic friend while a wedding party, including her ex-lover and his bride, enters a vine-covered church across the way.

To illustrate a variety of emotions as well as the faith of the Christian martyrs, Birney painted *The Last Token* (date and location unknown), which shows a young woman leaning down to pick up a rose in the midst of wild animals.

Birney drew his subject matter from everywhere—Germany, Italy, France, America and especially rural England. Wherever he happened to be, he painted his studies on the spot. Paintings of unusual roofs, castle kitchens, cottage and ale-cellar interiors were other subjects he explored. Authentic detail and expertise in color and composition gave his work strength.

Birney was born in Cincinnati, Ohio in 1858. He was educated in Washington, D.C., Boston, Philadelphia (the Pennsylvania Academy of the Fine Arts) and Munich (the Royal Academy). He died in 1909.

MEMBERSHIPS
Fine Arts Federation
Lotos Club
National Academy of Design
New York Watercolor Club
Salmagundi Club

10-Year Average Change From Base Years '78-'79: 46%

				-29%	83%	172%	32%	13%	51%

SEASON	75-76	76-77	77-78	78-79	79-80	80-81	81-82	82-83	83-84	84-85
Paintings				4	1	1	1	7	6	3
Dollars				$5,550	$1,100	$5,000	$1,900	$23,910	$12,450	$6,300

Record Sale: $9,500, SPB, 10/22/82, "The Ghost Story," 26 x 40 in.

HENRY WARD RANGER
(1858-1916)

A painter of idyllic landscapes, Henry Ward Ranger was born in Syracuse, New York. His formal training was in Paris at the Ecole des Beaux Arts, where he was attracted to genre painters Josef Israels and Anton Mauve, who practiced a style of heavily romantic realism. When Ranger returned to America, his dreamy New England scenes almost seemed to be replicas of the landscapes of Corot or Diaz in the late 1860s—an American adaptation of the barbizon style.

In 1884, Ranger set up a New York studio. Due to the vogue for landscapes at the turn of the century, he was soon very successful. In about 1900, the artist began spending half of his time in Old Lyme, Connecticut. There he founded the American Barbizon School, which produced no major American artists but which had a profound effect on early-twentieth-century landscapists and photographers.

Best known for woodland scenes, often in rich autumnal colors unified by controlled light and shade, Ranger excelled at creating an atmospheric effect. He arrived at an almost balletic compromise between descriptive realism and poetic vision. His approach to realism was direct only in that he sketched in the open air. He finished his work in the studio in the true academic manners usually including a dark foreground plane dappled with flecks of sunlight, an intermediate winding path or glade, and a misty, light-filled distance.

The Forest Road, Early Spring, 28 x 36 in., signed l.l. Courtesy of Connecticut Gallery, Marlborough.

Typical of Ranger's later period is *High Bridge, New York* (1905, Corcoran Gallery of Art). This romanticized interpretation of the urban landscape focuses upon the bridge itself, its curved forms mirrored in the water below. The Manhattan skyline in the distance is immersed in a luminous haze.

At Ranger's death, he bequeathed a sum of money to the National Academy of Design to create the Ranger Fund, allotted for the purchase of works by young artists.

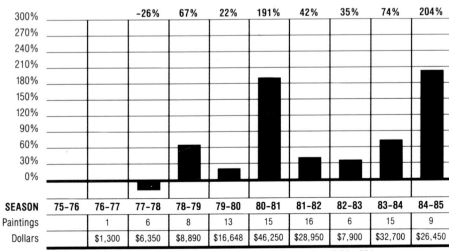

10-Year Average Change From Base Years '76-'77: 68%

		−26%	67%	22%	191%	42%	35%	74%	204%
SEASON	75-76	76-77	77-78	78-79	79-80	80-81	81-82	82-83	83-84	84-85
Paintings		1	6	8	13	15	16	6	15	9
Dollars		$1,300	$6,350	$8,890	$16,648	$46,250	$28,950	$7,900	$32,700	$26,450

Record Sale: $18,000, SPB, 6/4/81, "Harbour at Noank, Connecticut," 28×36 in.

MEMBERSHIPS
American Water Color Society
National Academy of Design

PUBLIC COLLECTIONS
Corcoran Gallery of Art,
   Washington, D.C.
Metropolitan Museum of Art, New York City
National Museum of American Art, Washington, D.C.

WILLARD LEROY METCALF

(1858-1925)

Willard Leroy Metcalf was a popular and successful painter, whose luminous and colorful New England landscapes were an extension of American impressionism.

Metcalf received encouragement in pursuing an artistic career from his parents. He was born in 1858 in Lowell, Massachusetts. At 17, he studied in Boston under landscape artist George Loring Brown and attended classes at the Lowell Institute and the School of the Museum of Fine Arts in Boston.

Accompanied by ethnologist Frank Cushing, Metcalf spent the years from 1881 to 1883 in the Southwest. Metcalf sketched illustrations of Indians and desert life in oil, watercolor and crayon. Their sale to *Harper's Magazine* enabled him to afford a trip to Europe in 1883.

At the time, impressionism was beginning to make its impact on European art. However, the instruction Metcalf received at the Academie Julien in Paris was stylistically conservative. One of the first Americans to visit the French village of Giverny where many impressionists worked, Metcalf would not incorporate their techniques in his paintings until the early 1900s.

Metcalf's one celebrated painting during his five years in Europe was *Ten Cent Breakfast* (1887, Denver Art Museum), a somber interior showing fellow artists and friends.

Settling in New York City in 1889, Metcalf supported himself primarily

Winter's Mantle, 1922, 26 x 29 in., signed l.r. Courtesy of Vose Galleries of Boston, Inc., Massachusetts.

through teaching at Cooper Union and selling illustrations to *Scribner's* and *Century.* He continued to paint.

A 1903 trip to Maine marked a decisive change in Metcalf's artistic style. His largely seasonal landscapes were infused with heightened color and luminosity and exhibited the broken brushstrokes characteristic of impressionism. As seen in *The North Country* (1923,

Metropolitan Museum of Art), many of Metcalf's landscapes attempt to convey a specific sense of place as well as atmospheric effect.

Enthusiastic about what Metcalf himself called his impressionist "renaissance," he became one of the founding members of The Ten American Painters. For 20 years, these artists popularized impressionism through frequent group exhibits. Metcalf also became an influential member of the art colony in Old Lyme, Connecticut.

Though he maintained a studio in New York City until his death there in 1925, Metcalf spent much of his time traveling and painting in New England.

MEMBERSHIPS
American Academy of Arts and Letters
American Watercolor Society
Century Association

PUBLIC COLLECTIONS
Art Institute of Chicago
Corcoran Gallery, Washington, D.C.
Metropolitan Museum of Art, New York City
Museum of Fine Arts, Boston
Museum of New Mexico, Santa Fe
National Gallery of Art, Washington, D.C.
Pennsylvania Academy of the Fine Arts, Philadelphia

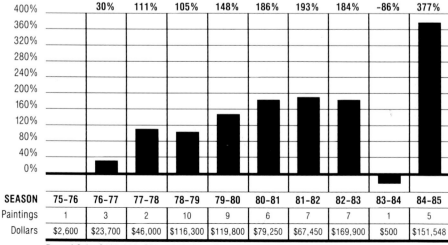

10-Year Average Change From Base Years '75-'76: 125%

	30%	111%	105%	148%	186%	193%	184%	-86%	377%

SEASON	75-76	76-77	77-78	78-79	79-80	80-81	81-82	82-83	83-84	84-85
Paintings	1	3	2	10	9	6	7	7	1	5
Dollars	$2,600	$23,700	$46,000	$116,300	$119,800	$79,250	$67,450	$169,900	$500	$151,548

Record Sale: $135,000, SPB, 12/6/84, ''The Landing Place,'' 26 x 29 in.

HENRY SIDDONS MOWBRAY
(1858-1928)

Idle Hours, 1895, 12 x 16 in., signed l.l. Courtesy of National Museum of American Art, Smithsonian Institution, Gift of William T. Evans.

Henry Siddons Mowbray was considered one of America's most versatile artists during the late nineteenth and early twentieth centuries.

Born in Alexandria, Egypt in 1858, he was brought to the United States the following year. He spent a brief and unhappy time at West Point Military Academy, where he did some illustrations for Homer Lee's *West Point Tic Tacs: A Collection of Military Verse* (1879).

After leaving the Academy, Mowbray received art instruction from Alfred Cornelius. In 1879, he went to Paris, where for the next seven years he studied under Leon Bonnat and was influenced by academic artists, particularly Jean Leon Gerome.

At first Mowbray painted genre scenes, and by 1883 his work had earned critical recognition and some commercial success. The following year, he began producing oriental figure paintings, which became his trademark for the next 15 years.

In 1886, Mowbray began a 15-year tenure as a teacher at the Art Students League.

Beginning in 1897, he devoted himself almost exclusively to painting murals, using an idealized figure style inspired by Renaissance art.

In the 1900s, Mowbray received many commissions for murals in public buildings and residences. He was so captivated by the murals and decorative designs of Pinturicchio that initially he produced close imitations; later he incorporated Pinturicchio's technique into his own style.

From 1924 until his death in 1928, Mowbray moved from decorative work to easel paintings depicting events in the life of Christ.

MEMBERSHIPS
American Academy in Rome
American Federation of Artists
National Institution of Artists

PUBLIC COLLECTIONS
Appellate Court House,
 New York City
Federal Court Room, Cleveland

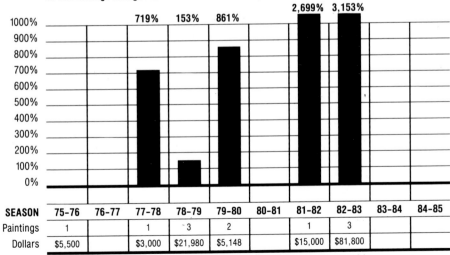

10-Year Average Change From Base Years '75-'76: 1,264%

SEASON	75-76	76-77	77-78	78-79	79-80	80-81	81-82	82-83	83-84	84-85
			719%	153%	861%		2,699%	3,153%		
Paintings	1		1	3	2		1	3		
Dollars	$5,500		$3,000	$21,980	$5,148		$15,000	$81,800		

Record Sale: $40,000, DM.D, 11/21/82, "Two Women in an Interior," 14 × 18 in.

544

JULIUS ROLSHOVEN
(1858-1930)

Julius Rolshoven became an award-winning painter who specialized in depicting the effects of light.

Born in 1858 in Detroit, Rolshoven attempted to enroll at the National Academy of Design in New York City, but was rejected because his work was considered unacceptable.

Undaunted, he attended Cooper Union night school in New York City in 1877. The next year he studied with Hugo Crola at the Academy of Dusseldorf, followed by three years of study with Loeffitz at the Royal Academy in Munich.

In 1812, Rolshoven studied in Paris with Robert-Fleury at the Academie Julien. He also studied briefly with Frank Duveneck in Florence.

The student turned teacher in 1890, when Rolshoven began to teach in Paris. Six years later, he taught in London.

Rolshoven traveled to Italy the next year and stayed there until World War I began, when he returned to the United States.

Having become known as one of the classic Eastern painters, Rolshoven moved West, setting up a studio in Santa Fe, New Mexico in 1916. He lived in Santa Fe for three years, and divided his final 11 years between Italy and New Mexico, until his death in 1930.

In New Mexico, Rolshoven made friends with many of the Indians by painting their portraits. He softened the harsh New Mexico light by setting up a tent as an outdoor studio. The romanticism and "old-master" look that he developed in Europe characterized his Western paintings. For example, *Sun Arrow* (date unknown, Museum of New Mexico) shows an Indian chief mounted on a prancing horse, suggesting the style of Velasquez or Rubens.

Indian Dancer, 27 x 15 in., signed l.l. Photograph courtesy of The Gerald Peters Gallery, Santa Fe, New Mexico.

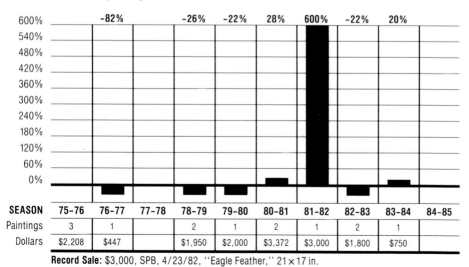

10-Year Average Change From Base Years '75-'76: 62%

		-82%		-26%	-22%	28%	600%	-22%	20%	
SEASON	75-76	76-77	77-78	78-79	79-80	80-81	81-82	82-83	83-84	84-85
Paintings	3	1		2	1	2	1	2	1	
Dollars	$2,208	$447		$1,950	$2,000	$3,372	$3,000	$1,800	$750	

Record Sale: $3,000, SPB, 4/23/82, "Eagle Feather," 21 x 17 in.

MEMBERSHIPS
Foreign Arts Club
International Art Congress
National Academy of Design
National Arts Club
Paris Society of Artists and Lithographers
Society Nationale des Beaux-Arts, Paris
Taos Society of Artists

PUBLIC COLLECTIONS
Baltimore Museum of Art
Brooklyn Museum
Cincinnati Museum of Art
Detroit Institute of Arts
Minnesota Museum of Art, St. Paul
Museum of New Mexico, Santa Fe

ROBERT WILLIAM VONNOH
(1858-1933)

Robert William Vonnoh was one of the earliest painters to introduce European impressionism to America. Vonnoh was a highly renowned academic portrait painter and an impressionist landscape painter. He won an impressive number of awards and was a member of a number of art organizations.

Born in Hartford, Connecticut in 1858, Vonnoh was raised in Boston. As a young man, he worked for a lithographic firm and studied with local artists. He studied at the Massachusetts Normal Art School from 1875 to 1881. From 1881 to 1883, Vonnoh studied under Gustave Boulanger and Jules Joseph Lefebvre at the Academie Julien. From 1884 to 1885, he taught at the Cowles Art School, and from 1885 to 1887, he taught at the School of the Museum of Fine Arts in Boston.

In 1887, Vonnoh returned to Paris and studied there for the next four years. He encountered French impressionism and was particularly fascinated by the work of Claude Monet. Monet's free, impressionistic style of painting strongly influenced Vonnoh's subsequent landscape paintings.

In 1891, Vonnoh returned to America and brought his enthusiasm for French impressionism to the Pennsylvania Academy of the Fine Arts. He was an instructor at the Academy until 1896; his pupils included William Glackens and Robert Henri.

Vonnoh's style was similar to that of Camille Pissarro; both preferred cool tones of muted colors and carefully balanced compositions. Vonnoh used spontaneous brushstrokes and pure colors in his realistic depictions of nature. He had the ability to capture natural light, color and atmosphere in a landscape.

In addition to his impressionistic landscapes, Vonnoh painted more than 500 commissioned portraits. Unlike his landscapes, these academic portraits were rather conventional and formal in style.

Indian Summer, 24 x 30 in., signed l.l. Courtesy of Connecticut Gallery, Marlborough.

In 1899, Vonnoh married sculptor Bessie Potter. From 1918 to 1920, he again served as an instructor at the Pennsylvania Academy of the Fine Arts. He died in Nice, France in 1933.

MEMBERSHIPS
Allied Artists of America
American Art Association of Paris
Architectural League of New York
Connecticut Academy of Fine Arts
Fellowship of the Pennsylvania Academy of the
    Fine Arts
National Academy of Design
National Association of Portrait Painters
Salmagundi Club
Society of American Artists

PUBLIC COLLECTIONS
Brooklyn Museum
Cleveland Museum of Art
Los Angeles County Museum of Art
Metropolitan Museum of Art, New York City
Pennsylvania Academy of the Fine Arts,
    Philadelphia
White House, Washington, D.C.

SEASON	75-76	76-77	77-78	78-79	79-80	80-81	81-82	82-83	83-84	84-85
Paintings		2	3	1	7	2	4	4	3	2
Dollars		$15,250	$13,600	$450	$59,050	$10,150	$21,600	$17,100	$7,900	$2,400

Record Sale: $15,500, SPB, 3/17/80, "Autumn Morning, Connecticut," 30 × 25 in.

CHARLES PARTRIDGE ADAMS
(1858-1942)

Mountain Landscape, 14 x 20 in., signed l.l. Courtesy of Grand Central Art Galleries, Inc., New York, New York.

The greater part of Charles Adams's career was devoted to capturing the drama of the Rocky Mountains and other scenes of the American West. Born in 1858, in Franklin, Massachusetts, Adams moved to Denver for health reasons in 1876; he soon became one of Colorado's favorite artists.

Employed first as an engraver in a bookstore, Adams advertised his services for landscapes and crayon portraits. He studied briefly at the Denver art school of Mrs. James Albert Chaim (or Chain), a former student of landscapist George Inness.

By the time Adams was 25, his work was in demand. He opened a summer studio, "The Sketch Box," in Estes Park near Longs Peak, Colorado—a center for his work, study and teaching for more than 40 years.

From it, he traveled to paint the Rockies, Estes Park, the Tetons and Yellowstone Park, the Spanish peaks, the San Juan and San Miguel Mountains and the New Mexico desert. With authoritative skill and realism, his work projects the natural atmosphere of these rugged Western landscapes, particularly in their changing, dramatic extremes.

Adams left the West once, to tour European galleries in 1914. He moved to California about 1916. In Laguna Beach, he turned to marine subjects, conveying the same realism and vitality his landscapes exhibited.

When Adams died in 1942, at age 84, he had completed some 800 paintings and numerous sketches.

MEMBERSHIPS
Denver Artists Club
Laguna Art Association

PUBLIC COLLECTIONS
Colorado State University, Boulder
Denver Art Association
Denver Art Museum
Kansas City Art Association, Missouri
San Diego Woman's Club

SEASON	75-76	76-77	77-78	78-79	79-80	80-81	81-82	82-83	83-84	84-85
Paintings				2	7	7	4	3	4	7
Dollars				$1,210	$8,050	$7,450	$3,700	$4,150	$4,350	$8,250

Record Sale: $2,800, CH, 12/5/80, "Near Silverton, Colorado," 10 × 14 in.

CHARLES VEZIN
(1858-1942)

Winter Day, The Palisades, 6⅛ x 8 in., signed l.r. Florence Griswold Museum, Lyme Historical Society, Old Lyme, Connecticut. Gift of Mrs. Robert D. Graff.

Sunlight in the Woods, 36 x 28 in., signed l.r. Courtesy of Marbella Gallery, Inc., New York, New York. Photograph by Richard Haynes.

Charles Vezin came late to the formal study of art, being nearly 40 when he enrolled at the Art Students League in New York City, but he brought to his avocation a worshipful attitude towards art, a tremendous enthusiasm, and a hearty, solid landscape style which earned him recognition and honor.

Vezin was born in Philadelphia in 1858. After military school, he studied in Germany. When he came back, he was first a salesman, then a dry goods entrepreneur.

At the same time Vezin started his business, he entered the Art Students League, studying with William Merritt Chase. He seems to have adopted some of Chase's methods, but rejected impressionism. Vezin became an energetic and controversial writer of articles outlining his theories of art and expressing his disgust for modernism.

He achieved swift success as a painter, specializing in New York cityscapes and Brooklyn waterfront scenes. His fellow artists recognized him by electing him president of the Art Students League in 1911 and of the Salmagundi Club in 1914, though he did not abandon the dry goods business for the full-time pursuit of painting until 1919.

Until his death in 1942 at his summer home in Coral Gables, Florida, Vezin exhibited widely, painted energetically, preached his gospel of art and thrived on controversy.

MEMBERSHIPS
American Federation of Arts
American Fine Arts Society
Art Alliance
Art Students League
Brooklyn Society of Artists
Century Club
National Academy of Design
New York Water Color Club
Painters and Sculptors of Brooklyn
Salmagundi Club

PUBLIC COLLECTIONS
Atlanta Art Gallery
High Museum, Atlanta
New-York Historical Society, New York City

SEASON	75-76	76-77	77-78	78-79	79-80	80-81	81-82	82-83	83-84	84-85
Paintings				1	1	2	2		1	
Dollars				$1,200	$5,500	$3,500	$5,200		$2,800	

Record Sale: $5,500, SPB, 3/17/80, "The Hudson," 28 × 36 in.

HENRY BAYLEY SNELL
(1858-1943)

Henry Bayley Snell was among the earliest artists to settle in the picturesque Delaware River Valley in Bucks County, Pennsylvania. Affiliated with the New Hope School of American impressionism, he was known throughout the region both as a painter of landscape and marine subjects and as a prominent instructor of art.

Born in Richmond, England in 1858, Snell came to New York City at age 17. He began his study at the Art Students League, supporting himself by working in the blueprint department of an engineering firm, and then by producing marine scenes for a lithography studio.

In 1888, Snell married artist Florence Francis. Before settling in New Hope, he taught art in New York City and Washington, D.C.

Snell and his wife first came to New Hope in 1898 to visit William Langson Lathrop, a prominent American tonalist painter and founder of the New Hope School. For many years Lathrop's home and studio served as the area's community center for art instruction and exhibition. Snell moved to New Hope in 1900.

He taught art at the Philadelphia School of Design for Women from 1899 to 1943. He also traveled extensively, as far as India, and regularly journeyed abroad with his students to France, England, Germany, Holland and Spain.

Snell is noted for his coastal scenes of St. Ives, Cornwall, England, a region which his New Hope colleague Walter Elmer Schofield also frequented. He also painted harbor scenes of Gloucester, Massachusetts and Boothbay Harbor, Maine. A great many of his works are of New Hope street scenes and landscapes of the rural Delaware River Valley.

Although he painted directly from nature, following the practice of New Hope painters, Snell's style is unusual; it

Late Twilight, 16 x 24 in., signed l.l. Courtesy of Marbella Gallery, Inc., New York, New York.

Near St. Ives, 11⅝ x 15⅝ in., signed l.l. Gift of the North Carolina Art Society, Raleigh, North Carolina. (Robert F. Phifer bequest.)

is not dynamic and bold like that of Edward Willis Redfield, nor is it akin to the sensitive, intricate brushwork of Daniel Garber. Instead, Snell's modest-sized canvases are painted with broad, flat passages of pigment, illuminated with soft, permeating hues.

Snell's work is not typical of the regional impressionistic style, with its emphasis on capturing seasonal and atmospheric conditions, yet he remains important as an early member of the

New Hope art colony, one whose reputation as a painter and teacher lured many younger artists to this Pennsylvania region.

SEASON	75-76	76-77	77-78	78-79	79-80	80-81	81-82	82-83	83-84	84-85
Paintings			1			1				
Dollars			$2,750			$700				

Record Sale: $2,750, SPB, 11/8/77, "Old Windjammer," 34 × 44 in.

MARY LOUISE FAIRCHILD MacMONNIES LOW
(1858-1946)

Mary Louise Fairchild MacMonnies Low, a portrait and mural painter, was born in 1858 in New Haven, Connecticut. A descendant of Governor Bradford of the *Mayflower,* she attended St. Louis Art Academy on a scholarship after her family moved to that city. She later studied under Carolus-Duran at the Academie Julien in Paris.

In 1888 in Paris, she married sculptor Frederick MacMonnies. As successful artists who each received acclaim at the 1893 Chicago Exposition, they were part of the circle that included James McNeill Whistler. They also summered at Giverny, a popular spot in the 1890s for American artists seeking the inspiration of Monet.

By 1909, the couple had divorced, and she married Will Hickok Low, an academic mural painter. She returned to the United States with her new husband, and lived in Bronxville, New York until her death in 1946. After the divorce, she dropped her earlier name, and avoided all references to MacMonnies.

The artist's work reflects several phases of development. At first, she painted in a sunlit style reminiscent of her teacher Carolus-Duran. She then entered a misty, tonal phase. She primarily painted dark, academic portraits after her marriage to Low, but in her final years, she returned to a lighter, impressionistic style.

MEMBERSHIPS
American Women's Art Association
National Academy of Design
Society of American Artists
Societe Nationale des Beaux-Arts
Womans Art Club
Womans International Art Club

PUBLIC COLLECTIONS
Art Institute of Chicago
Musee des Beaux-Arts, Rouen, France
St. Louis Art Museum
Union League Club, Chicago
Museum of Vernon, France

Portrait of Berthe Helene MacMonnies, 1896, 62 x 38 in., signed u.l. Private Collection. Photograph courtesy of Hirschl & Adler Galleries, Inc., New York, New York.

SEASON	75-76	76-77	77-78	78-79	79-80	80-81	81-82	82-83	83-84	84-85
Paintings							1			
Dollars							$16,000			

Record Sale: $16,000, P.NY, 12/14/81, "Portrait of Berthe Helene MacMonnies," 61 × 37 in.

550

ELBRIDGE AYER BURBANK
(1858-1949)

Elbridge Ayer Burbank created a great American heritage—an invaluable portrait gallery of American Indians of the West.

Beginning in 1895, Burbank drew and painted from life more than 1,200 pictures of leaders and members of some 125 Western tribes. He painted many chiefs, among them Geronimo, Joseph, Sitting Bull, Red Cloud and Rain in the Face. But hundreds of other subjects were chosen for their distinctive individual and tribal character. Born in 1858 at Harvard, Illinois, Burbank earned honors as a student at the Art Institute of Chicago. On graduation, an assignment from *Northeast Magazine* took him through the Rockies to the Washington State coast, painting Western scenes to promote land sales for the Northern Pacific Railway.

In 1886, Burbank went to Munich to study with Paul Nauen and Frederick Fehr. Four years later, he returned to Chicago and specialized in portraits, particularly of Negro subjects.

His major lifework was launched in 1895 by his uncle, Edward E. Ayer, first president of the Field Columbia Museum, trustee of the Newberry Library and collector of Indian lore. He commissioned Burbank to do portraits of living, prominent Indian chiefs.

Burbank traveled through Oklahoma, New Mexico and Arizona, among the Navajo, Hopi and Zuni. He portrayed numerous California tribes, and later, the Sioux, Crow, Nez Perce and Ute.

Chief Black-Coyote, 1901, 13 x 9 in., signed l.l. Courtesy of National Museum of American Art, Smithsonian Institution, Lent by Smithsonian Institution, National Museum of Natural History, Department of Anthropology.

Burbank liked the Indians; they were frequent guests at his table and in his home. Chief Geronimo, before his death in 1909, told Burbank he liked him better than any white man he had known.

Burbank's work displays not only technical maturity and extraordinary representational skill, but sympathy and genuine respect for his subjects. Working in oil, watercolor and crayon, with remarkably fresh effect, he produced strong, insightful portraits and scenes. They form the final poignant record of the proud Indian cultures on the eve of their dissolution.

Burbank died in San Francisco in 1949, at age 90.

PUBLIC COLLECTIONS
Field Museum, Chicago
Hubbell Trading Post Museum, Ganado, Arizona
National Gallery of Art, Washington, D.C.
Newberry Library, Chicago

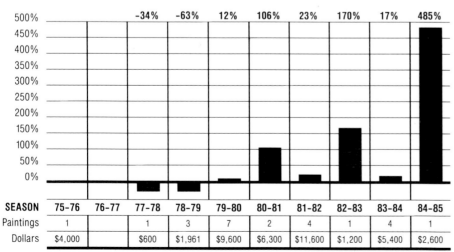

10-Year Average Change From Base Years '75-'76: 80%

	75-76	76-77	77-78	78-79	79-80	80-81	81-82	82-83	83-84	84-85
			-34%	-63%	12%	106%	23%	170%	17%	485%
SEASON	75-76	76-77	77-78	78-79	79-80	80-81	81-82	82-83	83-84	84-85
Paintings	1		1	3	7	2	4	1	4	1
Dollars	$4,000		$600	$1,961	$9,600	$6,300	$11,600	$1,200	$5,400	$2,600

Record Sale: $5,000, CH, 12/5/80, "Chief Stinking Bear Sioux," 15 x 14 in.

551

HELEN MARIA TURNER
(1858-1958)

Helen Maria Turner was an active member of the art colony in Cragsmoor, New York, particularly well known for her oil paintings of women in gardens and interiors.

Born in Louisville, Kentucky in 1858, Turner spent her childhood and early adulthood in New Orleans. She was orphaned at age 13 and grew up in genteel poverty.

Turner began painting at age 22; she took classes at the New Orleans Art Union around 1890. From 1893 to 1895, she was an instructor at an Episcopal school for girls in Dallas, Texas.

In 1895, Turner moved to New York City and enrolled in the Art Students League, where she studied under Kenyon Cox and Douglas Volk. In 1898, she also enrolled in the Women's Art School of Cooper Union in order to continue studying portraiture with Volk. She earned a diploma from Cooper Union. From 1899 to 1900, Turner was enrolled in the Fine Arts Department of the Teachers' College of Columbia University, where she was accepted as a temporary instructor and received a scholarship.

In 1902, Turner was hired as a teacher in the Art School of the New York City Young Women's Christian Association. She taught life drawing, drawing from casts, and costume drawing. She continued to teach for 17 years and retired in 1919.

Turner was a true American impressionist painter who chose to study with American instructors. Her early work included miniature portraits, pastels, watercolors and oils. From 1900 to 1910, she concentrated on landscapes.

From 1910, Turner worked almost exclusively in oils. Most of her paintings were done without the customary preliminary sketches and studies. She was most famous for her portraits of people in their homes or other intimate environments.

Lilies, Lanterns, and Sunshine, 1923, 35 x 43 in., signed l.l. Courtesy of The Chrysler Museum, Norfolk, Virginia. Gift of W.B.S. Grandy.

Turner spent almost every summer between 1906 and 1941 at the artists' colony in Cragsmoor, New York; she did spend several summers studying with William Merritt Chase in Italy. She died in 1958 in New Orleans.

MEMBERSHIPS
American Federation of Arts
Allied Artists of America
Association of American Women
 Painters and Sculptors
National Academy of Design
New York Water Color Club

PUBLIC COLLECTIONS
Chrysler Museum, Norfolk, Virginia
Corcoran Gallery of Art, Washington, D.C.
Detroit Institute of Arts
Museum of Fine Art, Houston
Metropolitan Museum of Art, New York City
New Orleans Museum of Art
Newark Art Museum, New Jersey
Phillips Collection, Washington, D.C.

SEASON	75-76	76-77	77-78	78-79	79-80	80-81	81-82	82-83	83-84	84-85
Paintings				1	1	1	2	1		1
Dollars				$750	$3,200	$2,800	$9,750	$2,400		$2,000

Record Sale: $6,750, SPB, 9/23/81, "Morning Call," 16 x 12 in.

552

JOHN HAUSER
(1859-1918)

As a painter of the American Indian, John Hauser gained recognition not only for his artistic ability, but also for the authenticity with which he recorded the details of a vanishing way of life. Among his many works are portraits of some of the most famous Indian chiefs of the day.

Born in 1859 in Cincinnati to German immigrant parents, Hauser showed an early talent for painting. He studied drawing at the Ohio Mechanics' Institute, then moved on to the Cincinnati Art Academy and the McMicken Art School.

In 1880, he went to Munich to study at the Royal Academy of Art under Nicholas Gysis. He came back to Cincinnati and taught in the public schools, but returned to Germany in 1885 for further training under Gysis and others in Munich and Dusseldorf. He finally attended the Ecole des Beaux Arts in Paris.

By the 1890s, Hauser had become interested in the American Indian; he traveled through reservation after reservation of the Apache and Pueblo Indians in Arizona and New Mexico, sketching and painting. He also came to know the Sioux. He continued these trips for more than 20 years and is credited with having done much to chronicle how the Indians lived and worshiped.

He painted a notable series of portraits of such legendary chiefs as Sitting Bull, Red Cloud, American Horse,

Sioux Encampment Porcupine, 1910, 12 x 18 in., signed l.l. Courtesy of Vose Galleries of Boston, Inc., Massachusetts.

Spotted Tail, High Horse and Lone Bear. He also did many large canvases of Indian hunters and village life, all painted in his careful, realistic style.

In 1901, in recognition of the trust the Indians had in him, Hauser and his wife were adopted by the Sioux nation. He was given the Indian name "Straight White Shield."

On his travels Hauser amassed a remarkable collection of Indian artifacts and art, most of which he had donated to the Cincinnati Art Museum before his death in 1918.

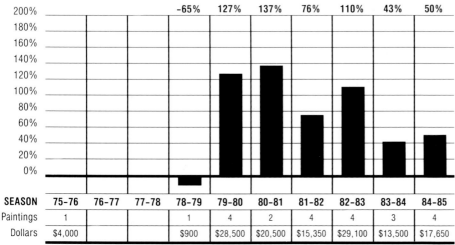

10-Year Average Change From Base Years '75-'76: 60%

			-65%	127%	137%	76%	110%	43%	50%

SEASON	75-76	76-77	77-78	78-79	79-80	80-81	81-82	82-83	83-84	84-85
Paintings	1			1	4	2	4	4	3	4
Dollars	$4,000			$900	$28,500	$20,500	$15,350	$29,100	$13,500	$17,650

Record Sale: $14,000, P.NY, 10/21/82, "In the Cheyenne Country," 11 x 18 in.

MEMBERSHIPS
Cincinnati Art Club
Muenchener Kunstler Club
Muenchener Kunstverein

PUBLIC COLLECTIONS
Cincinnati Art Museum
Thomas Gilcrease Institute of American History and Art, Tulsa

MAURICE PRENDERGAST
(1859-1923)

The Canal, Venice, 16½ x 10¾ in., signed l.l.
Photograph courtesy of Hirschl & Adler
Galleries, Inc., New York, New York.

Maurice Brazil Prendergast, known for his post-impressionist watercolors, monotypes and oil paintings, was a member of The Eight. His bright, watercolor scenes of urban life have a mosaic- or tapestry-like quality, achieved by presenting flat, bold areas of color in combination with a compression of perspective and scale.

Born in St. Johns, Newfoundland in 1859, Prendergast grew up in Boston. As a youth, he was apprenticed as a commercial artist, a trade he practiced into the 1880s. During this period, Prendergast sketched conventional watercolor landscapes.

Prendergast's determination to be an artist led him to the conclusion that he must study abroad. In 1886, he made his first of six trips to England, accompanied by his younger brother, Charles.

Charles, himself an artist and woodcarver, gave lifelong assistance and support to his brother's career. Upon their return to Boston in 1887, the two worked for four years to enable Maurice to travel to Paris in 1891.

During his three-year stay in France, Prendergast studied at Academie Colarossi and Academie Julien, immersing himself in contemporary art movements. At first, Prendergast was influenced by the work of James McNeill Whistler and Edouard Manet. But more important influences were the neo-impressionists, the symbolists and the nabis. Henceforth, Prendergast

would express his preference for boldly-colored, flat-patterned forms in techniques aligned with post-impressionisms.

By 1895, he had returned to his brother's home in Winchester, Massachusetts, where he assisted with Charles's picture-framing business and embarked on sketching trips to nearby beaches and parks.

During another European trip from 1898 to 1900, Prendergast was inspired by Italian Renaissance painters, particularly Vittore Carpaccio. Under this influence, he produced monotypes and watercolors with complicated compositions, such as *A Bridge in Venice* (1898, Cleveland Museum of Art) and *Piazza de San Marco* (ca. 1898, Metropolitan Museum of Art).

He continued to make periodic trips to Europe to gain exposure to fresh influences. By 1913, the year of the New York City Armory Show, in which he exhibited, Prendergast had moved to New York City with his brother.

Of The Eight, with whom he exhibited in 1908, only Prendergast had an international reputation. He stood apart from the group in style as well, although he agreed with their revolutionary intentions.

The group was criticized as being radical, though Prendergast's lively and decorative qualities won some praise. More sensational accounts called his work "unadulterated slop" and "an explosion in a color factory."

Prendergast's late work included portraits, imaginary landscapes, nudes and mural decorations. He explored a mosaic-like technique influenced by Paul Signac, and introduced white opaque into his watercolors, giving them a richness equaling oils. His later oils show increasingly thick pigment application.

Prendergast died in 1923.

PUBLIC COLLECTIONS
Barnes Foundation, Merion, Pennsylvania
Carnegie Institute, Pittsburgh
Cleveland Museum of Art
Corcoran Gallery of Art, Washington, D.C.
Detroit Institute of Arts
Lehigh University, Bethlehem, Pennsylvania
Metropolitan Museum of Art, New York City
Museum of Fine Arts, Boston
Whitney Museum of American Art,
  New York City
Worcester Art Museum, Massachusetts

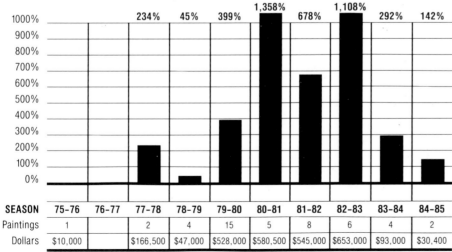

10-Year Average Change From Base Years '75-'76: 473%

	75-76	76-77	77-78	78-79	79-80	80-81	81-82	82-83	83-84	84-85
%			234%	45%	399%	1,358%	678%	1,108%	292%	142%
SEASON	75-76	76-77	77-78	78-79	79-80	80-81	81-82	82-83	83-84	84-85
Paintings	1		2	4	15	5	8	6	4	2
Dollars	$10,000		$166,500	$47,000	$528,000	$580,500	$545,000	$653,000	$93,000	$30,400

Record Sale: $410,000, SPB, 5/29/81, "The Flying Horses," 13 x 21 in.

BRYANT CHAPIN
(1859-1927)

Bryant Chapin is known for his many still lifes, although he also painted landscapes and portraits during his 40-year career. A member of the Fall River School of Massachusetts painters, he studied with Robert S. Dunning as a young man. Dunning's influence can be seen particularly in Chapin's early work.

Like Dunning, Chapin painted fruit on highly-polished tables with elaborately-carved edges and deep reflections. Grapes and peaches were favorite subjects, but Chapin also introduced the open orange. The palette in these early works is light, the forms rather hazy and the light soft.

Born in Fall River in 1859, Chapin spent most of his life there. He taught at the Evening Drawing School and lectured on art. He did travel several times, however, to paint landscapes in Europe. He died in Fall River in 1927.

Chapin was very conscientious about his paintings and imbued them with a wistful mysticism which made them popular. His later still lifes are more distinctive because they are set outdoors.

Many of these paintings are of berries, some in wooden berry boxes and some on the bare ground. The edges, especially of strawberries, were ideal for heavy highlights. Chapin's style was so fluid and soft, however, that the very paint surface suggests cushioning for the tender fruit.

Still Life with Apples, 1911, 9¾ x 12¾ in., signed l.l. Collection of James T. Duff.

PUBLIC COLLECTIONS
Fall River Public Library, Massachusetts

10-Year Average Change From Base Years '76-'77: 56%

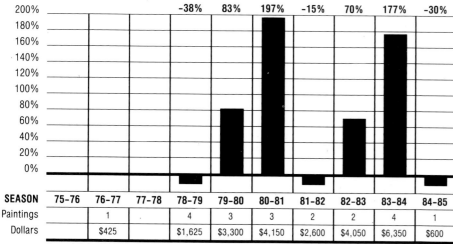

SEASON	75-76	76-77	77-78	78-79	79-80	80-81	81-82	82-83	83-84	84-85
				-38%	83%	197%	-15%	70%	177%	-30%
Paintings		1	.	4	3	3	2	2	4	1
Dollars		$425		$1,625	$3,300	$4,150	$2,600	$4,050	$6,350	$600

Record Sale: $2,750, BB.SF, 3/24/83, "Still Life," 24 × 19 in.

ELLIOTT DAINGERFIELD
(1859-1932)

The Grand Canyon, 36¼ x 38¼ in., signed l.c. Courtesy of North Carolina Museum of Art, Raleigh.

Elliott Daingerfield is best known for his paintings of landscapes and religious subjects. His works, described as "American decorative impressionism," offer poetic representations that often were painted from memory rather than from direct observation. He was called "master of the canyon" for his subtly toned, imaginative paintings of the Grand Canyon. Daingerfield also distinguished himself as an art teacher and critic.

Born in Harper's Ferry, Virginia in 1859, Daingerfield spent most of his early years in Fayetteville, North Carolina. He first learned watercolor, then oil painting and photography. He left the South at age 21 to study in New York City, first with Walter Satterlee and then at the Art Students League. That same year, 1880, he first exhibited paintings at the National Academy of Design.

In 1884, Daingerfield became acquainted with George Inness, the American landscape painter, who took an interest in him and promoted his work. Daingerfield's early work shows the barbizon influence, as well as ideas and techniques derived from Inness. He later wrote a biography, *George Inness* (1891), in which he praised "the principles underlying his composition, the science of his balances and rhythm, his knowledge and taste in truth of sky, of tree form, of ground construction."

In the 1890s, Daingerfield moved away from his soft landscapes to undertake rich, brightly-colored religious paintings, which reflect sixteenth-century Italian style. His *The Story of the Madonna* (ca. 1900, private collection) won the National Academy of Design's Thomas B. Clarke prize for figure painting in 1902. That same year, he received an important commission for a series of large murals in the Lady Chapel of the Church of Saint Mary the Virgin in New York City.

Daingerfield returned to his landscape painting during the early years of the twentieth century, when he executed a number of small oil sketches. Work from this period shows the influence of Arthur B. Davies in composition and painting style. However, his late work, dating from 1915 to 1924, again shows the influence of Inness in scale, mood, and color.

After a 1911 visit to the Grand Canyon, Daingerfield painted what he called his chief work, *The Grand Canyon* (1912, North Carolina Museum of Art). He used the canyon as the subject for many different paintings. Many are highly imaginative, depicting nude figures on the canyon ledge.

Though he resided in New York City, Daingerfield maintained a summer studio in Blowing Rock, North Carolina. He used the vistas near this resort town in the Blue Ridge Mountains in many of his paintings, including *Slumbering Fog* (date unknown, Metropolitan Museum of Art).

The artist visited Europe in 1897 and 1924. Following the second trip, he painted scenes of Venice.

Daingerfield suffered a decline in health in 1925 and painted little work of consequence from that date until his death in 1932.

MEMBERSHIPS
Lotus Club
National Academy of Design
National Arts Club
New York Water Color Club
Society of American Artists

PUBLIC COLLECTIONS
Art Institute of Chicago
Brooklyn Museum
Butler Art Institute, Youngstown, Ohio
City Art Museum, St. Louis
Los Angeles Museum
Metropolitan Museum of Art, New York City
National Gallery, Washington, D.C.
Toledo Museum, Ohio

10-Year Average Change From Base Years '76-'77: 102%

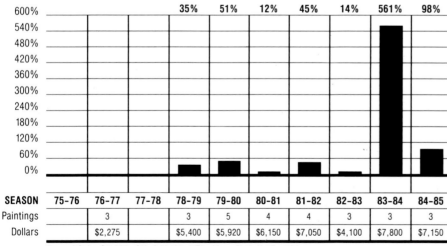

	35%	51%	12%	45%	14%	561%	98%

SEASON	75-76	76-77	77-78	78-79	79-80	80-81	81-82	82-83	83-84	84-85
Paintings		3		3	5	4	4	3	3	3
Dollars		$2,275		$5,400	$5,920	$6,150	$7,050	$4,100	$7,800	$7,150

Record Sale: $5,000, CH, 6/1/84, "The Moon Path," 16 × 12 in.

THEODORE WENDEL
(1859-1932)

Lady with Parasol, Ipswich, ca. 1889, 20 x 30¼ in. Courtesy of Vose Galleries of Boston, Inc., Massachusetts.

Theodore Wendel was one of the first American artists to embrace the form and technique of French impressionism.

He was born in Midway, Ohio in 1859. When he was 19, after a brief period of study at the University of Cincinnati, he and a friend, Joseph De Camp, went to Munich to continue their studies. At that time, Munich was a training ground for young American artists. Wendel attended the Royal Academy there, and in 1879 became a student of Frank Duveneck. Duveneck's paintings and teaching had no lasting effect on Wendel's painting, and none of his work from this period has survived.

In the 1880s, Wendel traveled to Paris, which changed the entire course of his artistic life. He attended the Academie Julien and began to use the techniques of the impressionists.

In the summer of 1886, he went to Giverny, the home of Monet, and joined an American colony of young artists, among them Louis Ritter, W.L. Metcalf, John Breck and Theodore Robinson. Wendel did not imitate Monet. However, he did use Monet's hazy impressionism, vigorous brushwork and strong colors. He continued to use these techniques for the rest of his life.

In 1889, he returned to America and settled in Boston. He taught at Wellesley College and Cowles Art School, and maintained a studio in Boston.

In 1898, he moved to Ipswich, Massachusetts. Here he devoted his time to painting the people, architectural features and countryside, as Monet had done at Giverny.

In 1914, Wendel joined the Guild of Boston Artists, an organization of 50 local painters and sculptors. The Boston Museum of Fine Arts sponsored the Guild's exhibitions in major museums across the country to show the fine work being done by Boston artists, and Wendel's paintings were among them.

Wendel died in 1932 at Ipswich.

MEMBERSHIPS
Guild of Boston Artists

PUBLIC COLLECTIONS
Cincinnati Museum of Art
Museum of Fine Arts, Boston
Pennsylvania Academy of the Fine Arts,
   Philadelphia

SEASON	75-76	76-77	77-78	78-79	79-80	80-81	81-82	82-83	83-84	84-85
Paintings				1	1	2	1		1	2
Dollars				$3,050	$600	$5,500	$37,000		$3,500	$14,500

Record Sale: $37,000, S.BM, 11/19/81, "Harbour Scene," 25 × 30 in.

JOHN FERY
(1859-1934)

Near Lost Lake, Wyoming, 18 x 35 in., signed l.r. Courtesy of Braarud Fine Art, La Conner, Washington.

John Fery was born in 1859 into a prominent and wealthy Austrian family, and grew up on his father's estate, located between Linz and Salzburg. He studied art in Vienna with Gripenkerl, in Dusseldorf with Peter Jansen, and in Karlsruhe with Schwenlehr.

Fery also studied in Munich. He declined a permanent position at the famous Dusseldorf Academy, preferring to come to the United States to practice his art and to follow his interest in wilderness scenery.

Fery came to America in 1886 and he lived on the Eastern seaboard for about five years. He quickly established himself as a successful painter of American landscape and hunting scenes, living for several years at Lake George and in the Catskill Mountain region, and later in Milwaukee, Wisconsin and New Jersey. Around 1890 he had a studio in Cleveland, Ohio. In 1891 he returned briefly to Europe.

It appears that the result of his return to Europe was the organization of a hunting party led by Fery, which spent the years 1892 and 1893 traveling through the Midwest and far West United States in search of wilderness scenery and wild game. An undated article from the *Milwaukee Journal* provides a glimpse of the tour: "John Fery, a native of Hungary (sic), and as such a sportsman of the word's best meaning, conceived the idea, of organizing a party

of lovers of the chase, selected from the European gentry and members of the aristocracy, for a hunting trip in the virgin hunting grounds of the Northern Rockies of America, which the completion of the Northern Pacific (Railroad) had brought into the lime-light of European notice at that time. A call issued to that effect by Mr. Fery in Hunter's Journals was soon answered by Count Bleuchar, by Count Zepplin, Harry Meisenback, inventor of the half-tone process, and four other persons who together with Mr. Fery made up a party of eight huntsmen and started for the U.S. in 1893."

The itinerary of the group included Lake Michigan, New Mexico, Arizona,

the Grand Canyon of the Colorado, California, Oregon and Wyoming. Fery published an article recounting his experiences in the European *Hunter's Journal* under the title "Eine Jagt in Wyoming." He led a second expedition to the West in 1895, and these adventures were the beginning of his career as a painter of the Western landscape.

Fery's greatest patron was the Great Northern Railroad. He was commissioned to do paintings of the scenery along the railroad's route through the West, particularly in Glacier National Park. He was an important artistic stimulant in the creation of Glacier National Park, just as Moran had been earlier in the creation of Yellowstone National Park and Grand Canyon of the Colorado Park.

Fery died in Everett, Washington in 1934.

Many of Fery's paintings were on a grand scale, as large as 10 by 12 feet in size, but his smaller works are still sought by collectors for their vivid rendering of the Western landscape. In 1944, the Great Northern did an inventory of works by Fery in its collection. Over the years, they had purchased 362 works by the artist; they were located in hotels, railway stations, travel and ticket offices and office buildings.

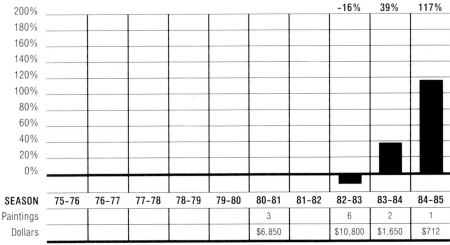

10-Year Average Change From Base Years '80-'81: 35%

SEASON	75-76	76-77	77-78	78-79	79-80	80-81	81-82	82-83	83-84	84-85
								-16%	39%	117%
Paintings						3		6	2	1
Dollars						$6,850		$10,800	$1,650	$712

Record Sale: $5,000, BB.SF, 3/24/83, "Iceberg Lake," 45 × 52 in.

ABBOTT FULLER GRAVES
(1859-1936)

Load of Poppies, 48¼ x 72¼ in., signed l.r. Photograph courtesy of Hirschl & Adler Galleries, Inc., New York, New York.

Abbott Fuller Graves was a renowned specialist in decorative open-air garden paintings and floral still lifes. His use of thick, impasto brushstrokes, bright colors and natural light, most evident in his later garden paintings, shows the influence of European impressionism.

Born in Weymouth, Massachusetts in 1859, Graves studied both in New England and abroad. He attended, but did not graduate from, the Massachusetts Institute of Technology. Although already considered one of the best flower painters in Boston, Graves went to Paris and Italy in 1884 to continue his studies. In Europe, he roomed with Edmund C. Tarbell and studied still-life painting.

After returning to Boston in 1885, Graves became an instructor at the Cowles Art School. Also teaching there was his close friend and colleague, Childe Hassam. The two painters undoubtedly influenced one another. In 1887, Graves returned to Paris to study figure painting at the Academie Julien. There he studied under Cromon, Laurens and Gervais until 1891.

After 1891, the majority of Graves's works depict gardens and floral landscapes. Often these oils, pastels and watercolors include female figures. Some portray exotic gardens of Spain and South America. The bright sunlight and bold use of color and paint, as well as the subject matter of the garden paintings, reflect the influence of European impressionism on Graves's work.

Throughout his career, Graves continued his travels between New England and Paris. In 1891, he opened his own art school in Boston. The school moved to Kennebunk, Maine and closed in 1902. From 1902 to 1905, Graves was employed as a commercial illustrator for magazines in Paris. When Graves died in 1936, he had achieved wide acclaim as a specialist in garden painting, both in New England and Paris.

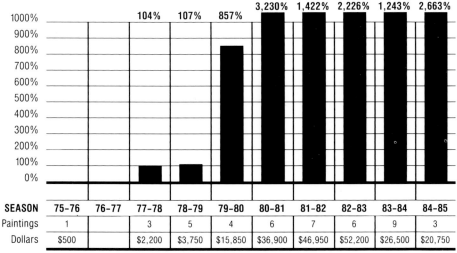

10-Year Average Change From Base Years '75-'76: 1,317%

SEASON	75-76	76-77	77-78	78-79	79-80	80-81	81-82	82-83	83-84	84-85
			104%	107%	857%	3,230%	1,422%	2,226%	1,243%	2,663%
Paintings	1		3	5	4	6	7	6	9	3
Dollars	$500		$2,200	$3,750	$15,850	$36,900	$46,950	$52,200	$26,500	$20,750

Record Sale: $21,000, S.BM, 5/20/82, "Afternoon at the Pond," 30 x 40 in.

MEMBERSHIPS
Allied Artists of America
American Art Association of Paris
Artists' Fund
Boston Art Club
Boston Society of Watercolor Painters
Connecticut Academy of Fine Arts
Copley Society of Boston
National Arts Club
National Academy of Design
North Shore Art Association
Salmagundi Club

PUBLIC COLLECTIONS
Art Museum, Portland, Maine
National Arts Club, New York City

CHILDE HASSAM

(1859-1935)

Landscape and cityscape painter Frederick Childe Hassam (he was later to drop Frederick) was born into a prominent Massachusetts family whose forebears came to New England in the seventeenth century. He received his early training in Boston and, during the 1880s and 1890s, did illustrations for publications such as *Scribner's* and *Harper's*. Meanwhile, he studied at the Boston Art Club and the Lowell Institute, and later with a young German painter, Ignaz Gaugengigl.

In 1886, he began a three-year sojourn in Paris, where he enrolled in the Academie Julien. While in Paris, Hassam fell under the spell of the French impressionists; his subsequent work bears testimony to his fascination with artists such as Claude Monet and Camille Pissarro.

Returning to the United States, Hassam settled in New York City, where he became one of the most successful of the American impressionists. Strangely, he disliked the term impressionism intensely, and never acknowledged his debt to French painting. Instead, he saw himself as a devotee of the English watercolorists, Turner and Constable. Yet, his light, sparkling palette, broken brushstrokes and unconventional subjects are unmistakably French-inspired, albeit with a generous helping of American realism. Hassam, for example, never stressed light vibrations to the detriment of form.

New York Street Scene, 1900, 24¼ x 20¼ in., signed l.r. Photograph courtesy of Hirschl & Adler Galleries, Inc., New York, New York.

After the turn of the century, Hassam's work increasingly began to show the effects of post-impressionism. His palette became harsher and more vivid, and he dropped the broken brushstrokes that characterized his earlier paintings in favor of firm contours. His underlying conservatism became more apparent as the years went on; although he was represented in the innovative 1913 New York City Armory Show, he later renounced its radical tendencies.

Besides his New England landscapes, Hassam is also noted for his views of New York City streets and apartment interiors. During 1917 and 1918, he turned out a series of lithographs reminiscent of the work of Whistler. His charming versions of rain-drenched cityscapes are among his most popular works.

At the height of his popularity, Hassam joined a number of other New York impressionists in forming a group called Ten American Painters or, more simply, The Ten. He was also a member of several artist's organizations. His work was honored by a number of prestigious institutions, including the National

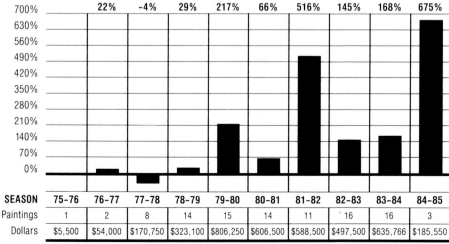

10-Year Average Change From Base Years '75-'76: 183%

		22%	-4%	29%	217%	66%	516%	145%	168%	675%
SEASON		75-76	76-77	77-78	78-79	79-80	80-81	81-82	82-83	83-84	84-85
Paintings		1	2	8	14	15	14	11	16	16	3
Dollars		$5,500	$54,000	$170,750	$323,100	$806,250	$606,500	$588,500	$497,500	$635,766	$185,550

Record Sale: $205,000, SPB, 4/25/80, "October Sundown Newport," 26 × 24 in.

Gloucester, ca. 1902, 27 x 27 in., signed l.r. Courtesy of
Vose Galleries of Boston, Inc., Massachusetts.

Academy of Design, the Carnegie Institute and the Pennsylvania Academy of the Fine Arts.
    Hassam died in 1935.

MEMBERSHIPS
American Academy of Arts and Letters
American Water Color Society
Boston Art Club
Munich Secession
National Academy of Design
National Institute of Arts and Letters
New York Water Color Club
Societe Nationale des Beaux Arts
Ten American Painters

PUBLIC COLLECTIONS
Albright-Knox Art Gallery, Buffalo
Art Institute of Chicago
Carnegie Institute, Pittsburgh
Cincinnati Art Museum
Corcoran Gallery of Art, Washington, D.C.
Detroit Institute of Arts
Los Angeles County Museum
Metropolitan Museum of Art, New York City
Minneapolis Institute of Art
Musee d'Orsay
Museum of Fine Arts, Boston
Pennsylvania Academy of the Fine Arts,
   Philadelphia
Phillips Academy, Andover, Massachusetts
St. Louis Art Museum
Toledo Museum of Art
Rhode Island School of Design, Providence
Worcester Art Museum, Massachusetts

Elms, East Hampton, N.Y., 1920, 16 x 20 in., signed l.l. Courtesy of
Vose Galleries of Boston, Inc., Massachusetts.

LEONARD PERCIVAL ROSSEAU
(1859-1937)

Leonard Percival Rosseau drew upon his lifelong passion for hunting and sports and his knowledge of animals to become America's foremost painter of field and hunting dogs.

Rosseau, a peripatetic adventurer, was born in 1859 in Louisiana. Before going abroad to study at age 35, Rosseau was a cowboy, cattle driver and commodities broker. Though he painted periodically, he received his first formal training at the Academie Julien in Paris, where he studied for six years under Jules Lefebvre, Tony Robert-Fleury and Herman Leon.

Like many academy-trained artists, Rosseau initially painted nudes. "All studying in an academy is done from the nude," he said, "except by those who are going in for landscape work." It was, in fact, a nude for which Rosseau received his first critical award in 1900.

Ironically, however, the artist found it difficult to find a market for his work. An artistic turning point came for Rosseau when, in 1904, he painted *Diana Hunting* (location unknown), in which he put animals on the canvas for the first time.

Immediately sensing that animals were his forte, Rosseau submitted pictures of two bird dogs in the field for the next Paris Salon opening. "The day after the Salon opened, I received 11 telegrams asking my price for the pictures, and I sold both in a few hours," Rosseau said.

From 1910 to 1914, Rosseau spent his winters in the United States. He was widely exhibited and worked largely on commissions for thoroughbred dog breeders. He returned permanently to the United States in 1915.

Rosseau contended that his knowledge of dogs ensured his success as an animal painter. "I have run hounds from childhood and have at my fingertips the thorough knowledge of dogs necessary to picture them faithfully. It takes years to acquire this," he claimed.

The artist also conceded that his subjects could sometimes be nervous and difficult to work with and said he never tried "to get them to 'sit' for a portrait." His paintings, therefore, were largely attitudinal reconstructions—an attempt, he said, to capture the dog's unique temperament.

Rosseau died in 1937 at his North Carolina summer home.

Hunting Dogs, 1908, 40 x 26 in., signed l.l. Courtesy of Connecticut Gallery, Marlborough, Connecticut.

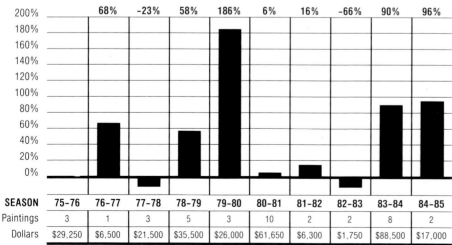

10-Year Average Change From Base Years '75-'76: 43%

SEASON	75-76	76-77	77-78	78-79	79-80	80-81	81-82	82-83	83-84	84-85
		68%	-23%	58%	186%	6%	16%	-66%	90%	96%
Paintings	3	1	3	5	3	10	2	2	8	2
Dollars	$29,250	$6,500	$21,500	$35,500	$26,000	$61,650	$6,300	$1,750	$88,500	$17,000

Record Sale: $22,000, BB.SF, 2/16/84, "Precision," 28 x 35 in.

MEMBERSHIPS
Lotus Club
Lyme Art Association
Pennsylvania Academy of the Fine Arts

HENRY OSSAWA TANNER
(1859-1937)

Henry Ossawa Tanner was a successful artist in a variety of forms, from landscapes to genre paintings to religious portraits. He was often considered the dean of American painters living in Paris during the early twentieth century.

Many artists sought Europe's creative freedom, patronage and well-developed exhibition system, over America's limited opportunities and conservative atmosphere. Tanner had an additional reason to stay abroad: racial prejudice.

Tanner was born in 1859 in Pittsburgh. He was raised in Philadelphia, where his father was an outspoken but respected bishop. Deciding to become an artist in 1872 after observing a landscape painter in the city's Fairmount Park, he spent considerable time sketching, sculpting and painting animals and seascapes.

In 1880, after meeting with resistance from both the white art community and his family, Tanner was accepted at the Pennsylvania Academy of the Fine Arts. He studied under Thomas Eakins, whose influence was evident in his work after he left the Academy. His paintings featured the realistic, somber tones often associated with Eakins.

Disheartened by his failures in Philadelphia, and later in Atlanta, Tanner all but gave up painting for a period. However, a trip to the mountains in North Carolina gave him renewed inspiration.

Tanner produced many sketches of blacks in the area, attracting the atten-

Annunciation, 1898, 57 x 71¼ in., signed l.l. Philadelphia Museum of Art, Pennsylvania. The W. P. Wilstach Collection.

tion of Bishop Joseph Hartzell, who became the first of several white benefactors. Through the financial support of various patrons, Tanner was able to study in Paris, a major turning point in his career.

Under Laurens and Constant at the Academie Julien, Tanner's approach became more personal. He created a series of poignant, sensitive paintings, based on his North Carolina sketches and the peasants around Brittany. He made good use of light modulation to define mood.

By 1893, Tanner had added religious scenes to the genre paintings that had

preoccupied him. His work received a great deal of acceptance at the Salon in Paris, and one Philadelphia patron, Rodman Wanamaker, sent Tanner to the Holy Land in 1897 to further his religious work.

After 1898, Tanner's style changed significantly. His Middle-Eastern experience, coupled with an appreciation of impressionist innovation in color, light and form, were the basis of his more mature religious paintings, such as *Abraham's Oak* (1905, location unknown).

Tanner remained in Paris, producing and refining large-scale religious paintings, until his death in 1937. He had returned to the United States for only a brief time in the early 1900s.

MEMBERSHIPS
National Academy of Design
Paris Society of American Painters
Pennsylvania Academy of the Fine Arts Fellowship
Societe International de Peinture et Sculpture

PUBLIC COLLECTIONS
Art Institute of Chicago
Carnegie Institute, Pittsburgh
Des Moines Association of Fine Arts, Iowa
Frederick Douglass Institute, Washington, D.C.
Hackley Art Gallery, Muskegon, Michigan
Hampton Institute, Hampton, Virginia
Louvre, Paris
Luxembourg Museum, Paris
Metropolitan Museum of Art, New York City
Pennsylvania Academy of the Fine Arts, Philadelphia
Philadelphia Museum of Art

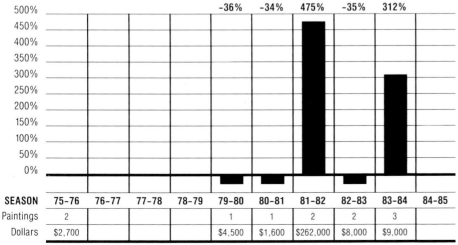

10-Year Average Change From Base Years '75-'76: 114%

					-36%	-34%	475%	-35%	312%	

SEASON	75-76	76-77	77-78	78-79	79-80	80-81	81-82	82-83	83-84	84-85
Paintings	2				1	1	2	2	3	
Dollars	$2,700				$4,500	$1,600	$262,000	$8,000	$9,000	

Record Sale: $250,000, SPB, 12/10/81, "The Thankful Poor," 35 × 44 in.

WILLIAM LANGSON LATHROP

(1859-1938)

Farm House, 22 x 35 in., signed l.r. Courtesy of Newman Galleries, Philadelphia, Pennsylvania.

A major figure of the American tonalist movement, William Langson Lathrop is credited with founding the New Hope School of American impressionism, which rose to prominence along the banks of the Delaware River in Bucks County, Pennsylvania. Painter, etcher, and dedicated art instructor, he devoted himself to painting the tranquil countryside of the Delaware River Valley, inspiring his many students to do the same.

Born in Warren, Illinois in 1859, Lathrop grew up on his grandparents' farm in Painesville, Ohio. He strengthened his inherent artistic abilities by painting the rugged Ohio landscape, and by producing detailed drawings of farm implements and machinery.

In 1874, Lathrop moved to New York City to seek employment as an artist. He first worked as a graphic assistant for *Harper's Monthly* and *Century Magazine,* and then for a photoengraving company during the 1880s.

Largely self-taught, Lathrop briefly studied at the Art Students League in New York City in 1886, under William Merritt Chase. In 1888, he traveled to England, France and Holland. He had little interest in cities and museums, but was captivated by Europe's quaint villages and rural landscapes.

Returning to New York City in 1889, Lathrop developed enduring friendships with many of the American impression-

ist artists who called themselves The Ten. He roomed that year with John Twachtman. In the late 1890s, he lived with Julian Alden Weir in Branchville, Connecticut.

Lathrop moved to New Hope in 1899. His home near the Delaware River soon became a flourishing art school, where he taught landscape painting. In 1929, he founded the Phillips Mill Community Association, and served as its first president. The Mill hosted annual exhibitions organized by Lathrop, Edward Willis Redfield and others.

Lathrop's art, eventually influenced by the lighter-color palette of impressionism, remained essentially tonalistic. Until the early 1920s, he preferred dominant, earth-colored tones, which gave his works a "poetic" richness likened to Corot and Daubigny. When tonalism fell out of vogue in the 1920s, Lathrop adopted the lighter hues characteristic of impressionism. Even then his works retained their subdued mood, with a seriousness which at times borders on melancholy.

Lathrop was an influential teacher, the founder of a legacy of New Hope artists who flourished for many years after his death in 1938.

MEMBERSHIPS
National Academy of Design
New York Watercolor Society
Rochester Art Club

PUBLIC COLLECTIONS
Bucks County Historical Society,
  Doylestown, Pennsylvania
Corcoran Gallery of Art, Washington, D.C.
Everson Museum of Art, Syracuse, New York
Metropolitan Museum of Art, New York City
Montclair Art Museum, New Jersey
National Academy of Design, New York City
National Museum of American Art, Washington, D.C.
New Hope Public Library, Pennsylvania
Pennsylvania Academy of Fine Arts, Philadelphia
Philadelphia Museum of Art
Phillips Collection, Washington, D.C.
Swarthmore College, Pennsylvania

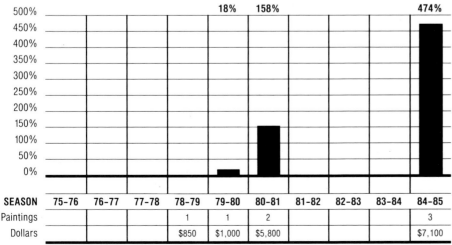

10-Year Average Change From Base Years '78-'79: 163%

SEASON	75-76	76-77	77-78	78-79	79-80	80-81	81-82	82-83	83-84	84-85
					18%	158%				474%
Paintings				1	1	2				3
Dollars				$850	$1,000	$5,800				$7,100

Record Sale: $3,500, D.NY, 4/24/85, "Little Will's Lime Kiln," 22×25 in.

564

ELIZABETH NOURSE

(1859-1938)

Born in Cincinnati, Elizabeth Nourse was trained in art at the Cincinnati School of Design. She studied under Thomas S. Noble and Louis T. Rebisso. In 1879, she became a member of the Cincinnati Pottery Club, and in 1881 she helped found the Cincinnati Etching Club.

Despite being offered a position as drawing instructor at the Cincinnati School of Design, Nourse left America to study in Paris. She expected to stay no more than a few years, but like many of her compatriots in the latter years of the nineteenth century, once settled in France she stayed for a lifetime.

Nourse's professor at the Academie Julien, Gustave Boulanger, found her much further advanced than most of his other students and advised her to work on her own. After only three months at the academy, she started painting independently, and within a year she had a painting accepted for hanging "on the line" (at eye level) at the Paris Salon. Soon, she was exhibiting regularly.

In 1885, Nourse became the first American woman accepted into the Societe National des Beaux Arts, and the first to have one of her paintings purchased by the French government for the permanent collection of the Luxembourg Museum. Before long, her work began to win many awards. On her only trip home, in 1891, she enjoyed a successful solo show at the Cincinnati Museum; two years later her paintings scored a hit at the Chicago Exposition.

Fisher Girl of Picardy, 1889, 46¾ x 32⅜ in., signed l.r. Courtesy of National Museum of American Art, Smithsonian Institution, Gift of Elizabeth Pilling.

Nourse painted landscapes and some portraits, but her favorite subjects were hard-working peasant women and their children. She was widely recognized as a major figure among the American expatriates, and her work has been described as being a forerunner of social realism.

MEMBERSHIPS
Cincinnati Etching Club
Cincinnati Pottery Club
National Association of Women Painters and
  Sculptors
Paris American Women's Art Association
Societe National des Beaux Arts

PUBLIC COLLECTIONS
Art Institute of Chicago
Cincinnati Art Museum
Musee d'Orsay, Paris
National Gallery of Art, Washington, D.C.
Newark Museum, New Jersey
Toledo Museum of Art, Ohio

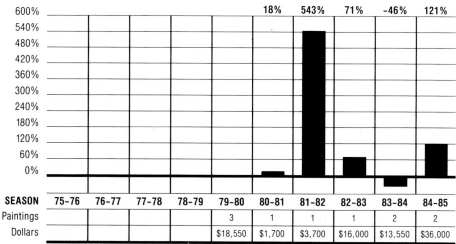

10-Year Average Change From Base Years '79-'80: 118%

					18%	543%	71%	-46%	121%
600%									
540%									
480%									
420%									
360%									
300%									
240%									
180%									
120%									
60%									
0%									

SEASON	75-76	76-77	77-78	78-79	79-80	80-81	81-82	82-83	83-84	84-85
Paintings					3	1	1	1	2	2
Dollars					$18,550	$1,700	$3,700	$16,000	$13,550	$36,000

Record Sale: $25,000, SPB, 12/6/84, "The Sewing Lesson," 47 x 31 in.

HENRY RANKIN POORE
(1859-1940)

Henry Rankin Poore was a spirited and versatile artist, able to paint on diverse themes and noted for his sporting pictures as well as genre and landscape paintings. His well-traveled and educated life, which he recorded as a painter, illustrator and writer, helped him become a respected teacher and critic.

Born in Newark, New Jersey in 1859, Poore was raised in California, expecting to become a minister. His plans changed, however, after he saw the Philadelphia Centennial art show.

He spent a year at the National Academy of Design, then trained with Peter Moran at the Pennsylvania Academy of the Fine Arts until 1880. During this period he was very popular for his paintings of dogs and hunting, as well as Western mining scenes.

After receiving a degree from the University of Pennsylvania in 1883, he studied for two and a half years with Luminais and Bouguereau in Paris.

Upon returning to his Philadelphia studio, Poore began to reevaluate his work. After a year in Paris in 1891, followed by a year of sketching foxhunting in England, he began to paint more humble and unassuming subjects. His work became suggestive of the work of J.F. Millet.

Poore became a professor at the Pennsylvania Academy of the Fine Arts around 1886, later writing a number of books on art criticism. He spent his

Canal Scene, ca. 1885, 23½ x 26 in. Florence Griswold Museum, Lyme Historical Society, Connecticut, Gift of Dr. and Mrs. Gerald Freedman.

final years at his studio in Orange, New Jersey, where he died in 1940.

MEMBERSHIPS
American Federation of Arts
National Academy of Design
Lotus Club
Pennsylvania Academy of Fine Arts,
    Fellowship
Philadelphia Art Club
Philadelphia Sketch Club
Salmagundi Club

PUBLIC COLLECTIONS
National Museum, New Zealand
Philadelphia Art Club
St. Louis Art Museum
Worcester Art Museum, Massachusetts

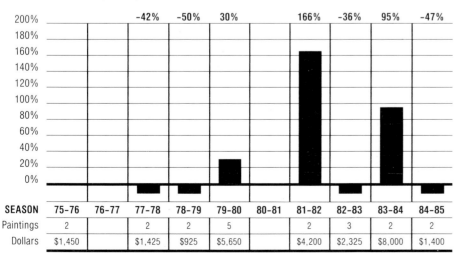

10-Year Average Change From Base Years '75-'76: 15%

			−42%	−50%	30%		166%	−36%	95%	−47%

SEASON	75-76	76-77	77-78	78-79	79-80	80-81	81-82	82-83	83-84	84-85
Paintings	2		2	2	5		2	3	2	2
Dollars	$1,450		$1,425	$925	$5,650		$4,200	$2,325	$8,000	$1,400

Record Sale: $7,250, SPB, 1/27/84, "Diana and the Hounds," 52 × 46 in.

JOSEPH HENRY SHARP
(1859-1953)

A painter, illustrator and teacher, particularly noted for his depictions of Indians, Joseph Henry Sharp was born in Bridgeport, Ohio in 1859.

In *El Palacio* in 1922, Laura H. Davies wrote of Sharp's portrayal of Indians: "He feels the thrill of things that thrill his subjects and so he puts the living spirit, not merely the technically exact portrait, upon his canvas."

Sharp was an avid student, first at the McMicken School of Design and then at the Cincinnati Art Academy. In 1881 he went to Europe, studying with Charles Verlat in Antwerp, and on successive trips with Carl Marr in Munich and Benjamin Constant and Jean Paul Laurens in Paris. From 1892 to 1902, he taught the life class at the Cincinnati Art Academy during the winter, leaving his summers free for sketching trips which covered the entire West.

Sharp's paintings of Indians are distinguished by their accuracy. The differences between various tribes—in facial structures, costumes, artifacts and ceremonials—are so carefully noted in his work that his paintings are prized by anthropologists and art lovers alike.

Just prior to 1900, Sharp went to Sioux country in Southeastern Montana, where he took copious notes on the ceremonies and lifestyles he observed. He transformed a shepherd's wagon into a studio and called it "The Prairie Dog."

"I guess it was Fenimore Cooper who first attracted me to the Indian," Sharp

Red Willow Camp in Winter, 19⅜ x 23⅜ in., signed l.l. Courtesy of Wunderlich and Company, Inc., New York, New York.

Old Chiefs Query, 30 x 40 in., signed l.r. Photograph courtesy of The Gerald Peters Gallery, Santa Fe, New Mexico.

said in an interview for *New Mexico Magazine.* "Perhaps they attracted me as subjects to paint because of their historical value as First Americans."

A year later, President Theodore Roosevelt had his Indian Commissioners build Sharp a studio and cabin at the Crow Agency on the old Custer battlefield. Despite the cold, Sharp traveled throughout the plains country doing hundreds of Indian paintings.

In 1902, Sharp began spending several months each year in Taos, New Mexico, painting the Pueblo Indians. In 1909, he acquired a permanent studio there, and became a charter member of the Taos Society of Artists in 1912.

Sharp's visits to Hawaii produced brilliant landscapes, seascapes and florals, known for their pastel shades and feathery touch. He died in Pasadena in 1953.

MEMBERSHIPS
American Federation of Artists
California Art Club
California Print Makers Society
Cincinnati Art Club
Salmagundi Club
Taos Society of Artists

PUBLIC COLLECTIONS
Academy of Natural Sciences, Philadelphia
Amon Carter Museum of Western Art, Fort Worth
Butler Museum, Youngstown, Ohio
Cincinnati Art Museum
Herron Art Institute, Indianapolis
Houston Museum of Fine Art
Museum of Santa Fe, New Mexico
Smithsonian Institution, Washington, D.C.

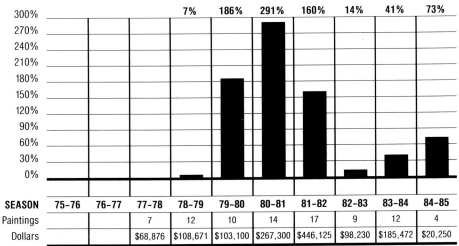

10-Year Average Change From Base Years '77-'78: 97%

	75-76	76-77	77-78	78-79	79-80	80-81	81-82	82-83	83-84	84-85
			7%	186%	291%	160%	14%	41%	73%	
SEASON	75-76	76-77	77-78	78-79	79-80	80-81	81-82	82-83	83-84	84-85
Paintings			7	12	10	14	17	9	12	4
Dollars			$68,876	$108,671	$103,100	$267,300	$446,125	$98,230	$185,472	$20,250

Record Sale: $100,000, SPB, 10/22/81, "Elk Foot Taos," 25 x 30 in.

ADDISON THOMAS MILLAR
(1860-1913)

Addison Thomas Millar was a painter and etcher, remembered chiefly as a student of William M. Chase and as a member of the Silvermine group of artists.

Millar was born, and began his artistic career, in Warren, Ohio. He studied under local artist John Bell. In 1877 and the next two years, he won prizes in a landscape competition sponsored by a young people's magazine, *The Youth's Companion*.

In 1879, Millar moved to Cleveland, where he studied under DeScott Evans and began painting portraits in addition to his landscapes. In 1883, he moved to New York City. He studied painting and etching at the Art Students League.

In 1892, Millar entered the Shinnecock School, conducted by noted landscapist William M. Chase. He exhibited his work regularly for the next three years at the National Academy of Design, the Society of American Artists, and private galleries in Boston, Philadelphia and Chicago.

In 1894, Millar opened a studio in Paris. He studied under Benjamin Constant, Henri Martin and Boldini, and exhibited a painting at the Salon Champs de Mars. Millar spent the following summer painting scenes of Holland; in 1895 he traveled to Spain, where he renewed his studies under Chase.

Returning to New York City, Millar continued to exhibit etchings and paint-

Still Life, 8 x 10 in., signed l.l. Photograph courtesy of M. Knoedler & Co., Inc., New York, New York.

ings at the National Academy of Design, until his death in an automobile accident in 1913.

MEMBERSHIPS
Salmagundi Club

PUBLIC COLLECTIONS
Detroit Institute of Arts
Library of Congress, Washington, D.C.
New York Public Library,
    New York City
Rhode Island School of Design,
    Providence

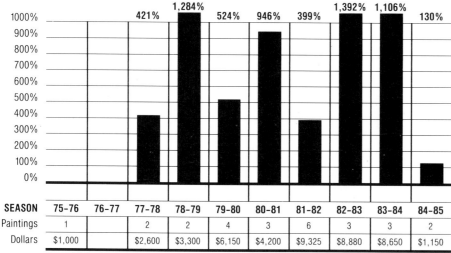

10-Year Average Change From Base Years '75-'76: 689%

SEASON	75-76	76-77	77-78	78-79	79-80	80-81	81-82	82-83	83-84	84-85
(% change)			421%	1,284%	524%	946%	399%	1,392%	1,106%	130%
Paintings	1		2	2	4	3	6	3	3	2
Dollars	$1,000		$2,600	$3,300	$6,150	$4,200	$9,325	$8,880	$8,650	$1,150

Record Sale: $7,000, CH, 6/1/84, "The Rug Merchant," 21 x 28 in.

HENRY JOSEPH BREUER

(1860-1932)

Henry Breuer was a California landscape painter and illustrator whose subject was the magnificent natural scenes of that state, particularly Yosemite Valley and the high Sierras. Breuer also painted coastal scenes of Morro Bay and the nearby Santa Inez Mountains, as well as California sunsets and the Busch gardens in Santa Barbara.

Born in Philadelphia, Breuer studied in Paris; he was influenced by Corot and the barbizon painters. His style, however, was more realistic than theirs. He began landscape painting in 1893, after his trip abroad. Before that, he worked as a Rookwood-pottery decorator and lithographic designer in Cincinnati, later moving to New York City as a mural decorator in the mid-1880s. In 1890,

he moved to California to become an artist on the *San Francisco Chronicle.* Later he was art editor of a California magazine.

Breuer was commissioned to paint views of the San Gabriel Valley in Southern California for the St. Louis Exposition in 1904.

His love affair with the State of California, particularly its mountains, was evident in many paintings of the Sierra Nevada Mountains. In 1926, Breuer lived in Lone Pine, California, a small town along the eastern edge of the mountain range, remote from any urban settlement but close to the grandeur of the granite peaks.

He died in 1932.

Moro Bay, 1919, 18 x 46 in., signed l.l.
Courtesy of Petersen Galleries,
Beverly Hills, California.

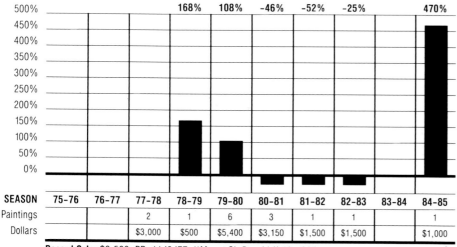

10-Year Average Change From Base Years '77-'78: 89%

SEASON	75-76	76-77	77-78	78-79	79-80	80-81	81-82	82-83	83-84	84-85
				168%	108%	-46%	-52%	-25%		470%
Paintings			2	1	6	3	1	1		1
Dollars			$3,000	$500	$5,400	$3,150	$1,500	$1,500		$1,000

Record Sale: $2,500, PB, 11/8/77, "Mount Sir Donald," 48 x 36 in.

569

GARI MELCHERS
(1860-1932)

Gari Melchers was a leading figure and genre painter who enjoyed considerable success, both in Europe and the United States. He is best known for the Dutch figure paintings of his early years, as well as for his later murals and portraits of prominent men, including Theodore Roosevelt, Lloyd George and Andrew Mellon.

Melchers was born in 1860 in Detroit, the son of Westphalian sculptor and woodcarver Julius Melchers. He received his earliest instruction from his father, then went to Germany in 1877 and studied under Karl von Gebhardt at the Dusseldorf Academy. In 1881, Melchers moved to Paris to study under Gustave Boulanger and Jules Lefebvre at the Academie Julien.

By 1884, Melchers had established a studio at the Dutch fishing village of Egmond-aan-Zee, where he enjoyed great success over the next 30 years.

Melcher's motto of this period, "true and clear," manifested itself in paintings of Dutch peasants, often mother and child, with frequent religious motifs. Stylistically, his paintings evolved over time from austere interior settings reminiscent of Vermeer, to more brightly colored plein-air scenes, painted in a decorative style, with impressionistic influences.

In 1914, Melchers returned to the United States, and for the remainder of his career proved adept as a painter of American themes. Settling down on the estate of "Belmont," near Fredericksburg, Virginia, he produced many fine paintings of regional and domestic scenes.

Melchers remained highly active throughout his later years, traveling widely to execute portraits of the rich and famous, as well as historical murals for the Detroit Public Library and the Missouri State Capitol. He died in 1932 at "Belmont," which remains open to the public today and houses an impressive collection of his work.

The Sermon, 1886, 62⅜ x 86½ in., signed l.r. Courtesy of National Museum of American Art, Smithsonian Institution, Bequest of Henry Ward Ranger through the National Academy of Design.

MEMBERSHIPS
National Academy of Design
International Society of Artists
National Institute of Arts and Letters

PUBLIC COLLECTIONS
Corcoran Gallery of Art, Washington, D.C.
Mary Washington College, Fredericksburg, Virginia
National Gallery, Washington, D.C.

SEASON	75-76	76-77	77-78	78-79	79-80	80-81	81-82	82-83	83-84	84-85
Paintings		1	1	1	2	1		2	2	1
Dollars		$900	$3,500	$1,000	$18,600	$800		$17,400	$28,800	$950

Record Sale: $26,000, CH, 12/9/83, "Young Mother," 25 × 21 in.

570

JOHN KANE
(1860-1934)

Day of Rest, ca. 1928, 15 x 20 in., signed l.l. Courtesy of La Salle University Art Museum, Philadelphia, Pennsylvania.

A legend in his own time, John Kane was a self-taught modern American primitive painter who spent most of his life as a manual laborer and was past age 65 before his first painting was accepted for exhibition. Then, almost overnight, he was recognized for what he was—a painter of raw power and originality. He recorded in painstaking detail the steel mills, structures and landscapes of Pittsburgh, where he spent much of his life.

Born in Scotland in 1860, he was baptized John Cain. Years later, when a bank teller made an error, he adopted the different spelling. After his father died, he left school at 10 to work in the coal mines and came to the United States at 19.

Kane was tall and strong but unskilled, and he took a long succession of tough, physical jobs, sometimes working seven days a week. Several times, he went back to mining coal.

At 31, he lost his left leg in a railroad accident, but learned to walk again with an artificial limb. In 1897, he married, and over the next few years fathered two daughters and a son. The son he had prayed for, however, lived only a day. In his grief, Kane began to drink heavily and his wife soon left him. They remained estranged for nearly 25 years.

For a time, he had a job painting railroad cars. During lunch he would paint landscapes on the sides of the cars, then paint them out. He also earned a few extra dollars by coloring photographs for working people, usually of dead loved ones.

In middle age, he learned carpentry and house painting. Salvaging scraps of beaverboard, he began to paint rather stiff but meticulously accurate landscapes and industrial scenes. Twice during all these years, he tried to enroll in art school, but each time he could not afford it.

After two previous rejections, in 1927 Kane finally had a painting accepted for the prestigious Carnegie International Exhibition in Pittsburgh. He was then 67. When word of his past became known, he became an instant celebrity, with dealers and the press courting him.

Kane, now reunited with his wife, continued to live in modest quarters in Pittsburgh until his death from tuberculosis in 1934. His paintings, however, now were exhibited regularly and were bought by wealthy collectors and museums. In all, 140 of his paintings have been recorded.

PUBLIC COLLECTIONS
Albright-Knox Art Gallery, Buffalo
Barnes Foundation, Merion, Pennsylvania
Carnegie Museum of Art, Pittsburgh
Chrysler Museum, Norfolk, Virginia
Detroit Institute of Arts
Metropolitan Museum of Art, New York City
Whitney Museum of American Art,
  New York City

SEASON	75-76	76-77	77-78	78-79	79-80	80-81	81-82	82-83	83-84	84-85
Paintings		1			2	4				
Dollars		$12,000			$7,750	$35,250				

Record Sale: $23,000, SPB, 5/29/81, "Scot's Day at Kennywood," 19 × 27 in.

THEODORE EARL BUTLER
(1860-1936)

Although Theodore Butler is considered an American impressionist, he spent his entire life—except for his youth and a few years during World War I—in Giverny, the town in the North of France that Claude Monet made famous. The lack of appreciation of Butler's work may possibly be ascribed to the fact that he was differently regarded on the two sides of the Atlantic, and to the fact that he became part of the Monet household. He married not one of the famous impressionist's step-daughters, but two of them.

Butler was born in Columbus, Ohio in 1860. He attempted to follow a business career like his father, and even took a job in a warehouse after graduating from Marietta College in 1880. But the experience ended badly, with Butler "defacing" the walls of the warehouse with paintings.

From 1882 to 1885, Butler studied at the Art Students League in New York. In 1885 he went to Paris, where he studied at the Academie Julien, the Atelier Colarossi and the Grande Chaumiere.

Butler began his artistic career as a rather conservative Salon painter, but was profoundly influenced by Monet's impressionism. After meeting Monet in Giverny, Butler lightened his palette, used thicker paint and adopted the technique of using broken color. In general, however, his subject matter differs from Monet's; Butler was much more a chronicler of Giverny itself, and especially of his own family life. (He had married one

Le Jeunes Peopliers, 22½ x 29 in., signed l.r. Courtesy of Henry B. Holt, Inc., Essex Fells, New Jersey.

of Monet's step-daughters in 1892. She died in 1899, and he married her sister in 1900.) *Bathing the Child* (1893, Janet Fleisher Gallery) is an example.

In a catalog of paintings in the collection of the Metropolitan Museum of Art, Butler's *Un Jardin, Maison Baptiste* (1895) is described as a scene similar to those painted by Monet, but "distinguished from that of his accomplished French mentor by its soft pastel palette, less forceful brushwork, and lack of an effective compositional focus."

He returned to New York City with his family in 1913 to install some historical murals he had completed, and also contributed two canvases to the Armory Show. Because of World War I, the Butlers remained in New York until 1921. While there, Butler organized the Society of Independent Artists with John Sloan.

The quality of Butler's paintings declined in the final 15 years of his life. He died in 1936 in Giverny.

MEMBERSHIPS
Societe des Artistes Independents
Societe du Salon d'Automne
Society of Independent Artists

PUBLIC COLLECTIONS
Metropolitan Museum of Art, New York City

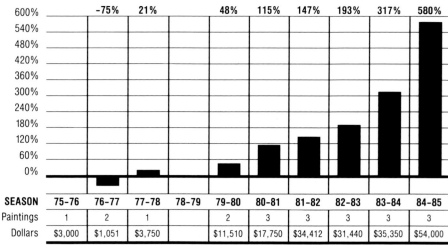

10-Year Average Change From Base Years '75-'76: 150%

				-75%	21%		48%	115%	147%	193%	317%	580%

SEASON	75-76	76-77	77-78	78-79	79-80	80-81	81-82	82-83	83-84	84-85
Paintings	1	2	1		2	3	3	3	3	3
Dollars	$3,000	$1,051	$3,750		$11,510	$17,750	$34,412	$31,440	$35,350	$54,000

Record Sale: $32,000, SPB, 12/6/84, "Mother and Child," 20 x 24 in.

CHARLES P. GRUPPE
(1860-1940)

Primarily a landscape artist, Charles Paul Gruppe is closely identified with the Dutch School of painting. His sympathetic portrayal of Hollanders and their muted, subtle environment is so authentic that Gruppe was elected into the exclusive Pulchre Studio in the Netherlands, an unusual honor for an American.

In the more than 20 years he lived in the Netherlands, Gruppe painted portraits of people, interiors, farms, boats, fishermen and coastal waterways, using a low-keyed, softly colored palette, with the rich, dark tonal qualities of the Netherlands.

Gruppe was born in 1860 in Picton, Ontario. When he was 10, his family moved to Rochester, New York following the death of his father. Gruppe had no training as an artist, but his innate drawing talent was nurtured by early employment as a sign painter. He learned to sketch; in his spare time, painting out-of-doors, he also learned to use water-colors and oils. His work was good and he began to sell.

At age 21, Gruppe went to Europe. Although he had no money for art school, he showed his work to the director of the academy in Munich, who told him his drawing was exceptional. Gruppe stopped in Holland and was captivated; thereafter, he began to live and paint like a Dutchman. Eight years later, he settled in The Hague and did not return permanently to the United

Old Lyme Landscape, 30 x 40 in., signed l.l. Courtesy of Henry B. Holt, Inc., Essex Fells, New Jersey.

States until 1914, when World War I broke out in Europe.

Gruppe's excellence as a landscape painter is based on his careful, fine drawing and subtle colors. As a colorist, he was thoroughly Dutch, full of harmonious effects that lend a soft atmosphere, as in his use of low-hanging, luminous clouds. Many of his paintings depict marine life on the Zuider Zee, and at Sheveningen where fishing boats dock. Gruppe built a villa there to be close to the fleet.

Very quickly, Gruppe was recognized as a painter of the Dutch School. Queen Emma and later Queen Wilhelmina bought his paintings. Of 18 artists who applied for membership in the Pulchre studio, Gruppe was the only one elected. The other 17 applicants were all Hollanders.

Because of his genuine identification with the mind and spirit of the Netherlands, Gruppe is sometimes mistakenly identified with the Hague School. His subject matter differs, however, from the domestic topics of Hague School artists, who depict primarily family scenes and children. Gruppe also did many portraits in oil, watercolor, chalk and pencil, but it is his landscape and marine painting for which he earned his lasting reputation.

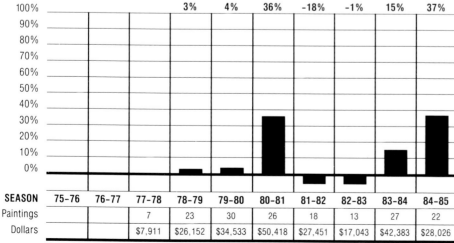

10-Year Average Change From Base Years '77-'78: 10%

			3%	4%	36%	-18%	-1%	15%	37%
SEASON	75-76	76-77	77-78	78-79	79-80	80-81	81-82	82-83	83-84	84-85
Paintings			7	23	30	26	18	13	27	22
Dollars			$7,911	$26,152	$34,533	$50,418	$27,451	$17,043	$42,383	$28,026

Record Sale: $9,000, BB.SF, 6/24/81, "Welcoming the Fishing Vessels Home," 31 x 41 in.

MEMBERSHIPS
American Federation of Arts
American Water Color Society
National Arts Club
New York Water Color Club
Philadelphia Art Club
Pulchre Studio
Rochester Art Club
Salmagundi Club

PUBLIC COLLECTIONS
Brooklyn Museum
Butler Institute of American Art,
  Youngstown, Ohio
Detroit Institute of Arts
Maryland Institute, Baltimore
National Arts Club, New York City
National Gallery of Art, Washington, D.C.
St. Louis Art Museum

EDWIN WILLARD DEMING

(1860-1942)

Edwin Willard Deming dedicated his life to the artistic preservation of American Indian culture. Primarily a painter, he was also a muralist, illustrator and sculptor of Indian and animal subjects.

He was born in Ashland, Ohio in 1860, but his family moved to Western Illinois while he was a boy. The area was still populated by Indians, and Deming grew up with Indian playmates. As a teenager, he traveled even further West, by train and stagecoach to Indian territory, to sketch the inhabitants.

His parents sent Deming to Chicago to study business law, but he was set on becoming an artist. He sold most of his possessions to get money for a trip to New York City and enrolled at the Art Students League. Next came a year in Paris at the Academie Julien.

Back in the United States, Deming began to paint cycloramas for a living. In 1887, he made the first of many trips to the Southwest to paint the Apache and Pueblo. He then traveled to Oregon to paint the Umatilla.

On a later trip he lived for a year with the Indians, learning their ways of life, their culture and their religion. It is said that no other painter knew more about the American Indian than Deming. In 1916, he painted murals of Indian life for the American Museum of Natural History in New York City.

When the United States entered World War I, Deming, though then 57, volunteered and was commissioned as a cap-

Bird Woman Meeting Lewis and Clark on the Upper Missouri, 27 x 34 in., signed l.l. Courtesy of Kennedy Galleries, New York, New York.

tain. He was active in camouflage work and also painted targets. After his return he lived and worked in New York City until his death in 1942.

MEMBERSHIPS
National Arts Club
National Society of Mural Painters
Washington Art Club

PUBLIC COLLECTIONS
American Museum of Natural History,
  New York City
Art Museum, Montclair, New Jersey
Brooklyn Museum
National Gallery of Art, Washington, D.C.

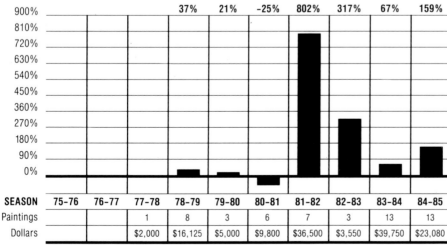

10-Year Average Change From Base Years '77-'78: 172%

| | | 37% | 21% | -25% | 802% | 317% | 67% | 159% |

SEASON	75-76	76-77	77-78	78-79	79-80	80-81	81-82	82-83	83-84	84-85
Paintings			1	8	3	6	7	3	13	13
Dollars			$2,000	$16,125	$5,000	$9,800	$36,500	$3,550	$39,750	$23,080

Record Sale: $30,000, SPB, 4/23/82, "Indian Horse Race," 20 × 36 in.

ARTHUR FRANK MATHEWS
(1860-1945)

A major turn-of-the-century painter of imaginative landscapes in Northern California, Arthur Frank Mathews was a highly versatile artist who also made an impact in crafts, furniture, interiors, mural painting, architecture and publishing. Through furniture designs, he developed a version of art nouveau called the California decorative style, which dominated Northern California art during the early twentieth century.

Mathews's paintings, primarily California landscapes, have a poetic, romantic quality, derived from his use of color tonalities. He emphasized the formal rather than the realistic qualities of his subject, using flat areas of color, closely related in tone and intensity. In this, Mathews was influenced by oriental art and by Puvis de Chavannes and Whistler. Like Whistler, Mathews believed that art represents a refinement of nature. Like Puvis, he drew themes from biblical and mythological sources.

Born in 1860 in Markesan, Wisconsin, Mathews moved as a child to Oakland, California with his family. His architect father enrolled him in private drawing lessons when Mathews was six and later took him on as an apprentice. In 1885, Mathews went to Paris, where he stayed for four years, studying under Jules Joseph Lefebvre and Gustave Boulanger at the Academie Julien. Upon his return to San Francisco, he was appointed director of the California School of Design, a position he held for 16 years.

Following the 1906 earthquake, Mathews and his wife, Lucia, opened the Furniture Shop, where they infused art nouveau with Western motifs—including the California poppy—carved into and painted on furniture and decorative objects. They also published a magazine, *Philopolis,* which helped give direction to the rebuilding of San Francisco.

Discovery of San Francisco Bay by Portola, 1896, 70¼ x 58½, signed l.l. Courtesy of John H. Garzoli Gallery, San Francisco, California.

Ladies of the Dance, 1926, 34½ x 59½ in., signed l.r. Courtesy of John H. Garzoli Gallery, San Francisco, California.

Among his several mural paintings, Mathews did 12 panels on California history for the state capitol building in Sacramento.

MEMBERSHIPS
Philadelphia Art Club

PUBLIC COLLECTIONS
Metropolitan Museum of Art, New York City
Oakland Museum, California

SEASON	75-76	76-77	77-78	78-79	79-80	80-81	81-82	82-83	83-84	84-85
Paintings				1	1	1			1	
Dollars				$17,000	$28,000	$2,000			$2,750	

Record Sale: $28,000, BB.SF, 1/10/80, "Ladies on the Grass," 48 × 52 in.

ANNA MARY ROBERTSON MOSES
("GRANDMA MOSES")
(1860-1961)

Red Barn #1745, 11 x 14 in., signed l.l. Courtesy of Henry B. Holt, Inc., Essex Fells, New Jersey.

Anna Mary Robertson Moses, or Grandma Moses, was the quintessential American folk artist. She was also the embodiment of the American success story.

In her late seventies, she began painting primitive scenes recalled from her youth. Within a few years her work was being bought by avid collectors and shown in museums.

Like Currier and Ives, who inspired some of her early work, her paintings evoked a nostalgic response from the public. In brightly-colored, well-organized compositions, she depicted a simpler way of life that had vanished.

Moses was born on a farm near Eagle Bridge in upstate New York in 1860. At age 12 she worked as a hired girl, housekeeping, cooking and tending the sick and elderly. After 15 years of this, she married farmhand Thomas Moses and moved to Virginia, where they rented a farm.

She bore 10 children, five of whom died in infancy. Her life was typical of a farmwife of the day—constant work. After 18 years, the family returned to Eagle Bridge and bought a dairy farm. The children grew up and married. In 1927, Thomas Moses died.

Grandma Moses stayed on the farm, now run by one of her sons. When she became too old to work outside, she

began stitching worsted-yarn pictures to pass the time; when arthritis made stitching too painful, her family suggested she try painting.

In 1938, three of her paintings in the window of a drugstore in nearby Hoosick Falls caught the eye of a knowledgeable collector. They launched her career as a painter.

At first her paintings were somewhat limited in scope, with few figures and the emphasis on content. By the 1940s, however, feeling more confident in her new medium, she became more expansive, painting landscapes with rolling hills and many small figures engaged in a variety of activities.

Grandma Moses was extraordinarily prolific, producing an estimated 1,600 paintings. With old-time frugality, she painted them in batches to avoid wasting paint. Sometimes she completed as many as five pictures in a single week.

She continued to paint until a few months before her death in 1961 at age 101.

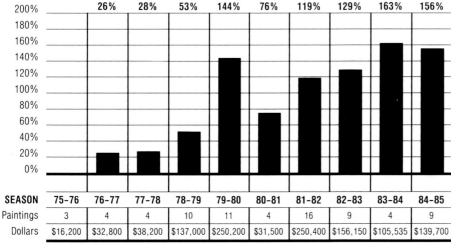

10-Year Average Change From Base Years '75-'76: 89%

SEASON	75-76	76-77	77-78	78-79	79-80	80-81	81-82	82-83	83-84	84-85
		26%	28%	53%	144%	76%	119%	129%	163%	156%
Paintings	3	4	4	10	11	4	16	9	4	9
Dollars	$16,200	$32,800	$38,200	$137,000	$250,200	$31,500	$250,400	$156,150	$105,535	$139,700

Record Sale: $121,000, SPB, 4/25/80, "One Little Hut Among the Bushes," 18 × 24 in.

PUBLIC COLLECTIONS
Bennington College Museum, Vermont
Phillips Collection, Washington, D.C.
White House, Washington, D.C.

576

DENNIS
MILLER
BUNKER
(1861-1890)

Although he did not live long—he died at age 29—Dennis Miller Bunker left enough portraits, landscapes and still lifes of sufficient merit to rank him as a painter of major significance. He did remarkably sensitive portraits of women, employing compositional elements from Whistler in some. Others were influenced more by Abbott Thayer, whom Bunker greatly admired. His early landscapes followed the style of Courbet and the barbizon painters, but after a summer of painting in England with John Singer Sargent, Bunker veered sharply toward impressionism in the last two years of his life.

Bunker was born in Garden City, Long Island in 1861. He studied at the National Academy of Design, at the Art Students League under William Merritt Chase and also for a time with Charles Dewey, a barbizon landscapist. In the summers of 1881 and 1882, he went to Nantucket to paint with his friends, Abbott Thayer and Joe Evans, both of whom had already studied in Paris. This convinced Bunker that he, too, should go to Paris.

In the fall of 1882, he left for France to study with Antoine Hebert at the Academie Julien and then with Gerome at the Ecole des Beaux Arts. In summer he traveled to Brittany to paint with other Americans. His early plein-air landscapes showed a marked talent for handling the play of light across green fields and coastal villages.

Back in Boston in 1885, he joined the faculty of the Cowles Art School. A one-man show of his work attracted the attention of Isabella Stewart Gardner, the noted collector, and he enjoyed her patronage for the remainder of his short life.

In 1887, Bunker met Sargent and the following year joined him for a summer

Roadside Cottage, Medfield, 1890, 18 x 24 in. Courtesy of Vose Galleries of Boston, Inc., Massachusetts.

Wild Asters, 1884, 25 x 30 in., signed l.r. Courtesy of Vose Galleries of Boston, Inc., Massachusetts.

of painting landscapes at Calcot, a village near Reading, England. Sargent, much taken with Monet's work at the time, was developing his own form of modified impressionism. Bunker's work turned in the same direction and he followed Sargent's lead in using a more open form of composition and a much brighter, though still limited, color palette. He carried this still further forward

the following summer in a group of charming landscapes painted at Medford, Massachusetts.

In 1889, Bunker became engaged and shortly afterward moved to New York, hoping to find more portrait commissions. They did not come easily, however, and worry and diminishing savings both took a toll on his health. He was married in the fall of 1890, but, while home in Boston for the Christmas holidays, he collapsed and died of heart failure.

PUBLIC COLLECTIONS
Fenway Court, Isabella Stewart Gardner Museum, Boston
Metropolitan Museum of Art, New York City
Museum of Fine Arts, Boston

SEASON	75-76	76-77	77-78	78-79	79-80	80-81	81-82	82-83	83-84	84-85
Paintings		1		2		1			1	1
Dollars		$18,000		$8,300		$10,000			$10,000	$40,000

Record Sale: $40,000, SPB, 12/6/84, "In the Greenhouse," 18 × 24 in.

FREDERIC REMINGTON

(1861-1909)

Frederic Sackrider Remington was a very significant artist, skilled as a writer and lauded as an illustrator, painter and sculptor. His subtle and powerful work made him the premier chronicler of the late-nineteenth-century American West.

The son of a newspaper publisher, Remington was born in Canton, New York in 1861. He began sketching as a boy. After attending a Massachusetts military academy from 1876 to 1878, he entered the newly formed Yale University Art School in New Haven, Connecticut. His father's death in 1880 induced him to leave school and briefly take on clerical work in Albany, New York.

During a short journey West in 1881, Remington received a glimpse of the life and land that would influence and inspire the rest of his life. The trip, consisting of sketching, prospecting and cowpunching from Montana to Texas, resulted in his first published illustration in *Harper's Weekly* in 1882.

In 1883, he bought a sheep ranch in Kansas, which served as a home base for more trips throughout the Southwest, where he sketched horses, cavalrymen, cowboys and Indians. Remington sold the ranch in 1884, and established a studio in Kansas City, Missouri.

Returning to New York City in 1885, Remington quickly became a successful illustrator, his work appearing in many publications. He began writing and illustrating his own books and articles as well, giving Eastern America what became the accepted vision of the American West.

Wanting greater acceptance as a fine artist, he studied at the Art Students League in New York City for a few months in 1886. Remington began submitting his paintings to exhibitions, but his illustrations remained the primary source of his remarkable reputation.

Remington did start winning prizes for his paintings in the early 1890s. His

If Skulls Could Speak (The Signal), 1900, 40 x 27 in., signed l.r., Courtesy of Wunderlich and Company, Inc., New York, New York.

work consisted of visual narratives of the old West, with landscape secondary to the figure.

In 1895, Remington produced his first bronze sculpture: *The Bronco Buster* (a cast in the Metropolitan Museum of Art), which immediately became popular and was followed by 24 other bronzes. His ability to exhibit a strong sense of life and movement in a three-dimensional work was recognized.

After moving to a farm in Connecticut, where he established an art gallery and library surrounded by collected Western memorabilia and artifacts, Remington began to experiment with a kind of impressionism around 1905. Many American artists were attracted to the style during that period, but

Remington never really ceased to be a realist.

Remington died in Ridgefield, Connecticut in 1909 after a sudden attack of appendicitis, leaving a legacy of more than 2,750 paintings and drawings and 25 sculptures from which multiple casts were made.

In addition, he had written eight books and numerous articles about the American West, and served in the Spanish-American War as a war correspondent. He was the most important artist ever to record the vanishing Western frontier.

MEMBERSHIPS
National Academy of Design
National Institute of Arts and Letters

PUBLIC COLLECTIONS
Amon Carter Museum, Fort Worth, Texas
Buffalo Bill Memorial Association,
   Cody, Wyoming
Metropolitan Museum of Art, New York City
Museum of Fine Arts, Houston
Remington Art Museum, Ogdensburg, New York
Rockwell Museum, Corning, New York
Whitney Gallery of Western Art,
   Cody, Wyoming

SEASON	75-76	76-77	77-78	78-79	79-80	80-81	81-82	82-83	83-84	84-85
Paintings	1		3	9	9	9	10	11	6	6
Dollars	$155,000		$164,000	$253,540	$396,800	$220,000	$228,250	$679,400	$568,700	$21,959

Record Sale: $500,000, SPB, 5/30/84, ''Coming to the Call,'' 27 × 40 in.

CHARLES SCHREYVOGEL

(1861-1912)

After years of struggle to make a living in art, Charles Schreyvogel was surprised by sudden nationwide success as he turned 40.

His reputation was made overnight by one oil painting, *My Bunkie* (date unknown, Metropolitan Museum of Art), a dramatic Western scene of a cavalryman rescuing an unhorsed comrade from pursing Indians. Schreyvogel had not been able to sell the painting or even give it away. On impulse, he entered it in the 1900 National Academy of Design exhibition. It captured first prize.

Catapulted into fame, Schreyvogel specialized in now-sought-after Western scenes of Indians and troopers. His work was compared favorably to that of the famous contemporary he admired, Frederic Remington, much to Remington's chagrin.

When Remington died in 1909, Schreyvogel wore the mantle of premier Western artist for the brief remainder of his life.

Born to German immigrants in New York City in 1861, Schreyvogel grew up poor. In his teens, he was a gold engraver's apprentice and a meerschaum carver.

He studied at the Newark Art League with portrait painter H. August Schwabe. In 1886, he began three years' study at the Royal Academy in Munich.

Back in New York City in 1890, Schreyvogel earned a meagre living with lithographs, portraits, landscapes and

The Triumph, 1908, 20 x 16⅛ in. Courtesy of Wunderlich & Company, Inc., New York, New York.

The Lost Dispatches, 1909, 25 x 34 in., signed l.r. Photograph courtesy of The Gerald Peters Gallery, Santa Fe, New Mexico.

ivory miniatures. Interested in Western themes, he sketched the 1890 Buffalo Bill show. With W.R. Fisher's patronage, he made his first trip West.

He spent five months in Colorado and Arizona, where he painted scenes of

cowboy and Indian life. But his Western paintings did not sell, and his straitened existence continued until he won the 1900 Academy prize.

Schreyvogel traveled West many times to research his paintings. His *Custer's Demand* (1903, Gilcrease Institute) was acclaimed. Some critics thought his composition and color sense superior to Remington's. Schreyvogel's flair for drama (some say melodrama), as well as the numerous reproductions of his work, gained him a wide following.

Schreyvogel died in Hoboken in 1912 of blood poisoning. In all, he left fewer than 100 known paintings and a few bronzes.

MEMBERSHIPS
National Academy of Design

PUBLIC COLLECTIONS
Library of Congress, Washington, D.C.
Metropolitan Museum of Art, New York City
National Cowboy Hall of Fame and Western
  Heritage Center, Oklahoma City
Thomas Gilcrease Institute of American
  History and Art, Tulsa

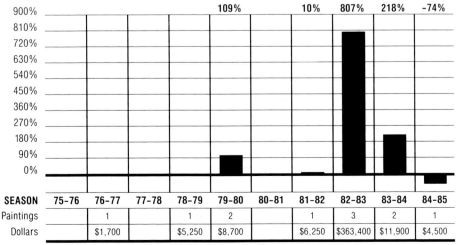

10-Year Average Change From Base Years '76-'77: 153%

				109%		10%	807%	218%	-74%

SEASON	75-76	76-77	77-78	78-79	79-80	80-81	81-82	82-83	83-84	84-85
Paintings		1		1	2		1	3	2	1
Dollars		$1,700		$5,250	$8,700		$6,250	$363,400	$11,900	$4,500

Record Sale: $180,000, SPB, 6/2/83, ''Doomed,'' 25 x 34 in.

GEORGE GARDNER SYMONS
(1861?-1930)

New Hope Winter Scene, 25 x 30 in., signed l.l. Courtesy of Henry B. Holt, Inc., Essex Fells, New Jersey.

Landscape and marine artist George Gardner Symons was one of the most successful of the plein-air painters, whose works were produced outdoors rather than in the studio. His style combined elements of impressionism and realism and was extremely popular.

Little is known of Symons's early life. The most likely date for his birth is 1861. He may have studied at the Art Institute of Chicago; he is known to have worked as a commercial artist in the Chicago area early in his career. He also studied in Paris, Munich and London.

Although he traveled and painted in California with artist William Wendt in 1886, Symons spent many years before 1906 in Europe, settling in St. Ives, Cornwall. There he adopted the plein-air technique of such artists as Julius Olsson, Adrian Stokes and Rudolph Hellwag. Elmer Schofield also joined the artists' colony at St. Ives, and he and Symons became friends. Their work bears comparison in many aspects.

Returning to the United States in 1906, Symons set up a studio near Laguna Beach, California, and became active in Western art societies. Most of his time, however, was spent in New York City or in Colerain, Massachusetts.

Symons believed in drawing his inspiration directly from nature. Particularly in California and the Southwest, he wandered considerable distances to paint scenes of the ocean coast or the Grand Canyon. He executed many snow scenes, for which he became especially well known, and views of the Berkshires.

Like Schofield, Symons used an impressionistic style, characterized by energy and simplicity. His canvases were usually large, and he favored sweeping, panoramic views with wide brushstrokes and large areas of bright color. Good examples of his snow scenes are *An*

Winter - New England, 16 x 20¼ in., signed l.r. Courtesy of John H. Garzoli Gallery, San Francisco, California.

Opalescent River (1908, Metropolitan Museum of Art), with thick impasto and coarse canvas imparting texture, and *The Winter Sun* (date unknown, Art Institute of Chicago).

Symons's greatest critical success occurred in the years immediately following 1909. He remained successful throughout his career, however, and exhibited widely in New York City, California and London. He died in 1930 in Hillside, New Jersey.

SEASON	75-76	76-77	77-78	78-79	79-80	80-81	81-82	82-83	83-84	84-85
Paintings		3	9	15	24	31	17	14	6	8
Dollars		$37,150	$34,350	$58,500	$89,699	$117,925	$59,150	$49,730	$13,300	$12,175

Record Sale: $33,200, PB, 10/28/76, "Winter Scene, Pennsylvania," 30 × 38 in.

WALTER P.S. GRIFFIN
(1861-1935)

Walter P.S. Griffin was an American impressionist whose work was strongly influenced by Childe Hassam.

He was born in Portland, Maine in 1861. He studied first at the Museum School of Art in Boston and then at the Art Students League in New York City. Later he went to Paris and studied at the Academie Colarossi under Collin and Laurens.

He then settled in Brittany for seven years to paint that rugged corner of France. His familiarity with and empathy for French art combined to give his work an authentic impressionist look—although it also displayed some traces of barbizon sentimentality.

On his return to the United States, Griffin divided his time between teaching and painting, first in Hartford, Connecticut for a year, and then at an art school he founded in Quebec. By the time he had moved to Old Lyme, Connecticut in 1905, however, he seems to have abandoned teaching to concentrate on painting.

It was in Old Lyme that he met and became a close friend of Hassam. Hassam's influence can be seen in Griffin's work of this period. The barbizon traces faded further.

In 1911, Griffin returned to Brittany and stayed until 1918, strengthening his impressionist technique. He also returned frequently during the post-war period and painted in Norway and Venice as well.

Beached Boats Finnisterre, France, 27 x 32 in. Courtesy of Vose Galleries of Boston, Inc., Massachusetts.

Old Lyme, 27 x 32 in., signed l.l. Courtesy of Vose Galleries of Boston, Inc., Massachusetts.

Shortly before his death in Maine in 1935, Griffin showed a growing interest in expressionism. His final paintings are rich with thick, bright colors, applied with a palette knife.

MEMBERSHIPS
Allied Artists of America
Allied Artists of Paris
American Art Club
American Water Color Society
National Institute of Arts and Letters
New York Water Color Club
Salmagundi Club

PUBLIC COLLECTIONS
Albright-Knox Art Gallery, Buffalo, New York
Brooklyn Museum
Luxembourg Gallery, Paris
Memorial Art Gallery, Rochester, New York

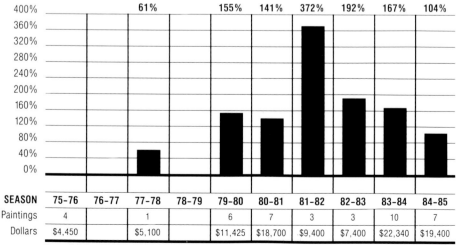

10-Year Average Change From Base Years '75-'76: 149%

SEASON	75-76	76-77	77-78	78-79	79-80	80-81	81-82	82-83	83-84	84-85
			61%		155%	141%	372%	192%	167%	104%
Paintings	4		1		6	7	3	3	10	7
Dollars	$4,450		$5,100		$11,425	$18,700	$9,400	$7,400	$22,340	$19,400

Record Sale: $7,000, W.W, 12/13/81, ''Rural Landscapes,'' 9 x 13 in.

FREDERICK JUDD WAUGH
(1861-1940)

Westerly, 40 x 50 in., signed l.r. Courtesy of Vose Galleries of Boston, Inc., Massachusetts.

Frederick Judd Waugh was among the most popular academic painters of marine subjects of his time. He painted approximately 2,500 seascapes and achieved international recognition.

Born in 1861 in Bordentown, New Jersey, Waugh was raised by an artistic family. His father, Samuel B. Waugh, was a portrait and landscape painter. His mother, Eliza Young Waugh, was a miniaturist. His half-sister, Ida Waugh, was a figure painter. Oddly, his father discouraged the young Frederick from becoming a painter, and it was only after a good deal of teenage protest that Frederick was permitted to attend the Pennsylvania Academy of the Fine Arts in Philadelphia.

From 1880 to 1883, Waugh studied at the Academy under Thomas Eakins and Thomas Anshutz. Waugh then went abroad and studied under Adolphe William Bougereau and Tony Robert-Fleury at the Academie Julien in Paris. In the summer, Waugh painted at an artists' colony near Fontainebleau.

Waugh's early work consisted of figurative compositions which were conventional and decorative in style. He first began painting the sea while in England, and it soon became his primary subject.

Waugh remained in Europe from 1892 to 1907, and then returned to the United States. From 1901 to 1907, he lived in England and worked as an illustrator for the *Graphic* and various London papers and magazines. There he gained success as a marine painter as well as an illustrator.

Already a renowned artist, Waugh returned to America in 1907 and settled in Provincetown, Massachusetts, on Cape Cod. In addition to Waugh's tremendous number of marine paintings, he also did some award-winning portraits and genre paintings.

Waugh worked with both watercolors and oils in a plein-air style. He applied heavy, impasto brushstrokes on the canvas. The colors were often applied directly out of the tubes without prior mixing. This use of pure unmixed colors added to the freshness of Waugh's paintings. The waves look bright and wet, and the quality of light in the seascapes is amazingly realistic. Through the years, Waugh's seascapes gradually progressed from realistic, clearly defined depictions of large panoramic views to more abstract, broadly defined portrayals of smaller areas of sea, rocks and sky.

Waugh received wide recognition and praise during his lifetime. He was elected an associate member of the National Academy of Design in 1909 and academician in 1911. He also won many prestigious awards, including the Popular Prize from the Carnegie International Exhibition of Paintings, in five consecutive years from 1934.

Waugh died in 1940 in Provincetown.

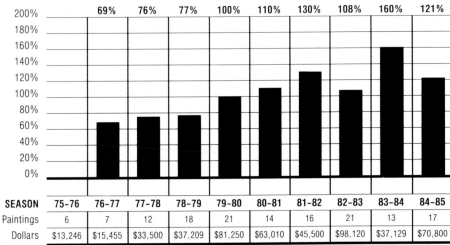

10-Year Average Change From Base Years '75-'76: 95%

SEASON	75-76	76-77	77-78	78-79	79-80	80-81	81-82	82-83	83-84	84-85
		69%	76%	77%	100%	110%	130%	108%	160%	121%
Paintings	6	7	12	18	21	14	16	21	13	17
Dollars	$13,246	$15,455	$33,500	$37,209	$81,250	$63,010	$45,500	$98,120	$37,129	$70,800

Record Sale: $37,000, SPB, 6/2/83, "Sympathie," 45 x 58 in.

MEMBERSHIPS
National Academy of Design

PUBLIC COLLECTIONS
Bristol Academy, England
City Art Museum, St. Louis
Metropolitan Museum of Art, New York City
National Gallery of Art, Washington, D.C.
Walker Art Gallery, Liverpool, England

CHARLES COURTNEY CURRAN
(1861-1942)

The Perfume of Roses, 29¼ x 23⅜ in., signed l.l. Courtesy of National Museum of American Art, Smithsonian Institution, Gift of William T. Evans.

Charles Courtney Curran, a prolific and popular painter all his life, was among the artists responsible for the rebirth of the genre tradition in late nineteenth century American art.

Born in 1861 in Hartford, Kentucky, Curran spent his formative years in Sandusky, Ohio, where his family had moved in 1881. Curran studied briefly at the Cincinnati School of Design.

The following year, Curran moved to New York City. There he enrolled in the National Academy of Design, worked under the tutelage of Walter Satterlee, and later attended the Art Students League.

Curran achieved early artistic recognition. He had his first exhibit at age 23 at the National Academy of Design. Five years later, the Academy awarded him Third Hallgarten Prize for *A Breezy Day* (date and location unknown), designated most "meritorious painting in oil."

Curran's two years of study at the Academie Julien in Paris, from 1889 to 1891, likely influenced the impressionistic use of form and light in his subsequent works.

He spent the remainder of his life dividing his time between New York City and his house and studio in the Cragsmoor region of New York State. Curran died in 1942.

In addition to teaching art and painting, Curran was a leader of the Cragsmoor Art Colony. For several years, he and his wife co-edited the art student publication *Palette and Brush*.

During his life, Curran received much recognition for his figure paintings, but his style was not limited exclusively to that genre. The widely traveled artist also painted landscapes, portraits and a series of views of the Imperial Temples of Peking.

He is perhaps best known for those works which combine sweeping vistas of the Cragsmoor area with the almost whimsical delicacy of the female form, as in *Two Women in a Landscape* (1916, location unknown).

MEMBERSHIPS
Allied Art Association
American Water Color Society
National Academy of Design
Lotos Club
MacDowell Club
National Arts Club
New York Water Color Club
Salmagundi Club
Society of American Artists

PUBLIC COLLECTIONS
Albright-Knox Art Gallery, Buffalo
Art Association of Richmond, Indiana
Columbus Museum of Art, Ohio
Dallas Museum of Fine Arts
Fort Worth Art Museum, Texas
Metropolitan Museum of Art, New York City
Montclair Art Museum, New Jersey
National Gallery of Art, Washington, D.C.
Pennsylvania Academy of the Fine Arts,
    Philadelphia
Toledo Museum of Art, Ohio
Witte Memorial Museum, San Antonio

10-Year Average Change From Base Years '75-'76: 274%

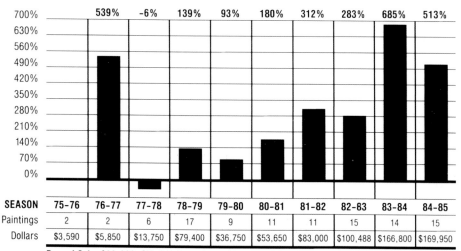

	75-76	76-77	77-78	78-79	79-80	80-81	81-82	82-83	83-84	84-85
		539%	-6%	139%	93%	180%	312%	283%	685%	513%
SEASON	75-76	76-77	77-78	78-79	79-80	80-81	81-82	82-83	83-84	84-85
Paintings	2	2	6	17	9	11	11	15	14	15
Dollars	$3,590	$5,850	$13,750	$79,400	$36,750	$53,650	$83,000	$100,488	$166,800	$169,950

Record Sale: $80,000, CH, 6/1/84, "Chrysanthemums," 9 × 12 in.

IRVING RAMSEY WILES
(1861-1948)

When Irving Ramsey Wiles painted a portrait of actress Julia Marlowe in 1901, he captured the essence of America's Gilded Age. The painting (National Gallery of Art) was as renowned as the actress herself.

Wiles delighted in portrait painting, and was best known for his elegant portraits of women and celebrities. President Theodore Roosevelt and William Jennings Bryant sat for Wiles, who was the son of landscape painter and art instructor Lemuel M. Wiles. His daughter, Gladys Wiles, also distinguished herself as a painter.

Born in Utica, New York in 1861, he was raised in New York City. He considered a career as a violinist; however, at age 17 he was studying art with his father, and by the next year he had exhibited at the National Academy of Design. He then studied at the Art Students League under James Carroll Beckwith and William Merritt Chase from 1879 to 1881. Chase not only influenced his style, but also became a lasting friend, choosing Wiles to complete the portrait commissions left unfinished at his death.

Wiles went to Paris in 1882, attending the Academie Julien, where Boulanger and Lefebvre taught him. He also studied under Carolus-Duran. Paris street scenes in watercolors were painted during his student years.

When Wiles returned to New York City in 1884, he found it necessary to divide his time between painting and illustrating for *Century, Harper's* and *Scribner's* magazines, since portrait work was not sufficiently lucrative. He also taught classes in his New York studio, and at his father's Silver Lake Art School in Ingham, New York in the summers.

More time was devoted to portraiture and oil figure studies after his election to the National Academy of Design in 1897. Wiles's technique followed that of

John Gellatly, 1930-1932, 79⅛ x 38½ in., signed l.r. Courtesy of National Museum of American Art, Smithsonian Institution, Washington, D.C. Gift of Irving R. Wiles.

Chase, who advocated a direct approach, in that he rarely made studies and painted directly on the canvas. He used fluid brushwork, illuminating colors brightly against dark backgrounds.

Peconic, Long Island, where his summer classes were moved during the late 1890s, eventually became his home. Many of the seascapes done at Peconic reveal a sense of freedom and informality. For recreation, Wiles sailed and collected model ships.

Wiles died at age 87 in 1948.

MEMBERSHIPS
Allied Artists of America
American Federation of Arts
American Water Color Society
Century Association
National Academy of Design
National Arts Club
National Association of Portrait Painters
National Institute of Arts and Letters
Society of American Artists

PUBLIC COLLECTIONS
Butler Art Institute, Youngstown, Ohio
Chase Bank, New York City
Corcoran Gallery of Art, Washington, D.C.
Metropolitan Museum of Art, New York City
National Gallery of Art, Washington, D.C.
West Point Military Academy, New York

SEASON	75-76	76-77	77-78	78-79	79-80	80-81	81-82	82-83	83-84	84-85
Paintings		1	2	5	10	8	5	7	2	3
Dollars		$2,600	$7,200	$19,750	$21,050	$23,050	$11,250	$16,100	$6,250	$2,827

Record Sale: $8,500, CH, 3/18/83, "In the Garden," 9 × 5 in.

CHARLES D. CAHOON
(1861-1951)

Charles Drew Cahoon flourished as a successful painter of Cape Cod landscapes, seascapes and vignettes during the first three decades of the twentieth century. Although his work is little known today, recognition and appreciation for it appear to be growing.

Cahoon was born in 1861 in Harwich, Massachusetts. His father was a sea captain and amateur artist; Cahoon gained drawing experience by copying some of his father's sketches. He also went to sea for a few years as a young man.

He studied the new art of photography and worked in Boston in 1886 as a photograph retoucher, a profession he followed until he was able to paint full-time in the early 1900s. It may be that his photographic work guided him toward his detailed, realistic painting style.

At first, Cahoon painted conventional subjects, such as his *Burning of the Exchange Building, Harwich* (date and location unknown), a depiction of a local tragedy. He also executed portraits, including one of New Hampshire governor Frank Rollins and one of General Ayling of Centerville, Massachusetts. He received commissions for copies of Gilbert Stuart's portraits of George and Martha Washington and of Franz Hals's *Laughing Cavalier.*

As Cahoon's style matured, he turned to the subject for which he was to become best known: gentle, carefully detailed pictures of Cape Cod sights—

Cape Cod Snowfall, 8 x 10 in., signed l.r. Courtesy of The Cahoon Museum of American Art, Cotuit, Massachusetts.

fishermen, boats, weather-beaten houses, all suffused with mellow light. He maintained a studio in Boston and painted there and in Harwich. Summer visitors to the Cape bought many of his paintings, and Cahoon prospered until the stock market collapse of 1929, in which he lost his investments. He returned to Harwich to live and contin-

ued to paint. According to his son, Alvin, Cahoon once described painting as "a poor man's career."

Cahoon died in Harwich in 1951. Alvin Cahoon, who also became a professional painter, estimates that his father produced between 2,500 and 3,000 paintings.

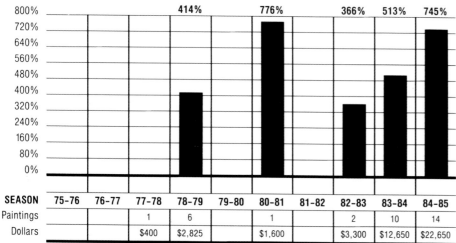

10-Year Average Change From Base Years '77-'78: 469%

SEASON	75-76	76-77	77-78	78-79	79-80	80-81	81-82	82-83	83-84	84-85
				414%		776%		366%	513%	745%
Paintings			1	6		1		2	10	14
Dollars			$400	$2,825		$1,600		$3,300	$12,650	$22,650

Record Sale: $3,800, RB.HM, 8/9/83, "Autumn Marsh, Massachusetts," 10 x 24 in.

585

MINA FONDA OCHTMAN
(1862-1924)

During her lifetime, Mina Fonda Ochtman's work was largely subordinated to, and eclipsed by, that of her husband, painter Leonard Ochtman. Now, however, critics regard her work as a fine blending of the American landscape with French impressionism.

Born in Laconia, New Hampshire in 1862, Ochtman moved to New York City when she was 24. She set up a studio with a friend, and took courses at the Art Students League, before meeting and marrying her husband in 1891.

Shortly after their marriage, the Ochtmans moved to the Greenwich, Connecticut area—their home for the remainder of their lives. There, each became active in the influential Cos Cob art colony.

For the next 20 years, Ochtman's time was devoted to raising the couple's three children and caring for their home. Her art was eclipsed by the work of her husband who, by 1910, had established a reputation as one of the foremost landscape painters in the United States.

In 1911, the Ochtmans founded the Greenwich Society of Artists. Mina Ochtman's work, which she resumed after her children were older and continued until her death in 1924, was exhibited at the Society, as well as at the National Academy of Design.

Although the couple frequently relied upon the same landscape setting for inspiration, Mina Ochtman's paintings were crisper and brighter than her husband's.

Before the 1920s, however, after the 1913 Armory Show, modernists trends superseded impressionism as practiced by Ochtman. Until recent revivals, often in joint exhibition, the paintings of both Ochtmans were either forgotten or disregarded.

Summer in Nearby Woods, 12 x 16 in. Courtesy of Connecticut Gallery, Marlborough, Connecticut.

MEMBERSHIPS
American Water Color Society
National Association of Women Painters and
  Sculptors
Greenwich Society of Artists

SEASON	75-76	76-77	77-78	78-79	79-80	80-81	81-82	82-83	83-84	84-85
Paintings								1		
Dollars								$800		

Record Sale: $800, P.NY, 6/1/83, "Forest Interior," 16 × 20 in.

ARTHUR B. DAVIES
(1862-1928)

A visionary painter of dancing nudes in mythical landscapes, Arthur Davies occupies an important position in American art. He is accorded a leading role both for his painting and for his brilliance in organizing the 1913 Armory Show in New York City. The historic show brought together on a grand scale 1,600 pieces of American and European art, exposing the public for the first time to the scope of modern trends. The show affected the course of art history in the United States.

Davies's own canvases, often described as "decorative," depict arcadian landscapes populated by Botticelli-like nudes and mythical unicorns. The paintings are considered to be in the symbolist tradition, comparable to the work of Pierre Puvis de Chavannes.

Born in Utica, New York, Davies worked in Mexico as an engineer before studying art with Dwight Williams, and later at the Chicago Academy of Design. In 1886, he moved to New York City, making a living as a magazine illustrator and gaining influence among wealthy women who liked his romantic, dreamlike paintings, untouched by realism or modernism. In two trips to Europe, Davies studied works by the Venetians, the pre-raphaelites and the German romantics.

In style, Davies's work bears some resemblance to the frescoes of Pompeii, which he admired. He used long, horizontal canvases, crossed by processions of nudes or dancing figures who seem to

Two Spirits, 21½ x 29 in. Courtesy of La Salle University Art Museum, Philadelphia, Pennsylvania.

be holding their breath. Davies believed this technique—painting figures at the moment of inhalation—would capture a lifelike quality that was present in Greek sculpture. Some authorities have described his figures and their poses as "eerie"; others say they are languorous.

Through the 1890s, Davies painted conventional landscapes, moving in 1913 to a cubist style in which his dancing nudes are presented as geometric forms with superficial facets. In 1918, he developed an interest in lithography, aquatint and etching, returning in his last decade of work to the misty romantic canvases of his early period.

Davies's personality was a study in

contrasts. His reclusive, romantic streak, revealed in the paintings, hid strong executive capabilities that emerged when he was given control of organizing the Armory Show.

Originally planned as an exhibit of American work, the show was expanded by Davies to include "a few" items of radical European art. Before he was done, he had launched one of the largest international exhibits of its kind, unerringly choosing the finest modern artists. His own work, in contrast, shows few signs of modernism, although he exhibited among the progressive painters called The Eight.

Davies liked fairy tales and baseball. He had an almost morbid dislike of crowds and led a secretive private life. Other artists did not even know the location of his studio, perhaps because for more than two decades Davies carried out a secret liaison with a mistress in New York City, who bore him a daughter. Davies spent weekends in rural Congers, New York, with his wife and two sons, who knew nothing of the second family until Davies's death in 1928 of heart failure.

MEMBERSHIPS
National Academy of Design

PUBLIC COLLECTIONS
Art Institute of Chicago
Metropolitan Museum of Art, New York City

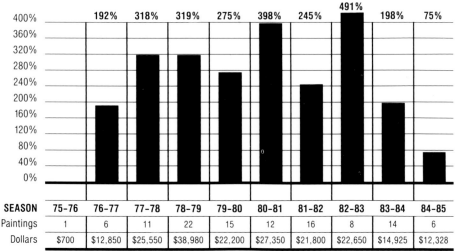

10-Year Average Change From Base Years '75-'76: 251%

SEASON	75-76	76-77	77-78	78-79	79-80	80-81	81-82	82-83	83-84	84-85
		192%	318%	319%	275%	398%	245%	491%	198%	75%
Paintings	1	6	11	22	15	12	16	8	14	6
Dollars	$700	$12,850	$25,550	$38,980	$22,200	$27,350	$21,800	$22,650	$14,925	$12,328

Record Sale: $13,000, SPB, 5/29/81, "Fantasy," 33 × 26 in.

CHARLES ROLLO PETERS
(1862-1928)

Charles Peters was a successful San Francisco landscape artist noted primarily for his nocturnal paintings. Throughout his career, he had the opportunity to study and exhibit both in the United States and Europe.

Born in 1862 to a wealthy family, Peters studied at the Urban Academy under Jules Tavernier and at the San Francisco Art Association's California School of Design under Virgil Williams and Chris Jorgensen.

In 1886, he went to Europe, attending the Ecole des Beaux Arts and the Academie Julien, studying with Boulanger and Lefebvre, among others. He returned to San Francisco in 1890, but made frequent trips to Europe. During these years, Peters began to paint night scenes.

He settled in Monterey, California in 1895, becoming part of the Carmel art colony, a loosely knit collection of free spirits, including Maynard Dixon and Jo Mora. At the urging of Alexander Harrison, Peters concentrated on the nocturnals, with which he ultimately achieved his greatest success. Many of his subjects were found among the adobe houses and old missions dotting the Bay area.

Peters's one-man exhibitions in New York City and London earned him enough to purchase the 32-acre Doud tract in 1900. There he built an estate which included a studio and gallery. Following the San Francisco earthquake in

Nocturne, ca. 1920, 19½ x 25¼ in., signed l.l. Photograph courtesy of Petersen Galleries, Beverly Hills, California.

1906, he cared for the homeless of the art community at the estate.

During the early 1900s, Peters joined William Keith and Eugene Neuhaus to found the Del Monte Art Gallery. Despite this, he suffered financial setbacks which forced him to sell his estate in 1911. He returned to San Francisco, where he organized the first exhibition

of painting and sculpture by California artists at the Golden Gate Park Memorial Museum.

Peters went to Europe again in 1923, and continued to paint there until illness caused a return to San Francisco in 1926.

MEMBERSHIPS
Lotos Club
Salmagundi Club

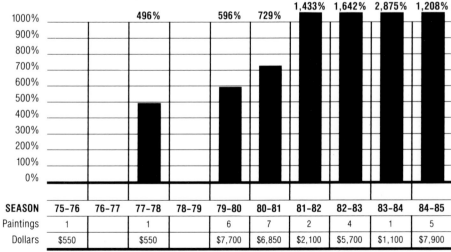

10-Year Average Change From Base Years '75-'76: 1,122%

SEASON	75-76	76-77	77-78	78-79	79-80	80-81	81-82	82-83	83-84	84-85
			496%		596%	729%	1,433%	1,642%	2,875%	1,208%
Paintings	1		1		6	7	2	4	1	5
Dollars	$550		$550		$7,700	$6,850	$2,100	$5,700	$1,100	$7,900

Record Sale: $4,250, BB.SF, 2/28/85, "Moonlight on the Adobe," 31 × 43 in.

ROBERT REID
(1862-1929)

The work of figure painter and muralist Robert Reid reveals an impressionistic use of light and vivid color. Reid was a founding member of Ten American Painters, a group formed to promote impressionism in the United States.

Reid was born in Stockbridge, Massachusetts in 1862. From 1880 to 1884, he was a student and assistant instructor at the school of the Museum of Fine Arts in Boston. (Fellow students Edmund Tarbell and Frank Benson were later to join him in the Ten American Painters.) He also studied at the Art Students League in New York City.

In 1886, Reid went to Paris, where he studied at the Academie Julien for three years. His instructors included Gustave Boulanger and Jules Lefebvre. He also exhibited annually in the Salon.

Returning to the United States, he gained a reputation for murals, which often featured neoclassical female figures and flowers. He painted a series of panels depicting the five senses for the Library of Congress, contributed to the decoration of numerous public and exposition buildings, and produced designs for 20 stained-glass church windows.

Reid's easel works, such as *Fleur-de-Lys* (ca. 1899, Metropolitan Museum of Art), *Violet Kimono* (ca. 1910, National Museum of American Art), and *The Mirror* (ca. 1910, National Museum of American Art), display greater boldness of design than

The Old Gardener, 36¼ x 40¼ in., signed u.l. Courtesy of The Brooklyn Museum, Gift of the Fellow Members in the Players and Lambs Clubs.

do his murals, although they employ the same conventional subjects. Brushwork is vigorous, usually on coarse canvas, and rich colors are used, especially strong blues.

In 1927, Reid moved to Colorado Springs, Colorado. There he worked as a portraitist and founded the Broadmoor Art Academy. After a paralyzing stroke in 1927, he learned to paint with his left hand. He exhibited in 1928, a year before his death.

MEMBERSHIPS
National Academy of Design
National Institute of Arts and Letters
Ten American Painters

PUBLIC COLLECTIONS
Albright-Knox Art Gallery, Buffalo
Brooklyn Museum
Cincinnati Art Museum
Corcoran Gallery of Art, Washington, D.C.
Library of Congress, Washington, D.C.
Massachusetts State House
Metropolitan Museum of Art, New York City
National Gallery of Art, Washington, D.C.
National Museum of American Art, Washington, D.C.

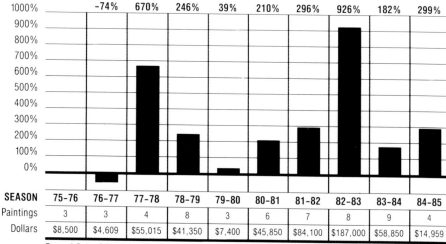

10-Year Average Change From Base Years '75-'76: 279%

	-74%	670%	246%	39%	210%	296%	926%	182%	299%

SEASON	75-76	76-77	77-78	78-79	79-80	80-81	81-82	82-83	83-84	84-85
Paintings	3	3	4	8	3	6	7	8	9	4
Dollars	$8,500	$4,609	$55,015	$41,350	$7,400	$45,850	$84,100	$187,000	$58,850	$14,959

Record Sale: $60,000, CH, 12/3/82, ''Tending the Garden,'' 22 × 19 in.

EDWARD PERCY MORAN
(1862-1935)

Edward Percy Moran, who preferred to be known as Percy Moran, was born in Philadelphia in 1862. His father, Edward Moran, was a well-known marine painter who emigrated to the United States with three brothers, also artists. Thomas Moran is known for his Rocky Mountain pictures, Peter was a painter, etcher, and illustrator, and John was a painter.

Percy Moran continued in the family tradition by excelling as a genre and landscape painter and as an etcher. He was equally adept in oil and watercolor.

Although he attended public school in Philadelphia, Moran spent most of his youth studying at his father's studio in New York City. In 1894, father and son traveled to Paris, where the young Moran attended and graduated from military school and then studied art for a year. Returning home, he continued his art studies at the National Academy of Design in New York City and then at the Pennsylvania Academy of the Fine Arts under S.J. Ferris. This was followed by four years of study in Paris and London.

Returning to New York City, Moran opened a studio and soon attracted notice with his watercolor sketches. His earliest work consists of scenes of children and peasant life, and portraits of pretty women. Later, he turned to the subject for which he is best remembered: the customs and homelife of colonial America. These quiet paintings, telling

The Lost Drummer Boy, ca. 1915, 24 x 36 in., signed l.l. Courtesy of Petersen Galleries, Beverly Hills, California.

stories of love or of domestic incidents, are distinguished by great attention to detail. Many were reproduced in colored etchings, photogravures and mezzotint, and were published in books and magazines.

Percy Moran died in New York City in 1935.

MEMBERSHIPS
National Water Color Society

PUBLIC COLLECTIONS
Philadelphia Museum of Art, Pennsylvania
Walker Art Center, Minneapolis, Minnesota

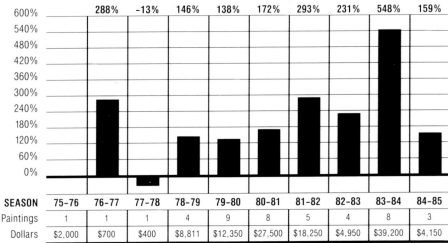

10-Year Average Change From Base Years '75-'76: 196%

	288%	-13%	146%	138%	172%	293%	231%	548%	159%

SEASON	75-76	76-77	77-78	78-79	79-80	80-81	81-82	82-83	83-84	84-85
Paintings	1	1	1	4	9	8	5	4	8	3
Dollars	$2,000	$700	$400	$8,811	$12,350	$27,500	$18,250	$4,950	$39,200	$4,150

Record Sale: $12,000, P.NY, 10/13/83, "Battle of New Orleans," 26 x 36 in.

WILL
SPARKS
(1862-1937)

Will Sparks was a multi-talented individual best known for his colorful landscapes of the West. Educated to enter the medical profession, Sparks instead chose art, and produced some 3,000 murals, portraits and oils in his 50-year career.

Sparks was born in St. Louis in 1862. He was educated in the public schools, at Washington University and at the St. Louis School of Fine Arts. He majored in anatomy at the St. Louis Medical College, and nearly chose a career in medicine. His innate abilities and inclinations led him back to art, however, and Sparks rapidly established himself as a local talent.

He went to New York City in 1884, then on to Paris, where he studied at the Academies Julien and Colarossi under Bouvert and Cazin. He met Louis Pasteur, and combined his medical and artistic skills to produce several anatomy drawings for the famous scientist.

Sparks returned to America and traveled West, working for various newspapers along the way. He arrived in California in 1888, and settled in San Francisco in 1891. He joined the San Francisco Bohemian Club, a carefree group of struggling local artists. To support his painting, he worked as a feature writer for the San Francisco *Evening Call* and, in 1904, joined the University of California faculty as a teacher of anatomical drawing.

Most of Sparks's paintings were scenes of California, New Mexico, Arizona and Mexico. His most significant work was a series of 36 paintings, done between 1887 and 1919, paying tribute to California's many original Spanish missions. He completed a second series of paintings in 1933.

Sparks died in San Francisco in 1937, survived by his second wife.

Jacklin House, 8 x 10 in., signed l.r. Photograph courtesy of George Stern, Fine Arts, Encino, California. Collection of James Zidell.

MEMBERSHIPS
San Francisco Art Association
San Francisco Bohemian Club
Sequoia Club
Society of California Artists

PUBLIC COLLECTIONS
Bohemian Club, San Francisco
Fine Arts Guild, San Diego
M.H. de Young Memorial Museum, San Francisco
St. Louis Art Museum
Toledo Museum of Art, Ohio

SEASON	75-76	76-77	77-78	78-79	79-80	80-81	81-82	82-83	83-84	84-85
Paintings					3	7		5		3
Dollars					$4,000	$9,400		$4,600		$2,450

Record Sale: $2,000, BB.SF, 5/4/80, "October Day," 20 × 28 in.

EDMUND C. TARBELL
(1862-1938)

At the turn of the century, Edmund C. Tarbell was the undisputed leader of the Boston School of impressionist painters—so influential, in fact, that those who comprised the inner circle of his many followers were often referred to as "Tarbellites."

Despite his predisposition toward impressionism, however, he never sacrificed precise realism in his work. Rendering the beauty of the thing seen, he believed its color, its drawing and its values were what counted in painting.

Some observers dubbed him the "impressionist Vermeer" because of his penchant for painting serene, light-filled interiors, with well-polished furniture and gleaming floors, peopled by genteel young ladies reading, sewing or chatting together. It was a well-bred world where nothing unseemly ever happened. Besides those genre scenes he also painted many portraits, usually of the rich and powerful.

Tarbell was born in West Newton, Massachusetts in 1862. When his father died young and his mother remarried, he was left with his grandparents in Boston. At age 15, he was apprenticed to a leading local lithographer.

Three years later he enrolled in the School of the Boston Museum to study under Otto Grundmann. There he met Frank Benson, who was to become another commanding figure in the Boston School of painters. He and Benson

Girl with Sailboat, 40 x 30 in., signed l.l. Courtesy of Vose Galleries of Boston, Inc., Massachusetts.

also attended the Academie Julien in Paris, and toured Europe together. During this trip, Tarbell's admiration for the French impressionists blossomed, although he was drawn more to the subtle tones of Degas than to the higher-keyed colors of Pissaro and Monet.

In 1889, Tarbell joined the faculty of the Boston Museum School, a position he held until 1913. Despite the placid nature of his paintings, he was a peppery, assertive man with strong opinions. He became one of the most respected and feared art instructors of his day, and his influence was felt far beyond Boston.

Tarbell's insistence on the all-importance of technique, however,

brought him into conflict with some of his noted contemporaries. John Singer Sargent, for one, sneered at the idea, even while seeking advice on painting from Tarbell.

In addition to his interior genre paintings, Tarbell also did many outdoor scenes, some of them reminiscent of Renoir.

By 1918, Tarbell's polished, well-crafted portraits were in such demand in Washington, D.C. that he moved there to work. Among others, he painted Presidents Wilson and Hoover. While in Washington, he also was asked to become director of the Corcoran School of Art.

In 1925, Tarbell retired to his summer home in New Castle, New Hampshire, where he continued to paint until his death in 1938.

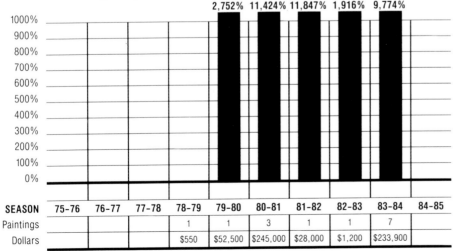

10-Year Average Change From Base Years '78-'79: 6,286%

SEASON	75-76	76-77	77-78	78-79	79-80	80-81	81-82	82-83	83-84	84-85
					2,752%	11,424%	11,847%	1,916%	9,774%	
Paintings				1	1	3	1	1	7	
Dollars				$550	$52,500	$245,000	$28,000	$1,200	$233,900	

Record Sale: $185,000, SPB, 12/4/80, "Child with Boat," 40 x 30 in.

FRANK WESTON BENSON
(1862-1951)

Frank Weston Benson was born in Salem, Massachusetts in 1862. One of the first American impressionists, he became known for his portraits of women and children, especially in outdoor settings. He was a member of Ten American Painters, a group of early impressionists.

Benson's early training was at the Museum of Fine Arts in Boston, followed by study with Boulanger and Lefebvre in Paris at the Academie Julien. He taught throughout his career, first in Portland, Maine, then in his own studio in Boston, and later at the Museum of Fine Arts, where he had first studied.

In contrast to the subdued interiors of his close friend, Edmund Tarbell, Benson painted women and children at play in cheerful, brightly colored outdoor settings. The subjects were rich, beautiful and leisurely, untouched by any unpleasant realism—they were people, as one critic commented, "on holiday."

One of his most frequently mentioned paintings, *Portrait in White* (1889, National Gallery), a first-anniversary portrait of his wife, is considered a study in tone similar to works by James Whistler—an "art-for-art's-sake treatment." The portrait is a special study of two types of white, the blue-white of his wife's dress and the yellow-white of the chair in which she poses.

Benson also painted some of the murals in the Library of Congress in Washington, D.C. In later life he turned to still lifes and sporting scenes, particularly depicting duck hunting and other waterfowl. He died in 1951 in Salem.

Ducks in Flight, 1937, 32 x 40 in., signed l.l. Courtesy of Vose Galleries of Boston, Inc., Massachusetts.

Summer, 1890, 50⅛ x 40 in., signed l.r.
Courtesy of National Museum of American Art, Smithsonian Institution, Gift of John Gellatly.

MEMBERSHIPS
American Academy of Arts and Sciences
Boston Guild of Artists
Chicago Society of Etchers
National Academy of Design
National Institute of Arts and Letters
Society of American Etchers
Ten American Painters

PUBLIC COLLECTIONS
Albright-Knox Art Gallery, Buffalo
Art Institute of Chicago
Butler Art Institute, Youngstown, Ohio
Carnegie Institute, Pittsburgh
Cincinnati Art Museum
Corcoran Gallery of Art, Washington, D.C.
Detroit Institute of Arts
Indianapolis Art Museum
Metropolitan Museum of Art, New York City
Museum of Fine Arts, Boston
National Gallery of Art, Washington, D.C.
Rhode Island School of Design, Providence
Worcester Art Museum, Massachusetts

SEASON	75-76	76-77	77-78	78-79	79-80	80-81	81-82	82-83	83-84	84-85
Paintings		1	1	2	7	4	7	5	2	2
Dollars		$24,000	$1,100	$16,000	$43,500	$66,500	$174,800	$24,000	$30,000	$80,700

Record Sale: $85,000, SPB, 12/10/81, "Portrait of Mary Sullivan," 84 × 54 in.

593

EDWARD AUGUST BELL
(1862-1953)

Painter Edward August Bell was born in New York City. He studied at the National Academy of Design between 1877 and 1879, then attended the Art Students League for two years, before sailing to Germany in 1881. There, he studied with Ritter L. von Loefftz at the Bavarian Royal Academy in Munich. He painted in Europe until his return to New York City in 1891.

Bell's work was usually symbolic or decorative. Early in his career, he stopped using models in an attempt to make his paintings creative rather than imitative.

He received many awards, including a silver medal from the Bavarian Royal Academy; the Second Hallgarten Prize from the National Academy in 1893; a bronze medal at the Paris Exposition of 1899; and silver medals at the Pan-American Exposition at Buffalo in 1901 and at the Louisiana Purchase Exposition at St. Louis in 1904.

Bell's work is held by the Cincinnati Art Museum and represented in several other institutions.

He died in Long Island, New York in 1953.

MEMBERSHIPS
Art Students League
National Academy of Design
Salmagundi Club
Society of American Artists

PUBLIC COLLECTIONS
Cincinnati Art Museum
Indianapolis Museum of Art
Smith College Museum of Art,
  Northampton, Massachusetts

At the Piano, 20 x 14 in., signed l.l. Courtesy of Grand Central Art Galleries, Inc., New York, New York.

SEASON	75-76	76-77	77-78	78-79	79-80	80-81	81-82	82-83	83-84	84-85
Paintings	1			2	1	4				
Dollars	$1,100			$6,250	$3,600	$6,700				

Record Sale: $3,600, CH, 3/20/80, "Dancers," 22 × 33 in.

594

JOHN MARSHALL GAMBLE

(1863-1937)

Poppies and Yellow Lupins, ca. 1959, 20 x 30 in., signed l.r. Collection of Paul Bagley. Photograph courtesy of Petersen Galleries, Beverly Hills, California.

Although he was also a successful portrait painter, John Marshall Gamble is best known for his landscapes of California wildflowers. They are admired today particularly because he painted them in the late nineteenth and early twentieth centuries, at a time when large-scale real estate development had not yet started, and he showed the flowers covering hillsides, canyons and dunes in all their original profusion. Whether it was the bright light blue of wild lilacs leaning over a footpath, or a golden-brown field of buckwheat blossoms stretching toward the mountains in the distance, Gamble caught the sunny splendor of the scene on his canvas.

He was born in Morristown, New Jersey in 1863, but moved to California when he was 20. He studied at the San Francisco School of Design with Emil Carlsen, who seemed to have a stronger influence on him than anyone else. Later, he went to Paris to study under Jean Paul Laurens and Benjamin Constant, and at the Academie Julien.

On his return to California, Gamble settled down to paint the wild beauty of the hills and coastline. After the contents of his studio in San Francisco were destroyed in the fire that followed the great 1906 earthquake, he moved to Santa Barbara and lived there until his death in 1937. When the noted Fox-

Arlington Theatre was built in Santa Barbara, Gamble painted an enormous California landscape on the stage curtain.

He was especially well known for his many paintings of the brilliant yellow California poppies that blanket the hills and valleys in the spring and contrast with the vivid hues of other wildflowers, such as the blue lupine. As a counterpoint to these floral paintings, he also did interesting studies of Pacific sunsets over the long stretches of gray sand that mark the mouths of rivers along the coast.

SEASON	75-76	76-77	77-78	78-79	79-80	80-81	81-82	82-83	83-84	84-85
Paintings					1	2	3	3	2	
Dollars					$750	$3,242	$3,700	$3,350	$2,250	

Record Sale: $2,600, SPB, 6/23/81, "California Coastline," 20 × 30 in.

MEMBERSHIPS
San Francisco Art Association
Santa Barbara Art League

PUBLIC COLLECTIONS
Museum of Art, Auckland, New Zealand

JEAN
MANNHEIM
(1863?-1945)

Jean Mannheim was one of the few Western landscape painters who continued to paint portraits and genre figure compositions throughout his career. His early work showed the influence of Bouguereau in its soft tones and delicate technique, but after he began to work in California, Mannheim's paintings became bolder and more expressive and his palette considerably brighter.

Mannheim was born in Kreuznach, Germany, probably in 1863, to a German father and a French mother. He had already been trained as a bookbinder when he was drafted into the German army. He hated the army and deserted, fleeing to France.

In Paris, Mannheim worked as a bookbinder to get money to study painting, first at the Ecole Delecluse, then at the Academie Colarossi and finally with Bouguereau and several others. In 1881, he came to the United States, the first of several trips, and stayed with a married sister in Chicago. There he painted portraits for prices ranging from $20 to $40 until he had saved enough to return to France for more study. Eventually he came to Illinois to stay, painting portraits and teaching.

A few years later, he moved his second wife and their two daughters to London, where he taught at the Brangwyn School of Art. It was a pleasant association for Mannheim, but the damp English climate was bad for his wife. After two years, he resigned and returned to the United States.

He taught briefly in Denver and then, in 1908, moved on to Pasadena, California. At first he had a studio in Los Angeles; when his wife died, he moved his studio close to home in Pasadena so he could look after his daughters.

In 1913, Mannheim founded the Stickney Memorial School of Art and took his students on regular trips to paint the surrounding farmland and

Laguna Seascape, 28 x 36 in., signed l.l. Courtesy of George Stern, Fine Arts, Encino, California.

coastal views. Mannheim himself was particularly struck by the rugged beauty of the coast around Monterey, where he often painted. His landscapes painted there and elsewhere in California were noted for their strength and simplicity.

He continued to combine portrait commissions and figure studies with plein-air landscape painting until his death in 1945.

MEMBERSHIPS
California Art Club
Laguna Beach Art Association
Long Beach Art Association
Pasadena Art Club

PUBLIC COLLECTIONS
Denver Art Museum
Laguna Beach Museum of Art, California
Long Beach Museum of Art, California
Springville Museum of Art, Utah

SEASON	75-76	76-77	77-78	78-79	79-80	80-81	81-82	82-83	83-84	84-85
Paintings					1	7	1	1		1
Dollars					$2,300	$9,200	$1,100	$800		$2,500

Record Sale: $3,000, SPB, 3/16/81, "Spirit of the Night," 30 × 36 in.

ALBERT STERNER
(1863-1957)

Although he executed and exhibited oil paintings throughout his career, Albert Sterner was recognized primarily as an illustrator and lithographer. His background combined training in the printing trade with academic European artistic study; both influences are visible in his work.

Sterner was born in London in 1863, of American parents. He attended drawing classes at the Birmingham Art Institute until his family moved to the United States in the late 1870s, leaving him in the care of relatives in Germany. After working as a clerk in Gaggenau, he lived for a time in Freiburg, then joined his family in Chicago sometime between 1879 and 1882. In Chicago, he worked for several lithographers, helped Walter Wilcox Burridge paint theater scenery, and collaborated on illustrated articles for a local paper.

Sterner settled in New York City in 1885, but spent much time in Europe during the following two decades. He studied under Gustave Boulanger and Jules Lefebvre at the Academie Julien in Paris in 1886, and executed numerous magazine illustrations. In 1892, he illustrated George Curtis's *Prue and I* with 100 pen-and-ink and wash drawings; many similar commissions followed.

Sterner strongly maintained that illustrators deserved credit as serious artists. He produced watercolors, red-chalk drawings, lithographs and monotypes.

Olivia, 1918, 30 x 40 in., signed c.r. Courtesy of Frank S. Schwarz & Son, Philadelphia, Pennsylvania.

His work shows strong draftsmanship, as well as suggestions of symbolist and expressionist influence. He also painted still lifes, portraits and landscapes, which took on a decorative quality late in his career.

Sterner continued to paint until his death in 1957 at age 94.

MEMBERSHIPS
American Water Color Society
Art Association of Newport
National Academy of Design
Painter-Gravers of America
Society of Illustrators

PUBLIC COLLECTIONS
Brooklyn Museum
Carnegie Institute, Pittsburgh
Kupferstitch Kabinet, Dresden
Kupferstitch Kabinet Pinakothek, Munich
Metropolitan Museum of Art, New York City
New York Public Library, New York City
Toronto Museum of Fine Arts

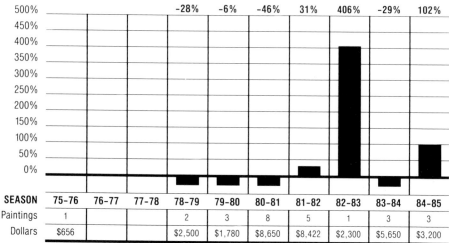

10-Year Average Change From Base Years '75-'76: 54%

SEASON	75-76	76-77	77-78	78-79	79-80	80-81	81-82	82-83	83-84	84-85
				-28%	-6%	-46%	31%	406%	-29%	102%
Paintings	1			2	3	8	5	1	3	3
Dollars	$656			$2,500	$1,780	$8,650	$8,422	$2,300	$5,650	$3,200

Record Sale: $4,000, CH, 6/1/84, "Self-Portrait," 24 x 19 in.

HENRY GOLDEN DEARTH
(1864-1918)

Henry Golden Dearth, noted as a great technician by American collectors, painted landscapes and figures.

Born in Bristol, Rhode Island in 1864, Dearth received early instruction in painting from Horace Johnson, a Connecticut portrait painter. Later he studied in Paris for about four years at the Ecole des Beaux-Arts and in the atelier of Aime Morot.

He returned to America briefly in 1887, and opened a studio in New York City the following year. He first exhibited at New York City's National Academy of Design in 1888. In 1896, he married Cornelia Van Rensselaer.

During the last two decades of his life, Dearth spent his winters in New York City and summers in Normandy. He had a summer studio at Montreuil-sur-Mer near Boulogne, which he used as headquarters for his sketching trips along the coasts of Normandy and Brittany.

Dearth's specialty became landscapes of the coast of Normandy. The keynote of his work was simplicity, suggesting detail, as in *Sunset in Normandy* (date and location unknown).

From about 1900 until his death, he changed his mode of expression drastically. He became a collector of oriental, Near Eastern and early European art, and often used items from his collection in his paintings. He devoted himself almost entirely to works featuring these objects and elegantly-dressed women painted in bright, broken colors.

A Farm in Summer, 1891, 18½ x 28¾ in., signed l.r. Photograph courtesy of Hirschl & Adler Galleries, Inc., New York, New York.

Dearth died at his home in New York City in 1918, at age 54. He was honored after his death by a memorial exhibition that traveled to 19 of the most important museums and galleries in America.

MEMBERSHIPS
National Academy of Design

PUBLIC COLLECTIONS
Art Institute of Chicago
Carnegie Institute, Pittsburgh
Detroit Institute of Arts
Indianapolis Museum of Art
Metropolitan Museum of Art, New York City
National Gallery of Art, Washington, D.C.
St. Louis Art Museum

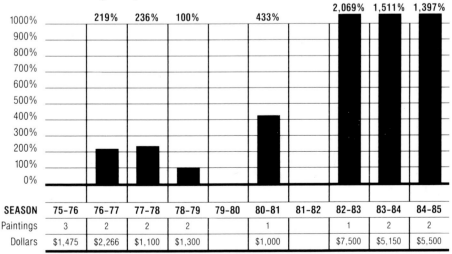

10-Year Average Change From Base Years '75-'76: 746%

SEASON	75-76	76-77	77-78	78-79	79-80	80-81	81-82	82-83	83-84	84-85
		219%	236%	100%		433%		2,069%	1,511%	1,397%
Paintings	3	2	2	2		1		1	2	2
Dollars	$1,475	$2,266	$1,100	$1,300		$1,000		$7,500	$5,150	$5,500

Record Sale: $7,500, CH, 12/3/82, "Dusk," 24 × 40 in.

598

PAUL CORNOYER
(1864-1923)

Paul Cornoyer's artistic legacy includes both his award-winning New York City scenes and the many grateful students to whom he gave his time, attention and affection.

Born in St. Louis, Missouri in 1864, Cornoyer went to Paris in 1889 to study in the Academie Julien, under painters Jules Lefebvre, Benjamin Constant and Louis Blanc. He remained in Paris until 1894, painting and exhibiting; he won a prestigious gold medal from the American Art Association.

He returned to St. Louis in 1894, and there won a gold medal from the St. Louis Association of Painters and Sculptors in 1895. However, it was when he went to New York City, teaching at the Mechanics' Institute, that he began to establish his lifelong reputation as teacher and painter.

Cornoyer's New York City street scenes, dispassionate and calm, capture overall light effects with a carefully limited range of colors. His technical skill and capacity for observation create striking effects.

Though his prestige as a painter was won in New York City, Cornoyer also taught summer courses in Connecticut and Massachusetts. In 1917, he moved to East Gloucester, Massachusetts, where he continued to paint and exhibit until his death in 1923. He was involved in setting up an exhibition for the local art association at the time of his death.

Missouri Landscape, 32 x 36 in., signed l.c. Courtesy of Raydon Gallery, New York, New York.

MEMBERSHIPS
Allied Artists Association
National Academy of Design
National Arts Club
Newark Art Association
North Shore Arts Association of Gloucester
Salmagundi Club
Society of Western Artists

PUBLIC COLLECTIONS
Brooklyn Museum
Dallas Art Association
Fine Arts Institute of Kansas City, Missouri
Newark Art Association, New Jersey
St. Louis Art Museum

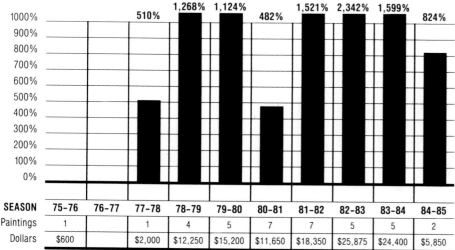

10-Year Average Change From Base Years '75-'76: 1,074%

SEASON	75-76	76-77	77-78	78-79	79-80	80-81	81-82	82-83	83-84	84-85
			510%	1,268%	1,124%	482%	1,521%	2,342%	1,599%	824%
Paintings	1		1	4	5	7	7	5	5	2
Dollars	$600		$2,000	$12,250	$15,200	$11,650	$18,350	$25,875	$24,400	$5,850

Record Sale: $20,000, SPB, 5/31/84, ''Rainy Day, Madison Square,'' 32 × 36 in.

CHARLES M. RUSSELL
(1864-1926)

Charles M. Russell lived the life he depicted during his prolific career as painter, sculptor and illustrator of Western scenes. He spent his youth living and working in the American West; the public grew to know him as the "Cowboy Artist."

Born in 1864 in what is now the Oak Hill section of St. Louis, Russell went to Montana at age 16. He worked as a sheepherder, trapper and cowboy. He had begun to draw many years earlier and to paint on wood and model figures for his own pleasure and that of his friends. He always thought of himself as a cowboy who painted.

In 1888, he rode to Canada with a friend, and on the return trip he wintered with a tribe of Blood Indians, members of the Blackfoot nation. He spent almost six months with the Blood, gaining a deep insight into Indian life, which was reflected in his later works.

Russell's artistic reputation was established in the 1890s when he displayed his works in frontier saloons throughout the Montana territory. In 1890, he published *Studies of Western Life,* a portfolio of 12 paintings. In 1893, he was commissioned by manufacturer and rancher William Niedringhaus to produce several paintings—his first serious art assignment.

When Russell married 18-year-old Nancy Cooper in 1896, she became the motivating force in his art career. They settled in Great Falls, Montana, which

Roping the Wolf, 18 x 24 in., signed l.l. Photograph courtesy of The Gerald Peters Gallery, Santa Fe, New Mexico.

was his permanent headquarters. "Mame," as he called her, insisted that he limit his cowboy-style drinking and observe regular working hours. She also encouraged him to write for magazines, as a way to sell the illustrations he painted. In 1903, he visited New York City and continued to do so annually. His first one-man show was held there in 1911.

That year, the Montana state legislature commissioned Russell to create two murals for its House of Representatives. In 1912, *Lewis and Clark Meeting the*

Indians at Ross' Hole was installed. The painting hints at the changes soon to come in the West.

Russell was also skilled in pen-and-ink drawing, watercolor and sculpture. He produced more than 100 bronze statues, a natural outcome of his practice of modeling in clay and wax for his paintings.

His work was often exhibited in New York City, Chicago and London; he held 28 one-man shows. In 1904, he exhibited at the St. Louis World's Fair, and in 1925, at the Corcoran Gallery of Art in Washington, D.C.

Magazines expanded Russell's popularity, and *Harper's Weekly* featured his illustrations as early as 1888. He was soon published in *McClure's* and in *Leslie's.* In addition, his works were reproduced on numerous calendars.

Widely acclaimed by critics and the public, Russell died in 1926 in Great Falls.

PUBLIC COLLECTIONS
Amon Carter Museum of Western Art, Fort Worth
Gilcrease Institute, Tulsa
Montana Historical Society, Helena
National Cowboy Hall of Fame, Oklahoma City
Norton Gallery, Shreveport, Louisiana
State Capitol Building, Helena, Montana
Trigg C. M. Russell Gallery, Great Falls, Montana
Whitney Gallery of Western Art, Cody, Wyoming
Woolaroc Museum, Bartlesville, Oklahoma

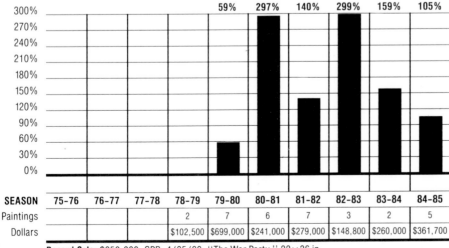

10-Year Average Change From Base Years '78-'79: 151%

			59%	297%	140%	299%	159%	105%

SEASON	75-76	76-77	77-78	78-79	79-80	80-81	81-82	82-83	83-84	84-85
Paintings				2	7	6	7	3	2	5
Dollars				$102,500	$699,000	$241,000	$279,000	$148,800	$260,000	$361,700

Record Sale: $250,000, SPB, 4/25/80, "The War Party," 22 × 36 in.

FRANZ ARTHUR BISCHOFF
(1864-1929)

Roses, ca. 1912, 40 x 50, signed l.r. Private Collection, Photograph courtesy of Petersen Galleries, Beverly Hills, California.

An early Southern California landscape painter, Franz Bischoff ranks among the best of the plein-air painters. His impressionistic studies of the region's scenery, particularly around his home in a wooded Pasadena canyon, won critical acclaim at a time when California was experiencing its first wave of impressionistic work, during the early years of the twentieth century.

Bischoff was born in Northern Bohemia, in what was then Austria. He immigrated to the United States as a young ceramic decorator in 1885 and took a job as a designer in a New York City china factory. During the next two decades, he owned and operated ceramics studios there and in Michigan, formulating many of his own colors and earning an award-winning reputation as "King of the Rose Painters."

Bischoff moved to California in 1906, after 20 years as a ceramicist and china painter. Like other artists who arrived in the benevolent, sun-kissed state at that time, Bischoff turned immediately to landscapes. His style ranged from impressionistic in the early works to post-impressionistic and somewhat expressionistic in later paintings. He is noted for his superb colors, a legacy of his years as a ceramicist.

He continued to do some ceramic work in a fully-equipped workshop he built into his home in Pasadena's Arroyo Seco canyon.

Besides the ceramics workshop, Bischoff also built a large gallery and a painting studio at his canyon home, which itself was a work of art, done in Italian Renaissance style. His environment was a superb, open-air studio; views of canyon and mountain were depicted in many of his paintings, which were sometimes oil and sometimes tempera on canvas.

Associated with the Eucalyptus School, Bischoff won critical and public recognition almost as soon as he set color to canvas. He gradually expanded his explorations of the natural environment to the Sierra Nevadas, the coastal region and Northern California. The year before he died, he painted his last canvas, a bold portrayal in stunning colors of Zion National Park in Utah.

PUBLIC COLLECTIONS
Laguna Beach Museum of Art, California
Oakland Museum, California
Terra Museum of American Art, Evanston, Illinois

SEASON	75-76	76-77	77-78	78-79	79-80	80-81	81-82	82-83	83-84	84-85
Paintings					3	1	3	4	2	2
Dollars					$2,350	$750	$9,200	$6,650	$3,950	$2,150

Record Sale: $4,250, SPB, 6/29/82, "Milking Time," 19 × 26 in.

ELMER WACHTEL
(1864-1929)

Upper Ojai Valley, California, 30 x 40 in., signed l.l. Courtesy of David and Sons Fine Arts, Laguna Beach, California.

Elmer Wachtel was one of the foremost Southern California landscape painters of the nineteenth and early twentieth centuries. Along with his wife, landscape painter Marion Kavanagh, Wachtel received an extraordinary amount of praise from contemporary critics.

Born in Baltimore in 1864, Wachtel was raised in Lanark, Illinois, and worked as a hired farm hand. In 1882, he moved to his brother's ranch in Los Angeles.

In Los Angeles Wachtel taught himself to play the violin and viola. By 1888,

he was the first violin in the Los Angeles Philharmonic Orchestra. Because he did not earn much as a violinist, he also worked as a store clerk in his brother's furniture store.

Wachtel began sketching still lifes in his spare time, and after saving enough money to go to New York, he studied at the Art Students League. He worked under William Merritt Chase, but left the school because he objected to its methods. He remained in New York and sketched the city streets, bringing his work in to be critiqued by Chase.

Wachtel then sailed to England and

completed his studies by working in a London art school for one year. When he returned to Los Angeles, he set up a studio in the back of his parents' house and began to devote himself to painting. In 1904, he married Marion Kavanagh and the two spent the next 25 years painting landscapes together.

Wachtel's subjects were usually the deserts, mountains and High Sierras of California, and occasionally the landscapes of other areas, such as Arizona and New Mexico. He painted primarily with oils and used impressionistic brushstrokes. His early works were tonalist with moody dark colors, while his later paintings were lighter in color and more decorative and lyrical in composition.

Wachtel died in 1929.

SEASON	75-76	76-77	77-78	78-79	79-80	80-81	81-82	82-83	83-84	84-85
Paintings							2	3	5	1
Dollars							$6,100	$4,650	$5,050	$800

Record Sale: $3,800, SPB, 10/3/81, "South Lake, High Sierras," 28 × 36 in.

PUBLIC COLLECTIONS
Laguna Beach Museum of Art, California

602

DE COST SMITH
(1864-1939)

De Cost Smith was one of the group of late-nineteenth- and early-twentieth-century illustrators who compiled an exceptionally valuable pictorial record of the life and ways of the American Indian.

As a result of growing up close to an Indian reservation and traveling among the Indians in the West while still a young man, Smith developed sympathy and understanding which won him their confidence and respect. This, in turn, enabled him to paint them with accuracy and candor. He made many trips to visit various tribes, and with Edwin Willard Deming, another noted painter of Indians, collaborated on a noteworthy series of articles for *Outing Magazine*.

Smith was born in Skaneateles in Western New York State in 1864. As a boy he came to know the Indians at the nearby Onandaga Reservation, and eventually was initiated into the tribe. He studied art in New York City. After seeing the Indian paintings of George De Forest Brush, he decided that he too would become a painter of Indians.

He made his first trip to sketch Indians in what was still the Dakota Territory in 1884. In time he became so interested in Indian culture that he learned to speak several dialects.

Later, Smith went to Paris to study at the Academie Julien. While there, he exhibited some of his earliest Indian paintings at the Paris Salon. Before his death in 1939, he illustrated many articles on the American West for such leading magazines as *Century*. It is for his Indian paintings, however, that he was best known.

War Party, 1904, 37¼ x 30½ in., signed l.l. Courtesy of Vose Galleries of Boston, Inc., Massachusetts.

Winter Hunt, 23 x 30 in., signed l.r. Courtesy of Vose Galleries of Boston, Inc., Massachusetts.

MEMBERSHIPS
American Ethnological Society
Salmagundi Club

PUBLIC COLLECTIONS
American Museum of Natural History,
New York City
Museum of the American Indian, New York City

SEASON	75-76	76-77	77-78	78-79	79-80	80-81	81-82	82-83	83-84	84-85
Paintings					1		1			
Dollars					$1,500		$800			

Record Sale: $1,500, SPB, 6/24/80, "Moving Camp," 15 × 21 in.

CHARLES HERBERT WOODBURY
(1864-1940)

Charles Herbert Woodbury, a marine painter and etcher, was born in Lynn, Massachusetts in 1864. He received an engineering degree from Massachusetts Institute of Technology in 1886, but abandoned the profession for painting soon after graduation.

He made several trips abroad, and studied under Boulanger and Lefebvre at the Academie Julien in Paris in 1891.

Woodbury established a studio in Boston. He also painted during the summer at Perkins Cove, near Ogunquit, Maine, where he conducted a school for more than 30 years. He also was a visiting lecturer at Dartmouth College, Wellesley College and the Art Institute of Chicago.

The coast near his summer studio inspired many of his seascapes, including *Ogunquit, Maine* (date unknown, Metropolitan Museum of Art) and *The North Atlantic* (date unknown, Worcester Art Museum).

Woodbury received many prizes and awards for his watercolors, oils and etchings. He won a gold medal in oil painting at the 1915 Panama-Pacific Exposition in San Francisco, as well as a medal of honor in watercolor. He was elected to full membership by the National Academy of Design in 1907.

Woodbury was a respected instructor and art educator. In 1919, he wrote *Painting and Personal Equation* with E.W. Perkins. He also wrote *The Art of Seeing* in 1925.

Woodbury died in Boston in 1940.

Boat in Marshy Inlet, 10 x 14 in., signed l.r. Courtesy of Arvest Galleries, Inc., Boston, Massachusetts.

Three Umbrellas, 20 x 27 in. Courtesy of Vose Galleries of Boston, Inc., Massachusetts.

MEMBERSHIPS
American Watercolor Society
Boston Water Color Club
National Academy of Design
New York Water Color Club
Society of American Artists
Society of American Etchers

PUBLIC COLLECTIONS
Carnegie Institute, Pittsburgh
Corcoran Gallery of Art, Washington, D.C.
Detroit Institute of Arts
Library of Congress, Washington, D.C.
Metropolitan Museum of Art, New York City
Museum of Fine Arts, Boston
Rhode Island School of Design, Providence
St. Louis Art Museum
Telfair Academy of Arts and Sciences, Savannah, Georgia
Worcester Art Museum, Massachusetts

SEASON	75-76	76-77	77-78	78-79	79-80	80-81	81-82	82-83	83-84	84-85
Paintings	1		1	1	6	4	5	2	4	10
Dollars	$2,600		$500	$325	$9,080	$6,800	$4,125	$1,200	$3,000	$15,850

Record Sale: $3,800, S.BM, 5/15/85, "View of Boston Common," 23 x 19 in.

JOHN LEON MORAN
(1864-1941)

Cabbage Pickers, 18 x 26 in., signed l.l. Photograph courtesy of Vose Galleries of Boston, Massachusetts.

It might be said that John Leon Moran, figure and landscape painter, came by his art naturally. His father and four uncles all were painters and etchers, as were his brothers, Percy and Peter.

Born in 1864 in Philadelphia, Moran received his first art instruction from his father, British-born painter Edward Moran. He then moved to New York City, where he studied at the National Academy of Design.

Moran made several trips to Europe in the late 1870s, before establishing a stu-

dio in New York City in 1883. The European trips enabled Moran to study art in innumerable continental studios, galleries and museums.

For a number of years, Moran painted exclusively in watercolor. In the mid-1880s, he traveled to Virginia, where, like artists Jacob O. Ward and David Johnson, he studied and painted that state's Natural Bridge. His *Natural Bridge, Virginia, 1885* hangs in the Governor's Mansion in Richmond.

However, Moran was best known as a

figure painter, and many of his early landscapes are critically regarded as inferior to the bulk of his work.

Frequently exhibited by the National Academy of Design and New York's American Water Color Society, Moran received his first artistic award in 1893 from the Art Club of Philadelphia. A second award followed 11 years later—a gold medal from the American Art Society in Philadelphia.

Moran died in Watchung, New Jersey in 1941.

SEASON	75-76	76-77	77-78	78-79	79-80	80-81	81-82	82-83	83-84	84-85
Paintings	2			1	2	1	1	1	2	2
Dollars	$1,850			$575	$7,800	$8,000	$4,500	$1,600	$2,000	$2,850

Record Sale: $8,000, BB.SF, 1/21/81, ''Gypsies,'' 30 × 48 in.

MEMBERSHIPS
American Water Color Society
Plainfield Art Association

LOUIS MICHEL EILSHEMIUS
(1864-1941)

The visionary paintings of Louis Michel Eilshemius attracted little notice until after he had stopped painting them.

The disciplined impressionist landscapes of his early career, in the 1880s and 1890s, gained some modest success. But shortly before 1900, Eilshemius's technique became sketchy, even feathery, representative of no artistic period or tradition. His increasingly eccentric subjects were drawn from dreams and nightmares, echoing the disintegration of his personality.

Eilshemius was born in 1864 at the family estate near Arlington, New Jersey. He was educated in Geneva, Switzerland and Dresden, Germany. He also studied agriculture at Cornell University from 1882 to 1884.

He studied art for the next four years, first at the Art Students League in New York City, later at the Academie Julien in Paris and with landscapist Joseph Van Luppen in Antwerp.

A few of Eilshemius's landscapes, whose effects of clear light are in the barbizon mode, were accepted for exhibit by the National Academy of Design and the Philadelphia Academy of the Fine Arts. However, Eilshemius did not receive the public and critical attention he thought he deserved. His entry for the 1893 World's Columbian Exposition was turned down and his 1897 gallery exhibition was ignored. His isolation and eccentricity, fed by bitterness, began to govern his work and life.

Three Girls and River, 1907, 23 x 27 in., signed l.r. Courtesy of National Museum of American Art, Smithsonian Institution, Gift of Louis and Annette Kaufman.

Eilshemius became obsessed with speed. It is said he completed 3,000 paintings between 1882 and 1920. He besieged dealers with paintings in the ever more exaggerated primitivism of his new style, signing them with a changed spelling, "Elshemius."

Periodically, Eilshemius was preoccupied with poetry, letters to newspapers and prose (he had 30 books printed at his own expense). Drawing his inheritance, he traveled extensively. The South Seas provided themes for paintings between 1905 and 1909.

After a failed studio exhibition in 1909, Eilshemius's delusions took over. He called himself "Mahatma, Mightiest of the Mighty," and passed out leaflets listing grandiose accomplishments.

Marcel Duchamp praised Eilshemius's *Supplication* (date and location unknown) at a 1917 exhibition, but the embittered artist stopped painting in 1921.

Recognition came in the early 1930s, when his work was acquired by several leading museums, but Eilshemius could not benefit from it. He was left an invalid by a 1932 automobile accident. Ill and impoverished, he died at New York City's Bellevue Hospital in 1941.

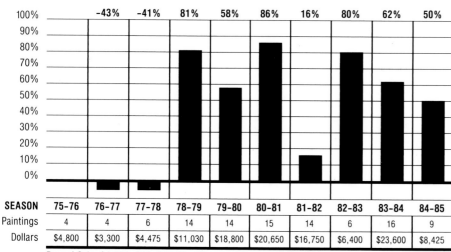

10-Year Average Change From Base Years '75-'76: 35%

	-43%	-41%	81%	58%	86%	16%	80%	62%	50%

SEASON	75-76	76-77	77-78	78-79	79-80	80-81	81-82	82-83	83-84	84-85
Paintings	4	4	6	14	14	15	14	6	16	9
Dollars	$4,800	$3,300	$4,475	$11,030	$18,800	$20,650	$16,750	$6,400	$23,600	$8,425

Record Sale: $4,000, SPB, 3/7/81, "Summer Afternoon," 30 × 20 in.

MEMBERSHIPS
Modern Art Association
American Federation of Arts
Salmagundi Club
Salons of America
Societe Anonyme

PUBLIC COLLECTIONS
Hirshhorn Museum and Sculpture Garden,
  Washington, D.C.
Metropolitan Museum of Art,
  New York City
Museum of Modern Art, New York City
Phillips Collection, Washington, D.C.
Whitney Museum of American Art,
  New York City

GEORGE HENRY BOGERT
(1864-1944)

George Henry Bogert, often confused with painter George Hirst Bogart (1864 to 1923), was a landscape artist, born in New York City in 1864.

He began his studies at the National Academy of Design in the early 1880s. In 1884, he traveled to Paris, where he studied with such prominent artists as Puvis de Chavannes, Raphael Collin and Aime Morot.

After a four-year hiatus he returned to the United States, continuing his studies under Thomas Eakins in New York from 1888 to 1895.

In the 1890s, Bogert again sojourned in Europe, painting landscapes of Venice, the Isle of Wight and particularly Etaples (in Northern France), where he was taught and influenced by plein-air landscapist Eugene Boudin.

Like Boudin, Chavannes and Turner, Bogert employed loose brushwork and the use of cool blue tones to achieve blurred form and soft half-light effects, further accentuated by the application of dense impasto.

Much of his later work seems to emulate the soft-focus photography which evolved at the turn of the century, demonstrating that either camera or brush could produce synthesized and interpretive views of nature.

Although his works were often romantic, Bogert did not execute his work with sentimental subjectivity. Nor did he adhere to stark objectivity. Rather, he incorporated elements of

Irish Seascape, 12 x 16 in., signed l.l. Courtesy of La Salle University Art Museum, Philadelphia, Pennsylvania, Given by Donald E. Smith.

each. Bogert identified himself with the barbizon landscape painters.

September Evening (1898, Metropolitan Museum of Art), one of Bogert's most successful works, is representative of his tonalist style. The *Art Interchange* of May 1899 said it was "one of the most tender and beautiful landscapes that has come from his easel."

Despite Bogert's growing appeal in the late 1880s, little is known of him

after the turn of the century, except that he made several summer painting expeditions to Holland. He finally settled into the artists' colony at Old Lyme, Connecticut.

Bogert died in New York City at age 80, after a brief illness.

MEMBERSHIPS
Artists Fund Society of New York
Lotos Club of New York
National Academy of Design
Pennsylvania Academy of the Fine Arts
Salmagundi Club
Society of American Artists
Society of Landscape Painters

PUBLIC COLLECTIONS
Albright-Knox Gallery, Buffalo
Art Institute of Chicago
Brooklyn Institute
Corcoran Gallery, Washington, D.C.
Dallas Museum of Fine Arts
Detroit Institute of Arts
Edinburgh Museum, Scotland
Huntington Museum, California
Metropolitan Museum of Art,
    New York City
Milwaukee Art Institute, Wisconsin
Minneapolis Institute of Arts, Minnesota
Museum of Fine Arts, Boston
National Gallery, Washington, D.C.
Newark Museum, New Jersey
Pennsylvania Academy of the Fine Arts,
    Philadelphia
St. Louis Museum, Missouri

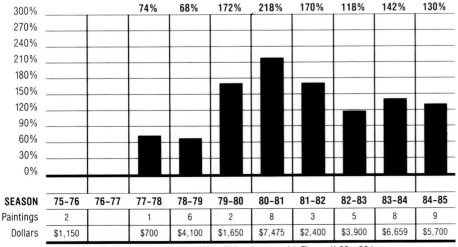

10-Year Average Change From Base Years '75-'76: 121%

	75-76	76-77	77-78	78-79	79-80	80-81	81-82	82-83	83-84	84-85
(%)			74%	68%	172%	218%	170%	118%	142%	130%
SEASON	75-76	76-77	77-78	78-79	79-80	80-81	81-82	82-83	83-84	84-85
Paintings	2		1	6	2	8	3	5	8	9
Dollars	$1,150		$700	$4,100	$1,650	$7,475	$2,400	$3,900	$6,659	$5,700

Record Sale: $1,600, W.W, 3/4/84, "Moonlit Landscape with Figure," 22 × 36 in.

607

WILLIAM RITSCHEL
(1864-1949)

Fishing Off the Coast, 14 x 26 in., signed l.r. Courtesy of Raydon Gallery, New York, New York.

William Ritschel was a noted marine painter whose seascapes drew on both his technical training as an artist and his experiences as a sailor.

Ritschel was born in Nuremberg, Germany in 1864. He studied under Friedrich August von Kaulbach and Karl Raupp at the Royal Academy in Munich for six years. He also traveled the world as a sailor. In 1895, he left Germany and, after spending time in France and Italy, settled in New York City.

Working first in watercolor and later in oil, Ritschel was exhibiting in national shows by 1914. He received a number of awards and was a member of many artists' organizations. His reputation was built on his expressive treatments of the sea, such as *Rocks and Breakers* (date unknown, Pennsylvania Academy of the Fine Arts) and *Inrush of the Tide* (date unknown, Albright-Knox Art Gallery).

By 1911, Ritschel was exhibiting in California; he may have moved to that state as early as 1909. By 1918, he had constructed a stone studio-home in Carmel Highlands, overlocking the Pacific Ocean, where he was to live for the rest of his life.

He was given a one-man exhibition in Oakland in 1931, and another in Los Angeles in 1942. Two paintings shown at the latter were singled out for special praise by Arthur Millier of the *Los Angeles Times: Song of the Sea* (date and location unknown) was described as "playful" and "lyrical," while *Carmel Highlands Coast* (date and location unknown) was termed "powerful" and "dramatic," and was cited for the painter's use of light to capture the conflict between sun and fog.

Ritschel traveled to the South Seas, the Orient and Capri. He continued to paint until his death in Carmel in 1949.

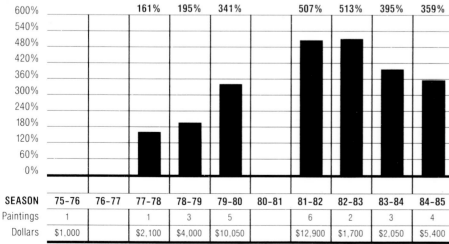

10-Year Average Change From Base Years '75-'76: 309%

SEASON	75-76	76-77	77-78	78-79	79-80	80-81	81-82	82-83	83-84	84-85
			161%	195%	341%		507%	513%	395%	359%
Paintings	1		1	3	5		6	2	3	4
Dollars	$1,000		$2,100	$4,000	$10,050		$12,900	$1,700	$2,050	$5,400

Record Sale: $6,250, SPB, 6/24/80, "Coral Reefs, Glorious Pacific," 30 × 40 in.

ERNEST L. MAJOR
(1864-1951)

Born in Washington, D.C. in 1864, Ernest L. Major studied at the Art Students League in New York City, and with Boulanger and Lefebvre in Paris. For most of his life he identified with Boston, where he maintained a studio and taught at the Massachusetts School of Art. His subjects included figure studies, portraits, still lifes and landscapes.

Among the characteristics of Major's work, his ability with composition and design was noted by critics. Contrived backgrounds lending themselves to flamboyant colors were used repeatedly. He strongly preferred artificial to natural light.

In *Nineteen-Nineteen* (date and location unknown), a mantel shelf with a porcelain parrot and other decorative ornaments are combined with the central subject, a colorfully dressed girl, while not overwhelming the subject.

His *Shower of Gold* (date and location unknown) utilizes many features of his distinctive style. The central subject is a nude reclining on a tiger-skin rug, positioned with her head toward the viewer. The foreshortening required in the face and body is nicely executed. The subject is endowed with a cascade of beautiful golden-red hair. The tiger's head is painted in excellent detail. Carefully detailed roses are scattered about. Lights and shadows are dramatic. Dark, spangled draperies are in the background.

Major's work could be termed dramatic and decorative, blended with colorful individuality. His long life ended in 1951.

MEMBERSHIPS
Boston Art Club
Guild of Boston Artists

Loire River, France, ca. 1890. Courtesy of Vose Galleries of Boston, Inc., Massachusetts.

SEASON	75-76	76-77	77-78	78-79	79-80	80-81	81-82	82-83	83-84	84-85
Paintings		1	1						13	
Dollars		$1,100	$1,400						$16,350	

Record Sale: $2,800, S.BM, 11/17/83, ''Portrait of Artist's Wife,'' 24 × 18 in.

CARLE J. BLENNER
(1864-1952)

Carle J. Blenner's enduring success, first as an international society portraitist and later as a painter of floral still lifes, rested firmly on a precocious talent and impeccable training.

Born in 1864 in Richmond, Virginia, Blenner was educated at Marburg, Germany and was graduated from the Yale University Art School.

He studied for six years at the Academie Julien in Paris, under Bouguereau, Robert-Fleury and Aman-Jean. He first exhibited at the Paris Salon in 1887, at age 23, and for the next three years. From the 1890s, he maintained a working studio for more than 50 years on 57th Street in New York City.

Blenner was in demand as a portraitist of the wealthy, titled and famous—particularly women. His subjects included Lady Hamilton, granddaughter of the Duke of Cambridge; Mrs. Raymond White; Lady Chetwynde; and Mme. Nordica, Isabel Irving and Evelyn Nesbitt of the theater. His male portraits were of such personages as the Duke of Cambridge, the Earl of Yarmouth, Richard Henning and Henry Clay Pierce.

Blenner turned to still-life studies of flowers, probably about 1915, and continued to reap awards for these and other works—the last in 1932, when he was 70.

His florals reflect his superb training. However, his own sense of textures and his superior use of pigment in the service

Portrait of Arturo Toscanini, 1902, 15½ x 11½ in., signed u.l. Photograph courtesy of Hirschl & Adler, Inc., New York, New York.

Studio Model, 28¾ x 25¾ in., signed l.r. Courtesy of Grand Central Art Galleries, Inc., New York, New York.

of light create not only unlabored representations, but revelations of the flowers' essence.

Blenner died in New Haven, Connecticut in 1952, at age 90.

MEMBERSHIPS
American Federation of Arts
Connecticut Academy of Fine Arts
Greenwich Art Association
New Haven Paint and Clay Club
Newport Art Association, Rhode Island
Salmagundi Club, New York City
Washington Arts Club, Washington, D.C.

PUBLIC COLLECTIONS
Fort Worth Art Museum
Houston Museum of Fine Arts
Rutgers University, New Brunswick, New Jersey
University of Vermont, Burlington

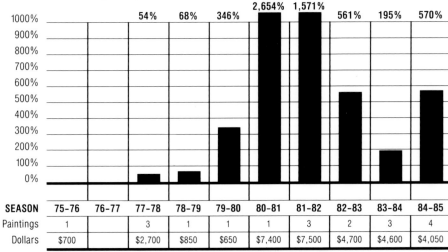

10-Year Average Change From Base Years '75-'76: 669%

| | | 54% | 68% | 346% | 2,654% | 1,571% | 561% | 195% | 570% |

SEASON	75-76	76-77	77-78	78-79	79-80	80-81	81-82	82-83	83-84	84-85
Paintings	1		3	1	1	1	3	2	3	4
Dollars	$700		$2,700	$850	$650	$7,400	$7,500	$4,700	$4,600	$4,050

Record Sale: $7,400, S.BM, 5/21/81, "Woman with Mirror," 24 × 20 in.

WARREN B. DAVIS
(1865-1928)

Like Frank W. Benson in Boston, Warren B. Davis had two careers in art, first as a painter and then, when he was past middle age, as an etcher. In his early years, he was known primarily for his paintings and pastels of neoclassical goddesses and dancing maidens, draped and undraped. Many of these were reproduced as covers and illustrations for *Vanity Fair*. He executed several murals on the same theme that were known for their rhythm, balance and beauty. His etchings followed in the same poetic vein, with such evocative titles as *Evening, Crescent* and *Nocturne.*

Davis was born in New York City in 1865. As a boy he studied the piano seriously, but gave it up in favor of painting. Throughout his life, however, he continued to devote most of his leisure hours to playing the piano. He got his training as a painter at the Art Students League.

Graceful, auburn-haired nymphs, dancing against backgrounds of russet, black or gold, early became his specialty. Some critics at the time thought that the fluidity with which he painted the filmy draperies of his female figures had never been equalled.

Davis never touched a copper plate or an etcher's needle until he was 50. When he decided to learn etching, however, he applied himself as seriously as he had with paint and pastels. His etchings

Studio Reflections, 26 x 20 in. Courtesy of Grand Central Art Galleries, Inc., New York, New York.

The Three Graces, 15½ x 11¾ in., signed l.l. Courtesy of Marbella Gallery, Inc., New York, New York. Photograph by Richard Haynes.

proved even more popular than his earlier work. They sold well both in this country and abroad.

Davis died at his home in Brooklyn in 1928.

MEMBERSHIPS
Allied Artists of America
Salmagundi Club

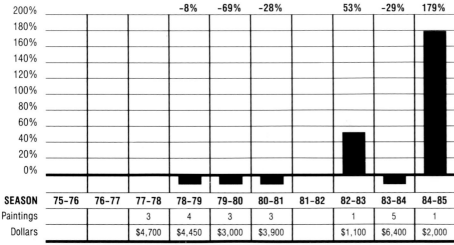

10-Year Average Change From Base Years '77-'78: 14%

	75-76	76-77	77-78	78-79	79-80	80-81	81-82	82-83	83-84	84-85
				-8%	-69%	-28%		53%	-29%	179%

SEASON	75-76	76-77	77-78	78-79	79-80	80-81	81-82	82-83	83-84	84-85
Paintings			3	4	3	3		1	5	1
Dollars			$4,700	$4,450	$3,000	$3,900		$1,100	$6,400	$2,000

Record Sale: $2,800, SPB, 10/27/78, "Woman in White," 14 × 10 in.

ROBERT HENRI
(1865-1929)

Robert Henri was an early-twentieth-century portrait and cityscape painter who, as the leader of the Ashcan School, inspired two generations of artists between the World Wars.

Henri was instrumental in breaking the hold of traditionalists on the world of art. He painted ordinary and exotic people, rather than the social elite, and his paintings of city streets and urban slums helped inaugurate the modern era.

Henri was born Robert Henry Cozad and given the name of Robert Henri by his father, a gambler who shot a man in a fight and had to flee for his life from a lynching mob. Henri revered his father and emulated his flair for life. His studio was not only a lecture hall where Henri espoused his philosophy of life and art, but a beer hall where he and his followers played poker and held indoor scrimmages with pots of spaghetti.

Raised in the midwestern states of Ohio and Nebraska, Henri later moved to Atlantic City, New Jersey. He trained at the Pennsylvania Academy of the Fine Arts, where he became a devotee of Thomas Eakins and a student of Thomas Anshutz, picking up the thread of realism started by Eakins.

In 1888, Henri traveled to Paris, where he studied at the Academie Julien and at the Ecole des Beaux-Arts. He temporarily adopted impressionistic techniques, but by the mid-1890s he had abandoned them for the darker tonal qualities of Hals, Velazquez and

Indian Portrait, 40 x 32 in., signed l.l. Photograph courtesy of The Gerald Peters Gallery, Santa Fe, New Mexico.

Rembrandt—colors more suited to the leader of the urban realists.

Despite their subject and tone, Henri's paintings are not morose, nor do they carry a social message. On the contrary, they sparkle with life, reflecting Henri's conviction that human dignity and joy can be found anywhere. Many of his portraits were of children.

Henri attacked his canvases aggressively, focusing on personality, gesture and glance, rather than anatomy. He painted as rapidly as he could with single, dramatic brushstrokes, suggesting rather than defining the forms. His aim was to capture feeling and sensation— the spirit of life—rather than to compose well-designed canvases.

Henri's landscape paintings express

the artist's emotional responses to the moods of nature. His portraits are marked by expressive faces and eyebrows; he could suggest a piece of clothing with a dab of color.

A vocal and forceful man, Henri led a generation of artists to break away from conservative traditions and to reject the elite, academic subject matter of his day. In Philadelphia and later in New York City, his studio became a center of activity, attracting Glackens, Luks, Sloan and Shinn, as well as many other young artists inspired by the new realism. He taught at the New York School of Art, among others, as well as at a school established under his own name.

In 1908, he organized an exhibition of paintings by The Eight, which shocked the conservative art world with its strong realism. Hundreds flocked to view the revolutionary work. Critics called the group the "black gang"; they were later to be known as the Ashcan School.

MEMBERSHIPS
National Academy of Design
Art Students League
National Institute of Arts and Letters

PUBLIC COLLECTIONS
Art Institute of Chicago
Brooklyn Museum
Carnegie Institute, Pittsburgh
Carolina Art Association, Charleston
Dallas Art Association
Fine Arts Gallery, Columbus, Ohio
Kansas City Art Institute
Metropolitan Museum of Art, New York City
New Orleans Art Association
Pennsylvania Academy of the Fine Arts,
   Philadelphia
San Francisco Institute

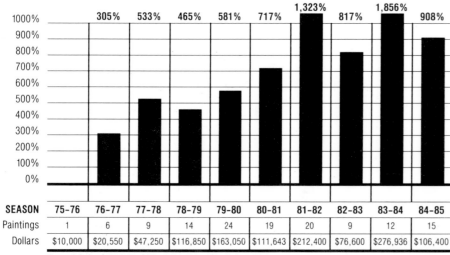

10-Year Average Change From Base Years '75-'76: 751%

	75-76	76-77	77-78	78-79	79-80	80-81	81-82	82-83	83-84	84-85
		305%	533%	465%	581%	717%	1,323%	817%	1,856%	908%
SEASON	75-76	76-77	77-78	78-79	79-80	80-81	81-82	82-83	83-84	84-85
Paintings	1	6	9	14	24	19	20	9	12	15
Dollars	$10,000	$20,550	$47,250	$116,850	$163,050	$111,643	$212,400	$76,600	$276,936	$106,400

Record Sale: $57,045, SPB, 5/30/84, "Sis," 24 × 20 in.

PHILIP L. HALE
(1865-1931)

Painter, teacher and writer, Philip Leslie Hale is recognized for his decorative paintings of the female figure. His technique is derived from the impressionists and suggests the influence of French impressionist Edgar Degas.

Born in Boston in 1865, he was the son of a clergyman and patriotic writer, the Reverend Edward Everett Hale.

Philip Hale studied with J. Alden Weir at the Art Students League in New York City, and then went to Paris for further studies at the Academie Julien and the Ecole des Beaux-Arts.

While in France, he lived at Giverny and knew Claude Monet well. Traveling throughout Europe, Hale visited the major museums, and copied the works of Ingres, Vermeer, Watteau and Michelangelo.

After studying abroad for 15 years, Hale returned to America around 1895, and was given a one-man show in New York City.

Like many artists, Hale underwent stages in his choice of subjects. In the 1890s, he painted sporting scenes. He then turned to studies of women and painted them in the nude, in landscapes and indoors. During the 1920s, he painted larger allegorical subjects, reflecting the theme of man versus the overwhelming forces of nature. He also painted portraits.

Hale taught at the Boston Museum School for many years, where he also studied with teacher and painter Edmund C. Tarbell. He also spent a few years teaching at the Pennsylvania Academy of the Fine Arts.

Hale was known as a teacher who did not encourage questions from his students about his paintings or private life. He was more interested in painting universal human situations than in the character of the individuals.

Grandmother's Birthday, 30 x 36 in., signed l.l. Courtesy of Vose Galleries of Boston, Inc., Massachusetts.

He died in Boston in 1931, of a ruptured appendix. Boston's famed Vose Galleries held a retrospective exhibition of Hale's work in 1966.

MEMBERSHIPS
Fellowship of the Pennsylvania Academy
  of the Fine Arts
Guild of Boston Artists
National Academy of Design
National Arts Club
National Association of Portrait Painters
Philadelphia Art Club
St. Bololph Club
San Francisco Art Club

PUBLIC COLLECTIONS
Cooper-Hewitt Museum, New York City
Corcoran Gallery of Art, Washington, D.C.
Delaware Art Museum, Wilmington
Pennsylvania Academy of the Fine Arts,
  Philadelphia

SEASON	75-76	76-77	77-78	78-79	79-80	80-81	81-82	82-83	83-84	84-85
Paintings		1	1	1	1		2		2	
Dollars		$9,500	$1,200	$2,000	$9,000		$9,700		$15,500	

Record Sale: $9,500, PB, 4/21/77, "The Rub Down," 48 × 30 in.

WILLIAM S. HORTON
(1865-1936)

William S. Horton was a gifted impressionist who was little-known in his time, but whose oils, pastels, watercolors and drawings are highly valued today. They are exhibited in leading American and European museums and art galleries.

Horton was born into a wealthy family in Grand Rapids, Michigan in 1865. While still in his early teens, he left his academic schooling to study at the Art Institute of Chicago, and then at the Art Students League and the National Academy of Design in New York City. Next, he studied under Benjamin Constant at the Academie Julien in Paris; it was under Constant that his unique style of impressionism began to emerge. Horton used vivid colors, while those of other impressionists were muted.

Horton first exhibited at the Salon des Artistes Francaises. He was encouraged when one of his paintings won a gold medal at Nantes in 1904 and a bronze at Orleans in 1905 in provincial salons.

Since he was financially secure, Horton was never forced to sell his paintings. He was, however, his own taskmaster, and painted on a strict schedule to satisfy his own sense of accomplishment.

Since Horton rarely sold a painting, when he died in Paris in 1936 a great many of his works were bequeathed to his son, W. Gray Horton, who had no need to sell them either. They were not put on the auction block, and for this reason the works of William S. Horton are modestly priced compared to those of other impressionists of his time. There is, however, a growing group of collectors who would prefer a Horton painting to one by one of his contemporaries.

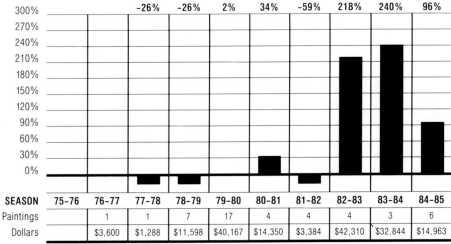

Beach Scene, signed l.r. Courtesy of Vose Galleries of Boston, Inc., Massachusetts.

MEMBERSHIPS
American Federation of Arts
Cercle Interallie
Cercle Volney
New York Water Color Club
Salon D'Automne
Societe Internationale
Societe Moderne

PUBLIC COLLECTIONS
Brooklyn Museum
Library, Museum and Art Gallery,
  Bootle, Liverpool, England
National Museum, Stockholm, Sweden
National Museum of American Art, Washington, D.C.

10-Year Average Change From Base Years '76-'77: 53%

	75-76	76-77	77-78	78-79	79-80	80-81	81-82	82-83	83-84	84-85
		-26%	-26%	2%	34%	-59%	218%	240%	96%	
SEASON	75-76	76-77	77-78	78-79	79-80	80-81	81-82	82-83	83-84	84-85
Paintings		1	1	7	17	4	4	4	3	6
Dollars		$3,600	$1,288	$11,598	$40,167	$14,350	$3,384	$42,310	$32,844	$14,963

Record Sale: $37,000, SPB, 6/2/83, "Concert on the Sand, Hythe," 25 × 30 in.

614

GRACE CARPENTER HUDSON
(1865-1937)

A genre painter who specialized in paintings and illustrations of American Indians, Grace Carpenter Hudson was born in Potter Valley, California.

She began studying art at age 13 and progressed so rapidly that two years later she won the Alvord Gold Medal from the San Francisco Art Association for a figure drawing. She continued to study at the Mark Hopkins Institute in San Francisco under Virgil Williams.

The artist settled in Ukiah, California, where she painted, taught and created illustrations for such magazines as *Sunset, Cosmopolitan* and *Western Field.* In 1890, she married John Hudson, a physician who eventually gave up his practice to do research and writing on the language and art of the Pomo Indians of Mendocino County. He also acted as Pacific Coast ethnologist for the Field Museum of Natural History in Chicago.

In 1893, Hudson exhibited paintings of her favorite Pomo subjects in the Women's Department of the California State Building at the World's Columbian Exposition in Chicago. In 1901, she spent nearly a year in Hawaii, painting native children.

Then, in 1904, Hudson was commissioned by the Field Museum in Chicago to paint a series of pictures of the Pawnee Indians of Oklahoma. Of this series, the best known was her portrait of Eagle Chief, the leader of four Pawnee tribes and an honored guest of Theodore Roosevelt at the White House. In 1905, she and her husband made the first of two extended tours of Europe to visit museums and galleries.

The artist had a special talent for capturing the volatile moods of childhood. Her work has a quiet enchantment and an abiding realism. It is also considered an important historical, if sometimes too sentimental, record of the Pomo Indians.

Indian Woman (A Daughter of the Quail-Woman), 1918, 22 x 16 in., signed l.l. Courtesy of Monterey Peninsula Museum of Art, California.

The Interrupted Bath—Quail Baby, 1892, 38 x 33 in., signed l.r. Courtesy of Monterey Peninsula Museum of Art, California.

PUBLIC COLLECTIONS
Field Museum of Natural History, Chicago
Oakland Museum, California
National Gallery of Art, Washington, D.C.

SEASON	75-76	76-77	77-78	78-79	79-80	80-81	81-82	82-83	83-84	84-85
Paintings		1	3	10	5	8	9	4	4	2
Dollars		$3,200	$34,500	$85,350	$5,235	$109,100	$143,500	$24,600	$10,700	$11,509

Record Sale: $33,000, SPB, 10/22/81, "Ray of Light," 16 × 10 in.

SYDNEY LAURENCE
(1865-1940)

Sydney Laurence was a painter and adventurer best known for his landscapes of Mt. McKinley and other scenes of the Alaskan frontier. Having painted most of his known work between 1912 and 1940, Laurence has been called one of the last of the Rocky Mountain School of landscape artists.

Born in Brooklyn, Laurence is said to have run off to sea in his teens, and to have returned to New York after several years as a seaman. Sometime in the 1880s, he enrolled in the National Academy of Design, where he studied under Edward Moran. In 1889, he traveled to Paris and entered the Ecole des Beaux Arts.

During the next 10 years, Laurence painted in both England and France, maintaining a residence at St. Ives, a fishing village on the coast of Cornwall. Working primarily as a marine painter, Laurence exhibited paintings at the Royal Academy of Arts in London and the Paris Salon of 1894, receiving an honorable mention at the latter for *Setting Sun, Coast of Cornwall* (date and location unknown).

By 1898, Laurence had returned to New York City, where he exhibited his work at the National Academy of Design. He became a war correspondent for several years, covering the Spanish-American War for the *New York Herald* and working for the English journal *Black and White* during the Boer War and the Boxer Rebellion.

Alaska Trail, 20 x 16 in., signed l.l. Courtesy of Green's Show Print, Los Angeles, California.

By 1903, Laurence had abandoned his correspondent's and painting careers to follow the gold rush to Alaska, where he supported himself for 10 years in odd jobs as cook, carpenter, photographer and part-time gold prospector.

Laurence renewed his career as a landscape painter only after 1912, when he was able to finance a painting expedition to Mt. McKinley, which was at that time unclimbed and unpainted. From this expedition, Laurence returned with some 40 color sketches, which he repainted on larger canvases over the following year.

Laurence exhibited his work successfully at the 1915 Panama-Pacific Exposition in San Francisco. The same year, his backers purchased two large canvases, which were subsequently hung in the National Museum of American Art of the Smithsonian Institution.

For the remainder of his career, Laurence enjoyed the patronage of art collectors on the East and West coasts. By 1925, he could afford to open a winter studio in Los Angeles, where he continued to paint much of his work on Alaskan subjects. He remained active until his death in 1940 in Seattle.

MEMBERSHIPS
Royal Society of British Artists
Salmagundi Club

PUBLIC COLLECTIONS
Anchorage Historical and Fine Arts Museum, Alaska
Alaska Bank of Commerce, Anchorage

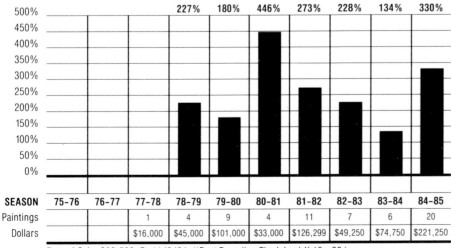

10-Year Average Change From Base Years '77-'78: 227%

SEASON	75-76	76-77	77-78	78-79	79-80	80-81	81-82	82-83	83-84	84-85
			227%	180%	446%	273%	228%	134%	330%	
Paintings			1	4	9	4	11	7	6	20
Dollars			$16,000	$45,000	$101,000	$33,000	$126,299	$49,250	$74,750	$221,250

Record Sale: $32,500, B, 11/8/84, "Boat Rounding Fire Island," 16 x 20 in.

RODERICK D. MacKENZIE
(1865-1941)

Roderick MacKenzie was a versatile painter whose work ranged from oil portraits, landscapes and scenes of the imperial splendor of British India in its heyday, to a series of pastels showing the industrial might of the steel mills of Alabama. He handled all subjects with equal finesse. He also did etchings, and was commissioned to do eight large murals and bas-relief panels for the Alabama State House.

MacKenzie was born in London in 1865. He came by his bent for colorful pageantry naturally because his father was a painter of heraldry and carriages. When he was seven, however, his family moved to Mobile, Alabama. He received his art training at the School of the Museum of Fine Arts in Boston, and then the Academie Julien and the Ecole des Beaux Arts, both in Paris.

From 1893 until 1913, MacKenzie lived and worked most of the time in India. His paintings of such splendid occasions as the coronation of King Edward VII and the state entry into Delhi during the durbar of 1903 were widely acclaimed. His portraits of various potentates were applauded when they were exhibited in London and Paris.

He left the pomp of India behind in 1913, however, and returned to Alabama, where he lived until his death in 1941. He was fascinated by the drama of the steel industry that was beginning to transform the South. Working at various sites at night, he caught the contrast of cavernous, dark interiors of mills suddenly brilliantly illuminated by white-hot molten metal being poured and shaped. His work was praised by art critics and steel industrialists alike.

From a mural in the rotunda of the Alabama State Capitol, *The Founding of Mobile,* featuring d'Iberville and Bienville. Courtesy of the Alabama Department of Archives and History, Montgomery, Alabama.

MEMBERSHIPS
Alabama Hall of Fame
American Federation of Arts
Royal Society of Arts, London

PUBLIC COLLECTIONS
Alabama State House, Montgomery
Indian Museum, Calcutta

SEASON	75-76	76-77	77-78	78-79	79-80	80-81	81-82	82-83	83-84	84-85
Paintings						1				
Dollars						$12,600				

Record Sale: $12,600, B, 6/18/81, "The State Entry into Delhi in 1902," 132 × 218 in.

WILLIAM WENDT
(1865-1946)

Serenity, 1934, 30 x 36 in., signed l.l. Courtesy of Petersen Galleries, Beverly Hills, California.

Called the dean of California artists, William Wendt spent his mature life painting landscapes of the rolling hills and arroyos of the Southern part of that state. At first he worked with rather tentative, feathery brushstrokes, but later he developed a bold, self-confident style which one critic termed "masculine impressionism." A deeply religious man, he found peace and satisfaction in painting lovely, natural settings.

Born in Germany in 1865, he came to the United States at age 15 to join an uncle in Chicago. His only art training was some evening classes at the Chicago Art Institute, but he managed to find work in a commercial art shop, painting formula pictures and display scenery.

In his free time he took up easel painting. When he won the second prize of $200 at the Chicago Society of Artists exhibition in 1893 it was enough, he decided, to allow him to work full-time as an easel painter.

He liked to sketch in the field and then return to his studio to paint large landscapes. In 1894, seeking new scenes to paint, he made his first trip to California. He returned there two years later, the second time with George G. Symons, another painter who became a long-time painting companion.

In 1898, the two went to England together, visiting galleries and painting for several months along the coast of Cornwall. Afterward, Wendt had an exhibition of his work from California

and England, which was enthusiastically received in Chicago. Over the next few years he made several other trips to California and Europe.

In 1906, Wendt married Julia Bracken, a sculptor from Chicago, and then settled into a combination home and studio he had bought in Los Angeles. The two worked harmoniously together, she in the studio and he wandering the hills sketching, then returning

to translate his sketches into finished landscapes.

Wendt painted exactly what he saw in nature with warm colors and outstanding effects of light and shadow. The tranquility, strength and sense of well-being of his work appealed to a wide audience. It had a sober sort of poetry about it, one critic wrote, like a fine, familiar hymn.

In 1912, Wendt built a studio in Laguna Beach, California, where he worked steadily until his death in 1946. He and his wife shared their knowledge with aspiring artists, and had much to do with the growth of Laguna Beach as a center of the arts.

MEMBERSHIPS
American Federation of Arts
California Art Club
Chicago Society of Artists
Laguna Beach Art Association
National Academy of Design
National Arts Club
Society of Western Artists

PUBLIC COLLECTIONS
Art Institute of Chicago
Cincinnati Art Museum
Des Moines Art Center, Iowa
Indianapolis Museum of Art
Los Angeles County Museum of Art

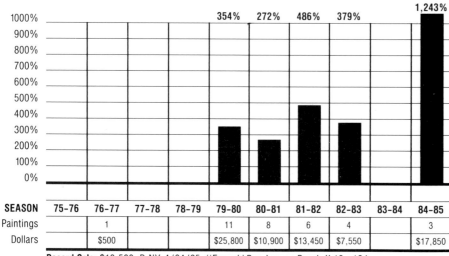

10-Year Average Change From Base Years '76-'77: 456%

SEASON	75-76	76-77	77-78	78-79	79-80	80-81	81-82	82-83	83-84	84-85
					354%	272%	486%	379%		1,243%
Paintings		1			11	8	6	4		3
Dollars		$500			$25,800	$10,900	$13,450	$7,550		$17,850

Record Sale: $10,500, D.NY, 4/24/85, "Emerald Bay, Laguna Beach," 12 x 16 in.

EANGER IRVING COUSE
(1866-1936)

Although trained in classical art in Paris, Eanger Irving Couse was bent on creating an art that was purely American in subject matter. He came home to make his reputation painting Indians, especially the Pueblo Indians around Taos, New Mexico.

Indians had long since lost their image as savages and Couse portrayed them almost poetically as tranquil, unthreatening, and indeed beautiful. Most of his work contains definite, recognizable characteristics. A sparsely-clad Indian crouches or squats on his heels, lit by firelight, sidelight or sometimes moonlight to accentuate his muscularity. Usually he is engaged in some domestic activity and has a pensive, withdrawn expression.

Couse came by his interest in Indians naturally. Born in Saginaw, Michigan in 1866, when it was still a remote logging center, he grew up surrounded by them.

Intent on becoming an artist, Couse first worked as a housepainter to earn money for study. In 1884, he was able to afford three months at the Art Institute of Chicago. Then it was back to housepainting for another season.

For two years he studied at the National Academy of Design in New York City, doing odd jobs to pay his way. Both years he won awards in student exhibitions.

Returning to Saginaw, Couse painted portraits of townspeople until he had enough money to go to Paris. There he studied at the Academie Julien under

At the Spring, 1918, 30 x 36¼ in., signed l.l. Courtesy of Wunderlich and Company, Inc., New York, New York.

Tony Robert-Fleury and Adolphe Bouguereau.

In Paris, Couse married a fellow student whose father had a ranch in Oregon. Visiting there, Couse delighted in painting the Indians in deep pastel hues reminiscent of the French barbizon painters.

Because there was as yet little interest in pictures of Indians, however, Couse returned to France and settled in a village on the English Channel, where he painted more marketable scenes of coastal fishing and shepherds.

Hearing of the isolation and pageantry of the Pueblo Indians from two Americans studying in Paris, Couse visited Taos in 1902. It was a turning point; he had found the subject matter that he would paint for the rest of his life.

In Taos he often sketched outdoors,

sometimes taking along one of his favorite Indian models, but his paintings were composed and executed on an easel in his commodious studio. The imprint of his French academic training never left him.

From 1922 until 1934, paintings by Couse were used on calendars distributed by the Santa Fe Railway and prints hung in every Santa Fe waiting room. They formed the nucleus of an impressive collection of his work owned by the railroad.

Couse's wife died in 1929. Although he continued to paint, friends say that he had lost his spark. He died in Taos in 1936.

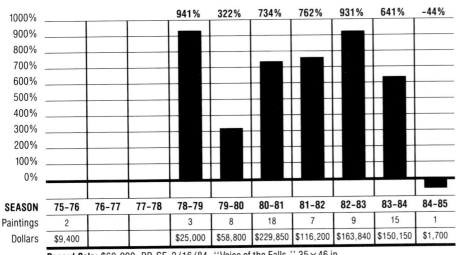

10-Year Average Change From Base Years '75-'76: 536%

| | | | 941% | 322% | 734% | 762% | 931% | 641% | -44% |

SEASON	75-76	76-77	77-78	78-79	79-80	80-81	81-82	82-83	83-84	84-85
Paintings	2			3	8	18	7	9	15	1
Dollars	$9,400			$25,000	$58,800	$229,850	$116,200	$163,840	$150,150	$1,700

Record Sale: $60,000, BB.SF, 2/16/84, "Voice of the Falls," 35 × 46 in.

ALLEN TUCKER
(1866-1939)

Architect and painter Allen Tucker was one of the founders of the Society of Independent Artists. His widely exhibited paintings are reminiscent, in their brushwork and use of light, of the work of Vincent Van Gogh.

Born in Brooklyn in 1866, Tucker graduated with a degree in architecture at Columbia University. While working as an architectural draftsman in New York City, he began studying painting under John H. Twatchman at the Art Students League. When he was 38, Tucker abandoned architecture altogether and devoted himself to painting full-time.

Tucker based his studio in New York City but spent summers traveling and painting in Europe, along the New England coast, in New Mexico or in the Canadian Rockies.

In 1911, Tucker secured his place in art history by becoming a charter member of the Association of American Painters and Sculptors. The Association was responsible for a major exhibition— the 1913 New York City Armory Show—which included five paintings by Tucker. Six years later, he helped found the Society of Independent Artists.

Tucker's first comprehensive one-man show was held in 1918 at the Whitney Studio Club (later the Whitney Museum of American Art). He was subsequently exhibited in the Paris Salon and in Philadelphia.

Washington Crossing the Delaware, 1931, 20 x 36 in., signed l.l. Courtesy of Collection The Whitney Museum of American Art, New York, New York, Purchase.

As exemplified by his *A Book of Verse* (1916, The Allen Tucker Memorial), the artist's crude but passionate use of light, inspired by Van Gogh, was stylistic pioneering in American art.

From 1920 to 1928, Tucker was a teacher and lecturer at the Art Students League, and until his death in New York in 1939 he published extensively.

MEMBERSHIPS
Architectural League of New York
Association of American Painters and Sculptors

PUBLIC COLLECTIONS
Albright-Knox Art Gallery,
 Buffalo, New York
Art Institute of Chicago
Brooklyn Museum
Metropolitan Museum of Art, New York City
Phillips Collection, Washington, D.C.

10-Year Average Change From Base Years '76-'77: 311%

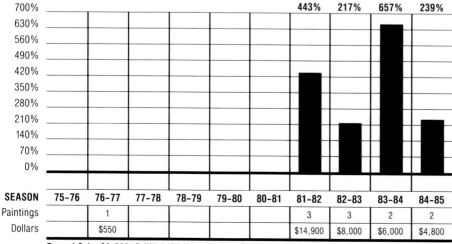

SEASON	75-76	76-77	77-78	78-79	79-80	80-81	81-82	82-83	83-84	84-85
							443%	217%	657%	239%
Paintings		1					3	3	2	2
Dollars		$550					$14,900	$8,000	$6,000	$4,800

Record Sale: $9,500, D.NY, 4/21/82, "Fir Tree Shadows," 28 x 34 in.

ARTHUR CLIFTON GOODWIN
(1866-1929)

Arthur Clifton Goodwin, a little-known American impressionist, is considered the painter par excellence of the city of Boston.

Born in 1866 in Portsmouth, New Hampshire, Goodwin grew up in Chelsea, Massachusetts. Known as the "Beau Brummel of Chelsea," he worked as a salesman in a wholesale paper establishment, and often drank to excess. He began to paint at age 30.

With the help of Louis Kronberg, who allowed him to use his studio and colors, Goodwin remained in Boston until 1920, painting the city in all its moods and colors. One of his favorite subjects was "T" wharf, a pier at which the boats of many Portuguese and Italian fishermen were docked. In 1914, Goodwin was admitted to membership in the Guild of Boston Artists, which gave him an opportunity to exhibit his work.

He continued to drink, and his erratic lifestyle—his appearance alternated between that of a tramp and a dandy—caused him to lose patrons frequently. He was always able to sell his paintings, but his fees were inconsistent.

Between 1902 and 1920, the painter's style changed slowly; it was a process of perfecting his vision rather than changing direction. His delicate sensitivity to nuances of light and color allowed him to blend his human figures into the natural landscape, to achieve an unusual harmony between man and his surroundings. His vigorous, spontaneous and optimistic paintings were owned by such notables as John Singer Sargent.

Goodwin was particularly fascinated by those places where the city abruptly meets the natural landscape, and preferred to paint piers, plazas and river bridges. One of the few American impressionists who chose urban subjects, he never experienced the influence of the French masters directly. Rather, he absorbed the already common idiom

T. Wharf Basin, Boston, 29 x 36 in., signed l.r. Courtesy of Arvest Galleries, Inc., Boston, Massachusetts.

without reflecting a specific artist's style.

In 1920, the artist moved to New York City and married. He lived with his wife on a farm in Chatham, New York. In 1929, Goodwin returned to Boston alone, and also returned to his bohemian way of life. He died unexpectedly that year and was discovered in his home by friends, his trunk packed and a steamship ticket to France propped up next to it.

MEMBERSHIPS
Guild of Boston Artists

PUBLIC COLLECTIONS
Addison Gallery of Arts, Andover, Massachusetts
Colby College Art Museum

SEASON	75-76	76-77	77-78	78-79	79-80	80-81	81-82	82-83	83-84	84-85
Paintings	1	3	8	12	26	18	13	9	14	3
Dollars	$1,400	$6,700	$15,100	$28,508	$59,675	$109,550	$61,100	$25,900	$43,775	$4,900

Record Sale: $26,000, SPB, 5/29/81, ''Boston, Arlington Street in Winter,'' 25 × 30 in.

ALBERT LOREY GROLL
(1866-1952)

The traditional poverty of the art student prevented Albert Lorey Groll from being a figure painter: he could not afford to pay for models, so he turned to landscape. He was to become a master painter of the American desert.

Groll's origins were urban, his training academic and European. Born in 1866 in New York City, he studied art in London and in Munich, where his teachers were Nickolaus Gysis and Ludwig Von Loefftz.

When he returned to the United States, he painted on the Northeast coast for a time. He lived in New York City all his life, but when he accompanied a Brooklyn Museum of Arts and Sciences expedition to the Southwest, he discovered the Arizona desert.

Groll's sketches from that trip led to a painting which won him a gold medal from the Pennsylvania Academy of the Fine Arts. He returned many times to Arizona and New Mexico for the source material of his paintings and etchings. Much respected and rewarded as "America's sky painter," he died in New York City in 1952.

Albert Groll produced poetry from the arid desert landscape. The sweep of his skies awakened Americans to the grandeur of the Southwest. The Pueblo Indians of New Mexico particularly respected his accuracy and sensitivity, bestowing on him the name "Chief Bald Head—Eagle Eye."

Flying Clouds, Navajo Desert, Arizona, 28 x 36 in., signed l.r. Courtesy of National Academy of Design, New York, New York.

MEMBERSHIPS
Allied Art Association
American Water Color Society
Artists' Fund Society
Lotos Club
National Academy of Design
National Arts Club
New York Water Color Club
Salmagundi Club
Society of Painters of New York

PUBLIC COLLECTIONS
Brooklyn Museum
Carnegie Institute, Pittsburgh
Corcoran Gallery of Art, Washington, D.C.
Lotos Club, New York City
Metropolis Institute of Arts, Minnesota
Montclair Art Museum, New Jersey
Museum of Fine Arts, Boston
National Gallery of Art, Washington, D.C.
St. Louis Art Museum

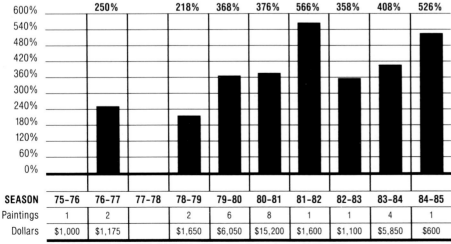

10-Year Average Change From Base Years '75-'76: 341%

	250%		218%	368%	376%	566%	358%	408%	526%
SEASON	75-76	76-77	77-78	78-79	79-80	80-81	81-82	82-83	83-84	84-85
Paintings	1	2		2	6	8	1	1	4	1
Dollars	$1,000	$1,175		$1,650	$6,050	$15,200	$1,600	$1,100	$5,850	$600

Record Sale: $3,750, SPB, 6/19/81, "Horsemen in Landscape," 25 x 35 in.

622

WILLIAM ROBINSON LEIGH
(1866-1955)

Waiting, 1914, 16 x 24 in., signed l.l. Courtesy of Vose Galleries of Boston, Massachusetts.

William Robinson Leigh was one of the most prolific and accomplished painters of the American West. He is especially well known for his dramatic paintings of Western plains, mountains, canyons, cavalry, cowboys and Indians.

Born near Falling Waters, West Virginia in 1866, Leigh spent his childhood on a farm. He began his artistic training at age 14, when he went to study under Hugh Newell at the Maryland Institute in Baltimore. Despite Leigh's poverty, he was able to go to Europe, and he spent 12 years studying at the Royal Academy in Munich. He studied under Raupp, Gysis, Von Lindenschmidt and Von Loefftz.

The painting technique that Leigh learned and mastered in Germany remained with him throughout his career. He began with a detailed charcoal drawing and painted over it. Starting with the most distant objects, such as the horizon and sky, Leigh slowly painted each object until he reached the foreground.

Leigh's bold colors and clear lighting add to the dramatic intensity of his works. Because he used traditional European techniques in painting the American West, he was known as the "Sagebrush Rembrandt."

Although Leigh had always wanted to paint the American West, it was not until he was around 40 years old that he finally realized his dream. He traveled to Chicago and offered the Santa Fe Railroad Company a painting of the Grand Canyon in exchange for a ride to New Mexico. The company was so pleased with the finished painting that they commissioned five more pictures, giving Leigh more time to roam the West before he was forced to return to New York City to earn a living. Leigh returned to the West to paint whenever he could.

Back in New York City, Leigh supported himself by illustrating scenes from American history for *Scribner's* and *Collier's.* In 1921 he married Ethel Traphagen, a women's-clothing designer, and together they founded the Traphagen School of Fashion in New York City.

After Leigh's death in 1955, his widow gave his entire collection of work to the Gilcrease Institute of American History and Art in Tulsa, Oklahoma.

MEMBERSHIPS
Allied Art Association
American Watercolor Society
Salmagundi Club

PUBLIC COLLECTIONS
Academy of Natural Sciences, Philadelphia
American Museum of Natural History, New York City
Thomas Gilcrease Institute of American History and Art, Tulsa, Oklahoma

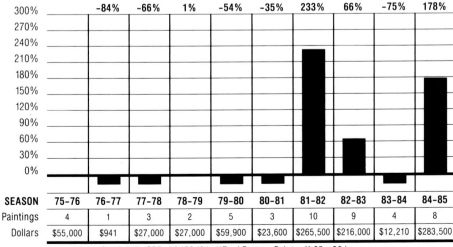

10-Year Average Change From Base Years '75-'76: 16%

	-84%	-66%	1%	-54%	-35%	233%	66%	-75%	178%

SEASON	75-76	76-77	77-78	78-79	79-80	80-81	81-82	82-83	83-84	84-85
Paintings	4	1	3	2	5	3	10	9	4	8
Dollars	$55,000	$941	$27,000	$27,000	$59,900	$23,600	$265,500	$216,000	$12,210	$283,500

Record Sale: $135,000, SPB, 10/22/81, "Zuni Pottery Painter," 25 x 30 in.

623

PINCUS MARCIUS-SIMONS
(1867-1909)

Pincus Marcius-Simons (popularly known as "Pinkey") was an expatriate painter and one of the few American symbolist artists exhibited in the Paris salons.

Born in 1867 in New York City, Marcius-Simons was taken to Europe while still an infant, returning to the United States only once before he was 25. After spending part of his childhood in Spain and Italy, he was educated at Vaugirard College in Paris, and studied art under J.G. Vibert.

Marcius-Simons's earliest paintings were historical and sentimental genre scenes. He exhibited them at the Paris Salon in 1882.

By his twenties, however, Marcius-Simons abandoned his earlier, academic style, turning to a near-poetic style reminiscent of Turner and the French symbolists. Whether landscapes or more imaginative, mystical subjects, Marcius-Simons's works were characterized by their remarkable coloration.

Although he was regarded in Paris as the standard-bearer of the symbolist movement in America, Marcius-Simons did not follow the restrictions of subject matter decided by the leaders of that movement in France, despite the fact that he occasionally borrowed from their symbolism and was exhibited in their galleries.

Victory, 1904, signed l.l. Courtesy of the National Park Service, Sagamore Hill National Historic Site, Oyster Bay, New York.

Beginning in 1894, he turned his attention to illustrating operatic themes. He worked as a set designer in Bayreuth, Germany at the Wagner Theatre until his death there in 1909.

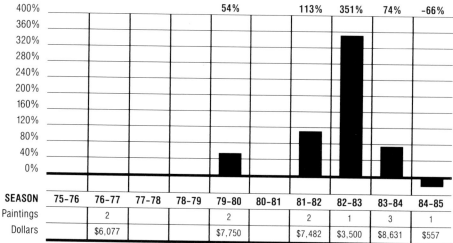

10-Year Average Change From Base Years '76-'77: 88%

SEASON	75-76	76-77	77-78	78-79	79-80	80-81	81-82	82-83	83-84	84-85
					54%		113%	351%	74%	−66%
Paintings		2			2		2	1	3	1
Dollars		$6,077			$7,750		$7,482	$3,500	$8,631	$557

Record Sale: $5,250, SPB, 6/12/80, "Parsifal & the Knights of the Holy Grail," 44 × 57 in.

624

GUY ROSE
(1867-1925)

Guy Rose was a successful painter and teacher in the early 1900s. His major contribution was introducing and developing the French impressionistic style among California painters.

Rose, the son of a wealthy rancher, was born in San Gabriel, California in 1867. He revealed a skill for drawing during a convalescence from a near-fatal gun accident, and developed this talent by studying with Emil Carlsen at San Francisco's California School of Design. Lefebvre, Constant and Doucet were Rose's instructors when he traveled to France to study at the Academie Julien.

In 1891, Rose worked as a magazine illustrator in New York City. He made the first of many return trips to France in 1893.

In 1894, Rose's *One Flight Into Egypt* (date and location unknown) won an honorable mention in an exhibition at the Paris Salon. His citation made Ross the first Californian to receive a Salon honor.

A severe attack of lead poisoning interrupted Rose's career in 1894. Unable to paint for years, he lived first in Los Angeles, then in New York City, for the next five years.

In New York Rose taught at Pratt Institute, and illustrated for *Harper's, Scribner's, Century* and *Youth's Companion.*

His love of French impressionist painting never dimmed and he returned to Paris in 1899. Although he was not a

Coastal Scene, 10½ x 14 in., signed l.r. Courtesy of Maxwell Galleries, LTD., San Francisco, California.

formal student of Monet, Rose met the French impressionist and received his critical evaluation.

In France, Rose produced luminous, lightly brushed paintings. He crossed the Atlantic for the last time in 1914, and returned to California.

In California Rose painted scenes of Carmel, Point Lobos, Laguna Beach and San Gabriel. He became an instructor, and later director, of the Stickney Memorial School of Art in Pasadena. In Southern California between 1914 and 1920, Rose was considered the equal of any American painter of his time.

Another attack of lead poisoning ended his career in 1921, and he died four years later. However, his influence had spread throughout California.

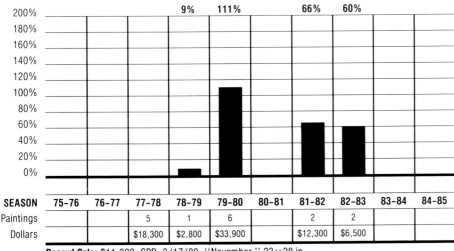

10-Year Average Change From Base Years '77-'78: 49%

SEASON	75-76	76-77	77-78	78-79	79-80	80-81	81-82	82-83	83-84	84-85
				9%	111%		66%	60%		
Paintings			5	1	6		2	2		
Dollars			$18,300	$2,800	$33,900		$12,300	$6,500		

Record Sale: $11,000, SPB, 3/17/80, "November," 23 × 28 in.

MEMBERSHIPS
California Art Club

PUBLIC COLLECTIONS
Cleveland Museum of Art
Laguna Beach Museum of Art, California
Oakland Museum, California

625

GEORGE B. LUKS

(1867-1933)

George Luks's lack of sentimentality and his understanding of the cruder and coarser strata of civilization made him one of the most powerful realists of the Ashcan School, the group of painters who were tremendously influential in creating realism in twentieth-century American painting.

Luks's habit of embroidering or even manufacturing his past makes it difficult to trace his life. The son of two amateur painters, he was born in Williamsport, Pennsylvania in 1867. His father was a doctor. In 1884, he attended the Pennsylvania Academy of the Fine Arts in Philadelphia, where he studied under Thomas Anshutz. He then proceeded to Europe to study in Dusseldorf, Paris and London.

In 1894, Luks joined the art department of the Philadelphia *Press.* He covered the Cuban front as artist correspondent for the Philadelphia *Evening Bulletin* in 1896. He also did comic strips and caricatures.

With Everett Shinn, William Glackens, John Sloan and their mentor, Robert Henri, Luks became one of the famous Eight. This group was later known as the Ashcan School, for the darkness of their palette and the urban dinginess of their subject matter. Luks drew his technique from Frans Hals and Rembrandt, and his subjects from the city streets.

He continued to work as a newspaper artist, the equivalent of today's news photographer. As one by one his fellow artists left Philadelphia for New York City, he joined the New York *World* as a cartoonist.

Simultaneously, Luks developed into an accomplished painter, working swiftly and with great energy. His street urchins, wrestlers and coal miners were painted with brutal vitality and uncompromising affection. *The Wrestlers* (1905, location unknown), perhaps his most widely-reproduced work, illus-

The Polka Dot Dress, 1927, 58⅛ x 37 in. Courtesy of National Museum of American Art, Smithsonian Institution, Gift of Mrs. Howard Weingrow.

trates both his ability to capture with absolute clarity the essence of a moment, and his reckless and slapdash approach to technique and anatomy.

In 1908, with Maurice Prendergast, Ernest Lawson and Arthur B. Davies, Luks and the other members of his group exhibited at the Macbeth Gallery in New York City, a show which was intended as a rebuke to the conservative art establishment. This show by The Eight became a rallying point for the forces of change, which eventually resulted in the Armory Show of 1913, in which Luks also exhibited. Ironically, the vigor and new ideas of the modernist foreign painters who participated in the Armory Show overshadowed the American realists who had organized it, and Luks and his friends were passed by.

Luks taught for several years at the Art Students League, and then founded his own school, where the students divided their time between painting under his inspiration and keeping their bellicose master under control. He was found dead in a New York street at age 66.

MEMBERSHIPS
American Painters and Sculptors
National Association of Portrait Painters
New York Water Color Club

PUBLIC COLLECTIONS
Addison Gallery of American Art, Andover, Massachusetts
Barnes Museum, Merion, Pennsylvania
Brooklyn Museum
Chattanooga Art Association
Cleveland Art Museum
Delgado Museum, New Orleans
Detroit Art Institute
Harrison Gallery, Los Angeles
Metropolitan Museum of Art, New York City
Milwaukee Art Institute
Munson-Williams-Proctor Institute, Utica, New York
Museum of Fine Arts, Boston
National Gallery, Washington, D.C.
New York Public Library, New York City
Phillips Gallery, Washington, D.C.
Whitney Museum of American Art, New York City

SEASON	75-76	76-77	77-78	78-79	79-80	80-81	81-82	82-83	83-84	84-85
Paintings	1	2	15	15	16	10	14	8	15	7
Dollars	$13,000	$11,250	$74,300	$41,144	$61,900	$37,100	$345,150	$53,600	$111,100	$82,650

Record Sale: $235,000, SPB, 12/10/81, "Lily Williams," 40 × 39 in.

WILLIAM DE LEFTWICH DODGE

(1867-1935)

Early in the twentieth century, William de Leftwich Dodge was one of the most prominent muralists in America. His works were created on the grand scale for buildings as distinguished as the Library of Congress, the Brooklyn Academy of Music, New York City's Surrogate Court Building and the Waldorf-Astoria Hotel. At that time murals were considered an essential ingredient in the architectural planning of theaters, world's-fair exposition halls, and many private homes.

Dodge was also commissioned for portraits and murals by such notables as King Faisal I, railroad-car designer George Pullman and art critic Sadakichi Hartmann.

Dodge's style was midway between classical academic and impressionistic modes, as might be expected from his American and European training.

He was born in 1867 in Bedford, Virginia; but he grew up in Munich and Paris where his mother had gone to study painting.

In 1885, Dodge was admitted to the Ecole des Beaux-Arts in Paris, where he studied under Jean Leon Gerome. Students' work was expected to conform to the academic style of the master, but Dodge managed to adapt his style in some ways. In many of his early paintings—*The Conquest of Mexico* (date and location unknown), for instance—he departed from the usual classical mythological pictures fashionable at the time.

One of Dodge's best-known works was done in 1885 when he was only 19 years old: *The Death of Minnehaha,* an 8-by-10-foot painting that, when shipped to New York, earned him a gold medal from the American Art Association.

In 1893, for the Columbian Exposition held in Chicago, Dodge was responsible for decorating the interior of the

Forest with Wild Laurels, 43 x 34 in., signed l.r. Photograph courtesy of Balogh Gallery, Inc., Charlottesville, Virginia.

dome—100 feet in diameter—atop the administration building. This commission helped him decide to be a muralist.

Dodge had settled in New York City by 1900; he had a studio on West Fourteenth Street. He had also married in 1897.

Dodge's style was in transition in 1900, when he painted the beautiful *La Sainte Ivresse.* It is a celebration of young love, a mixture of flowery beaux-arts realism and the free palette and shorter strokes of impressionism.

All of Dodge's work was done from life, including his working drawings. He researched everything for historical accuracy (probably not an onerous task, as archaeology and history were two of his passions). Dodge was also an inventor; the Smithsonian Institution owns one of his model helicopters.

At the same time he was at work on large murals, Dodge executed smaller watercolors and oils: landscapes and family portraits, book illustrations and magazine covers. *The Southern Pine* (date and location unknown), with its aquamarine sky, slender dark green trees and russet shadows, is typical of his paintings.

In 1907 Dodge moved into the "Villa Francesca," in Setauket, Long Island. It was an elaborate building in the classical tradition, with Ionic columns and caryatids, which he had designed.

Dodge died in New York City in 1935.

MEMBERSHIPS
American Watercolor Society
Beaux Arts Society
Fencers Club
Players Club
Society of Mural Painters

PUBLIC COLLECTIONS
Metropolitan Museum of Art, New York City
National Academy of Design, New York City
Smithsonian Institution, Washington, D.C.

SEASON	75-76	76-77	77-78	78-79	79-80	80-81	81-82	82-83	83-84	84-85
Paintings			1	1	1	2	3	1	1	2
Dollars			$1,300	$525	$1,600	$7,500	$12,850	$550	$3,800	$4,000

Record Sale: $7,500, S.W, 6/6/82, "Georgette in Giverny, 1900," 39 × 24 in.

OSCAR FLORIANUS BLUEMNER
(1867-1938)

Oscar Bluemner's training as an architect in Germany, where he was born in 1867, influenced his later work as an early modernist painter.

Bluemner studied at the Academy of Fine Arts in Berlin, and was awarded a royal medal for an architectural painting in 1892. Reportedly, a disagreement on art with Emperor William II led Bluemner to emigrate to America in that same year; he sought commissions at the Columbian Exposition of 1893.

By 1901, Bluemner was living in New York City, where he won a competition for the design of the Bronx Borough Courthouse. Disillusioned with architecture after a disagreement with his partner, he then made painting his major career.

Visiting Europe in 1912, Bluemner was honored by Berlin's Gurlitt Galleries with a one-man show. He became known as "the vermillionaire" because of his liking for bright reds and greens. Often painting houses, barns and buildings, he possessed the touch of a draftsman.

Exposure to cubism could have occurred during his European trip, when his style changed; however, he never became radically cubist. His *Cubistic Village* (1918, Metropolitan Museum of Art) shows the influence of analytical cubism. *Old Canal Port* (1914, Whitney Museum of American Art) expresses his changing style.

In 1913, Bluemner showed five

Blue Above, 51 x 36 in., signed l.r. Photograph courtesy of Hirschl & Adler Galleries, Inc., New York, New York.

brightly-colored landscapes at New York City's Armory Show. By 1915, he was intermittently part of the Stieglitz group of painters, and Stieglitz sponsored his first American one-man show. Bluemner shared an interest, with the Stieglitz painters like Dove, O'Keeffe and Hartley, in emotionally-charged forms of abstraction. He wrote: "Every color has a specific effect on our feelings. . . . A color and shape produces an emotion."

Another important show was the Forum Exhibition of Modern American Painters in March of 1916, where Bluemner was one of 16 artists featured. The Bourgeois Gallery in New York regularly showed his work from 1917 to 1923.

Despondent over his financial situation, compounded by failing eyesight, Bluemner ended his life by suicide in 1938.

PUBLIC COLLECTIONS
Museum of Fine Arts, Boston
Museum of Modern Art, New York City
Phillips Gallery, Washington, D.C.
Whitney Museum of American Art,
  New York City

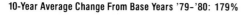

10-Year Average Change From Base Years '79-'80: 179%

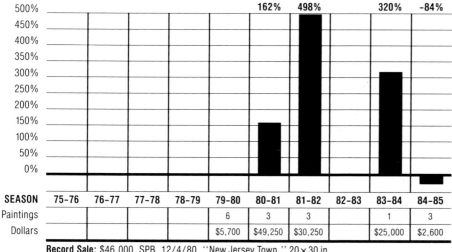

SEASON	75-76	76-77	77-78	78-79	79-80	80-81	81-82	82-83	83-84	84-85
(% change)						162%	498%		320%	-84%
Paintings					6	3	3		1	3
Dollars					$5,700	$49,250	$30,250		$25,000	$2,600

Record Sale: $46,000, SPB, 12/4/80, "New Jersey Town," 20 × 30 in.

628

PAUL
KING
(1867-1947)

Peggy's Cove, Nova Scotia. Courtesy of Vose Galleries of Boston, Inc., Massachusetts.

Versatility, artistic maturity, and mastery of technique and medium are hallmarks of Paul King's art. His diverse works—portraits, landscapes, seascapes, rural scenes and illustrations—established his reputation in the first quarter of the century.

In every canvas, technique and approach are adapted to the subject with great confidence and naturalness. Each of King's paintings reflects the artist's distinctive personality, style and sensitive perceptions, as well as his fine draftsmanship.

From 1906, when his oil *Hauling in the Anchor Line* (date and location unknown) captured the Salmagundi Club's two top prizes, King regularly received prestigious recognition. His merit was freely acknowledged by his artist peers, as well as by critics and the public.

King was born in 1867 to a Buffalo, New York goldsmith. Apprenticed there to the lithography firm of Cosack & Company, he became an accomplished lithographer while still in his teens.

King later studied at the Art Students League of Buffalo and, from 1901 to 1904, at the New York Art Students League with H. Siddons Mowbray. While still a student, he was an illustrator for *Life* and *Harper's* magazines and for American Book Company publications.

For almost two years, in 1905 and 1906, King studied in Holland with Willy Sluiter, Evert Pieters and Bernard Bloomers.

From 1908 to 1921, King was a board member of the Philadelphia School of Design for Women, serving as vice president and acting president from 1915 to 1918. During World War I, he worked in the camouflage unit. King's pictures,

often of everyday outdoor life or common rural scenery, are invested with freshness and insight. His landscapes, especially his winter scenes, became particular favorites. In 1923, *Early Winter* won the National Academy of Design Altman prize. King was named an academician in 1933.

He moved in 1921 from his long-time home in the Germantown section of Philadelphia to Stony Brook, Long Island, where he died in 1947.

MEMBERSHIPS
Allied Artists of America
American Federation of Arts
Artists Aid Society
Artists Fund Society
International Society of Arts and Letters
National Academy of Design
National Arts Club
Pennsylvania Academy of the Fine Arts
Philadelphia Art Club
Salmagundi Club

PUBLIC COLLECTIONS
Albright-Knox Gallery, Buffalo
Butler Art Institute, Youngstown, Ohio
National Gallery of Art, Washington, D.C.
Reading Museum, Pennsylvania

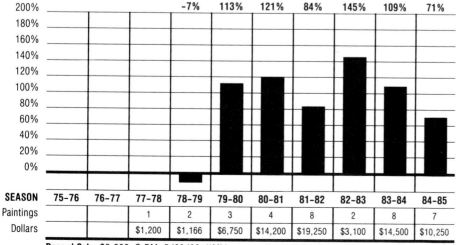

10-Year Average Change From Base Years '77-'78: 80%

			-7%	113%	121%	84%	145%	109%	71%

SEASON	75-76	76-77	77-78	78-79	79-80	80-81	81-82	82-83	83-84	84-85
Paintings			1	2	3	4	8	2	8	7
Dollars			$1,200	$1,166	$6,750	$14,200	$19,250	$3,100	$14,500	$10,250

Record Sale: $6,000, S.BM, 5/20/82, "Midsummer, Keene Valley," 32 × 40 in.

629

JEROME MYERS
(1867-1940)

A painter allied with the New York realists, Jerome Myers depicted slum life on the Lower East Side with a sentimentality that belies the oppressive conditions of the ghetto. His forms are soft, his settings picturesque and his colors muted, with light, jewel-like touches. The subjects—Italian and Jewish immigrants—resemble European peasants rather than the inhabitants of a New York City slum.

Myers began painting lower-class life in 1887, 20 years before the Ashcan School had its impact on American art. He chose to depict market scenes, children at play and people enjoying a summer's concert. His work possesses a light-hearted quality, leading some critics to accuse him of trivializing his subjects.

Born in 1867 in Petersburg, Virginia, Myers moved with his family to Philadelphia and then to Baltimore, where he worked as a sign painter. In New York City, after 1886, he studied at night at the Cooper Union and the Art Students League, earning a living during the day by painting theater sets and working in the art department of the *Herald Tribune*. He traveled to Paris briefly in 1896 and again in 1914. He held his first one-man show in 1908.

Myers became associated with the emergent realists. Despite his urban subject matter, however, he was not considered one of The Eight. Although he depicted the poor with dignity, his can-

Children in Playground, 19½ x 23½ in., signed l.r. Photograph courtesy of Kennedy Galleries, New York, New York.

vases lack the powerful dark colors and psychological insight of the Ashcan painters.

His early work is composed primarily

of drawings, pastels and watercolors. In mid-career, he turned increasingly to oil painting and then to etching. He illustrated numerous articles and he exhibited in the 1913 New York City Armory Show—an idea that was hatched in his studio.

A few years before his death in 1940, Myers published his autobiography, *Artist in Manhattan.*

MEMBERSHIPS
National Academy of Design
New Society of Artists

PUBLIC COLLECTIONS
Art Institute of Chicago
Brooklyn Museum
Delaware Art Museum, Wilmington
Los Angeles County Museum of Art
Metropolitan Museum of Art, New York City
Milwaukee Art Museum, Wisconsin
Memorial Art Gallery of the University of
    Rochester, New York
New Orleans Museum of Art
Phillips Collection, Washington, D.C.

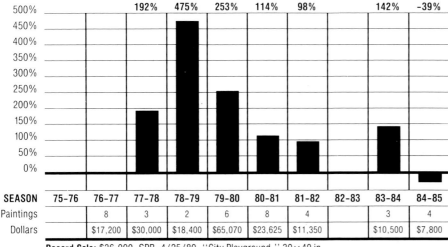

10-Year Average Change From Base Years '76-'77: 154%

	192%	475%	253%	114%	98%		142%	-39%

SEASON	75-76	76-77	77-78	78-79	79-80	80-81	81-82	82-83	83-84	84-85
Paintings		8	3	2	6	8	4		3	4
Dollars		$17,200	$30,000	$18,400	$65,070	$23,625	$11,350		$10,500	$7,800

Record Sale: $36,000, SPB, 4/25/80, "City Playground," 30 x 40 in.

630

HERMANN DUDLEY MURPHY
(1867-1945)

With his subtle, harmonious land-scapes and beautiful floral paintings, Hermann Dudley Murphy was a major figure in the Boston School, the painter who comes closest to its aesthetic ideals. A portraitist turned landscape artist, Murphy was successful early in his career, and his canvases, particularly the later floral still lifes, are still in great demand. His approach combines realism with the quest for ideal beauty, expressed through the harmony of color and design.

Born in 1867 in Marlboro, Massachusetts, Murphy studied at Boston's Museum School under Tarbell and Benson. In 1891, he traveled to Paris, where he became a student of Laurens at the Academie Julien. But the strongest influence on his work came from Whistler; Murphy's early portraits and landscapes show a concern for delicate color tonalities and careful compositions. The compositions are simplified, conveyed through graduated bands of color.

Also like Whistler, Murphy believed that the frame should harmonize with the painting in size and color. He became a leading frame manufacturer in Boston, producing many hand-carved, gold-leaf frames of his own design.

In his early period, Murphy concentrated on portraits and figure studies, but his aesthetic touch and soft colors were not particularly well suited for the

Zinnias and Marigolds, 30 x 20 in., signed l.l. Courtesy of the Museum of Fine Arts, Boston, Massachusetts, Charles Henry Hayden Fund.

boardroom. He turned to sea views and landscapes with large skies and cloud formations. They are marked by beautiful, almost abstract patterns of line and color.

In mid-career, Murphy went to the tropics, finding there a new, sun-drenched environment of sea, sky and flowers. His landscapes from that

period demonstrate greater color range and vibrancy. In the 1920s, he entered his last and most successful period, with floral and still-life canvases. Impressionistic principles can be seen in his work, especially in this late phase.

Murphy worked from his house and studio, "Carrig Rohane," in Winchester, Massachusetts, taught at Harvard University and was an avid canoeist. He died in 1945.

MEMBERSHIPS
Boston Society of Arts and Crafts
Boston Society of Water Color Painters
Boston Water Color Club
Copley Society
Guild of Boston Artists
Massachusetts State Art Commission
National Academy of Design
National Arts Club
New York Water Color Club
Painters and Sculptors Gallery Association
Salmagundi Club

PUBLIC COLLECTIONS
Albright-Knox Art Gallery, Buffalo
Art Institute of Chicago
Cleveland Art Museum
Dallas Museum of Fine Arts
Museum of Fine Arts, Boston
National Academy of Design, New York City
Springville Museum of Art, Utah
St. Louis Art Museum

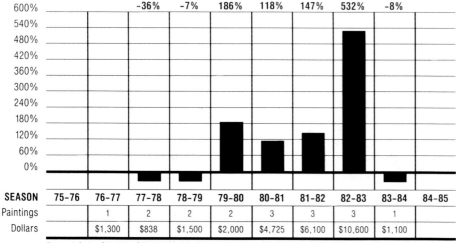

10-Year Average Change From Base Years '76-'77: 117%

		−36%	−7%	186%	118%	147%	532%	−8%	

SEASON	75-76	76-77	77-78	78-79	79-80	80-81	81-82	82-83	83-84	84-85
Paintings		1	2	2	2	3	3	3	1	
Dollars		$1,300	$838	$1,500	$2,000	$4,725	$6,100	$10,600	$1,100	

Record Sale: $7,000, CH, 3/18/83, "Along the Venetian Canal," 20 × 27 in.

WALTER ELMER SCHOFIELD
(1867-1944)

Landscape, 50 x 58 in., signed l.r. Courtesy of Newman Galleries, Philadelphia, Pennsylvania.

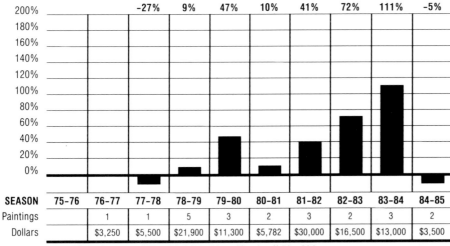

10-Year Average Change From Base Years '76-'77: 29%

		-27%	9%	47%	10%	41%	72%	111%	-5%

SEASON	75-76	76-77	77-78	78-79	79-80	80-81	81-82	82-83	83-84	84-85
Paintings		1	1	5	3	2	3	2	3	2
Dollars		$3,250	$5,500	$21,900	$11,300	$5,782	$30,000	$16,500	$13,000	$3,500

Record Sale: $15,000, SPB, 12/10/81, ''June Morning,'' 50×60 in.

Walter Elmer Schofield painted powerful impressionistic landscapes of the Bucks County, Pennsylvania countryside, as well as turbulent seascapes of the Cornish coast of England. His most popular works, dramatic snow scenes of the hills and woodlands of Bucks County, established Schofield as a prominent member of that region's New Hope School of American impressionism.

Born in Philadelphia in 1867, Schofield attended Swarthmore College. He then enrolled at the Pennsylvania Academy of the Fine Arts, where he studied with Thomas Anshutz from 1889 to 1892.

At the Academy he met Edward Willis Redfield, the acknowledged leader of the New Hope School, and Robert Henri, leader of a group of urban real-

632

ists who later would exhibit with others as "The Eight." Along with Redfield, Schofield began attending meetings at Henri's studio, where he became friendly with other future members of The Eight, including John Sloan, Everett Shinn and William Glackens.

In Paris at the Ecole des Beaux Arts and the Academie Julien from 1892 to 1895, Schofield studied in the ateliers of William Adolphe Bouguereau, Gabriel Ferrier and Henri Lucien Doucet. Like other American artists of that time, Schofield considered Paris training essential to his career, but his work never assumed the elevated subject matter and degree of technical refinement characteristic of Salon painting. Like Redfield, who also studied under Bouguereau, Schofield soon tired of this strict, academic training and retreated to the Forest of Fontainbleau to paint directly from nature.

After 1902, Schofield spent the months of October through April in Philadelphia, and the remainder of the year with his wife in England. Enamored of the rugged English coastline, he traveled throughout the country and lived in Southport, Yorkshire, Bedfors and Otley. Schofield's favorite painting spot was St. Ives, Cornwall, which was an established artists' colony in his time. A considerable portion of his work consists of bold coastal scenes of St. Ives, with the sea battering against massive cliff formations.

Schofield was familiar with New Hope, Bucks County from an early age, as the region is located just north of Philadelphia. Although he did not live in New Hope, and never exhibited at the community center, Phillips Mill, he did exhibit with Redfield, Daniel Garber, and other regional impressionist painters at the Pennsylvania Academy annual shows. While visiting Bucks County, Schofield often stayed with his old Academy colleague, Redfield, at his home in Center Bridge. This friendship, which ended in rivalry in 1904, was essential to the development of Schofield's mature style. He adopted Redfield's technique of completing a large canvas in a single sitting and applying paint in thick, long brushstrokes. Schofield's canvases were enormous,

and it was quite a feat to keep them anchored in stormy weather, part of the challenge Schofield loved in plein-air painting.

Schofield's landscapes were executed with lavish amounts of paint, enthusiastically applied. Detail was suppressed in favor of general atmospheric effect. He often employed a high horizon line which emphasized the active surface brushwork and imparted a bold, decorative quality to the picture plane.

A unique combination of the realist tradition of direct observation of nature with the broken brushwork and vivid hues of impressionism, Schofield's style remains the most dashing of the New Hope School. He died in 1944.

MEMBERSHIPS
Century Association
Chelsea Arts Club
Fellowship of the Pennsylvania Academy of the
   Fine Arts
Institute of Arts and Letters
National Academy of Design
National Arts Club
National Institute Arts League
Philadelphia Art Club
Royal Society of British Artists
Royal Society of Oil Painters
Salmagundi Club
Society of American Artists
St. Ives Arts Club

PUBLIC COLLECTIONS
Albright-Knox Art Gallery, Buffalo, New York
Art Institute of Chicago
Brandywine River Museum, Pennsylvania
Brooklyn Museum
Carnegie Institute, Pittsburgh
Cincinnati Art Museum
Corcoran Gallery of Art, Washington, D.C.
Delaware Art Museum, Wilmington
Fine Arts Museum of San Francisco
Indianapolis Museum of Art
Metropolitan Museum of Art, New York City
National Academy of Design, New York City
National Arts Club, New York City
National Museum of American Art, Washington, D.C.
Pennsylvania Academy of the Fine Arts,
   Philadelphia

JULES EUGENE PAGES
(1867-1946)

Jules Eugene Pages, an impressionist painter, was born in San Francisco in 1867. He first studied art at the San Francisco Art Association's California School of Design. By about 1888, Pages made his first trip to Paris, where he studied at the Academie Julien with Constant, Lefebvre and Robert-Fleury.

Pages financed his study trips to Paris by working in San Francisco as a newspaper illustrator. However, by the mid-1890s, he lived permanently in Paris and only visited California. Pages frequently traveled to Brittany, Spain and Belgium on sketching trips. Other subject matter included Paris street scenes, and the people and vistas of California.

Pages's work incorporates the pure colors and broad brushstrokes of impressionism with drawing, and is characterized by a sensitivity to natural form and effects of light. He believed that impressionism was the renaissance of modern art.

In 1902, he became an instructor at the Academie Julien. Five years later, he became an administrator. He also began to win numerous awards at the Paris Salons, and was named a chevalier in the French Legion of Honor in 1910.

Pages's work was exhibited in both Europe and California. He participated as a member of the International Jury of Award and as an exhibitor at the 1915 Panama-Pacific International Exposition in San Francisco. He was made a member of the Bohemian Club of San

Zinnias in Crock, 16¼ x 13 in., signed l.r. Private Collection Photograph courtesy of WIM Fine Arts, Oakland, California.

Interior of St. Marco, Venice, ca. 1906-1908, 24 x 18¼ in., signed l.r. Courtesy of WIM Fine Arts, Oakland, California.

Francisco, and was honored with a one-man exhibition there in 1924.

Pages left Paris permanently in 1941, in advance of the Nazi occupation. He lived in San Francisco until his death in 1946.

MEMBERSHIPS
International Society of Paris
 Painters and Sculptors

PUBLIC COLLECTIONS
Fine Arts Museum of San Francisco
Luxembourg Museum, Paris
Museum of Pau, France
Museum of Toulouse, France
Oakland Art Museum, California

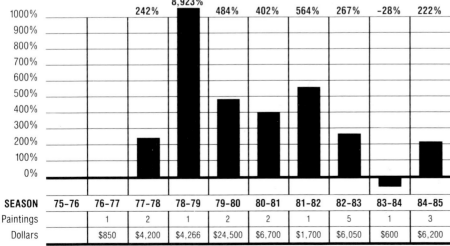

10-Year Average Change From Base Years '76-'77: 1,231%

| | 242% | 8,923% | 484% | 402% | 564% | 267% | -28% | 222% |

SEASON	75-76	76-77	77-78	78-79	79-80	80-81	81-82	82-83	83-84	84-85
Paintings		1	2	1	2	2	1	5	1	3
Dollars		$850	$4,200	$4,266	$24,500	$6,700	$1,700	$6,050	$600	$6,200

Record Sale: $17,000, BB.SF, 6/18/80, ''Washington Alley, Charcuterie Chinoise,'' 40 × 31 in.

REYNOLDS BEAL

(1867-1951)

American impressionist Reynolds Beal had a gift for capturing air movement and seasonal quality in his lively watercolors and crayon drawings.

Born in New York City in 1867, Beal showed early artistic talent, but attended Cornell University and graduated with a degree in naval architecture. Although he retained a lifelong interest in the sea and in yachts, he turned permanently to the fine arts after his 1887 graduation.

With the encouragement of his younger brother, well-known painter Gifford Beal, he studied in Europe, primarily in Madrid. In 1890, he began the formal study of art under William Merritt Chase in Chase's Long Island school.

Beal's work has none of the bravura of technique or dark palette of Chase. Beal's colors are fresh, light and juicy. His fascination with boats and with the sea is evident. Although he was intimately acquainted with yacht construction, his artist's eye was less concerned with the seaworthiness of a vessel than with its evanescent wind-governed relationship to water and air. Another favorite Beal subject was the circus.

A man of independent means, Beal was able to travel through the waterways of the world all his life, painting and drawing to his heart's content until his death in 1951. In spite of this relative ease, Beal was no dilettante Sunday painter; he had his first one-man show in 1905 at the Clauson Gallery in New York

Provincetown Waterfront, 1916, 29 x 36 in., signed l.l. Courtesy of Vose Galleries of Boston, Inc., Massachusetts.

City, and was elected an associate member of the National Academy of Design in 1909. He was involved in founding the Society of Independent Artists and the New Society of Artists.

Beal's traveling companions included, at one time or another, the well-known American impressionist painters Ernest Lawson and Childe Hassam, as well as

H. Dudley Murphy and Henry Ward Ranger. He visited the Caribbean Islands and Central America, the West Coast of America and all of Europe, but much of his work was done in the Northeastern United States. His bright, cheerful palette was well suited to the crisp colors and brisk skies of the Atlantic seashore; but even in his most landlocked landscape, water usually appeared somewhere.

MEMBERSHIPS
American Watercolor Society
Boston Art Club
Century Club
Lotos Club
National Academy of Design
National Arts Club
New Society of Artists
New York Water Color Club
Salmagundi Club
Society of Independent Artists
Worcester Art Museum

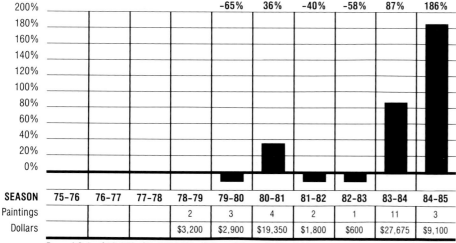

10-Year Average Change From Base Years '78-'79: 21%

| | | -65% | 36% | -40% | -58% | 87% | 186% |

SEASON	75-76	76-77	77-78	78-79	79-80	80-81	81-82	82-83	83-84	84-85
Paintings				2	3	4	2	1	11	3
Dollars				$3,200	$2,900	$19,350	$1,800	$600	$27,675	$9,100

Record Sale: $12,000, CH, 3/23/84, "View of Essex," 18 x 24 in.

635

LOUIS PAUL DESSAR
(1867-1952)

Called the "Millet of America" by contemporaries because of his tonalist, pastoral landscapes with workers and animals, Louis Paul Dessar was known to spend as long as two years perfecting a canvas.

Born in Indianapolis, Indiana in 1867, Dessar graduated from City College in New York City and then from the National Academy of Design in the same city. He journeyed abroad to Paris, where he studied under Bouguereau and Tony Robert-Fleury. Dessar became a competent story-painter and portraitist, and upon his return to New York City in 1892 proceeded to earn his living in that way for nearly 10 years.

Dessar's artistic conversion came as he was painting a portrait of the wife of a prominent art collector, posing in a room full of landscapes by the barbizon painters. Surrounded by those paintings, Dessar decided that in comparison his portraits and genre pieces had only ephemeral value; that landscape, modified by human and animal presence and rendered in the wisest traditions of art, contained the seeds of more lasting excellence. After finishing that portrait, Dessar returned to France to immerse himself in his chosen subject.

Back in the United States once more, he became one of a number of artists who were called tonalists, including Kost, Minor and Bogert.

The Wood Chopper, 1906, signed l.l. Florence Griswold Museum, Lyme Historical Society, Old Lyme, Connecticut.

Dessar spent his winters in New York and summered in Becket Hill near Old Lyme, Connecticut, part of the artists' colony that, while under leader Henry Ranger, concentrated on painting directly from nature in the barbizon ton-alist mood (soon eclipsed by artists of impressionist persuasion). His canvases embody the values he sought to convey; they combine a lucid peacefulness with an impersonal perspective, and his interminable search for perfection of light and color produced a diffused brightness that seems to come from beyond the picture plane.

Dessar worked slowly and exhibited rarely; he taught at the National Academy of Design in 1946, not long before his death in 1952, but most of his time was spent in his studio working on his paintings.

MEMBERSHIPS
Artists Fund Society
Lotos Club
Lyme Art Association
National Academy of Design
Salmagundi Club
Society of American Artists

PUBLIC COLLECTIONS
City Art Museum, St. Louis
Lyons Art Museum, France
Metropolitan Museum of Art, New York City
Montclair Art Museum, New Jersey
National Gallery of Art, Washington, D.C.
Omaha Museum, Nebraska

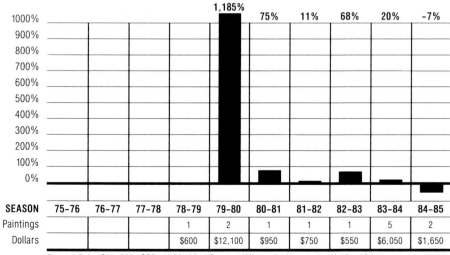

10-Year Average Change From Base Years '78-'79: 193%

					1,185%	75%	11%	68%	20%	-7%
1000%										
900%										
800%										
700%										
600%										
500%										
400%										
300%										
200%										
100%										
0%										
SEASON	75-76	76-77	77-78	78-79	79-80	80-81	81-82	82-83	83-84	84-85
Paintings				1	2	1	1	1	5	2
Dollars				$600	$12,100	$950	$750	$550	$6,050	$1,650

Record Sale: $11,500, SPB, 1/30/80, "Peasant Woman by Haystacks," 18 × 13 in.

636

ALFRED H. MAURER
(1868-1932)

Alfred H. Maurer is known as one of the very first American modernist painters. A transitional figure in American art, Maurer was already producing mature paintings in a Whistlerian mode at the time of his conversion, first to fauvism, then to cubism.

Alfred Maurer was born in New York City, the son of successful lithographer and genre painter Louis Maurer. After studying for several years at the National Academy of Design, Maurer traveled to France, where he worked for most of the next 14 years.

In France, he studied briefly at the Academie Julien. By 1901, he was winning medals at major exhibitions in Europe and the United States for his Whistlerian studies of women, decoratively posed, and following Japanese motifs.

Around 1905, Maurer became acquainted with Leo and Gertrude Stein and their circle of friends in Paris, and soon thereafter began painting in a brightly-colored fauvist manner inspired by the work of Paul Cezanne. Maurer's paintings of this period were exhibited in New York City at Alfred Stieglitz's Photo-Secession Gallery in 1909 and at the New York City Armory Show in 1913.

Maurer returned to New York City permanently in 1914. By the end of World War I he was painting still lifes and figure studies in a cubist manner, employing flattened planes and distorted shapes. His studies of twinned and inter-

A French Cafe, 1901, 24 x 20 in., signed l.l. Courtesy of Wunderlich and Company, Inc., New York, New York.

penetrating heads have been said to reflect his unhappy relationship with his father. Maurer committed suicide in 1932 at his home in New York City.

MEMBERSHIPS
Paris Society of American Painters

PUBLIC COLLECTIONS
Barnes Collection, Merion, Pennsylvania
Museum of Modern Art, New York City
Phillips Collection, Washington, D.C.

10-Year Average Change From Base Years '75-'76: 77%

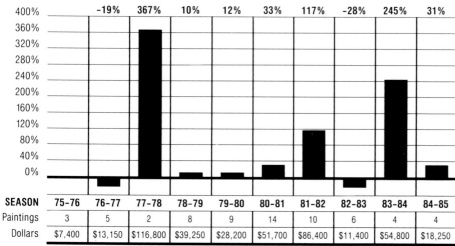

	-19%	367%	10%	12%	33%	117%	-28%	245%	31%

SEASON	75-76	76-77	77-78	78-79	79-80	80-81	81-82	82-83	83-84	84-85
Paintings	3	5	2	8	9	14	10	6	4	4
Dollars	$7,400	$13,150	$116,800	$39,250	$28,200	$51,700	$86,400	$11,400	$54,800	$18,250

Record Sale: $115,000, PB, 3/22/78, "Jeanne," 74 x 37 in.

GEORGE OVERBURY ("POP") HART
(1868-1933)

Mexican Port, 9½ x 13 in., signed l.l. Courtesy of Marbella Gallery, Inc., New York, New York, Photograph by Richard Haynes.

George Overbury Hart, known simply as "Pop," was a largely self-taught painter and etcher who wandered the world, recording scenes of everyday life with a deft hand.

He preferred watercolors to oils and, when he was past 50, turned to prints, lithographs and etchings. His drypoint prints, in particular, were admired because of his handling of dark-light contrasts.

Hart was born in Cairo, Illinois in 1868. Two brothers, both much older, were artists; this probably kindled a desire in him to be one. He struck out on his own at an early age, supporting himself as best as he could. His only formal training was a brief stint at the Chicago Art Institute and another at the Academie Julien in Paris.

From 1907 to 1912, Hart painted signs for amusement parks around New York City and then, until 1920, painted stage sets for the motion picture studios in Fort Lee, New Jersey. Between jobs, however, he managed to travel to Europe, Egypt, the South Seas, Mexico and South America, sketching and painting wherever he happened to be.

Hart was the classic wandering bohemian. Much of his work was undisciplined—genre scenes of the every-day folk he encountered on his travels. Some of it was racy, some poignant, but he knew how to capture the revealing gesture and the flavor of a locale to make his work interesting.

It was not until the 1920s that his work began to be regarded seriously. His reputation continued to grow until his death in New York City in 1933.

MEMBERSHIPS
American Watercolor Society
Brooklyn Society of Etchers
New York Water Color Society
Society of Independent Artists

PUBLIC COLLECTIONS
Art Institute of Chicago
British Museum, London
Brooklyn Museum
Cincinnati Art Museum
Los Angeles County Museum of Art
Metropolitan Museum of Art, New York City
National Museum of American Art, Washington, D.C.
Newark Museum, New Jersey
New York Public Library, New York City

SEASON	75-76	76-77	77-78	78-79	79-80	80-81	81-82	82-83	83-84	84-85
Paintings					3	1	1	2	2	1
Dollars					$1,950	$1,300	$2,400	$1,800	$1,200	$600

Record Sale: $2,400, SPB, 12/10/81, "Summer Weekend," 14 x 22 in.

WILLIAM HENRY SINGER, JR.
(1868-1943)

Although he was considered an American impressionist, William H. Singer, Jr. spent nearly all of his life as a painter in Europe, especially in Norway. Most of his work was devoted to capturing on canvas the solitude and majestic grandeur of the Norwegian mountains and fjords. His landscapes were notable on two counts: first for the vitality of the brushwork and vibrancy of color; and second, for the absence of any figures in them. It was nature that interested Singer, not man.

He was born to a prosperous steelmaking family in Pittsburgh, Pennsylvania in 1868. He showed an early interest in art, but his father insisted that he enter the family business, where he stayed for 11 years.

In his free time, however, he sketched and painted in the countryside and studied with Martin Borgord, a Norwegian painter then living in Pittsburgh who later was to introduce Singer to Norway. When two of his paintings were accepted for the Carnegie International Exhibition in 1900, Singer was sufficiently encouraged to leave his job and go to Monhegan Island, off the coast of Maine, to paint.

The following autumn Singer, his wife and Borgord sailed for Paris. He enrolled at the Academie Julien, but disliked the emphasis on figure painting and left after a few months. He also studied with Jean-Paul Laurens, but left for the same reason.

Village of Olden, Norway, 1919, 18¼ x 22 in., signed l.r. Florence Griswold Museum, Lyme Historical Society, Gift of Joseph and Renate Szymanski.

The Singers and Borgord went to Laren, a small artists' community in Holland, called the "Dutch Barbizon" of its day. There, he was able to concentrate on developing his technique as a landscape painter. After a few years, however, he wearied of the flatness of the Dutch countryside, and he longed for something different.

It was Borgord who suggested a trip to Norway, and this proved to be the turning point in Singer's career. He was overwhelmed by the vastness of the mountains and the stillness of the valleys

and fjords. Here were all the elements of solidity, majesty and timelessness that he had been searching for.

At first the Singers spent springs and summers in Norway, and returned to Holland for the winters. Later, after building a mansion near Olden, a fishing village on the West coast, they lived there all year.

Singer inherited a considerable fortune, and he and his wife were known for their generosity to the Norwegians. During World War II, when the Germans occupied Norway, the Olden villagers cared for them and prevented Germans from imprisoning them. In 1943, however, Singer suffered a heart attack at his home there and died before a doctor could reach him.

MEMBERSHIPS
Allied Artists of America
American Art Association
National Academy of Design
Pittsburgh Art Society
St. Lucas Art Association

PUBLIC COLLECTIONS
Art Institute of Chicago
Brooklyn Museum
Delgado Museum, New Orleans
Gemeente Museum, The Hague
Metropolitan Museum of Art, New York City
Musee du Luxembourg, Paris
Pennsylvania Academy of the Fine Arts, Philadelphia
Royal Museum, Antwerp, Belgium
Stedelijk Museum, Amsterdam

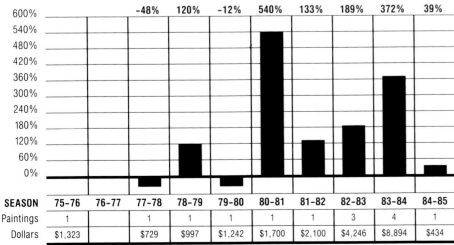

10-Year Average Change From Base Years '75-'76: 148%

			-48%	120%	-12%	540%	133%	189%	372%	39%

SEASON	75-76	76-77	77-78	78-79	79-80	80-81	81-82	82-83	83-84	84-85
Paintings	1		1	1	1	1	1	3	4	1
Dollars	$1,323		$729	$997	$1,242	$1,700	$2,100	$4,246	$8,894	$434

Record Sale: $6,500, BB.SF, 2/16/84, "End of the Fjord," 18 × 22 in.

639

CHAUNCEY FOSTER RYDER
(1868-1949)

Mt. Lafayette, 45 x 60 in. Courtesy of Vose Galleries of Boston, Inc., Massachusetts.

Chauncey Foster Ryder was a prolific and active artist, skilled as an etcher and lithographer and very respected as a landscape painter. His early desire to become a portraitist, which gave way to specializing in landscape compositions, gave an added dimension to his work.

Born in Danbury, Connecticut in 1868, Ryder decided to become an artist before he entered his teens. To fulfill that goal, he later took night courses at the Art Institute of Chicago while working by day as an accountant to support himself. In 1892, he married Mary Keith Dole in Chicago, and soon started working as an illustrator.

Wanting to learn more of portrait painting, he attended the Academie Julien in Paris in the early 1900s, training with Raphael Collin and Jean Paul Laurens as well. However, Ryder's interest in landscapes steadily grew as he traveled in France, Italy and Holland. He won a Paris Salon award in 1907, and returned to the United States in 1908, establishing his studio in New York City.

His favorite place, however, was his summer home in Wilton, New Hampshire, where he could spend all of his time painting much of the relatively untouched New England countryside. Ryder, a modest man, found solace in depicting the idyllic aspects of nature.

He applied paint to canvas thickly, with sweeping strokes of color, frequently using a palette knife to shape the subject matter. Ryder's work was always a spaciously solid depiction of nature's lasting attributes. That same spaciousness and concern also applied to his prints, notwithstanding the confining boundaries of the copper plates.

Ryder died in Wilton, New Hampshire in 1949, leaving numerous examples of his work in Europe and the United States.

MEMBERSHIPS
Allied Artists of America
American Federation of Arts
American Water Color Society
Brooklyn Society of Artists
Chicago Society of Etchers
Lotos Club
National Academy of Design
National Arts Club
New York Water Color Club
Salmagundi Club

PUBLIC COLLECTIONS
Art Institute of Chicago
Brooklyn Museum
Corcoran Gallery, Washington, D.C.
Dayton Museum of Arts, Ohio
Metropolitan Museum of Art, New York City
National Gallery, Washington, D.C.
St. Louis Art Museum

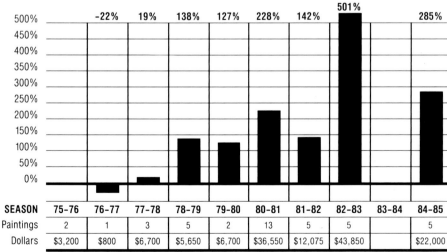

10-Year Average Change From Base Years '75-'76: 158%

	-22%	19%	138%	127%	228%	142%	501%		285%

SEASON	75-76	76-77	77-78	78-79	79-80	80-81	81-82	82-83	83-84	84-85
Paintings	2	1	3	5	2	13	5	5		5
Dollars	$3,200	$800	$6,700	$5,650	$6,700	$36,550	$12,075	$43,850		$22,000

Record Sale: $32,000, CH, 6/3/83, "Road to Raymond," 28 x 36 in.

640

HARRY ROSELAND
(1868-1950)

Genre painting enjoyed tremendous popularity in nineteenth-century America. It was a style that allowed a painter to tell a story, evoke an emotion, tell a joke, or educate. Largely superseded in the twentieth century by changes in popular taste and improvements in photographic technology, genre painting nevertheless remains a strong subcurrent in popular taste. One of the most notable painters in this mode was Harry Roseland.

Roseland, born in Brooklyn, New York in 1868, matured as an artist while waves of change were sweeping over the art world. Largely self-taught, he chose to paint what he saw.

He received some education in art under J.B. Whittaker in Brooklyn, and at first painted some landscapes and still lifes, but his natural flair was for telling a story in his paintings.

His subject matter was at first highly sentimental and heavily influenced by fashionable taste: smartly turned-out young women, old folks, and idealized farm scenes. He abandoned the mawkishness that is the downfall of so many self-educated artists when he found a topic that was close to home and yet largely unnoticed: the post-Civil War blacks who formed the underpinnings of Northeastern society.

Roseland's clever, skillful scenes of homely activities—such as checker-playing or letter-reading—were remarkably dispassionate and candid for the

A Bright Future, 1906, 14 x 20 in., signed u.l. Courtesy of Henry B. Holt, Inc., Essex Fells, New Jersey.

time, though to modern eyes they seem condescending and dated. The capture with gentle humor of a way of life that existed through the first half of the twentieth century and has now vanished.

Roseland never left his native Brooklyn, dying in New York in 1950, but he enjoyed a remarkable success as an artist in his chosen specialty, improving and maturing continually. The archetype of the independent American artist, he never even traveled to Europe to study or observe, choosing to carve his own path.

MEMBERSHIPS
Brooklyn Arts Club
Brooklyn Society of Artists
Brooklyn Painters Society
Salmagundi Club

PUBLIC COLLECTIONS
Brooklyn Institute of Arts and Sciences
Brooklyn Museum
Charleston Art Museum
Heckscher Museum, Long Island, New York

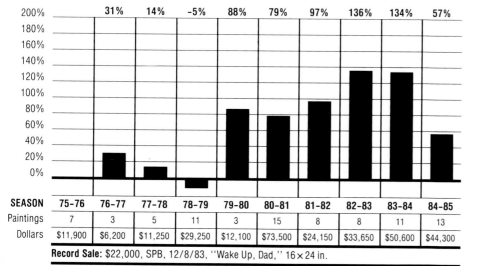

10-Year Average Change From Base Years '75-'76: 63%

	31%	14%	-5%	88%	79%	97%	136%	134%	57%
SEASON	75-76	76-77	77-78	78-79	79-80	80-81	81-82	82-83	83-84	84-85
Paintings	7	3	5	11	3	15	8	8	11	13
Dollars	$11,900	$6,200	$11,250	$29,250	$12,100	$73,500	$24,150	$33,650	$50,600	$44,300

Record Sale: $22,000, SPB, 12/8/83, ''Wake Up, Dad,'' 16 × 24 in.

BERT GREER PHILLIPS
(1868-1956)

Although he was not the first artist to visit Taos, New Mexico, Bert Greer Phillips was the first to settle there permanently.

Some fellow members of the famed Taos Society of Artists became modernists. But Phillips portrayed his beloved pueblo people and landscapes in an idealized, traditional style. He was successful, and a mainstay of the society, but he did not attain the level of celebrity and affluence of other Taos artists.

Born in Hudson, New York in 1868, Phillips won art prizes as a child. In 1884, at age 16, Phillips began five years' study at the Art Students League and the National Academy of Design in New York City.

An established artist by 1889, he was a successful Western illustrator before he had set foot in the West.

In 1894, Phillips traveled abroad, painted some appealing watercolor English landscapes, and arrived in Paris in 1895 to study at the Academie Julien. There he met American artists Joseph Sharp, who had visited Taos, and Ernest Blumenschein.

Back in New York City, Phillips and Blumenschein shared a studio. In the summer of 1898, they headed West. Stranded on the way to Mexico by a broken wagon wheel, they stayed in Taos to paint. In the fall, Blumenschein returned to New York, but Phillips remained in Taos.

Indian Portrait, 16 x 12 in., signed l.l. Photograph courtesy of The Gerald Peters Gallery, Santa Fe, New Mexico.

Phillips painted his Indian subjects in their own pueblos. He was one of the few non-Indians invited to share their pastimes, and accumulated a museum-quality collection of Indian art and artifacts. He also championed Indian causes, and worked successfully to restore Indian rights to traditional lands near Taos.

Other artists came to live in Taos. In 1912, Phillips was among the six founders of the Taos Society. Others were Blumenschein, Sharp, Oscar Berninghaus, Herbert Dunton and Irving Couse.

Phillips's romance with "pure-aired" Taos never flagged, and his paintings reflect it. They have a visionary, dreamy quality, possessing lyrical charm.

Phillips died in 1956, in San Diego, California.

MEMBERSHIPS
Chicago Gallery
Salmagundi Club
Society of Western Artists
Taos Society of Artists

PUBLIC COLLECTIONS
Museum of New Mexico, Santa Fe
Polk County Courthouse, Des Moines, Iowa
San Marcos Hotel, Chandler, Arizona
State Capitol, Jefferson City, Montana

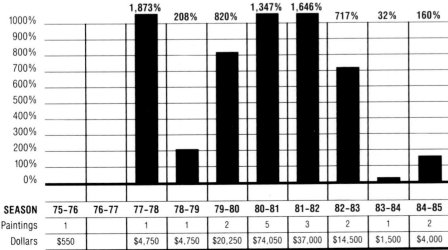

10-Year Average Change From Base Years '75-'76: 756%

| | 1,873% | 208% | 820% | 1,347% | 1,646% | 717% | 32% | 160% |

SEASON	75-76	76-77	77-78	78-79	79-80	80-81	81-82	82-83	83-84	84-85
Paintings	1		1	1	2	5	3	2	1	2
Dollars	$550		$4,750	$4,750	$20,250	$74,050	$37,000	$14,500	$1,500	$4,000

Record Sale: $47,000, SPB, 6/23/81, "By the Campfire," 30×20 in.

642

Spectators at Winter Ceremonial, Taos Pueblo, 24⅞ x 46¾ in., signed l.l. Courtesy of Stark Museum of Art, Orange, Texas.

Scene Near Arroyo Seco, Taos, N.M., 12 x 16 in., signed l.r. Photograph courtesy of The Gerald Peters Gallery, Santa Fe, New Mexico.

LAWTON S. PARKER
(1868-1954)

A portrait and landscape painter, Lawton S. Parker was a member of the Giverny Group, six relatively young American painters who, after study in Paris, fell under the spell of Claude Monet and lived and worked for a time near his studio-home in Giverny, France. A solid, academic painter to begin with, Parker adopted what some called a new kind of impressionism. Despite Monet's influence, he did not see nature the same way as did the major French impressionists, nor did he use broken colors to convey a sense of light as they did. His was a more conventional approach, with his colors matched as closely as possible to those of nature.

Parker was born in Fairfield, Michigan in 1868. He started his long training at the Art Institute of Chicago, then went to Paris in 1889 to study at the Academie Julien with Bouguereau and Tony-Fleury. Back in New York City, he enrolled at the Art Students League and studied with Mowbray and William Merritt Chase. Then it was back to Paris for training in mural painting with Besnard and finally, in 1897, a stint at the Ecole des Beaux Arts under Gerome. He also studied for a time with Whistler.

His life was not all uninterrupted study, however. To support himself Parker also taught at the St. Louis School of Fine Arts, at Beloit College in Wisconsin and at the New York School of Art. And in 1900 he opened his own academy of painting in Paris.

In 1902, Parker arrived in Giverny to join the succession of American artists who had lived there since 1887. Guy Rose, Frederick Frieseke and Richard Miller were there at the time. The four became close friends, criticized each other's work and eventually exhibited together in New York as impressionists,

although some critics at the time referred to them as luminists.

Determined to become an even better portrait painter than he already was, Parker's purpose in coming to Giverny was to get his models out of the studio and into the sunlight. While he painted colors as he saw them, his work showed how varied color can be when viewed at different angles or in different positions in relation to the sun. His flesh tones, so conventional when seen in the subdued light of his studio, became refreshingly alive when seen in this new environment.

In 1913, Parker was the first American to be awarded the coveted Gold Medal at the Paris Salon. He died in Pasadena in 1954.

MEMBERSHIPS
Allied Artists of America
Chicago Society of Artists
National Academy of Design
National Arts Club

PUBLIC COLLECTIONS
Art Institute of Chicago
Los Angeles County Museum of Art
National Collection, France

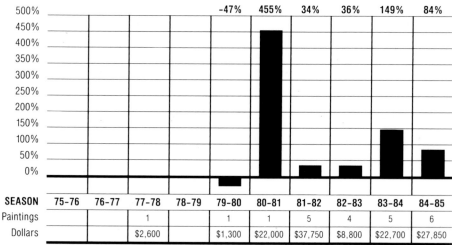

10-Year Average Change From Base Years '77-'78: 102%

| | | | -47% | 455% | 34% | 36% | 149% | 84% |

SEASON	75-76	76-77	77-78	78-79	79-80	80-81	81-82	82-83	83-84	84-85
Paintings			1		1	1	5	4	5	6
Dollars			$2,600		$1,300	$22,000	$37,750	$8,800	$22,700	$27,850

Record Sale: $23,000, S.W, 2/3/85, "Alfresco Tea," 41 × 37 in.

644

LEON DABO
(1868-1960)

An eminent academician is said to have remarked at an exhibition of Leon Dabo's paintings, "Surely these glorious things have never been rejected by an intelligent jury." In fact, the works had been consistently spurned by juries of which the speaker had been a member. Leon Dabo—painter of landscapes and murals, illustrator, lithographer, lecturer—was recognized and honored abroad before he was appreciated in his own country.

Born in Grosse Pointe, Michigan in 1868, of French parents, Dabo was introduced to art by his father, who had been a professor of aesthetics in France and who owned a substantial art collection.

In 1884, Dabo studied with John La Farge in New York City. In 1885, he went to Paris, studying architecture and decoration at the Ecole des Arts Decoratifs, working under Puvis de Chavanne, Daniel Vierge and Pierre Galland, and attending the Ecole des Beaux-Arts and the Academie Julien.

Dabo studied under Galliardi in Rome in 1887, and also copied the masters in Florence and Venice. In 1888, he went to London, where he often visited Whistler's studio. Returning to the United States in 1890, he was assistant to La Farge, learning stained-glass techniques. He painted in the mornings and evenings.

In the work of Whistler, of Redon and the French impressionists, and of the

Evening on the Hudson, 1909, 27⅛ x 36⅛ in., signed l.l. Courtesy of National Museum of American Art, Smithsonian Institution, Gift of William T. Evans.

great Japanese masters, the young artist discovered intellectual and emotional stimuli that fused to become uniquely Dabo. And the time spent painting every morning and evening improved his technique. Over the years, his painting evolved from tight, rather ordinary work, to impressionistic studies of light and atmosphere, to the relationships of color, line and arrangement that are Dabo's own.

Called "the poet in color" by Bliss Carman, Dabo saw nature with the poet's eye. His landscapes convey the broad and powerful in nature, as well as the sensitive and intimate. His color effects are luminous and transparent.

There are no violent contrasts, only nuances of light and color, harmonious tones that blend. Hardly a brushstroke shows.

Dabo described his landscapes as pretexts for beautiful color arrangement; their purpose was to evoke feelings. His depictions of nature have a sense of mystery suggestive of great spiritual power.

Dabo's career spanned 76 years. He died in New York City in 1960 at age 92.

MEMBERSHIPS
Allied Artists Association Limited of London
Brooklyn Society of Artists
Hopkin Club of Detroit
Les Amis des Arts
Les Mireilles
National Academy of Design
National Arts Club
National Society of Mural Painters
Royal Society of Arts and Sciences
School Art League of New York
Society des Amis du Louvre
Society of Pastellists
Three Arts Club

PUBLIC COLLECTIONS
Art Institute of Chicago
Baltimore Art Association
Brooklyn Museum
Delgado Museum, New Orleans
Detroit Institute of Arts
Imperial Museum of Art, Tokyo
Metropolitan Museum of Art, New York City
Minneapolis Art Museum
Montclair Art Museum, New Jersey
National Arts Club, New York City
National Gallery, Ottawa, Canada
National Gallery, Washington, D.C.
Newark Museum, New Jersey
Reading Art Gallery, Pennsylvania
Toledo Museum of Art, Ohio

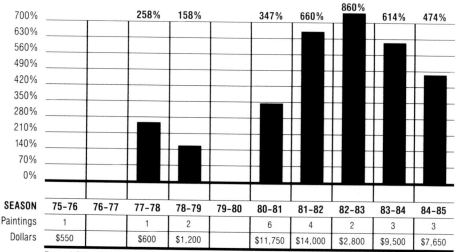

10-Year Average Change From Base Years '75-'76: 421%

SEASON	75–76	76–77	77–78	78–79	79–80	80–81	81–82	82–83	83–84	84–85
			258%	158%		347%	660%	860%	614%	474%
Paintings	1		1	2		6	4	2	3	3
Dollars	$550		$600	$1,200		$11,750	$14,000	$2,800	$9,500	$7,650

Record Sale: $7,000, CH, 6/1/84, "Long Island Sound," 30 × 34 in.

PERCY GRAY
(1869-1952)

Percy Gray was a California landscape painter who, in his mature years, specialized in watercolor and became known for his distinctive perspectives, as well as for a unique technique he developed for building up paint to capture the essence of the scene he was painting. He worked in other media as well—pencil, oils, etching and lithography—but it was watercolor that he liked best.

Gray was born in San Francisco in 1869. He attended the California School of Design, worked as a stockbroker's clerk for a time and then became a newspaper sketch artist. After moving to New York in 1895, he joined the staff of the *Journal* as a sketch artist, and soon became head of the whole art department.

After hours, he studied at the Art Students League under William Merritt Chase, whose ideas on landscape painting influenced Gray for the rest of his life. Following the earthquake and fire in San Francisco in 1906, Gray returned home to work for the *Examiner,* again as a sketch artist. After four years he was able to give it up and concentrate on his painting.

Most of his scenes were of the countryside immediately surrounding San Francisco. Very occasionally he would travel to the deserts of Arizona and the mountains of Oregon and Washington. At one time he also did 20 portraits of

Bridge in Landscape, 1929, 15 x 21½ in., signed l.l. Courtesy of Maxwell Galleries, Ltd., San Francisco, California.

American Indians, but for the most part he eschewed portrait work; he did not like it.

Gray loved to roam the hills and meadows of the San Francisco Bay area, sketching the essential elements of a scene on the spot. Back in his studio, he would lightly pencil in the outline of his composition, then set to work with his watercolors.

In the last few years before his death in 1952, Gray lost much of his flair for color-filled landscapes, however, and his work took on a more somber, contemplative quality.

MEMBERSHIPS
Bohemian Club
San Francisco Art Association
Society of Western Artists

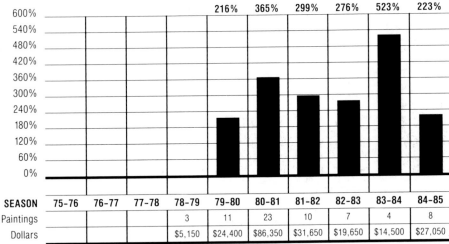

10-Year Average Change From Base Years '78-'79: 272%

SEASON	75-76	76-77	77-78	78-79	79-80	80-81	81-82	82-83	83-84	84-85
					216%	365%	299%	276%	523%	223%
Paintings				3	11	23	10	7	4	8
Dollars				$5,150	$24,400	$86,350	$31,650	$19,650	$14,500	$27,050

Record Sale: $9,500, BB.SF, 6/24/81, ''Oak Grove in Blue Mist,'' 22 × 30 in.

WILSON H. IRVINE
(1869-1936)

Wilson Henry Irvine, known primarily for his landscapes, was a prolific master of a variety of subjects and media. Never one to be content with the traditional, he is known for his experimentation during the 1920s and 1930s.

Born in Byron, Illinois in 1869, Irvine took up journalism after high school. It wasn't until he moved to Chicago that he developed an interest in art. He acquired a job as manager of the art department of the Chicago Portrait Company and attended classes at the Art Institute of Chicago at night. During this time, he specialized in recording on canvas the rural Illinois where he grew up.

In 1917, Irvine and his wife spent more than a year traveling around Britain and France. There he expanded his repertoire, painting the quaint fishing villages that dotted the British and French coasts.

Irvine returned to the United States and settled in Old Lyme, Connecticut. He became associated with Guy Wiggins and Everett Warner as part of the Old Lyme Art Colony. In these years, he pursued pure landscape painting.

Irvine was always on the cutting edge of the art world until his death in 1936. In 1927, he successfully mastered the technique of etching in aquatint. Three years later, Irvine began producing what he termed prismatic painting—landscapes and still lifes as seen through a glass prism. This accentuated the

Spring Landscape, Old Lyme, 24¼ x 30 in., signed l.l. Courtesy of Henry B. Holt, Inc., Essex Fells, New Jersey.

effect of light on the edges of any object viewed.

The style was slow to find acceptance, but Irvine kept with it. In 1934, he won the best-picture award in the annual exhibition of the Lyme Art Association with *Indolence* (date and location unknown), a prismatic rendering of a nearly life-size nude.

MEMBERSHIPS
Allied Artists of America
Chicago Society of Artists
Chicago Water Color Club
Cliff Dwellers
Lyme Art Association
National Academy of Design
Palette and Chisel Club
Salmagundi Club
Society of Western Artists

PUBLIC COLLECTIONS
Art Institute of Chicago
Corcoran Gallery of Art, Washington, D.C.
Sears Memorial Museum, Elgin, Illinois
Union League Club, Chicago

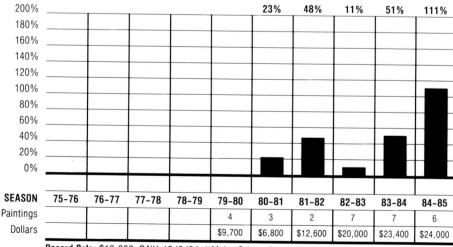

10-Year Average Change From Base Years '79-'80: 41%

| | 23% | 48% | 11% | 51% | 111% |

SEASON	75-76	76-77	77-78	78-79	79-80	80-81	81-82	82-83	83-84	84-85
Paintings					4	3	2	7	7	6
Dollars					$9,700	$6,800	$12,600	$20,000	$23,400	$24,000

Record Sale: $13,000, P.NY, 10/3/84, "Maine Street, Essex," 24 x 27 in.

647

MARIE DANFORTH PAGE
(1869-1940)

Marie Danforth Page was a noted portraitist who resided in Boston all her life. Daughter of a prominent Boston businessman and wife of a physician, she was trained in the conservative Boston tradition of painting, but she carved a distinct niche for herself with her sensitive portraits of children and her perceptive treatment of the mother-and-child theme.

Danforth's art training began in 1886 when she took drawing lessons from Helen Knowlton, a pupil of Boston's leading artist, William Morris Hunt. From 1890 to 1896, Danforth studied at the School of the Museum of the Fine Arts in Boston, under Frank Benson and Edmund Tarbell.

Tarbell's influence is evident in her modified impressionist color palette and in the broad, soft brushstrokes of her early works. However, unlike Tarbell, she seldom painted women quietly engaged in some domestic activity. Instead, she concentrated on portraits and, in time, developed the theme of mother and child.

Danforth lived in an age when the only career deemed proper for a married woman (especially an upper-class woman) was that of homemaker. Nevertheless, even after her 1896 marriage to Dr. Page, her career as a portraitist grew ever more successful.

Her paintings were characterized by simplified settings, shallow space and few accessories. She specialized in children and young girls, but from 1914 on, Page returned again and again to the mother-and-child theme. Her best-known painting on this subject, *The Tenement Mother* (ca. 1914, George Walter Vincent Smith Art Museum, Springfield, Massachusetts), was critically acclaimed and established her position.

After 1917, Page's work underwent significant changes. Her colors became brighter, with lighter flesh tones and

The Gay Gown, 45 x 35 in., signed u.r. Courtesy of Vose Galleries of Boston, Inc., Massachusetts.

patchy brushwork. This was due in part to her exposure to European modernism. Still, she maintained the solid, straightforward approach to painting admired by her following.

Page died in 1940.

MEMBERSHIPS
Boston Guild of Artists
Copley Society
National Academy of Design

PUBLIC COLLECTIONS
Erie Museum of Art, Pennsylvania
George Walter Vincent Smith Museum, Springfield, Massachusetts
Harvard University, Cambridge, Massachusetts
Montclair Art Museum, New Jersey
Santa Barbara Museum of Art, California

SEASON	75-76	76-77	77-78	78-79	79-80	80-81	81-82	82-83	83-84	84-85
Paintings							1	1	1	
Dollars							$11,000	$3,500	$4,000	

Record Sale: $11,000, S.BM, 5/20/82, "The Gay Gown," 45 × 33 in.

WILLIAM McGREGOR PAXTON
(1869-1941)

Prominent Boston painter William McGregor Paxton is known for his portraits, murals and genre paintings, although he experimented widely in other media, including etching and lithography.

Born in 1869 in Baltimore, Paxton grew up in Newton, Massachusetts. He studied art at the Cowles School in Boston under Dennis Miller Bunker and then at the Ecole des Beaux-Arts in Paris with Jean-Leon Gerome.

Returning to Boston, Paxton supplemented his income by designing newspaper ads while studying with Edmund Tarbell, Frank Benson and Joseph DeCamp; he then joined them on the faculty at the school of the Museum of Fine Arts of Boston.

Paxton, well known for his portraits, was dubbed the "court painter of Philadelphia" for those he painted during the brief period he lived there. Among his prominent works are portraits of Presidents Grover Cleveland and Calvin Coolidge. Also notable are murals he executed for the Army and Navy Club of New York City and for the St. Botolph Club of Boston.

However, it is his paintings of attractive young women of the leisure class, presented in an artful and idealized fashion, for which he is best remembered. These paintings recall the works of Jan Vermeer in their extraordinary

The String of Pearls, 1908, signed u.r. Courtesy of Vose Galleries of Boston, Inc., Massachusetts.

attention to details of flesh and textiles and the effects of reflected light, and are characterized by highly finished surfaces in the beaux-arts manner. While these paintings focused on the content of daily life, the emphasis on the details of material surroundings was criticized as imitating the superficiality of society pictures by European painters, which were fashionable at the time.

However, this emphasis on detail resulted from Paxton's theory of "bin-ocular vision," a way of seeing about which he commented: ". . . a man looking out through two eyes sees things with a certain single focus, and outside that focus, all vertical lines and vertically inclined spots double." This led him to paint objects outside his focus by slightly blurring them.

Always academically oriented, Paxton became a full member of the National Academy of Design in 1928. He died in Boston in 1941.

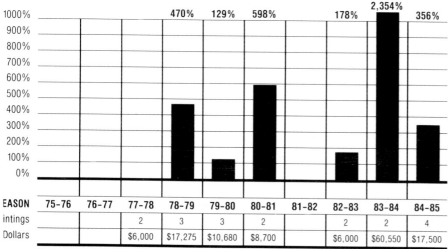

10-Year Average Change From Base Years '77-'78: 584%

	75-76	76-77	77-78	78-79	79-80	80-81	81-82	82-83	83-84	84-85
% change				470%	129%	598%		178%	2,354%	356%
EASON	75-76	76-77	77-78	78-79	79-80	80-81	81-82	82-83	83-84	84-85
intings			2	3	3	2		2	2	4
Dollars			$6,000	$17,275	$10,680	$8,700		$6,000	$60,550	$17,500

Record Sale: $60,000, SPB, 12/8/83, "Reverie," 36 × 29 in.

MEMBERSHIPS
Allied Artists of America
American Federation of Arts
Beachcombers Club
Boston Arts Club
Copley Society of Boston
Guild of Boston Artists
National Academy of Design
National Arts Club
North Shore Art Association
Pennsylvania Academy of the Fine Arts
Philadelphia Art Center

PUBLIC COLLECTIONS
Army and Navy Club, New York City
Cincinnati Art Museum
Corcoran Gallery of Art, Washington, D.C.
Delaware Art Museum, Wilmington
Detroit Institute of Arts
Metropolitan Museum of Art, New York City
Museum of Fine Arts, Boston
Pennsylvania Academy of the Fine Arts, Philadelphia
Wadsworth Atheneum, Hartford, Connecticut

CARL RUNGIUS
(1869-1959)

Carl Clemens Moritz Rungius was a spirited and effective artist, skilled as a draftsman and hightly esteemed as a visual historian and naturalist. His full knowledge of anatomy, coupled with distinct composition and color sense, made him the foremost painter of Western North American big-game subjects.

Born near Berlin, Germany in 1869, Rungius was fascinated with big-game animals from childhood. He started painting in 1889, attending the Berlin Art School. His boyhood dream of studying and painting American big game was realized in 1894 when he emigrated to the United States, establishing a winter studio in New York City, and a summer studio in Banff, Alberta, Canada.

Rungius spent most of his time in the wilderness, and always painted directly from nature. His first sketching expedition was to Yellowstone Park and other parts of Wyoming in 1895, which he followed by over 50 years of stalking and painting wildlife from Arizona to Alaska.

Rungius documented the life and habitat of the antelope, elk, deer, goat and mountain sheep, as well as his favored larger subject matter—the grizzly bear, moose and caribou. These works are still considered to be important natural-history records.

Occasionally, he crossed the path of cowboys on a roundup or cattle drive. His depictions of their life-style were executed with immediacy and honesty.

In 1913, Rungius was elected an associate of the National Academy, becoming an academician in 1920.

Among his friends and admirers was Theodore Roosevelt, who purchased many Rungius paintings. Rungius apparently died in New York City at age 90 in 1959, leaving behind an opulent and unsurpassed record of North American big-game animals.

Moose Near Long Lake, ca. 1925, 30 x 45 in., signed l.r. Courtesy of Wunderlich and Company, Inc., New York, New York.

MEMBERSHIPS
American Federation of Arts
Lotus Club
National Academy of Design
National Arts Club
Salmagundi Club
Society of American Animal Painters
  and Sketchers
Society of Men Who Paint the Far West

PUBLIC COLLECTIONS
Glenbow Museum, Calgary, Alberta, Canada
New York Zoological Society, New York City
Shelburne Museum, Vermont

10-Year Average Change From Base Years '77-'78: 54%

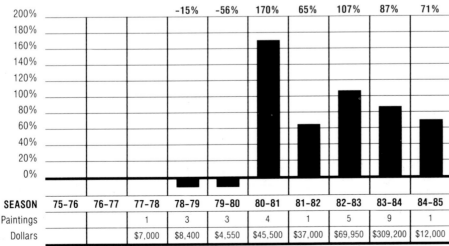

SEASON	75-76	76-77	77-78	78-79	79-80	80-81	81-82	82-83	83-84	84-85
				-15%	-56%	170%	65%	107%	87%	71%
Paintings			1	3	3	4	1	5	9	1
Dollars			$7,000	$8,400	$4,550	$45,500	$37,000	$69,950	$309,200	$12,000

Record Sale: $70,000, SPB, 5/30/84, ''The Challenge,'' 35 × 56 in.

HENRY HOBART NICHOLS
(1869-1962)

Subtle and muted, the landscapes of Henry Hobart Nichols are not exaggerated, outrageous or faddish. They exhibit a truly personal style. Yet he was a supportive comrade to his more radical artistic peers, and a man respected by all.

Born in Washington, D.C. in 1869, Nichols studied at the Art Students League and under Howard Helmick in Washington, then traveled to Paris to attend the Academie Julien and train with Claudio Castellucho. When he returned to the United States he based himself in New York City, although he painted in upper New York State and in New England.

He also devoted himself all his life to the welfare and promotion of his fellow artists. In 1900, he was involved with United States support for the Paris Exposition. From 1939 to 1949, he was president of the National Academy of Design. He was also a director and trustee of the Tiffany Foundation, and a trustee of the Metropolitan Museum of Art in New York. He died in New York City in 1962 at age 93.

In an age when traditional formulas are often rejected, the richness and diversity possible within a formal manner may not be fully appreciated. Hobart Nichols painted for the love of painting and the love of the landscape; his quiet paintings and illustrations, spare and academic as they are, have poetry and truth in them.

The Brook—Winter, 22 x 17¾ in., signed l.l. Courtesy of Grand Central Art Galleries, Inc., New York, New York.

10-Year Average Change From Base Years '78-'79: 46%

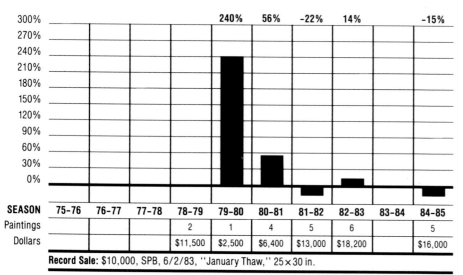

				240%	56%	–22%	14%		–15%

SEASON	75-76	76-77	77-78	78-79	79-80	80-81	81-82	82-83	83-84	84-85
Paintings				2	1	4	5	6		5
Dollars				$11,500	$2,500	$6,400	$13,000	$18,200		$16,000

Record Sale: $10,000, SPB, 6/2/83, "January Thaw," 25 x 30 in.

EDWARD WILLIS REDFIELD
(1869-1965)

Edward Willis Redfield was the acknowledged leader of the New Hope School of American impressionism. His bold and vigorous landscape paintings, especially his snow scenes of Bucks County in the Delaware River Valley of Pennsylvania, distinguished him as one of this country's foremost painters. Redfield's exuberant, impressionistic style was emulated by several generations of New Hope artists, many of whom settled in this picturesque area due to his tremendous influence.

Born in Bridgeville, Delaware in 1869, Redfield moved to Philadelphia at an early age. He soon became familiar with Bucks County, just a short jaunt North of the city. Determined to become an artist, he studied painting under a Mr. Rolf, in preparation for entrance into the prestigious Pennsylvania Academy of the Fine Arts.

From 1885 to 1889, Redfield followed a traditional course of study at the Academy under Thomas Anshutz, James Kelley and Thomas Hovenden. He developed a lifelong friendship with fellow student Robert Henri, an influential teacher and founder of the Ashcan School.

Redfield sailed with Henri for Paris in 1889, where he continued his studies at the Academie Julien and Ecole des Beaux Arts. He received rigorous training as a figure painter and portraitist under Adolphe William Bouguereau and Tony Robert-Fleury.

Old Stover Mill, 50 x 56 in., signed l.r. Courtesy of Newman Galleries, Philadelphia, Pennsylvania.

Valley of the Delaware, 50 x 56 in., signed l.r. Courtesy of Newman Galleries, Philadelphia, Pennsylvania.

Stifled within this rigid academic system, Redfield retreated from Paris to the village of Brolles in the Forest of Fountainebleu, where he pursued landscape painting.

Redfield and his French wife returned to Pennsylvania in 1898, settling in Center Bridge, near New Hope. Particularly taken with the rolling hills and graceful woodlands of the region, he worked in semi-isolation on his farm, situated near the Delaware River. Here, he gradually developed his own original, impressionistic style.

Like the French impressionists, Redfield was interested in capturing the effects of atmosphere and light, although his technique did not depend on the juxtaposition of contrasting colors to stimulate the picture surface. He applied his paint in long brushstrokes of

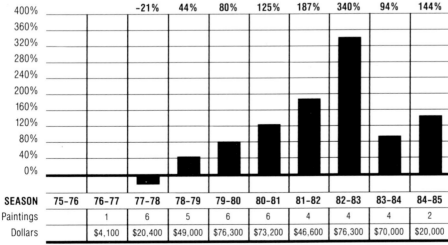

10-Year Average Change From Base Years '76-'77: 110%

		−21%	44%	80%	125%	187%	340%	94%	144%
SEASON	75-76	76-77	77-78	78-79	79-80	80-81	81-82	82-83	83-84	84-85
Paintings		1	6	5	6	6	4	4	4	2
Dollars		$4,100	$20,400	$49,000	$76,300	$73,200	$46,600	$76,300	$70,000	$20,000

Record Sale: $48,000, CH, 3/18/83, ''The Ferry Road at Point Pleasant,'' 32 × 40 in.

652

The Brook at Carversville, 28 x 32⅛ in., signed l.r. Courtesy of National Museum of American Art, Smithsonian Institution, Bequest of Henry Ward Ranger through the National Academy of Design.

thick impasto, rather than with the short, feathery brushstrokes characteristic of French impressionism.

He developed a method of painting which enabled him to complete a large (50-by-56-inch) canvas in a single day's work. This technique, achieved after years of formal study, allowed Redfield to record the ever-changing weather and atmospheric conditions.

Celebrated as a painter of the winter landscape, Redfield was exposed to every harshness the season could muster. A plein-air painter, he often stood knee-deep in snow, his canvas strapped to a tree, in order to work directly from nature.

Like Monet, whom he greatly admired, Redfield painted relentlessly throughout his long life, which ended in 1965. His influence, particularly upon younger New Hope impressionists, has proven enduring; today, traces of his style appear in the works of contemporary artists of the region.

MEMBERSHIPS
American Federation of Arts
National Institute Artists League
Pennsylvania Academy of the Fine Arts
Philadelphia Art Club
Salmagundi Club
Society of American Artists

PUBLIC COLLECTIONS
Albright-Knox Art Gallery, Buffalo
Art Institute of Chicago
Brooklyn Museum
Carnegie Institute, Pittsburgh
Cincinnati Art Museum
Corcoran Gallery of Art, Washington, D.C.
Dallas Museum of Fine Arts
Detroit Institute of Arts
Los Angeles County Museum of Art
Metropolitan Museum of Art, New York City
Minneapolis Institute of Arts, Minnesota
Musee d'Orsay, Paris
National Gallery of Art, Washington, D.C.
New Jersey State Museum, Trenton
Pennsylvania Academy of the Fine Arts,
   Philadelphia
Philadelphia Museum of Art
St. Louis Art Museum

BEN AUSTRIAN
(1870-1921)

Hailed in London as "the Landseer of chickens," Ben Austrian may be the only American artist whose reputation was built on paintings of chickens. One of his early depictions of a baby chick, just hatched from its shell, caught the eye of a director of a new soap company. Along with the slogan "Hasn't Scratched Yet!!!," it became the trademark for Bon Ami cleanser. In the years that followed, Austrian painted all the chicks featured in Bon Ami advertisements. He enlisted his wife as the model for the contented housewife shown using the product for household cleaning chores.

Austrian was born in Reading, Pennsylvania in 1870. He showed an early aptitude for drawing and was given his first box of watercolor paints when he was only five. Except for a brief time as a student of local artist Frederick Spang, however, he was entirely self-taught.

After working as a salesman in Williamsport, Pennsylvania, Austrian returned to Reading as a traveling representative for one of his father's businesses. In return for an order, Austrian would give customers one of his own early paintings.

When his father died in 1897, Austrian had to take over the operation of the family steam laundry. He despaired of ever becoming a painter. Before long, however, he persuaded his mother to let him sell the laundry, giving her the proceeds, so that he could paint full-time.

He hatched three chicks in his studio and, as they grew, trained them to pose for him. These were the first models for his many paintings of chickens. He also painted some trompe l'oeil paintings of game hanging after the hunt which attracted considerable attention. *A Day's Hunt* (1898, location unknown), was purchased by a Reading industrialist in 1904 for $2,500, a high price at that time.

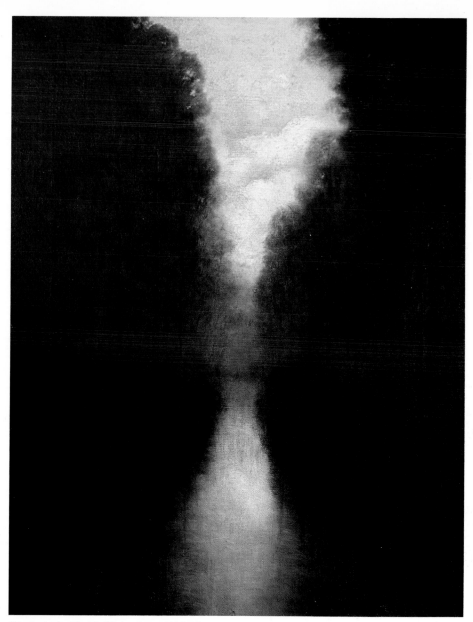

Sunrise in the Florida Wetlands, ca. 1915, 19½ x 15½ in., signed l.r. Courtesy of Private Collection, Radnor, Pennsylvania.

From the 1890s on, Austrian regularly did paintings for Bon Ami advertisements and later formed his own lithographic printing company to sell reproductions of them. In 1902, he went to Paris to paint and then to London for several years. It was then that his work was compared to Landseer's.

Austrian had a winter studio in Palm Beach, Florida. He died there of a stroke in 1921.

PUBLIC COLLECTIONS
Historical Society of Berks County, Pennsylvania
Kutztown State University, Pennsylvania
Walker Art Museum, Liverpool, England

SEASON	75-76	76-77	77-78	78-79	79-80	80-81	81-82	82-83	83-84	84-85
Paintings						1		1		1
Dollars						$850		$3,750		$800

Record Sale: $3,750, S.BM, 5/12/83, "The Stranger," 20 x 26 in.

Motherhood, 1897, 29½ x 30 in., signed l.r.
Courtesy of the Reading Public Museum, Pennsylvania.

Chicks, 1901, 11 x 9½ in., signed l.r.
Courtesy of Henry B. Holt, Inc., Essex Fells, New Jersey.

Sunrise Near Palm Beach, Florida, 1918,
25½ x 35½ in., signed l.r.
Courtesy of Private Collection, Radnor, Pennsylvania.

ALEXANDER JOHN DRYSDALE
(1870-1934)

A true product of the South, Alexander Drysdale spent all of his adult life in and around New Orleans, painting the bayous in moody, misty tones much like those of the symbolists. He was greatly influenced by George Inness, whose "transitory effects of nature" he much admired.

Drysdale was born in Marietta, Georgia in 1870, but moved to New Orleans when his father was appointed dean of Christ Church Cathedral there. He gave up a budding career as an accountant to study painting with Paul Poincy in New Orleans. Later he studied at the Art Students League in New York under Charles Curran and Frank Vincent Dumond.

On his return to New Orleans, Drysdale devoted himself to landscapes, capturing in soft, evocative tones the mystery of moss-draped oaks and still bayou waters. He developed a distinctive technique, using kerosene-thinned oil paint almost as if it were watercolor.

Drysdale was a prolific painter, sometimes finishing two paintings in a single day. He was sensitive to the criticism that much of his work was repetitive, but he pointed out that the same could be said about other artists of the day— John Singer Sargent, Robert Henri and William Merritt Chase among them. When he died in 1934, so much of his work existed that its value plunged.

Audubon Park, 17½ x 23½ in., signed l.l. Courtesy of Raydon Gallery, New York, New York.

Drysdale was his own best salesman, frequently persuading wealthy women and successful cotton brokers to invest in his work. One of his paintings hangs in "Sagamore Hill," Theodore Roosevelt's summer home on Long Island.

MEMBERSHIPS
Artists Association of New Orleans
Arts & Crafts Club of New Orleans

PUBLIC COLLECTIONS
Louisiana State Museum
New Orleans Museum of Art
Sagamore Hill National Historic Site, Oyster Bay, New York

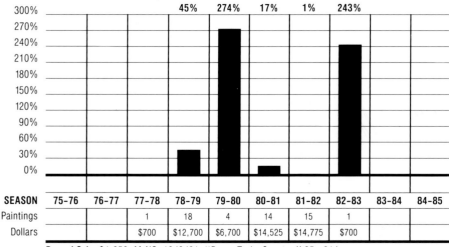

10-Year Average Change From Base Years '77-'78: 97%

			45%	274%	17%	1%	243%		

SEASON	75–76	76–77	77–78	78–79	79–80	80–81	81–82	82–83	83–84	84–85
Paintings			1	18	4	14	15	1		
Dollars			$700	$12,700	$6,700	$14,525	$14,775	$700		

Record Sale: $4,250, M.NO, 10/2/81, "Bayou Teche Country," 35×91 in.

656

WILLIAM GLACKENS
(1870-1938)

William Glackens was a painter and illustrator, one of The Eight who transformed American art with their new realism in the early twentieth century.

Glackens painted middle-class urban subjects—usually well-dressed people in restaurants, cafes, parks and clothing stores—people who were enjoying their lives in the city. There is pleasure in his work and a touch of elegance. In his later career, Glackens—influenced by the impressionistic style of Renoir—painted nudes, portraits of women, and summer landscapes in shimmering brushstrokes of red, green, orange and yellow. He has been called "the American Renoir."

Like other members of the Ashcan School who congregated around Robert Henri, Glackens began as a newspaper artist, working in his hometown for the *Philadelphia Press* and *Record*. He was extremely talented at drawing, with a near-photographic memory for detail, working quickly and rarely lingering over an assignment. Friends used to play a game with Glackens, asking him to describe a room they had just left—which he would do, down to the last detail, including the style of molding on the ceiling. It was said that he never bothered to sketch a scene on the spot because he could remember it so well.

In 1891, the year he began as an artist-reporter, Glackens met Henri, who urged him to take up painting. The young illustrator attended night classes

Beach Umbrellas at Blue Point, ca. 1915, 26 x 32 in., signed l.l. Courtesy of National Museum of American Art, Smithsonian Institution, Gift of Mr. and Mrs. Ira Glackens.

at the Pennsylvania Academy of the Fine Arts. In 1895, he went to Europe with Henri and Elmer Schofield to travel and paint. On his return, Glackens settled in New York City, earning his living with magazine illustrations and devoting his free time to painting. For Glackens the city represented, not ashcans and squalor, but the good life of restaurants, theaters and entertainment.

In 1905, he produced his masterpiece, *Chez Mouquin* (1905, Chicago Art Institute)—a picture of a couple seated in a French cafe that rivals the best of

the impressionists. The work shows Glackens's extraordinary drawing ability and his exquisite sense of detail. Until 1905, Glackens painted in the dark tones of the new realism; but after another visit to France, he adopted vivid rainbow colors. He liked bright sunlight and increasingly turned away from urban scenes to breezy, lyrical landscapes and seaside paintings.

Glackens was a quiet man who did what he wanted with apparent ease. Good-humored and tolerant, he lived in Greenwich Village with his wife, a daughter of William Merritt Chase, and his children. Good meals and good times are reflected in the family groups Glackens painted.

In 1912, Glackens went abroad with $20,000 from his friend, Albert C. Barnes, to purchase a series of paintings that would become the nucleus of the distinguished Barnes Foundation collection in Merion, Pennsylvania. Glackens chose works by the major impressionists: Renoir, Degas, Van Gogh and Cezanne.

He died in 1938.

MEMBERSHIPS
National Academy of Design

PUBLIC COLLECTIONS
Art Institute of Chicago
Detroit Museum of Arts
Metropolitan Museum of Art, New York City

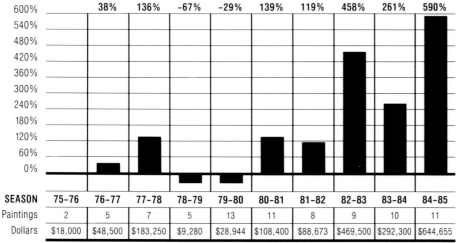

10-Year Average Change From Base Years '75-'76: 165%

	75-76	76-77	77-78	78-79	79-80	80-81	81-82	82-83	83-84	84-85
		38%	136%	-67%	-29%	139%	119%	458%	261%	590%
SEASON	75-76	76-77	77-78	78-79	79-80	80-81	81-82	82-83	83-84	84-85
Paintings	2	5	7	5	13	11	8	9	10	11
Dollars	$18,000	$48,500	$183,250	$9,280	$28,944	$108,400	$88,673	$469,500	$292,300	$644,655

Record Sale: $345,455, CH, 12/7/84, "Beach at Annisquam," 25 x 30 in.

657

HENRY SALEM HUBBELL
(1870-1949)

A portrait and still-life painter influenced by French impressionists, Henry Salem Hubbell was born in Paola, Kansas in 1870. He studied at the Art Institute of Chicago. Later Hubbell went to Paris; he worked with Whistler, Constant, Collin and Laurens, and exhibited at the famed Paris Salon.

American author Booth Tarkington saw Hubbell's painting *The Goldfish* (date and location unknown) in the Paris Salon of 1910; his purchase of the painting enabled Hubbell to take his family to Venice for a holiday.

Returning to the United States in the early part of the twentieth century, Hubbell worked as an illustrator for *The Women's Home Companion.* Later he was named professor of painting and director of the School of Painting and Decoration at Carnegie Institute of Technology in Pittsburgh, where he served from 1918 to 1921.

At the invitation of the federal government, Hubbell painted the official portraits of 15 secretaries of the interior. He also painted a portrait of President Franklin D. Roosevelt.

In 1924, Hubbell decided to make Miami his home, and a year later became a founding member of the Board of Regents of the University of Miami. He spent the next 25 years in Miami and died there in 1949.

In 1971, three of his works were included in an exhibition of American artists who were influenced by French impressionists, held at the University's Lowe Art Museum in Coral Gables, Florida.

Black Fan, 33 x 22 in., signed l.l. Courtesy of Grand Rapids Art Museum, Michigan.

SEASON	75-76	76-77	77-78	78-79	79-80	80-81	81-82	82-83	83-84	84-85
Paintings							1	1	3	1
Dollars							$750	$32,000	$5,400	$13,000

Record Sale: $32,000, SPB, 6/2/83, "Tea Time," 33 × 22 in.

HARRIET RANDALL LUMIS
(1870-1953)

American impressionist Harriet Randall Lumis painted bucolic landscape scenes and the harbors of New England. Although she never studied in Europe, she began her career when impressionism was an avant-garde movement in the United States. Lumis remained faithful to the tenets of impressionism, and did not adopt the style of the modern abstractionists who exhibited at the New York Armory Show in 1913.

Born in Salem, Connecticut in 1870, Lumis evidenced an interest in art at an early age. She married at 22 and moved to Springfield, Massachusetts with her draftsman-architect husband. There she studied drawing with Mary Hubbard and James Hall, and painting with tonalist Willis S. Adams. Under his tutelage, Lumis's first serious landscapes evoked the tonalists' mistiness and poetic mood, which often contrasted with colorful sky effects.

Lumis later studied with tonalist painters Leonard Ochtman and Edward Parker Hayden. Then, trying to free herself from the dark tonalist palette, she enrolled in the New York Summer School in Connecticut.

Influenced by French impressionist Claude Monet's work, Lumis learned to dissolve form in light by breaking up her daubs of color. She used a high-key palette, almost monochromatic, as in *A Wet Day Gloucester* (ca. 1917, private collection).

In the 1920s, she exhibited at local and national shows. Her brushwork became looser, her palette brighter, and her canvases larger. At age 50, she studied with Hugh Breckenridge; her technique became still freer, yet she remained true to the tenets of basic composition and accurate draftsmanship.

Gloucester, ca. 1918, 24 x 28 in., signed l.l. Photograph courtesy of R.H. Love Galleries, Inc., Chicago, Illinois. Private Collection.

During the Depression, sales of Lumis's paintings dropped. She produced little work and her husband died in 1937. To keep herself solvent, Lumis began to teach.

In 1949, she and other painters formed the American Artists Association to promote traditional or realistic styles of painting, rather than modern abstraction.

Although Lumis continued teaching and painting until her death in 1953, she received little recognition later in her career, and there was little demand for her work.

In 1977 and 1978, Lumis was rediscovered. Her work was shown at an exhibit which traveled to museums in Missouri, Wisconsin and Ohio.

MEMBERSHIPS
Connecticut Academy of Fine Arts
Gloucester Society of Artists
National Association of Women Painters
  and Sculptors
Philadelphia Art Alliance
Springfield Art League

PUBLIC COLLECTIONS
Museum of Fine Arts, Springfield,
  Massachusetts

SEASON	75-76	76-77	77-78	78-79	79-80	80-81	81-82	82-83	83-84	84-85
Paintings							2	1	1	1
Dollars							$21,000	$650	$2,200	$4,700

Record Sale: $19,000, SPB, 6/4/82, "Gloucester," 24 × 28 in.

JOHN MARIN
(1870-1953)

John Marin was an important early American modernist, widely regarded as the best American watercolorist since Winslow Homer. His paintings are notable for their expression of dynamic forces in collision, whether the forces are man-made Manhattan skyscrapers or natural rocks and waves.

Marin was born in 1870 in Rutherford, New Jersey, and received early training as an architect before deciding to pursue a career in art. Having worked for several years as an architect, in 1899 Marin enrolled at the Pennsylvania Academy of the Fine Arts, where he studied for two years under Thomas Anshutz. Subsequently, Marin spent another two years studying under Frank DuMond at the Art Students League in New York City.

In 1905, Marin sailed to Europe, where he spent most of the next six years working in Paris and touring extensively in Italy, Belgium, Holland and Austria. His paintings of this period show the predominant influence of Japanese painting and of James A.M. Whistler, especially in their emphasis on soft forms, their reserved tonality, and an economy of brushwork resembling calligraphy.

In 1909, Marin had his first New York City show at Alfred Stieglitz's Gallery 291, the most progressive gallery of its time in the United States. Stieglitz thought well of Marin's work, and did

Region of Brooklyn Bridge Fantasy, 1932, 18¾ x 22¼ in., signed l.r. Courtesy of Collection The Whitney Museum of American Art, New York, New York.

much to promote him throughout his career.

In 1911, Marin returned to the United States, dividing the next 20 years between New York City and the coast of Maine, both of which he painted with vigor and an increasing taste for experimentation. This period marks the beginning of Marin's modernism, which is most apparent in his portrayal of Manhattan skyscrapers painted in the cubist or futurist manner.

Marin's paintings of the coast of Maine share with his cityscapes such modernist techniques as sight lines, contrasting weights and rapid brushwork in order to represent the flux and collision of natural elements, such as waves and rocks. In contrast to his Maine pieces, Marin also painted a series of New Mexico landscapes in 1929 and 1930, notable for their desert ambience.

Having begun his formal career late in life, at age 40 Marin began to achieve the success that eluded many of his contemporaries among the first generation of American modernists. With Alfred Stieglitz as his faithful dealer, Marin's work sold well and at high prices from the mid-1920s on. He was honored with a retrospective exhibit at the Museum of Modern Art in 1936, and remained active until his death at age 83 at his home in Cape Split, Maine.

MEMBERSHIPS
American Academy of Arts and Letters

PUBLIC COLLECTIONS
Art Institute of Chicago
Museum of Modern Art, New York City
National Gallery of Art, Washington, D.C.

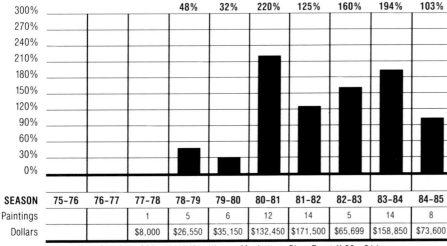

10-Year Average Change From Base Years '77–'78: 110%

			48%	32%	220%	125%	160%	194%	103%
SEASON	75-76	76-77	77-78	78-79	79-80	80-81	81-82	82-83	83-84	84-85
Paintings			1	5	6	12	14	5	14	8
Dollars			$8,000	$26,550	$35,150	$132,450	$171,500	$65,699	$158,850	$73,600

Record Sale: $36,000, SPB, 12/10/81, "Lower Manhattan, River Front," 26 × 21 in.

MAXFIELD PARRISH
(1870-1966)

Maxfield Parrish was an enterprising and prosperous artist, skilled as a painter and highly esteemed as an illustrator. His decorative and whimsical works, which grew from his early interest in the English pre-raphaelite tradition, made him one of the most popular and sought-after illustrators in the history of American art.

Born in Philadelphia in 1870, the son of successful painter Stephen Parrish, he was exposed to art from childhood. His first intention was to be an architect, but his talent and love for art intervened and he entered the Pennsylvania Academy of the Fine Arts in 1889. He studied with renowned illustrator Howard Pyle at the same time.

In 1894, he exhibited at the Pennsylvania Academy of the Fine Arts. One of his drawings was featured on the cover of *Harper's Weekly* in 1895; his penchant for combining sentiment, naturalism and fantasy soon had many publishers wanting Parrish illustrations.

A bout with typhoid fever in the late 1890s sent Parrish on a trip to recuperate; it included Arizona, where he honed his colorist ability in 1902, and Italy, where he worked on his first published color illustrations for Edith Wharton's *Italian Villas* in 1903.

Thereafter, making his studio in Windsor, Vermont, he illustrated many magazine covers and children's books, sold millions of color prints and became a popular muralist. His most famous murals are in the St. Regis Hotel in New York City and the Palace Bar in San Francisco.

Parrish left illustration in 1930 to paint landscapes, which he did for the following 30 years. Two years before his death in 1966, there was a strong revival of interest in, and sales of, his early works. Decorative compositions with fantasy-laced photographic details, characterized by meticulous draftsmanship and a perfect finish, were the legacy of Maxfield Parrish.

Lady Ursula Informs the King, 20½ x 16¼ in., signed l.l. Courtesy of Vose Galleries of Boston, Inc., Massachusetts.

MEMBERSHIPS
National Academy of Design
National Institute Art League
Pennsylvania Academy of the Fine Arts
Society of American Artists
Union Internationale des Beaux
  Arts et Lettres

PUBLIC COLLECTIONS
Brandywine River Museum,
  Chadds Ford, Pennsylvania
Delaware Art Museum, Wilmington
Hotel Sherman, Chicago
Palace Hotel, San Francisco
St. Regis Hotel, New York City

SEASON	75-76	76-77	77-78	78-79	79-80	80-81	81-82	82-83	83-84	84-85
Paintings		2	4	5	4	3	4	9	7	4
Dollars		$77,500	$92,000	$51,250	$115,750	$51,000	$115,000	$135,050	$82,400	$36,800

Record Sale: $62,500, SPB, 10/25/79, ''Egypt,'' 33 × 21 in.

FRANK P. SAUERWEIN
(1871-1910)

Frank P. Sauerwein, or Sauerwen, as he signed most of his work, painted landscapes, Indian scenes and genre scenes of the American Southwest. He worked in both watercolor and oil.

Sauerwein was born in 1871. Sources differ as to whether he was born in Maryland, New York or New Jersey. His father was Charles D. Sauerwein, a European-trained artist and his son's first teacher.

Sauerwein was raised in Philadelphia and graduated from the Philadelphia Museum School of Art in 1888. He also studied at the Pennsylvania Academy of the Fine Arts, the Philadelphia School of Industrial Arts, and the Art Institute of Chicago.

Seeking a healthier climate for his tuberculosis, Sauerwein moved to Denver in 1891; his sister, also tubercular, lived there. He became involved in the artistic life of the city and sketched in the Rockies. With artist Charles Craig, Sauerwein visited a Ute Indian reservation in Colorado Springs in 1893; he also traveled throughout the West as he became interested in Western subjects.

Sauerwein and his sister moved to California in 1901. After her death, he traveled in Europe. Upon his return to the United States, he lived at various times in Denver, California and New Mexico, eventually settling in Taos.

He became known for his realistic, competent renderings of Western landscapes and Indian life. His work was straightforward, with well-handled brushstrokes and color. One of his paintings was purchased by the Santa Fe Railway; others were sold by the El Tovar Hotel at the Grand Canyon.

Finally too ill to paint, Sauerwein moved to Connecticut in the hope of a cure. He died in Stamford in 1910.

Firelight, 10 x 13½ in., signed l.r. Photograph courtesy of The Gerald Peters Gallery, Santa Fe, New Mexico.

PUBLIC COLLECTIONS
Museum of New Mexico, Santa Fe
Panhandle-Plains Historical Museum,
    Canyon, Texas
Southwest Museum, Los Angeles

SEASON	75-76	76-77	77-78	78-79	79-80	80-81	81-82	82-83	83-84	84-85
Paintings				1	3	2			2	
Dollars				$4,250	$3,950	$12,500			$1,650	

Record Sale: $9,000, SPB, 10/17/80, "Taos Indians Bathing," 18 × 26 in.

GRANVILLE REDMOND

(1871-1935)

A California artist known primarily for his poppy scenes and brilliant sunsets, Grenville Richard Seymour Redmond was born in Philadelphia. Deaf by age three from scarlet fever, he attended the California School for the Deaf, where Theophilius Hope, a deaf philosopher and teacher, encouraged him to study art.

Redmond studied under Arthur Mathews and Amedee Joulin at the San Francisco Art Association's California School of Design for three years. He then worked under Benjamin Constant and Jean-Paul Laurens at the Academie Julien in Paris. Upon his return to Los Angeles in 1889, Redmond changed his first name to Granville and opened a studio, painting scenes of Laguna Beach, San Pedro and Catalina Island.

In the years between 1908 and 1917, the artist moved between Northern and Southern California. In Los Angeles in 1917, he met Charlie Chaplin, who sponsored his work in film. Chaplin gave Redmond a studio on the movie lot, and utilized his skills both for his private collection and for cinematic scenery work. He also cast his friend as the sculptor in *City Lights.*

Characterized as a colorist and delineator of nature's moods, Redmond had a distinctive style akin to pointillism in feeling. Considered California's first resident impressionist, the artist believed that details should be realistic, but that the whole should reflect a personal con-

ception of form, design and color. He said, in a 1931 interview with Arthur Miller, "Fifteen minutes. No one should sketch longer than that from nature. By that time everything has changed."

California Beauties, 30 x 40 in., signed l.l. Courtesy of Maxwell Galleries, LTD., San Francisco, California.

MEMBERSHIPS
Bohemian Club
California Art Club
Laguna Beach Art Association
San Francisco Art Association

PUBLIC COLLECTIONS
Laguna Beach Museum of Art, California
Los Angeles County Museum of Art
Museum of the City of New York
Oakland Museum, California
San Diego Museum of Art, California
Stanford Museum of Art, California
Washington State Capitol, Olympia

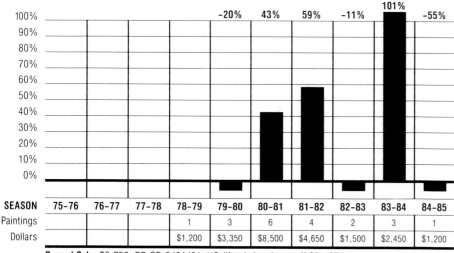

10-Year Average Change From Base Years '78-'79: 17%

SEASON	75-76	76-77	77-78	78-79	79-80	80-81	81-82	82-83	83-84	84-85
					-20%	43%	59%	-11%	101%	-55%
Paintings				1	3	6	4	2	3	1
Dollars				$1,200	$3,350	$8,500	$4,650	$1,500	$2,450	$1,200

Record Sale: $2,750, BB.SF, 6/24/81, "California Landscape," 20 x 27 in.

GEORGE ELMER BROWNE
(1871-1946)

George Elmer Browne was a popular American impressionist of the late nineteenth and early twentieth centuries. He was also a skilled teacher and administrator, active in many capacities in the international art world.

Browne was probably influenced by Constable. His skies were always interesting; typically his landscapes are two-thirds sky, with much cloud movement. He had a strong and innate sense of composition.

Color and force were other dominant elements in Browne's work. He used wide masses of color, with only suggestions of detail in the foreground. He liked to stress the use of keynotes to his students: picking one idea or color and carrying it out to completion.

Browne was born in Gloucester, Massachusetts in 1871. After attending public school in Salem and revealing artistic talent at an early age, he studied at the Museum of Fine Arts and the Cowles School of Art in Boston. This was the time of the great artistic exodus to Paris, and Browne went to study at the Academie Julien with Jules Lefevbre and Tony Robert-Fleury.

When he returned to this country, he set up a studio in New York City and began painting. He won his first award—a bronze medal—at the Mechanics Fair in Boston in 1895. He founded the Browne Art Classes. Many summers were spent at Provincetown, Massachusetts. A famous quote of

Haying, 20½ x 25¾ in., signed l.l. Courtesy of Arvest Galleries, Inc., Boston, Massachusetts.

Browne's: "Drawing should be like writing a letter to a friend. It should aim more at conveying a personal reaction to the subject matter rather than a display of virtuosity."

According to an article that appeared in the *American Magazine of Art* in November 1926, "Browne's sympathies are wholly academic. . . . Cubism and futurism he regards as merely 'Faddism.' The idea of the Faddist, 'that an

egg is square,' he thinks, is analogous with the primitive faith of the ancients that the earth was flat."

Browne was highly regarded in France, where he was named Officer of Public Instruction and Fine Arts. In 1926, he was made Chevalier of the French Legion of Honor. One of his paintings, *Bait Sellers of Cape Cod* (date and location unknown), was bought in 1904 in the Paris Salon by the French Government.

Browne died in Provincetown in 1946.

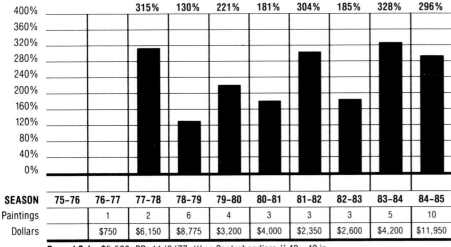

10-Year Average Change From Base Years '76-'77: 218%

SEASON	75-76	76-77	77-78	78-79	79-80	80-81	81-82	82-83	83-84	84-85
			315%	130%	221%	181%	304%	185%	328%	296%
Paintings		1	2	6	4	3	3	3	5	10
Dollars		$750	$6,150	$8,775	$3,200	$4,000	$2,350	$2,600	$4,200	$11,950

Record Sale: $5,500, PB, 11/8/77, "Les Contrabandiers," 49 × 49 in.

664

JOHN SLOAN
(1871-1951)

John Sloan loved ordinary people; as a member of the Ashcan School in the early twentieth century, he painted and sketched hundreds of them in the rhythms of private life—hanging out the wash, drying their hair or sleeping on rooftops during a summer's night in New York City.

The most politically active of the American realists, Sloan joined the Socialist Party and served for a period as art editor of *The Masses,* a literal magazine. His drawings and paintings, however, are apolitical, revealing only a strong and often joyous interest in city life. He never made a good living from his art; academics recoiled from his intimate recordings of ordinary events, and it wasn't until the last decade of his life that Sloan could support himself by painting.

Like other painters who gathered around Robert Henri to revolutionize artistic tastes, Sloan, born in 1871 in Lock Haven, Pennsylvania, began as a newspaper illustrator for the Philadelphia *Inquirer* and the *Press.* He entered the Pennsylvania Academy of the Fine Arts in 1892 to study for a year under Thomas Anshutz. The same year he met and was captivated by Henri and the new realism. Thereafter, he began painting dark, warm, almost monochromatic scenes of city life, using the color scheme of Franz Hals, recommended by Henri, that was characteristic of the Ashcan artists.

Toward Evening, Gloucester, 24 x 20 in., signed l.r. Courtesy of Arvest Galleries, Inc., Boston, Massachusetts.

In 1904, Sloan settled in New York City, developing skills as an etcher. His vignettes of backyards, restaurants, bars, street corners and parks on Fifth Avenue and in the tenderloin district were the first of their kind in this country.

The American Water Color Society returned four of his etchings as "too vulgar." Barred from exhibiting in conventional channels, Sloan joined his friends in the 1908 showing by The Eight, which turned the art world upside down overnight. Recognized then as a prominent artist, praised as an "American Hogarth," Sloan still did not sell a painting until he was 40. "The only reason I am in this profession is because it's fun," he once said.

After the showing by The Eight, Sloan adopted the color theory of Hardesty Maratta, and his palette brightened with new, colorful landscapes painted in Gloucester, Massachusetts. He also made summer painting trips to Santa Fe,

New Mexico from 1919 on. Although he painted the glorious Western environment, Sloan maintained his predilection for people. Much of his Santa Fe work focuses on Mexican-Americans and American Indians.

Beginning in 1928, Sloan turned increasingly to figure studies and nudes, using oil glazes over tempera, overlaid with a network of red lines. The result was an almost metallic or plastic surface, highly personal and not very popular with the public, who by now wanted his early work.

Sloan taught for most of his career, associated with the Art Students League, where he was elected director in 1931. In 1939, he painted a mural for the Bronxville, New York post office, entitled *The First Mail Arrives at Bronxville, 1846.* That same year he published a treatise on his field, *Gist of Art.*

Depending upon the observer, Sloan was either a judicious man who weighed every action, or he was hard-bitten and unbending. But his etchings of New Yorkers, seen from the rear window of his studio, reveal a warm and generous heart. He died in 1951.

MEMBERSHIPS
American Academy of Arts and Letters
New Society of Artists
Society of Independent Artists

PUBLIC COLLECTIONS
Art Institute of Chicago
Barnes Foundation, Merion, Pennsylvania
Brooklyn Museum
Carnegie Institute, Pittsburgh
Cincinnati Museum of Art
Delaware Art Museum, Wilmington
Detroit Institute of Arts
Hood Museum, Dartmouth College
Museum of New Mexico, Santa Fe
Newark Museum, New Jersey
Phillips Gallery, Washington, D.C.
Whitney Museum of American Art, New York City

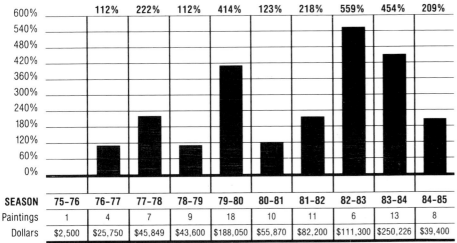

10-Year Average Change From Base Years '75-'76: 242%

	112%	222%	112%	414%	123%	218%	559%	454%	209%

SEASON	75-76	76-77	77-78	78-79	79-80	80-81	81-82	82-83	83-84	84-85
Paintings	1	4	7	9	18	10	11	6	13	8
Dollars	$2,500	$25,750	$45,849	$43,600	$188,050	$55,870	$82,200	$111,300	$250,226	$39,400

Record Sale: $130,000, SPB, 4/25/80, "Spring Planting, Greenwich Village," 26 x 32 in.

WILLIAM KAULA
(1871-1953)

The Upper Connecticut, 10 x 13 in., signed l.l. Courtesy of Arvest Galleries, Inc., Boston, Massachusetts.

William Kaula, who specialized in painting New England landscapes, was born in Boston in 1871. He studied at the Massachusetts Normal Art School and the Cowles Art School in Boston and at the Academy Colarossi and the Academie Julien in Paris. Around the turn of the century he became a student of Edmund Tarbell, a fellow Bostonian who remained a major influence on

Kaula's work throughout his life.

Best known for his striking interpretations of cloud-filled skies and broadly-defined New Hampshire hills, Kaula seldom ventured far from his beloved New England.

In 1902 he married painter Lee Lufkin, and in 1904 the two participated in a joint exhibition at the Cobb Gallery in Boston. Kaula also had one-man

shows at the prestigious Copley Gallery in Boston and at the Christopher Hungington Gallery in Mt. Vernon, Maine.

He served for a time as president of the Boston Society of Water Color Painters and was a member of the Boston Art Club and the New York Water Color Club. Besides watercolors, Kaula also painted in oils and pastels. He died in 1953 at age 82.

MEMBERSHIPS
American Art Association of Paris
Boston Art Club
Boston Guild of Artists
Boston Society of Water Color Painters
Boston Water Color Club
New York Water Color Club

PUBLIC COLLECTIONS
Museum of Fine Arts, Boston

10-Year Average Change From Base Years '78-'79: 4%

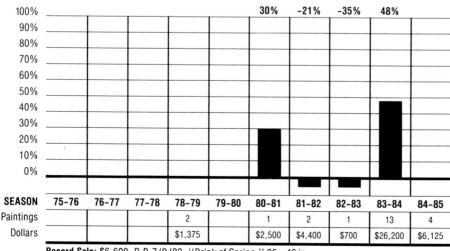

SEASON	75–76	76–77	77–78	78–79	79–80	80–81	81–82	82–83	83–84	84–85
Paintings				2		1	2	1	13	4
Dollars				$1,375		$2,500	$4,400	$700	$26,200	$6,125

Record Sale: $6,600, B.P, 7/9/83, "Brink of Spring," 35 × 46 in.

666

LYONEL
FEININGER
(1871-1956)

Dead End, 1951, 17 x 24 in., signed l.r. Courtesy of Kennedy Galleries, New York, New York.

Born in New York City, the son of distinguished concert artists, Lyonel Feininger first planned to be a musician, and music was profoundly important in his artistic career. Feininger said, "The whole world is nothing but order," and cited Johann Sebastian Bach as the most important artistic influence in his life.

In 1887, Feininger traveled to Germany to study music, but soon switched to painting. He studied at the Kinstgewerbeschule in Hamburg, at the Berlin Academy and at the Academie Collarossi in Paris. From 1883 until 1907, he was an illustrator and satirical cartoonist for many German periodicals, as well as a comic-strip artist for the *Chicago Sunday Tribune.* He also illustrated children's books. His style at this time was flat and decorative.

In 1907, he met Jules Pascin and Robert Delaunay in Paris and, inspired by their avant-garde example, began to devote himself to serious painting influenced by Van Gogh, Cezanne, Delaunay and cubisn. While the effects of cubism were apparent in his work, his emotive experimentation with light, color and space added a dimension of depth and lyricism.

In 1918, the artist began doing woodcuts, some of his most spontaneous and delightful work. In 1919, he joined architect Walter Gropius at the Bauhaus, the German center for design studies. He was on the faculty with Paul Klee and Vasily Kandinsky, and later became an artist-in-residence, remaining there until 1933.

By 1921, Feininger had perfected a romantic style that fused aspects of cubism and expressionism. In 1924, he joined Klee, Kandinsky and Alexij von Jawlensky in the group known as "the Blue Four," and participated with them in many exhibitions in New York City and Germany.

In the mid 1930s, Feininger returned to America because of the political situation in Germany, where, under Hitler, his works were to be characterized as "degenerate art." He taught at Mills College for a year in 1936, and then settled in New York City until his death in 1956.

SEASON	75-76	76-77	77-78	78-79	79-80	80-81	81-82	82-83	83-84	84-85
Paintings								34	37	25
Dollars								$607,641	$500,795	$158,240

Record Sale: $220,000, CH, 11/3/82, "Gelmeroda III," 39 × 31 in.

FREDERICK BALLARD WILLIAMS
(1871-1956)

A Glade by the Sea, 1908, 30⅛ x 45⅛ in., signed l.r. Courtesy of National Museum of American Art, Smithsonian Institution, Gift of William T. Evans.

Landscape and figure painter Frederick Ballard Williams combined romantic subjectivity with representational execution to produce an original statement, which sought to elevate nature to a status it did not hold in itself. Decorative in appearance, his works were modern in sentiment and spontaneity.

Williams was born in 1871 in Brooklyn, New York. He was educated in the public schools of Bloomfield and Montclair, New Jersey, and studied art in night classes at the Cooper Union in New York City and at the New York Institute of Artists and Artisans. Williams studied briefly under John Ward Stimson, described as "an idealist," before attending the School of the National Academy of Design.

He traveled to England and France, then settled in Glen Ridge, New Jersey. He had his first exhibition at the National Academy in 1901, and won a bronze medal at the Pan-American Exposition in Buffalo the same year.

Williams basically produced two types of paintings. Many of them, such as *The Rendezvous* (date and location unknown), portrayed nature peopled by idealized figures—usually women—who were present only to add beauty. He was best known for landscapes like *Garrets Mountain, N.J.* (date and location unknown), a broad vista, seen from an elevated perspective.

Williams was the recipient of many medals and awards throughout his career, including the Isidor Gold Medal of the National Academy of Design in 1909 for his figure painting *Chant d'Amour* (date and location unknown). In 1910, he was part of a group of artists who went West to paint the Grand Canyon and other Western sites. He later spent a summer producing a series of paintings of California landscapes.

Although Williams was a representational painter, he did not paint from nature. He studied nature, as one might study a language, but his paintings were produced in the studio. This physical separation reveals Williams's philosophy: the technical craft of painting, and even the subject itself, is distinct from and subservient to the artistic vision. However, Williams also believed that the subject was served by the art, that the artistic vision of beauty elevated and completed the object of its expression.

After a productive and successful career, Williams died in Glen Ridge in 1956.

MEMBERSHIPS
American Federation of Arts
Lotus Club
Montclair Art Association
National Academy of Design
National Arts Club
New York Water Color Club
Salmagundi Club

PUBLIC COLLECTIONS
Albright-Knox Art Gallery, Buffalo
Art Institute of Chicago
Atlanta Art Museum
Brooklyn Museum
City Art Museum, St. Louis
Dallas Art Association
Harrison Gallery, Los Angeles Museum
Metropolitan Museum of Art, New York City
Milwaukee Art Institute
Montclair Art Museum, New Jersey
National Gallery of Art, Washington, D.C.

SEASON	75-76	76-77	77-78	78-79	79-80	80-81	81-82	82-83	83-84	84-85
Paintings	1		1	1	1	2	2		6	1
Dollars	$301		$600	$650	$1,800	$1,800	$1,780		$5,600	$575

Record Sale: $1,800, S.W, 6/8/80, "Ladies in a Garden," 16 × 24 in.

CHARLES W. HAWTHORNE
(1872-1930)

Portrait and genre painter Charles W. Hawthorne continued to work in the solid, disciplined style of the academicians long after other artists had turned to modernism in revolt against academic strictures. Hawthorne is frequently called a conservative. His careful, well-painted portraits reflect the influence of his teacher, William Merritt Chase.

But there is another side to this important painter, for his primary subjects were the rugged Yankee and Portuguese fishermen of New England, and Hawthorne's naturalistic depiction of their harsh life places him within the traditions of realism. Hawthorne was not one of the New York realists; rumor has it that Robert Henri rejected Hawthorne from The Eight. Nevertheless, he took his share of abuse from critics for his "brutal" paintings of Provincetown fishermen. It was several years before these paintings—treatments of a strong but sad people, struggling to make a meager living—were critically accepted. They are now considered Hawthorne's most important work, and he is credited with establishing the Cape Cod School of Art.

Born in 1872 in Lodi, Illinois, Hawthorne grew up in Richmond, Maine, a small town on the Kennebec River. His father was a sea captain and Hawthorne's youth was spent among the seafaring people he later depicted.

The School, 48 x 60 in., signed l.l. Courtesy of Vose Galleries of Boston, Inc., Massachusetts.

He moved to New York City, enrolling in the Art Students League as a night student in 1894, working during the day at menial jobs. Later he studied with Chase; as an associate, he helped Chase organize his New York school. In 1898, Hawthorne went to Holland, and was strongly influenced by the tonal style of Franz Hals.

Hawthorne's portraits, primarily of women and children, reflect an introspective, sometimes sad mood. Faces are solidly modeled in a conservative style.

Around 1910, Hawthorne picked up traces of impressionism, but the bright, happy face of impressionism did not suit the tragic look of people who daily risked their lives on the sea. Hawthorne remained a realistic painter, acutely observing and representing the nature and people. His depictions of fishermen were so exact that a medical doctor once used a Hawthorne canvas to illustrate skin cancer caused by exposure to the elements.

Hawthorne won numerous awards and made a comfortable living from his painting. He died in 1930.

MEMBERSHIPS
American Water Color Society
Century Association
National Academy of Design
National Arts Club
National Institute of Arts and Letters
Salmagundi Club

PUBLIC COLLECTIONS
Brooklyn Museum
Carnegie Institute, Pittsburgh
Corcoran Gallery of Art, Washington, D.C.
Metropolitan Museum of Art, New York City
Museum of Fine Arts, Boston

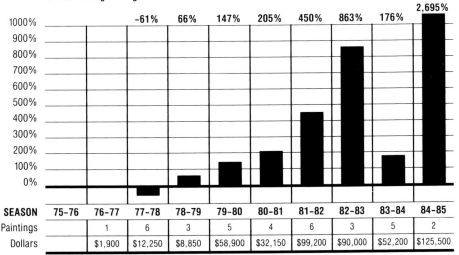

10-Year Average Change From Base Years '76-'77: 505%

	-61%	66%	147%	205%	450%	863%	176%	2,695%

SEASON	75-76	76-77	77-78	78-79	79-80	80-81	81-82	82-83	83-84	84-85
Paintings		1	6	3	5	4	6	3	5	2
Dollars		$1,900	$12,250	$8,850	$58,900	$32,150	$99,200	$90,000	$52,200	$125,500

Record Sale: $110,000, CH, 12/7/84, "June," 24 x 20 in.

AARON HARRY GORSON
(1872-1933)

Industrial Night Scene, 36 x 42 in., signed l.l. Courtesy of Kennedy Galleries, New York, New York.

Aaron Harry Gorson was a landscape artist best known for his paintings of the steel mills around Pittsburgh, Pennsylvania. Gorson enjoyed a successful career from around 1902 until his death in 1933, and is remembered today as one of the pioneers of the American industrial landscape.

Gorson was born in Lithuania, and emigrated to the United States at age 18. He began his formal studies at the Pennsylvania Academy of the Fine Arts under Thomas Anshutz, and in 1899 went to Paris, where he studied under Benjamin Constant at the Academie Julien and Jean Paul Laurens at the Academie Colarossi.

In 1903, Gorson returned to Pittsburgh, where he established his home for the next 18 years, and became well known for his dramatic portrayals of the smelting and manufacturing processes of the steel industry, and for his glowing nocturnes of Pittsburgh and the Monongahela Valley.

Gorson himself testified eloquently in his own writings to the beauty and excitement that he found in the surroundings of the Monongahela Valley—in the gracefully curving Monongahela and Allegheny Rivers, framed by dark hills and lit by millions of lights, and in the variegated clouds of smoke.

Gorson found enthusiastic patronage for his work in Pittsburgh, New York City, Philadelphia and other major art centers. For the next 30 years, his paintings were exhibited widely in major American art museums, including the Pennsylvania Academy of the Fine Arts, the Corcoran Gallery of Washington, D.C., the Art Institute of Chicago and the National Academy of Design.

In 1921, Gorson moved to New York, where he continued to enjoy an active social life and professional career until his death of pneumonia in 1933.

MEMBERSHIPS
Art Alliance of America
Associated Artists of Pittsburgh
Brooklyn Art Association
L'Union Internationale des Beaux Arts
  et Lettres

PUBLIC COLLECTIONS
Heckscher Museum, Huntington, Long Island
Newark Museum, New Jersey
Worcester Art Museum, Massachusetts

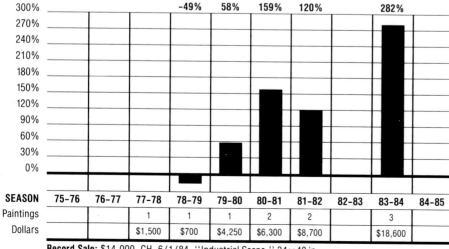

10-Year Average Change From Base Years '77-'78: 95%

				-49%	58%	159%	120%		282%	
300%										
270%										
240%										
210%										
180%										
150%										
120%										
90%										
60%										
30%										
0%										

SEASON	75-76	76-77	77-78	78-79	79-80	80-81	81-82	82-83	83-84	84-85
Paintings			1	1	1	2	2		3	
Dollars			$1,500	$700	$4,250	$6,300	$8,700		$18,600	

Record Sale: $14,000, CH, 6/1/84, "Industrial Scene," 34 x 42 in.

670

GEORGE AMES ALDRICH

(1872-1941)

Landscape painter and etcher George Ames Aldrich was born in Worcester, Massachusetts in 1872. As a member of the Chicago Galleries Association, he was established as a Chicago talent and exhibited there regularly. His early art experience was as a magazine illustrator in the 1890s, when he did illustrations for *The London Times* and *Punch* magazine.

Aldrich was enrolled at the Art Students League in New York City and at the Massachusetts Institute of Technology, where he may have studied architecture. His art studies continued in Paris, where he was a pupil at the Academies Julien and Colarossi.

Aldrich won four prizes from the Hoosier Salon in Chicago, the first in 1923 for a snow scene. Many of his landscapes were painted in Normandy and Brittany, probably in 1909 and 1910, when he lived in Dieppe.

A critic who saw Aldrich's works in a Chicago show wrote that his painting had "... a sense of a romantic approach to each subject, a spirit of adventure in painting it...." His American landscapes were painted with imagination and "faithful observance of the original."

In 1924, Aldrich received an architectural-club traveling scholarship for a European study trip. During that time he spent six months in residence at the American Academy in Rome, and three months at the Fontainebleau School of Fine Arts in France. He then

Nocturne, Montreuil sur Mer, 20 x 24¼ in., signed l.r. Courtesy of Marbella Gallery, Inc., New York, New York.

traveled and sketched in Italy, France, Spain, Germany and England.

Aldrich died at his home in Chicago in 1941, at age 68.

MEMBERSHIPS
Chicago Society of Painters and Sculptors
Chicago Gallery of Art
Hoosier Salon, Chicago
Societe des Artistes Francais

PUBLIC COLLECTIONS
Ball States Teachers College, Muncie, Indiana
Decatur Museum, Illinois
Houston Museum of Fine Arts
Musee de Rouen

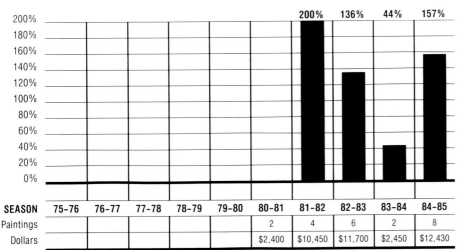

10-Year Average Change From Base Years '80-'81: 107%

SEASON	75-76	76-77	77-78	78-79	79-80	80-81	81-82	82-83	83-84	84-85
							200%	136%	44%	157%
Paintings						2	4	6	2	8
Dollars						$2,400	$10,450	$11,700	$2,450	$12,430

Record Sale: $5,500, D.NY, 9/23/81, "Millstream in Summer," 36 x 36 in.

671

EDWARD BOREIN
(1872-1945)

The Trail Boss, 22 x 28 in., signed l.r. Courtesy of Wunderlich and Company, Inc., New York, New York.

Vigor and authenticity characterize the thousands of etchings, drawings and paintings of Western life created by Edward Borein during his long and successful career. A native Californian and a cowboy in his youth, Borein was self-taught. He drew from direct observation the horses, cattle drives, cowhands, Indians and ranch life he found fascinating.

The son of a county politician in San Leandro, California, Borein attended grade schools in Oakland and began to draw at an early age. At age 17, he became a ranch hand. For the next 13 years, he developed his skills as a cowboy, sketching whenever he could on the cattle ranges of California and Mexico.

In 1891, Borein briefly attended the San Francisco Art Association School, where he met artists James Swinnerton and Maynard Dixon, who became his lifelong friends. Borein made his first sale in 1896, to Charles Lummiss, who also became a close friend.

After a sketching trip to Mexico with Dixon, Borein became a staff artist on the *San Francisco Call* in 1900. He also opened an Oakland studio. With Dixon, he took another sketching trip through the Sierra Mountains, Oregon and Idaho in 1901. On a 1903 trip to Mexico and through Pueblo Indian country, he began painting watercolors. In these Oakland years, Borein also produced oils described as uneven in quality.

In 1907, Borein went to New York City, where he remained to work and study until 1919, with brief trips to the West. He became an illustrator for *Harper's, Collier's, Western World* and *Sunset* magazines, and was in demand for other commissions and for advertising work.

It was in this period, considered by some to be his finest and most produc-tive, that Borein began to etch, studying under Childe Hassam and later with Preisig at the Art Students League of New York. He is best known for his etchings, a medium he chose in order to make his portrayals of the Western way of life most accessible to a wide audience.

Borein returned to Oakland in 1919; married in 1921; and settled in Santa Barbara. He continued until his death in 1945 to produce an abundance of etchings, drawings and watercolors.

Many biographies note Borein's great personal popularity, stemming from an unaffected simplicity of manner and an attractive personality.

Borein was friendly with many prominent artists of the day, as well as with such celebrities as Will Rogers and Theodore Roosevelt.

He died in 1945.

MEMBERSHIPS
Art Students League of New York City
Brooklyn Society of Etchers
Print Makers Society of California

PUBLIC COLLECTIONS
Gallery of Western Art,
    Montana Historical Society
New York Public Library, New York City

10-Year Average Change From Base Years '78-'79: 98%

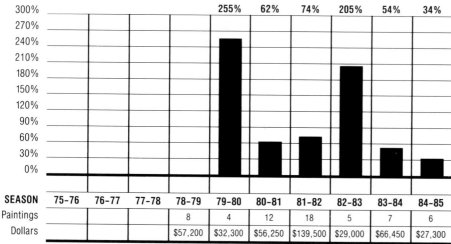

SEASON	75-76	76-77	77-78	78-79	79-80	80-81	81-82	82-83	83-84	84-85
					255%	62%	74%	205%	54%	34%
Paintings				8	4	12	18	5	7	6
Dollars				$57,200	$32,300	$56,250	$139,500	$29,000	$66,450	$27,300

Record Sale: $26,000, CH, 6/1/84, "Trail Boss," 15 × 20 in.

672

JOSEPH RAPHAEL
(1872-1950)

Although he spent much of his working life in Europe, Joseph Raphael was considered essentially a California painter because his work was exhibited there regularly. His early work was academic, very much in the vein of Dutch genre painting. Later he developed a style that was basically impressionist, but with elements of pointillism and expressionism as well. The result was paintings that brimmed with color and light.

Raphael was born in Jackson, California in 1872. He studied first at the California School of Design. Then, thanks in part to support from a wealthy patron, he went to Paris to study at the Ecole des Beaux Arts and the Academie Julien. During World War I, he spent part of the war years in Belgium and the rest in Holland.

He was thoroughly Europeanized by the end of the war and continued to live abroad, sending his paintings back to his agent in San Francisco. Besides oils, he also did watercolors, etchings, pen-and-ink drawings and wood-block prints.

Raphael's work was vigorous and fresh. In his floral paintings, for instance, details of individual flowers are overwhelmed in lavish explosions of color.

Just as in World War I he had been stranded in Europe, so Raphael was in San Francisco on a visit when World War II broke out in Europe and he had to remain in the United States. He con-

The Garden, ca. 1915, 28 x 30 in., signed l.l. Courtesy of John H. Garzoli Gallery, San Francisco, California.

tinued to live in San Francisco until his death in 1950.

PUBLIC COLLECTIONS
Fine Arts Museum of San Francisco

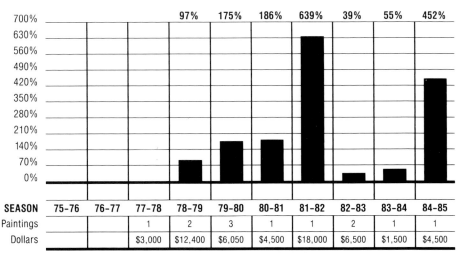

10-Year Average Change From Base Years '77-'78: 205%

SEASON	75-76	76-77	77-78	78-79	79-80	80-81	81-82	82-83	83-84	84-85
				97%	175%	186%	639%	39%	55%	452%
Paintings			1	2	3	1	1	2	1	1
Dollars			$3,000	$12,400	$6,050	$4,500	$18,000	$6,500	$1,500	$4,500

Record Sale: $18,000, BB.SF, 3/17/82, "Tulip Field," 26 x 31 in.

673

EDWARD DUFNER
(1872-1957)

A Morning in June, 14 x 14 in., signed l.r. Courtesy of Henry B. Holt, Inc., Essex Fells, New Jersey.

Along the Bay, 14 x 14 in., signed l.r. Courtesy of Henry B. Holt, Inc., Essex Fells, New Jersey.

Edward Dufner was an art instructor and prolific painter, whose work was critically recognized and widely displayed during his lifetime.

Born in Buffalo, New York in 1872, Dufner entered the Buffalo Art Students' League when he was 18 years old. Three years later, he received an Albright Scholarship, enabling him to move to New York City. He studied there and worked as a magazine illustrator for four years, before traveling to Paris.

During his five years abroad, Dufner traveled through England, France and Spain, and studied under Jean Paul Laurens and James McNeill Whistler. Whistler significantly influenced Dufner with his artistic balance and his unique color harmonies.

Dufner exhibited in the Paris Salon annually while he lived abroad. In 1900, he received the first Wanamaker prize at the American Art Association in Paris.

In 1903, Dufner became an instructor at the Art Students' League in Buffalo, where he taught for three years. As a teacher, he disdained academic art and conventional composition, focusing instead on encouraging individual expression in his students.

Dufner was elected an associate member of the National Academy of Design in 1910, and subsequently taught at the Art Students League in New York City, where he lived until his death in 1957.

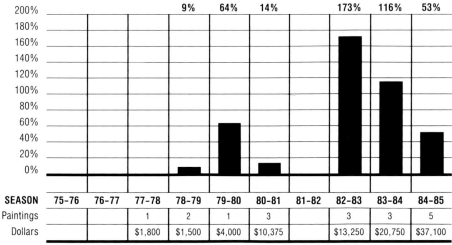

10-Year Average Change From Base Years '77-'78: 61%

SEASON	75-76	76-77	77-78	78-79	79-80	80-81	81-82	82-83	83-84	84-85
				9%	64%	14%		173%	116%	53%
Paintings			1	2	1	3		3	3	5
Dollars			$1,800	$1,500	$4,000	$10,375		$13,250	$20,750	$37,100

Record Sale: $18,000, D.NY, 10/24/84, "Evening Song," 40 × 50 in.

MEMBERSHIPS
Allied Artists of America
National Academy of Design
National Arts Club
New York Watercolor Club
Paris Allied Artists of America
Salmagundi Club

PUBLIC COLLECTIONS
Albright-Knox Art Gallery, Buffalo, New York
Milwaukee Art Museum, Wisconsin
National Academy of Design, New York City

HOWARD LOGAN HILDEBRANDT
(1872-1958)

Howard Hildebrandt was known primarily as a portrait painter, whose clients included many prominent politicians, business executives and intellectuals. The artist also painted a lesser number of still lifes, landscapes and genre paintings, in oil and watercolor.

Hildebrandt was born in 1872 in Allegheny, Pennsylvania, the son of a tailor. After receiving his early education in the Allegheny public schools, Hildebrandt studied painting at the National Academy of Design in New York City, at the L'Ecole des Beaux Arts in Paris, and at the Academie Julien in Paris under Benjamin Constant and Jean Paul Laurens.

In 1904, Hildebrandt returned to the United States. He maintained a studio in Pittsburgh until 1906, after which he worked primarily in New York City and New Canaan, Connecticut.

Hildebrandt's portraits are notable for their naturalistic modeling. His portrait of W.B. Thayer, chairman of the board of American Telephone and Telegraph, depicts the subject relaxing out-of-doors, seated in a lawn chair, before an impressionistic background dappled with sunlight.

Hildebrandt died in a rest home in Stamford, Connecticut at age 86 in 1958.

Eliot Clark, 1947, 32¼ x 25⅞ in., signed l.l. Courtesy of National Museum of American Art, Smithsonian Institution, Washington, D.C. Gift of Mrs. Eliot Clark.

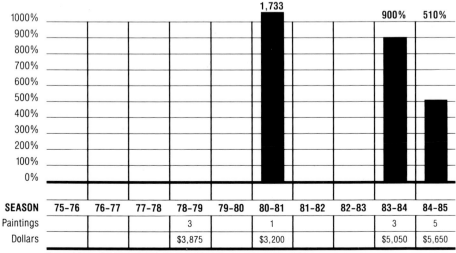

10-Year Average Change From Base Years '78-'79: 786%

SEASON	75-76	76-77	77-78	78-79	79-80	80-81	81-82	82-83	83-84	84-85
Paintings				3		1			3	5
Dollars				$3,875		$3,200			$5,050	$5,650

Record Sale: $3,500, S.BM, 11/17/83, "Esmeralda," 27 x 27 in.

MEMBERSHIPS
Allied Artists of America
American Federation of Arts
American Water Color Society
Artist's Fellowship, Inc.
Century Club
Lotus Club
National Arts Club
National Academy of Design
New York Water Color Society
Pittsburgh Art Association
Salmagundi Club
Society of Independent Artists

PUBLIC COLLECTIONS
Butler Art Institute, Youngstown, Ohio
Herron Art Institute, Indianapolis
Lotus Club, New York City
National Academy of Design, New York City

675

LOUIS KRONBERG
(1872-1964)

Louis Kronberg, popular portraitist of the early twentieth century, became best known for his specialty: pictures of the theater and its performers, particularly dancers and dancing.

Kronberg, who lived for many years in Paris, was born in 1872 in Boston. He attended the School of the Museum of Fine Arts in Boston, and the Art Students League in New York City, where he studied under William Merritt Chase.

A Longfellow traveling scholarship enabled him to study abroad for three years. From 1894 to 1897, he attended the Academie Julien in Paris, studying under Benjamin Constant, J.P. Laurens and Raphael Collin. In Paris, stimulated by the original works of the impressionists, he began to paint in a freer, lighter mode.

Kronberg's early oil paintings were in the academic mode, somewhat dark, with a subdued tonal effect. However, influenced by the techniques of James McNeill Whistler, the composition of Edgar Degas, and his own interest in oriental woodcuts and engravings, Kronberg evolved a new personal style—animated, dramatic, adventurous in design.

He worked increasingly in watercolors and pastels to create portraits and scenes of the ballet. A trip to Spain in 1921 and 1922 led to a renowned series of Spanish and Gypsy folk dancers, in watercolor, pastel and oil.

Popular well into the first third of the

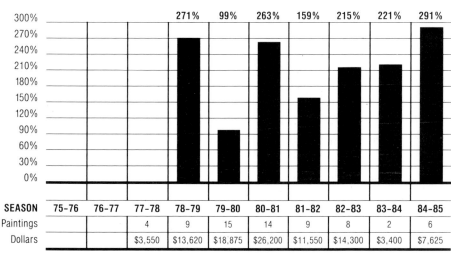

Before the Dance, 24 x 20 in., signed l.r. Courtesy of Maxwell Galleries, LTD., San Francisco, California.

twentieth century, Kronberg made portraits of many notables of the United States and Europe. His paintings were shown in important exhibitions and acquired by leading museums.

MEMBERSHIPS
American Water Color Society
Boston Art Club
Boston Society of Water Color Painters
Copley Society
London Pastel Society
New York Water Color Club
Society of Odd Brushes

PUBLIC COLLECTIONS
Albright-Knox Art Gallery, Buffalo
Butler Institute of American Art, Youngstown, Ohio
Isabella Stewart Gardner Museum, Boston
Indianapolis Museum of Art, Indianapolis
Metropolitan Museum of Art, New York City
Musee d'Orsay, Paris, France
Museum of Fine Arts, Boston
Pennsylvania Academy of the Fine Arts, Philadelphia
San Diego Museum of Art

10-Year Average Change From Base Years '77-'78: 190%

SEASON	75–76	76–77	77–78	78–79	79–80	80–81	81–82	82–83	83–84	84–85
				271%	99%	263%	159%	215%	221%	291%
Paintings			4	9	15	14	9	8	2	6
Dollars			$3,550	$13,620	$18,875	$26,200	$11,550	$14,300	$3,400	$7,625

Record Sale: $5,000, CH, 12/3/82, ''The Ballerina,'' 52 × 34 in.

676

ERNEST LAWSON
(1873-1939)

Ernest Lawson was an American impressionist who was attracted to such unconventional landscape subjects as squatters' huts, railroads and bridges across New York's Harlem River. He preferred landscapes to city streets and painted them in thick, smooth impasto, applied with a palette knife. His highly-personal use of color led one critic to comment that he seemed to paint from "a palette of crushed jewels."

Lawson was born in Nova Scotia in 1873, the son of a doctor. When his father went to practice in Kansas City, Missouri, young Lawson was left behind and raised by an aunt in Ontario.

He rejoined his parents in Kansas City when he was 15, and accompanied his father on a trip to Mexico in 1889. Once there, he worked as a draftsman and studied at the Santa Clara Art Academy in his spare time. This was followed by study at the Art Students League in New York City, and then by work in Connecticut with impressionists John Twachtman and J. Alden Weir.

Lawson also studied at the Academie Julien in Paris, but for most of his two-year stay in France, he painted on his own. While there he met Alfred Sisley, who advised him to be more assertive in his brushwork. For a time his work wavered between the conflicting influences of Sisley and Twachtman.

After settling in New York City, Lawson met Robert Henri and was invited to participate in the exhibition of The Eight

The Old Mill, 25 x 30 in., signed l.r. Courtesy of John H. Garzoli Gallery, San Francisco, California.

held in 1908. Lawson also was involved in planning the 1913 New York City Armory Show, where the work he exhibited brought him national recognition.

Like Monet, Lawson often selected a single subject and painted it in different lights and different weather conditions. Early on, he painted many such views of the Harlem River.

Troubled with arthritis in his later years, Lawson moved to Florida where he died in 1939.

MEMBERSHIPS
Century Association
National Academy of Design
National Arts Club
National Institute of Arts and Letters

PUBLIC COLLECTIONS
Art Gallery of Toronto
Art Institute of Chicago
Barnes Foundation, Merion, Pennsylvania
Brooklyn Museum
Corcoran Gallery of Art, Washington, D.C.
Delaware Art Museum, Wilmington
Detroit Institute of Arts
Metropolitan Museum of Art, New York City
Nelson-Atkins Museum of Art, Kansas City, Missouri
Whitney Museum of American Art, New York City

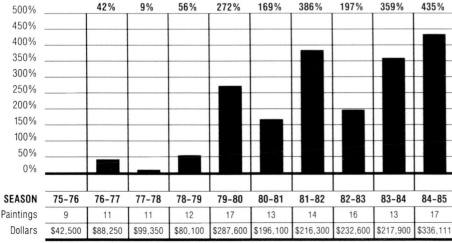

10-Year Average Change From Base Years '75-'76: 193%

	42%	9%	56%	272%	169%	386%	197%	359%	435%

SEASON	75-76	76-77	77-78	78-79	79-80	80-81	81-82	82-83	83-84	84-85
Paintings	9	11	11	12	17	13	14	16	13	17
Dollars	$42,500	$88,250	$99,350	$80,100	$287,600	$196,100	$216,300	$232,600	$217,900	$336,111

Record Sale: $110,000, CH, 12/7/84, "Across the Hudson to Yonkers," 25 × 30 in.

JACK WILKINSON SMITH
(1873-1949)

Jack Wilkinson Smith was one of the earliest and most successful painters of Southern Californian scenery. He is best known for his impressive depictions of valleys, mountains and seascapes.

Born in Paterson, New Jersey in 1873, Smith was the son of a painter. He studied at the Cincinnati Art Institute with Frank Duveneck, and at the Art Institute of Chicago.

Smith was a commercial artist before he became a fine artist. He worked as a scene painter in Chicago, and as a scene and sign painter in Lexington, Kentucky. As a staff artist for the *Cincinnati Enquirer,* in 1898 Smith won national recognition for his front-line sketches of the Spanish-American War. In 1906, he went to California and settled in Alhambra.

While Smith's early paintings were primarily watercolors of landscapes and figures, his later works were almost all oil landscapes. His style was impressionistic in the sense that he painted from life and emphasized the natural light, colors and atmosphere of the countryside. However, unlike the European impressionists' paintings, Smith's landscapes were more sharply defined by light and shadow. This caused them to have a somewhat photographic quality.

Smith was a very active member of the Southern Californian art community. He was a founding member of the California Art Club, the Laguna Beach Art

Thundering Surf, ca. 1925, 25 x 30 in., signed l.l. Courtesy of Petersen Galleries, Beverly Hills, California.

Association, and the Sketch Club. He was the recipient of numerous awards before his death in 1949.

MEMBERSHIPS
Allied Artists of America
California Art Club
California Water Color Society
Laguna Beach Art Association
Salmagundi Club

PUBLIC COLLECTIONS
Laguna Beach Museum of Art, California
Springville Museum of Art, Utah

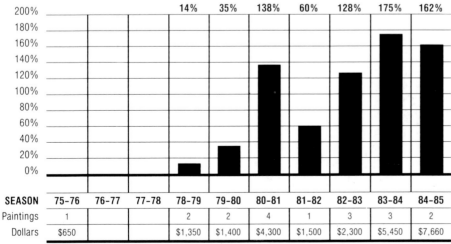

10-Year Average Change From Base Years '75-'76: 89%

				14%	35%	138%	60%	128%	175%	162%

SEASON	75-76	76-77	77-78	78-79	79-80	80-81	81-82	82-83	83-84	84-85
Paintings	1			2	2	4	1	3	3	2
Dollars	$650			$1,350	$1,400	$4,300	$1,500	$2,300	$5,450	$7,660

Record Sale: $7,000, CH, 3/15/85, "Mountain Trail," 28 x 34 in.

678

HOWARD CHANDLER CHRISTY
(1873-1952)

Women in Fanciful Garden Setting (open front), 66 x 72 in., signed l.r. Private Collection, Photograph courtesy of Kennedy Galleries, New York.

Howard Chandler Christy, while notable as a painter, achieved his greatest acclaim as a book and magazine illustrator. Christy exhibited tremendous range in his drawings—from action-filled wartime depictions to the rendering of a woman who would become the prototype of femininity in the early 1900s.

Christy left his native Ohio in 1893, at age 20, to study under William Merritt Chase at the Art Students League in New York City. He chose illustration as his artistic focus.

Christy's trip to Cuba in 1898, and his subsequent action renderings of Theodore Roosevelt's "Rough Riders" in the Spanish-American War, first brought him recognition. The drawings, along with Christy's narrative, were published in *Scribner's Magazine.* The military motif was also exhibited in a later series, "Men of the Army and Navy."

It was not long before Christy was a regular artistic contributor to the most popular publications of his day, among them *Harper's Magazine* and *Collier's Weekly.* In these periodicals, Christy introduced a feminine figure of striking beauty and luminescence; known as the "Christy Girl," she captured the style and standard of a decade.

During that period, Christy's work was not solely restricted to magazines.

He also illustrated books by James Whitcomb Riley and Richard Harding Davis.

From 1920 until his death in New York City in 1952, Christy turned his attention to portrait painting. Many of his subjects were notable contemporaries, including aviator Amelia Earhart, Prince Humbert of Italy, and the wife of newspaper magnate William Randolph Hearst.

One of Christy's most impressive and ambitious works, *Signing of the Constitution* (date unknown), is hung in the House of Representatives of the United States Capitol in Washington.

MEMBERSHIPS
Society of Illustrators

PUBLIC COLLECTIONS
United States Capitol, Washington, D.C.

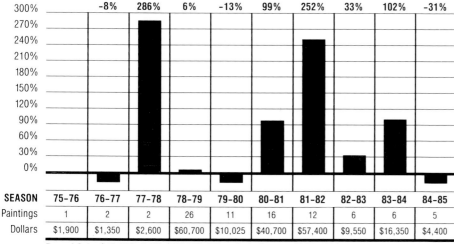

10-Year Average Change From Base Years '75-'76: 73%

	-8%	286%	6%	-13%	99%	252%	33%	102%	-31%

SEASON	75-76	76-77	77-78	78-79	79-80	80-81	81-82	82-83	83-84	84-85
Paintings	1	2	2	26	11	16	12	6	6	5
Dollars	$1,900	$1,350	$2,600	$60,700	$10,025	$40,700	$57,400	$9,550	$16,350	$4,400

Record Sale: $19,000, D.NY, 4/21/82, "Nymphs in Summer," 24 × 28 in.

LOUIS BETTS
(1873-1961)

Louis Betts is known for his sensitive portraits of prominent individuals in public and professional life. In a long and productive career that began with his first painting at age 14, Betts did portraits of Hamlin Garland, Booth Tarkington, George Eastman, the Mayo brothers and many others in Chicago, New York and Europe.

Born in 1873 in Little Rock, Arkansas, Betts grew up in Chicago. He was the son of a landscape painter, who gave him his first artistic training. He was nearly 30 when he enrolled in the Pennsylvania Academy of the Fine Arts to study for a year under William Merritt Chase.

In 1902, the Academy awarded Betts a travel fellowship and he left for Europe to travel and study art, particularly the work of Hals and Velasquez. Betts stayed in Holland and Spain for several years, engaged in a lucrative portrait business based on contacts provided by Chase.

On his return to the United States, Betts found himself in constant demand as a portraitist. He devoted himself very seriously to this art form, never deviating into other channels or following up the landscape painting he had done earlier. In the next 25 years, he produced a succession of important portraits of men, women and children, many of which won awards from major art institutions in the United States.

Demoiselle Barthe, 32 x 24 in., signed u.l. Courtesy of Grand Central Art Galleries, Inc., New York, New York.

Betts possessed an extraordinary ability to portray character. The personality of his subject radiates from the canvas through the gleam in the eyes and the posture of the body, as though the person were present in the room. That presence is no accident of talent; Betts's stated ambition was to capture the physical and spiritual character of his subjects, and he would labor for hours to absorb and convey those features.

Betts and his wife, also an artist, lived in a heady world in Chicago and New York City, on intimate terms with other artistic celebrities. Betts was a violinist and an avid fisherman, drawing inspiration from his retreats into nature. He died in 1961.

MEMBERSHIPS
National Academy of Design
National Art Club
National Institute of Arts and Letters
Salmagundi Club
Union League Club

PUBLIC COLLECTIONS
Art Institute of Chicago
Corcoran Gallery, Washington, D.C.
Little Rock Art Museum, Arkansas
Mayo Foundation, Rochester, Minnesota
Toledo Museum, Ohio

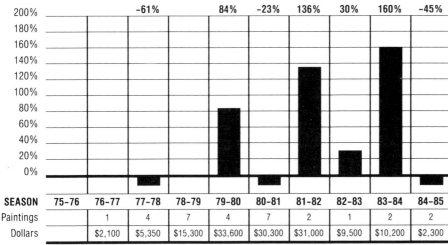

10-Year Average Change From Base Years '76-'77: 31%

SEASON	75-76	76-77	77-78	78-79	79-80	80-81	81-82	82-83	83-84	84-85
			-61%		84%	-23%	136%	30%	160%	-45%
Paintings		1	4	7	4	7	2	1	2	2
Dollars		$2,100	$5,350	$15,300	$33,600	$30,300	$31,000	$9,500	$10,200	$2,300

Record Sale: $25,000, SPB, 12/10/81, "Ladies in the Garden," 40 × 30 in.

LOUIS AGASSIZ FUERTES
(1874-1927)

Louis Agassiz Fuertes is considered to be the foremost American illustrator of birds, surpassing even John James Audubon.

Named after the great naturalist of the nineteenth century, Louis Agassiz of Harvard, Fuertes was born in Ithaca, New York in 1874. He graduated from the College of Architecture at Cornell University in 1897. Rather than pursue the engineering career his father had intended for him, he went on to study art with Abbot Thayer.

In addition to illustrating numerous books, pamphlets and magazines, including several series in *National Geographic,* Fuertes prepared habitat groups for the American Museum of Natural History in New York City and painted murals. He is best known for his series of plates entitled *The Birds of New York* (1910), which includes most species native to Eastern North America. At the time of his death in 1927, Fuertes was at work on a complementary series entitled *The Birds of Massachusetts.*

The material for Fuertes's illustrations was drawn from his ornithological expeditions throughout North America, Mexico, Colombia, the West Indies, Europe and Africa. The life studies of birds made during his 1926 expedition to Ethiopia, sponsored by the Field Museum of Natural History in Chicago, are among his best work.

Fuertes's meteoric career was the result of his extraordinary ability to observe and re-create from memory all aspects of a bird's appearance and behavior. Ornithologists praised his illustrations for their accurate representation of anatomy and pose, while others drew attention to their strength of composition and effective use of color and light. His work amply demonstrates his extensive knowledge of birds and their environs, his fidelity to nature and his

Bald Eagle Juvenile. Photograph courtesy of the Brandywine River Museum, Chadds Ford, Pennsylvania, Collection of Laboratory of Ornithology, Cornell University.

great technical skills, as well as his particular gift of investing these technical studies with a sensitive and subjective sense of a bird's individual characteristics.

PUBLIC COLLECTIONS
Academy of Natural Sciences, Philadelphia
American Museum of Natural History,
  New York City
Field Museum of Natural History, Chicago
New York State Museum, Albany

SEASON	75-76	76-77	77-78	78-79	79-80	80-81	81-82	82-83	83-84	84-85
Paintings				2				1	2	1
Dollars				$2,650				$1,000	$15,800	$14,000

Record Sale: $15,000, SPB, 1/27/84, ''Northern Phalarope; Flickers,'' 8 × 13 in.

FRANCIS JOHN McCOMAS
(1874-1938)

Francis McComas was an Australian-born painter who came to be regarded as one of the best watercolorists in the United States during the early twentieth century. Although he is remembered chiefly as a painter of the American Southwest, McComas also traveled and painted many works in Europe, Mexico and the South Seas.

McComas was born in Tasmania, and educated at the Sydney Technical Institute. He came to America in 1898, studying briefly with Arthur Matthews at the San Francisco School of Design. In 1899, he traveled to Paris for an additional year of study at the Academie Julien.

In 1907, McComas painted studies in Greece, and exhibited them to critical praise in London the following year. Returning to the United States, the artist began painting his landscapes of the American Southwest, for which he soon became well known. Some of his better-known subjects from this period include the mesas of New Mexico, scenes from Navajo country and California oaks and gnarled cypresses.

McComas participated in the 1913 New York Armory Show, and was appointed a jurist for the art competition of the 1915 Panama-Pacific Exposition held in San Francisco. Although best known for his American landscapes, he is said to have produced some of his best works on trips to Tahiti in 1927, Spain in 1928 and Mexico in 1932 and 1935.

McComas's work sold readily and at good prices throughout his career. Among his better-known commissions were works painted for the Metropolitan Museum of Art in New York, and for the private collections of Marshall Field and Irenee Dupont. The artist remained professionally active until his death in Monterey, California in 1938.

Hawaii, 1898, 14½ x 20¾ in., signed l.r. Courtesy of John H. Garzoli Gallery, San Francisco, California.

MEMBERSHIPS
American Water Color Society
Bohemian Club of San Francisco
Philadelphia Water Color Club

PUBLIC COLLECTIONS
Metropolitan Museum of Art, New York City
Portland Art Society, Oregon

SEASON	75-76	76-77	77-78	78-79	79-80	80-81	81-82	82-83	83-84	84-85
Paintings					2		7		2	
Dollars					$1,850		$37,100		$2,117	

Record Sale: $18,000, BB.SF, 10/3/81, "Monterey, California," 42 × 61 in.

FREDERICK CARL FRIESEKE
(1874-1939)

Frederick Carl Frieseke was one of the leading American impressionists. Until the early 1930s, the expatriate's international reputation was such that he was called "America's best-known contemporary painter." His relative anonymity today is due to the prettiness and sentimentality of his canvases; his work fell out of favor because his subject matter was considered cloying by post-World War I sensibilities.

Born in Owasso, Michigan in 1874, Frieseke went to France in 1898. He remained there until his death in 1939. Though Frieseke preferred to say that he was self-taught, he actually studied at the Art Institute of Chicago and the Art Students League in New York City before entering the French Academie Julien.

It was the study of the work of other artists that enriched Frieseke, rather than the academic routine. He spent time in the atelier of Constant and Laurens, and in Paris received criticism from James Abbott McNeill Whistler. Whistler's influence can be seen in Frieseke's dark, early work. The contemporary art nouveau movement, with its strong linear emphasis and decorative style, was a continuing influence on his paintings.

In 1906, Frieske moved to Giverny, where Monet was his neighbor. Under the influence of Monet, Frieseke began to use the prismatic, rich color spectrum of the impressionists in garden and inte-

The Blue Garden, 32 x 32 in. Photograph courtesy of Hirschl & Adler Galleries, Inc., New York, New York.

rior scenes. His choice of subject matter was more similar to Renoir's, though: voluptuous, sensuous female nudes.

But Frieseke borrowed from the post-impressionists as well, by enveloping his figures in patterns made by colored flowers, garden furniture and sunlight. *Lady Trying on a Hat* (1909, Art Institute of Chicago) and *On The Bank* (ca. 1915, Art Institute of Chicago) exemplify his technique.

Frieseke's adopted impressionist style never compromised his solid sense of composition. He was apt to unify the whole with a dominant color, as in *The Yellow Room* (date and location unknown). Another example is the lavender hue that permeates every other

color in *Memories, 1915* (location unknown).

In particular, Frieseke was fascinated by the effects of sunlight. In a 1914 interview he said, "It is sunshine, flowers in sunshine, girls in sunshine, the nude in sunshine, which I have been principally interested in. . . ."

He thought of himself as a realist, reproducing on canvas what he saw in nature. However, some of his contemporaries regarded his paintings as "tea cakes," or "confections."

Frieseke enjoyed acclaim during his life. His paintings were purchased for the French National Collection, and he was represented at the Venice Bienniale with 17 pictures. He was commissioned to paint several large murals for buildings in New York City and Atlantic City. At the Panama-Pacific International Exposition of 1915 in San Francisco, Frieseke received the grand prize.

MEMBERSHIPS
National Academy of Design
Societe National des Beaux Arts, Paris
Paris Art Association
New York Water Color Club
Chevalier of the Legion of Honor

PUBLIC COLLECTIONS
Art Institute of Chicago
Cincinnati Art Museum
Corcoran Gallery of Art, Washington, D.C.
Los Angeles County Museum of Art
Metropolitan Museum of Art, New York City
Minneapolis Institute of Arts, Minnesota
Musee d'Orsay, Paris
Museum of Odessa, Soviet Union
Telfair Academy of Arts and Sciences,
   Savannah, Georgia

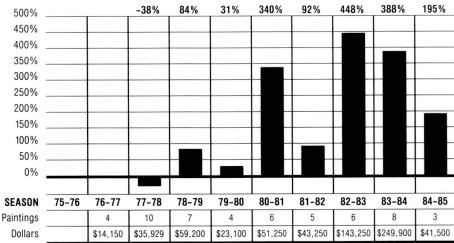

10-Year Average Change From Base Years '76-'77: 171%

		-38%	84%	31%	340%	92%	448%	388%	195%

SEASON	75-76	76-77	77-78	78-79	79-80	80-81	81-82	82-83	83-84	84-85
Paintings		4	10	7	4	6	5	6	8	3
Dollars		$14,150	$35,929	$59,200	$23,100	$51,250	$43,250	$143,250	$249,900	$41,500

Record Sale: $85,000, CH, 6/1/84, "Woman Sewing in Garden," 28 × 36 in.

683

FRANK TENNEY JOHNSON
(1874-1939)

Frank Tenney Johnson was one of the most successful early-twentieth-century frontier painters and illustrators. He specialized in painting cowboys, Indians and early settlers.

Born in 1874, Johnson apprenticed himself at age 14 to panoramic painter F.W. Heine in Milwaukee. A year later, Johnson was greatly influenced while studying under Richard Lorenz.

Johnson then painted portraits and worked on the staff of a Milwaukee newspaper. In 1902, he went to New York City and studied under Robert Henri at the Art Students League. He soon became a newspaper and fashion artist.

The desire to return West never left him, and after improving his skills, he settled on a ranch in Colorado, where he painted the Western subjects he liked best.

Johnson's Western work began receiving notice from New York City publishers. He established himself as a successful illustrator for magazines and for books by such prominent writers as Zane Grey.

In the 1920s, Johnson and his friend Clyde Forsythe formed a studio which attracted many noted artists, including Charles Russell, Ed Borein, Dean Cornwell and Norman Rockwell. During this era, Johnson and Forsythe founded the Biltmore Art Gallery in the Biltmore Hotel in Los Angeles.

Johnson, who won numerous awards

Don, The Horse Wrangler, 1935, 24 x 30 in., signed l.l. Collection of S. Hallock duPont, Jr., Photograph courtesy of Kennedy Galleries, New York, New York.

during his career, was celebrated for his paintings of cowboys under stars; his treatment was termed the Johnson "moonlight technique."

His career was ended in 1939, when he died of spinal meningitis. He had contracted the disease from kissing his hostess at a dinner party; both died within two weeks.

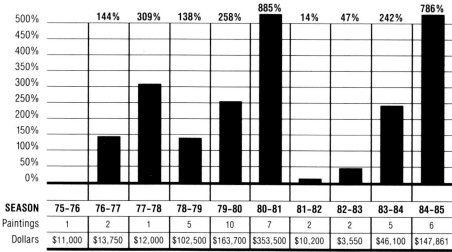

10-Year Average Change From Base Years '75-'76: 282%

SEASON	75–76	76–77	77–78	78–79	79–80	80–81	81–82	82–83	83–84	84–85
		144%	309%	138%	258%	885%	14%	47%	242%	786%
Paintings	1	2	1	5	10	7	2	2	5	6
Dollars	$11,000	$13,750	$12,000	$102,500	$163,700	$353,500	$10,200	$3,550	$46,100	$147,861

Record Sale: $120,000, SPB, 10/17/80, "Pack Horses from Rim Rock Ranch," 36 × 46 in.

MEMBERSHIPS
American Federation of Artists
Allied Artists of America
American Water Color Society
California Art Club
Laguna Beach Art Association
National Academy of Design
New York Water Color Club
Painters of the West
Salmagundi Club
Society of Painters

PUBLIC COLLECTIONS
Dallas Art Association
Fort Worth Art Center, Texas
National Gallery of Art, Washington, D.C.
Phoenix Museum of Art, Arizona

684

FRANCIS LUIS MORA
(1874-1940)

Francis Luis Mora, son of one painter and sculptor and brother of another, was an illustrator, muralist and portraitist whose work reflects a blend of Spanish and modern-American influences.

Mora was born in 1874 in Uruguay. His father, Domingo Mora, was a well-known artist who gave Mora his early artistic training. The family moved to the United States, and Mora attended school in New Jersey, New York City and Boston. He studied drawing and painting under Frank Benson and Edmund Tarbell at the Boston Museum of Fine Arts School; later he studied under H. Siddons Mowbray at the Art Students League in New York City. He also traveled to Europe to study the great paintings of the old masters.

By age 18, Mora was illustrating for leading periodicals. He began exhibiting two years later, and in 1900 he received a commission for a mural in the public library of Lynn, Massachusetts. In 1904, he painted the Missouri State Building mural for the Louisiana Purchase Exposition in St. Louis. He also painted portraits of Andrew Carnegie and President Warren G. Harding; the latter hangs in the White House.

Mora worked in oil, watercolor, charcoal and pastel; in addition, he produced etchings and sculpture. His subjects were generally interiors, seascapes and landscapes with figures. Like Tarbell and Benson, Mora captured the flavor of leisured life, particularly in outdoor scenes. He also painted Indian and Western scenes (his brother, Joseph Jacinto Mora, also received considerable recognition for his paintings and sculptures of Western subjects).

Mora taught at the Art Students League, the Grand Central School of Art and the New York School of Art, all in New York City. He died in 1940.

Mrs. Francis Luis Mora (Sophia Brown Compton), ca. 1900, 84 x 41½ in., signed l.r. Courtesy of Kennedy Galleries, New York, New York.

MEMBERSHIPS
Allied Artists of America
American Federation of Arts
American Water Color Society
Architectural League of New York
Art Students League
Ceramic Society
National Academy of Design
National Arts Club
National Association of Portrait Painters
New York Water Color Club
Salmagundi Club
Society of American Artists
Society of American Etchers
Society of Illustrators

PUBLIC COLLECTIONS
Butler Institute of American Art,
   Youngstown, Ohio
Museum of Modern Art,
   New York City
National Academy of Design,
   New York City
National Gallery of Canada, Ottawa
Newark Museum, New Jersey
Oakland Museum, California
Toledo Museum of Art, Ohio
White House, Washington, D.C.

SEASON	75-76	76-77	77-78	78-79	79-80	80-81	81-82	82-83	83-84	84-85
Paintings		3	3	6	9	14	19	10	8	4
Dollars		$12,100	$6,100	$13,990	$9,500	$52,950	$50,500	$21,620	$13,800	$4,350

Record Sale: $15,000, D.NY, 9/24/80, "The Sun Screen," 48 × 36 in.

JOHN F. CARLSON
(1874-1945)

Across the Meadow, 18 x 24 in., signed l.r. Courtesy of Henry B. Holt, Inc., Essex Fells, New Jersey.

Prolific nature painter John F. Carlson is recognized as one of America's foremost landscape artists. As founder of the John F. Carlson School of Landscape Painting, he was known for teaching his students to juxtapose tone, light and shadow to reflect the myriad moods of nature.

His work was characterized by crisp form, intense color and complex webs of swirling shapes. The overall effect was realistic.

Carlson acquired a predilection for trees and winter as a child in Kalmar Lan, Sweden, a sylvan land of snow-crested mountains. His early interest in art developed as he gazed, transfixed, while his uncle painted idyllic landscapes.

The family immigrated to America when Carlson was 10 or 11. They settled first in Brooklyn, New York, where Carlson attended public schools, and then in Buffalo. Carlson's afterschool hours were often spent sketching scenes of Sweden from memory.

To support his son's interest in art, Carlson's father hired a private tutor, John Mayer, who provided lessons in life drawing and nature sketching. Carlson later attended Buffalo's Albright Art School, where he trained under Lucius Hitchcock.

In 1902, Carlson was awarded a scholarship to study at the Art Students League in New York City. His instructors were Frank V. Dumond and Birge

Harrison. Harrison became not only Carlson's mentor, but a good friend. In 1903, Carlson received his first honor, the Ralph Radcliffe Whitehead Prize.

The same year, Harrison was asked to teach at Byrdcliffe, a newly-founded arts and crafts community in Woodstock, New York, and Carlson was granted a scholarship to the school. Woodstock was at first enchanting to the young student, but the regimented lifestyle of the community was anathema to Carlson's creativity; he re-established quarters in nearby Rock City, New York.

In 1906, Carlson came back to Woodstock as Harrison's assistant. Three years later, he held his first one-man show at Katz Gallery in New York City. In 1911, he was elected an associate of the National Academy of Design and also became director of the Art Students League summer school, a position he held until 1918.

Carlson traveled through the United States, capturing its beauty on canvas, before returning to Woodstock in 1922 to found his own school. He often spent hours painting in sub-freezing conditions without mittens. During this period, he also helped found the Broadmoor Art Academy in Colorado Springs.

The years after Carlson's reappearance at Woodstock were busy, fruitful and happy. In 1925, he was made a full academician of the National Academy. Three years later, he completed his famous book, *Elementary Principles of Landscape Painting,* later changed to *Carlson's Guide to Landscape Painting.*

Carlson continued his painting and teaching careers in Woodstock, New York City, the Canadian Rockies and Gloucester, Massachusetts until his death in 1945.

MEMBERSHIPS
American Artists Professional League
American Water Color Society
Connecticut Academy of Fine Arts
National Academy of Design
National Arts Club
Painters and Sculptors Gallery Association
Salmagundi Club
Washington Water Color Club

PUBLIC COLLECTIONS
Art Association, Lincoln, Nebraska
Baltimore Museum
Brooks Memorial Gallery, Memphis, Tennessee
Butler Art Institute, Youngstown, Ohio
Carnegie Institute, Pittsburgh
Corcoran Gallery, Washington, D.C.
Fort Worth Art Association, Texas
Metropolitan Museum of Art, New York City
Montclair Art Museum, New Jersey
National Academy of Design, New York City
Randolph-Macon Women's College, Lynchburg, Virginia
Toledo Museum of Art, Ohio
Virginia Museum of Fine Arts, Richmond

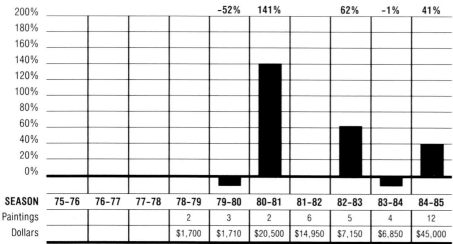

10-Year Average Change From Base Years '78-'79: 27%

| | -52% | 141% | | 62% | -1% | 41% |

SEASON	75-76	76-77	77-78	78-79	79-80	80-81	81-82	82-83	83-84	84-85
Paintings				2	3	2	6	5	4	12
Dollars				$1,700	$1,710	$20,500	$14,950	$7,150	$6,850	$45,000

Record Sale: $13,000, D.NY, 9/24/80, "Spring Thaw," 30 x 40 in.

JOSEPH CHRISTIAN LEYENDECKER
(1874-1951)

Joseph Christian (J.C.) Leyendecker generated a rich heritage of Americana by illustrating hundreds of magazine covers. From 1899 to 1943, he painted 322 covers for the *Saturday Evening Post*. His original symbol for the New Year, a cherubic baby, was immortalized on *Post* covers. Creator of some of the most popular advertisements and poster designs of his time, he was regarded as one of America's most talented illustrators.

Born in 1874 in the German village of Montabour, Leyendecker and his family emigrated to Chicago when he was nine. His brother, Frank Xavier Leyendecker, was also an artist; later they studied and worked together.

At age 16, Leyendecker, who had busied himself since age eight painting on oilcloth, landed an unpaid apprentice's job at J. Manz & Company, a Chicago engraving house. Soon he earned two dollars weekly as artist/errand boy, which enabled him to attend the Art Institute at night. He studied for five years with John H. Vanderpoel. At age 20, he completed 60 illustrations for an edition of the Bible, published in 1894.

Leyendecker made an outstanding impression in Paris, where the brothers studied at the Academie Julien in 1896 and 1897. He was awarded four prizes by the Academie, and in 1897 had a one-man exhibition at the Salon Champs du

Baby Mechanic, 1925, 28 x 20 in. Photograph courtesy of Borghi & Co. Fine Art Dealers, New York, New York.

Mars. Undoubtedly, the Parisian period was important in forming the distinct Leyendecker style.

Recognition as a successful poster designer came when Leyendecker's

poster won *The Century* magazine's 1896 contest; well-known Maxfield Parrish placed second.

J.C. Leyendecker had great versatility, varying his themes to play upon sentiments of the occasion. His abandoned, spontaneous freedom of style accentuated the muscles of the young men in his posters. He created the popular "Arrow Collar Man" advertisement in 1905; it was followed by work for many well-known companies.

He did covers for *Collier's, The American Weekly* and *Inland Printer*. His work during the World Wars included allegorical posters from 1917 to 1919 and a series of war bond posters in 1944.

A private person who shied from publicity, J.C. Leyendecker died in New Rochelle, New York in 1951.

MEMBERSHIPS
Salmagundi Club

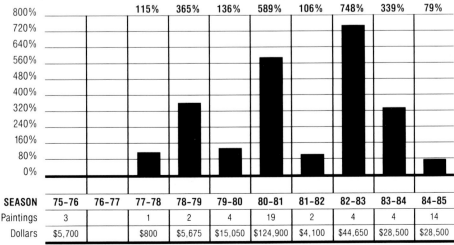

10-Year Average Change From Base Years '75-'76: 275%

	75-76	76-77	77-78	78-79	79-80	80-81	81-82	82-83	83-84	84-85
			115%	365%	136%	589%	106%	748%	339%	79%
SEASON	75-76	76-77	77-78	78-79	79-80	80-81	81-82	82-83	83-84	84-85
Paintings	3		1	2	4	19	2	4	4	14
Dollars	$5,700		$800	$5,675	$15,050	$124,900	$4,100	$44,650	$28,500	$28,500

Record Sale: $26,000, P.NY, 4/2/81, "Yule," 30 × 22 in.

OSCAR E. BERNINGHAUS
(1874-1952)

Oscar Edmund Berninghaus worked successfully as both a fine artist and a commercial artist during most of his life. He divided his time between his hometown of St. Louis, Missouri and Taos, New Mexico. As one of the founders of the Taos Society of Artists, he believed that the Southwest, and Taos in particular, would figure prominently in the development of a uniquely American art.

Berninghaus trained as a lithographer for a large St. Louis printing firm, while taking night art classes at Washington University and the St. Louis School of Fine Arts.

At age 25, while on vacation, he discovered Taos in a most unorthodox manner: from the top of a railroad car. Fascinated by Berninghaus's station-side sketches, a railroad employee had arranged for a chair to be lashed to the train's roof, to afford Berninghaus an unparalleled view of the New Mexico landscape.

Often compared to Western painters Charles M. Russell and Frederic Remington, Berninghaus was best known for his paintings of horses and Indians. He painted the Indians of Taos in natural, unsentimentalized settings, revealing an understanding of their life in a twentieth-century world. In his paintings, man never occupied a dominant position relative to the natural landscape, and in later years

Indians Returning to Taos (after Trading Expedition), 30 x 36 in., signed l.r. Photograph courtesy of The Gerald Peters Gallery, Santa Fe, New Mexico.

Berninghaus still further reduced man's participation in his scenes.

As an independent commercial artist, Berninghaus was most successful with the advertisements he illustrated for the Anheuser-Busch Brewery. Berninghaus called this work "common commercialism," but it is now known as the Berninghaus collection, 50 of his works donated by the Busch family to the St. Louis City Art Museum.

In the 1920s, Berninghaus moved to Taos permanently, changing his style somewhat to employ deeper pigmentation and more complicated composition. As he grew older, he abandoned his camping and sketching trips in favor of painting from memory. Because of the flux of colors in spring and fall, Berninghaus most often used those seasons for his landscapes.

He died in Taos in 1952.

MEMBERSHIPS
National Academy of Design
2 x 4 Club
Salmagundi Club
St. Louis Art Guild
Taos Art Association
Taos Society of Artists
Taos Students' Association

PUBLIC COLLECTIONS
Anschutz Collection, Denver
City Art Museum, St. Louis
Cowboy Hall of Fame, Oklahoma City
Erie Museum, Pennsylvania
Fort Worth Museum, Texas
Gilcrease Institute of Art, Tulsa
Harrison Eiteljorg Collection, Indianapolis
Los Angeles County Museum
Museum of New Mexico, Santa Fe
San Diego Museum

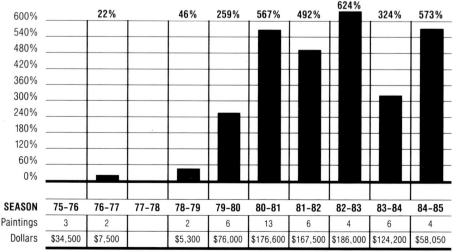

10-Year Average Change From Base Years '75-'76: 323%

SEASON	75-76	76-77	77-78	78-79	79-80	80-81	81-82	82-83	83-84	84-85
(% change)		22%		46%	259%	567%	492%	624%	324%	573%
Paintings	3	2		2	6	13	6	4	6	4
Dollars	$34,500	$7,500		$5,300	$76,000	$176,600	$167,500	$186,000	$124,200	$58,050

Record Sale: $75,000, SPB, 4/23/82, "Domain of Their Ancestors," 25 × 30 in.

A

Abstraction. Art which makes no direct, immediately discernible reference to recognizable objects. In abstract art, the formal arrangement of colors and forms is independent of, and more important than, the subject matter.

Academic. Pertaining to the arts as taught in academies and schools of art according to established rules. Since the high tide of conservatism in the late nineteenth century, the term has become synonymous with traditional thinking and opposition to fresh and innovative ideas in art.

Acrylic. A widely used water-based polymer paint. Because of its chemical composition, it combines the characteristics of traditional oil and watercolor paints and can be used for washes and for heavy impasto. It is relatively odorless, quick-drying and extremely resistant to deterioration.

Action painting. The vigorous, often improvisatory, gestural slash and drip paintings made most notably by Jackson Pollock, Willem de Kooning and Hans Hofmann. The term is often used to describe the entire abstract expressionist movement, including the more consciously planned canvases of Mark Rothko, Barnett Newman and others.

Aquatint. Like etching, a method of engraving which uses acid to eat into a metal plate. Unlike etching, however, it is a tone, rather than a line, process. The porous ground of the plate allows the acid to form a network of extremely fine lines, creating transparent effects comparable to those of watercolor painting.

Armory Show. The International Exhibition of Modern Art held in 1913 at the 69th Regiment Armory in New York City and later in Boston and Chicago. It introduced avant-garde European and contemporary American painting to the American public and critics. Enormous in scope (approximately 1,600 paintings) and highly controversial, it proved to be the turning point in the development and appreciation of modern art in the United States.

Art Institute of Chicago. Established in 1879 as an art school, it has grown into one of the major art institutions of the United States. Approximately 4,000 students attend its classes annually. Its collections—particularly of Spanish, Flemish, Dutch, French and American paintings and of Near Eastern and oriental decorative arts—place it among the outstanding museums of the world.

Art nouveau. A decorative linear style which appeared in all media throughout Europe and in the United States at the end of the nineteenth century. Characterized by sinuously curving organic forms, it was often used to depict mysterious landscapes, women and symbolist subjects.

Ashcan School. The work of a group of late-nineteenth- and early-twentieth-century realist American painters who, disdaining the prevailing aestheticism of the academics, determined to bring painting back into touch with the life of the common man. Often collectively called The Eight, they depicted the seamy life of the streets, taverns and prize-fight rings, thus gaining the distinctly derogatory designation of their school.

Assemblage. Mixed-media combinations of found objects (rather than traditional art objects of paint, canvas, carved stone and cast bronze). Primarily assembled, rather than painted, modeled or carved, these works question the nature of art and often break down the traditional distinctions between painting and sculpture.

B

Barbizon. The style developed by a group of landscape painters in mid-nineteenth-century France who lived and worked in Barbizon, a village on the edge of the forest of Fountainebleau. Opposed to the prevailing classical conventions of landscape painting, they strove to depict peasant life and the surrounding country-side exactly as it was, without prettification. The best-known of the group were Millet and Rousseau.

Baroque. An opulent style, religious in origin, that prevailed in the Roman Catholic countries of Europe, particularly in France and Italy, from the end of the sixteenth century until the early eighteenth century. In its truest form it was a union of architecture, painting and sculpture, all designed to evoke a strong emotional response. Through skillful use of substance, light, color and texture, baroque artists sought to create an illusion of the actuality and truth of a subject.

Bauhaus. A utopian school founded in 1919 in Weimar, Germany to promote the unity of the arts and harmony between craftsmanship and artistry in a modern technological society. The school moved to Dessau in 1925, was closed by Hitler in 1933, and has been continued in the United States at Harvard University and the Illinois Institute of Technology. The teachings of Josef Albers, first at the Black Mountain School and later at Yale University, promoted the Bauhaus ideal.

Blaue Reiter (Blue Rider). A pre-World War I artistic alliance established in Munich in 1911, it was founded by Vasily Kandinsky and Franz Marc, who also published the *Blaue Reiter Almanac*. The style of the group, which turned toward the symbolic semi-abstraction of bold and strident color, was used by American painter Marsden Hartley for his "German Officer" series. Together with Die Bruecke (the Bridge), established in Dresden in 1905, the Blaue Reiter composed the foundations of German expressionism.

Boston School. A group of American impressionist painters who studied or worked in Boston around 1900, several of whom were also members of The Ten. The dominant figures were Edmund C. Tarbell and Frank W. Benson. Although impressionist landscape paintings were popular in Boston as early as the late 1880s, the impressionist figure paintings of the Boston School were not well received there until after 1900.

Brandywine School. Initially a term used to denote the work of Howard Pyle and the many illustrators he taught and influenced through his hand-picked classes in Wilmington, Delaware and Chadds Ford, Pennsylvania, both located on the Brandywine River. Because several of the progeny of N.C. Wyeth, perhaps Pyle's best-known student, have continued to live in the area and paint in a distinctive representational manner, the term now has come also to include succeeding generations of the Wyeth family, most notably Andrew Wyeth, and similarly influenced local painters as well.

C

Ca. Abbreviation for circa, meaning "about" or "approximately."

Century Association. An organization founded in New York City in 1847 when members of the Sketch Club asked 100 men (hence the name) to form a new club oriented toward the arts. Its membership now includes educators and other professionals in addition to practicing artists. Its clubhouse, which includes galleries for frequent exhibitions, is at 7 West 43rd Street in Manhattan.

Chromolithography. A method of surface-printing lithographs in many colors which involves no engraving. A different stone or plate is used for each color and each is printed in exact register with the others. It is widely used, particularly for posters and other forms of commercial art.

Classical. A term used to describe art which conforms to the standards and principles established in ancient Greece and Rome. Generally speaking, such work is characterized by its simplicity, symmetry and dignity.

Color field. Organic, sensuous and joyous abstract painting developed in the United States during the 1960s in which color is both the form and the subject (also identified with post-painterly abstraction). The very large, fluid, stained or sprayed areas of color often allude to landscapes; some of them seem devoid of passion or emotional expression.

Constructivism. A radical movement begun in Russia by 1917 by the brothers Naum Gabo and Antoine Pevsner, who used industrial materials in three-dimensional sculpture. Transplanted to Paris and Germany, it was picked up by American artists; its formal anti-expressionism dominated American abstract art of the early 1930s.

Conte crayon. A proprietary name for a man-made chalk which is widely used in sketching. It is available in black, brown and red and was named for Nicholas Conte, who developed the first lead pencil in 1790.

Cos Cob, Connecticut. One of several communal art colonies which were developed by plein-air American impressionists in picturesque locales accessible by railroad (and later by automobile) from New York City. Other such colonies included Old Lyme, Connecticut, Appledore, Isle of Shoals, New Hampshire, and the Shinnecock Hills of Long Island, New York.

Cubism. A style which originated in the search by Picasso and Braque for methods of representation to replace the sensuous pictorial realism of the impressionists. Derived from the perceptual realism of Cezanne, cubism developed into an austere, very logical technique by which the permanent structure of an object was analyzed and then fragmented into planes to reveal its whole structure. Rather than depicting objects as they appear, the cubists superimposed several different views of the same object to express the idea of the object instead.

D

Dada, New York. A 1915 forerunner of the irreverent international avant-garde dada movement, led by French-born Marcel Duchamp, Cuban-born Francis Picabia and American-born Man Ray. The concepts underlying their activities, publications, paintings and readymades (nihilistic or ironic sculptures based on manufactured objects) became the basis for later pop and conceptual art.

Daguerrotype. The earliest successful photographic process. Developed in France by Louis Daguerre in the mid-nineteenth century, it made use of a silver or silver-covered copper plate which was made sensitive to light through the use of chemicals.

Decorative. A general term for all arts in which decoration is added to a functional object. In the context of painting, it frequently is applied to work that is intended to embellish or ornament a given space. Purists traditionally disdain decorative work as not a part of the fine arts of painting and sculpture.

Dusseldorf. Between 1840 and 1860 many prominent American artists—including Albert Bierstadt, George Caleb Bingham, Eastman Johnson, Emmanuel Leutze and Richard Caton Woodville—were attracted to the study of sentimental genre painting at the Dusseldorf Academy. The Dusseldorf style is typically hard and dry. After the Civil War, a shift toward realism led younger students to Munich and Paris instead.

E

The Eight. A group of eight relatively dissimilar realist painters, led by Robert Henri, who banded together in 1908 to exhibit their work independently after the work of three of them had been rejected for exhibition at the National Academy of Design. They exhibited together only once, but the name remained with them; they were also known as members of the Ashcan School. The Eight were Henri, William Glackens, George Luks, Everett Shinn, John Sloan, Arthur Davies, Ernest Lawson and Maurice Prendergast.

Encaustic. An ancient painting technique, mentioned by Pliny, in which colors were mixed with wax which in turn was heated so that the colors were absorbed into the wall. The same technique was used for a time in Egypt in the first century A.D. for small portraits on mummy cases. Leonardo da Vinci attempted without success to revive the process in the early sixteenth century, and several artists also attempted to use the method in the late nineteenth century.

Engraving. A term which has come to refer to all the processes for multiplying prints. While there are distinct differences between individual methods of engraving, the chief difference is between reproductive and original engravings. The former reproduce an idea or work of an artist other than the engraver, while original engravings are unique works of art created by engraver himself.

Etching. A widely used form of engraving in which the etcher draws on a copper plate which has been covered with an acid-impervious resinous ground, exposing the copper wherever he wants a line. When the plate is placed in an acid bath, the exposed parts are eaten away. By controlling the depth of the acid "bite," subtle variations in the strength of lines may be achieved. Prints are then made by inking the plate, removing the ink from its surface, and pressing paper onto the plate; the picture is made by the ink in the etched-away lines.

Expressionism. A late-nineteenth- and early-twentieth-century northern European movement away from the representation of the observed world to the expression of personal emotional intensity. Its subjective, exaggerated and distorted colors and forms were further developed in the abstract expressionism of Willem de Kooning and others and, in the 1980s, in the work of the neo-realists.

F

Fauvism. The spontaneous use of pure bright color (rather than tone), expressively applied with distortions in flat patterns. Work in this style by Henri Matisse and others was first exhibited in the Paris Salon d'Automne of 1905; the furor it aroused caused a critic to label these artists the "fauves" (wild beasts). Max Weber helped Matisse organize a short-lived school in 1907, which was attended by Patrick Henry Bruce and other Americans.

Federal period. A phase of neo-classicism in design and architecture in the United States which lasted from approximately 1780 until approximately 1820. It was based primarily on the work of Robert and James Adam in England. Its most distinguishing features were: graceful, slender proportions; small but delicate ornaments; and curvilinear elements, such as eliptical rooms and sweeping circular staircases.

Folk art. Paintings, objects and decorations made in a distinctive or traditional manner by artists or craftsmen who have had no formal training. In general, it is looked upon as an autonomous tradition which is seldom affected by changes in fashion or trends in professional art.

Fourteenth Street School. A relatively small group of realist painters who, in the late 1920s and 1930s, had studios in the vicinity of Union Square and 14th Street in New York City. In sharply different styles they continued in the tradition of the Ashcan School and portrayed boisterous, vulgar crowds, lonely individuals and the hopelessness of people in breadlines. The group was founded by Kenneth Hayes Miller, but its most substantive work was done by Reginald Marsh, Raphael and Moses Soyer and Morris Kantor.

Futurism. An artistic program which arose in Italy shortly before the outbreak of World War I and sought to simulate the dynamism of the modern urban technological world through exploding faceted cubist form. Joseph Stella used the style for his monumental depictions of the Brooklyn Bridge.

G

Gouache. An opaque watercolor paint. The effects achieved with it are closer to those of oil paint than of watercolor. A disadvantage of gouache is the fact that it lightens as it dries.

H

Hudson River School. A succession of American painters who, between 1840 and the late nineteenth century, established for the first time a true tradition of landscape painting in the United States. Many of the scenes they painted were in the Hudson River Valley and the adjoining mountains of New York State and Vermont. Their work, derived from European romantic landscape painting, was marked by a meticulous rendering of detail and by an almost religious reverence for the magnificence of the American wilderness.

I

Impasto. A thick application of oil paint on canvas or a panel. The heaviness of the paint, often clearly showing the marks of individual brushstrokes, is thought to add character and vigor to the painting.

Impressionism. One of the most important artistic movements of the nineteenth century in France and in many ways the precursor of much of modern art. It began as a loose association of brilliantly innovative painters, such as Monet, Renoir and Sisley, whose primary purpose was to record their immediate emotional responses to a scene, rather than to create a conventional record of nature. The styles of impressionist painters varied widely, but they were united by their desire to capture the spontaneity of the moment and to avoid the constrictions of formal compositions.

L

Limner. A designation used originally in the Middle Ages for an illuminator of manuscripts. Beginning in the sixteenth century it took on new meaning to include painters of miniature portraits and sometimes painters in general. In this last context the term has been obsolete since the nineteenth century. Early American folk artists were sometimes called limners.

Lithography. The only major process of surface printing in which no engraving or cutting-out of the surface of the plate is involved. The design is put on the surface of a stone with a greasy chalk; the stone is wetted and then covered with a greasy ink, which is rejected by the wet surface and clings only to those areas which already are greasy.

Lotos Club (also Lotus Club). A New York City club dedicated to the cultivation of the arts. Since its founding in 1870 it has honored many distinguished writers, musicians, actors and others in the arts with testimonial dinners. Its quarters are at 5 East 66th Street.

Luminism. An effect that is obtained in painting when a light or reflective undercoat of paint is visible through a thin or transparent outer layer. The technique was developed in the mid-nineteenth century in America by painters, such as George Caleb Bingham, who had a particular interest in the character of light as an element in painting.

M

Macchiaioli. An important school of Italian painters who worked in Florence between 1850 and approximately 1865. In revolt against academic painting and influenced by the realism of Corot and Courbet, they employed individual touches or daubs of color to achieve their desired effect. Some of the group were landscape and genre painters, while others did costumed history scenes.

Magic realism. An American variant of surrealism which uses sharp focus and precise representation to portray imaginary subjects.

Mannerism. A sophisticated, sixteenth-century, elongated style used most elegantly in Italy and elsewhere for international court portraits. Seventeenth-century colonial portraits were often based on English prints of mannerist portraits and on Italian mannerist treatises filtered through England.

Minimal art. Reductive movements of the 1960s, including color-field painting, op art, hard-edge painting and serial imagery. They arose as a further development of the cool, formal, abstract expressionist art of Mark Rothko, Barnett Newman and others, and as a reaction against autobiographical gestural action painting.

Modernism. A term used to describe innovations in art brought about by two factors: a strong sense of detachment from the past and a deliberate desire to replace past aesthetic concepts with an artistic expression more in accord with the contemporary ideas and beliefs. Sometimes reaction to prevailing aesthetic concepts can take the form of a return to those of an earlier period. Although the requisite sense of detachment from the past has been especially strong through much of the twentieth century, the term "modernism" can be applied to innovations in any art period.

Munich School. A group of radical young German painters under the leadership of Wilhelm Liebl in Munich in the latter half of the nineteenth century. Their work was characterized by a choice of commonplace subject matter, loose and vigorous brushwork and a relatively dark and restricted palette. This style had a strong influence on many young Americans who came to Munich to study in the 1870s, notably Frank Duveneck and William Merritt Chase.

N

Nabis. Young French painters between 1889 and 1899 who were influenced by Eastern motifs, esoteric ideas and the art of Paul Gauguin. Their goal was to devise decorative techniques to adorn "a plane surface covered with colors brought together in a certain order." Their name comes from the Hebrew word for "prophet."

National Academy of Design. Founded in New York City in 1826 by Samuel F.B. Morse and others as a rebellion against the dictatorial administration of an earlier American Academy of Fine Arts. Over the years the National

Academy became a bastion of conservatism and the works of innovative young artists were frequently excluded from its exhibitions. Most trends in twentieth-century American art have developed independently of the Academy.

Neoclassicism. An eighteenth-century attempt to revive the classical art—and thereby the glory—of ancient Greece and Rome. In the United States it was consciously adopted for the art (especially the architecture) of the early republic.

New Deal Art. Art produced between 1933 and 1943 under the auspices of various government programs, including the Works Progress Administration's Federal Art Project (WPA/FAP) and the Treasury Relief Administration Project (TRAP), which employed more than 5,000 artists. The subject matter of most of the thousands of murals and easel paintings these programs generated was interpretations of the prescribed American scene.

New Hope School (Pennsylvania impressionists). A group of American landscape painters with strong inclinations toward impressionism who settled and painted in the region around New Hope, a small town on the Delaware River in rural Bucks County, Pennsylvania, for several generations beginning in 1898. Although he did not live in New Hope, Edward Redfield is considered the leader of the group. Because of their focus on scenes of the countryside and country life, the group now is looked upon as a rural counterpart to the urban Ashcan School of painters, with whom they were contemporaries.

New York School. The name given to the group of bold, highly innovative painters who lived and worked in New York City during the 1940s and 1950s and who collectively developed abstract expressionism. Also known as action painting, the work of this school had as far-reaching an effect on artists as cubism had had on earlier generations of painters.

O

Old Lyme impressionists. A loosely defined group of early-twentieth-century American impressionist landscape painters who worked in the area of Old Lyme, Connecticut, a picturesque old town at the mouth of the Connecticut River. Childe Hassam was one of the early members and the catalyst around whom the group coalesced. Several other members of The Ten, among them J. Alden Weir and John H. Twachtman, were also considered Old Lyme impressionists.

Op art. An abbreviation for optical art, a term first used to define work in "The Responsive Eye" exhibition at the Museum of Modern Art in 1965. It covers a broad range of sophisticated, geometric, abstract painting styles which exploit perceptual ambiguities and shock or distort what is perceived by the viewer.

Orientalism. In its earliest connotation, the interest in the exotic colors and savage passions of the Middle East and North Africa that first appeared in the work of Delacroix in the 1820s and later became an important element in romantic painting. In a later context, it refers to the influence of oriental art and design, particularly of Japanese prints, on the work of such painters as Whistler, Van Gogh and Gauguin after the United States gained access to Japanese ports in 1854. The universal values embodied in oriental art, calligraphy and philosophy have been adapted or reflected in American painting most recently in action painting and the work of some painters of the Northwest.

Orphism. A completely abstract type of color painting created by French artist Robert Delaunay in 1912-1913. His work contained no reference to the visual world; he believed that "color alone is form and subject."

P

Painterly. The tendency to depict form as patches of colored light and shade, in which edges merge into the background or into one another, best exemplified by the work of Rembrandt. Its opposite, linear, which denotes an emphasis on outline and drawing, is considered characteristically American.

Panorama. A complete depiction of a landscape or historical scene, often mounted on the inside of a large cylindrical surface, such as a curved wall or round room. It may also be a scene that is passed before a spectator in such a way as to show the various parts of the whole in continuous succession.

Pennsylvania Academy of the Fine Arts. The oldest continuously operative art institution in the United States. Modeled after the Royal Academy in London, it was founded in Philadelphia in 1805 by Charles Willson Peale, sculptor William Rush and a group of prominent local business and professional men. In addition to the Academy's continuing teaching functions, its museum is recognized for its comprehensive collection of American painting.

Photo-realism. Also known as superrealism, a style of figurative painting and sculpture of photographic exactitude that gained prominence in the United States and England during the 1960s and 1970s. It was usually characterized by banal contemporary subject matter and a glossy finish. Unlike naturalism, however, its aim was to create a sense of unreality through an almost hallucinatory wealth of detail and sometimes through altered scale.

Plein-air. The French phrase for "open air." The term refers to painting which is done outdoors, directly from nature. It is also used sometimes to describe a style of painting which conveys a feeling of openness and spontaneity.

Pop art. Art which uses symbols, images and objects of mass production and contemporary popular culture—normally seen on supermarket shelves, in mass-media advertising and in comic strips—in the context of the fine arts. It appeared in England in the mid-1950s, but reached its apex in the United States during the 1960s in the work of painters like Andy Warhol, Jasper Johns and Robert Rauschenberg and sculptors like Claes Oldenburg. Much of its effect on the viewer is based on the shock value of seeing the commonplace displayed as serious art.

Post-impressionism. A term invented by English art critic Roger Fry when he organized an exhibition in London of such modern French masters as Cezanne, Manet and Matisse in 1910. The term underscored the fact that these painters had rejected the principles of impressionism and had instead focused their attention on creating form rather than imitating natural form.

Post-modernism. A general term used to cover such contemporary phenomena as pop art and pop design, which appeared in the 1960s as a reaction against the values established by the acknowledged masters of modern art. The initiators of post-modernism felt that modern art and the functionalism of modern design did not fulfill the psychological and emotional needs of ordinary people as they were reflected in the popularity and near-universal acceptance of mass-produced consumer goods.

Pre-raphaelitism, American. An association, organized in 1863 in emulation of John Ruskin's British Pre-Raphaelite Brotherhood in order to promote landscape, still-life and nature painting with the photograph as a standard of accuracy. John William Hill and William Trost Richards were two of the members of the Association for the Advancement of Truth in Art who published the American pre-raphaelite manifesto in *The New Path*.

Precisionism. Known in the 1920s and the 1930s as cubist realism, the work of Charles Sheeler and other "immaculate" painters featured indigenous American subject matter executed in a sharp, precise linear manner, without figures or anecdotal elements.

Primitive art. A term which often is applied to paintings and other art in three distinctly different categories: 1) Dutch and Italian painters working before the Renaissance, or before about 1500 A.D. 2) The work of peoples, such as African blacks, Eskimos and Pacific islanders, whose art matured unaffected by any influence from the traditional great centers of culture. 3) The work of artists, primarily European and American, who have received little or no formal training, yet have developed their own unsophisticated, nontraditional style.

R

Realism. In one context, this term refers to the depiction of life as it is—even the squalid and ugly—instead of conventionally beautiful or idealized subjects. In another context, it means representational painting, as against that painting which is deliberately abstract or distorted. In the late nineteenth and early twentieth centuries, the term "social realism" was coined to apply to representational painting which contained a specific political or social message.

Regionalism. Associated with the patriotic efforts of Thomas Hart Benton and others, especially in the 1930s, to communicate something significant about America by making the legends of a region's shared past the subject matter of their art. Various areas of the country, including the Midwest, the Pacific Northwest and New York City, had their own brands of regionalism.

Rococo. A graceful, yet florid, style of interior decoration and ornamentation that replaced the excessive ostentation associated with Louis XIV and the Palace of Versailles after his death in 1715. It was characterized by curves and counter-curves, prettiness and gaiety. The style lasted in France only until the mid-eighteenth century, but flourished longer in Germany and Austria.

Romanticism. A cult of feeling and individual imagination which originated in mid-eighteenth-century English philosophy and spread throughout the arts in Europe. America's first romantic, Washington Allston, brought to the United States the inspiration to paint seascapes and landscapes imbued with the sublime power of nature, as well as moralistic history paintings.

S

Salon. For many years the only officially recognized exhibition of paintings in Paris. It derived its name from the fact that it was originally held in the Salon d'Apollon in the Louvre. It has undergone many transformations over the years, but for the most part its organizers have been traditionalists who have been hostile to and have excluded new and innovative paintings. In 1863, the outcry from those whose work had not been accepted was so vehement that Napoleon III ordered a special Salon des Refuses which was equally controversial and was held only once.

Scumbling. A technique in painting of softening or modifying the color of a surface by applying an upper layer of opaque color. The upper layer is thin or irregular enough to allow some of the color beneath to show through.

Serigraphy. A stenciling process more commonly known as silk-screen printing. Paint or ink is brushed over unmasked areas of stretched silk on which the design has been fixed. By using successive masks on the same screen, multi-colored prints can be achieved. The process is widely used in commercial art and in the textile industry.

Social realism. Direct and critical portrayals of social, political and economic issues in art works, particularly during the 1930s.

Surrealism. Based on the depiction of dreams and the subconscious, and founded by Frenchman Andre Breton in 1924, surrealistic art aims for "the systematic dismantling of establishment values." Its principle of automatism (the depiction of pure thought) helped pave the way for the improvisatory character of American action painting.

Synchromism. The sole modern movement founded by American artists before World War I. Synchromism means "with color," and Morgan Russell and Stanton MacDonald-Wright used color alone to generate form, meaning and composition. Their work was based in part on the color theory of French painter Robert Delaunay.

T

Tachism. A term coined in 1952 by French art critic Michel Tapie to describe paintings in which dabs and splotches of color appear to have been applied at random, with no regard for form or construction. It is now frequently applied to action painting and to any painting technique that strives to be completely spontaneous and instinctive.

Taos Colony. An art colony in Taos, New Mexico, which began in 1912 when a small group of painters, led by Henry Sharp, formed the Art Society of Taos. Tired of European traditions, these artists sought intrinsically American subjects to paint and found them in the local Spanish and Pueblo Indian cultures and in the spectacular scenery of the Southwest. Members of the original group continued to work until 1927, and Taos continues today as a popular center for artists.

Tempera. A method of painting on surfaces prepared with gesso in which dry pigments are mixed with egg yolks, whites or sometimes whole eggs to form a water-soluble yet binding medium. It was the commonest painting technique until the late fifteenth century. The medium dries almost immediately and is permanent.

The Ten. A group of 10 late-nineteenth-century Boston painters who exhibited together from 1898 until 1918. Initially they banded together to protest what they considered to be the too-strict academic tastes of the city. While the styles of these painters varied widely (some were not American impressionist painters at all), as a group they are now thought of generally as the Boston School of American impressionists.

Tonalism. A poetic, meditative style developed primarily between 1880 and 1910. Tonalist paintings often used intimate interiors or sylvan settings, depicted as if photographed behind a veil or shrouded in mist.

Trompe l'oeil. French for "deceive the eye." The term is applied to easel or decorative painting whose purpose is to fool the eye as to the composition or the reality of the objects represented—as with painted money that appears to be real, and the like. In easel painting the technique is normally restricted to surfaces in or near the plane of the picture.

SELECTED BIBLIOGRAPHY

AUCTION RECORDS

Hislop, Richard, ed. *Annual Art Sales Index*. Weybridge, Surrey, England: Art Sales Index Ltd. (Published annually.)

Leonard's Annual Index of Art Auctions. Newton, Massachusetts: Leonard's Index of Art Auctions. (Published annually.)

Mayer, E. *International Auction Records*. New York: Editions Publisol. (Published annually.)

DICTIONARIES

Baigell, Matthew. *Dictionary of American Art*. Reprint with corrections. New York: Harper and Row, 1982.

Brewington, Dorothy E.R. *Dictionary of Marine Artists*. Peabody Museum of Salem, Massachusetts and Mystic Seaport Museum, Connecticut, 1982.

Cummings, Paul. *Dictionary of Contemporary American Artists*. New York and London: St. Martin's and St. James, 1977.

Groce, George C., and David H. Wallace. *The New York Historical Society's Dictionary of Artists in America*. New Haven: Yale University Press, 1957.

Mantle Fielding's Dictionary of American Painters, Sculptors and Engravers. Revised by Glenn B. Opitz. Poughkeepsie, N.Y.: Apollo Book, 1983.

Murray, Peter and Linda. *Penguin Dictionary of Art & Artists*. Penguin Books, 1959.

Samuels, Peggy and Harold. *Illustrated Biographical Encyclopedia of Artists of the American West*. New York: Doubleday, 1976.

HISTORIES AND GENERAL REFERENCES

Ashton, Dore. *The New York School: A Cultural Reckoning*. New York: Viking Press, 1972.

Baigell, Matthew. *The American Scene: American Painting of the 1930s*. New York: Praeger, 1979.

_____. *A Concise History of American Painting and Sculpture*. New York: Harper and Row, 1984.

Barker, Virgil. *American Painting: History and Interpretation*. New York: Macmillan, 1951.

Berman, Greta, and Jeffrey Wechsler. *Realism and Realities: The Other Side of American Painting, 1940-1960*. New Brunswick: Rutgers University Art Gallery, 1981.

Bermingham, P. *American Art in the Barbizon Mood*. Washington, D.C., 1975.

Bizardel, Y. *American Painters in Paris*. New York, 1960.

Boyle, Richard. *American Impressionism*. Boston: New York Graphic Society, 1974.

Broder, Patricia Janis. *The American West: The Modern Vision*. Boston: New York Graphic Society/Little, Brown and Co., 1984.

_____. *Great Paintings of the Old American West*. New York: Abbeville Press, 1981.

Brown, Milton H. *American Art to 1900*. New York: Harry N. Abrams, 1978.

_____. *American Painting from the Armory Show to the Depression*. Princeton, N.J.: Princeton University Press, 1955.

Campbell, Mary Schmidt. *Tradition and Conflict: Images of a Turbulent Decade, 1963-1973*. New York: Studio Museum in Harlem, 1985.

Cohen, George M. *A History of American Art*. New York: Dell, 1971.

Corn, Wanda M. *Grant Wood: The Regionalist Vision*. New Haven: Yale University Press for the Minneapolis Institute of the Arts, 1983.

Czestochowski, John S. *The American Landscape Tradition: A Study and Gallery of Paintings*. New York: E.P. Dutton, 1982.

Davidson, Abraham A. *Early American Modernist Painting 1910-1935*. New York: Harper and Row, 1981.

Dunlap, William. *A History of the Rise and Progress of the Arts and Design in the United States*. New York, 1934. 2 Vols. Edited by Rita Weiss. Introduction by James T. Flexner. 3 Vols. New York: Dover Publications, 1969.

Fine, Elsa Honig. *The Afro-American Artists: A Search For Identity*. New York: Holt, Rinehart and Winston, 1973.

Flexner, James T. *American Painting: First Flowers of Our Wilderness*. Boston: Houghton and Mifflin, 1947.

_____. *American Painting: The Light of Distant Skies, 1760-1835*. New York: Harcourt Brace, 1954.

_____. *America's Old Masters: First Artists of the New World*. New York: Viking Press, 1939.

_____. *Nineteenth-Century American Painting*. New York: Putnam's, 1970.

_____. *That Wilder Image: The Painting of America's Native School from Thomas Cole to Winslow Homer*. Boston: Little, Brown, 1962.

Frankenstein, Alfred V. *After the Hunt: William Michael Harnett and Other American Still Life Painters, 1870-1900*. 2nd Edition. Berkeley and Los Angeles: University of California Press, 1969.

Hassrick, Peter. *Treasures of the Old West*. New York: Harry N. Abrams, Inc., 1984.

_____. *The Way West: The Art of Frontier America*. New York: Harry N. Abrams, Inc., 1977.

Hills, Patricia. *Social Concern and Urban Realism: American Painting of the 1930s*. Boston: Boston University Art Gallery, 1983.

Hoopes, Donelson. *The American Impressionists*. New York: Watson-Guptill, 1973.

Geldzahler, Henry. *American Painting of the Twentieth Century*. New York: The Metropolitan Museum of Art, distributed by the New York Graphic Society, 1965.

Gerdts, William. *American Impressionism*. New York: Abbeville Press, 1984.

Gerdts, William H., and Russell Burke. *American Still Life Painting*. New York: Praeger, 1971.

Gerdts, William H. *Down Garden Paths: The Floral Environment in American Art*. London and Toronto: Associated University Presses, 1983.

_____. *Painters of the Humble Truth: Masterpieces of American Still Life 1801-1939*. Columbia, Missouri: University of Missouri Press, 1981.

Goodrich, Lloyd, and John I. H. Baur. *American Art of Our Century*. New York: Praeger, 1961.

Greenberg, Clement. *Art and Culture: Critical Essays*. Boston: Beacon Press, 1961.

Harmsen, Dorothy. *American Western Art*. Harmsen Publishing Co., 1977.

Homer, William I. *Alfred Stieglitz and the American Avant-Garde*. Boston: New York Graphic Society, 1977.

Howat, John K. *The Hudson River and Its Painters*. New York: Viking Press, 1972.

Kenin, Richard. *Return to Albion: Americans In England, 1760-1940*. New York: Holt, Rinehart and Winston; Washington, D.C.: The National Portrait Gallery, Smithsonian Institution, 1979.

Larkin, Oliver W. *Art and Life in America*. New York: Holt, Rinehart and Winston, 1966.

Levin, Gail. *Synchromism and American Color Abstraction*. New York: Braziller, 1978.

Lewis, Samella. *Art: African American*. New York: Harcourt, Brace, Jovanovich, 1978.

Lipman, Jean, and Tom Armstrong, eds. *American Folk Painters of Three Centuries*. New York: Hudson Hills Press/Whitney Museum of American Art, 1980.

Marling, Karal Ann. *Wall-to-Wall America: A Cultural History of Post Office Murals in the Great Depression*. Minneapolis: University of Minnesota Press, 1983.

Meixner, Laura. *An International Episode: Millet, Monet and Their North American Counterparts*. Exhibition catalog. Memphis, Tennessee: Dixon Gallery and Gardens, 1982.

Miles, Ellen, ed. *Portrait Painting in America: The Nineteenth Century*. New York: Main Street/Universe Books, 1977.

Novak, Barbara. *American Painting of the 19th Century*. 2nd Edition. New York: Harper and Row, 1979.

_____. *Nature and Culture: American Landscape and Painting, 1825-1875*. New York: Oxford University Press, 1980.

Park, Marlene, and Gerald E. Markowitz. *New Deal for Art: The Government Art Projects of the 1930s With Examples from New York City and State*. Hamilton,

New York: The Gallery Association of New York State, Inc., 1977.

Porter, James A. *Modern Negro Art*. New York: Dryden Press, 1943.

Portraits from "The Americans": The Democratic Experience—An Exhibit at the National Portrait Gallery Based on Daniel J. Boorstin's "The Americans". New York: Random House, 1975.

Portraits USA 1776-1976: An Exhibition Celebrating the Nation's Bicentennial. University Park, Pennsylvania: Museum of Art, Pennsylvania State University, 1976.

Prown, Jules D. *American Painting: From Its Beginnings to the Armory Show*. Cleveland, Ohio: World Publishing, 1969.

Quick, M. *American Expatriate Painters of the Late Nineteenth Century*. Dayton, Ohio, 1978.

Richardson, Edgar P. *American Romantic Painting*. Edited by Robert Freund. New York: E. Weyhe, 1944.

_____. *Painting In America, From 1502 to the Present*. New York: Thomas Crowell, 1965.

Ritchie, Andrew C. *Abstract Painting and Sculpture in America*. New York: Museum of Modern Art, 1969.

Rose, Barbara. *American Painting: The Twentieth Century*. Cleveland, Ohio: World Publishing, 1969.

Rossi, Paul, and David Hunt. *The Art of the Old West*. New York: Alfred A. Knopf, 1971.

Sandler, Irving. *The Triumph of American Painting: A History of Abstract Expressionism*. New York: Harper and Row, 1970.

Seitz, William C. *Abstract Expressionist Painting in America*. Cambridge, Massachusetts: Harvard University Press, 1983.

Sellin, David. *Americans in Brittany and Normandy, 1860-1910*. Phoenix Art Museum, 1982.

Shapiro, David. *Social Realism: Art as a Weapon*. Critical Studies in American Art. New York: Frederick Unger, 1973.

Sheldon, George W. *American Painters*. New York, 1879.

Soria, Regina. *Dictionary of Nineteenth Century American Painters in Italy: 1760-1914*. East Brunswick, New Jersey: Fairleigh University Press, 1982.

Stein, Roger B. *Seascape and the American Imagination*. New York: The Whitney Museum of American Art, 1975.

Sweeney, J. Gray. *Great Lakes Marine Painting of the Nineteenth Century*. Washington, D.C.: National Gallery of Art, 1980.

Tuckerman, Henry T. *The Book of the Artists: American Artist Life*. New York: Putnam's, 1867. Reprint. New York: James F. Carr, 1966.

Wein, Frances Stevenson, ed. *National Portrait Gallery Permanent Collection Illustrated Checklist.* Washington, D.C.: Smithsonian Institution Press, 1980.

Wilmerding, John. *American Art.* London and New York: Penguin Books, 1976.

_____, et al. *American Light: The Luminist Movement, 1850-1875.* Washington, D.C.: The National Gallery of Art, 1980.

_____. *A History of American Marine Painting.* Salem, Massachusetts: Little, Brown for the Peabody Museum of Salem, 1968.

Wynne, G. *Early Americans in Rome.* Rome, 1966.

PERIODICALS

American Art Journal, New York, New York.

Antiques, New York, New York.

Art & Antiques, New York, New York.

Art & Auction, New York, New York.

Art in America, New York, New York.

Art Journal, New York, New York.

ARTnews, New York, New York.

Art Students League News, New York, New York.

Maine Antique Digest, Waldoboro, Maine.

Winterthur Portfolio, Chicago, Illinois.

AUCTION HOUSES

CODE	AUCTION HOUSE
A	Aldridges—Bath
A.D	Adams—Dublin
A.R	D'Anjour—Rouen
A.T	Arnaune—Toulouse
AAA.S	Australian Art Auctions—Sydney
AG	Anderson & Garland— Newcastle
AMG.C	Appay, Mainon- Gairoared et G.— Cannes
AN.Z	Auktionshaus Am Neumarkt—Zurich
AW.H	Arno Winterberg— Heidelberg
B	Bonham—London
B.A	Paul Brandt— Amsterdam
B.G	Blache—Grenoble
B.M	Boscher—Morlaix
B.P	Barridoff Galleries— Portland
B.S	Bukowski—Stockholm
B.T	Beaumont—Tours
B.V	Blache—Versailles
BB	Richard Baker & Baker—Birkenhead
BB.SF	Butterfield & Butterfield—San Francisco
BC	Bannister & Co.— Haywards Heath
BFA	Barber's Fine Art— Woking
BL.N	Bailly, Loevenbruck— Nancy
BMM	Button, Menheinett & Mutton— Wadebridge
BR	Bracketts—Tunbridge Wells
BR.CS	Bretaudiere et Raynaud—Chalon- sur-Saone
BV	Bradley & Vaughan— Haywards Heath
BW	Biddle & Webb— Birmingham
C	Christie, Manson Woods—London
C.A	Campo—Antwerp
C.LIA	Calvet—L'Isle Adam
C.V	Chapelle—Versailles
CB	Charles Boardman & Son—Haverhill
CBS	Chrystal Brothers—Isle of Man
CE	Christie Edmiston— Glasgow
CG.P	Charles Galleries— Pontiac

CODE	AUCTION HOUSE
CG.V	Champion-Gondran— Vienna
CH	Christie—New York
CJ.N	Courchet, Palloc & Japhet—Nice
CL.E	Champin & Lombrail—Enghien
CR.T	Chassaing, Rivet— Toulouse
CS.L	Chenu & Scrive—Lyon
CSK	Christie's, South Kensington— London
D.B	Commissaires- Priseurs—Bordeaux
D.H	Dupuy—Honfleur
D.NY	William Doyle—New York
D.R	Denesle—Rouen
D.V	Dorotheum—Vienna
DA.B	Darmancier—Bourges
DA.R	Dapsens—Reims
DH	Dacre, Son & Hartley—Ilkley
DL.Se	Delpeint & Lemaitre— Saint Etienne
DM.D	Du Mouchelle— Detroit
DO.H	Dorling—Hamburg
DV.G	De Vos—Ghent
DWB	Dreweatt, Watson & Barton—Newbury
E	Edmiston—Glasgow
E.EDM	Eldred—East Dennis, Mass.
EC	Entwistle—Southport
EG	Elliott Green— Lymington
F.M	Finarte—Milan
F.P	Freemans— Philadelphia
F.R	Finarte—Rome
FB.M	Fraser Bros.— Montreal
FO.R	Fournier—Rouen
G	Grant—Stourport
G.G	Gaucher—Grenoble
G.L	Galateau—Limoges
G.S	Goodman—Sydney
G.SB	Guichard—Saint Brieuc
G.Z	Germann—Zurich
GA.L	Guillaumot & Albrand—Lyon
GC	Geering & Colyer— Hawkhurst
GD.B	Galerie Dobiaschofsky— Bern
GDA.G	Galerie D'Horlogerie Ancienne—Geneva

CODE	AUCTION HOUSE
GF.L	Galerie Fischer— Lucerne
GG.S	Geoff. Gray—Sydney
GG.TA	Gordon Galleries—Tel Aviv
GGL.L	Genin, Griffe, Leseuil—-Lyon
GK.B	Galerie Kornfeld— Bern
GK.Z	Galerie Koller—Zurich
GM.B	Galerie Moderne— Bruxelles
GS.B	Galerie Stuker—Bern
GSP	Graves, Son & Pilcher—Hove
GT	Garrod Turner— Ipswich
GT.A	Gerrard-Tasset— Angouleme
GV.G	Goteborgs Auktionsverk— Goteborg
GV.P	Gilles Vergnault— Parthenay
H.AP	Hours—Aix-en- Provence
HB	Heathcote Ball— Leicester
HG.C	Hanzell Galleries— Chicago
HMA.L	Herment-Mochon & Anaf—Lyon
HN.H	Hauswedel & Nolte— Hamburg
HS	Henry Spencer— Retford
J	Jollys—Bath
J.M	Joel—Melbourne
JSS	Jackson, Stopps and Staff—London
JT	James Thompson— Kirkby
K.B	Kaczorowski—Brive- La Gaillarde
K.BB	Kohn—Bourg-en- Bresse
K.N	Klinger—Nurnberger
K.S	Kvalitetsauktion— Stockholm
KC	King & Chasemore— Pulborough
KC.R	King & Chasemore— Roermond
KF.M	Karl & Faber—Munich
KH.K	Kunsthallens Kunstauktioner— Copenhagen
KK.B	Kornfeld & Klipstein— Bern
KM.K	Kunsthaus Am Museum—Cologne

CODE	AUCTION HOUSE	CODE	AUCTION HOUSE	CODE	AUCTION HOUSE
KV.L	Kunstgalerij De Vuyst—Lokeren	PC	Phillips—Chester	VT.M	Villebrun & Tournel—Marseilles
KV.S	Kvalitetsauktion—Stockholm	PE	Phillips—Edinburgh	W.M	Weinmuller—Munich
L	Lane & Sons—Penzance	PG	Phillips—Glasgow	W.T	Waddington—Toronto
		PJ.M	Phillips-Jacoby—Montreal	W.W	Weschler—Washington
L.C	Lelieve—Chartres	PK	Phillips—Knowle	WA.B	Watine & Arnault—Berthune
L.K	Lempertz—Cologne	PL	Phillips—Leeds	WK.M	Galerie Wolfgang Ketterer—Munich
L.SG	Louiseau—Saint Germain-en-Laye	PS	Phillips In Scotland—Edinburgh	WSW	Warner, Sheppard & Wade—Leicester
L.SM	Lerond—Saint Maur	PWC	Parsons, Welsh & Cowell—Sevenoaks	WW	Woolley & Wallis—Salisbury
LE	Locke & England—Leamington Spa	PX	Phillips—Exeter	WWL	Warren & Wignall—Leyland
LM	Lalonde Martin—Bristol	R.G	Rosset—Geneva	YG.P	Youngs Gallery—Portsmouth, N.H.
LP	Lalonde Brothers & Parham—Bristol	R.I	Renner—Issoudon	12.P	De Cagny—Paris
LS	Love & Sons—Perth	R.K	Rasmussen—Copenhagen	15.P	Cornette De St. Cyr—Paris
M.LA	Massart—L'Isle Adam	R.M	Regis—Marseilles	16.P	Ferri—Paris
M.LF	Manson—La Fleche	R.V	Rijaud—Vernon	17.P	Lemee—Paris
M.NO	Mortons—New Orleans	RB.HM	Richard Bourne—Hyannis, Mass.	21.P	Pillias—Paris
M.V	Martin—Versailles	RG	Rowland Gorringe—Lewes	23.P	Jozon—Paris
MA.V	Maynards—Vancouver			28.P	Morelle—Paris
MC.A	Martin & Courtois—Angers	RG.M	Raynaud & Gamet—Marseille	29.P	Ledoux-Lebard—Paris
MCB	McCartney, Morris & Barber—Ludlow	S	Sotheby—London	32.P	Chalvet De Recy—Paris
		S.BM	Skinner—Bolton, Mass.	33.P	Boisgirard—Paris
MCC	McCartney, Morris & Barker—Ludlow	S.D	Sadde—Dijon	35.P	Ader, Picard & Tajan—Paris
MM	Morrison, McChlery—Glasgow	S.J	Sausverd—Joigny	36.P	Deurbergue—Paris
		S.O	Savot—Orleans	37.P	Englemann—Paris
MMB	Messenger, May & Baverstock—Godalming	S.Tr	Strange—The Rocks, Australia	4.P	Le Blanc—Paris
		S.W	Sloan—Washington	40.P	Tilorier—Paris
MS.P	Martinot & Savignat—Pontoise	SB	Sotheby Belgravia—London	42.P	Libert—Paris
MV.LH	Mabile-Vankemriel—Le Havre	SBA	Sotheby Beresford Adams—Chester	45.P	Oger—Paris
MVT.L	Mercier, Velliet & Thullier—Lille	SKC	Sotheby, King & Chasemore—Pulborough	50.P	Binoche—Paris
				54.P	Delaporte—Paris
MW.A	Mak Van Waay—Amsterdam	SMG	Shakespear, McTurk & Graham—Leicester	56.P	Ribault-Menetiere—Paris
N	Neale & Son—Nottingham	SPB	Sotheby—USA	6.P	Audap, Godeau & Solanet—Paris
N.M	Neumeister—Munich	SY	Sotheby Parke Bernet, O/S of USA & UK	60.P	Rogeon—Paris
O	Oliver—Sudbury	SYB	Sotheby Bearnes—Torquay	61.P	Millon—Paris
O.F	Osenat—Fontainebleau	T.B	Thierry—Brest	62.P	Renaud—Paris
OL	Outhwaite & Litherland—Liverpool	TH.B	Thelot—Blois	63.P	Laurin, Guilloux & Buffetaud—Paris
		TL	Lawrence—Crewkerne	66.P	Loudmer & Poulain—Paris
OT	Osmond, Tricks—Bristol	TRS	Thomson Rose & Spenser—York	7.P	Robert—Paris
P	Phillips—London	UA.Z	Uto Auktions A.G—Zurich	73.P	Labat—Paris
P.LF	Pillet—Lyons-La-Foret	V	Vost's—Colchester	75.P	Couturier & Nicolay—Paris
P.M	Phillips Ward Price—Montreal	V.LH	Viel—Le Havre	77.P	Delorme—Paris
P.NY	Phillips—New York	V.P	Verhaeghe—Poitiers	81.P	Boscher—Paris
P.T	Phillips Ward Price—Toronto	VMB.H	Van Marle & Bignell—The Hague		
PB	Sotheby Parke Bernet—USA	VN.R	Vendu Notarishuis—Rotterdam		

INDEX

Pages 1-330 are found in Volume I; pages 355–688, in Volume II; and pages 713–1046, in Volume III. Where more than one page number is cited for an artist, the first citation refers to the main biographical entry; subsequent citations refer to additional color plates.